All in One

Recommended by Teachers Trusted by Toppers

LEGAL STUDIES

Class 11

EVERYTHING YOU NEED TO SCORE

- Simplified Theory
- CBSE Textbook & other Important Questions
- CBQs; MCQs, A-R, Case Based
- Sample Question Papers

CBSE Exams 2026

All in One®

Recommended by **Teachers** Trusted by **Toppers**

LEGAL STUDIES

Class 11

EVERYTHING YOU NEED TO SCORE

- Simplified Theory
- CBSE Textbook & other Important Questions
- CBQs; MCQs, A-R, Case Based
- Sample Question Papers

CBSE Exams 2026

Author
Manik Chaubey

arihant
SUCCESS AND NOTHING LESS

arihant
SUCCESS AND NOTHING LESS

ARIHANT PRAKASHAN
(School Division Series)

卐 *ADMINISTRATIVE & PRODUCTION OFFICES*

Regd. Office

'Ramchhaya' 4577/15, Agarwal Road, Darya Ganj, New Delhi -110002
Tele: 011- 47630600, 43518550; Fax: 011- 23280316

卐 *Head Office*

Kalindi, TP Nagar, Meerut (UP) - 250002, Tel: 0121-7156203, 7156204

卐 *SALES & SUPPORT OFFICES*

Agra, Ahmedabad, Bengaluru, Bareilly, Chennai, Delhi, Guwahati, Hyderabad, Jaipur, Jhansi, Kolkata, Lucknow, Nagpur & Pune.

PO No : TXT-XX-XXXXXXX-X-XX

Published By Arihant Publications (India) Ltd.

For further information about the books published by Arihant, log on to www.arihantbooks.com or e-mail at info@arihantbooks.com

Follow us on

卐 *PRICE* ₹350.00

PRODUCTION TEAM

Publishing Managers	*Cover Designer*	*Inner Designer*
Mahendra Singh Rawat & Keshav Mohan	Salman Shaikh	Ankit Tyagi
Project Head	*Page Layouting*	*Proof Reader*
Monika Bhasin	Chintoo Kumar	Anurag Vashist

Index *cum* Study Planner

Index *cum* Study Planner

Index *cum* Study Planner

Unit 5 Family Justice System

Studied | Revised | Exam ready

One Book- Endless Features
to Help you Succeed

Complete Theory in Each Chapter

Each chapter has Complete, Easy to Understand and Simplified theory covering latest syllabus and rationalised CBSE Textbook. Theory is developed in such a way that it perfectly rectifies the complexity of CBSE Text making it suitable for all types of students.

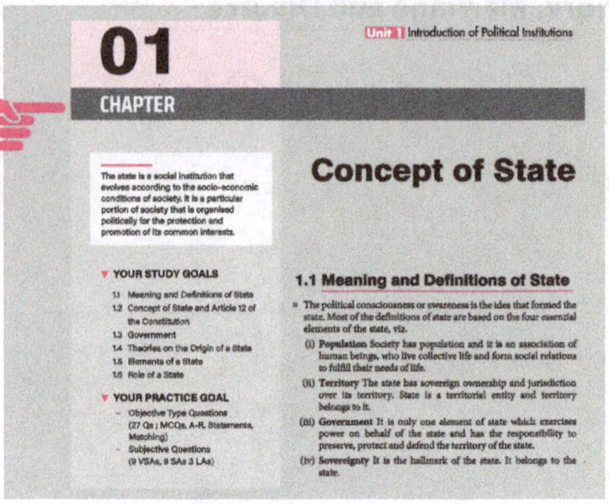
Unit 1 Introduction of Political Institutions

01 CHAPTER

Concept of State

The state is a social institution that evolves according to the socio-economic conditions of society. It is a particular portion of society that is organised politically for the protection and promotion of its common interests.

YOUR STUDY GOALS
1.1 Meaning and Definitions of State
1.2 Concept of State and Article 12 of the Constitution
1.3 Government
1.4 Theories on the Origin of a State
1.5 Elements of a State
1.6 Role of a State

YOUR PRACTICE GOAL
- Objective Type Questions (27 Qs ; MCQs, A-R, Statements, Matching)
- Subjective Questions (9 VSAs, 9 SAs 3 LAs)

1.1 Meaning and Definitions of State

- The political consciousness or awareness is the idea that formed the state. Most of the definitions of state are based on the four essential elements of the state, viz.
  (i) **Population** Society has population and it is an association of human beings, who live collective life and form social relations to fulfill their needs of life.
  (ii) **Territory** The state has sovereign ownership and jurisdiction over its territory. State is a territorial entity and territory belongs to it.
  (iii) **Government** It is only one element of state which exercises power on behalf of the state and has the responsibility to preserve, protect and defend the territory of the state.
  (iv) **Sovereignty** It is the hallmark of the state. It belongs to the state.

CBSE TEXTBOOK FOLDER

1 Write short notes on the following
(i) Patriarchal Theory
(ii) Social Contract Theory
(iii) Article 12 of the Constitution of India

Ans (i) According to this theory, in the origin and development of the state, the eldest male descendant of the family had an important role to play. This theory finds its support from Sir Henry Maine. This theory rests on the following assumptions
- The concept of permanent marriages was prevalent in ancient times.
- Paternity was an established fact/reality.

CBSE Textbook Folder

Complete explanations of all the questions of CBSE Textbook Exercises.

Quick Test 1

1 How can state be defined as a social institution?
2 What does Article 12 of the Indian Constitution mention?
3 What do you understand by the term 'local authorities' as mentioned under the Article 12 of Indian Constitution?
4 Define any one social relations which are formed by human beings to fulfill their needs of life?

Quick Test

A set of 3-5 Questions given in between the text, helps students to remain connected with the text while studying. They can instantly assess themselves for their understanding.

One Book- Endless Features

to Help you Succeed

Exam Pattern Question

Exam Pattern exercise have all types of questions; Objective Type Questions, SA & LA Type Questions.

Exam Pattern Questions

Objective Type Questions

Multiple Choice Questions (MCQs)

1. Kishwar Chand has planned to launch a political party and he admired Black's theory of political organisation. Identify the reference in which Black gave his theory. **Competency Based Que**
   (a) State (b) Government
   (c) People (d) Legislature
2. Which of the following articles defines state under the Indian Constitution?
   (a) Article 12 (b) Article 13
   (c) Article 14 (d) Article 15
5. The origin of state is traced to the authority of the eldest male descendant of the family in which of the following theories?
   (a) Matriarchal Theory
   (b) Patriarchal Theory
   (c) Divine Theory
   (d) Kinship Theory
6. Pradeep, a Ph.D. Scholar in Delhi University, has submitted his thesis related to Indian society largely driven by patriarchal system.
   Who among the following has supported patriarchal system? **Competency Based Que**

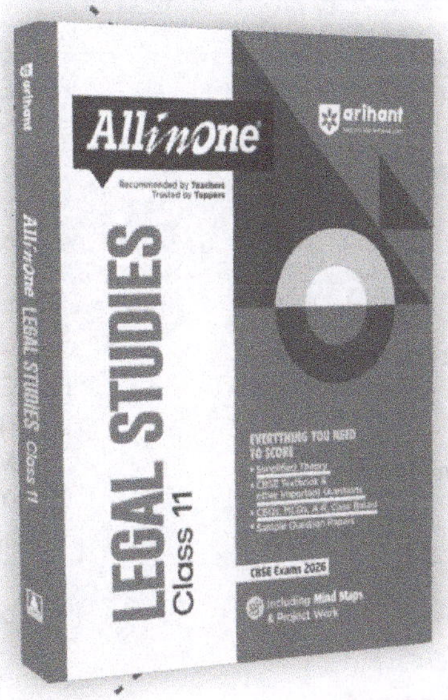

Self Assessment Test

Complete Test of chapter in Exam format.

SELF ASSESSMENT TEST

Objective Type Questions

1. Who defines state as "The political system of a body of people who are politically organised; the system of rules by which jurisdiction and authority are exercised over such a body of people"?
   (a) Salmond (b) Black (c) Laski (d) Plato
2. What does territory of the state include?
   (a) Internal waters (b) Airspace (c) Land (d) All of these
3. ……… is the hallmark of the state.
   (a) Government (b) Sovereignty (c) Society (d) None of these
4. Under which articles are Fundamental Rights contained?
   (a) Articles 12-35 (b) Articles 10-35 (c) Articles 1-5 (d) None of these
5. Mater familias is a concept defined under which among the following?
   (a) Matriarchal theory (b) Patriarchal theory (c) Both (a) and (b) (d) None of these

Very Short Answer Type Questions

6. Name some sub-state governing authorities at the local and regional levels.
7. Who are the proponents of the following theories of origin of the state?
   (i) Patriarchal theory
   (ii) Divine theory
8. State any two assumptions of the patriarchal theory.
9. 'Matriarchal state is based on the basis of equality'. Justify the statement. **Competency Based Que**

SAMPLE QUESTION PAPER 1

A Highly Simulated Sample Question Paper for CBSE Class XI

LEGAL STUDIES

General Instructions

- This question paper contains 4 sections – A, B, C and D.
- Section A contains 20 multiple choice questions for 20 marks.
- Section B contains 8 short answer type questions for 2 marks each.
- Section C contains 8 questions for 3 marks each.
- Section D contains 4 long answer type questions for 5 marks each.

Time : 3 hours *Max. Marks : 80*

SECTION A

1 A Law student, Manu, has briefed his junior fellows about the concepts of Locke, that laws could only be designed in the name of the common good. Identify the related concept, as given by Locke. (1)
(a) Divine Power
(b) Limited Government
(c) Sovereign Government
(d) Self-Preservation

2 Which of the following deals with legal issues related to use of inter-networked information technology? (1)
(a) Cyber crime (b) Cyber law
(c) Internet (d) None of these

3 Which Act was enacted to ban the employment of children, who have not completed their fourteenth year, in specified occupations and processes? (1)
(a) The Child Labour (Prohibition and Regulation) Act, 1986
(b) Child Protection Act, 1990
(c) Child labour Prevention Act, 1992
(d) None of the above

4 Sanjay is very radical about the fundamental changes in the legal system of India and actively asks for reforms in laws as it was brought in the past. Who has introduced legal reform in India? (1)
(a) British East India Company
(b) Mughal Era
(c) Harsha Dynasty
(d) Dutch

5 Dr. Satya Prakash sends his servant Aditya to receive the guests at railway station and however the driver accidentally injures a pedestrian. Name the law that shall be imposed by the injured or the aggrieved party against the accused in this situation. (1)
(a) Personal Law
(b) Law of Obligations
(c) Constitutional Law
(d) Law of Torts

6 The term property is derived from which word?
(a) Propertietat (b) Propertat (1)
(c) Propertiat (d) None of these

7 Ved Prakash, a law student was asked in the compus placement about the subordinate legislation and its origin is India. Which of the following is/are the parts of Subordinate Legislation? (1)
(i) Obiter dicta (ii) Judicial Rules
(iii) Colonial Law (iv) Local Law
Codes
(a) (i), (ii) and (iv) (b) (ii), (iii) and (iv)
(c) (i), (ii) and (iii) (d) All of the above

Sample Question Papers

To make students practice of examination in real sense, there are 3 Sample Question Papers at the end. All these Sample Question Papers are exactly prepared on the latest syllabus & pattern of examination.

Latest Course Structure

S. No.	Units	Marks
1	Introduction of Political Institutions	15
2	Basic Features of the Constitution of India	15
3	Jurisprudence, Nature and Sources of Laws	15
4	Judiciary: Constitutional, Civil and Criminal Courts and Processes	20
5	Family Justice System	15
6	Project	20
	Total	100

Unit 1 Introduction of Political Institutions

1. Concept of State

i. What is a State?
ii. The concept of State and Article 12 of the Indian Constitution
iii. What is Government?
iv. Emergence of the State from Society
v. Definition of State
vi. Theories on the Origin of State
vii. Elements of a State
viii. Role of a State

2. Forms and Organs of Government

i. Introduction to the Organs of Government
ii. Forms of Government
  a. Monarchy
  b. Aristocracy
  c. Dictatorship
  d. Democracy
iii. Main organs of Government and its Functions
  a. General Functions of Legislature as Organ of Government
  b. General Functions of Executive as Organ of Government
  c. General Functions of Judiciary as Organ of Government

3. Separation of Powers

i. Concept of Separation of Powers
ii. Historical Background and Evolution of Montesquieu's Doctrine of Separation of Powers
  a. Montesquieu's Doctrine of Separation of Powers
  b. Basic Features of the Doctrine of Separation of Powers as Enunciated by Montesquieu
  c. Checks and Balances of Power
  d. Impact of the Doctrine
iii. Evaluation of The Doctrine of Separation of Powers
  a. Key Benefits and Advantages of the Doctrine of Separation of Powers
  b. Defects of the Doctrine
iv. Separation of Powers in Practice
  a. Separation of Powers in Britain
  b. Separation of Powers in the United States of America
  c. Separation of Powers in India

vii. Cyber Law in India
viii. Scope or Extent of The Information Technology Act, 2000 (IT Act)
ix. What was Section 66A IT Act, 2000?

Unit 4 Judiciary: Constitutional, Civil and Criminal Courts and Processes

1. Judiciary: Constitutional, Civil and Criminal Courts and Processes

i. Introduction: Establishment of the Supreme Court and High Courts
ii. Constitution, Roles and Impartiality
  a. Independence and Impartiality of the Supreme Court
  b. Structure and Hierarchy of the Courts in India
  c. The Civil Process and Functioning of Civil Courts
iii. The Civil Court Structure
  a. Common Legal Terminologies
  b. Types of Jurisdictions
  c. Res subjudice and Res judicata in Code of Civil Procedure, 1908
iv. Structure and Functioning of Criminal Courts in India
  a. Types of Offences
  b. Criminal Investigations and First Information Report (FIR)
  c. Criminal Process- Investigation and Prosecution
  d. Doctrine of autrefois acquit and autrefois convict (i.e. previously acquitted and previously convicted)
  e. Function and Role of Police
v. Other Courts in India
  a. Family Courts
  b. Administrative Tribunals

Unit 5 Family Justice System

1. Institutional Framework, Marriage and Divorce

i. Nature of Family Laws in India
ii. Human Rights and Gender Perspective
iii. Institutional Framework- Family Courts
iv. Role of Women in the Creation of Family Courts
v. Role of Lawyers and Counselors in Family Courts
vi. Role of Counselors and Gender Issues
vii. Marriage and Divorce

2. Child Rights

i. Child Rights
ii. Right to Education
iii. Right to Health
iv. Right to Shelter
v. Child Labour
vi. Sexual Abuse
vii. Juvenile Justice

3. Adoption

i. Adoption
ii. Minor custody and Guardianship

4. Property, Succession and Inheritance

i. Concept of Property: Joint Family Property and Separate Property
ii. Inheritance and Succession
iii. Intestate Succession
iv. Rules relating to Intestate Succession
v. Testamentary Succession

5. Prevention of Violence Against Women

i. What is Domestic abuse / violence?
ii. International Legal Framework
iii. Laws in India on Prevention of Violence against Women

01 CHAPTER

Concept of State

The state is a social institution that evolves according to the socio-economic conditions of society. It is a particular portion of society that is organised politically for the protection and promotion of its common interests.

YOUR STUDY GOALS

YOUR PRACTICE GOAL

- Objective Type Questions (27 Qs ; MCQs, A-R, Statements, Matching)
- Subjective Questions (9 VSAs, 9 SAs 3 LAs)

1.1 Meaning and Definitions of State

- The political consciousness or awareness is the idea that formed the state. Most of the definitions of state are based on the four essential elements of the state, viz.
  - (i) **Population** Society has population and it is an association of human beings, who live collective life and form social relations to fulfill their needs of life.
  - (ii) **Territory** The state has sovereign ownership and jurisdiction over its territory. State is a territorial entity and territory belongs to it.
  - (iii) **Government** It is only one element of state which exercises power on behalf of the state and has the responsibility to preserve, protect and defend the territory of the state.
  - (iv) **Sovereignty** It is the hallmark of the state. It belongs to the state.

Some definitions of state are

- According to **Black's Law dictionary**, state has been defined as "The political system of a body of people who are politically organised; the system of rules by which jurisdiction and authority are exercised over such a body of people".

- According to **J.W. Garner,** "State is a community of persons, more or less numerous, permanently occupying a definite portion of territory, independent or nearly so, of external control and possessing an organised government to which the great body of inhabitants render habitual obedience".
- According to **Aristotle**, "State is a body of citizens sufficing for the purposes of life".
- According to **Bluntschli,** "State is the politically organised people of a definite territory".

1.2 Concept of State and Article 12 of the Constitution

- **Article 12** of the Indian Constitution states that "In this part, unless the context otherwise requires, the state includes the Government and Parliament of India and the Government and the Legislature of each of the states and all local or other authorities within the territory of India or under the control of the Government of India".
- Thus, according to **Article 12** of the Constitution, state includes the following
  - The Government and the Parliament of India, i.e. the Union Legislature and Executive.
  - The Government and Legislature of each state, i.e. Executive and Legislature of state.
  - All local and other authorities within the territory of India.
  - All local and other authorities under the control of the Government of India.

Facts about Article 12

- Article 12 defines the term 'state' which is included in Part III of the Constitution while mentioning the significance of the provisions of Fundamental Rights of the Indian Citizen.
- Article 12 is not a Fundamental Right in itself. However, it defines the term 'state' for the Fundamental Rights entailed in Articles 14-35.
- In Article 12, there is no mention of judiciary (Supreme Court, High Courts, or Lower Courts) as a 'state', but judiciary cannot make rules that are violative of Fundamental Rights.

1.3 Government

According to Black's Law dictionary, definition of government, 'The structure of principle and rules determining how a state or organisation is regulated'.

The main differences between state and government are as follows

State	Government
A state has four essential elements population, territory, government and sovereignty.	Government is only one element of the state.
Sovereignty is the hallmark of the state. It belongs to the state.	The government exercises power on behalf of the state.
The state has sovereign ownership and jurisdiction over its territory. State is a territorial entity and territory belongs to it.	The government has the responsibility to preserve, protect and defend the territory of the state.

Emergence of State from Society

- Society is an association of human beings, who live a collective life and form social relations to fulfill their needs of life i.e. physical, emotional, intellectual or spiritual. It includes all the social relationships based on kinship' affinity, language affinity, religious affinity, common conscience of individuals and territorial affinity.

- A society qualifies for being a state when it is governed by common set of laws, rules, regulations and obeys a supreme authority.
- Thus, it is clear that
  - Society is the primary association.
  - A state is formed out of a society and it is described as a **society** which is, **politically organised**.
  - A state is formed to regulate the political activity of individuals for social order.
  - The state depends on society for its existence and not vice-versa.
- **Aristotle** (384-322 BCE) in his treatise politics where he observed that **Man is a social animal, Man is a political animal.**
- **R.M. MacIver** (1882-1970) in his famous work **The Modern State** has thus observed, 'There are social forms like the family or church or the club which work neither for their origin nor for their inspiration to the state, and social forces, like custom or competition', which the state many protect or modify, but it does not create. According to him, 'The state is a word, which regulates the external relationship of a man in society'.

Quick Test 1

1. How can state be defined as a social institution?
2. What does Article 12 of the Indian Constitution mention?
3. What do you understand by the term 'local authorities' as mentioned under the Article 12 of Indian Constitution?
4. Define any one social relations which are formed by human beings to fulfill their needs of life?

1.4 Theories on the Origin of a State

Different theories have been given by different philosophers regarding the origin of state. Some of the theories are discussed below

Theory of Kinship

- This theory is based on sociological facts. **Aristotle** (384-322 BC) was the earliest advocate of this theory.
- In his treatise, 'Politics' Aristotle state, 'Society of many families is called a village and a village is most naturally composed of the descendants of one family, the children and the children's children...., for every family is governed by the elder, as are the branches thereof, on account of their religion there unto... and when many villages so entirely join themselves together as in every respect to form but one society, that society is state and contains in itself that perfection of government'.
- According to this theory, state originated in the following ways
  - Family was the basic unit of society in the very beginning. Blood relationship and kinship brought all members of the family together and they accepted the authority of the head of the family.
  - Name of the common ancestor became the symbol of **kinship**[1].
  - Kinship created society and society in turn, created the state.
  - Expansion of family gave rise to new families and the multiplication of families led to the formation of clans. Further, the expansion of clans led to the existence of tribes and ultimately to the existence of the state.
- According to **R.M. MacIver** (1882-1970), family, discipline, command and obedience are supposed to represent the origin of government. The curbs and controls that constitute the nature of the government is first identified in the family.

1 **Kinship** It is a system of social organisation based on real family ties.

Patriarchal Theory

- According to this theory, the eldest male descendant of the family had an important role in the origin and development of the state. This theory is supported by Sir Henry Maine (1822-1888).
- In his book **'The Spirit of Laws' (1861),** Maine explained that the state developed through uncontrolled autocracy[2] of the family head (**patria potestas**) in the following ways
  - Under patria potestas, the eldest male parent of the family had the final and unqualified authority over the family and the household.
  - The eldest male expanded the family ties by polygamy[3] and thus created the bond among the individuals on the basis of kinship to form a state.
  - The congregation of families formed villages, and extension of villages formed tribes or a clan, that later formed the state.
- Patriarchal theory is based on the following assumptions
  - The concept of permanent marriages was prevalent in ancient times.
  - Paternity was an established fact/reality.
  - In a family, the line of descent was traced through males only and not females.

Matriarchal Theory

- This theory was given by political thinkers like **McLennan** (1827-1881) and **Edward Jenks** (1861-1939). According to them, patriarchal families did not exist in the primitive ages. Polyandry[4] was the highest authority of the household.
- McLennan had described **mater familias** (mother as the head of the family) as the **martia protestas** (mother as the final authority) in matters of possession and disposal of property of the family.
- Edward Jenks has described this theory from his studies of the primitive tribes in Australia. Australian tribes were organised into some sort of tribe called the **Totem group.**
- These groups were not organised on the basis of blood relationship. Instead, they were united by a common symbol like a tree or an animal. The men of one totem group would marry all the women of their generation belonging to another totem group. Thus, polygamy as well as polyandry were included in the system of marriage.
- The important points of Jenks' matriarchal theory are
  - Tribe was the oldest and primary social group. It constituted the earliest form of society.
  - In due course of time, tribes break down into clans and clans in turn evolved into households. Further, households evolved into modern families.
  - Kinship was traced through females.
  - Conjugal (marital) relationships were transient (temporary) in nature.
  - Only the females succeeded in power and property.
  - The matriarchal society evolved into patriarchal society with the passage of time and beginning of pastoral stage in human civilisation.
- The largest matriarchal society in the world is **Minangkabau,** an indigenous tribe of the Sumatra region of Indonesia. Ownership of land and family name is passed from mother to daughter in this tribe.

---

2 **Autocracy** It is the system of government by one person with absolute power.
3 **Polygamy** It means marrying more than one woman.
4 **Polyandry** It means a woman having more than one husband.

Criticism of Patriarchal and Matriarchal Theories

- Patriarchal and Matriarchal theories have been criticised on the basis that the authority of a state as a political institution over its individuals is not dependent on nature but on the choice of individuals.
- The purpose of forming a state also differs to a great extent from that of a family.
- The authority to run a state is provided to the ruler not because of his seniority, but on account of his status and competence.

Divine Theory

- This theory was supported by political thinkers such as **James I** (1556-1625) and **Sir Robert Filmer** (1588-1653). According to the divine theory of kinship, state is established and governed by either of the following
  - God
  - Some superhuman power
  - King as the agent of God and the religious scriptures
- Divine theory suggested that individuals should obey and support some definite ruler with a high moral status which is equivalent to God. This theory adds moral character to state functions.
- Thus, the main features of divine theory are
  - Monarchy is divinely appointed and the king derives his authority from God.
  - Monarchy is hereditary and it must go from father to son.
  - King is only answerable to God.
  - Opposition to the lawful authority of a king is a sin.
- Hindus, Christians, Muslims, Jews and many other faiths of this world hold a similar view, that the origin of polifical authority it had divine saction.

Social Contract Theory

- According to this theory, the **mutual agreement and mutual consent** of the people are required to form a state. **Thomas Hobbes** and **John Locke** from England and **Jean Jacques Rousseau** from France are the supporters of this theory.
- According to them, individuals entered into a social contract to escape from the pre-political condition of society.
- The pre-political condition of mankind was described as the state of nature.
- These theories served as the basis of modern democracy.

Thomas Hobbes and His Social Contract Theory

Hobbes (1588-1679), in his literary work, **Leviathan**, explained the origin of the state. The main points of his theory are

- Human beings were in the state of nature before the emergence of a civil state.
- Hobbes characterised the pre-social phase as the 'State of nature' in which human lives were in constant struggle with nature. It was a state of constant war 'Where every man was enemy to every other man'.
- In order to evade the state of nature and to secure their natural rights of life, liberty and property as civil rights, individuals entered into a social contract to establish a state.
- The people authorised the right of governing themselves to the sovereign (king), which came into being as a result of the contract.
- The person or group of persons to whom the rights or authority were surrendered became the sovereign and the people who agreed to give the authority to be governed became the subjects.

- The ruler was not a party to this social contract and thus was not bound by any terms of social contract. He was free to rule according to his desires and beliefs.
- The commands of the sovereign were laws for the governed (people or subjects) and the sovereign was not accountable to the people. People gave their ruler unquestioned obedience.

Criticism of Hobbes' Theory

Hobbes' theory was **criticised by R.G. Gettle** in the following ways

- Hobbes created an all-powerful sovereign on the belief that law, order, peace and security could not be maintained in society without such sovereign power.
- He deprived the people of their right to revolt against the sovereign.
- He allowed individuals to disobey the commands only when
  - the sovereignty deprived individuals of their right to self-preservation.
  - the ruler got conquered and submitted authority to a new emperor.
- He did not maintain the difference between state and government as a political institution. He believed that a change in the government led to the dissolution of the state.

John Locke and His Social Contract Theory

- **John Locke** (1632-1704) in his book **Two Treatises of Government** explained that the state of nature was not a state of war; it was a state of peace, natural rights, preservation, goodwill and mutual assistance.
- His state of nature was pre-political where people were social and had rights and liberties. The main points of Locke's Social Contract theory are
  - The state of nature ensured **three rights** to individuals relating to life, liberty and property.
  - There were inconveniences in the state of nature, where men considered them as judges in their own disputes.
  - Life was inconvenient because each individual had to interpret the law of nature for himself. They also had to enforce the law of nature without the help of any other authority.
  - The state of nature lacked the machinery to enforce the natural rights of individuals.
  - Two contracts were made to preserve a state of affairs, which were social and governmental.

    (i) **Social Contract** It led to the formation of a civil society. Social contract (among individuals) required the individuals to surrender their natural rights in exchange of civil rights.

    (ii) **Governmental Contract** It led to the establishment of the government. It was between the individuals and the ruler, to establish a system of law and justice in the form of a state. The ruler was a party to the contract and was thus bound by its terms.

    (a) Unlike Hobbes, Locke traced the sources of government's authority to the consent of the community.

    (b) He **introduced the concept of limited government**, in terms of the rulers, their powers, functions and tenure.

    (c) **Locke believed in limited monarchy** where the king was the trustee of the people.

    (d) If the ruler abused his powers and broke the trust, he may be changed through revolt by the people.

Jean-Jacques Rousseau and Social Contract Theory

- According to **Rousseau** (1712-1779), the general will of the people led to the creation of the institution called the state. Rousseau, in his literary work, **The Social Contract** described the state of nature as a state of bliss and happiness.

- According to him, with the passage of time, life became intolerable with increase in population and disparity of wealth and power. Simplicity and happiness disappeared. Thus, human beings started to build their relations on co-operation and dependency. They entered into a social contract to preserve their natural rights without submitting or sub-ordinating to any ruler or authority.

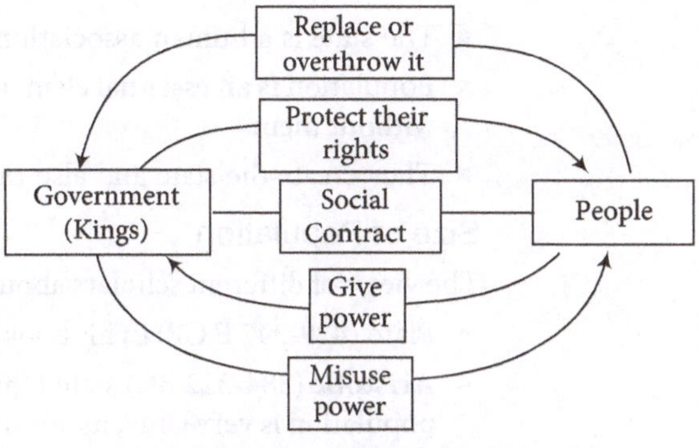

▲ *Rousseau's Social Contract Theory*

- The main points of Rousseau's Social Contract theory are
  - Rousseau regarded the general will of the people as sovereign. Individuals surrendered their rights to the general will and they were themselves a part of it. Thus, they shared the rights even after transferring them.
  - Individuals were governed by a new authority in the name of general will (common good) of the people in the form of direct democracy.
  - The common good depends upon the prevailing circumstances in the society.
  - The government is only the tool to execute the popular will. Thus, sovereignty remain in continuous exercise and there is no scope of revolt in Rousseau's theory.

Criticism of Rousseau's Theory

Rousseau's theory has been criticised on the following grounds

- Individuals who did not know about the concept of political authority and civil rights could not reach an agreement in any particular point of time and start living a collectivised civil life.
- If **the existence of state is based on agreement** of the members of a society, the **old agreement** may be revoked[5] for new according to the self-interests of the members. Thus, a mechanically originated state will run under the constant fear of destabilisation.

Quick Test 2

1. How was family the basic unit of society?
2. What is the major theme of the book 'The Spirit of Laws'?
3. Give any one criticism of patriarchal theory.
4. What is the ruler's stand on social contract, according to Thomas Hobbes?

1.5 Elements of a State

- There are **four essential elements** of a state, i.e. population, territory, government and sovereignty.
- Apart from these, **international recognition** is also considered as an essential element of the state. It means the recognition of the sovereignty of a state including its territory and population by other states.

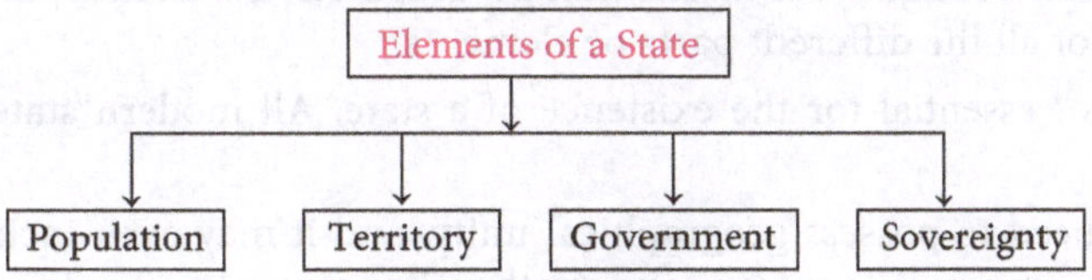

5 **Revoke** It means to officially cancel the power or effect of something.

Population

- The state is a human association formed by the people living in it.
- Population is an essential element of a state as it is the people who make a state and there can be no state without them.
- They create the state and also maintain the resources, live on the land and form the government.

Size of Population

The views of different scholars about the size of population are

- Plato (429-347 B CE) in his book **The Laws**, Plato suggested that 5040 citizens can make an ideal state.
- **Aristotle** (384-322 BC) stated that the population of a state should neither be so large nor so small. If the population is very large, its administration may be inconvenient, and if the population is so small, people may not be able to lead a life of peace and security.
- **Stephen Leacock** (1869-1944) stated that the population must be sufficient in number to maintain a state organisation. It should not be greater than the territory and the resources of the state.

Nature of Population

The nature of population may be homogeneous or heterogeneous in respect of race, religion, language or culture. Countries such as India, United States of America and Canada have a population marked with such diversity.

Territory

A state is a territorial institution. The fixed territory and population of a state gives it a physical identity in the view of municipal law (or domestic law) and international law.

Aristotle (384-322 BCE) favoured the state having moderate size. According to Montesquieu (1689-1755) 'There is a necessary connection between the size of the state and the form of the government'.

The first thing to be exercised in a given territory are the functions of a state as a political and legal community of human beings.

Some of the major features of territory as an element of a state are

- Territory is a geographical area that is owned and controlled by a government or country to exercise state sovereignty.
- It is generally described as land which belongs to the state and individuals, internal waters and territorial sea (straits).
- The airspace above this territory (land, bodies of water, atmosphere and natural resources) also belongs to the state.
- Territories include the physical basis of the state.
- Nomads and gypsies can have no state because they lead a wandering life.
- It should have territorial contiguity. It means that geographically, a territory should be one composite whole, i.e. consisting of all the different parts or elements.
- A fixed territory is not essential for the existence of a state. All modern states are contained within territorial limits.
- A territory does not need to possess geographical unity, and it may even include the territorial areas which lack connection, or are distant from one another. For example, islands or other territories which are part of the mainland, are also included in the territory of a state.

Government

Government is the political and administrative organ of a state. The state operates through its government. The features of the government as an element of a state are

- The state include all its citizens, and is a broader concept.
- The government is the sum total of legislative, executive and judicial activities of a state. The legislatures makes laws, the executive enforces laws and the judiciary solves the disputes.
- Government also includes internal bodies and sub-state governing authorities at the local and regional levels. For example, the Municipal Corporations, Municipal Councils, Panchayats and Gram Sabhas in India.
- The government of a state makes provisions for the services of defence, foreign relations, levy of taxes, issue of currency, building of roads, bridges, transportation, communication, water supply, electricity, health education, and other types of social and physical infrastructure.
- The government of a state enforces law to maintain order, peace and security.
- The role of government changes with the changes in the role of a state.

Sovereignty

- Sovereignty[6] is an important factor that distinguishes the state from other associations.
- Without sovereign, there is no existence of a state.
- Sovereignty is the most essential characteristic in the formation of the state. No state can exist without internal and external sovereignty. These are discussed below
  - **Internal Sovereignty** It means that the people residing within the territory of the state give their unqualified obedience and support to the authority of the state. It is because the state has the supreme authority in all its internal matters.

    By its sovereignty, the state makes laws and decisions and issue commands which are binding on all its citizens. The right to use legitimate force is exclusive right of a state. Internal revolts or external aggressions may disturb a state but the state continues to exist as long as it has legitimate sovereignty.
  - **External Sovereignty** It means the freedom of state from external control and influence. The state should be equal to other states and should not be assigned any inferior position. The state should be free to enact its own laws as well as foreign policy without any external pressure.

1.6 Role of a State

- Political thinkers have different opinion regarding the role of the state. In the words of Professor **MacIver**, "The state has no finality, can have no perfected form. The state is an instrument of social man". To many scholars the functions of the state are also different. Some consider state as a moral and ethical institution whereas others consider it as an evil institution.
- MacIver has referred to different notions of the state such as class organisation, legal institution, mutual insurance agency, unnecessary evil, necessary evil, the march of God on the Earth, welfare system, power system, state as an organism etc.
  - **Minimal State** The idea is to ensure the widest possible individual liberty. The state's role is to protect individuals from interference in their liberty and that transactions between private individuals are voluntary and free.
  - **Developmental States** The term 'developmental state' describes the state's essential role in harnessing national resources and directing incentives through a distinctive policy-making process. A state that is focused on economic development and takes necessary policy measures to accomplish that objective.

6 Sovereignty It means the power of a country to control its own government.

- **Social Democratic State** This state functions on the principle of fairness, equality, equal distribution of wealth to achieve social, political, economic justice and empowerment of its people. It is considered necessary to promote the economic growth and the social well being of its people.
- **Collectivised State** They undertake the control of economic life, by bringing common ownership of all economic resources under their own control for the welfare of all. The state makes laws to control the private property of its citizens. The state takes care of the economic needs of its citizens i.e provides food, shelter, employment and the citizens must not act against the government policies.
- **Totalitarian State** The state must have absolute powers and individuals have no right against the state. According to this view, the state can do no wrong. The whole life of an individual is within the jurisdiction of the state. Dictators like Hitler and Mussolini are the examples of this state.
- **Modern Welfare State** Irrespective of the classification, functions of a modern welfare state includes the maintenance of law and order, establishment of justice, defense, public security, foreign relations, maintenance of public health, sanitation, water supply, transport, communication system, supply of power, electricity, essential commodities, control of banking, currency and inflation, preservation of forests, checking of trading, control of prices and measurements, etc.

Quick Test 3

1. What is international recognition as an element of a state.
2. How population give state a physical identity?
3. Name any one element of the government that make it an organ of a state.
4. Mention any two examples of totalitarian state?

Mind Map

CONCEPT OF STATE

1 Definitions of State

- According to Bluntschli, 'State is the politically organised people of a definite territory.'
- According to Aristotle, "State is a body of citizens sufficing for the purposes of life".

Concept of State and Article 12 of the Constitution

- Article 12 of the Constitution, includes.
- The Government and Legislature of each state.
- All Local and other authorities within the territory of India.

- All local and other authorities under the control of the Government of India.

2 Government

- Government is only one element of the state.
- The government exercises power on behalf of the state.

Emergence of State from Society

- Society is an association of human beings, who live a collective life and form social relations to fulfill their needs of life.
- A society qualifies for being a state when it is governed by common set of laws, rules, regulations and obeys a supreme authority.
- It is clear that
  - Society is the primary association.
  - A state is formed out of society and it is described as a society politically organised.
  - Regulate the political activity of individuals for social order.
  - The state depends on society for its existence and not vice-versa.

3 Theories on the Origin of a State

Theory of Kinship

- This theory is based on sociological facts.
- State originated in the following ways
  - Family was the basic unit of society in the very beginning.
  - Name of the common ancestor became the symbol of kinship.
  - Kinship created society and society in turn, created the state.

Patriarchal Theory

- According to this theory, the eldest male descendant of the family had an important role in the origin and development of the state. This theory is supported by Sir Henry Maine (1822-1888).
- Patriarchal theory is based on the following assumptions
  - The concept of permanent marriages was prevalent in ancient times.
  - Paternity was an established fact/reality.
  - In a family, the line of descent was traced through males only and not females.

Matriarchal Theory

- Patriarchal families did not exist in the primitive ages. Polyandry was the highest authority of the household.

Important Points

- Tribe was the oldest and primary social group.
- Tribes break down into clans and clans in turn evolved into households.
- Matriarchal society evolved into patriarchal society with the passage of time and beginning of pastoral stage in human civilisation.

Divine Theory

- According to the divine theory of kinship, state is established and governed by either of the following
  - King as the agent of God and the religious scriptures.
  - God
  - Some superior power

Social Contract Theory

- According to this theory, the mutual agreement and mutual consent of the people are required to form a state.
- Thomas Hobbes, John Locke, Rousseau propounded this theory.
- The pre-political condition of mankind was described as the state of nature.
- This is the basis for modern democracy.

4 Elements of a State

- **Population** It is an essential element of a state as it is the people who make a state and there can be no state without them.
- **Territory** The first thing to be exercised in a given territory are the functions of a state as a political and legal community of human beings.
- **Government** It is the political and administrative organ of a state.
- **Sovereignty** It is the most essential characteristic in the formation of the state. No state can exist without internal and external sovereignty.

5 Role of a State

- Political thinkers have different opinion regarding the role of the state.
- MacIver has referred to different notions of the state such as class organisation, legal institution, mutual insurance agency, unnecessary evil, necessary evil, the march of God on the Earth, welfare system, power system, state as an organism etc.
- **Classification of Role of the State** Minimal States, Developmental States, Social Democratic States, Collectivised States, Totalitarian States, Modern Welfare States.

CBSE TEXTBOOK FOLDER

1. Write short notes on the following

(i) Patriarchal Theory
(ii) Developmental States
(iii) Social Contract Theory
(iv) Totalitarian States
(v) Article 12 of the Constitution of India

Ans. (i) According to **the patriarchal** theory, in the origin and development of the state, the eldest male descendant of the family had an important role to play. This theory finds its support from Sir Henry Maine. This theory rests on the following assumptions

- The concept of permanent marriages was prevalent in ancient times.
- Paternity was an established fact/reality.
- In a family, the line of descent was traced through males only and not females.
- The head male member possessed unlimited powers over the other family members.

(ii) **Developmental States** A developmental state is characterised by having strong state intervention, as well as extensive regulation and planning. The term 'developmental state' describes the states' essential role in harnessing national resources and directing incentive through a distinctive policy-making process.

The first person to seriously conceptualise the developmental state was Chalmers Johnson (1931-2010). Johnson defined the developmental state as a state that is focused on economic development and takes necessary policy measures to accomplish that objective.

(iii) According to **the social contract** theory, the mutual agreement and mutual consent of the people are required to form a state.

Thomas Hobbes and John Locke from England and Jean Jacques Rousseau from France are the propounders of this theory. According to them, to escape from the pre-political condition of society, individuals entered into a social contract.

(iv) **The Totalitarian States** must have absolute power and individuals have no right against the state.

According to this view, the state can do no wrong. The whole life of an individual is within the jurisdiction of the state. Dictators like Hitler and Mussolini are the examples of this state.

(v) **Article 12 of the Constitution of India** Clarifies and defines the term 'State' occuring in any provision concerning Fundamental Rights in Part III. According to it, state includes the following

- The Government and the Parliament of India, i.e. the Union Legislature and Executive.
- The Government and Legislature of each state, i.e. Executive and Legislature of state.
- All local and other authorities within the territory of India.
- All local and other authorities under the control of the Government of India.

2. Write one point of difference between the following

(i) Internal and External Sovereignty
(ii) Matriarchal and Patriarchal Theory of the State
(iii) Minimal and Collectivised State
(iv) Social Contract Theory by Hobbes and Locke
(v) State and Government

Ans. (i) **Internal Sovereignty** It means that the people residing within the territory of the state give their unqualified obedience and support to the authority of the state, and further that the state is supreme in all its internal matters.

External Sovereignty It is understood as the freedom of state from external control and influence.

(ii) **Matriarchal Theory** In this theory, kinship was traced through females.

Patriarchal Theory In this theory, kinship was traced through males.

(iii) **Minimal state** advocates for little involvement and relies on market mechanisms.

Collectivised state emphasises centralised planning and control over economic activity.

As a result, the key difference between the two is the extent of government intervention in the economy.

(iv) **Social Contract Theory of Hobbes** According to Hobbes' Social Contract theory, the ruler was not a party to this social contract and thus was not bound by any terms of social contract. He was free to rule as per his whims and fancies.

The sovereign's commands were laws for the governed (people or subjects) but the sovereign was not accountable to the people. People gave their ruler unquestioned obedience.

Social Contract Theory of Locke According to Locke's Social Contract Theory, social contract led to the formation of a civil society and government contract led to the establishment of the government.

Social contract (among individuals) required the individuals to surrender their natural rights in exchange of civil rights.

Governmental contract was between the individuals and the ruler to establish a system of law and justice in the form of a state. The ruler was a party to the contract and was thus bound by its terms.

(v) **State** The state is a social institution that evolves according to the socio-economic conditions of society.

Government Government is only one organ of a State. The government exercises power on behalf of the state.

3. Answer the following questions briefly

(i) List down the various theories on the origin of the state.

(ii) Briefly explain the elements of a state.

(iii) What are the various states on the basis of its role?

Ans. (i) Different theories have been given by different philosophers regarding the origin of the state. Some of them are

(a) **Theory of Kinship** This theory is based on sociological facts. Aristotle was the earliest advocate of this theory.

This theory is based on the following assumptions

- Family was the basic unit of society in the very beginning. Blood relationship and kinship brought all members of the family together and they accepted the authority of the head of the family.
- Name of the common ancestor became the symbol of kinship. Thus, kinship created society and society in turn, created the state.
- With the expansion of family, new families arose and the multiplication of families led to the formation of clans. Further, the expansion of clans brought tribes into existence and ultimately the state.

(b) **Patriarchal Theory** Refer to Q. No. 1(i) of CBSE Textbook Folder.

(c) **Matriarchal Theory** This theory finds support from political thinkers like McLennan and Edward Jenks. According to them, patriarchal families were non-existent in the primitive ages. Polyandry was the highest authority of the household. The important points that can be seen from Jenks' theory are given below

- Kinship was traced through females.
- Conjugal relationships were transient in nature. Polyandry was the earliest form of marriage.
- Only the females succeeded in power and property.
- Matriarchal authority was an established fact in this theory.
- According to Jenks, with the passage of time the matriarchal society evolved into the patriarchal one.

(d) **Divine Theory** This theory was supported by political thinkers such as James I (1556-1625) and Sir Robert Filmer (1588-1653). According to the divine theory, the state is established and governed by either of the God, or some superior power, or king as the agent of God and the religious scriptures.

(e) **Social Contract Theory** Refer to Q. No. 1(iii) of CBSE Textbook Folder.

(ii) The following are the essential elements of a state

Population The state is a human association constituted by the people living there. Population is an essential element of a state. It is the people who make a state, without them there can be no state.

They also maintain the resources, live on the land, and form the government. The population must be large enough to make a state and sustain it.

Territory A state is a territorial institution. The fixed territory and population of a state gives it a physical identity in the view of municipal law (or domestic law) and international law.

The functions of a state, as a political and legal community of human beings, must first of all be exercised in a given territory.

In brief, a territory does not need to possess geographical unity, and it may even consist of territorial areas which lack connection, or are distant from one another. For example, islands or other territories which are part of the mainland still constitute the territory of a state.

Government It is the political and administrative organ of a state. The state operates through its government. The state consists of all its citizens, and is a broader concept. The government is the sum total of legislative, executive and judicial activities of a state.

It also includes internal bodies and sub-state governing authorities at the local and regional levels, such as the Municipal Corporations, Municipal Councils, Panchayats and Gram Sabhas in India.

The government of a state makes provisions for the services of defence, foreign relations, levy of taxes, issue of currency, etc. The government of a state shall be so organised that it enforces law to maintain order, peace and security.

Sovereignty It is the significant factor that distinguishes the state from other associations. Without sovereignty, there can be no state in the technical sense of the term. Sovereignty is the most essential ingredient and characteristic in the formation of the state. No state can exist without internal and external sovereignty.

(iii) For answer refer to text under the heading Role of a State on page no. 9 and 10.

4. Answer the following questions in about 200 words.

(i) Explain the comparative views on social contract theory.

(ii) Define state.

(iii) Explain the emergence of the state.

Ans. (i) The social contract theory is linked with morality and political theories which were presented by Thomas Hobbes, Jean Jacques Rousseau and John Locke.

The three theorists agreed that human beings are equal by nature and therefore no one has a right to control others unless there is a collective agreement to give authority to an individual or individuals to govern.

However, Hobbes believes that the government should have absolute authority over the people it governs while Locke and Rousseau urge that the government should govern as long as it does not infringe the liberty of the people.

This means that the laws drawn in society should be agreed upon by all. Hobbes believed the social contracts were created because man wanted to escape the brutal society in the state of nature. On the other hand, Locke states that the need was to improve the society in terms of peace and security though it was there in the state of nature due the natural law.

Rousseau, on the other hand, believed the need was to restore freedom to the human beings. In fact, he says that human beings should be forced to be free. This is done through the laws that govern people and define their character.

(ii) The state is a particular portion of society organised politically for the protection and promotion of its common interests. The political consciousness or awareness is the idea that formed the state.

It does not have an exact definition and has been given varied meanings by varied scholars. Most of the definitions of state are based on the four essential constituents of the state, viz. population, territory, government and sovereignty.

According to Black's Law dictionary, state has been defined as "The political system of a body of people who are politically organised; the system of rules by which jurisdiction and authority are exercised over such a body of people".

(iii) A state is formed out of a society and it is described as a society which is politically organised. Society is an association of human beings, who live a collective life and form social relations to fulfill their needs of life, i.e. physical, emotional, intellectual or spiritual.

It includes all the social relationships based on kinship, affinity, language affinity, religious affinity, common conscience of individuals and territorial affinity.

A society qualifies for being a state when it is governed by common set of laws, rules, regulations and obeys a supreme authority.

Thus, it is clear that

- Society is the primary association of a state.
- A state is formed to regulate the political activity of individuals for social order.
- The state depends on society for its existence, and not vice-versa.

5. Patria, a locatable place on the world map, having a considerable territory under its control, consisted of a population of 1 million people. It was ruled by Col. George however the place did not gain any international political recognition as one of the major elements was missing. Identify and explain all the elements of state. **Competency Based Que**

Ans. In the given situation, one of the major elements needed to constitute a state is missing and that element is sovereignty. There are four essential elements of a state such as

(i) Population (ii) Territory

(iii) Government (iv) Sovereignty

For explanation of these elements, refer to Q. No. 3 (ii) of CBSE Textbook Folder.

6. How has the concept of state been defined in the Constitution of India? Why do you think it has been included in Part III of the Constitution?

Ans. In the Indian Constitution, a state has been defined in simple words, as a community formed by people within a specified territory. The state included the government, the Parliament, State Legislature and other authorities.

Article 12 in the Part III of the Indian Constitution defines the term 'State'. The concept of 'State' has been included because it is integral to the application of the provisions concerning Fundamental Rights, also included in Part III of the Indian Constitution.

7. How would you differentiate between India as a state and the various states in India?

Ans. India as a state has all the features of a valid state, i.e. population, territory, government and sovereignty. However, the other states in India miss out a very essential feature of a state, which is the element of sovereignty.

The various states in India are not free to govern their internal and external affairs independently without any interference from the union.

Sovereignty is the crucial factor that distinguishes the state from other associations. Without a sovereign, there can be no state in the technical sense of the term. Sovereignty is the most essential ingredient and characteristic in the formation of the state. No state can exist without internal and external sovereignty.

Internal sovereignty means that the people residing within the territory of the state give their unqualified obedience and support to the authority of the state, and further that the state is supreme in all its internal matters. External sovereignty is understood as the freedom of state from external control and influence. The state should be treated as equal with other states and should not be assigned any inferior position. The state should be free to enact its own laws as well as foreign policy without any external pressure.

Exam Pattern Questions

Objective Type Questions

Multiple Choice Questions (MCQs)

1. Kishwar Chand has planned to launch a political party and he admired Black's theory of political organisation. Identify the reference in which Black gave his theory. **Competency Based Que**

(a) State (b) Government
(c) People (d) Legislature

2. Which of the following articles defines state under the Indian Constitution?

(a) Article 12 (b) Article 13
(c) Article 14 (d) Article 15

3. Article 12 is a part of which of the following parts of the Indian Constitution?

(a) Part I (b) Part II
(c) Part III (d) Part IV

4. Which of the following is defined as a 'Society politically organised'?

(a) Government (b) Society
(c) State (d) Both (a) and (c)

5. The origin of state is traced to the authority of the eldest male descendant of the family in which of the following theories?

(a) Matriarchal Theory
(b) Patriarchal Theory
(c) Divine Theory
(d) Kinship Theory

6. Pradeep, a Ph.D. Scholar in Delhi University, has submitted his thesis related to Indian society largely driven by patriarchal system.
Who among the following has supported patriarchal system? **Competency Based Que**

(a) Henry Maine (b) Hugo Grotius
(c) Harold Laski (d) John Salmond

7. The idea that the king derives his authority from God is a hallmark of ....

(a) Social Contract theory
(b) Divine theory
(c) Matriarchal theory
(d) Patriarchal theory

8. **The kings's authority is derived from God, and rebellion against the king is equivalent to rebellion against God.**

Which theory of government is illustrated by the statement given? **Competency Based Que**

(a) Social Contract Theory
(b) Divine Right Theory
(c) Natural Law Theory
(d) Absolutist Theory

9. **Rahul, a resident of a newly formed nation ,was wondering how his country came into existence .His friend explained that the people of their nation had mutually agreed to form a state, surrendering some of their rights to a sovereign in exchange for protection and stability. This sovereign in exchange for protection and stability. This sovereign was not born by any contract and was free to rule as they wished.**

What theory does this illustration describe? **Competency Based Que**

(a) Divine Right Theory
(b) Social Contract Theory
(c) Markist Theory
(d) Liberal Theory

10. **Who among the following thinkers is not associated with the social contract theory?**

(a) Hobbes (b) Locke
(c) Rousseau (d) Plato

11. **A Law student, Manu, has briefed his junior fellows about the concept of Locke, that laws could only be designed in the name of the common good. Identify the related concept, as given by Locke.** **Competency Based Que**

(a) Divine Power
(b) Limited Government
(c) Sovereign Government
(d) Self-Preservation

12. **Which of the following is NOT an essential element of a state?**

(a) Population (b) Territory
(c) Authority (d) Government

13. **Which of the following is a political and administrative organ of the state?**

(a) Sovereignty (b) Territory
(c) Government (d) All of these

14. **Which of the following refers to the freedom of state from external control and influence?**

(a) Internal Sovereignty
(b) External Sovereignty
(c) International Recognition
(d) None of the above

15. Preeti and Kaushal were in a discussion that how Thomas Hobbes and John Locke, well- known English philosophers, helped to establish political ideas of Western democracy and shape the societies across the world.

Which among the following factors provides law and is comprehensible through the rationality of human mind? **Competency Based Que**

(a) God (b) Constitution
(c) Equality (d) Power

16. **Which of the following statement is TRUE regarding the collectivised states ?**

(a) They undertake the control of economic life, by bringing common ownership of all economic resources.
(b) They undertake the control of social life, by bringing common ownership of all social resources.
(c) They undertake the control of personal life, by bringing common ownership of all personal resources.
(d) They undertake the control of political life, by bringing common ownership of all political resources.

17. **Match the following.**

	Cloumn I (Theory)		**Column II** (Name)
A.	Family was the unit of society in the beginning.	1.	Matriarchal theory
B.	Martia potestas	2.	Patriarchal theory
C.	Patria potestas	3.	Divine theory
D.	State is established and governed by God.	4.	Theory of kinship

Codes

	A	B	C	D		A	B	C	D
(a)	4	1	2	3	(b)	1	3	2	4
(c)	3	1	2	4	(d)	2	1	4	3

18. **Match the following.**

	Thinker		**Work**
A.	Plato	1.	Two Treatises of Government
B.	Aristotle	2.	The Laws
C.	Rousseau	3.	Politics
D.	Locke	4.	The Social Contract

Codes

	A	B	C	D		A	B	C	D
(a)	2	3	4	1	(b)	1	4	3	2
(c)	4	1	3	2	(d)	3	4	1	2

19. **Statement I** Thomas Hobbes believed that humans are inherently self-interested and that the state of nature is a war of 'all against all'.

Statement II John Locke argued that individuals have inherent rights to life, liberty and property, which government must protect.

Which of the following is correct?
(a) Both the Statement are correct.
(b) Both the Statement are incorrect.
(c) Statement I is correct, but Statement II is not correct.
(d) Statement I is not correct, but Statement II is correct.

20. Consider the following statements.
Statement I According to Thomas Hobbes, individuals in the state of nature lived a life that was 'solitary, poor, nasty, brutish and short'.
Statement II Hobbes believed that individuals had the right to revolt against the sovereign.
Which of the following is correct?
(a) Both the Statement are correct.
(b) Both the Statement are incorrect.
(c) Statement I is correct, but Statement II is not correct.
(d) Statement I is not correct, but Statement II is correct.

21. **Statement I** Stephen Leacock, an English political writer had stated that the population must be sufficient in number to maintain a state organisation.
Statement II Montesquieu said that there is a necessary connection between the size of the state and the form of the government.
Which of the following is correct?
(a) Both the Statement are correct.
(b) Both the Statement are incorrect.
(c) Statement I is correct, but Statement II is not correct.
(d) Statement I is not correct, but Statement II is correct.

22. Consider the following statements.
Statement I John Locke believed in the concept of absolute monarchy.
Statement II According to Locke, the ruler was a party to the social contract and was bound by its terms.
Which of the following is correct?
(a) Both the Statement are correct.
(b) Both the Statement are incorrect.
(c) Statement I is correct, but Statement II is not correct.
(d) Statement I is not correct, but Statement II is correct.

Assertion-Reason Questions

Directions (Q.Nos. 23-27) In the questions given below, there are two statements. Read the statements and choose the correct option from the following codes.

Codes
(a) Both A and R are true and R is the correct explanation of A.
(b) Both A and R are true, but R is not the correct explanation of A.
(c) A is true, but R is false.
(d) A is false, but R is true.

23. **Assertion** (A) Matriarchal theory traces the line of descent through males only.
Reason (R) In patriarchal theory, the head male possessed unlimited powers over the other members of the family.

24. **Assertion** (A) Rousseau belongs to the social contract tradition.
Reason (R) He explains the origin of the state through enactment of a social contract.

25. **Assertion** (A) Population is an essential element of a State.
Reason (R) It is the people who make a state, without them there can be no state.

26. **Assertion** (A) Sovereignty is the crucial factor that distinguishes the state from other associations.
Reason (R) Without sovereign, there can be no state in the technical sense of the term.

27. **Assertion** (A) Internal sovereignty means that the people residing within the territory of the state give their unqualified obedience and support to the authority of the state.
Reason (R) External sovereignty is understood as the freedom of state from external control and influence.

Answers

1. (a) State
2. (a) Article 12
3. (c) Part III
4. (c) State
5. (b) Patriarchal Theory
6. (a) Henry Maine
7. (b) Divine theory
8. (b) Divine Right Theory
9. (b) Social Contract Theory
10. (d) Plato
11. (b) Limited Government
12. (c) Authority
13. (c) Government
14. (b) External Sovereignty

15. (b) Constitution
16. (a) They undertake the control of economic life, by bringing common ownership of all economic resources.
17. (a) 4 1 2 3
18. (a) 2 3 4 1
19. (a) Both the Statement are correct.
20. (a) Both the Statement are correct.
21. (a) Both the Statement are correct.
22. (b) Both the Statement are incorrect.
23. (d) A is false, but R is true.
24. (a) Both A and R are true and R is the correct explanation of A.

    According to Rousseau, individuals surrender their rights to the general will of which individuals themselves were a part.

    Thus, they shared the rights even after transferring them. Individuals were governed by a new authority in the name of general will (common good) of the people in the form of direct democracy.
25. (a) Both A and R are true and R is the correct explanation of A. The state is a human association constituted by the people living there. Population is an essential element of a state. It is the people who make a state, without them there can be no state.
26. (a) Both A and R are true and R is the correct explanation of A. Sovereignty is the most essential ingredient and characteristic in the formation of the state. No state can exist without internal and external sovereignty.
27. (b) Both A and R are true, but R is not the correct explanation of A.

Subjective Questions

Very Short Answer Type Questions

1. 'The theory of kinship on the origin of state is based on sociological facts'. Identify who was the proponent of the kinship theory of state and explain.

Competency Based Que

Ans. Aristotle was the earliest proponent of the kinship theory of state. According to his theory, family was the basic unit of society in the very beginning. Blood relationship and kinship brought all members of the family together Moreover, they had to accept the authority of the head of the family.

2. 'Patriarchal and Matriarchal theories are criticised'. Justify the given statement. **Competency Based Que**

Ans. Patriarchal and Matriarchal theories are criticised on the following grounds

(i) The authority of a state as a political institution over its individuals is not by nature but by the choice of individuals.

(ii) The purpose of forming a state also differs to a great extent from that of a family.

3. 'The state originate as per the divine theory. Comment'?

Competency Based Que

Ans. According to the divine theory of kinship, state is established and governed by God or some superior power or king as the agent of God and the religious scriptures.

The supporter of divine theory believed that the state doesn't come into being by the people but it is the handiwork of God on the Earth.

4. In a small island community, residents agree to establish rules and a governing council to ensure mutual protection and resolve disputes.

They collectively decide to surrender some individual freedoms in exchange for stability and security.

This voluntary agreement is renewed anually, allowing residents to modify or dissolve the council of it fails to serve their interests.

Identify which philosopher's Social Contract theory is best exemplified by this illustration and explain it?

Competency Based Que

Ans. John Locke's Social Contract theory emphasises voluntary consent, protection of individual rights and the right to dissolve the government if it fails to serve the people's interests.

The illustration reflects locke's ideas, as the community voluntarily establishes a governing council, surrenders some freedoms and retains the right to modify or dissolve it annually. Locke's theory prioritises individual consent and protection of natural rights.

5. Who are the major proponents of the Social Contract theory?

Ans. Hobbes, Locke and Rousseau are the major proponents of the Social Contract theory.

6. State the essential elements to constitute a state.

Ans. The essential elements to constitute a state are

(i) Population (ii) Territory

(iii) Government (iv) Sovereignty

7. Imagine a world without rules or laws, where individuals are free to do as they please. This chaotic state often referred to as the "State of nature", is characterised by fear, uncertainty and a constant struggle for survival. To escape this precarious condition, individuals come together and agree to form a government, surrendering some of their individual freedoms in exchange for security, order and protection of their rights.

(i) **Identify the theory which is discussed in the above passage.**

(ii) **How does the theory explain the origin of political authority?** **Competency Based Que**

Ans. (i) This is the social contract theory discussed in the above passage.

(ii) The social contract theory posits that political authority originates from a voluntary agreement among individuals. To escape the chaotic state of nature, individuals surrender some of their natural rights to a sovereign power in exchange for protection and the maintenance of social order. This mutual agreement forms the basis of the state and legitimises the authority of the government.

8. It is estimated that India shall become world's largest populated country by 2025. Why is population an essential element to constitute a state? **Competency Based Que**

Ans. Population is an essential element of a state as it is the people who make a state and there can be no state without them.

They create the state and also maintain the resources, live on the land and form the government.

9. Rahul learnt from his tutor that most countries in the world are sovereign. What do you understand about 'sovereignty'? **Competency Based Que**

Ans. Sovereignty is the significant factor that distinguishes the state from other associations. Without sovereign, there is no existence of a state. Sovereignty is the most essential characteristic in the formation of the state. No state can exist without internal and external sovereignty.

Short Answer Type Questions

1. Write a short note on the meaning and definition of state. Why is Garner's definition important?

Ans. The state is a particular portion of society that is organised politically for the protection and promotion of its common interests.

According to J.W. Garner, 'State is a community of persons, more or less numerous, permanently occupying a definite portion of territory, independent or nearly so, of external control and possessing an organised government to which the great body of inhabitants render habitual obedience'.

Garner's definition is important because it covers all the essential elements to constitute a state. These four elements include population, territory, government and sovereignty.

2. Name the authorities that are included under the ambit of Article 12 of the Indian Constitution.

Ans. According to the Article 12 of the Indian Constitution, state includes the following

- The Government and the Parliament of India, i.e. the Union, Legislature and Executive.
- The Government and Legislature of each state, i.e. Executive and Legislature of state.
- All local and other authorities within the territory of India.
- All local and other authorities under the control of the Government of India.

3. "Men are social animals. They live in association with each other. These associations are formed due to relationships/bonds created by marriage, birth, common language or religious beliefs and common goals". **Competency Based Que**

(i) **In the light of the statement, explain the emergence of the state from society.**

(ii) **Explain territory as an important element to constitute a state.**

Ans. (i) For answer, refer to text under the heading the Emergence of the State from Society, on page no. 2 and 3.

(ii) A state is a territorial institution. The fixed territory and population of a state gives it a physical identity in the view of municipal law (or domestic law) and international law.

The first thing to be exercised in a given territory are the functions of a state as a political and legal community of human beings.

4. Radical feminists around the world, emphasised that patriarchal states are resultant of gender inequality. Briefly discuss the patriarchal and matriarchal theories with respect to the origin of the state. **Competency Based Que**

Ans. For answer, refer to text under the heading Patriarchal and Matriarchal Theories, on page no. 4.

5. Hobbes' Social Contract theory is criticised by R.G. Gettle'. Analyse. **Competency Based Que**

Ans. Hobbes' theory was criticised by R.G. Gettle in the following ways

- Hobbes created an all-powerful sovereign on the belief that law, order, peace and security could not be maintained in society without such sovereign power.
- He deprived the people of their right to revolt against the sovereign.
- He allowed individuals to disobey the commands only when the sovereignty deprived individuals of their right to self-preservation.
- He did not maintain the difference between state and government as a political institution.
- He believed that a change in the government led to the dissolution of the state.

6. John Locke (1632-1704) in his book, 'Two Treatises of Government' explained that the state of nature was not a state of war, but a state of peace, natural rights, preservation, goodwill and mutual assistance. In the light of the statement, state the features of Locke's theory. **Competency Based Que**

Ans. The features of Locke's theory are

(i) His state of nature was pre-political where people were social and had rights and liberties.

(ii) The state of nature ensured three rights to individuals relating to life, liberty and property.

(iii) There were inconveniences in the state of nature, where men considered them as judges in their own disputes.

(iv) According to John Locke, two contracts were made to preserve a state of affairs, which were social and governmental. The two contracts are-social contract and government contract.

7. What are the features of Rousseau's Social Contract theory?

Ans. The features of Rousseau's Social Contract theory are

(i) Rousseau regarded the general will of the people as sovereign.

(ii) Individuals surrender their rights to the general will of which individuals themselves were a part. Thus, they shared the rights even after transferring them.

(iii) Individuals were governed by a new authority in the name of general will (common good) of the people in the form of direct democracy.

(iv) The common good depends upon the prevailing circumstances in the society.

(v) According to him, the government is merely the tool to execute the popular will.

(vi) Sovereignty remain in continuous exercise and there is no scope of revolt in his theory.

8. "The Government is the sum total of Legislative, Executive and Judicial activities of a state".

(i) What is the role of government?

(ii) What are the other three elements of state? **Competency Based Que**

Ans. (i) The roles of government are

- The government of a state makes provisions for the services of defence, foreign relations, levy of taxes, issue of currency, building of roads, bridges, transportation, communication, water supply, electricity, health education, and other types of social and physical infrastructure.
- The government of a state enforces law to maintain order, peace and security.

(ii) The other three elements of state include

(a) Sovereignty (b) Territory (c) Population

9. Ramesh, a resident of a small village, was struggling to make ends meet. He was working as a daily wage laborer and was finding it difficult to provide for his family. The government intervened and established a minimum wage system, provided pension and education facilities, and also initiated social security schemes for the elderly and disabled.

(i) What role did the government play in Ramesh's life?

(ii) What functions did it perform as a welfare state? **Competency Based Que**

Ans. (i) The government played a crucial role in Ramesh's life by establishing a minimum wage system, providing pension and education facilities, and initiating social security schemes.

(ii) As a welfare state, the government performed various functions, including the protection of workers, provision of social security, and promotion of social unity and harmony. The government's intervention improved Ramesh's standard of living and provided him with a sense of security and dignity.

Long Answer Type Questions

1. In a debate organised in a law school, a group of students were agruing and trying to explain the origin of state, though there was no valid answer regarding the same. Like them, political philosophers and thinkers have also tried and attempted to trace out and explain the origin of the state in various methods. There were various beliefs regarding the origin of the state, some believe that the origin of the state lie in the hands of God whereas others believe that they are based on social contract and some trust on single force, the family, etc.

(i) Explain the origin of the state by the "Hands of God". **Competency Based Que**

(ii) How is population an important element of state?

(iii) What are the functions of a government in a state?

Ans. (i) The origin of the State by the "Hands of God" is based on the divine theory of State. It states that state is established and governed by God and the king as its agent to rule over its subjects.

(ii) Population is an essential element of a state as it is the people who make a state and without them, there can be no state. The people also maintain the resources, live on the land, and form the government. The population must be large enough to make a state and sustain it.

(iii) The functions of a government in a state are

- Government is the political and administrative organ of a State. The state operates through its government.
- The government is the sum total of Legislative, Executive and Judicial activities of a state.
  It also includes internal bodies and sub-state governing authorities at the local and regional levels, such as the Municipal Corporations, Municipal Councils, Panchayats and Gram Sabhas in India.
- The government of a state makes provisions for the services of defense, foreign relations, levy of taxes, issue of currency, building of roads, bridges, transportation, communication, water supply, electricity, health education, and other types of social and physical infrastructure.
- The government of a state shall be so organised that it enforces law to maintain order, peace and security.

2. How does social contract theory explain the origin of the state? Briefly describe the theories of different thinkers of social contract tradition as far as the state of nature and need of social contract is concerned.

Ans. The social contract theory traces the origin of the state to the mutual agreement and mutual consent of the people to form a state. According to social contract theory, individuals enter into a social contract to escape from the pre-political condition of society.

This theory established the obedience to political authority and that ultimate political authority rested with the consent of the people. The pre-political condition of mankind was described as the state of nature.

Three different thinkers of social contract tradition described the reality of state of nature and need of social contract in three different ways. These are Thomas Hobbes, John Locke and Jean-Jacques Rousseau.

For explanation of 'Social Contract Theories' of these thinkers, refer to text on page no. 5.

3. He characterised the pre-social phase as the 'State of nature' in which human lives were in constant struggle with nature. It was a state of perpetual (constant) war 'Where every man was enemy to every other man'. The life of a human being was 'solitary, poor, nast, brutish and short'. **Competency Based Que**

(i) Identify who is being talked about in the paragraph given above?

(ii) What do you understand by the concept of social contract?

(iii) What are the views of the given personality about social contract theory?

Ans. (i) The political philosopher Thomas Hobbes is being talked about in the given paragraph.

(ii) According to the social contract theory, the mutual agreement and mutual consent of the people are required to form a state.

(iii) Thomas Hobbes and John Locke from England and Jean Jacques Rousseau from France are the propounders of this theory. According to them, to escape from the pre-political condition of society, individuals entered into a social contract.

For answer refer to the text under the heading Thomas Hobbes and His Social Contract Theory, on page no. 5 and 6.

SELF ASSESSMENT TEST

Objective Type Questions

1. Who defines state as "The political system of a body of people who are politically organised; the system of rules by which jurisdiction and authority are exercised over such a body of people"?
   (a) Salmond (b) Black (c) Laski (d) Plato
2. What does territory of the state include?
   (a) Internal waters (b) Airspace (c) Land (d) All of these
3. .... is the hallmark of the state.
   (a) Government (b) Sovereignty (c) Society (d) None of these
4. Under which articles are Fundamental Rights contained?
   (a) Articles 12-35 (b) Articles 10-35 (c) Articles 1-5 (d) None of these
5. Mater familias is a concept defined under which among the following?
   (a) Matriarchal theory (b) Patriarchal theory (c) Both (a) and (b) (d) None of these

Very Short Answer Type Questions

6. Name some sub-state governing authorities at the local and regional levels.
7. Who are the proponents of the following theories of origin of the state?
   (i) Patriarchal theory
   (ii) Divine theory
8. State any two assumptions of the patriarchal theory.
9. 'Matriarchal state is based on the basis of equality'. Justify the statement. **Competency Based Que**

Short Answer Type Questions

10. Is Article 12 a Fundamental Right in itself? Justify.
11. State the three difference between state and government.
12. In the Mosuo community, women are the heads of households and inherit property. Men reside in their mother's or sister's household, playing a significant role in childcare and household chores. Women control economic decisions and children are raised collectively. Men's roles are fluid, with no formed authority or ownership. **Competency Based Que**
13. Briefly discuss Locke's Social Contract theory.
14. There are two kinds of sovereignty. Explain. **Competency Based Que**
15. Write three differences between territory and government.

Long Answer Type Questions

16. Explain in detail Thomas Hobbes, John Locke and Rousseau's understanding of the social contract and origin of the state.
17. Which theory, according to you, is the most convincing in historically explaining the origin of the state? Give reasons for your answer.
18. How is state defined differently by different thinkers? What are the essential elements of a state and of a nation?

02 CHAPTER

Forms and Organs of the Government

Government is a set of institutions which exercises control through legal devices and imposes penalties on those who break the law.

▼ **YOUR STUDY GOALS**

▼ **YOUR PRACTICE GOAL**

- Objective Type Questions (29 Qs ; MCQs, A-R, Statements, Matching)
- Subjective Questions (8 VSAs, 16 SAs, 3 LAs)

Government is an essential element of state and carries out its functions. **State remains constant while the government changes** from time to time. The policies of the state which are mentioned in the Constitution, are implemented by the government.

In modern democracies, **governments are not above the law.** They exercise their power within the permissible limits as mentioned in the Constitution (the supreme law of the country). For example, the Indian Government cannot make any law which violates the Fundamental Rights of the people.

2.1 Forms of Government

A government can be of various types. They are

Monarchy

- The form of government which is **ruled by a single person** (called monarch) is known as monarchy.
- Monarchy is the **oldest form of government.** In a monarchy, the state machinery functioned according to the orders and rule of the monarch. In this form of government, **the will of the monarch ultimately prevails** in all matters of governance.

- According to **J.W. Garner** (1871-1938), "Any government in which the supreme and final authority is in the hands of a single person is a monarchy, without regard to the source of his election or the nature and duration of his tenure".
- In a monarchy, the king's son succeeds him and the right to rule remains in the family. Monarchs generally surround themselves with people and advisors who help them to perform their functions.
- The monarchial form of government declined with the development of republican and democratic forms of government. For example, in the United Kingdom, monarchs are only retained as **'ceremonial'**[1] head with no real political power.
- According to **C.C. Rodee,** "Constitutional monarchs are loved and respected by their people as the symbols of unity of the nation or empire, but are **devoid**[2] of political power".

Aristocracy

- The form of government which is ruled by **a small group of people or few people,** is known as aristocracy.
- The word 'Aristocracy' originates from two Greek words, **aristo** which means 'the best' and **kratein,** which means 'to rule'.
- According to **Garner**, aristocracy is the form of government "In which relatively a small portion of citizens have a voice in choosing public officials and in determining public policies".
- In an aristocratic form of government, political power in the state is controlled by a few people.
- This small group of people is chosen from among the people of the state on different basis, such as wealth (land owning class), education (nobles), religious positions (priestly class), family, succession, physical force, etc. The ruler is considered as a class which is separate and superior from the ruled.

Dictatorship

- The form of government in which a **single person** (called dictator) exercises complete authority over others **with the help of military** is known as dictatorship.
- According to **Alfred Cobban** (1901-1968), "It is the **government of one man** who has not obtained the position by inheritance, but either by **force or consent** or a combination of both".
- The dictator controls and exercises the political powers of the state. Like a monarch, a dictator does not come to power through elections, instead he occupies the position by force, invasion, intervention and militarism. The orders of the dictator are the laws of the land. He puts them into action and makes decisions based on his will.
- The dictator holds **absolute power**. He is not accountable or answerable to the citizens of the state. Thus, citizens are deprived of their human rights, personal liberty, etc. Totalitarian state is an example of modern dictatorship.

Democracy

- According to **Abraham Lincoln** (1809-1865), a former President of the US, democracy is a **government of the people, by the people and for the people.**
- 'Government of the people' means equal distribution of political powers and influence among the citizens of the state. 'Government by the people' means participation of all citizens in forming a government. 'Government for the people' means the rule of government for the promotion of public welfare.

1 **Ceremonial** It means of a post or role conferring or involving only nominal authority of power.
2 **Devoid** It means entirely lacking or free from.

- The word, 'democratic' originated from the Greek word, **Demos meaning people** and **Kratia meaning rule,** i.e. rule by a popular vote. This form of government is the most popular form in the modern civilised states.
- Some other definitions of democracy are
  - According to Greek leader, **Pericles** (495-429 BC), democracy is a form of government in which people are powerful.
  - According to **Bryce** democratic form of government is one where the ruling power of the state was vested not in a particular class or classes but in the community as a whole.

Types of Democracy

There are two types of democracy as

(i) Direct or Pure Democracy

- According to **Garner,** "A pure democracy so called is one in which the will of the state is formulated or expressed directly and immediately through the people in mass meetings or primary assembly, rather than through the medium of delegates or representatives chosen to act for them".
- In a direct democracy, people exercise their power directly. They vote in open assemblies on different issues.
- In this form of democracy, there are three forms of popular action. These are
  - **Initiative** It means by which a specified number of voters prepare a bill for acceptance or approval by legislature or general public.
  - **Referendum** It means by which the bill passed by the legislature is forwarded to the voters for final ratification[3].
  - **Plebiscite** It means by which an important issue is decided by the votes of the people, instead of the government.
- Direct or pure form of democracy is not possible for the states which have a large population and territory.
- In this kind of democracy, the following steps are followed
  - First, laws are prepared in a draft form.
  - Second, this draft goes to people for an opinion poll.
  - The result of opinion poll is discussed in the Parliament and then, the law is made accordingly. All laws are subject to the veto[4] power of the people.
- Direct or pure democracy was practiced in **Greek city state, Athens** during 4th and 5th century BC.
- It was also practiced in Rome during the early stages of the Roman polity as an ideal system of popular participation. In contemporary times, it is practiced in Switzerland.

(ii) Indirect or Representative Democracy

- According to Garner, "This kind of democracy resembles its pure form in the sense that **political power remains vested in the people,** but the two differ in respect to their exercise".
- This form of government is based on universal suffrage i.e. citizens of the country elect their representatives on the basis of votes.
- The representatives establish a law-making and law-enforcing agency for a specific period of time. The representatives are answerable and accountable to the general public on the matters of governance.

---

3 Ratification It means the action of signing or giving formal consent to a treaty, contract or agreement making it officially valid.
4 Veto It means a Constitutional Right to reject a decision or proposal made by a law-making body.

- In case the laws violated the Constitutional provisions, people have an option to move to the Supreme Court for getting declared such laws as void. There is no provision for referendum or plebiscite in this form of democracy.
- All the citizens of the state have equal opportunity of participation in the political affairs of the state as in this form of democracy as compared to monarchy or dictatorial form of government.

Forms of Democratic Systems

- Basically, there are two forms of democratic government systems i.e. Presidential form of government and Parliamentary form of government.

(i) Parliamentary Form of Government

- In this form of government, the legislature and the executive are related to each another through membership in the two bodies and their accountability.
- The executive is accountable to the legislature while implementing laws and discharging its responsibilities like health, education, food and public distribution, defence, and police services, among others.
- This form of government is termed as **cabinet government** by **Sir Ivor Jennings** (1903–65), an English academic and lawyer, and Prime Ministerial government by **Richard Crossman** (1907–74), an English author and politician.
- According to **Professor M.P. Jain,** the principle of collective responsibility is an important principle of this form of government. It represents the ministerial accountability to the legislature. This principle means that Council of Minister works as a unit and is responsible for the general conduct of the government affairs.
- India and the United Kingdom both have Parliamentary form of government.

(ii) Presidential Form of Government

- According to **Garner**, Presidential government is that form of government in which the chief executive is independent of the legislature as to his tenure and, to a large extent, as to his policies and acts.
- In this system, the real executive is also the nominal head of state.
- In this form of government, the President is elected by the people, either directly or indirectly, for a pre-determined period of time, unless he/she is impeached by the legislature on the grounds mentioned in the country's Constitution. This form of government works on the principles of **checks and balances** and **separation of powers.**
- Argentina and the United States of America both have Presidential from of government.

Difference between Parliamentary and Presidential form of Government

Parliamentary form of Government	Presidential form of Government
The President is indirectly elected.	People directly elect the President.
The President is the nominal head of the state while the Prime Minister is the head of the government as well as the state.	The President is the real head of the state and the government.
The Prime Minister and the Council of Ministers are answerable to the legislature.	The President and the secretaries are not answerable to the legislature.
The Council of Ministers may be removed by a no-confidence motion in the Parliament before the expiry of his term.	President can only be removed by the process of impeachment before the expiry of his/her term.

Parliamentary form of Government	Presidential form of Government
The powers of the Prime Minister are limited in the choice of ministers. He/She can only choose from the members of the Parliament.	The President has very wide powers and can appoint anyone in the government.
This form of government is found in the UK and India.	This form of government is found in USA and Argentina.

Democratic Systems on the basis of Distribution Powers

On the basis of distribution of powers between the centre and states, there are two forms of democratic government i.e. **Federal and Unitary** form of government. These are discussed below

(i) Unitary Form of Government

- In this form of government, the state along with its provinces and units, is **governed by a single Central Government**. The Central Government establishes local and provincial governments as subordinates for better administration. It gives the powers and authority to the local or provincial governments.
- According to Garner, in this form of government, there is no Constitutional division or distribution of powers between the Central Government and sub-ordinate local governments of the state.

(ii) Federal Form of Government

- This is a form of government, in which all the governmental powers are divided or distributed between a Central Government and the governments of individual states.
- The issues of national significance, such as international relations, war and peace, atomic energy, etc that are included in the **Seventh Schedule**[5] of the Indian Constitution is managed by the Central Government.
- The State Governments have the power to enact legislation regarding the issues of importance to the region and the community that are included in the state list.
- The Central and State Governments are both authorised to make laws on the matters included in **concurrent list**.
- Local and provincial governments are regarded as a part of the federal government but have complete autonomy.
- The Indian Constitution has adopted federal features but it does claim to establish India into a federation of states. Thus, according to **K.C. Wheare**, India's system of government is federal in character and unitary in spirit.

Difference between Unitary and Federal form of Government

Unitary Form of Government	Federal Form of Government
The centre has great authority whereas states have lesser autonomy in a unitary system of government.	The centre has lesser powers whereas the states have greater autonomy.
Powers were concentrated in one single authority.	Power was divided between the centre and states.
This system provided for single citizenship.	This system provided for dual citizenship.
Its examples are UK, France, Italy and Japan.	Its examples are USA and Canada.

5 **Seventh Schedule** of Indian Constitution defines the division of power between the Union and State Governments.

Quick Test 1

1 Name the nation where monarchs are only retained as 'ceremonial' head.
2 Which form of government is a rule by few people?
3 How 'Totalitarian' is one form of dictatorship in the modern world?
4 Name any two countries where the Parliamentary form of government is found.

2.2 Main Organs of the Government

Government generally functions by distributing its functions between its three organs i.e. Legislature, Executive and Judiciary.

A government achieves the purpose of a state by performing these functions as they constitute the minimal requirements of any form of government. This system of distribution of powers is called **separation of powers.**

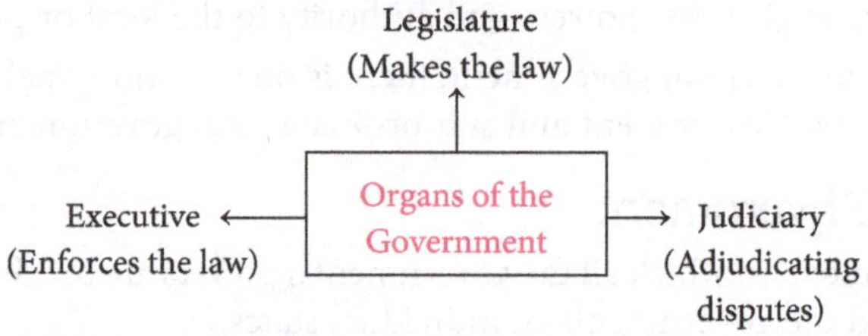

The functions of the organs of the government are

Composition of the Legislature

In a democracy, the legislature can either be unicameral or bicameral. These are discussed below

Bicameral Legislature

- In a bicameral legislature, there are **two houses or chambers.** Indian Parliament is a bicameral legislature, consisting of two houses, i.e. **House of People** (Lok Sabha) and **Council of States** (Rajya Sabha).
- The members of the Lok Sabha consists of the representatives of citizens of entire country, who are directly elected by the people. The members of Rajya Sabha consists of the representatives elected by the Legislative Assemblies of the states and other nominated members from the field of art, culture, academics, sports, literature science and social service.
- The purpose and functions of Rajya Sabha are to check quick and ill-considered legislations with advice of experts and eminent person. This makes possible to examine issues from different perspectives and to safeguard the interests of states in a federal system.
- In the states of the Indian Union, the legislature consists of the **Vidhan Sabha** (lower house) and **Vidhan Parishad** (upper house). There are **6 states** which have a bicameral legislature, they are Andhra Pradesh, Bihar, Karnataka, Maharashtra, Telangana and Uttar Pradesh.

Unicameral Legislature

- In a unicameral system, there is only one house of the legislature. It is cost-effective and suitable for countries with a smaller population. This system of legislature is present in Turkey, by the name of Grand National Assembly of Turkey and in Bangladesh by the name of House of Nation, etc.
- This system is supported by the reason that the legislative body representing people's interest must be one, and if this fails, then delays and conflicts may arise in the enactment of legislation.

- There are **24 states** which have a unicameral legislature. These are Arunachal Pradesh, Assam, Chhattisgarh, Delhi, Goa, Gujarat, Haryana, Himachal Pradesh, Jharkhand, Kerala, Madhya Pradesh, Manipur, Meghalaya, Mizoram, Nagaland, Odisha, Puducherry, Punjab, Rajasthan, Sikkim, Tamil Nadu, Tripura, Uttarakhand and West Bengal.

Facts about the Parliament

- The Parliament of India is circular which represents 'continuity'.
- The Halls of two Houses of the Parliament i.e. Lok Sabha and Rajya Sabha are horse shoe in shape.
- The **green carpet** laying in Lok Sabha **represents agriculture.**
- The **red carpet** laying in Rajya Sabha **represents royalty and sacrifice done by the freedom fighters.**
- The library of the Parliament is second largest in India.
- The circumference of the Parliament is 1/3 of a mill, i.e. 536.33 m.

General Functions of Legislature

In various nations, the term Legislature is used interchangeably with the terms Parliament, Assembly and Congress. Parliament means meeting for discussion.

Following are the functions of legislature

- **Law-making Function** The primary function of the Legislature is to make the laws. The Legislature amends and repeals the outdated laws and also makes new laws to meet the present requirements. Laws, when enacted by the legislature, are called **Acts.** These acts are the direct source of law to control and regulate the institutions running in a state and society. All legislations are enacted for the achievement of certain objectives and purposes. For example, the Indian Legislature enacted the Consumer Protection Act, 1986. This act was replaced by the Consumer Protection Act, 2019, with the purpose of protecting the interest of consumers and the speedy settlement of their disputes.

Parliamentary Procedure and Enactment of Laws

- A bill is a statute in draft that cannot become law until it has been approved by both the Houses of Parliament and received the President's assent. When a bill is introduced by a minister, it is known as a **Government Bill;** whereas when a bill is introduced by a member other than minister, then it is known as a **Private Member's Bill.**
- In the case of introduction and passing of ordinary bills, the Indian Constitutions **Articles 107-108** outline the procedure for introducing and passing bills and in the case of money bills, **Articles 109 and 110** outline this procedure. The specifics of the Presidents assent to bills are outlined in **Article 111.**
- Ordinary bills may originate in either House of the Parliament. A money bill, on the other hand, can only be introduced in the House of People (Lok Sabha), not the Council of States (Rajya Sabha).
- A money bill includes
  - the imposition, abolition, modification, or regulation of any tax.
  - custody of the Consolidated Fund or Contingency Fund of India.
  - payment into money or withdrawal of money from any such fund and other related matters.
- The government's estimated receipts and expenditures for the following fiscal year are presented in the Annual Financial Statement each year. According to **Article 112** of the Indian Constitution, the President ensures the statement to be presented to both Houses of the Parliament. The provisions of the proposed bill are discussed by the members of the Parliament. A bill is **generally passed after three readings.**

- **Ensures Accountability of the Executive** According to **Article 75(3)** of the Indian Constitution, the Council of Ministers are collectively accountable to the House of the People. The Parliament checks and ensures the executive and administrative accountability through its control over finances. It assesses the policies of the government and performance of administration through procedures like questions, calling attention motion, etc.

In the Lok Sabha, the motion of no-confidence can be moved and passed against the Council of Ministers.

- **Judicial Functions** The legislature acts as a judge in impeachment cases (removal from office before the end of a term). The procedure for impeaching the Chief Election Commissioner, judges of the Supreme Court and High Court, the President and Vice-President of India is outlined in the Indian Constitution. It also performs judicial function when it decides on the privileges of the Members of the House.
- **Electoral and Administrative Functions** The Speaker and Deputy Speaker of Lok Sabha are elected by the members of Lok Sabha amongst them. The Deputy Chairman of Rajya Sabha is elected by the member of Rajya Sabha.
- In India, an electoral college[6] is formed by the elected members of both Houses of Parliament and Legislative Assemblies of the states, to elect the President. The Vice-President is elected by an electoral college consisting of the elected member of both the Houses of Parliament.
- **Expressing and Formulating the Will of the State** The legislature formulates and expresses the will of the state. In a representative democracy, the will of the state is the opinion and sentiments of its citizens and the public issues concerning them.

General Functions of Executive

Executive is often referred to as the 'government' of a state. In a representative democracy, the term executive has a broad meaning. It executes or implements the laws made by the legislature or interpreted by the judiciary. Following are the functions of executive

- **Internal and External Administration of the State** The main function of the executive is the maintenance of internal and external administration.
  - Internal administration include
    - (i) maintenance of law and order
    - (ii) financial matters
    - (iii) infrastructure and industrial development
    - (iv) welfare and development of the people (health, education, labour, employment, rural and local development)
    - (v) environment and forests
    - (vi) natural resource management
    - (vii) trade and commerce
  - External administration includes defence, foreign affairs, international relations, etc.
- **Legislative Functions** The executive performs the following legislative functions
  - **Delegated Legislation** It is an enactment made by an individual or body other than Parliament. Executive can frame orders, rules, regulations, ordinances, by-laws[7] and circulars. They carry equal force of law if framed within the sphere and policy of the parent legislation.
  - **Ordinance** The executive has the power to issue ordinances when the Parliament is not in session. Under **Article 123** of the Constitution of India, the President has the power to promulgate an ordinance during the recess of Parliament.

    An ordinance is a law that is made by the President of India only when the Indian Parliament is not in session. The President make an ordinance on the recommendation of the union cabinet. Immediate legislative actions can be taken using ordinances. However, it must be noted that for an ordinance to exist, it should be approved by the Parliament **within six weeks** of being introduced. The Parliament is required to sit within 6 weeks from when the ordinance was introduced.

6 Electoral college is a body of electors chosen or appointed by a larger group.
7 By-laws are generally what institution or a community defines for its governance and these are the rules to be followed by it's members.

- **Financial Functions** The executive imposes and collects taxes and incurs expenditure on the various activities of the state. It prepares the budget of the financial year, maintains accounts of government departments and prepares national policies. It also arranges financial grants from international entities like the International Monetary Fund, World Bank, etc.
- **Judicial Functions** The executive has the power to grant pardon (Presidential), to suspend or lessen the punishment on special grounds,

General Functions of Judiciary

Following are the functions of judiciary

- **To Hear and Decide Disputes** The main function of the judiciary is to hear and decide a case, according to the laws of the land. Disputes may arise among citizens of a state, between citizens and state, among the federal units, between the various departments of the executive and in international relations. They call for intervention by the judiciary. Judiciary is required to be independent from the political influence or interference, in order to settle disputes and pass judgement. Impartial and time bound justice delivery are essential requirements for the judiciary.
- **Power of Judicial Review** Judicial review is a type of court proceeding in which a judge reviews or examines the legal validity of a decision/action, made by a government body. The judiciary can examine legislative enactments (approved) and executive orders.

  It can declare the order invalid if it violates the provisions of the Constitution. The power granted to the judiciary by the Constitution is judicial review.
- **Interpretation of Laws** Judges determine the meaning of a law made by the legislature, wherever it is confusing or not clear, or appears to be inconsistent with other laws of the land. The meaning given by the judiciary to the statutory law is considered final and binding on the parties.
- **Advisor to the President** The Supreme Court has special advisory jurisdiction in matters, which may be referred by the President of India to the Supreme Court under **Article 143** of the Constitution.
- **Role of Judiciary as an Activist** In India, the first instance of the activist role of the judiciary was seen after the emergency, when the **Supreme Court introduced Public Interest Litigation (PIL)** a tool meant to ensure justice for the under-privileged and the marginalised.
- **Legislative and executlive function** The judiciary has been given powers to frame rules and execute them for the smooth functioning of its own administration. This is also done to ensure independence of the judiciary.

Judiciary and Its Jurisdiction

- Judiciary refers to the set of courts having civil and criminal jurisdiction. Tribunals and various forms have also become part of the conventional judicial system, with the expansion and diversification of state and its agencies, and expansion of arbitration and conciliation.
- Such as the motor accident claim Tribunal and Redresal forms under the Consumer Protection Act, 1986.
- The judiciary exercises jurisdiction on the basis of territorial limits, pecuniary/financial limits, appealable matters, matters for review and revision. The judiciary consists of Magisterial Courts, District and Sub-District Courts at the lower level and the higher judiciary comprising High Courts and the Supreme Court. Decisions given by them is known as **judgement, decree, order** or **award.**

Quick Test 2

1. Name the four states of India where bicameral structure of legislature exists.
2. Name any one primary function of a State Legislature.
3. What do you understand by a government bill?
4. In which circumstances, the executive has the power to issue ordinance?
5. On what basis, judiciary exercises it's jurisdiction?

Mind Map

FORMS AND ORGANS OF THE GOVERNMENT

1 Definition and Forms of Government

- Government is a set of institutions that exercises control through legal devices and imposes penalties on lawbreakers.
- It is an essential element of the state, carrying out its functions while the state remains constant.

Forms of Government

- Governments can take various forms, including monarchy, aristocracy, dictatorship and democracy.
- Each form has distinct characteristics and methods of government.

Monarchy

- A monarchy is ruled by a single person, known as a monarch, and is considered the oldest form of government.
- Monarchs often inherit their position, and their authority prevails in governance.

Aristocracy

- Aristocracy is governed by a small group of people, often based on wealth, education, or social status.
- This form of government emphasises the rule the 'best' or elite class.

Dictatorship

- In a dictatorship, a single individual or a small group holds absolute power, often obtained through force rather than election.
- Dictators are not accountable to the public, leading to the suppression of individual rights.

Democracy

- Democracy is defined as government by the people, for the people, and of the people, emphasising equal participation in governance.
- It can be further divided into direct and indirect (representative) democracy.

Types of Democracy

- **Direct Democracy** Citizens directly participate in decision-making, often through referendums or plebiscites
- **Indirect Democracy** Citizens elect representatives to make decisions on behalf, which is more practical for larger their populations.

2 Forms of Democratic Systems

Parliamentary Form of Government

- In a Parliamentary system, the executive is accountable to the legislature, and the two branches are interconnected
- The Prime Minister is the head of government, while the President serves as the nominal head of state.

Presidential Form of Government

- The Presidential system features a clear separation between the executive and legislative branches.
- The President is elected independently and holds significant powers, including the ability to appoint officials.

Democratic Systems on the basis of Distribution Powers

Unitary Form of Government

- A unitary government is governed by a single central authority, with local governments acting as subordinates .
- There is no Constitutional division of powers, allowing for centralised decision-making.

Federal Form of Government

- In a federal system, powers are divided between a Central Government and individual State Governments.
- Both levels of government can legislate on concurrent matters, allowing for regional autonomy.

3 Main Organs of the Government

Overview of Government Function

- The government functions through three main organs: Legislature, Executive and Judiciary.
- This distribution of powers is known as the separation of powers, which is crucial for maintaining checks and balance.

Legislature

- The Legislature is responsible for making laws and can be unicameral or bicameral.
- In a bicameral legislature, there are two houses. such as the Indian Parliament, which consists of the Lok Sabha and Rajya Sabha.

Functions of the Legislature

- Law-making
- Financial
- Deliberative
- Electoral

Executive

- The Executive enforces laws and administers the state .
- It is responsible for both internal and external administration, including law and order, defense and foreign affairs.

Functions of the Executive

- **Internal Administration** Maintains law and order, manages financial matters, and oversees welfare programmes.
- **Legislative Function** Can issue ordinances when Parliament is not in session, allowing immediate legislative action.
- **Financial Functions** Imposes and collects tax\es, expenditures, prepares the budget, and manages government expenditures.
- **Judicial Functions** Has the power to grant pardons and suspend punishments unspecific circumstances.

Judiciary

- The Judiciary interprets laws and resolves disputes, ensuring justice is served.
- It operates independently from the other branches of government to maintain impartiality.

Function of Judiciary

- **Dispute Resolution** Hears and decides cases based on the laws of the land.
- **Judicial Review** Examines the legality of legislative and executive actions, ensuring they comply with the Constitution.
- **Interpretation of Laws** Clarifies the meaning of laws, providing final and binding interpretations.
- **Protection of Rights** Safeguards the fundamental rights of citizens against violations by other government organs .

4 Conclusion

- Understanding the forms and organs of government is essential for comprehending how political power is structured and exercised in different countries.
- Each form of government has its unique characteristics, advantages, and challanges influencing the governance and rights of citizens.

CBSE TEXTBOOK FOLDER

1. Provide one point of difference between the following

(i) Monarchy and democracy

(ii) Parliamentary and Presidential form of government

(iii) Direct and indirect democracy

(iv) Lok Sabha and Rajya Sabha

(v) Unicameral and bicameral legislature

Ans. (i)

Monarchy	Democracy
The monarch is not answerable to the people for his actions.	The government is accountable to the people for all its actions and policies.

(ii)

Presidential Form of Government	Parliamentary Form of Government
People directly elect the President and he/she is the real head of the state.	The President is indirectly elected and he/she is the nominal head of the state.

(iii)

Direct Democracy	Indirect Democracy
In a direct democracy, people exercise their sovereignty and powers directly and vote in open assemblies on different issues.	In an indirect democracy, people exercise their sovereignty and powers indirectly, through their chosen representatives.

(iv)

Lok Sabha	Rajya Sabha
The members of the Lok Sabha consists of the representatives of citizens of entire country ,who are directly elected by people.	The members of Rajya Sabha consists of the representatives elected by the legislative assemblies of the states and other nominated members.

(v)

Unicameral Legislature	Bicameral Legislature
In unicameral legislature, there is only one chamber/body that makes law/policy.	In bicameral legislature, there are two chambers/bodies that makes law/policy.

2. Give an example for the following

(i) A country where a unicameral legislature exists.

(ii) A country where Presidential form of government prevails.

(iii) A country where the monarch enjoys the absolute power.

(iv) A country where direct democracy exists.

(v) A country where constitutional monarchy exists.

Ans. (i) Turkey (ii) USA (iii) Saudi Arabia

(iv) Switzerland (v) UK

3. Write brief notes on the following

(i) Money Bill

(ii) Annual Financial Statement.

(iii) Democracy

(iv) Unitary form of Government

(v) Judicial function of Executive

Ans. (i) **Money Bill** A money bill contains provision for imposition, abolition, alteration or regulation of any tax, custody of the consolidated fund or contingency fund of India, payment of money into or withdrawal of money from any such fund and related matters. However, a money bill shall be introduced only in the House of People and not in the Council of States.

(ii) **Annual Financial Statement** It is the annual statement of estimated receipts and expenditure of the government for ensuring the financial year. Article 112 of the Constitution of India states that the President shall cause the statement to be laid before both the houses of Parliament. Generally, a bill is passed after three readings

(iii) The word, 'democratic' originated from the Greek word, Demos meaning people and Kratia meaning rule, i.e. rule by a popular vote. According to Abraham Lincoln (1809-1865), democracy is a government of the people, by the people and for the people.

(iv) In unitary form of government, the state along with its provinces and units, is governed by a single Central Government. The Central Government establishes local and provincial governments as sub-ordinates for better administration.

(v) The judicial functions of the executive include power to grant pardon (Presidential), to suspend or lessen the punishment on special grounds, or to exchange one form of punishment for another on the petition of a person who is convicted of any offence by the court.

4. Explain the role of the following organs of government.

(i) Legislature (ii) Executive (iii) Judiciary

Ans. (i) A legislature primarily performs the following functions

- **Law-making Functions** The primary role of the legislature is to make the laws. The legislature amends and repeals the outdated laws and also makes new laws to meet the present requirements. Laws, when enacted by the legislature, are called 'Acts'. These acts are the direct source of law to control and regulate the institutions running in a state and society.
- **Deliberative Function** The legislature also deliberates or discusses the bills before they become laws.
- **Financial Functions** The legislature acts as the manager of the financial requirements of the nation. Money or taxes can neither be collected nor spent by the government without approval of the legislature.
- **Electoral Functions** The Speaker and Deputy Speaker of Lok Sabha are elected by the members of Lok Sabha amongst them. The Deputy Chairman of Rajya Sabha is elected by the member of Rajya Sabha.
- **Judicial Functions** The legislature performs judicial functions while hearing and trying cases of impeachment (removal from office before term).

(ii) The executive performs the following functions

- **Internal and External Administration of the State** The main function of the executive is the maintenance of internal and external administration. Internal administration include maintenance of law and order, financial matters, infrastructure and industrial development, welfare and development of the people (health, education, labour, employment, rural and local development), environment and forests, natural resource management, trade and commerce, etc. External administration include maintenance of defence, foreign affairs, international relations, etc.
- **Issue Ordinances** The executive has the power to issue ordinances when the Parliament is not in session. An ordinance is a law that is made by the President of India on the recommendation of the Union Cabinet and only when the Indian Parliament is not in session.
- However, it must be noted that for an ordinance to exist, it should be approved by the Parliament within six weeks of being introduced. Parliament is required to sit within 6 weeks from when the ordinance was introduced.

(iii) The primary functions of judiciary as an organ of the government are

- **To Hear and Decide Disputes** The first and the foremost function of the judiciary is to hear and decide a case, according to the laws of the land. The role of the judiciary is expanding with the expanding role of the executive. Disputes may arise among citizens of a state, between citizens and state, among the federal units, between the various departments of the executive and in international relations, calling for intervention by the judiciary.
- **Interpretation of Laws** Judges determine the meaning of a law made by the legislature wherever it is not clear. The meaning given by the judiciary to the statutory law is Considered final and binding on the parties.
- **Protecting the Rights of the People** Judiciary acts as the protector of the Fundamental Rights of the people. It ensures that constitutional rights of the people are not violated by any other organ of the government.
- **Safeguarding the Constitution** The judiciary also acts as the guardian of the Constitution. It is responsible for upholding the Constitution as the fundamental law of the land.

5. A country, Amerintina was governed by representatives on behalf of the citizens. Another country, Plicia was governed by the citizens themselves by various methods.

Identify the above two forms of government and differentiate between their processes. **Competency Based Que**

Ans. The two forms of the government as discussed in the passage are indirect democracy and direct democracy. The country Amerintina was governed by the process of indirect democracy wherein elected representatives of the people governed the state on their behalf. On the other hand, the country Plicia was governed through the process of direct democracy wherein the citizens themselves take part in decision-making.

Another major key difference between the direct and indirect forms of democracy is the speed at which decisions can be taken. In a direct democracy, decisions can be made quickly, as the people are directly involved in the process.

In contrast, in indirect democracy, there may be long delay in decision process, as they must be made by the representatives who have been elected by the people.

Exam Pattern Questions

Objective Type Questions

Multiple Choice Questions (MCQs)

1. The functions of the state are carried on by the ....

(a) Government (b) Legislature
(c) Judiciary (d) None of these

2. Which of the following is the oldest form of government?

(a) Monarchy (b) Democracy
(c) Aristocracy (d) All of these

3. A monarchy is a system of government where the head of the state is hereditary position, typically held for life.

Which of the following is TRUE regarding the characteristics of a monarchy? **Competency Based Que**

(a) A system of government where head of the state is elected for a fixed term.
(b) A system of government where the head of state is a hereditary position, but their powers are limited by Constitution.
(c) A system of government where the head of the state is a hereditary position, typically held for life, and has absolute powers.
(d) A system of government where the head of state is appointed by separate head of government.

4. Which of the following is the form of government in which relatively a small portion of citizens have a voice in choosing public officials and in determining public policies?

(a) Monarchy (b) Aristocracy
(c) Democracy (d) None of these

5. A state has a specific form of government where the ruler controls all aspects of the life of its citizens. The citizens do not have freedom of speech and expression and all the major and minor decisions pertaining to people are taken according to the whims and fancies of the ruler.

Which form of government is being talked about in the above described situation? **Competency Based Que**

(a) Monarchy (b) Aristocracy
(c) Dictatorship (d) Democracy

6. Who defined democracy as the "Government of the people, by the people, for the people"?

(a) Lincoln (b) Garner
(c) Laski (d) Aristotle

7. In a country 'X', people exercise their power directly. People vote in open assemblies on different issues. This is known as a referendum or plebiscite. The outcome of the voting here becomes the law. **Competency Based Que**

Identify which kind of democracy is being discussed here?

(a) Direct democracy
(b) Indirect democracy
(c) Aristocratic democracy
(d) None of the above

8. Which of the following countries does not follow a Parliamentary form of government?

(a) United States (b) United Kingdom
(c) India (d) Nepal

9. Under this form of government, the whole state with all its units and provinces is organised under a single Central Government. The local/provincial governments are created by the Central Government as its subordinates for better administration. The Central Government delegates powers and authority to the local/provincial government.

Which form of government is being talked about here?

(a) Federal (b) Unitary
(c) Presidential (d) Parliamentary

10. A bicameral legislature is a system of government where the legislative power is divided between two separate assemblies, typically an upper house and a lower house.

Which of the following is TRUE regarding the characteristic of bicameral legislature.

(a) A system of government where the legislative power is held by single assembly.
(b) A system of government where the legislative power is divided between two separate assemblies, with the upper house representing the interest of the people.
(c) A system of government where the legislative power is divided between two separate assemblies, with the upper house representing the interest of the state or regions.
(d) A system of government where the legislative power is held by executive branch.

11. In a country with bicameral legislature, there are two houses of the Legislative Assembly. The House of People (Lok Sabha) consists of the representatives of citizens of the entire country living in states and union territories. Council of States (Rajya Sabha) consists of the representatives elected by the Legislative Assemblies of the states, and other nominate members from the field of art, culture, academics, sports, literature science and social service. **Competency Based Que**

Which country is being talked about here?

(a) India (b) Nepal
(c) Bangladesh (d) Bhutan

12. Which of the following state does NOT have bicameral legislature?

(a) Andhra Pradesh
(b) Karnataka
(c) Maharashtra
(d) Uttarakhand

13. In which of the following countries legislature is known as House of Nation?

(a) Turkey (b) Ghana
(c) Romania (d) Bangladesh

14. Which among the given statements is TRUE about the separation of power in government?

(a) The legislature enforces the laws.
(b) The executive interprets the laws.
(c) The judiciary formulates laws.
(d) The legislature formulates and expresses the will of the state.

15. Which statement best reflects the responsibility to act as the guardian of the Constitution?

(a) The Judiciary interprets the Constitution and protects the Fundamental Rights.
(b) The Judiciary creates the political offices as these offices are the guardian of the Constitution.
(c) The Judiciary only secures, social justice, social equality to protect the rights of the people.
(d) The Judiciary regulates the institutions across the world to guard the Constitution.

16. There is a country which has bicameral legislature. The legislative organs has two houses called the House of Lords and the House of Commons. The House of Lords is the upper house while the House of Commons is the lower house. The country is a Constitutional monarchy where the head of the state is hereditary queen.

Identify the country which is being talked about here. **Competency Based Que**

(a) India (b) Bangladesh
(c) Iran (d) United Kingdom

17. Match the following.

Column I (Form of Government)	Column II (Description)
A. Monarchy	1. Rule by people
B. Aristocracy	2. Rule by a single person wearing a crown
C. Dictatorship	3. Political power in hands of few people
D. Democracy	4. Rule by dictator

Codes

	A	B	C	D		A	B	C	D
(a)	3	2	4	1	(b)	1	2	4	3
(c)	2	3	4	1	(d)	4	3	1	2

18. Match the following.

Column I (Form of Government)	Column II (Description)
A. Parliamentary Form	1. Executive is independent of legislature.
B. Unitary Form	2. All provincial units are under single Central Government.
C. Presidential Form	3. Power is divided between center and state.
D. Federal Form	4. Legislature and executive related to each other through Parliament.

Codes

	A	B	C	D		A	B	C	D
(a)	3	2	4	1	(b)	2	3	4	1
(c)	1	3	2	4	(d)	4	2	1	3

19. Match the following.

Column I (Organ of the Government)	Column II (Function)
A. Legislature	1. Adjudication of disputes
B. Executive	2. Enactment of laws
C. Judiciary	3. Maintenance of internal and external administration

Codes

	A	B	C		A	B	C
(a)	3	1	2	(b)	2	3	1
(c)	1	2	3	(d)	3	2	1

20. Arrange the marginal heading as per the Articles of the Constitution in chronological order .

I. Assent to bills by the President

II. Legislative procedure for introduction of ordinary bills

III. Legislative procedure for introduction of money bills

IV. Annual financial statement

Choose the correct option

(a) IV, I, III, II (b) II, III, I, IV
(c) I, II, III, IV (d) II, IV, III, I

21. Russia is a federal Semi-Presidential republic state. President Vladimir Putin is currently serving his fourth term as President of Russia. Putin forwarded a 2020 Constitutional Amendment enabling him to remain in power until 2036. Whether or not Putin is a dictator is a matter of some debate. Those who believe that he is a dictator argue that he imprisons his opponents, removed freedom of speech and has restructured the government to give himself long lasting power.

Identify the philosopher who supported and held that the state must have absolute powers and individuals have no right against the state? **Competency Based Que**

(a) Aristotle (b) Montesquieu
(c) Hegel (d) Pericles

22. Minister of transport has been granted the authority to create laws regarding road safety, as long as they are within the boundaries set by the road safety act. The minister creates a law requiring all drivers to wear seatbelts, which is within the scope of authority granted. **Competency Based Que**

What does this situation represent? Choose the correct option explaining the situation.

(a) An example of delegated, legislation, where the minister has been granted the authority to create laws within specified boundaries.
(b) An example of judicial review, where the minister's law is being reviewed by the courts.
(c) An example of legislative supremacy, where the minister has absolute power to create laws.
(d) An example of executive overreach where, the minister has exceeded their authority.

23. Consider the following statements.

Statement I Direct democracy is not possible in states with large populations and territories.

Statement II Representative democracy is based on universal suffrage, where citizens elect their representatives.

Which of the following is correct?

(a) Both the Statement are correct.
(b) Both the Statement are incorrect.
(c) Statement I is correct, but Statement II is not correct.
(d) Statement I is not correct, but Statement II is correct.

24. Consider the following statements.

Statement I In direct democracy, citizens elect their representatives to make decisions on their behalf.

Statement II In representative democracy, the will of the state is formulated and expressed through the representatives elected by the people.

Which of the following is correct?

(a) Both the Statement are correct.
(b) Both the Statement are incorrect.
(c) Statement I is correct, but Statement II is not correct.
(d) Statement I is not correct, but Statement II is correct.

Assertion-Reason Questions

Directions (Q. No. 25-29) In the questions given below, there are two statements. Read the statements and choose the correct option.

Codes

(a) Both A and R are true and R is the correct explanation of A.
(b) Both A and R are true, but R is not the correct explanation of A.
(c) A is true, but R is false.
(d) A is false, but R is true.

25. Assertion (A) Dictatorial form of government is the rule by a single person or a determined set of individuals.

Reason (R) Dictator controls and exercises the political powers of the state.

26. Assertion (A) Dictatorial form of government respects individual liberty.

Reason (R) In a democracy, people have a huge say in decision-making of the government.

27. Assertion (A) The United States has a Presidential form of government.

Reason (R) India has a Parliamentary form of government.

28. Assertion (A) Delegated legislation is an enactment made by an individual or body other than Parliament.

Reason (R) By delegating the power to make a legislation to the executive, the Parliament empowers different people or bodies to integrate more details to an act of Parliament.

29. Assertion (A) In a direct democracy, people exercise their power directly.

Reason (R) People vote in open assemblies on different issues.

Answers

1. (a) Government
2. (a) Monarchy
3. (b) A system of government where the head of state is a hereditary position, but their powers are limited by Constitution.
4. (b) Aristocracy
5. (c) Dictatorship
6. (a) Lincoln
7. (a) Direct democracy
8. (a) United States
9. (b) Unitary
10. (c) A system of government where the legislative power is divided between two separate assemblies, with the upper house representing the interest of the state or regions.
11. (a) India
12. (d) Uttarakhand
13. (d) Bangladesh
14. (d) The legislature formulates and expresses the will of the state.
15. (a) The Judiciary interprets the Constitution and protects the Fundamental Rights.
16. (d) United Kingdom
17. (c) 2 3 4 1
18. (d) 4 2 1 3
19. (b) 2 3 1
20. (b) II, III, I, IV
21. (c) Hegel
22. (a) An example of delegated legislation, where the minister has been granted the authority to create laws within specified boundaries.
23. (a) Both the Statements are correct.
24. (d) Statement I is not correct, but Statement II is correct.
25. (a) Both A and R are true and R is the correct explanation of A.
26. (d) A is false, but R is true. A dictatorial form of government does not respect individual liberty. It is a democratic government that does so.
27. (b) Both A and R are true, but R is not the correct explanation of A.
28. (a) Both A and R are true and R is the correct explanation of A.
29. (a) Both A and R are true and R is the correct explanation of A.

Subjective Questions

Very Short Answer Type Questions

1. What do you understand by separation of powers?

Ans. The legislature makes laws ,the executive implements the law and the judiciary interprets laws and adjudicates disputes. This system of distribution of powers among the three organs of the government is called separation of powers.

2. 'It is a form of political regime in which the supreme and final authority is in the hands of a single person'. Identify the form of the government and explain. **Competency Based Que**

Ans. Monarchy is the oldest form of government. In a monarchy, the state machinery functions according to the commands and rule of the monarch. Monarchy, thus, refers to a rule by one. It is the will of one person which ultimately prevails in all matters of governance.

3. State the origin of the term 'Aristocracy'.

Ans. The word 'Aristocracy' originated from the Greek words, 'aristo' which means 'the best' and 'kratein', which means 'to rule'.

4. 'This form of the government is vested in the hands of a few people'. Identify the form of government and analyse. **Competency Based Que**

Ans. This is an aristocracy form of government, in which political powers of the state are vested in the hands of a few people. It is a form of government in which a relatively small proportion of people determine the policies of the government and determines the public policies. In this form of government ruler is considered superior.

5. Which is the most popular form of government in modern states? What are the two kinds of this form of government?

Ans. Democracy is the most popular form of government in modern states. There are two types of democracy

(i) Direct democracy (ii) Indirect democracy

6. A member of Parliament, Ms. Smith, introduced a bill to amend the Education Act to include climate change education in the national curriculum. The bill is not sponsored by the government, but has gained support from opposition parties and civil society organisations. What type of bill is this an example of and how? **Competency Based Que**

Ans. This is an example of private member's bill because it is introduced by an individual member of parliament rather than the government. Private number's bill are often used to raise awareness about specific issues or to propose changes to existing laws.

7. Imagine a country where the Central Government holds supreme power and can create or dissolve local governments at will. The Central Government has the authority to make laws and policies that apply to the entire country, and local governments must adhere to these laws. Based on the illustration, what is the key characteristic of a unitary government? **Competency Based Que**

Ans. A unitary government is characterised by a centralised authority where the Central Government holds supreme power. It has the authority to create and dissolve local governments, and the powers of local governments are derived from and sub-ordinate to the Central Government.

8. What are the three organs of the government?

Ans. The three organs of the government are

(i) **Legislature** It makes the laws.

(ii) **Executive** It implements the law.

(iii) **Judiciary** It acts as the interpreter and arbiter in disputes.

Short Answer Type Questions

1. Japan, Britain and some others are oldest monarchies of the world. They have survived with several changes according to the time and period. How does power flow in a monarchial form of government? **Competency Based Que**

Ans. In a monarchy, the king's son succeeded him and the right to rule remained in the family. The power remained concentrated in the hands of the king whose authority prevails in all matters of the state. Monarchs generally surrounded themselves with people and advisors who help them perform their functions.

2. In the Indian sub-continent there were many ruling classes existed with hereditary social class and upper class of people. How does a monarchial form of government differ from an aristocratic form of government? **Competency Based Que**

Ans. Monarchy is a form of political regime in which the supreme and final authority is in the hands of a single person wearing a crown, irrespective of whether his office is hereditary or elective. On the other hand, aristocracy is the form of government in which political powers of the state are vested in the hands of a few people.

3. Explain the democracy as a form of government in which people are powerful.

Ans. Democratic form of government is the most popular form in the modern civilised states. It refers to a system of government in which the people play a very important role in electing their government.

They also enjoy a variety of rights. Bryce defined democratic form of government as one where the ruling power of the state is vested not in a particular class or classes but in the community as a whole.

4. In India, a poor person can not be deprived from the injustice and equality. The judiciary ensures that no one must be left out. What is the role of courts in an indirect form of democracy? **Competency Based Que**

Ans. In an indirect democracy, courts play a very important role. In this kind of democracy, judges are supposed to be independent and impartial. The representatives, in this case, are chosen by the process of universal adult suffrage.

Thus, all the citizens of the state have equal opportunity of participation in the political affairs of the state in contrast to monarchy or dictatorial form of government. The political power remains in the hands of the people.

5. In South Africa, the President is elected by the Parliament and he/she is the head of the government. What are the two kinds of democracy that prevail in modern societies? **Competency Based Que**

Ans. The two kinds of democracies that prevail in modern societies are

(i) **Direct Democracy** In a direct democracy, people exercise their power directly. People vote in open assemblies on different issues. The outcome of the voting here becomes the law.

(ii) **Indirect Democracy** In an indirect democracy, power vests in people, however, they exercise their power through their chosen representatives. In this kind of democracy, the representatives are chosen for a definite term during which they make and implement laws.

6. Ramesh, a resident of Uttar Pradesh, was curious about how the Indian Government functioned. He noticed that while the Central Government handled matters like international relations and atomic energy, the State Government dealt with regional issues like education and agriculture. He also observed that both the Central and State Governments had the authority to make laws on certain matters like trade and commerce. Identify the type of government does India have, and how does it function? **Competency Based Que**

Ans. India has a government that is federal in character and unitary in spirit. The Central Government handles matters of national importance, while State

Governments deal with regional issues. There is also a concurrent list where both Central and State Governments have the authority to make laws. This system allows for a balance of power between the Central and State Governments.

7. State any two major characteristics of a Parliamentary form of government.

Ans. Two characteristics of a Parliamentary form of government are

(i) In the Parliamentary system, the legislature and the executive are related to each other, by way of membership in the two bodies and their accountability.

(ii) The executive is accountable to the legislature while implementing laws and discharging its responsibilities.

8. After the Second World War, many countries opted for democratic form of government where people directly or indirectly participate in government. State any three differences between a Presidential and a Parliamentary form of government.

Ans. Differences between a Presidential and a Parliamentary form of government are

Parliamentary form of Government	Presidential form of Government
The President is indirectly elected.	People directly elect the President.
The President is the nominal head of the state while the Prime Minister is the head of the government as well as the state.	The President is the real head of the state and the government.
The Prime Minister and the Council of Ministers are answerable to the legislature.	The President and the secretaries are not answerable to the legislature.
The Council of Ministers may be removed by a no-confidence motion in the Parliament before the expiry of his term.	President can only be removed by the process of impeachment before the expiry of his term.
The powers of the Prime Minister are limited in the choice of ministers. He can only choose from the members of the Parliament.	The President has very wide powers and can appoint anyone in the government.
This form of government is found in the UK and India.	This form of government is found in USA and Argentina.

9. The United States is the most popular country in the world, where Presidential form of the government functions. State any two major characteristics of a Presidential form of government. Competency Based Que

Ans. Two characteristics of a Presidential form of government are

(i) In the Presidential system, the executive branch of the government is independent of the legislature for its tenure and actions.

(ii) In this form, the President is elected by the people, whether directly or indirectly, for a fixed period unless removed on impeachment by the legislature on the grounds stated in the Constitution of the country.

10. In a country 'A', the Legislative Assembly follows a bicameral system. In another country 'B', the President is directly elected by the people. In another country 'C', the Prime Minister is elected by the people while the President is indirectly elected by the elected representatives of the people. All the three countries follow a democratic form of government. Competency Based Que

(i) What form of government exists in country 'B'?

(ii) What form of government exists in country 'C'?

Ans. (i) Presidential form of government exists in country 'B'.

(ii) Parliamentary form of government exists in country 'C'.

11. State any four differences between Unicameral legislature and Bicameral legislature.

Ans. Difference between Unicameral legislature and Bicameral legislature

Difference	Unicameral	Bicameral
Number of House	One	Two
Sharing of Power	Concentrated in one house	Shared between two houses
Decision-Making	Flexible and efficient as bills are introduced and passed in only a single house.	Time-consuming as both the houses have to pass the bill hence, their approval is a tedious task.
Suitability	A unicameral legislature is best suited to smaller states.	Bicameral legislature is more suited to larger states

12. Indian democracy is considered as the world's largest democracy where every organ of the government work independently and co-operatively. What are the two ways in which a legislature can be organised in a democratic form of government? Competency Based Que

Ans. In a democracy, the legislature can either be unicameral or bicameral

(i) **Unicameral Legislature** In a unicameral system, there is only one house of the legislature. It is cost-effective and suitable for countries with a smaller population.

It also allows for a faster decision-making process. This system of legislature is seen in Turkey, which is known by the name of Grand National Assembly of Turkey; in Bangladesh by the name of House of Nation etc.

(ii) **Bicameral Legislature** In a bicameral legislature, there are two houses or chambers. Indian Parliament is a bicameral legislature, consisting of two houses, i.e. House of people (Lok Sabha) and Council of States (Rajya Sabha).

13. The primary function of the legislature is to make the laws. The legislature amends and repeals the outdated laws and also makes new laws to meet the present requirements.

(i) Name the article of the Constitution that states that the Council of Ministers responsible to the House of the People. Competency Based Que

(ii) State any other function of the legislature.

Ans. (i) Article 75(3) of the Constitution of India states that the Council of Ministers shall be collectively responsible to the House of the People.

(ii) The legislature also performs deliberative functions. It deliberates on the bills before they become laws.

14. In a country 'Zarebia', the legislature allows the executive to make laws on its behalf. Based on this power, the executive frames orders, rules, regulations, ordinances, by-laws and circulars. They carry equal force of law as if framed within the sphere and policy of the parent legislation.

Which form of legislation has been followed in Zarebia? Explain. Competency Based Que

Ans. The system of delegated legislation has been followed in Zarebia. Delegated legislative functions are performed by the executive. Delegated legislation is an enactment made by an individual or body other than Parliament.

By delegating the power to make a legislation to the executive, the Parliament empowers different people or bodies to integrate more details to an Act of Parliament. Parliament along these lines, authorises the executive to make laws and guidelines through delegated legislation.

Executive frames orders, rules, regulations, ordinances, by-laws and circulars. They carry equal force of law, if framed within the sphere and policy of the parent legislation.

15. Right to Education is renowned as a milestone law for the betterment of society as a whole, introduced by the legislature. Discuss the law-making function of the legislature. Competency Based Que

Ans. The primary function of the legislature is to make the laws. The legislature amends and repeals the outdated laws and also makes new laws to meet the present requirements. Laws, when enacted by the legislature, are called 'Acts'.

These Acts are the direct source of law to control and regulate the institutions running in a state and society. All legislations are enacted for the achievement of certain objectives and purposes.

For example, the Indian legislature enacted the Consumer Protection Act, 2019 with the purpose of protecting the interest of consumers and the speedy settlement of their disputes.

16. The judiciary acts as the guardian of the Constitution. It is vested with the duty to uphold the Constitution as the fundamental law of the land.

(i) What is the most important function of the judiciary?

(ii) How does the Judiciary protect the rights of the people? Competency Based Que

Ans. (i) The first and the foremost function of the judiciary is to hear and decide a case, according to the laws of the land. The role of the judiciary is expanding with the expanding role of the executive.

(ii) Judiciary acts as the protector of the Fundamental Rights of the people. It ensures that Constitutional Rights of the people are not violated by any other organ of the government.

Long Answer Type Questions

1. Briefly describe different forms of governments that exist at different locations in the world.

Ans. The different forms of government that exist in the world are as below

(i) **Monarchy** Refer to Q. No. 2 of Very Short Answer Type Questions.

(ii) **Aristocracy** Refer to Q. No. 3 of Very Short Answer Type Questions.

(iii) **Dictatorship** In this form of government, a single person or a small group of people exercise complete authority over others. The dictator controls and exercises the political powers of the state. He does not come to power through elections, instead he occupies the position by force, invasion, intervention and militarism, in contrast to a monarch.

His dictates are the laws of the country. He implements them and pass judgement according to his will. He holds absolute power. He is not accountable or answerable to the citizens of the state.

(iv) **Democracy** Refer to Q. No. 3 of Short Answer Type Questions.

2. There are two countries, one of which is located in Europe and the other one in North America. Historically, one of them has been the colony of the other. The political systems existing in these two countries are two of the most widely prevalent form of governments in modern times. The political system followed in one of these is also practiced in India.

(i) Identify the two countries and explain the forms of governments which are prevalent in these countries.

(ii) Distinguish between the two distinct forms of government that prevail in these countries.

Competency Based Que

Ans. (i) These two countries are the United Kingdom, situated in Europe and the United States, situated in North America.

The United Kingdom follows a Parliamentary form of government while the United States follows the Presidential form of government.

For Parliamentary form of government, refer to Q. No. 7 of Short Answer Type Questions.

In Presidential form of government, people directly elect the president and the president is the real head of the state and the government. The President has very mide powers and can appoint anyone in the government.

(ii) For difference between Parliamentary and Presidential form of governments, refer to Q. No. 8 of Short Answer Type Questions.

3. Write a note on the different organs of the government and its functionalities.

Ans. There are three main organs of government, which are the Legislature, the Executive and the Judiciary.

Some of the major functions of three organs are

Major Functions of Legislature

(i) The legislature formulates and expresses the will of the state. The will of state in a representative democracy is the will, opinion and sentiments of its citizens and the public issues concerning them.

(ii) Article 75(3) of the Constitution of India states that the Council of Ministers shall be collectively responsible to the House of the People. Parliament exercises check and ensures executive and administrative accountability.

Major Functions of Executive

(i) The main function of the executive is the maintenance of internal and external administration.

(ii) The executive performs certain legislative functions such as delegated legislative functions are performed by the executive. Delegated legislation is an enactment made by an individual or body other than Parliament.

Major Functions of Judiciary

(i) The main function of the judiciary is to hear and decide a case according to the substantive and procedural laws of the land. The role of the judiciary is expanding with the expanding role of the executive.

(ii) Judicial review is the power provided upon the judiciary by the Constitution, under it, judiciary can examine legislative enactments and executive orders of the governments, whether it be state or central, and declare them invalid, if they violates the provisions of Constitution.

SELF ASSESSMENT TEST

Objective Type Questions

1. "It is the government of one man who has not obtained the position by inheritance, but either by force or consent or a combination of both". In the above definition, Albert Cobban talks about which form of government? **Competency Based Que**

   (a) Dictatorship (b) Democracy (c) Aristocracy (d) Oligarchy

2. In which of the following forms of government is the executive independent of the legislature?

   (a) Presidential form of government (b) Parliamentary form of government
   (c) Both (a) and (b) (d) None of these

3. Which among the following is not a function of the legislative organ of the government?

   (a) Formulation of will of the state (b) Enactment of laws
   (c) Adjudication of laws (d) Classification of laws

4. Identify a function of the judicial organ of the government.

   (a) Controls the financial purse (b) Executes the laws
   (c) Guardian of the Constitution (d) All of these

Very Short Answer Type Questions

5. Which form of government prevails in India? Define briefly.
6. What do you understand by a dictatorial form of government?
7. In the city of Athens, citizens gather in a town hall meeting to vote directly on a proposed to increase funding for public transportation. In contrast, in the city of sparta citizens elect representatives to a city council which then votes on the same proposal. Which from of democracy is illustrated in each city and also explain that form of government? **Competency Based Que**
8. Which system provides people the right to choose their government? Identify the system and explain.
9. What are the two kinds of legislature? Which kind of legislature prevails in the Indian Parliament?

Short Answer Type Questions

10. Give three differences between a unitary and federal system of government.
11. Give three differences between unicameral and bicameral legislature.
12. State any four general functions of legislature as an organ of government.

Long Answer Type Questions

13. State the general functions of executive as an organ of the government.
14. In a landmark case, the Supreme Court of a country rules that the government's decision to deny citizenship to a marginalised community is unconstitutional and orders the government ot grant citizenship to all members of community. The courts' decision is based on the principles of equality and justice and is seen as a major victory for human rights activity.

    (i) What role is the judiciary playing in the above situation? Explain.
    (ii) Analyse the power of Supreme Court to interpret the laws. **Competency Based Que**

03

CHAPTER

For preserving the political liberty of individuals and democracy, it is important for the state to establish special organs for the exercise of powers.

Separation of Powers

YOUR STUDY GOALS

YOUR PRACTICE GOAL

- Objective Type Questions (36 Qs ; MCQs, A-R, Statements, Matching)
- Subjective Questions (8 VSAs, 17 SAs, 7 LAs)

The powers of the government have been divided into its **three organs** on the basis of powers exercised by them.

The powers have been divided among the following organs of the government.

(i) **Legislature** It is entrusted with the power of **enacting laws.**

(ii) **Executive** It is entrusted with the power of **implementing laws.**

(iii) **Judiciary** It is entrusted with the power of **solving disputes.**

3.1 Concept of Separation of Powers

- The theory of separation of powers implies the division of powers of the government among its three organs.
- The three organs of the government have to be kept separate and distinct.
- The organs must be independent of the one another's control.
- Each organ must exercise its powers within its own sphere.
- This means that each organ shall not interfere with the powers and independence of other organs of government.
- If any organ interferes in the functioning of the other organ, it shall be checked by another organ of the government.
- No new organ is created over and above the existing organs of government, to check encroachment or interference.
- The separation of powers requires the **presence of a written Constitution** to define the formal powers of each organ.
- The powers shall be defined and divided in a way so as to create a system of checks and balances of powers among the organs.

- This view is supported by the writings of **Carl J Friedrich (1901-1984)**, a German-American political theorist.
- According to **Wade** and **Phillips**, separation of powers may mean three different conditions which are
  (i) Same persons should not form part of more than one of the three organs.
  (ii) One organ of the government should not control or interfere in the function of another organ.
  (iii) One organ of the government should not exercise the functions of another.

3.2 Evolution of Montesquieu's Doctrine of Separation of Powers

- The French philosopher, **Baron De Montesquieu, (1689-1755)** has been credited with the creation of the concept of separation of powers.
- He was the first political thinker to present a detailed political account of this doctrine in his book, **Spirit of the Laws**. His theory on separation of powers has become the model of governance for all democracies.

Historical Background

- During his time, Montesquieu saw the **oppressive and despotic**[1] **rule of French King Louis XIV** (1661-1715).
- During that period, the ruler enjoyed the absolute powers of state and proclaimed, 'I am the State'. People's liberty was suppressed under the despotic rule of the King and his administrators.
- During his visit to England, Montesquieu experienced the **sense of liberty and freedom** enjoyed by the citizens of England.
- He was very impressed with the thoughts of Locke. He compared their system of governance with the system prevailing in his country.
- He examined the separation of powers of the government in England and their exercise by separate organs of the government namely, the King, Parliament and the law courts.
- Thus, the doctrine of the separation of powers emerged as a distinct doctrine in his famous book **Esprit Des Lois** (The Spirit of Laws), published in 1748.
- Montesquieu advocated that the separation of powers helps in ensuring political liberty. It is a state of peace of mind that arose from people's opinion of each other's safety. To have political liberty, the government should be constituted in a way that people need not be afraid of one another.
- According to Montesquieu, if the power has not been divided, it can cause tyranny (cruel and oppressive rule) in the name of law and justice.

Basic Features of the Montesquieu's Doctrine of Separation of Powers

The following are the basic features of the Montesquieu's doctrine of separation of powers.

- Montesquieu advised that the **division of powers is necessary** in between the legislative, the executive and the judicial system.
- He provided the reason for the division of powers between the three branches of the government as follows
  - When the legislative and executive powers are concentrated in the same persons, there cannot be liberty. It may lead to fear that the monarch may enact harsh laws and execute them in a cruel manner.
  - When the legislature have judicial powers, the life and liberty of the subjects would be exposed to absolute control, as the judge would be the legislator or law maker.

---

1 **Despotic** It means using of power over other people in a very unfair or cruel way.

- Where the judicial power is combined with the executive power, the judge might behave in a oppressive manner. If powers are vested in one organ, or exercised without separation, governance would not be effective.

- It is an essential attribute of any authority to abuse the powers, unless some limitations are imposed on it.
- To safeguard the liberty of the people, each organ of the government shall have the **obligation to act within its own sphere** and not beyond it. If the authority acts beyond the permissible limits, it would be checked by the other organs. This means that
  - the executive organ shall exercise some control over legislative and judiciary.
  - the legislative exercise some control over executive and judiciary.
  - the judiciary exercise some control over legislative and executive.
  - The system of checking the encroachment of powers by each organ and thus balancing the division of powers is termed as the system of **checks and balances.**

Checks and Balances of Power

- Montesquieu is credited with the creation of the system of checks and balances. This system provides for a system based regulation wherein one branch is allowed to limit another.
- The given diagram explains the operation of the check and balance mechanism between different organs of the government in the United States.
- The legislature, executive and judiciary are **controlled and blocked by each other.** On one hand, judiciary has the power to declare any acts unconstitutional which are passed by legislature and executive.
- On the other hand, the executive and legislature has power to appoint and impeachment of judges.

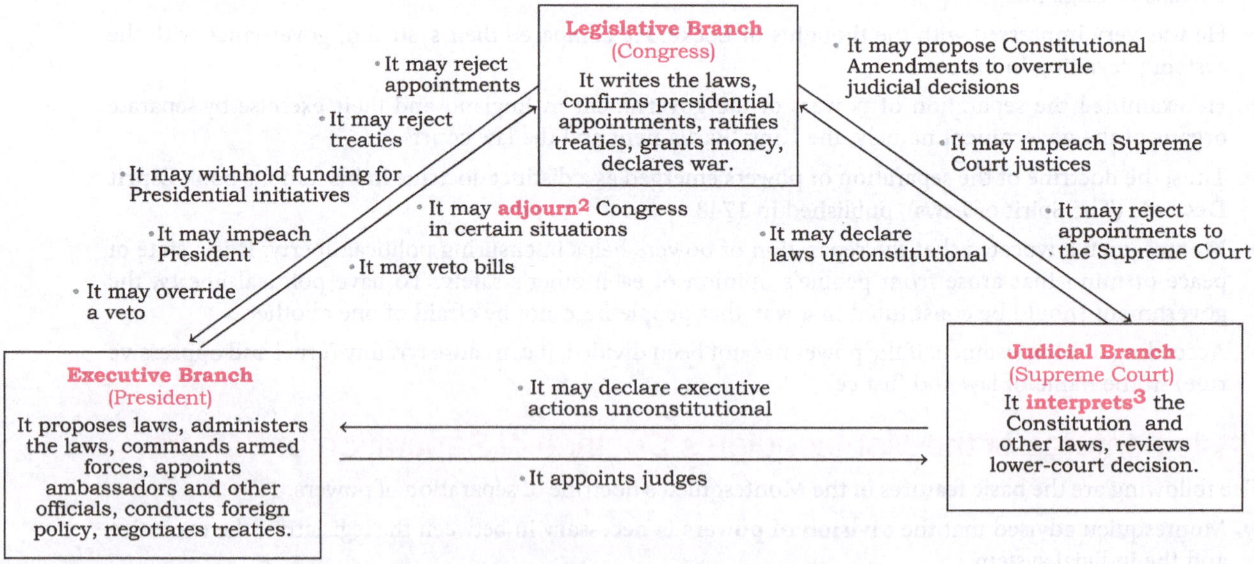

▲ *Separation of Power and Checks and Balances*

2 **Adjourn** It means to break off any meeting with the intention of resuming it later.
3 **Interprets** It means to explain the meaning of something.

Impact of the Doctrine of Separation of Powers

Montesquieu's doctrine was adopted in his country's political system. This doctrine had the following impacts

- It gave a boost to the **French Revolution** and further led to the adoption of the **Declaration of Rights in 1789.** The declaration provided that 'every society in which separation of powers is not determined has no Constitution'.
- The French Constitution, 1791 made executive, legislative and judiciary independent of one another'.
- James Madison (1751-1836) the 4th President of United State of America wrote in the federalist that the accumulation of power, legislative, executive and judiciary in the same hands, whether of one, a few or many, and whether hereditary, self-appointed or elective, many justly be pronounced the very definition of tyranny.
- **Montesquieu became the intellectual father of the American Constitution** because the doctrine of separation of powers forms the foundation on which the entire structure of the American (US) Constitution 1787 is based.

3.3 Evaluation of the Doctrine of Separation of Powers

The doctrine of separation of powers can be better understood in two ways

(i) It implies that concentration of all power in the hands of one single person or group, should be avoided.

(ii) It also implies division of those powers which essentially and primarily belong to one organ and not the other.

Key Benefits and Advantages of the Doctrine

- The benefits and advantages of doctrine of separation of powers are
  - It helps in making the organs more efficient in their performance of the functions.
  - It helps in safeguarding the liberty of the individuals as it requires each organ to function within its own sphere of law.
  - It seeks to establish an independent judiciary which is free from any bias. Montesquieu was interested in setting the judicial power as a check on and as arbiter between the other two organs.
  - It helps in providing stability to the government by protecting the state's sovereignty.

Defects of the Doctrine

- According to Montesquieu, there was no separation of powers under the British Constitution.
- **AV Dicey** had observed that the British Constitution had 'a weak separation of powers'.
- According to **Barnett** in Constitutional and Administrative Law (2005), 'Britain has an uncodified or unwritten Constitution'.
- Much of the British Constitution is expressed in written documents, within statutes, court judgements and treaties as the supreme and final sources of law.
- The statutes of Parliament can change the Constitution by passing new legislations. The British Constitution has other unwritten sources including 'Parliamentary Constitutional conventions'.
- Some defects of the doctrine of separation of powers are
  - It is difficult to divide the three organs of the government and their functions as they are inter-connected in some way even though their mode of action can differ.

- An extreme or rigid separation of powers can also destroy the unity and co-ordination which are required to run a state smoothly. Further, such a rigid separation can also create deadlocks and conflict among the organs.
- The functions performed by each organ are not unique. A judge makes law in the form of precedents. The executive legislates in the form of framing subordinate legislation, such as rules, bye-laws, regulations, policies, schemes, etc. The legislature acts judicially in deciding the breach of its privileges. Thus, an absolute separation of powers may even prove hazardous in the smooth functioning of the government.
- According to **John Emerich Edward Dalberg** (1834-1902), an English historian, politician and writer, popularly known as **Lord Acton**. "Power tends to corrupt, and absolute power corrupts absolutely".
- There is a confusion in the idea of 'function' with the idea of 'power' in Montesquieu's doctrine of separation of powers. Its meaning can be better analysed if the use of the word powers of the organs is substituted by functions. The word 'functions' implies the attitude of service while the word 'powers' implies force. The government performs activities to serve the purpose of the state and its individuals through its classified functions for which the different organs are created.
- This doctrine cannot be applied practically in a Parliamentary form of government where the executive and legislative function together.

Growth of the Executive Organ of the Government in a Welfare State

- Montesquieu had proposed that all the three organs of the government would be given equal and independent position in the political organisation of the country. However, it is not so in reality.
- The concept of welfare state demands more and more action and services from the government such as health, education, food and public distribution, public transport and supply of electricity.
- It tends to increase the powers of the executive, and develop it as a multifunctional organ.
- Today, the executive legislates, exercises judicial jurisdiction and plans the future activities of the government.
- According to **Barker,** if the growth of legislative organ, due to the cabinet system, was the notable feature of 18th century, then the growth of executive organ, due to the extension of rights and the corresponding extension of services, is the notable feature of the 20th century.

Quick Test 1

1. What does the theory of separation of powers suggest?
2. Why must one organ of the government not interfere in the another organ's functions?
3. Where did Montesquieu experience sense of liberty and freedom?
4. Name the doctrine which gave boost to the French Revolution.
5. Which country has an uncodified or unwritten Constitution?

3.4 Separation of Powers in Practice

- There is an overlap of powers among the different organs of the government, depending on the form of government prevalent in a particular state.

Separation of Powers in Britain

- Britain follows a Parliamentary system of government wherein there is a uniting of powers rather than a separation of powers. On top of the three organs is the **Crown**. He/She functions as the **ceremonial head** of the state.

- The Crown only signs the bills passed by the Parliament to make them laws.

Organs of the Government in Britain

- Executive (British Monarch)
- Legislature (House of Commons and House of Lords)
- Judiciary

The three organs of the government functioning in Britain are discussed below

Executive

- The British Queen/King acts as the nominal executive head without any real political powers. She/He holds office by the virtue of **hereditary succession**[4]. The real executive powers are vested with the Prime Minister and the Council of Ministers. The Queen/King exercises powers on the advice of the Council of Ministers.

Legislature

- The UK Parliament consists of two Houses i.e. the **House of Commons** and the **House of Lords**. Their work is similar like
  - making laws (legislation)
  - checking the work of the government (scrutiny)
  - debating on current issues
- The Prime Minister and his Council of Ministers are part of the legislature. They are collectively responsible to it and play an important role in legislative activities.
- They remain in office as long as they enjoy the confidence of the House of Commons. They make subordinate legislation. They perform judicial functions by being the members of Administrative Boards and Tribunals. The House of Commons performs judicial function in case of violation of its own privileges.

Judiciary

- The highest judicial court in the UK is the Supreme Court. Earlier, Appellate Committee of the House of Lords was the highest court in the United Kingdom.
- The judges of the Supreme Court are known as **Justices** of the Supreme Court or **Privy Counselors**. Justices of the Supreme Court are granted the courtesy title Lord or Lady for life.
- The head of the Appellate Committee were known as **Law Lords.** They were the final judges of judicial disputes in Britain. They sat simultaneously in the House of Lords, the upper house of the legislature. This arrangement ceased in October, 2009.

Constitutional Reform Act, 2005

- The Supreme Court of the United Kingdom was established in October 2009 after the Constitutional Reform Act, 2005. Until the Constitutional Reform Act, 2005, the **Lord Chancellor** was the head of the judiciary in Britain. He was attached to the legislature, executive and judiciary.
- The Lord Chancellor sat as a judge on the Judicial Committee of the House of Lords.
- **The Constitutional Reform Act, 2005** separated the powers of judiciary exclusively from both government and the Parliament.
- The Lord Chancellor was replaced by the Lord Speaker. The Lord Chief Justice is now head of the judiciary, and the Lord Chancellor may no longer sit as a judge.

---

4 **Hereditary Succession** It means a person who inherits an indivisible title or office after the death of the previous title holder.

- Therefore, legislative functions are now vested with an elected Lord Speaker and the judicial functions are vested with the Lord Chief Justice.
- The Lord Chancellor's Department was replaced with a Ministry of Justice and the Lord Chancellor. It is currently serves in the position of secretary of state for justice.

Separation of Powers in the US

- The US Constitution has adopted the presidential form of government wherein the theory of separation of powers has been adopted in letter and spirit.

Organs of the Government in the US

- **The Congress with two houses** (Legislative Organ)
  - Senate (the Upper house)
  - The House of Representatives (the Lower house)
- **President** (Executive Organ)
- **Supreme Court and the Subordinate Courts** (Judicial Organ)

- The American Constitution did not mention that the powers must be separated. It simply distributed the powers among the three organs of the government.
- While it give a **major share of powers to one organ** of government, instead smaller shares of powers to each of the other organs. This was done to avoid concentration and consequent abuse of power.
- The fathers of the Constitution considered that power should be limited, controlled and diffused.

Legislature

- The US Congress is the legislative organ with two Houses-the Senate and the House of Representatives.
- Congress is vested with the law making power and it is elected by the people.
- The tenure of the Congress is **6 years for Senate and 2 years for the House of Representatives.**
- The bills passed by the legislature in US, except money bills, are subject to ratification (change) or veto of the President.
- The powers of the Congress are
  - The Senate has equal power like the President to make appointments, declare war and ratify treaties.
  - The Congress acts as a judiciary in cases of impeachment of the President and Supreme Court judges.
  - Congress delegates law-making powers to the executive after laying down the legislative policy and principle.
  - Certain Constitutional provisions empower the Congress to override the veto power of the President. **The President cannot dissolve the Congress.**

Executive

- The President is the executive organ. The President is elected by the people who remains in power for 4 years.
- The President has the following powers
  - To recommend measures.
  - To summon Congress in special session.
  - To veto bills (except money bills) passed by the Congress.
  - To make appointments but these have to be ratified by the Senate.
  - The President appoints secretaries, with the approval of the Congress as executive heads of the departments. The President and secretaries are not members of the legislature.
  - The President formulates national policy, mobilises military troops and can declare state emergency.

  - The President can declare war only with the approval of both the Houses of the Congress.
  - The President could also intervene in the business of the court through his power of pardon for all offences, except treason.
- Executive in the US works on the principle of 'separation of powers' and 'checks and balances'.
- The President is not responsible to the Congress and the Congress is not responsible to the President.

Judiciary

- The Supreme Court and Subordinate Courts are the judicial organ in the US. The Supreme Court judges are appointed by the President but they have to be ratified by the Senate.
- In certain circumstances, the Senate may refuse to ratify the choices made by the President.
- The Supreme Court has the following powers
  - The US Supreme Court has the power under the Constitution to cancel or declare void the acts and actions of the legislature and executive.
  - The Supreme Court has the power of judicial review. It can declare them null and void (invalid), if they **contravenes**[5] the provisions of the US Constitution.

Separation of Powers in India

- In India, the governing system is similar to Britain. It has a Parliamentary system of government.
- Under the Constitution of India, the three organs of government are the legislature, executive and the judiciary.

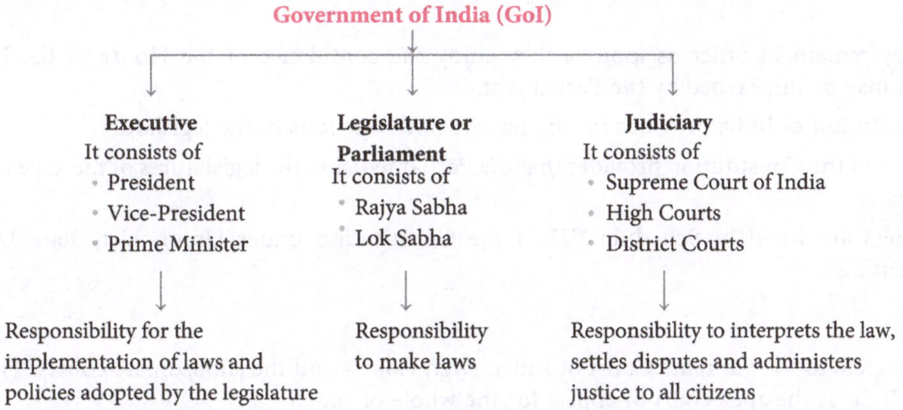

- The Indian Constitution has not adopted the doctrine of separation of powers in its strict sense.
- However, it has sufficiently differentiated the essential functions of the organs and no organ shall assume to itself the functions that belongs to the other organ.

Executive

- The President of India is the nominal executive head.
- The President is elected by the Electoral College consisting of the elected members of both Houses of Parliament and the elected members of the legislative assemblies of the state.
- He/She is appointed for a fixed term of **5 years**.
- The real power vests in the Prime Minister and his Council of Ministers. The President exercises his/her powers/functions with the aid and advice of the Prime Minister and his/her Council of Ministers.
- Usually the advice of Prime Minister and Council of Ministers is binding on the President.

---

5 **Contravenes** It means conflict with a right, principle etc., or to do something that is not allowed by a law or rule.

Powers of the President of India

- The President has wide legislative powers to issue ordinances for immediate action during the recess of the legislature. An ordinance issued shall have the force and effect as that of an act by Parliament.
- The President has the power to dissolve the House of People.
- The President has the power to declare National Emergency, State Emergency and Financial Emergency.
- The President is authorised to exercise legislative powers in case of State Emergency.

Legislature

- According to **Article 79** of the Constitution of India, the legislature (the Parliament) consists of the **President** and two Houses known as the **Council of States** (Rajya Sabha) and the **House of the People** (Lok Sabha).
- The term fixed for the **Lower House** (Lok Sabha) is **5 years** and **6 years** is fixed for the **Upper House** (Rajya Sabha). It is important to note that while the Lower House get dissolved after its term, the Upper House never get dissolved.
- **One-third of the total members** of the Upper House retires and new members get elected every two years gap.
- The Prime Minister and his/her council are normally the members of the Parliament. They play an active role in proposing a bill and voting a bill in the Parliament. A bill becomes an act when the President gives his/her assent to it.
- The Council of Ministers including the Prime Minister is **collectively responsible** to the House of the People.
- Thus, they remain in office as long as they enjoy the confidence of the House of the People. The President may be impeached by the Parliament.
- The Constitution of India provides for the powers and functions of the legislature.
- **Article 246** of the Constitution provides that the Parliament and the legislatures of the states have power to make laws.
- The matters are listed in **Schedule VII** of the Constitution under Union List, State List and the Concurrent List.

Judiciary

- Judiciary refers to the Supreme Court of India, High Courts and the subordinate courts. The Supreme Court of India is the apex court of appeal for the whole of India.

Independence of Judiciary

- **Article 50** of the Constitution of India provides that the state shall take steps to separate the judiciary from the executive in the public services of the state.
- The objective of Article 50 is to provide for the independence of the judiciary.
- According to **Article 124 (2)** of the Constitution, the Supreme Court and High Court judges shall be appointed by the President after consultation with such judges of the Supreme Court and of the High Courts in the states.
- The norms and requirements of consultation process were laid down in a nine-judge Constitution Bench of the Supreme Court (In re-Presidential Reference, AIR 1999 SC 1).
- The privileges and the allowances of a judge cannot be changed after his appointment. No discussion shall take place in Parliament with respect to the conduct of any judge of the Supreme Court or of the High Court, except when a proceeding of impeachment is initiated against him.

- The judges of the Supreme Court and High Court can be removed on impeachment by the legislature, only on the grounds of proven misbehaviour or incapacity.

Judicial Review and Basic Structure of the Constitution

- The Supreme Court of India exercises its power of judicial review in **Kesavananda Bharati case** popularly known as Fundamental Rights case.
- It held that the Parliament, by exercising its amending power under **Article 368**, could not alter the basic structure of the Constitution.
- Thus, the basic structure limits the amending power of the Parliament.
- After reviewing the different cases decided by the Supreme Court, the following features emerge as the basic structure, which are excluded from the amending power of the Parliament under **Article 368**
  - Supremacy of the Constitution.
  - Republic and democratic form of government.
  - Secular character of the Constitution and state.
  - Sovereignty of India.
  - Judicial review and jurisdiction of courts under Article 32 and Article 226.
  - Separation of powers and independent judiciary (In the case of State of Bihar Vs. Bal Mukund Shah.
  - Right to Equality and Rule of Law.
- Thus, the Supreme Court of India finally determines the essential features constituting the framework of the Constitution.
- In other words, the Supreme Court has assumed to itself, the constituent power in exercise of judicial review.

Role of Judiciary

The judiciary play the following roles

- Judiciary **acts as an interpreter** of the Constitution. It is authorised to inspect the legislation and administrative process, and assess whether or not they conform to the Constitution.
- It provides remedies for the enforcement of Fundamental Rights. For example, a writ jurisdiction can be invoked to take action against the Supreme Court under Article 32 and High Court under Article 226 of the Constitution.
- It plays the role of legislature while laying its own procedures for providing justice.
- It supervises, administers and controls the subordinate judiciary and thus performs an administrative function.

Quick Test 2

1. Why does Britain have fusion of powers rather than a separation of powers?
2. What do you understand the term 'Appellate'?
3. Which organ of the government give the power of pardon to the President of the USA?
4. What is the main responsibility of legislature/Parliament?
5. What do you understand by writ jurisdiction?

Mind Map

SEPARATION OF POWERS

1 Concept of Separation of Powers

Definition
- Division of government powers among distinct organs: Legislature, Executive and Judiciary.
- **Aim** Prevent concentration of power and ensure liberty and accountability.

Principles
- **Independence** Each organ operates independently.
- **Non-interference** No organ should encroach upon the functions of another.
- **Checks and Balances**
  - Mechanism to prevent abuse of power.
  - Requires mutual oversight among organs.
- **Written Constitution**
  - Clearly defines the powers and responsibilities of each organ.

2 Evolution of Montesquieu's Doctrine

Background
- The first political thinker to present a detailed political account of this doctrine in his book, 'Spirit of the Laws'.
- Separation of powers has become the model of governance for all democracies.
- Montesquieu's saw oppressive and despotic rule of French King Louis XIV.
- He was inspired by the English governance system and John Locke's ideas.

Montesquieu's Contributions
- Published 'The Spirit of Laws' in 1748.
- Advocated the separation of powers as essential for liberty.
- **Prevents**
  - **Legislative-Executive Combination** May lead to oppressive laws.
  - **Legislative-Judiciary Combination** Risk of arbitrary rulings.
  - **Executive-Judiciary Combination** Potential for judicial tyranny.

Impact
- Became the foundation for modern democracies.
- Key influence on the U.S. Constitution and the French Revolution.

3 Core Principles of Checks and Balances

Mechanism
- Prevents overreach by one branch.
- Allows limited control by one organ over others.

For examples
- **Legislature**
  - Impeachment powers (President/Judges).
  - Overrides executive veto.
- **Executive**
  - Veto legislative bills.
  - Appoints judges.
- **Judiciary**
  - Judicial review powers.
  - Declares laws unconstitutional.

4 Separation of Powers in Practice

United States Presidential System
- Clear division of powers.
- No overlap between Legislature (Congress), Executive (President) and Judiciary (Supreme Court).

For examples
- President can veto Congress bills.
- Congress can override veto and impeach.
- Supreme Court can invalidate unconstitutional acts.

Britain Parliamentary System
- Fusion of powers between legislature and executive.
- Monarch as a ceremonial head.

Changes
- Constitutional Reform Act, 2005
- Established an independent Supreme Court.
- Separated the judiciary from the legislature and executive.

Indian Parliamentary System
- Modeled after Britain.
- No strict separation but functional independence.

Features
- **Legislature** Parliament (Lok Sabha, Rajya Sabha).
- **Executive** President, Prime Minister, and Council of Ministers.
- **Judiciary** Supreme Court, High Courts, Subordinate Courts.

Judicial Independence
- **Article 50** Separation of judiciary from executive.
- Judicial review ensures laws conform to the Constitution.

5 Impact on Global Systems

France
- Doctrine inspired the French Revolution.
- Basis for the Declaration of Rights (1789).

USA
- Rigid separation forms the cornerstone of the Constitution.
- Emphasis on checks and balances.

India
- Not rigidly applied but ensures functional differentiation.
- Judiciary plays a vital role in maintaining the balance of power.

6 Criticism of the Doctrine

- Absolute separation is neither practical nor desirable.
- Co-ordination and overlap are necessary for governance.
- Can create inefficiency and conflict among organs.

7 Summary of Organ Roles Across Countries

Country	Legislature	Executive	Judiciary
USA	Congress (Senate & House)	President	Supreme Court
Britain	House of Commons & House of Lords	Monarch (Ceremonial)	Supreme Court
India	Parliament (Lok Sabha & Rajya Sabha)	President & Prime Minister	Supreme Court, High Courts

CBSE TEXTBOOK FOLDER

1. Write a short notes on the following
  (i) Article 368
  (ii) Concept of separation of powers
  (iii) Separation of powers in Britain
  (iv) Separation of powers in USA

Ans. (i) Article 368 of the Constitution provides for constituent powers of the Parliament and lays down the procedure for amendment of the Constitution. In the exercise of its power of judicial review, the Supreme Court of India in Kesavananda Bharati case popularly known as Fundamental Right's case, held that the Parliament in exercise of its amending power under Article 368 could not alter the basic structure of the Constitution. Thus, the basic structure limits the amending power of the Parliament.

(ii) The concept of separation of powers implies the division of the powers of the government among the three organs of the government. These three organs have to be kept separate and distinct. The organs must be independent of the other's control. These organs are

(a) **Legislature** It is entrusted with the power of enacting laws.

(b) **Executive** It is entrusted with the power of implementing laws.

(c) **Judiciary** It is entrusted with the power of adjudicating disputes.

(iii) Britain follows a Parliamentary system of government wherein there is a fusion of powers rather than a separation of powers. On top of the three organs is the Crown. He/She functions as the ceremonial head of the state. The Crown merely signs the bills passed by the Parliament to make them laws.

The three organs of the government functioning in Britain are

(a) Executive head (British Monarch)

(b) Legislature (House of Commons + House of Lords)

(c) Judiciary

The British Queen/King acts as the nominal executive head devoid of any real political powers. She/He holds office by virtue of hereditary succession.

The real executive powers vest with the Prime Minister and the Council of Ministers. The Prime Minister and his Council of Ministers are part of the legislature. They are collectively responsible to it and play an important role in legislative activities.

They perform judicial functions by being the members of Administrative Boards and Tribunals. The House of Commons performs judicial function in case of breach of its own privileges.

The highest judicial court in the UK is the Supreme Court. The judges of the Supreme Court are known as Justices of the Supreme Court or Privy Counselors. Justices of the Supreme Court are granted the courtesy title Lord or Lady for life.

(iv) In the US, the power of government is divided among three organs. The three organs of the government are

(a) **Legislature** The legislative or law making powers are provided to the Congress which have two houses, the Senate (the Upper House) and the House of Representative (the Lower House). The Senate shared his powers with the President to make appointments, declare war and ratify treaties. The Senate can refuse the choices made by the President. Congress is elected by the people. The Congress acts in a judicial capacity in cases of impeachment of the President and Supreme Court Judges.

(b) **Executive** The executive powers are provided to the President, who is elected by the people. The President formulates national policy, mobilise military troops and can declare state emergency.

The President's policies and treaties making decisions are subject to be ratification by the senate.

(c) **Judiciary** The Supreme Court has the power of judicial review. The judges of the Supreme Court are nominated by the President, but their appointments have to be ratified by the Senate. The court has the power to examine the laws passed by the Congress and the executive orders issued by the President and declare them null and void if it violates the provisions of the US Constitution.

2. Answer the following questions briefly.
  (i) Enumerate a few features that come under basic structure of the Constitution of India which are beyond the amending power of the Parliament under Article 368.

(ii) **How did Wade and Phillips interpret the separation of powers in their 1960 work?**

(iii) **What were the reasons that led Montesquieu to advocate the doctrine of separation of powers?**

(iv) **List down a few powers of the following**

(a) **The President of USA**

(b) **The Indian President**

(c) **The British Monarch**

Ans. (i) The following features emerge as the basic structure which are beyond the amending power of the Parliament under Article 368

- Supremacy of the Constitution
- Republic and democratic form of government
- Secular character of the Constitution and state
- Sovereignty of India
- Judicial review and jurisdiction of courts under Article 32 and Article 226
- Separation of powers and independent judiciary (In the case of State of Bihar Vs. Bal Mukund Shah)
- Right to Equality and Rule of Law

(ii) According to Wade and Phillips, separation of power may mean three different conditions, which are

- Some persons should not form part of more than one of the three organs.
- One organ of the government should not control or interfere in the function of another organ.
- One organ of the government should not exercise the functions of another.

(iii) The reasons that led Montesquieu to advocate the doctrine of separation of powers were

- During his time, Montesquieu saw the oppressive and despotic rule of French King Louis XIV (1661-1715). In that period, the ruler enjoyed the absolute powers of state and proclaimed, 'I am the State'. People's liberty was suppressed under the despotic rule of the King and his administrators.
- During his visit to England, Montesquieu experienced the sense of liberty and freedom enjoyed by the citizens of England. He was very impressed with the thoughts of Locke. He compared their system of governance with the system prevailing in his country.
- He examined the separation of powers of the government and their exercise by separate organs of the government namely, the King, Parliament and the law courts in the governance structure in England.

Thus, the doctrine of the separation of powers emerged as a distinct doctrine in his famous book 'Esprit Des Lois' (The Spirit of Laws) published in 1748.

(iv) (a) Some of the powers of the US President are

- The President receives his share of powers to recommend measures.
- He can summon the Congress in a special session.
- He has the power to veto bills (except money bills) passed by the Congress.
- The President has the powers of making appointments but these have to be ratified by the Senate.
- The President appoints secretaries, with the approval of the Congress as executive heads of the departments. The President and secretaries are not members of the legislature.
- The President formulates national policy, mobilises military troops and can declare state emergency.

(b) The powers of the Indian President are

- All the actions and decisions of the government are taken in the name of the President.
- The President has the power to appoint many constitutional officers and the members of the Union Government like the Prime Minister, Chief Justice of India, etc.
- The President has the power to summon either or both the Houses.
- The President also has the power to dissolve the House of People in some cases.
- The President has the power to summon a joint sitting of the house in cases of a deadlock, in which both houses sit together and the conflict is resolved.

(c) The British Queen/King acts as the nominal executive head without any real political powers. She/He holds office by virtue of hereditary succession. The real executive powers are vested with the Prime Minister and the Council of Ministers. The Queen/King exercises powers on the advice of the Council of Ministers.

3. Answer the following questions in about 200 words.

(i) **Evaluate the doctrine of separation of powers by providing a few advantages and defects of the doctrine.**

(ii) **Explain how the doctrine of separation of powers is exercised in India.**

Ans. (i) The advantages and defects of the doctrine of separation of powers

Advantages of the Doctrine

- It helps in making the organs more efficient in their performance of the functions.
- This doctrine helps in safeguarding the liberty of the individuals as it requires each organ to function within its own sphere of law.
- This doctrine seeks to establish an independent judiciary which is free from any bias.

Defects of the Doctrine

- It is difficult to divide the three organs of the government and their functions into water-tight compartments.
- An extreme or rigid separation of powers can ruin the unity and co-ordination which are required to run a state smoothly.
- Such a rigid demarcation can also create deadlocks and conflicts among the organs.
- This doctrine cannot be applied practically in a Parliamentary form of government where the executive and legislative function together.

(ii) The governing system in India is similar to Britain. Both have a Parliamentary system of government. Though the Indian Constitution has not adopted the doctrine of separation of powers in its strict sense, it has sufficiently differentiated the essential functions of the organs and no organ shall assume to itself what essentially belongs to the other.

Under the Constitution of India, the three organs of government are the legislature, executive and the judiciary. According to Article 79 of the Constitution of India, the Parliament consists of the President and two Houses known as the Council of States (Rajya Sabha) and the House of the People (Lok Sabha).

4. Can Montesquieu's separation of powers be applied in countries like India and the UK?

Ans. One may be inclined to say that the doctrine of separation of powers is accepted in India and UK after having a glance at the provisions of the Constitution of India and the system prevalent in Britain.

Under the Indian Constitution, executive powers are with the President, legislative powers with the Parliament and judicial powers with judiciary (Supreme Court, High Courts and Subordinate Courts). Similarly, the executive powers in the UK are with the monarch, legislative powers with the Parliament and judicial powers with judiciary.

In India, the President's function and powers are enumerated in the Constitution itself. Parliament is competent to make any law subject to the provisions of the Constitution and there is no other limitation on its legislative power.

The judiciary is independent in its field and there can be no interference with its judicial functions either by the executive or by the legislature. The Supreme Court and High Courts are given the power of judicial review and they can declare any law passed by the Parliament or the legislature unconstitutional.

Taking into account these factors, some jurists are of the opinion that the doctrine of separation of powers has been accepted in the Indian Constitution. However, it cannot be as rigid as the separation of powers in the US.

5. Explain why America is the best example of separation of powers.

Ans. America is the best example of separation of powers due to the following reasons

- The United States Constitution has a more rigid separation of powers than the Constitutions of other democracies.
- The Supreme Court of USA holds a check and balances that allow for a system based regulation.
- The American Constitution did not exclusively stated that powers ought to be separate. It simply distributed the powers.
- The legislative powers are vested in the Congress, the executive powers in the President, and the judicial powers in the court.
- The Supreme Court puts and allows one branch to limit another, such as the power of Congress to alter the composition and jurisdiction of the federal courts.

6. In USA, 'While apportioning the lion's share of powers to one organ of government, the Constitution gave smaller slices to each of the other organs. This was done to avoid concentration and consequent abuse of power'.

(i) Which organ of the government has maximum power in the USA?

(ii) Comment whether power should be limited, controlled and diffused equally among the three organs of the government and support your argument with relevant doctrine.

(iii) Of the three countries USA, UK and India where is the power most evenly divided amongst the three organs of the government?

Ans. (i) The executive organ of the government has the maximum power in the USA.

(ii) To preserve the political liberty of individuals and democracy, it is important for the state to establish special organs for the exercise of powers. The powers of the government have been divided into its three organs based on the powers which are to be exercised by them.

Each organ must exercise its powers within its own sphere. This doctrine entails that each organ shall not encroach upon or interfere with the powers and independence of other organs of government. If any organ encroaches into the domain of the other organ, it shall be checked by another organ of the government. Thus, no new organ is created over and above the existing organs of government, to check encroachment.

Further, the separation of powers requires the presence of a written Constitution to define the formal powers of each organ. The powers shall be defined and divided in a way so as to create a system of checks and balances of powers among the organs.

(iii) Of the three given countries, power is most evenly divided in the USA among the three organs of the government.

Exam Pattern Questions

Objective Type Questions

Multiple Choice Questions (MCQs)

1. Which among the given statements is TRUE for the Legislature?
(a) The Legislature is responsible for enforcing laws.
(b) The Legislature interprets laws as part of its function.
(c) The Legislature is responsible for enacting laws.
(d) The Legislature primarily checks encroachments.

2. Which among the following is NOT a function of the Judiciary?
(a) Interpreting laws and ensuring their correct application in legal cases.
(b) Enforcing laws passed by the Legislature.
(c) Resolving disputes and protecting Fundamental Rights.
(d) Reviewing the constitutionality of laws and government actions.

3. On the whole, separation of powers requires the existence of a written Constitution to define the formal powers of each organ. The powers shall be so defined and divided to create a system of checks and balances of powers among the organs. This view finds support from the writings of which German-American political theorist?
(a) James Madison
(b) Herman Finer
(c) Carl Friedrich
(d) Karl Popper

4. Who gave the most original, systematic as well as scientific elaboration of the concept of 'separation of powers'?
(a) Locke (b) Lord Atkin
(c) Montesquieu (d) Aristotle

5. Which French ruler enjoyed the absolute powers of state and gave the dictum was,'I am the State'?
(a) James I (b) Elizabeth
(c) Louis V (d) King Louis XIV

6. Who has written the book 'Esprit Des Lois' published in 1748?
(a) Lord Acton (b) Aristotle
(c) Montesquieu (d) Locke

7. Which statement best reflects the historical inspiration for Montesquieu's doctrine of separation of powers?
(a) Montesquieu was influenced by the American Revolution, which demonstrated the need for checks and balances.
(b) The French Revolution inspired Montesquieu to advocate for limiting the powers of the monarchy.
(c) The despotic rule of King Louis XIV motivated Montesquieu to propose separating powers to prevent absolute authority.
(d) Montesquieu's ideas were based on the principles outlined during the drafting of the US Constitution.

8. The origin of the concept of .... is originally credited to Montesquieu.
(a) sovereignty (b) checks and balances
(c) government (d) federalism

9. Montesquieu's teachings gave a boost to the French Revolution and led to the adoption of ....

(a) Universal Declaration of Human Rights
(b) US Constitution
(c) French Declaration of Rights
(d) None of the above

10. Who is the executive head of the British Government?

(a) President (b) Parliament
(c) Prime Minister (d) Monarch

11. Which of the following countries does not have a written Constitution?

(a) India (b) United States
(c) Germany (d) Britain

12. Lord Chancellor was the head of the judiciary in Britain, until the enactment of which act?

(a) Anti-Abolishment Act, 1955
(b) Government of Britain Act, 2002
(c) Constitutional Reform Act, 2005
(d) None of the above

13. Which of the following Constitutions has adopted a Presidential form of government?

(a) Indian (b) American (c) British (d) None of these

14. Who among the following is vested with the legislative powers in the USA?

(a) President (b) Congress
(c) White House (d) None of these

15. The entire structure of US Constitution is based on doctrine of ....

(a) separation of power (b) dissolution of power
(c) distilled sovereignty (d) diverse population

16. Who is the real executive head of the Government of India?

(a) President (b) Prime Minister
(c) Governor (d) None of these

17. Which article of the Indian Constitution provides that the Parliament consists of the President and two houses known as the Council of States and the House of the People?

(a) Article 79 (b) Article 80
(c) Article 81 (d) Article 82

18. Which of the following is the final court of appeal in India?

(a) High Court (b) Supreme Court
(c) District Court (d) Sessions Court

19. Which article of the Indian Constitution provides that the state shall take steps to separate the judiciary from the executive in the public services of the state?

(a) Article 50 (b) Article 51
(c) Article 52 (d) Article 53

20. Ramesh and his son Umesh had planned to visit the Supreme Court of India that is located in Delhi. The father told his son that the apex court is one of the organ of the government. Competency Based Que

Identify the other organ among the following options.

(a) Subordinate Courts (b) Local Body
(c) Executive (d) RBI

21. Kavya, a MBA aspirant, has learnt that England shall be the best place since it is most liberal and citizens enjoys larger freedom right at there, which was also described by Montesquieu. Name the despotic ruler, who was contemporary of Montesquieu. Competency Based Que

(a) Louis XIV (b) Louis XV
(c) Louis XVI (d) Louis XVII

22. In Britain the three organs of government are the executive head (the hereditary monarch), legislature (comprises House of Commons and House of Lords) and the judiciary.

Identify which among the following is the lower house of the Parliament in Britain? Competency Based Que

(a) House of Lords (b) House of Commons
(c) Both (a) and (b) (d) None of these

23. Among the all democracies across the world, India is best known for well and smooth functions of all organs of the government as per the principle of separation of power. Under which article of the Constitution of India does the Parliament consist of the President and two houses known as the Council of States and the House of the People?

(a) Article 76 (b) Article 77
(c) Article 78 (d) Article 79

24. One day Rajiv, who is himself a lawyer by profession, was asked by his teenage son about the history and formation and uniqueness of Indian Constitution. Which among the following is not a doctrine of basic structure of Indian Constitution? Competency Based Que

(a) Supremacy of the Parliament
(b) Republic and democratic form of government
(c) Secular character of the Constitution and state
(d) Sovereignty of India

25. Mr. 'A' is a member of the legislature of country 'X'. He is also a minister in the executive organ of country 'X'. 'A', along with other ministers, is collectively responsible to the lower house of the legislature for all acts done by him as a minister. Competency Based Que

Which form of government prevails in country 'X'?

(a) Parliamentary
(b) Presidential
(c) Can't say
(d) Both (a) and (b)

26. Arrange the following documents in chronological order.

I. US Constitution
II. Constitution of India
III. Declaration of human rights
IV. The French Constitution

Choose the correct option

(a) II, III, I, IV (b) I, III, IV, II
(c) I, IV, III, II (d) IV, III, I, II

27. Match the following.

Column I (Article)	Column II (Provision)
A. Article 50	1. Power to move to the High Court for enforcement of Fundamental Rights
B. Article 32	2. Separation of judiciary from executive
C. Article 226	3. Composition of Parliament
D. Article 79	4. Power to move to the Supreme Court for enforcement of Fundamental Rights

Codes

	A	B	C	D
(a)	1	2	3	4
(b)	2	4	1	3
(c)	3	2	1	4
(d)	4	2	3	1

28. **Statement I** Montesquieu's doctrine of separation of power emphasises the division of government into three branches legislature, executive and judicial.

Statement II According to Montesquieu each branch of the government should have a separate and independent role, and no one branch should dominate the others.

Which of the following is correct?

(a) Both the Statement are correct.
(b) Both the Statement are incorrect.
(c) Statement I is correct, but Statement II is not correct.
(d) Statement I is not correct, but Statement II is correct.

29. **Statement I** A declaration of rights is a formal statement that outlines the Fundamental Rights and freedoms of individuals, such as right of life, liberty and property.

Statement II The purpose of a declaration of rights is to protect individuals from government abuse and ensure that the government respects and upholds their rights.

Which of the following is correct?

(a) Both the Statement are correct.
(b) Both the Statement are incorrect.
(c) Statement I is correct but, Statement II is not correct.
(d) Statement I is not correct but, Statement II is correct.

30. Consider the following statements.

Statement I The judiciary in India has the power to scrutinise legislations and administrative processes to assess their conformity to the Constitution.

Statement II The Parliament has unlimited power to amend the Constitution, including its basic structure.

Which of the following is correct?

(a) Both the Statement are correct.
(b) Both the Statement are incorrect.
(c) Statement I is correct, but Statement II is not correct.
(d) Statement I is not correct, but Statement II is correct.

31. Consider the following statements.

Statement I The Supreme Court of India has the power to determine the essential features constituting the framework of the Constitution.

Statement II The Judges of the Supreme Court and High Court can be removed by the President without impeachment by the legislature.

Which of the following is correct?

(a) Both the Statement are correct.
(b) Both the Statement are incorrect.
(c) Statement I is correct, but Statement II is not correct.
(d) Statement I is not correct, but Statement II is correct.

Assertion-Reason Questions

Directions (Q. Nos. 32-36) In the questions given below, there are two statements. Read the statements and choose the correct option.

Codes

(a) Both A and R are true and R is the correct explanation of A.
(b) Both A and R are true, but R is not the correct explanation of A.
(c) A is true, but R is false.
(d) A is false, but R is true.

32. **Assertion** (A) Montesquieu has written the book called 'Spirit of Laws'.

Reason (R) The doctrine of separation of power has nothing to do with Montesquieu.

33. **Assertion** (A) The United States has a Presidential form of government.

Reason (R) In the United States, the President is the executive head of the state.

34. **Assertion** (A) In the United States, Congress is the executive organ, while the President is the legislative organ.

Reason (R) Both President and Congress are elected by people.

35. Assertion (A) India has a bicameral legislature.
Reason (R) Indian Parliament has two houses called Lok Sabha and Rajya Sabha.

36. Assertion (A) Kesavananda Bharati case provided the doctrine of basic structure of Indian Constitution.
Reason (R) There is no restriction on the amending power of Parliament as far as the amendment of Indian Constitution is concerned.

Answers

1. (c) The Legislature is responsible for enacting laws.
2. (b) Enforcing laws passed by the Legislature.
3. (c) Carl Friedrich
4. (c) Montesquieu
5. (d) King Louis XIV
6. (c) Montesquieu
7. (c) The despotic rule of King Louis XIV motivated Montesquieu to propose separating powers to prevent absolute authority.
8. (b) checks and balances
9. (c) French Declaration of Rights
10. (d) Monarch
11. (d) Britain
12. (c) Constitutional Reform Act, 2005
13. (b) American
14. (b) Congress
15. (a) separation of power
16. (b) Prime Minister
17. (a) Article 79
18. (b) Supreme Court
19. (a) Article 50
20. (c) Executive
21. (a) Louis XIV
22. (b) House of Commons
23. (d) Article 79
24. (a) Supremacy of the Parliament
25. (a) Parliamentary
26. (b) I, III, IV, II
27. (b) 2 4 1 3
28. (a) Both the Statement are correct.
29. (c) Statement I is correct, but Statement II is not correct.
30. (a) Both the Statement are correct.
31. (a) Both the Statement are correct.
32. (c) A is true, but R is false. The given book has been written by Montesquieu. However, Reason (R) is incorrect because Montesquieu is credited with the formulation of the separation of powers doctrine and the statement says the opposite here.
33. (a) Both A and R are true and R is the correct explanation of A. The United States follows the Presidential system of government wherein the President is the elected and the executive head of the state.
34. (d) A is false, but R is true. Assertion (A) is false because in the US, Congress is the legislative organ and President is the executive organ of the state.
35. (a) Both A and R are true and R is the correct explanation of A. A bicameral legislature implies the presence of two Houses in the legislature. The Indian Parliament is bicameral because it has two Houses namely, the Lok Sabha and the Rajya Sabha.
36. (c) A is true, but R is false. The doctrine of basic structure was formulated in the Kesavananda case; however, it is wrong to say that there is no restriction on the amending power of the Parliament.

Subjective Questions

Very Short Answer Type Questions

1. Who has been credited with the creation of the concept of separation of powers?

Ans. Montesquieu has been credited with the creation of the concept of separation of powers.

2. Why was division of powers important according to Montesquieu?

Ans. According to Montesquieu, if the power has not been divided, it can cause tyranny (cruel and oppressive rule) in the name of law and justice.

3. 'Montesquieu become the intellectual father of the US Constitution'. Explain Why? **Competency Based Que**

Ans. Montesquieu became the intellectual father of the American Constitution as his doctrine of separation of powers forms the foundation on which the entire structure of the US Constitution 1787 is based.

4. A local council in a city has three departments: a legislative body that makes laws, an executive that implements them, and a judicial authority that interprets them. However, there is a case where the executive department has been creating laws and implementing them at the same time.

I. Identify what is the issue when the executive department creates and implements laws simultaneously in a local council?

II. State the significance of maintaining a separation of powers in a democratic system.

Competency Based Que

Ans. (i) The issue is a violation of the separation of powers, as the executive department is overstepping its role by making laws, which should be the responsibility of the legislative body.

(ii) The significance of maintaining a separation of powers in a democratic system are

Maintaining a separation of powers ensures that no single branch of government becomes too powerful. Each branch (legislative, executive and judicial) operates independently, preventing the abuse of power and protecting individual freedoms and democracy.

5. 'We can not apply the principle of separation of powers in practice'. Where and Why? **Competency Based Que**

Ans. The principle of separation of powers cannot be fully applied in countries with a Parliamentary system, like the UK or India. In these systems the executive (Prime Minister and Cabinet) is drawn from the legislature, blurring the lines between the legislative and executive branches. This integration is essential for efficient governance but compromises strict separation.

6. Which article of the Indian Constitution provides for the appointment of High Court and Supreme Court judges, and what is the process for their appointment?

Ans. Article 124 of the Indian Constitution deals with the appointment of Supreme Court judges, while Article 217 addresses the appointment of High Court judges. Judges are appointed by the President of India, based on recommendations from the collegiums system, which consists of the Chief Justice of India and senior judges of the Supreme Court.

7. Which article provides for the amending procedure of the Constitution?

Ans. Article 368 of the Constitution provides for constituent powers of the Parliament, and lays down the procedure for amendment of the Constitution.

8. Rohan, a law student, was studying the Indian Constitution. He noticed that the Constitution divided the powers of the government among the legislature, executive, and judiciary. The legislature made laws, the executive enforced them, and the judiciary interpreted them. This division of powers ensured that no one organ became too powerful.

What is the main purpose of the separation of powers in a government? **Competency Based Que**

Ans. The main purpose of the separation of powers is to prevent any one organ of the government from becoming too powerful, and to create a system of checks and balances among the organs.

Short Answer Type Questions

1. State the different organs of the government along with their functions.

Ans. The three organs of the government along with their functions are

(i) **Legislature** It is entrusted with the power of enacting laws.

(ii) **Executive** It is entrusted with the power of implementing laws.

(iii) **Judiciary** It is entrusted with the power of adjudicating disputes.

2. 'The separation of powers is necessary in between the legislative, the executive and the judicial system.'

Explain the concept of separation of power.

Competency Based Que

Ans. The concept of separation of powers is a fundamental principle in modern democratic systems, where the powers of government are divided into three distinct branches: the legislative, the executive, and the judicial. Each branch has its own specific role and responsibilities. The legislature is responsible for making laws, the executive implements and enforces those laws, and the judiciary interprets and applies the laws in legal matters.

3. How does Montesquieu explain separation of powers?

Ans. Montesquieu explained the separation of powers in the following ways

(i) The theory of separation of powers in its simplest form implies that all the above functions should be entrusted to three different authorities.

(ii) The three organs of the government should be kept separate and distinct.

(iii) One organ should be independent of the control of others.

(iv) Each organ shall exercise its powers within its own sphere.

(v) Each organ shall not interfere with the powers and independence of other organs of government. If any organ interferes in the functions of the other organ, it shall be checked by another organ of the government.

4. What were the conditions in England which inspired Montesquieu to formulate the doctrine of separation of powers for remedying the conditions of France?

Ans. The conditions in England which inspired Montesquieu to formulate the doctrine of separation of powers for remedying conditions of France were

(i) Montesquieu experienced the sense of liberty and freedom enjoyed by the citizens of England. He was very impressed with the thoughts of Locke. He compared their system of governance with the system prevailing in France.

(ii) He examined the separation of powers of the government and their exercise by separate organs of the government namely, the king, Parliament and the law courts in the governance structure in England.

5. "Power corrupts and absolute power corrupts absolutely".

(i) Who made the above statement?

(ii) This theory is in support of which doctrine?

(iii) Why is the doctrine a protest against absolute power?

Competency Based Que

Ans. (i) Lord Acton made the above statement.

(ii) This theory is in support of the doctrine of separation of powers.

(iii) Separation of powers is in itself a protest against absolute power. Its meaning can be better analysed if the use of the word powers of the organs is substituted by functions. The word 'functions' implies the attitude of service while the word 'powers' implies force. The government performs activities to serve the purpose of the state and its individuals through its classified functions for which the different organs are created.

6. Briefly mention the essential conditions required for the enactment of the doctrine of separation of powers. Who is specifically credited to the origin of the concept of checks and balances?

Ans. Separation of powers requires the existence of a written Constitution to define the formal powers of each organ. The powers shall be defined and divided in a way so as to create a system of checks and balances of powers among the organs. The origin of the concept of check and balances is specifically credited to Montesquieu. This concept provides a system-based regulation that allows one branch of the government to limit another.

7. State the key advantages of the doctrine of separation of powers.

Ans. Separation of powers has the following advantages

(i) It helps in making the organs more efficient in their performance of the functions.

(ii) This doctrine helps in safeguarding the liberty of the individuals as it requires each organ to function within its own sphere of law.

(iii) This doctrine seeks to establish an independent judiciary which is free from any bias. Montesquieu was interested in setting the judicial power as a check on and as arbiter between the other two organs.

(iv) This system helps in providing stability to the government by protecting the state's sovereignty.

8. What are the key disadvantages of the doctrine of separation of powers?

Ans. The key disadvantages of the doctrine of separation of powers are

(i) The major disadvantage of the concept of separation of powers is that if it is strictly applied, it can lead to frictions among the various arms of government. This is true because where there is the need for co-ordination, the arms of government may stick to their role and refuse to co-operate.

(ii) Another disadvantage of the separation of power is that in practical, the organs of government must be independent of each other but in nations, where the ruling government has majority in parliament, the executive organ is able to control the legislature through its members in Parliament.

9. What importance does Constitutional Reform Act hold in establishing separation of powers between different organs of the British Government?

Ans. The Constitutional Reform Act, 2005 separated the powers, with legislative functions vested with an elected Lord Speaker and the judicial functions vested with the Lord Chief Justice. Until the Constitutional Reform Act, 2005, the Lord Chancellor was the head of the judiciary in Britain. He was the ex-officio Speaker of the House of Lords, a Government Minister who sat in cabinet and was head of the Lord Chancellor's Department, which administered the courts, the justice system and appointed judges.

He sat as a judge on the Judicial Committee of the House of Lords, the highest domestic court in the entire United Kingdom, and the Judicial Committee of the Privy Council, the senior tribunal court for parts of the commonwealth.

10. 'Powers are distributed in Britain among the three organs of the government'. Explain the three organs of the goverment in Britain. **Competency Based Que**

Ans. In Britain, the powers of the government are divided among three organs: the legislature, the executive, and the judiciary.

Legislature The British legislature is called Parliament, which is made up of two houses – the House of Commons and the House of Lords. The primary role of Parliament is to make and pass laws. Members of the House of Commons are elected, while members of the House of Lords are appointed or inherit their positions.

Executive The executive is headed by the Prime Minister, who leads the government. The Prime Minister and his cabinet are responsible for implementing and enforcing laws passed by Parliament. The Monarch also plays a ceremonial role in the executive, but their powers are mostly symbolic.

Judiciary The judiciary interprets and applies the law. It ensures that laws passed by Parliament are consistent with the Constitution and protects citizens' rights. The judiciary in Britain is independent of both the legislature and the executive to maintain fairness and justice.

The purpose of separating these powers is to prevent any one branch from becoming too powerful or abusing its authority. It ensures a system of checks and balances, where each branch can limit the powers of the others.

11. State the three organs of the government in the USA.

Ans. In the United States, the government is divided into three main organs: the legislative, the executive and the judicial branches.

Legislative The legislative branch is called Congress, which is made up of two houses – the Senate and the House of Representatives. Its main function is to make laws, approve budgets, and represent the interests of the people. Senators and Representatives are elected by citizens.

Executive The executive branch is led by the President, who serves as both the head of state and government. The President is responsible for enforcing and implementing laws, overseeing the military, and handling foreign relations. The executive branch also includes the Vice President and various government departments.

Judicial The judicial branch is responsible for interpreting laws and ensuring justice. It is led by the Supreme Court, and includes lower courts. The judiciary ensures that laws comply with the US Constitution and resolves legal disputes fairly.

12. What is the tenure of the President of the United States? Mention his powers as an executive organ of the government.

Ans. The President of the United States is elected for a tenure of four years. As per the Constitution of United States, the President has the following powers

(i) The President has been given the powers of making appointments but these have to be ratified by the Senate.

(ii) The President can declare war but he can do so only if he has got the approval of both the Houses of the Congress.

(iii) The President could intervene in the business of the court through his power of pardon for all offences except treason.

(iv) The US President appoints the members of the Cabinet with the approval of the Congress as executive heads of the departments.

(v) The President has the power to call special sessions of Congress and veto the bills, (except money bills) passed by the Congress.

13. Which form of government is practiced in India? What are the different organs of the Indian Government?

Ans. The Indian government is divided into three main organs : the legislative, the executive, and the judicial branches.

Legislative The legislative branch is known as the Parliament and consists of two houses–the Lok Sabha (House of the People) and the Rajya Sabha (Council of States). Its main responsibility is to make laws, discuss national issues, and approve budgets. Members of the

Lok Sabha are elected, while Rajya Sabha members are appointed or elected by state assemblies.

Executive The executive branch is headed by the President of India. The President is the ceremonial head of state, while the Prime Minister and the Council of Ministers manage the day-to-day functioning of the government. The executive is responsible for implementing laws and policies.

Judicial The judiciary is independent and ensures that laws are interpreted and applied correctly. The Supreme Court of India is the highest court, followed by high courts and lower courts. The judiciary safeguards citizens' rights and upholds the Constitution.

14. Define Article 50 of Indian Constitution. What is its significance?

Ans. Article 50 of the Indian Constitution provides that the state shall take steps to separate the judiciary from the executive in the public services of the state.

The objective of Article 50 is to provide for the independence of the judiciary. The judiciary in India interprets the Constitution.

15. Explain in brief the process of election, tenure and powers of the President of India.

Ans. The President of India is elected by the Electoral College consisting of the elected members of both Houses of Parliament and the elected members of the Legislative Assemblies of the state.

The President of India is appointed for a fixed term of 5 years. The President of India is the nominal executive head. The real executive is the Prime Minister and his/her Council of Ministers.

The President exercises his/her powers/functions with the aid and advice of the Prime Minister and his/her Council of Ministers. Usually the advice of the Prime Minister and Council of Minister is binding on the President.

16. The Government of India seeks to amend the Indian Constitution in a manner that the country changes from a republican form of government into a monarchial one. Several protests were observed against this, resulting in a petition before the Supreme Court stating the government does not have the power to amend the Constitution in this manner. Decide.

(i) **Do you think that the protests are justified?**

(ii) **Which article provides for the amending power of the Parliament? Explain.** **Competency Based Que**

Ans. (i) The protests are justified because the government does not have the power to alter the basic structure of the Constitution. Republican government is one of the basic feature of the Indian Constitution.

(ii) Article 368 provides for the amending power of the Parliament.

17. Mahesh, a law graduate, was appointed as a judge in the High Court. He was relieved to know that his privileges and allowances could not be varied after his appointment. He also felt secure knowing that no discussion could take place in Parliament regarding his conduct, except in case of impeachment proceedings.

What provisions are incorporated in the Constitution to establish an independent judiciary, and how do they protect judges like Mahesh? **Competency Based Que**

Ans. The Constitution incorporates provisions like Article 50, which separates the judiciary from the executive, and Article 124(2), which outlines the appointment process for judges. Additionally, the Constitution protects judges' privileges and allowances, and prohibits discussions in Parliament about their conduct, except in impeachment proceedings. These provisions ensure the independence and security of judges, allowing them to perform their duties impartially.

Long Answer Type Questions

1. Explain in detail the basic features of the doctrine of separation of powers as enunciated by Montesquieu.

Ans. For answer, the Basic Features of Montesquieu's Doctrine, refer to text on pg. 45 and 46.

2. Discuss the concept of checks and balances as propounded by Montesquieu. Also explain its impact.

Ans. Montesquieu is credited with the origin of the system of checks and balances. This system provides for a system based regulation wherein one branch is allowed to limit the other. This doctrine was adopted by Montesquieu in his country's political system. His teachings also gave a boost to the French Revolution and further led to the adoption of the Declaration of Rights in 1789.

The Declaration provided that every society in which Separation of Powers is not determined, has no Constitution.

The French Constitution, 1791 made executive, legislative and judiciary independent of one another. The doctrine of separation of powers forms the foundation on which the entire structure of the US Constitution 1787 is based. Thus, Montesquieu became the intellectual father of the American Constitution.

3. Critically evaluate the doctrine of separation of powers, analysing its advantages and disadvantages.

Ans. For answer refer to the text under the heading Advantages or Benefits of the Doctrine of Separation of Powers, on page no. 47.

For answer refer to the text under the heading Disadvantages or Defects of the Doctrine of Separation of Powers, on page no. 47 and 48.

4. How has the role of the executive organ of the government increased in a welfare state? Discuss.

Ans. Montesquieu had proposed that all the three organs of the government would be given equal and independent position in the political organisation of the country. However, it is not so in reality.

The concept of welfare state demands more and more action and services from the government such as health, education, food and public distribution, public transport and supply of electricity. It tends to increase the powers of the executive, and develop the executive as a multifunctional organ. Today, the executive legislates, exercises judicial jurisdiction and plans the future activities of the government.

According to Barker, if the growth of legislative organ, due to the cabinet system, was the notable feature of 18th century, then the growth of executive organ due to the extension of rights and the corresponding extension of services is the notable feature of the 20th century.

5. What do you understand about the doctrine of basic structure? Explain in detail.

Ans. The doctrine of basic structure is a key principle in Indian constitutional law, established by the Supreme Court in the Kesavananda Bharati case (1973). It asserts that although Parliament has the power to amend the Constitution under Article 368, it cannot alter or destroy its basic structure. This means that while Parliament can make changes to the Constitution, such changes cannot undermine its fundamental principles.

The idea behind the doctrine is to protect the Constitution's core values and ensure that any amendment does not harm its essential framework.

The basic structure includes principles like democracy, rule of law, separation of powers, Fundamental Rights, and judicial review. For instance, Parliament cannot amend the Constitution in a way that would alter the balance of power between the legislature, executive and judiciary, or infringe upon the rights of the people.

The doctrine acts as a safeguard to prevent any potential misuse of the amending power. It ensures that while the Constitution can evolve, its foundational principles remain intact, preserving the integrity of India's democratic system.

6. There are three countries 'A', 'B' and 'C' all of them are democracies but differ in the forms of government that exist in these countries. In country 'A', the Presidential form of government is followed, while in the other two countries 'B' and 'C', Parliamentary form of government exists.

While one of the countries is located in the sub-continent of Asia, the other one is located in North America and Europe. One of the countries 'A' is the oldest democracy of the world while the other 'C' is the largest democracy of the world. The other one 'B' is a Constitutional monarchy. **Competency Based Que**

(i) Identify the three countries discussed in the case.

(ii) How is power separated in the government of one of the countries discussed in the case, situated in Asia?

Ans. (i) Based on the above description, the three countries are

(a) America (b) UK (c) India

(ii) The Asian country described in the case is India. For answer, answer refer to the text under the heading the Governing System of Separation of Powers in India, on page no. 51.

7. Imagine a country where the executive branch, headed by a powerful leader, can pass laws without any checks or balances. This leader also controls the judiciary, ensuring that any legal challenges to their authority are dismissed. In this scenario, the fundamental principles of separation of powers are violated, leading to a concentration of power and potential abuse.

Based on the illustration, how does the separation of powers contribute to the protection of individual liberties and the prevention of authoritarianism?

Competency Based Que

Ans. The separation of powers is a fundamental principle in democratic governance that ensures a system of checks and balances. By dividing the powers of government into three distinct branches—legislative, executive and judicial—it prevents the concentration of power in the hands of a single individual or group.

The legislative branch, responsible for lawmaking, is kept separate from the executive branch, which enforces the laws. This division prevents any one branch from becoming too powerful. The judicial branch, independent of the other two, interprets laws and ensures that they are applied fairly. This system of checks and balances safeguards individual liberties by limiting the power of government and preventing arbitrary actions.

Moreover, the separation of powers promotes accountability and transparency. Each branch is accountable to the others and to the people. This helps to prevent corruption and abuse of power. By upholding the principles of the separation of powers, a democratic government can safeguard individual freedoms and maintain a balance of power.

SELF ASSESSMENT TEST

Objective Type Questions

1. The doctrine of separation of powers forms the foundation on which the entire structure of the .... is based.

   (a) British Constitution (b) Indian Constitution
   (c) Irish Constitution (d) American Constitution

2. Who observed that the British Constitution had a weak separation of powers?

   (a) Dicey (b) Montesquieu (c) Acton (d) None of these

3. In Britain, the three organs of government are the executive head (the British monarch), legislature composed of .... and .... and the judiciary.

   (a) House of Lords, House of Commons (b) Lok Sabha, Rajya Sabha
   (c) Senate, Congress (d) None of these

4. According to which article, the judges of the Supreme Court and High Courts shall be appointed by the President after consultation with such judges of the Supreme Court and of the High Courts in the states?

   (a) Article 121 (b) Article 124 (2) (c) Article 123 (d) Article 125

Very Short Answer Type Questions

5. 'The separation of powers may mean three different things'. Analyse. **Competency Based Que**
6. 'The British monarch a ceremonial head'. Explain why? **Competency Based Que**
7. Mention the names of the two houses of the US Congress and state their role.
8. To whom are the Ministers responsible in a Parliamentary system of government?
9. What do you understand by the doctrine of basic structure?

Short Answer Type Questions

10. Who is credited with the doctrine of separation of powers? What are its basic features?
11. Analyse the impact of the concept of separation of power given by Montesquieu.
12. Describe the major advantages of the theory of separation of power.
13. The Constitutional Reform Act 2005, is a landmark legislation that reformed the British Constitution. One of its key provisions is the establishment of the Supreme Court. Which replaced the House of Lords as the Highest Court in UK. A group of citizens challenges the government's decision to restrict freedom of speech in a particular province. They argue that the restrictions violates their Fundamental Rights. Examine the role of the Constitutional Reform Act 2005, in this scenario. **Competency Based Que**
14. Distinguish between the form of governments and separation of power existing in the United States, Britain and India.

Long Answer Type Questions

15. Out of the three countries: US, UK and India, which form of government seems the most democratic to you? Give reasons for your answer. **Competency Based Que**
16. How is the independence of the judiciary ensured by the Indian Constitution?
17. Discuss the role of judiciary in the Indian context.

04 CHAPTER

Salient Features of the Constitution

The Constitution is a fundamental law of a state. It establishes the relationship among the organs and the state and its citizens.

YOUR STUDY GOALS

YOUR PRACTICE GOAL

- Objective Type Questions (40 Qs ; MCQs, A-R, Statements, Matching)
- Subjective Questions (16 VSAs, 11 SAs, 5 LAs)

4.1 Meaning and Definition of the Term Constitution

- A Constitution is an agreed upon document, which establishes the basis on which people shall govern themselves.
- The term 'Constitution' is derived from the Latin term **'constitutio'** which means **'to establish'**.
- Some important definitions of Constitution are
  - According to **Oxford Dictionary**, the Constitution is a 'body of fundamental principles or established precedents according to which a state or other organisation is acknowledged to be governed'.
  - According to **Aristotle**, the Constitution is 'the way of life which the state has chosen for itself'.
  - According to **Wade and Phillips** in their book 'Constitution and Administrative Law', the 'Constitution of a country seeks to establish its fundamental or basic or apex[1] organs of government and administration. It also describes government and administration's structure, composition, powers and principal functions. The Constitution also defines the inter-relationship of these organs with one another, and regulates their relationship with the people, more particularly the political relationship'.

1 Apex It means the top or highest part of something, especially one forming a point.

Distinctive Features of the Constitution

The Constitution of a state may have the following distinctive features

- It is a fundamental legal document (body of rules).
- It may be written or unwritten.
- It prescribes the nature of the state (unitary or federal, etc.).
- It establishes the manner or procedure in which power is transferred from one government to another.
- It determines the powers and responsibilities of state and organs of the government.
- It can either be written in a single document or can be a compilation of multiple documents.
- It determines the rights and duties of the citizens of the state and lays down the procedure for enforcement of those rights.

4.2 Historical Perspective of the Indian Constitution

India was a colony (part of the British Empire) of Britain before independence. The authority of the British Crown prevailed over India. Several legislations were enacted by the British Parliament for India's governance.

Some significant legislations among these were

- Government of India Act, 1858
- Indian Councils Act, 1861
- Indian Councils Act, 1892
- Indian Councils Act, 1909
- Government of India Act, 1919
- Government of India Act, 1935

The Government of India Act, 1919 and 1935 have played significant role in the formation of Indian Constitution.

The Government of India Act, 1919

The Government of India Act, 1919, also known as the Montagu-Chelmsfords reforms. The features of this act are

- It introduced a **bicameral**[2] **legislature** at the centre and created two houses, i.e.
  (i) Legislative Assembly or the Lower House (ii) Council of States or the Upper House
- The Public Service Commission was established under the act for the first time in India.
- The act also raised the number of Indian members in the Executive Council of the Governor General from 1 to 3.
- Direct election was introduced in India through this act.

Constituent Assembly

- On 9th December, 1946, the Constituent Assembly, a body elected by members of the Provincial legislatures and State legislatures, met for the first time and formally commenced the task of 'Constitution-making'.
- Most of the members of the Constituent Assembly were from the Congress Party and some were communists and independents. **Allan Octavian Hume**, an Englishman, formed the Congress Party in 1885 to enable Indian participation in the British Government.
- In 1921, after World War I, Mohandas Karamchand Gandhi (Mahatma Gandhi) assumed the leadership of the Congress Party and led the movement for India's independence.
- The Constituent Assembly also included eminent members from law and public affairs.
- The Constituent Assembly had two roles that were governance and the framing of the Constitution.
- In the morning, it dealt with the governance matters and in the afternoon, it drafted the Constitution.

2 **Bicameral** It means a legislature body having two chambers or houses that make laws.

Sources of the Constitution of India

The framers of the Constitution of India, i.e. the Constitution Assembly, drew upon three sources to draft the Constitution.

The Government of India Act, 1935

- This act was the basis for the government and was in force in India from 1935 until 1950 when the Constitution of India was adopted.
- This act was passed in August, 1935. It contained 321 Sections and 10 Schedules. **Durga Das Basu** mentioned in his book **'Introduction to the Constitution of India'** that the Indian Constitution draws much of its source from the Government of India Act, 1935. This act has provided the administrative details and language to the provisions of the Constitution.
- The main features of this act are
  - The Government of India Act, 1935 referred to India as a **federation of provinces** and Indian states.
  - The provinces were given autonomy by dividing legislative and executive powers between the provinces and the centre. The provinces were under the executive authority of the Governor appointed by the Crown. Provinces were the autonomous units of administration.
  - Governor exercised the powers on the advice of ministers, who were in turn responsible to Provincial legislature.
  - Governor was given power to carry out certain functions, independent of the Ministerial advice, but subject to the control of the Governor-General.
  - At the central level, Government of India was under the executive authority of Governor- General.
  - Governor-General was to act on the advice of Ministers of Central Legislature, who were in turn responsible to the Central Legislature.
  - The **Executive Council** which was formed under Government of India Act, 1919, **functioned as the Council of Ministers**.
  - Governor-General also had discretionary functions but these were subject to the control of the secretary of state.
  - The Indian Government assumed the role of Federal Government. The Central Legislature was bicameral which consisted of Federal Assembly and Council of States. Some of the provincial legislatures had bicameral legislature and other provinces had unicameral legislature.

Divisions of Legislative Powers According to Government of India Act, 1935

- The legislative powers and matters were divided between Central Legislature and Provincial Legislatures.
- The powers assigned to the Central Legislatures and Provincial Legislatures were included in the Federal List and Provincial List, respectively.
- The centre and provinces could exercise their combined authority on matters included in the concurrent list.
- These lists dealt with the following matters
  - **Federal List** It dealt with matters such as currency, external affairs, armed forces, etc. on which only Central legislature had the authority to legislate.
  - **Provincial List** It dealt with matters such as education, public health and agriculture, etc. on which only Provincial legislature had the authority to legislate.
  - **Concurrent List** It dealt with matters such as marriage and divorce, criminal law, civil law and procedure, etc. on which both federal and provincial legislatures had authority to legislate.

Limitations on Legislative Powers

- The legislative powers were divided among Central and Provincial Legislatures but their exercise was subject to various limitations which were
  - The Governor-General and the Crown had the power to veto a bill passed by the legislature.
  - The Governor-General had the power to issue ordinance and permanent acts when the legislative house was not in session.
  - The Governor-General had the power to suspend legislature if the proceedings would affect the discharge of his special responsibilities.
  - No bill could be introduced in Legislature without the previous sanction of Governor- General, which aims to amend or repeal the law of British Parliament as applicable in India.
- Thus, the Central and Provincial legislatures were to act under the instructions of Governor- General, Secretary of State and ultimately the sovereign powers of the British Crown. Indians were given very limited rights of self-governance.
- The dissatisfaction over granting of limited governing rights to India under 1935 Act led to widespread protests.
- Finally, the Colonial Government accepted that the Constitution of India should be framed by an elected Constituent Assembly consisting of Indian people.

Constitutions of Other Countries

- Constitutions of other countries were used mostly with respect to the two chapters of the constitution namely, the Fundamental Rights and Directive Principles of State policy.
- **Fundamental Rights** largely deal with civil and political rights of citizens (for example, right to life, freedom of speech and expression).
- **Directive Principles** deal largely with the economic, social and cultural rights of the citizens (for example, right to health and livelihood).

Objective Resolution

- Adopted in the December 1946 Assembly Session, the Constitution derived its spirit from this source.
- It laid down the philosophy and the Constitution expressed it through its many lengthy and detailed provisions.
- **Jawaharlal Nehru,** the first Prime Minister of India, had drafted the objectives resolution drawing upon the Congress Party documents of the previous two decades.
- It called for the integrity of the Indian Union and that its authority and power were derived from the Indian people.
- It stated that all the people should be secured with regards to justice, social, economic and political, equality of status, of opportunity and before the law; freedom of thought, expression, belief, faith, worship, vocation, association and action, subject to law and public morality.
- It provided for adequate safeguards for minorities, depressed and backward classes and underdeveloped and tribal areas.
- It can be summarised to consist of three interdependent salient features
  - Protecting and enhancing national unity and integrity;
  - Establishing the institutions and spirit of democracy; and
  - Promoting a social evolutions for the betterment of the citizens.

The Indian Independence Act, 1947

- The Indian Independence Act, 1947 was enacted by the British Parliament on 18th July, 1947. According to the Act, from 15th August, 1947, two independent dominions to be known as India and Pakistan would be established.
- The Constituent Assembly of each dominion was to have unlimited power to frame and adopt from any Constitution. It had all authority to repeal any Act of British Parliament including the Indian Independence Act.
- The date of 15th August, 1947 was referred to as **'appointment date'** under the Government of India Act, 1935.

Making of the Constitution

- On 15th August, 1947, the last Viceroy of British India, Lord Mountbatten, declared India and Pakistan two independent countries.
- After this, the Constituent Assembly created a new Constitution for India.
- India's first Law Minister, **Dr. B.R. Ambedkar,** is considered to be the Principal Architect of the Constitution of India. He is known as **Modern Manu.**
- He was appointed as the Chairman of the Constitution Drafting Committee.
- Under the Chairmanship of **Dr. Bhim Rao Ambedkar**, the Drafting Committee worked from **15th August, 1947 to 26th January, 1950.** A proposal on Draft Constitution of India was prepared after many discussions and deliberations to improve the existing system of administration, geographical compulsions, social and cultural diversities and historical precedents.
- The draft was passed on 26th November, 1949 after receiving the assent from the President of the Assembly, **Dr. Rajendra Prasad.**
- The Constituent Assembly held **11 sessions** and took a period of **2 years, 11 months and 18 days** to make the Constitution in Hindi by the name of 'Bhartiya Sanvidhan' and in English by the name of 'The Constitution of India'.
- The original Constitution of India is hand-written with beautiful calligraphy[3] **by Prem Behari Narain Raizada.** The Constitution **came into effect on 26th January, 1950.** This date is referred to as the date of commencement under Article 394 of the India Constitution.

Quick Test 1

1. Mention any one feature of the Constitution.
2. Name the two acts passed by the British Government which played significant role in the making of the Indian Constitution.
3. What happened on the 9th December, 1946 in Indian history?
4. Who is known as Modern Manu?

4.3 Salient Features of the Constitution of India

The Indian Constitution came into effect on 26th January, 1950. The salient features of the Constitution of India are mentioned below

Modern Constitution

The Indian Constitution was modern in appeal even at the time when it was drafted. It reflected the thoughts and values of independent India.

3 **Calligraphy** It is the art of producing decorative hand-writing or lettering with pen or brush.

Preamble to the Constitution

- Preamble is an introductory statement.
- The Constitution of India starts with the Preamble. The Preamble includes the guiding principles and the philosophy of the Constitution. It provides **unity** and **integrity** of the country.
- The objectives specified in the Preamble contain the basic structure of the Constitution. It is the guide to interpret the provisions of the Constitution.
- The Preamble proclaims India to be a Sovereign, Socialist, Secular, Democratic and Republic country. There are also various other terms in the Preamble which ensure equality and protect people.
- The various other terms are Justice, Liberty, Equality and Fraternity.
- The Supreme Court of India in the Fundamental Rights case (**Kesavananda Bharati Vs. Union of India, 1973 SC)** held that Preamble does form part of the Constitution.

Preamble

We, the people Of India, having solemnly resolved to Constitute India into a **Sovereign Socialist Secular Democratic Republic** and to secure to all its citizens;

Justice, social, economic and political; liberty of thought, expression, belief, faith and worship;

Equality of status and of opportunity; and to promote among them all;

Fraternity assuring the dignity of the individual and the unity and integrity of the nation;

In our Constituent Assembly this 26th, November, 1949, do **hereby adopt;**

Enact and give to **ourselves this Constitution.**

- The Preamble to the Constitution reaffirms that the people of India have adopted, enacted and given to themselves the Constitution. Supreme Court in **Charan Lal Sahu Vs. Union Of India (AIR 1990 SC 1480)** popularly known as **Bhopal Gas Leak Tragedy case** held that sovereign denotes that India is not subject to any external authority and that India as a state has the power to legislate on any subject in conformity with Constitutional limitations.
- The Preamble to the Constitution states that India's governing system is based on Republican and Democratic principles. In **S. R. Bommai Vs. U.O.I. (AIR 1994 SC 1918),** the Supreme Court held that the word 'democratic' signifies that "India has a responsible Parliamentary form of government, which is accountable to the elected legislature".
- Republic denotes that the head of the state is an elected person and not a hereditary monarch.
- The Preamble seeks to achieve for all citizens, social, economic and political justice; liberty of thought, expression, belief, faith and worship; equality of status and opportunity; fraternity, unity and integrity of the nation.
- The Preamble and the Constitutional provisions aim to secure to its citizens equality of status and opportunity in state affairs such as elections and in state employment without any special privilege or discrimination based on the ground of religion, race, caste, sex, place of birth.
- The word **'Socialist'** was added by the **Constitution (forty-second Amendment) Act, 1976.**
- The Supreme Court in the case of **S.R. Bommai Vs. Union of India (AIR 1994 SC 1918)** held that the principal aim of socialism is to eliminate inequality of income, status, standards of life and to provide a decent standard of life to working people.
- The Preamble establishes India as a Secular State. India as a Union of States has no official religion.
- The state does not identify itself with or favour any particular religion.
- The word **'Secular'** was added by the **Constitution (forty-second Amendment) Act, 1976**. Even before the Amendment, operation of the concept of secularism was visible in the Fundamental Rights and Directive Principles. This has also been given the status of basic structure of the Constitution in Kesavananda Bharati's case.

Sovereign

- The term 'Sovereign' was incorporated in the Preamble to provide supreme power to the government.
- The term 'Sovereign' implies that India is free from any kind/form of foreign interference in its domestic affairs and matters.
- The state has the power to legislate on any subject in accordance with Constitutional limitations.

Secularism

- Secularism promotes the development and unity of various religions.
- India is a country of various religions, beliefs and sects. Its people profess and practice different religions.
- There is no state-recognised place of worship.
- State laws and policies prohibit any discrimination on the grounds of religion.
- It treats all religious equally.
- It provides protection to citizens to profess, propagate and practice their religions.

Democracy

- The word 'Democratic' signifies that India has a Parliamentary form of government, which is accountable to the elected legislature.
- The main reason for incorporating democracy is to provide freedom to the people to choose their own representatives and to save them from the tyrant (cruel) leaders.

Socialist

Generally, it means a system under which the means of production and distribution are owned by the State.

Republic

- The concept of 'Republic' was borrowed from the **Constitution of France**.
- Any Indian can contest for Presidential elections without any discrimination, if he/she fulfills the eligibility conditions as provided by the Constitution.

Justice

- The Preamble to the Constitution of India guarantees three types of justice to its citizens. They are
  - (i) **Social Justice** The concept of social justice promotes equal treatment of citizens and promotes the rule of law. This term ensures that there would be no discrimination among the citizens on any ground. The Fundamental Rights, provided in Part III of the Constitution, also ensures social justice.
  - (ii) **Economic Justice** The concept of economic justice avoids discrimination between genders, provides **equal opportunity to work** and ensures the **equal distribution of wealth.**
  - (iii) **Political Justice** The concept of political justice provides all citizens to participate in the political proceedings.

Liberty and Fraternity

- The terms 'Liberty' and 'Fraternity' are provided in the Preamble to the Indian Constitution.
- These terms were used in the French Revolution.
- Liberty refers to **freedom on people's actions** while enabling them to develop their own identities.
- Fraternity refers to a **spirit of brotherhood** among the people of the land.

Lengthiest Constitution

- According to **Durga Das Basu,** "The Constitution of India has the distinction of being the lengthiest, most detailed, elaborate Constitutional document the world has so far produced".
- The Indian Constitution is one of the lengthiest Constitutions in the world.

- It is also very detailed. Originally, the Constitution had **395 Articles and 8 Schedules.**
- The Indian Constitution has incorporated various articles by taking inspiration from various Constitutions around the world.

Quick Test 2

1. Mention the purpose behind including the words 'Socialist' in the Indian Constitution.
2. How 'political justice' can be provided as mentioned in the Preamble to the Indian Constitution?
3. What do you understand by the term 'fraternity' as mentioned in the Preamble of India's Constitution?
4. Why is Indian Constitution called the lengthiest Constitution of the world?

4.4 Fundamental Rights, Directive Principles of State Policy and Fundamental Duties

Fundamental Rights

- **Part III** of the Indian Constitution ensures some rights for the Indian citizens which are referred to as Fundamental Rights.
- These rights are **enforceable against the state** and the state cannot take them away.
- People have a **right to directly appeal** to the Supreme Court or High Courts for the violation of Fundamental Rights.
- In fact, the right to move or appeal to the Supreme Court or High Court is itself a Fundamental Right.
- It the Articles 12 to 35 of Part III in the Constitution list, the Fundamental Rights are
  - (i) Rights to Equality
    - Equality before laws (different point) prohibition of discrimination on grounds of religion, race, caste, sex or place of birth
    - Equality of opportunity in matters of public employment
    - **Abolition**[4] of untouchability and titles
  - (ii) Right to Freedom
    - Right to freedom of speech and expression
    - Right to free movement, to form associations, to practice any trade or occupation
    - Protection in respect to conviction for offences
    - Protection of life and personal liberty
    - Protection against arrest and detention in certain cases
  - (iii) Right against Exploitation
  - (iv) Right to Freedom of Religion
  - (v) Cultural and Education Rights
  - (vi) Right to Constitutional Remedies
- In addition to these rights, the **Right to Education** was inserted as **Article 21A** by the **86th Constitutional Amendment Act, 2002,** as a Fundamental Right.
- Moreover, Fundamental Rights stated under Articles 14 and 21 are even **conferred to non-citizens.**

4 **Abolition** It means the act of stopping or ending something.

Right to Property was originally a Fundamental Right, but after the 44th Constitutional Amendment Act, 1978, it ceased to be a Fundamental Right. Instead, the Right to Property is mentioned under 300 A of the Constitution of India which states that no person can be deprived of his property save by law.

- The Supreme Court shall have power to issue directions or orders or writs for the enforcement of Fundamental Rights under Article 32, and the High Courts have this power under Article 226 of the Constitution. Thus, the **Fundamental Rights are termed justiciable[5] rights.** The writs include habeas corpus, mandamus, prohibition, quo-warranto and certiorari.
- These writs are explained below

Type of Writ	Origin	Literal Meaning	Objective
Habeas Corpus	Latin	You may have the body	It is issued to produce a person who has been detained, whether in prison or in private custody, before a court and to release him/ her if such detention is found illegal.
Mandamus	Latin	We command	It is an order by a superior court commanding a person or a public authority to do something in the nature of public duty.
Quo Warranto	Latin	By what warrant or authority	It is an order issued by the court to prevent a person from holding office to which he/she is not entitled and to remove him/her from that office.
Certiorari	Latin	To be more fully informed	It is a writ issued by a higher court to a lower court. It is issued to seek the judicial review of a decision of a lower court.
Prohibition	English	To forbid or to stop	It is issued by a superior court to an inferior court in order to prevent the inferior court from dealing with a matter out of its jurisdiction. The aim of this writ is to keep the inferior courts within the limits of their jurisdiction.

Difference between Writ Jurisdiction of Supreme Court and Hight Court

Difference	Supreme Court	High Court
Purpose	To only enforce Fundamental Rights	To enforce Fundamental Rights as well as ordinary legal rights
Power	Article 32 is a Fundamental Right. The Supreme Court cannot refuse to exercise its power to issue the writs.	Article 226 it is not a Fundamental Right. High Court may refuse to exercise its power to issue writs.

Directive Principles of State Policy (DPSP)

- The Directive Principles of State Policy are included in **Part IV** of the Indian Constitution. These are the guiding principles that govern state policies in the social sector. They are **socialist in nature** and fulfill the social revolution agenda of the Preamble.
- The Directive Principles are **not enforceable** by any court of law
- **Articles 36-51** of the Constitution cover the Directive Principles of State Policy.
- These principles mandate the state to provide
  - free legal aid
  - organise village panchayats
  - ensure right to education
  - ensure humane conditions for work
- The concept of DPSP has been inspired by the **Irish Constitution.**
- Some of the important Directive Principles are
  - The right to an adequate means of livelihood for citizens

5 **Justiciable** It means cases which are capable of being decided according to the legal principles by a court.

- Equal pay for equal work for both men and women
- Equal justice and free legal aid
- Organisation of village panchayats
- Provision of just and humane conditions of work and maternity relief
- Uniform civil code for citizens
- Promotion of educational and economic interests of Scheduled Castes, Scheduled Tribes and other weaker sections
- Duty of the state to raise the level of nutrition and to improve public health
- Protection and improvement of environment and promotion of international peace and security

■ A large number of laws have been enacted and adopted to implement the Directive Principles of State Policy. For example, the Legal Services Authority Act 1987, Right to Free and Compulsory Education 2009, Child Labour Prohibition Act 1986, Environment Protection Act 1986, Wildlife Protection Act 1972, Minimum Wages Act 1948, Equal Pay for Equal Work Act, etc.

■ The **73rd and 74th Constitutional Amendment** Acts, 1992 led to the establishment of Panchayati Raj Institutions and Urban Local Bodies, based on democratic principles.

■ The Supreme Court of India while interpreting Constitutional provisions **raised some Directive Principles to the status of Fundamental Rights.** For example

- Right to **Equal Pay for Equal Work** in the case of **Randhir Singh Vs. UOI.**
- Right to **Clean and Healthy Environment in** the case of **M.C. Mehta Vs. Kamal Nath.**
- Right to **Free Legal Aid** in the case of **Hussainara Khatoon Vs. Home Secretary.**

■ In the view of comparison between Fundamental Rights and Directive Principles, the Fundamental Rights represents the Political and Civil Rights and the Directive Principles embody Social and Economic Rights.

Difference between Fundamental Rights and Directive Principles of State Policy

Fundamental Rights	Directive Principles of State Policy
Part III of the Constitution of India contains the Fundamental Rights. They are given in Articles 12-35 of the Constitution of India.	Part IV of the Constitution of India contains Directive Principles of State Policy. They are given in Articles 36-51 of the Constitution of India.
These are basic, inalienable rights that are guaranteed to Indian citizens by the Constitution of India.	Directive Principles of the Constitution of India are guidelines to be followed by the government while framing policies.
They are civil and political in nature, i.e. they help the citizens in enjoying their life under a government.	They are social and economic in nature.
Fundamental Rights are justiciable as they can be enforced legally by the courts by way of writs.	Directive Principles are not justiciable as they cannot be enforced by the courts if there is a violation. They can be enforced either by passing a legislation or by judicial process where they are linked to a Fundamental Right.
The concept of Fundamental Rights was borrowed from the Constitution of the United States of America.	The concept of Directive Principles of State Policy was borrowed from the Constitution of Ireland which was copied from the Constitution of Spain.

Fundamental Duties

- **Part IV-A** of the Constitution contains only one Article, i.e. **Article 51A.**
- This Article provides **11 Fundamental Duties** for the Indian citizens.
- It was added by **the 42nd Constitutional Amendment** Act, 1976.
- According to Article 51A, it shall be the duty of every citizen of India
  - to abide by the Constitution and respect its ideals and institutions, the National Flag and the National Anthem.
  - to cherish and follow the noble ideals which inspired our national struggle for freedom.
  - to uphold and protect the sovereignty, unity and integrity of India.
  - to defend the country and render national service when called upon to do so.
  - to promote harmony and the spirit of common brotherhood amongst all the people of India ignoring religious, linguistic and regional or sectional diversities, and to promote the dignity of women.
  - to value and preserve the rich heritage of our composite culture.
  - to protect and improve the natural environment including forests, lakes, rivers and wildlife, and to have compassion for living creatures.
  - to develop the scientific temper, humanism and the spirit of inquiry and reform.
  - to safeguard public property and to renounce/ reject violence.
  - to strive towards excellence in all spheres of individual and collective activity so that the nation constantly rises to higher levels of endeavour and achievement.
  - to provide (for a parent or guardian) opportunities for education of the child or ward between the age of six and fourteen (added by the 86th Constitutional Amendment Act, 2002).
- There is no provision in the Constitution to enforce Fundamental Duties.
- However, according to the judgement of the Supreme Court in the case of **Bijoe Emmanuel Vs. State of Kerala,** the duties imposed on the citizens may be enforced through the enactment of legislations.
- For example, 'The Prevention of Insult to National Honors Act, 1971' punishes a person who insults the national honors.

Constitutional Provision for Amendment of the Constitution of India

- Part XX of the Constitution of India provides the procedure for amendment of the Constitution in detail.
- Article 368 specifies the powers of the Parliament to amend the Constitution and lays down the procedure.
- There is no limitation on the constituent power of the Parliament for amending the Constitution by adding, removing or improving the provisions in the Constitution.
- The initial step of an amendment is the introduction of a bill in either House of Parliament.
- The bill has to be passed in each house by a majority of the total membership of that house and by a **majority of not less than two-thirds** of that house present and voting.
- The bill is then sent for the President's assent.
- Some amendments also require to be approved by the Legislature of **not less than one-half of the states** but it must be passed before presenting to the President for assent.
- The powers of Parliament to amend the Constitution of India, in respect of its basic structure, has been restricted by the Supreme Court in the case of Kesavananda Bharati Vs. The State of Kerala.

Adult Suffrage

- **Article 326** provides Indian citizens with the **Right to Vote** in the general elections to the House of People and to the Legislative Assemblies of States.
- Every citizen who is not less than 18 years of age (reduced from 21 years by the Constitutional Amendment Act, 1988) is eligible to exercise his/her voting right.

- However, the person can be disqualified as a voter under the Constitution or any other law, on the basis of unsoundness of mind, non-residence, crime or corrupt or illegal practice.
- According to **Article 326,** there is one general electoral roll for every territorial constituency for election to either House of Parliament or to the House or Houses of State Legislature.
- This article further specifies that no person shall be ineligible for inclusion to the electoral roll on the basis of religion, race, caste, sex or any of them.
- **Articles 330** and **332** provide for reservation of seats for the Scheduled Castes and Scheduled Tribes in the House of People and Legislative Assemblies respectively.
- **Article 331** provides for representation for members of the Anglo-Indian[6] community in the House of People. The right to free and fair elections has been declared to constitute the basic structure of the Constitution in the case of **Indira Nehru Gandhi Vs. Raj Narain,** popularly known as **Election case.**

Single Citizenship

- In a **federal state,** the citizens generally enjoy **double citizenship** like in the USA. In India, there is only **single citizenship** according to the Constitution. **Part II** of the Constitution of India contains provisions regarding citizenship. Single citizenship means that every Indian is a citizen of India, irrespective of the place of his/her residence or place of birth. He/She is not a citizen of the constituent state like Jharkhand, Uttarakhand or Chhattisgarh to which he/she may belong.
- The Constitution makers opted for single citizenship to eliminate regionalism and other disintegrating[7] tendencies. Single citizenship has promoted a sense of unity among the people of India.
- The Indian citizenship can be acquired in four ways which are listed under the Citizenship Act, 1955. These are
  - **By Birth** Every person who takes birth in India and whose parents are not illegal migrants is entitled to Citizenship by birth.
  - **By Registration** Citizenship can also be acquired by registration. It usually requires residence of atleast 7 years.
  - **By Descent** Citizenship can be acquired if either of the parents of a person is a citizen of India.
  - **By Naturalisation** A person can acquire citizenship by naturalisation if he/she is ordinarily a resident of India for 12 years.

Independent Judiciary

India has a single integrated judicial system. The Indian judiciary is free from the influence of the executive and the legislature. It functions according to the principles of the Constitution.

Emergency Provisions

- The makers of the Constitution believed that there could be situations in the future when the government could not be run as in ordinary times.
- Thus, to cope with such situations, the Constitution incorporated some emergency provisions.
- There are three types of emergency
  (i) Emergency caused by war, external aggression or armed rebellion (Article 352).
  (ii) Emergency arising out of the failure of Constitutional machinery in states (Articles 356 and 365).
  (iii) Financial emergency (Article 360).
- These provisions are incorporated to safeguard the sovereignty, unity, integrity and security of the country, the democratic political system and the Constitution.

---

6 Anglo Indian it is a person relating to both Britain and India.
7 Disintegrate It means break up into small parts as the resuet of impact or decay.

- During an emergency, the Central Government becomes all-powerful and the states are controlled by the centre. This kind of transformation of the political system from federal (during normal times) to unitary (during emergency) is a unique feature of the Indian Constitution.

Federal in Form, Unitary in Character

The Constitution of India establishes a federal system of government. It contains all the usual features of a federation, such as

- two governments
- division of powers
- written Constitution
- the supremacy of the Constitution
- the rigidity of the Constitution
- independent judiciary
- bicameralism

However, the Indian Constitution also contains a large number of **unitary or non-federal features,** such as

- a strong centre
- single Constitution
- appointment of State Governor by the centre
- All India Services
- integrated judiciary

Article 1 describes India as a **'Union of States'** which implies two things

(i) Indian Federation is not the result of an agreement by the states.

(ii) No State has the right to break away from the federation.

Division of Power (Centre-State Relations)

- The **Seventh Schedule** contains three legislative lists.
- These three lists define the legislative jurisdictions. These are discussed below
  - **Union List** The Central Government has the exclusive legislative authority to frame laws over matters listed in the union list. Matters of national importance are included in this list. There are **99 subjects** in the union list that include foreign affairs, defense, armed forces, communications, posts and telegraph, foreign trade, etc.
  - **State List** The State Governments have the authority on matters stated in the state list. There are **61 subjects** in the state list that include public order, police, administration of justice, prison, local governments, agriculture, etc.
  - **Concurrent List** Both Parliament and State Legislatures have powers over matters enumerated in the concurrent list. However, the Parliament has supremacy in this list. There are **52 subjects** in the concurrent list that include criminal and civil procedure, marriage and divorce, economic and special planning, trade unions, electricity, newspapers, books, education, population control and family planning, etc.

Schedules in the Constitution

- Originally, there were 8 Schedules but now **12 Schedules** are included in the Constitution of India.
- They provide necessary administrative details to the functioning of the organs of government. These schedules are **amendable**[8] by Parliament.

Quick Test 3

1. What do you understand by the term 'protection against arrest' as described under Fundamental Rights?
2. What are the basic principles mandate for the State to provide under DPSPs?
3. How many Fundamental Duties are included in the Article 51 A?
4. What are the types of emergency as per the Indian Constitution?

8 **Amendable** It means something that can be changed, revised or altered.

Mind Map

SALIENT FEATURES OF THE CONSTITUTION OF INDIA

1 Meaning and Definition of the Constitution

Definition
- Derived from Latin 'Constitutio,' meaning to establish.'
- A legally binding document establishing governance.
- Establishes the basis on which people shall govern themselves.

Key Definition
- **Oxford Dictionary** "Body of fundamental principles or established precedents governing a state."

2 Historical Perspective

Pre-Independence Laws
- Government of India Acts, 1858, 1919, 1935.
- Indian Councils Acts, 1861, 1892, 1909.

Key Contributions
- 1919 Act introduced bicameral legislature, direct elections.
- 1935 Act influenced the Constitution, introducing federal structures and legislative lists.

3 Constituent Assembly

Formation
- Established on December 9th, 1946.
- Members elected by provincial legislatures.
- Met for the first time and formally commenced the task of Constitution making.

Key Figures
- **Dr. B.R. Ambedkar** Principal architect.
- Drafting Committee chaired by Ambedkar.
- **Timeline** Worked from August 15th, 1947, to January 26th, 1950.

4 Primary Influences

- **Government of India Act, 1935**
- India as a federation of provinces and Indian States.
- Exercised the powers on the advice of Ministers
- Constitutions of other countries (e.g., USA, Ireland, France).
- Fundamental Rights largely deal with civil and political rights of citizen.
- Directive Principles deal largely with the economic, social and cultural rights.

5 The Preamble

Introduction
- Preamble is an introductory statement.
- Outlines philosophy and guiding principles.
- Declares India as Sovereign, Socialist, Secular, Democratic, Republic.

Values
- Secularism (development and unity of various religions, equality, propagate and practice their religions).
- Justice (Social, Economic, Political).
- Liberty (Thought, Expression, Belief, Faith).
- Equality (Status and Opportunity).
- Fraternity (Unity and Integrity).

6 Fundamental Rights (Part III, Articles 12–35)

Rights Provided
- Equality before law (Article 14).
- Freedom of speech, movement, profession (Articles 19–22).
- Protection against exploitation (Articles 23–24).
- Religious freedoms (Articles 25–28).
- Cultural and educational rights (Articles 29–30).
- Right to constitutional remedies (Article 32).

Amendments
- Right to Property removed (44th Amendment, 1978).
- Right to Education added (86th Amendment, 2002).

7 Directive Principles of State Policy (DPSP, Part IV, Articles 36-51)

Purpose
- Non-justiciable principles guiding state policies.
- Fulfill the social revolution agenda of the Preamble.
- Not enforceable by any court of law.
- Inspired by Irish Constitution.

Judicial Elevation
- Certain DPSPs elevated to Fundamental Rights in landmark cases.

8 Fundamental Duties (Part IV-A, Article 51A)

Introduction
- Added by the 42nd Amendment (1976).

Duties Includes
- Respect the Constitution, national flag and anthem.
- Protect the sovereignty, unity and integrity of India.
- Safeguard public property and to renounce.
- Improve the natural environment including forests, lakes, rivers etc.
- Provide education for children (86th Amendment, 2002).

9 Landmark Cases and Judgements

Kesavananda Bharati Case (1973)
- Established the basic structure doctrine.

S.R. Bommai Case
- Defined federal principles and scope of state emergencies.

M.C. Mehta Case
- Environmental protection elevated to Fundamental Rights.

10 Key Articles and Amendments

Amendments
- 42nd (Socialist, Secular added to Preamble).

Notable Articles
- **Article 32** Right to Constitutional Remedies.
- **Article 368** Constitutional Amendments.
- **Article 326** Universal Adult Suffrage.

11 Contemporary Relevance

- **Dynamic Document** Responsive to social, economic, and political changes.
- **Global Inspiration** Adopted best practices from other Constitutions.
- **Safeguard of Democracy** Ensures checks and balances.

CBSE TEXTBOOK FOLDER

1. Briefly write the facts/observation of the court with regards to the following cases

(i) Charan Lal Sahu Vs. Union of India

(ii) S.R. Bommai Vs. Union of India

(iii) Randhir Singh Vs. Union of India

(iv) M.C. Mehta Vs. Kamal Nath

(v) Ashok Kumar Thakur v Union of India

Ans. (i) The Supreme Court in the case of Charan Lal Sahu Vs. Union of India, popularly known as Bhopal Gas Leak Tragedy case, provided that India is not subject to any external authority and India as a state has the power to legislate on any subject in conformity with Constitutional limitations.

(ii) The Supreme Court in the case of S.R. Bommai Vs. Union of India provided that the principal aim of socialism is to eliminate inequality of income, status, standards of life and to provide a decent standard of life to working people.

(iii) The Supreme Court elevated the status of Right to Equal Pay for Equal Work from that of DPSP to that of Fundamental Rights in the case of Randhir Singh Vs. Union of India.

(iv) The Supreme Court elevated the status of Right to Clean and Healthy Environment from that of DPSP to that of Fundamental Rights in the case of M.C. Mehta Vs. Kamal Nath.

(v) The Supreme Court in the case of Ashok Kumar Thakur Vs. Union of India provided that no distinction can be made between the two sets of rights. The Fundamental Rights represents the political and civil rights and the Directive Principles embody social and economic rights. As the directive principles are non-justiciable by the judicial process, it does not mean that they are of subordinate importance.

2. Write brief notes on

(i) Fundamental Rights (ii) Fundamental Duties

(iii) Preamble

(iv) Directive Principles of State Policy

Ans. (i) Part III of the Indian Constitution ensures some rights for the Indian citizens. These rights are referred to as 'Fundamental Rights'. These rights are enforceable against the state and the state cannot take them away. People have a right to directly move to the Supreme Court or High Courts for the infringement of these rights. In fact, the right to move to the Supreme Court or High Court is itself a Fundamental Right. These rights are mentioned in Articles 12-35. The Fundamental Rights are

(i) Rights of Equality

(ii) Right to Freedom

(iii) Right against Exploitation

(iv) Right to Freedom of Religion

(v) Cultural and Education Rights and

(vi) Right to Constitutional Remedies

(vii) The Right to Education which was inserted as Article 21A by the 86th Constitutional Amendment Act, 2002.

(ii) Part IV-A of the Constitution contains only one Article, i.e. Article 51A. This Article provides 11 Fundamental Duties for the Indian citizens. It was added by the 42nd Constitutional Amendment Act, 1976. According to Article 51A, it shall be the duty of every citizen of India.

(iii) The Preamble refers to the introduction or preface to the Constitution containing the summary or essence of the Constitution. The Preamble to the Indian Constitution proclaims India to be a Sovereign, Socialist, Secular, Democratic and Republic Country. There are also various other terms in the Preamble which ensure equality and protection of people. These are Justice, Liberty, Equality and Fraternity.

(iv) The concept of DPSPs has been inspired from the Irish Constitution. The Directive Principles of State Policy are included in Part IV of the Indian Constitution. These are the guiding principles governing state policies in the social sector. They are interpreted as economic and social rights and are classically socialist in nature and fulfill the social revolution agenda of the Preamble.

The DPSPs are not enforceable by any court of law but provide guidance in carrying out and drafting laws regarding human and social development. Articles 36-51 of the Constitution cover the Directive Principles of State Policy.

These principles act as a direction to the state to promote social, economic and political justice in order to secure the welfare of the people.

These principles mandate the state to provide the following

- Free legal aid
- Organise village panchayats
- Ensure right to education
- Ensure humane conditions for work

3 Give one point of difference between the following

(i) Unicameral and Bicameral Legislature
(ii) Fundamental Rights and Fundamental Duties
(iii) Sovereign and Secular
(iv) Article 32 and Article 226
(v) Original and advisory jriadication of the Supreme Court

Ans. (i)

Unicameral Legislature	Bicameral Legislature
A unicameral legislature has only one house, which is the best suited to smaller states.	A bicameral legislature have two houses, which is the best suited to larger states.

(ii)

Fundamental Rights	Fundamental Duties
These are enforceable through courts.	These are not enforceable through courts.

(iii)

Sovereign	Secular
Authority of the state to conduct its own affairs without any external or internal interference.	The term 'secular' implies that there is no state religion and every religion is treated at par with one another.

(iv)

Article 32	Article 226
Article 32 is a Fundamental Right. It entitles the citizens of India to move the Supreme Court or High Courts for the enforcement of these rights.	Article 226 is not a Fundamental Right. It gives the power to High Court to issue writs to enforce any of the basic Fundamental Rights guaranteed by the Constitution.

(v)

Original Jurisdiction	Advisory Jurisdiction
The Supreme Court has the sole authority to hear certain cases, such as disputes between the government and state, or between states.	The president can refer a question of law or fact to the Supreme Court for an opinion. This Supreme courts's advice is not binding on the President or government.

4. Answer the following questions briefly.

(i) Why would one term the Constitution of India as a 'living document'?
(ii) Briefly describe the three sources of the Constitution of India.
(iii) How was the Constituent Assembly formed? What was its purpose?
(iv) When can the President of India proclaim a state of emergency? What happens during such a situation?
(v) Can the basic structure of the Constitution be amended? Why/ Why not?

Ans. (i) As the Indian Constitution keeps responding to the emerging circumstances and situations from time to time, almost like a human being, the Indian Constitution is termed as a living document. The Indian Constitution continues to be effective, as it is able to respond to changing situations, is dynamic and open to interpretations. It not only protects democracy, but also allows for evolution of new Practices.

(ii) The framers of the Constitution of India, i.e. the Constituent Assembly, drew upon three sources to draft the Constitution.

These are

(a) The first source was the foundation document or the base text the Government of India Act of 1935, which was passed by the Parliament in London. This act was the basis for the government and was in force in India from 1935 until 1950 when the Constitution of India was adopted.

(b) The second source was the Constitutions of other countries. They were used mostly with respect to the two chapters of the Constitution namely, the Fundamental Rights and the Directive Principles of State Policy.

(c) The third source was the Objectives Resolution adopted in the December, 1946 Assembly Session. The Constitution derived its spirit from this source. The Objectives Resolution laid down the philosophy and the Constitution expressed it through its many lengthy and detailed provisions.

(iii) The idea of a Constituent Assembly was put forward for the first time by M.N. Roy.

In 1935, the Indian National Congress (INC), for the first time, officially called for a Constituent Assembly to frame the Constitution for India.

(iv) The President can proclaim an emergency in the following situations

- Emergency caused by war, external aggression or armed rebellion (Article 352).
- Emergency arising out of the failure of Constitutional machinery in states (Articles 356 and 365).
- Financial emergency (Article 360).

During an emergency, the Central Government becomes all powerful and the states are controlled by the centre.

(v) The basic structure of the Constitution cannot be amended by the Parliament. This is because it is the very essence of the Constitution. The Supreme Court in the case of Kesavananda Bharati Vs. The State of Kerala has restrained the powers of Parliament to amend the Constitution of India in respect of its basic structure.

5. Answer the following questions in about 200 words.

(i) Describe any six features of the Constitution of India.

(ii) What is the importance of Fundamental Rights in a democratic country like India?

Ans. (i) The six features of the Indian Constitution are given below

(a) **Lengthiest Constitution** The Indian Constitution is one of the lengthiest Constitutions in the world. It is very detailed. Originally, the Constitution had 395 Articles and 8 schedules.

(b) **Fundamental Duties** Part IV-A of the Constitution contains only one Article, i.e. Article 51A. This Article provides 11 Fundamental Duties for Indian citizens. It was added by the 42nd Constitutional Amendment Act, 1976.

(c) **Independent Judiciary** India has a single integrated judicial system. The Indian judiciary is free from the influence of the executive and the legislature.

(d) **Fundamental Rights** Part III of the Indian Constitution ensures some rights for the Indian citizens which are referred to as Fundamental Rights. These rights are enforceable against the state and the state cannot take them away.

(e) **Directive Principles of State Policy** (DPSP) The Directive Principles of State Policy are included in Part IV of the Indian Constitution. These are the guiding principles that govern state policies in the social sector. They are interpreted as economic and social rights.

(f) **Single Citizenship** In India, there is only single citizenship according to the Constitution. Part II of the Constitution of India contains provisions regarding citizenship. Single citizenship means that every Indian is a citizen of India, irrespective of the place of his/her residence or place of birth.

(ii) The Fundamental Rights are essential for the physical, moral and financial development of any country. These are important not only to maintain the order in the society but also for proper functioning of the government. They are intended to advance the ideal of political democracy. They prevent the establishment of authoritarian and despotic rule in the country and defend the people's liberties and freedoms from invasion by the state. They serve as checks on the executive's tyranny and the legislature's arbitrary laws.

6. When can the President run the country in a unitary fashion? What are the three conditions under which it can happen? Explain.

Ans. The President can run the country in a unitary fashion in cases of emergency. The emergency provisions are incorporated to safeguard the sovereignty, unity, integrity and security of the country, the democratic political system and the Constitution. During an emergency, the Central Government becomes all powerful and the states are controlled by the centre.

The President can proclaim an emergency in the following situations

(i) Emergency caused by war, external aggression or armed rebellion (Article 352).

(ii) Emergency arising out of the failure of Constitutional machinery in states (Articles 356 and 365).

(iii) Financial emergency (Article 360).

7. Ajit was arrested by the police without giving any ground nor was he granted other basic rights behind the bars. Identify and explain the remedy available to him.

Ans. The remedy available for Ajit is that he can file a writ of Habeas Corpus. The writ of Habeas Corpus can be used to produce a person who has been detained, whether in prison or in private custody, before a court and to release him/her if such detention is found to be illegal.

8. On the question of inter-relationship between Fundamental Rights and Directive Principles, the Supreme Court in a landmark judgement held that 'Fundamental Rights and Directive Principles constitute the conscience of the Constitution'. In light of the above passage, answer the following questions.

(i) What are Fundamental Rights and Directive Principles?

(ii) Which is the landmark judgement mentioned above?

(iii) Evaluate the inter-relationship between Fundamental Rights and Directive Principles.

Ans. (i) Refer to Q. 2 (i) and (iv) of CBSE Textbook Folder.

(ii) The landmark judgement mentioned is that in the case Kesavananda Bharati Vs. State of Kerala (1973).

(iii) On the question of inter-relationship between Fundamental Rights and Directive Principles, the Supreme Court in the case of Kesavananda Bharati provided that Fundamental Rights and Directive Principles constitute the conscience of the Constitution. There is no opposition between the Fundamental Rights and Directive Principles and one supplements the other.

9. You may identify the invocation of particular writ remedy from the judgements of the Supreme Court of India or any High Court.

Ans. The judiciary provides for remedies for enforcement of Fundamental Rights of citizens, guaranteed by the Constitution.

Only the Supreme Court and the High Courts have the power to exercise writ jurisdiction. Article 32 of Indian Constitution gives the Supreme Court this authority while this power is provided to the High Courts by Article 226.

Exam Pattern Questions

Objective Type Questions

Multiple Choice Questions (MCQs)

1. Which among the given statements is TRUE about the Constitution?

(a) The Constitution is a collection of economic policies.
(b) The Constitution is an agreed-upon document for governance.
(c) The Constitution is a list of cultural norms and traditions.
(d) The Constitution is a set of military regulations.

2. Who defined the Constitution as 'the way of life which the state has chosen for itself'?

(a) Salmond (b) Laski (c) Aristotle (d) Plato

3. Which of the following are the features of the Constitution?

I. It determines the rights and duties of the citizens of a State.
II. It is a fundamental law of a state.
III. It is only in a written form.

Codes
(a) Both I and II (b) Both II and III
(c) Both I and III (d) All of these

4. Which of the following acts was passed by the British Parliament?

I. Government of India Act, 1919
II. Indian Councils Act, 1861
III. Government of India Act, 1935

Codes
(a) Both I and III (b) Only II
(c) Both II and III (d) All of these

5. .... increased the number of non-official members of the legislative councils.

(a) Government of India Act, 1858
(b) Indian Councils Act, 1861
(c) Indian Councils Act, 1892
(d) Indian Councils Act, 1909

6. The Indian Councils Act, 1909 introduced separate electorates for the ....

(a) Muslims
(b) Sikhs
(c) Christians
(d) Depressed Classes

7. Which of the following is/are the feature(s) of the Government of India Act, 1919?

I. It has increased the number of Indian members in the executive council of Governor General from 1 to 3.
II. The system of direct election was also introduced.
III. It introduced dyarchy.

Codes
(a) Only I (b) Only II
(c) Both I and II (d) All of these

8. Which of the following scenarios best demonstrates the primary purpose of the Objectives Resolution?

(a) Establishing a committee to draft the Constitution.
(b) Defining the principles and philosophy of the Constitution.
(c) Outlining the administrative structures of governance.
(d) Resolving disputes with the British Government.

9. Who was the chairman of the Drafting Committee?
(a) Maulana Abul Kalam Azad
(b) Dr. Bhimrao Ambedkar
(c) Sardar Vallabhbhai Patel
(d) Acharya J.B. Kriplani

10. Which of the following provisions of the Indian Constitution is not based on the 'quality principle'?
(a) Abolition of untouchability.
(b) Equality of opportunity in matters of public or state employment.
(c) Prohibiting state from discriminating against anyone based on grounds of religion, race, caste or place of birth.
(d) Prohibiting human trafficking, beggary and forced labour.

11. Right to Property ceased to be a Fundamental Right through which amendment?
(a) 42nd Amendment (b) 44th Amendment
(c) 54th Amendment (d) 56th Amendment

12. A person of 62 years has been appointed to fill a public office whereas the retirement age is 60 years. Which immediate remedy is available before the High Court? **Competency Based Que**
(a) Writ of quo-warranto (b) Writ of habeas corpus
(c) Writ of mandamus (d) Writ of prohibition

13. It is a writ issued by a superior court to an inferior court or body exercising judicial or quasi-judicial powers to remove a suit and adjudicate upon the validity of the proceedings or body exercising judicial or quasi-judicial functions.
(a) Prohibition (b) Certiorari
(c) Mandamus (d) Quo-warranto

14. Ink Pvt. Ltd. was a public authority that refused to perform its legal duty. Due to this, the High Court issued an order directing Ink Pvt. Ltd. commanding it to do its public duty. **Competency Based Que**
Which remedy was issued in this case?
(a) Mandamus (b) Habeas corpus
(c) Prohibition (d) Certiorari

15. According to Article 326 of the Indian Constitution, every citizen of India who is 18 years old or above is not otherwise disqualified can vote in elections. Which of the following is primary implication of Article 326?
(a) Only people above 21 years of age can vote in elections.
(b) People from certain castes and religion are not allowed for vote.
(c) Every citizen of India who is above 18 years of age has the right to vote.
(d) People with criminal records are not allowed to vote.

16. If a pesson is arrested and not produced before the magistrate within 24 hours, they are entitled to be released on the writ of ....
(a) quo-warranto (b) certiorari
(c) prohibition (d) habeas corpus

17. Directive Principles of State Policy (DPSP) are provided under which part and article of the Indian Constitution?
(a) Part IV A, Article 51 A (b) Part III, Article 51 A
(c) Part IV, Articles 36 to 51 (d) Part III, Articles 12 to 35

18. Arrange the following in the ascending order on the basis of enactment.
I. Legal Services Authority Act
II. Right to Free and Compulsory Education
III. Child Labour Prohibition Act
IV. Environment Protection Act
V. Wildlife Protection Act
Select the correct option.
(a) II, I, III, V, IV (b) I, III, V, II, IV
(c) V, III, IV, II, I (d) V, IV, III, I, II

19. Right to free legal aid was held in the case of
(a) Hussainara Khatoon Vs. Home Secretary
(b) Kesavananda Bharati Vs. Union of India
(c) Hinsa Virrodhak Sangh Vs. M.M.K. Jamat
(d) M.C. Mehta Vs. Kamal Nath

20. Which of the following words were added to the Preamble through the 42nd Amendment Act, 1976?
I. Socialist **II. Secular**
III. Republic **IV. Unity and integrity**
Select the correct option.
(a) I, II and III (b) II, III and IV
(c) I, II and IV (d) All of these

21. Arrange the following cases as per chronological order
I. S.R. Bommai Vs. Union of India
II. Charan Lal Sahu Vs. Union of India
III. Ashok Kumar Thakur Vs. Union of India
IV. Bijoe Emmanuel Vs. State of Kerala
Choose the correct option.
(a) I, II, III, IV (b) II, I, III, IV
(c) IV, I, II, III (d) IV, II, I, III

22. The idea of DPSP is borrowed from the ....
(a) Irish Constitution (b) Japanese Model
(c) US Constitution (d) Government of India Act, 1935

23. Which of the following articles specifies the powers of the Parliament to amend the Constitution?
(a) Article 376 (b) Article 365
(c) Article 368 (d) Article 386

24. Rehana, who just turned eighteen years this year, is very excited about her role in voting and election procedures. Which among the following articles, states about Adult Suffrage? **Competency Based Que**

(a) Article 321 (b) Article 324
(c) Article 326 (d) Article 327

25. Tanmay is a social media influencer who speaks about the topics related to current affairs and people's rights. He advocates about the better co-ordination in power-sharing mechanism in centre-state relations. Identify the schedule of the Indian Constitution that contains three legislative lists that describe the division of powers. **Competency Based Que**

(a) 3rd Schedule (b) 4th Schedule
(c) 5th Schedule (d) 7th Schedule

26. Robert Williams, a renowned of the Indian classical philosophy' is staying in India for a quite long period. He now wants to obtain Indian citizenship. How many years of residence in India is required to acquire citizenship by registration in India?

(a) 5 Years (b) 7 Years
(c) 6 Years (d) 12 Years

27. It dealt with matters such as marriage and divorce, criminal law, civil law and procedure. The above mentioned sentence is related to ....

(a) federal list (b) provincial list
(c) concurrent list (d) None of these

28. Which among the following is NOT a subject addressed by the Constitution of India?

(a) Functions and powers of the executive
(b) Official language
(c) Military strategy
(d) Emergency provisions

29. Consider the following statements and choose the correct option.

I. The Directive Principles of State Policy shall not be enforceable in any court.
II. The Fundamental Duties shall be enforceable in any court.

Codes

(a) Only I (b) Only II
(c) Both I and II (d) None of these

30. Which of the following parts of the Indian Constitution deal with the provisions regarding citizenship?

(a) Part I (b) Part II (c) Part VI (d) Part IX

31. The original Constitution of India contained .... Schedules.

(a) 8 (b) 9
(c) 11 (d) 12

32. Statement I Dr. B.R. Ambedkar is widely regarded as the Principal Architect of the Indian Constitution, which was adopted on 26th November, 1949.
Statement II Dr. B.R. Ambedkar played a pivotal role in drafting the Constitution of India, and was instrumental in shaping the document's final form.

Choose the correct option.

(a) Statement I is correct and Statement II is incorrect.
(b) Statement I is incorrect and Statement II is correct.
(c) Both the Statement are correct.
(d) Both the Statement are incorrect.

33. Match the following.

Column I		Column II
A.	Habeas corpus	1. By what warrant
B.	Certiorari	2. You may have the body
C.	Quo-warranto	3. To be more fully informed

Codes

	A	B	C		A	B	C
(a)	1	3	2	(b)	2	3	1
(c)	2	1	3	(d)	3	1	2

34. Match the following.

Column I		Column II
A.	Part III of the Constitution	1. DPSPs
B.	73rd and 74th Amendment Acts, 1993	2. Fundamental Rights
C.	Part XIV-A of the Indian Constitution	3. Panchayats and Municipalities
D.	Part IV of the Indian Constitution	4. Tribunal

Codes

	A	B	C	D		A	B	C	D
(a)	2	3	4	1	(b)	1	3	4	2
(c)	1	2	3	4	(d)	3	2	4	1

35. Match the following.

Column I		Column II
A.	Parliamentary form of government	1. US Constitution
B.	Special provisions for promoting freedom of trade and commerce	2. Australian Constitution
C.	Fundamental Rights	3. Irish Constitution
D.	Directive Principles of State Policy	4. British Constitution

Codes

	A	B	C	D		A	B	C	D
(a)	4	2	1	3	(b)	1	2	3	4
(c)	4	2	3	1	(d)	3	2	1	4

Assertion-Reason Questions

Directions (Q. Nos. 36-40) In the questions given below, there are two statements. Read the following statements and choose the correct option.

Codes

(a) Both A and R are true and R is the correct explanation of A.
(b) Both A and R are true, but R is not the correct explanation of A.
(c) A is true, but R is false.
(d) A is false, but R is true.

36. **Assertion** (A) Wade and Phillips in their book, 'Constitution and Administrative Law' defined Constitution 'as the way of life which the state has chosen for itself'.

Reason (R) A Constitution is a legally binding document which 'establishes' the basis on which consenting people shall govern themselves.

37. **Assertion** (A) Government of India Act, 1919 introduced a bicameral legislature at the center.

Reason (R) It aimed to create an Indian Federation.

38. **Assertion** (A) Colonial government conceded that the Constitution of India would be framed by an elected Constituent Assembly consisting of Indian people.

Reason (R) Growing dissatisfaction over limited governing rights granted to Indians under 1935 Act led to widespread protests.

39. **Assertion** (A) Preamble can be amended by the Parliament without any change to its basic structure.

Reason (R) Basic structure is defined by the Supreme Court in Kesavananda Bharati case.

40. **Assertion** (A) The Constitution of India provides single citizenship to its citizens.

Reason (R) Indian Federation is the result of an agreement between the two or more states.

Answers

1. (b) The Constitution is an agreed-upon document for governance.
2. (c) Aristotle
3. (a) Both I and II
4. (d) All of these
5. (c) Indian Councils Act, 1892
6. (a) Muslims
7. (d) All of these
8. (b) Defining the principles and philosophy of the Constitution
9. (b) Dr. Bhimrao Ambedker
10. (d) Prohibiting human trafficking, beggary and forced labour.
11. (b) 44th Amendment
12. (a) Writ of quo-warranto
13. (b) Certiorari
14. (a) Mandamus
15. (c) Every citizen of India who is above 18 years of age has the right to vote.
16. (d) habeas corpus
17. (c) Part IV, Articles 36 to 51
18. (d) V, IV, III, I, II
19. (a) Hussainara Khatoon Vs. Home Secretary
20. (c) I, II and IV
21. (d) IV, II, I, III
22. (a) Irish Constitution
23. (c) Article 368
24. (c) Article 326
25. (d) 7th Schedule
26. (b) 7 Years
27. (c) concurrent list
28. (c) Military strategy
29. (a) Only I
30. (b) Part II
31. (a) 8
32. (c) Both the Statement are correct.
33. (b) 2 3 1
34. (a) 2 3 4 1
35. (a) 4 2 1 3
36. (d) A is false, but R is true.
37. (b) Both A and R are true, but R is not the correct explanation of A.
38. (a) Both A and R are true and R is the correct explanation of A.
39. (a) Both A and R are true and R is the correct explanation of A.
40. (b) Both A and R are true, but R is not the correct explanation of A.

Subjective Questions

Very Short Answer Type Questions

1. What is a Constitution?

Ans. The term 'Constitution' is derived from the Latin word 'constitutio' which means 'to establish'. A Constitution is a legally binding document, which 'establishes' the basis on which consenting people shall govern themselves.

2. Write any three main features of the Constitution.

Ans. The three main features of the Constitution are

(i) It is a body of rules, which contains the rules to govern the nation.

(ii) It may be in a written or unwritten form. It may be written in a single document or in several documents.

(iii) It determines the powers and responsibilities of state and organs of government.

3. "The British Parliament has enacted several legislations". In this context, discuss the main features of the Indian Council Act, 1909. Competency Based Que

Ans. The Indian Councils Act, 1909, commonly known as the Morley-Minto or Minto-Morley Reforms had the following features

(i) It increased the involvement of Indians in the governance of British India.

(ii) It introduced separate electorates for the Muslims.

4. 'The Government of India Act, 1935 was the longest act passed by the British Parliament'. Write any two salient features of this act.

Ans. The two main salient features of the Government of India Act are

(i) It ended a system of dyarchy at the center which was established by the Government of India Act, 1919.

(ii) It divided the power by creating Federal List, Provincial List and Concurrent List.

5. When was the term 'Socialist' incorporated into the Indian Constitution and Why?

Ans. The term 'Socialist' was incorporated by the 42nd Amendment in 1976. The inclusion of the term 'socialist' in the Preamble was introduced to reflect the government's commitment to socialism and to promote the idea of a more equitable distribution of wealth and resources which aims to reduce social and economic inequalities in Indian society.

6. 'The Concept of Republic has been borrowed from the French Constitution'. Justify. Competency Based Que

Ans. The Concept of Republic in the Indian Constitution has been borrowed from the French Constitution. In a republic, the head of state is elected, not a monarch. This idea was adopted to ensure that leadership is based on democracy, where power rests with the people, and the President is elected, reflecting the values of liberty, equality, and fraternity.

7. Why is the Indian Constitution considered to be the world's longest written Constitution?

Ans. Indian Constitution is the longest written Constitution in the world, with 395 original Articles, 12 Schedules and 105 Amendments. The Indian Constitution drafted in the mid-20th century, has contained the best features gathered from the existing Constitutions in the world to suit the existing conditions and needs of the country.

8. State the various rights entailed in the right to equality.

Ans. Right to equality contains the (new point) following rights

- equality before laws
- prohibition of discrimination on grounds of religion, race, caste, sex or place of birth
- equality of opportunity in matters of public employment
- abolition of untouchability and titles

9. Name the writs that can be issued by the Supreme Court.

Ans. The Supreme Court shall have power to issue directions or orders or writs, including writs in the nature of habeas corpus, mandamus, prohibition, quo-warranto and certiorari.

10. What is the purpose of writ jurisdiction of High Courts?

Ans. The purpose of the writ jurisdiction of High Courts is to protect Fundamental Rights and ensure justice. Under Article 226 of the Indian Constitution, High Courts can issue writs to enforce rights, direct the government or authorities, and correct unlawful actions. It serves as a tool for individuals to seek legal remedies when their rights are violated.

11. Which part of the Indian Constitution is responsible for the welfare state? Is it justiciable in nature?

Ans. The Directive Principles of State Policy, enshrined in Part IV of the Indian Constitution, reflect that India is a welfare state. It is a positive obligation on the state. DPSPs are not enforceable in a court of law. They can be enforced either by passing a legislation an by judicial process where they are linked to a Fundamental Right and hence its status is elevated.

12. Write any two important Directive Principles.

Ans. The two important Directive Principles are

(i) The right to an adequate means of livelihood for citizens

(ii) Equal pay for equal work for both men and women

13. State any two difference between Fundamental Rights and DPSPs.

Ans. The difference between Fundamental Rights and Directive Principles is

Fundamental Rights	Directive Principles of State Policy
Part III of the Constitution of India contains the Fundamental Rights. They are given in Articles 12-35 of the Constitution of India.	Part IV of the Constitution of India contains Directive Principles of State Policy. They are given in Articles 36-51 of the Constitution of India.
They are civil and political in nature, means they help the citizens in enjoying their life under a government.	They are social and economic in nature.

14. These provisions are not enforceable by any court of law, but provide guidance in carrying out and drafting laws regarding human and social development.

(i) Which provisions are being discussed here?

(ii) These provisions are contained in which part of the Constitution? Competency Based Que

Ans. (i) Directive Principles of State Policy are being discussed here.

(ii) These provisions are contained in Part IV of the Constitution.

15. Which part of the Indian Constitution provides the procedure for the amendment of the Constitution? Also mention the relevant provision.

Ans. Part XX of the Constitution of India provides in detail the procedure for amendment of the Constitution, under Article 368. This article specifies the powers of the Parliament to amend the Constitution and lays down the procedure.

16. Country 'X' was primarily a federal state with a Parliamentary form of government wherein the powers were divided between the centre and states. However, certain provisions in the Constitution empowered the President to run the state in a unitary manner in certain cases. Competency Based Que

(i) Which provisions are being discussed here?

(ii) Which part of the Constitution contains such provisions?

Ans. (i) Emergency provisions are being discussed here.

(ii) Part XVIII of the Constitution contains the emergency provisions.

Short Answer Type Questions

1. Mohit and Shivangi, brother and sister, are doing research on the process of Constitution making in India. What do you understand about the term 'Constitution'? State some definitions given by different philosophers. Competency Based Que

Ans. The term 'Constitution' is derived from the Latin term 'Constitution' which means to set up. Some definitions of Constitution by different philosophers are

- According to Oxford Dictionary, the Constitution is a body of fundamental principles or established precedents according to which a state or other organisation is acknowledged to be governed.
- Aristotle defined the Constitution as 'the way of life which the state has choosen for itself'.
- Wade and Phillips, in their book 'Constitution and Administrative Law', state that the Constitution of a country seeks to establish its fundamental or basic or apex organs of government and administration, describe their structure, composition, powers and principal functions, define the inter-relationship of these organs with one another, and regulate their relationship with the people, more particularly the political relationship.

2. During the British rule in India, many positive changes were introduced in India for better administration. List down the features of the Government of India Act, 1919. Competency Based Que

Ans. The features of the Government of India Act, 1919 are

(i) It introduced a bicameral legislature at the Centre and created two houses

(a) Legislative Assembly or the Lower House

(b) Council of States or the Upper House

(ii) Term for the Legislative Assembly was 5 years while that for the Council of States was three years.

(iii) The Public Service Commission was established under the Act.

(iv) The Central Legislature had the power to pass legislation even though the Governor-General had vast powers in law-making.

(v) Final approval of legislation had to come from the Governor-General.

(vi) The Act raised the number of Indian members in the Executive Council of the Governor-General from 1 to 3.

(vii) Direct election was introduced in India through this Act.

3. Raj Narayan, a Ph. D Scholar from Delhi University, wrote a thesis paper about how there were many drawbacks in the Government of India Act 1935, which was overlooked by British. What were the limitations on exercising legislative powers under the Government of India Act, 1935? **Competency Based Que**

Ans. The legislative powers were divided among Central and Provincial legislatures but their exercise was subject to various limitations which were

(i) The Governor-General and the Crown had the power to veto a bill passed by the legislature.

(ii) The Governor-General had the power to issue ordinance and permanent acts when the legislative house was not in session.

(iii) The Governor-General had the power to suspend legislature if the proceedings would affect the discharge of his special responsibilities.

(iv) No bill could be introduced in legislature without the previous sanction of Governor-General, which aims to amend or repeal the law of British Parliament as applicable in India.

4. Before Independence India was under the control of the British Government. During their time, the British Parliament has enacted several legislations. **Competency Based Que**

(i) Name any few laws enacted by the British Parliament.

(ii) Write any two features of the Government of India Act, 1858.

(iii) Which act is known as Act for the Better Government of India?

Ans. (i) Laws enacted by the British Parliament are

- Government of India Act, 1858
- Indian Councils Act, 1861
- Indian Councils Act, 1892
- Indian Councils Act, 1909
- Government of India Act, 1919
- Government of India Act, 1935

(ii) The two features of Government of India Act, 1858 are

(a) It ended the dual government scheme initiated due to Pitt's India Act.

(b) The powers of the Company's Court of Directors were transferred to the Secretary of State for India. He was going to be a member of the British Parliament.

(iii) The Government of India Act, 1858, known as Act for the better government of India.

5. India's Constitution was prepared through the unique composition of scholars from different fields of study and expertise in the Constituent Assembly. Write a short note on Constituent Assembly. **Competency Based Que**

Ans. The Constituent Assembly was a body elected by members of the provincial legislatures and state legislatures. It met for the first time and formally commenced the task of 'Constitution-making'.

Most of the members of the Constituent Assembly from the Congress Party and some were communists and independents. The Constituent Assembly also included eminent members from law and public affairs. The Constituent Assembly had two roles that were governance and the framing of the Constitution. In the mornings it dealt with the governance matters and in the afternoon, it drafted the Constitution.

6. Scotland is unique in the sense that it is not sovereign state but included within a larger country i.e. UK. Write a short note on the term 'Sovereign' and 'Democratic' as stated in the preamble of the Indian Constitution. **Competency Based Que**

Ans. The term 'Sovereign' implies that India is free from any kind/form of foreign interference in its domestic affairs and matters. The state has the power to legislate on any subject in accordance with Constitutional limitations.

The word 'Democratic' signifies that India has a Parliamentary form of government, which is accountable to the elected legislature.

The main reason for in-corporating democracy is to provide freedom to the people to choose their own representatives and to save them from the tyrant leaders.

7. Ravi Shankar, who spent 20 years in imprisonment, has appealed in the Ahmedabad Civil Court for mercy petition but his appeal has not been considered yet. Briefly discuss the writ jurisdiction of the Supreme Court and High Courts. Also state the difference between the two. **Competency Based Que**

Ans. The Supreme Court shall have power to issue directions or orders or writs for the enforcement of Fundamental Rights under Article 32, and the High Courts have this power under Article 226 of the Constitution. Thus, the Fundamental Rights are termed justiciable rights. The writs include habeas corpus, mandamus, prohibition, quo warranto and certiorari.

The differences between Supreme Court and High Court are

Basis	Supreme Court	High Court
Purpose	To only enforce Fundamental Rights.	To enforce Fundamental Rights as well as ordinary legal rights.
Power	Article 32 is a Fundamental Right. The Supreme Court cannot refuse to exercise its power to issue the writs.	Article 226 is not a Fundamental Right. High Court may refuse to exercise its power to issue writs.

8. The government of a state made a rule to make it discretionary to grant dearness allowance to its employees. One of the employees filed a writ petition seeking a mandamus to compel the government to grant dearness allowance. **Competency Based Que**

(i) What is the writ of mandamus?

(ii) Will the writ of mandamus be granted in this case?

Ans. (i) A writ of mandamus is a command issued by the court to any public or quasi-public legal body that has refused to perform its legal duty. It is an order by a superior court commanding a person or a public authority to do something in the nature of public duty.

(ii) Writ of mandamus will not be granted in this case as no legal duty was imposed on the government to grant dearness allowance.

9. Bhola is a poor man who wants to avail legal services. His Fundamental Right to free speech and expression has been violated. However, he does not have the money to go to the court. He approaches the state to get free legal aid. **Competency Based Que**

(i) Is the state mandated to provide free legal aid?

(ii) Which part of the Constitution contains this provision? Also, discuss this provision in brief.

Ans. (i) Yes, the state is mandated to provide free legal aid to individuals who cannot afford legal services. This is a part of the right to access justice, which is crucial for ensuring equality before the law.

(ii) The provision is found in Article 39A of the Indian Constitution, which is part of the Directive Principles of State Policy. It directs the state to promote justice by providing free legal aid to ensure that opportunities for securing justice are not denied to any citizen due to economic or other disabilities. This reflects the aim of creating a fair and just society by helping those who cannot afford legal representation.

10. Kamla Devi filed a petition in the local court to provide protection for her ancestral property as a Fundamental Right but court refused to pass the order. In this context, state any four points of difference between Fundamental Rights and DPSPs. **Competency Based Que**

Ans. For answer refer to text under the heading differences between Fundamental Rights and DPSPs, on page no. 77.

11. Shiv Kumar was ordered by the Supreme Court that despite being disabled he is eligible for state jobs, whereas the State Public Service Commission withdrew its case in the High Court.

How can you say that the Indian judiciary is integrated in nature? **Competency Based Que**

Ans. The Indian Judiciary is considered integrated in nature because it operates as a unified system where all courts, from the Supreme Court down to the District Courts, are interconnected and work under a single legal framework. In this case, the Supreme Court's ruling ensured that Shiv Kumar, despite being disabled, was eligible for state jobs, demonstrating the judiciary's power to make binding decisions on the entire country, irrespective of the actions of individual state bodies like the Public Service Commission. The withdrawal of the case by the State Public Service Commission in the High Court further reflects how the decisions of higher courts (like the Supreme Court) are respected and followed by lower courts and authorities, reinforcing the unity and integration of the judicial system.

Long Answer Type Questions

1. Sapna in her classroom lecture has explained that the Directive Principles of State Policy were adopted from Ireland's Constitution, but it was originally derived from Spanish Constitution.

What are Directive Principles of State Policy? State any two features of DPSP. Also give three differences between Fundamental Rights and Directive Principles of State Policy. **Competency Based Que**

Ans. For answer refer to text under the heading Directive Principles of State Policy and their features, on page no. 76 and 77.

For answer refer to text under the heading Difference Between Fundamental Rights and Directive Principles, on page no. 77.

2. Sunderlal is a hawker who sells vegetables and fruits in the nearby locality. However, he also encourages people not to use plastic bags and should not litter here and there. In this context, explain what are 'Fundamental Duties'. State their salient features.

Ans. For answer refer to text under the heading Fundamental Duties and their Features, on page no. 78.

3. Shekher and Manoj were in discussion about the Constitution amendment procedures. They were impressed with the flexibility of Indian Constitution with comparison to United States. Discuss the Constitutional provisions for amending the Constitution. **Competency Based Que**

Ans. For answer refer to text under the heading Constitutional Provision and Amendment of Constitution, on page no. 78.

4. What do you understand by single citizenship? How is it relevant to India? How can Indian citizenship be acquired?

Ans. For answer refer to text under the heading the Single Citizenship acquired, on page no. 79.

5. How is Indian Constitution both federal and unitary?

Ans. For answer refer to text under the heading Federal in Form and Unitary in Character on page no. 80.

SELF ASSESSMENT TEST

Multiple Choice Questions

1. .... is also known as the Minto–Morley Reforms.
   (a) Government of India Act, 1861
   (b) Government of India Act, 1909
   (c) Government of India Act, 1919
   (d) Government of India Act, 1935
2. Which of the following acts was the longest act passed by the British Parliament?
   (a) Government of India Act, 1861
   (b) Government of India Act, 1909
   (c) Government of India Act, 1919
   (d) Government of India Act, 1935
3. Which of the following terms has been in-corporated in the Preamble?
   (a) Socialist (b) Secular (c) Democratic (d) All of these
4. Identify the Article that provides for the representation for members of the Anglo-Indian community in the House of People.
   (a) Article 330 (b) Article 331 (c) Article 332 (d) Article 333

Very Short Answer Type Questions

5. When did the Indian Constitution come into effect?
6. The term 'liberty' been used in the Constitution. Justify? **Competency Based Que**
7. What do you understand by the writ of habeas corpus?
8. Which article deals with the writ jurisdiction of the Supreme Court?
9. In a country, only people who our property and are above 25 years old are allowed to vote in elections. However, a new government comes to power and introduces a Constitutional Amendment that grants the right to vote of all citizens above 18 years old, regardless of their peoperty ownership or social status. What do we call this expansion of voting rights? **Competency Based Que**

Short Answer Type Questions

10. What is the meaning of the term 'Constitution'? What are the distinctive features of the Constitution of a state?
11. Give any three difference between Fundamental Rights and Directive Principles of State Policy.
12. What are writs? Why are they used? List the various types of writs and also give the purpose of their issue.
13. The Indian Constitution provides for a federal system with 28 states and 8 union territories, each with its own elected government . However certain subjects like defense, foreign affairs and accuracy are exclusively handled by the Cenral Government. Additionally, the Constitution also provide for a unified judiciary, a single currency and a single citizenship. What is the nature of Indain judiciary explain. **Competency Based Que**

Long Answer Type Questions

14. What is the significance of Preamble to the Indian Constitution?
15. Discuss the various Fundamental Rights under the Indian Constitution.
16. Discuss the Constitutional provisions on
    (i) Single citizenship (ii) Adult suffrage

05
CHAPTER

Administrative Law

Administrative Law aims to ensure that the policies, rules, regulations and legislations formulated for public good are not misused.

▼ **YOUR STUDY GOALS**

▼ **YOUR PRACTICE GOAL**

- Objective Type Questions (18 Qs ; MCQs, A-R, Statements, Matching)
- Subjective Questions (10 VSAs, 7 SAs, 3 LAs)

5.1 Growth, Development and Study of Administrative Law

There were several reasons for the growth of Administrative Law. These were

- In the 21st century, developing countries like India expect a very proactive state for their own welfare.
- As the states changed their nature from laissez-faire[1] to that of a welfare state, government activities increased and these were required to be regulated, hence Administrative Law was adopted.
- The legislature has no time to legislate upon the day-to-day ever-changing needs of the society.
- The governance will cease to function, if the sanction of the legislature is compulsorily required for all kinds of administrative actions.
- Thus, delegation (transfer of responsibility) is needed which is the single most important factor which led to the growth of Administrative Law.
- Administrative Law is the body of law that governs the administration and regulation of authorities created by the governement.
- Article 12 of the Constitution of India mentions 'any other authority', while defining 'State'.

1 **Laissez-faire** It means the policy of leaving things to take their own course, without interfering.

- These 'other authorities' are all part of the state. These included
  - authorities created by law
  - authorities which are agencies and instrumentalities of the state
  - authorities which are essentially discharging public functions which have an impact on the common people.

Administrative Law and Constitutional Law

- Before the 21st century, Administrative Law was considered a part of Constitutional Law.
- However, there has been a clear distinction in the subject matter of their respective studies in recent times.
- Administrative Law **aims to keep a check on the actions of the government** when dealing with the procedures affecting the rights of citizens. On the other hand, Constitutional Law clarifies the **scope of rights and duties of citizens and the government**.
- For example, the powers of the Parliament and of the different branches of the state, how elections are held and how the Parliament is formed.
- The questions in the scope of Constitutional Law are essential in the scheme of any democratic Constitution.
- Whereas, when a minister is finally appointed and his actions affect the general public good, then we can categorise the study of these actions as a core constituent of Administrative Law.

Types of Administrative Action

Administrative action can be of four types

(i) **Administrative Legislative Action** When the administration exercises **law-making power delegated** to it by the legislature, it is referred to as an administrative legislative action.
  - The power is delegated because it is not practically possible for any legislature in the world to legislate so perfectly that their laws are able to cover the possibility of all kinds of conflicts, which can arise out of a decision.
  - Administrative legislative action includes rule-making action as well as delegated legislation.

(ii) **Quasi-judicial Action or Administrative Adjudicatory Action** When the administration exercises judicial powers, it is referred to as quasi-judicial action, e.g. Tribunals.

(iii) **Simply Administrative Action** The administrative actions besides administrative legislative action and quasi-judicial action, that deal with execution of crucial administrative decisions, are referred to as simply administrative actions. In simply administrative action, **there is discretion** to the administrative authority i.e. the authority has the right to exercise his/her own understanding and discretion in dealing with the matter.

(iv) **Ministerial Action/Purely Administrative Action** Actions which are copybook action and actions in which no discretion is vested with the authority i.e. there is only one way of performing that action, such actions are referred to as purely administrative action or ministerial action.
For example, the law which created a university, mandates that the university open a bank account with a particular bank.

Quick Test 1

1. State any one reason for the growth of Administrative Law.
2. What is the aim of Administrative Law?
3. Mention any two types of Administrative Law.
4. What do you mean by ministerial action?

5.2 Fundamental Principle of Administrative Law

- It essentially deals with the doctrine of Constitutional **morality**[2]. Constitutional morality states that an administrative action must always be fair and reasonable, even in doing something legal.
- For example, a university guidelines read that you can appoint any person as the Professor of Law and no other qualification for such is laid down. University appoints a person who has no qualification of law and has no teaching experience. Hence in this case, it is the principle of administrative morality which operates and vitiates such appointment.
- In a democratic society, fundamental principles of Administrative Law are **transparency or openness,** the principle of participation, of **impartiality**[3] and objectivity, reasoned decisions, legality, effective review of administrative rules and administrative decisions, accountability and **non-arbitrariness**[4].
- All these principles are broadly encompassed under the Rule of Law, Doctrine of Separation of Powers and Principles of Natural Justice.

Rule of Law

- Rule of law is an essential tool to protect the freedom and dignity of individuals against organised powers.
- In the case of Kesavananda Bharati Vs. State of Kerala, 'Rule of Law' was categorised as a **'Basic Structure'** of the Constitution. Basic structure means those basic characters/attributes which are enshrined in the heart of the Constitution and which **cannot be repealed/replaced** by any Parliament.
- There was opposition to the doctrine of Rule of Law in the days of monarchy as it limits the powers of the monarch or king to change laws and rules according to his own desire.
- Hence, Rule of Law as a principle is essentially based only in democratic societies and is not a known feature of monarchies.

Separation of Power

- Separation of powers refers to the division of a State's Government into branches, each with separate, independent powers and responsibilities, so that the powers of one branch are not in conflict with those of the other branches.
- 'Separation of powers' was meant to create divisions within the government setup to create better administration within the state.
- The powers are separated into three branches i.e. legislature, executive and judiciary. It is known as the **triaspolitica**[5] model.
- The intention behind a system of separated powers is to **prevent the concentration of power** by providing for checks and balances.

Principles of Natural Justice

- Natural justice is an expression of English Common Law, and involves a procedural requirement of fairness.
- The principles of natural justice have great significance in the study of Administrative Law. It is also known as substantial justice or fundamental justice or universal justice or fair play in action.
- The principles of natural justice are not embodied rules and are not codified. They are rules made by judge and are regarded as counterparts of the American procedural due process.

---

2 **Morality** It means principles concerning the distinction between right and wrong or good and bad behaviour.
3 **Impartiality** It means equal treatment of all rivals or diputants, fairness.
4 **Non-arbitrariness** It means not subject to individual determination or preference.
5 **Trias politica** It is the philosophy that there has to be a strict separation between three independent powers in every nation.

- **Articles 14 and 21** of the Indian Constitution has strengthened the concept of natural justice. The principles of natural justice are based on two Latin maxims.
- In simple words, English Law recognises two principles of natural justice as stated below
  (i) **NemoJudex in Causasua or Nemodebetessejudex in Propriacausa** or **Rule against bias** which means no man shall be a judge in his own cause.
  (ii) **Audi Alterampartem** or the **Rule of Fair Hearing** (hear the other side) which means no one shall be unheard, both the parties have an opportunity of being heard.

Rule against Bias or Bias of Interest

- Bias means deciding a case otherwise than on the principles of evidence.
- The judiciary must be free from bias and should deliver pure and impartial justice. Judges must act judicially and decide the case without considering anything other than the principles of evidence.
- **This principle is based on the following rules**
  - No one should be judge in his own cause.
  - Justice should not only be done, but manifestly and undoubtedly -be seen to be done.

Kinds of Bias

The rule against bias may be classified into the following

- **Pecuniary Bias** Pecuniary bias arises, when the **judge has monetary/economic interest** in the subject matter of the dispute/case.

  The judge, while deciding a case should not have any pecuniary or economic interest. In other words, pecuniary interest in the subject matter of litigation disqualifies a person from acting as a judge.
- **Personal Bias** Personal bias arises from **near and dear** i.e. from friendship, relationship, business or professional association. Such a relationship disqualifies a person from acting as a judge.
- **Bias as to Subject Matter (official bias)** When the judge has **general interest in the subject matter** in dispute due to his association with the administration or private body, he will be disqualified on the ground of bias if he has personally identified himself with the issues in dispute.

Rule of Fair Hearing

- According to this principle, reasonable opportunity must be given to a person before taking any action against him.
- This rule insists that the affected person must be given an opportunity to produce evidence in support of his case.
- He should disclose the evidence to be utilised against him and should be given an opportunity to invalidate the evidence produced by the other party.

Essentials of Fair Hearing

A hearing will be treated as fair hearing if the following conditions are satisfied

- Adjudicating authority receives all the relevant material produced by the individual.
- The adjudicating authority discloses to the individual the concerned evidence or material which it wishes to use against him.
- The adjudicating authority provides the person concerned an opportunity to invalidate the evidence or material which the authority wants to use against him.

The essentials of fair hearing are

- **Notice** There is a duty on the part of the deciding authority to give notice to a person before taking any action against him. The notice must be reasonable and must contain the time, place, nature of hearing and other particulars.
- **Hearing** It is a code of procedure, which has no definite content, but varies with the facts and circumstances of the case. The following procedure is involved in hearing of a person against whom an order is passed.
  - He should be informed about the charges against him.
  - He should be given an opportunity to submit his explanation.
  - He should have a right to know the evidence both oral and documentary, by which the matter is proposed to be decided.
  - The witnesses should be examined in his presence and he should have the right to cross examine them and to lead his own evidence both oral and documentary in his defence.

Maneka Gandhi Vs. Union of India

- In Maneka Gandhi's case, the petitioner's passport was confiscated by the Union Government under Section 10(3) (c) of the Passport Act, 1967. The provision under which impoundment (seizure) took place authorises the Central Government to carry out the same if it was necessary for the interest of the general public at large. But the government did not provide any reasons for carrying out the same.
- The petitioner filed a writ petition under Article 32 of the Constitution which mentioned the following things
  - Section 10(3) (c) of the Passport Act, 1967 was in violation with Article 14 of the Constitution for it vested excessive discretionary (non-mandatory) powers in the hand of the passport authority.
  - Section 10(3) (c) did not align with the principles of natural justice because it did not provide any space for allowing the passport holder to be heard.
  - There was a lack of reasonable procedure by Section 10(3) (c) which also led to the same contravening (violate/disobey) with Article 21 of the Constitution.
  - Section 10(3) (c) was also in vialation with Article 19(1) (a) and (g)

Post Decisional Hearing

- Post decisional hearing can be identified as a harmonising tool to balance between administrative efficacy and fair procedures governing an individual.
- Post decisional hearing is a demand when immediate decisions are to be taken in relation to the public interest.
- In the case of post decisional hearing, an individual is provided with an opportunity to be heard after a decision has been adopted by the concerned authorities, within a specific time frame.
- The usage of post decisional hearing is restricted to exceptional usage only which include deprivation of property, liberty, livelihood or any other public interest that any individual can demand and is relevant by nature.
- The important feature of this kind of hearing is that the decision taken by the concerned authorities are not permanent and final by nature.
- Due to the conflict between pre-decisional hearing and post decisional hearing, the courts developed a test, which is divided into three parts to determine which is mandated. They are
  (i) The public interests that are involved need to be considered.
  (ii) Association of the risks that are involved in allowing the adoption of pre-decisional hearing needs to be taken care of, along with the values of the Constitution that are involved.
  (iii) Government's administrative and economic implications need to be considered.

5.3 Droit Administrative Law

- Droit Administrative Law means a body of rules which determine the organisation, powers and duties of public administration and regulate the relation of the administration with the citizen of the country.
- Droit Administrative Law does not represent the rules and principles enacted by Parliament.
- It contains the rules developed by administrative courts.
- In the late 18th century, when **Napoleon** took over the power of **French administration** and became the Consul General, there existed the king's court called **Conseil Du Roi** to exercise the judicial powers.
- This court only played an advisory role to the king.
- On the other hand, ordinary courts were neglected and their salary was dependent on the fee collected.
- Thus, they started discouraging the schemes and programmes of the government. As a result of this, reforms were brought about by Napoleon in the administration of justice which had two objectives
  (i) To assist socio-economic movements in the country.
  (ii) If there is any dispute between an individual and the government departments, it should be decided as quickly as possible.
- Hence, the ordinary courts were disallowed from interfering in administration.
- Similarly, the king's powers were also curtailed and the king's court was abolished.
- A new system evolved in which special courts had been established to quickly dispose of the pending matter.
- These were administrative courts which decided a dispute between a private individual and government departments. The highest administrative court was Counseil de' Etat.

Napoleon Bonaparte (1769-1821) was a French general, first consul, and emperor. He is known for revolutionising the military, creating the Napoleonic Code, reforming education, and making an agreement with the Catholic Church. His military expansions were a major focus, and he was widely admired during his life and even after, especially under his nephew Napoleon III.

Quick Test 2

1. What are the fundamental principles of Administrative Law?
2. State any one principle of natural justice.
3. Name the three kind of bias.
4. Give the name of the highest administrative court of france.

Mind Map

ADMINISTRATIVE LAW

1 Introduction to Administrative Law

Definition

- Governs administration and regulation of authorities created by the government.
- Aims to ensure policies, rules, and legislations are not misused.

Scope

- Focus on public good.
- Monitoring government actions affecting citizens' rights.

2 Growth and Development of Administrative Law

Reasons for Growth

- Transition from laissez-faire to welfare state.
- Increasing government activities needing regulation.
- Legislatures unable to address daily changing societal needs.
- Need for delegation to manage governance effectively.

Key Provision

- Article 12 of the Indian Constitution includes "other authorities" as part of the state.

3 Administrative Law Vs. Constitutional Law

Administrative Law

- Monitors government procedures impacting citizens' rights.
- Includes quasi-judicial and legislative functions.

Constitutional Law

- Clarifies rights and duties of citizens and government.
- Defines powers of Parliament and state branches.

For example

- **Administrative Law** Actions of ministers impacting public welfare.
- **Constitutional Law** Formation of Parliament and elections.

4 Types of Administrative Actions

Administrative Legislative Action

- Law-making powers delegated to the administration.

Examples

- Rule-making, delegated legislation.

Quasi-Judicial Action

- Exercise of judicial powers by administrative authorities.

For example

- Tribunals.

Simply Administrative Action

- Execution of administrative decisions.
- Discretionary powers are involved.

Ministerial Action

- Actions with no discretion; purely mechanical.

For example

- Opening a bank account for a university as mandated by law.

5 Fundamental Principles of Administrative Law

Fundamental Principles Transparency, participation, impartiality, reasoned decision, legality etc.

Rule of Law

- Protects freedom and dignity against organised powers.
- Recognised as a basic structure in Keshavananda Bharati Vs. State of Kerala.

Separation of Powers

- Divides government into Legislature, Executive, and Judiciary.
- Prevents concentration of power, ensures checks and balances.

Principles of Natural Justice

- **Nemo Judex in Causa Sua** No one shall be a judge in their cause.
- **Audi Alteram Partem** Right to a fair hearing.

6 Natural Justice: Detailed Overview

Principles

- Fairness in administrative decisions.
- Opportunity for affected individuals to present their case.

Types of Bias

- **Pecuniary Bias** Monetary interest.
- **Personal Bias** Relationships or associations.
- **Subject-Matter Bias** Judge's involvement in the matter.

Fair Hearing Essentials

- Reasonable notice of action.
- Right to present evidence and rebut opposing claims.
- Opportunity to cross-examine witnesses.

7 Post-Decisional Hearing

Definition

- Hearing granted after administrative decisions.

Purpose

- Balances administrative efficiency and individual rights.

Applications

- Scenarios involving public interest or deprivation of property.

Limitations

- Used only in exceptional cases.

8 Droit Administrative Law

Concept

- French system governing public administration.
- Rules developed by administrative courts.

Napoleon's Reforms

- Established specialised courts for disputes involving individuals and government departments.
- **Dual Justice System** Civil courts and administrative courts.

Significance

- Accelerated socio-economic progress.
- Efficient resolution of administrative disputes.

9 Landmark Cases

Kesavananda Bharati Vs. State of Kerala

- Established Rule of Law as a basic structure of the Constitution.

Maneka Gandhi Vs. Union of India

- Emphasised fairness and reasonableness in administrative decisions.
- Highlighted violations under Articles 14, 19 and 21.

10 Summary of Administrative Law Features

Key Characteristics

- Monitors delegated legislation.
- Ensures fairness, accountability and transparency.

Impact on Governance

- Balances government efficiency and citizens' rights.
- Serves as a check on arbitrary administrative actions.

Exam Pattern Questions

Objective Type Questions

Multiple Choice Questions (MCQs)

1. When a minister is finally appointed and his actions affect the general public good, we can categorise the study of these actions as a core constituent of which of the following?

(a) Administrative Law
(b) Constitutional Law
(c) Both (a) and (b)
(d) Neither (a) nor (b)

2. Which of the following is/are the aims of Administrative Law?

(a) To keep a check on the actions of the government when dealing with the procedures affecting the rights of citizens.
(b) To clarify the scope of rights and duties of citizens and the government.
(c) Both (a) and (b)
(d) Neither (a) nor (b)

3. If we were to examine the scheme of our Constitution, while defining 'State', which of the following articles of the Constitution of India mentions 'any other authority'?

(a) Article 13 (b) Article 15
(c) Article 12 (d) Article 11

4. Which among the following is TRUE for administrative legislative action?

(a) It includes adjudication of disputes similar to judicial functions.
(b) It is the execution of policies without any discretion.
(c) It involves rule-making and delegated legislation by the administration.
(d) It is solely procedural and does not impact public policies.

5 Quasi judicial action refers to the power of an adminisatrative agency or government official to make decisions that have the force of law.

Which of the following is an example of quasi-judicial action?

(a) A judge issuing a court order.
(b) An administrative agency issuing a regulation.
(c) A government official issuing a building permit.
(d) A hearing officer deciding dispute between two parties.

6. Which of the following is called administrative action?

(a) Administrative Legislative Action
(b) Simply Administrative Action
(c) Administrative Adjudicatory Action
(d) None of the above

7. Ministerial Action is also known as ....

(a) Administrative Legislative Action
(b) Simply Administrative Action
(c) Purely Administrative Action
(d) None of the above

8. Which among the following is NOT a feature of ministerial action in Administrative Law?

(a) The action involves no discretion by the authority
(b) It follows a predetermined procedure or guideline
(c) The action includes adjudication of legal rights
(d) It is a purely administrative task

9. A state 'X' has three separate organs of government, executive, legislature and judiciary. Competency Based Que

Which of the following principles is being followed by 'X'?

(a) Monarchy
(b) Separation of powers
(c) Delegated legislation
(d) None of the above

10. Which of the following is NOT a fundamental principle of Administrative Law?

(a) Rule of law
(b) Doctrine of separation of powers
(c) Doctrine of judicial review
(d) Principles of natural justice

11. Which statement best explains the principle of administrative morality in Administrative Law?

(a) Administrative morality ensures that all administrative actions are strictly legal, regardless of fairness.
(b) Administrative morality allows the discretionary powers of the executive to override constitutional provisions.
(c) Administrative morality mandates that administrative actions must always be fair and reasonable, even if they are legal.
(d) Administrative morality allows appointments without any qualifications or experience in exceptional cases.

12. Which of the following statements is TRUE regarding the Rule of Law in India?
(a) Rule of Law was introduced in India by the Government of India Act, 1935.
(b) Rule of Law is a feature of monarchies and not democratic societies.
(c) Rule of Law is considered a basic structure of the Constitution of India.
(d) Rule of Law allows Parliament to make laws without any restrictions.

13. The state of Kerala passes a law granting absolute power to the Chief Minister to appoint university professors without considering their qualifications or experience. The law is challenged in court, citing the principles of Administrative Law.
What principle of Administrative Law is most likely to be violated by this law? **Competency Based Que**
(a) Doctrine of Separation of Powers
(b) Principles of Natural Justice
(c) Rule of Law
(d) Administrative Morality

14. The Supreme Court of India rules in the case of Kesavananda Bharati Vs. State of Kerala that the 'Rule of law' is a 'basic structure' of the Constitution. The court holds that this principle cannot be repealed or replaced by any Parliament.
What does the term 'basic structure' refer to in this context? **Competency Based Que**
(a) A set of laws that can be amended by Parliament.
(b) A bundle of characteristics of the Constitution that cannot be repealed or replaced.
(c) A principle of Administrative Law that applies only to certain states.
(d) A doctrine that separates powers between the judiciary and the legislature.

15. Statement I Administrative legislative action refers to the power of the executive branch to make laws without the direct involvement of the legislative branch.
Statement II This type of option is often used in emergency situation where swift action is necessary and the legislative process would be too slow.
Choose the correct option.
(a) Both Statements are correct.
(b) Both Statements are incorrect.
(c) Statement I is correct, but Statement II is not correct.
(d) Statement II is correct, but Statement I is not correct.

16. Match the following.

Column I	Column II
A. Bias as to subject matter	1. No one shall be unheard.
B. Audi alteram partem	2. Strengthen natural justice.
C. Nemo debet esse judex in propria causa	3. No man shall be a judge in his own cause.
D. Articles 14 and 21	4. The judge has general interest in the case.

Codes

	A	B	C	D		A	B	C	D
(a)	2	4	1	3	(b)	4	1	3	2
(c)	2	3	1	4	(d)	2	3	4	1

Assertion-Reason Questions

Directions (Q. Nos 17-18) In the questions given below, there are two statements marked as Assertion (A) and Reason (R). Read the statements and choose the correct option.

Codes
(a) Both A and R are true and R is the correct explanation of A.
(b) Both A and R are true, but R is not the correct explanation of A.
(c) A is true, but R is false.
(d) A is false, but R is true.

17. Assertion (A) The legislature has no time to legislate upon the day-to-day ever-changing needs of the society.
Reason (R) The executive is given the power to legislate and use its discretionary powers.

18. Assertion (A) Personal bias arises from near and dear i.e. from friendship, relationship, business or professional association.
Reason (R) Such a relationship disqualifies a person from acting as a judge.

Answers

1. (a) Administrative Law
2. (a) To keep a check on the actions of the government when dealing with the procedures affecting the rights of citizens.
3. (c) Article 12
4. (c) It involves rule-making and delegated legislation by the administration.
5. (d) A hearing officer deciding dispute between two parties.
6. (b) Simply Administrative Action

7. (c) Purely Administrative Action
8. (c) The action includes adjudication of legal rights.
9. (b) Separation of power
10. (c) Doctrine of judicial review
11. (c) Administrative morality mandates that administrative actions must always be fair and reasonable, even if they are legal.
12. (c) Rule of Law is considered a basic structure of the Constitution of India.
13. (c) Rule of Law
14. (b) A bundle of characteristics of the Constitution that cannot be repealed or replaced.
15. (a) Both Statements are correct.
16. (b) 4 1 3 2
17. (b) Both A and R are true, but R is not the correct explanation of A.
18. (b) Both A and R are true, but R is not the correct explanation of A.

Subjective Questions

Very Short Answer Type Questions

1. What has led to the growth of Administrative Law?

Ans. The need for delegation is often pointed out as the single most important factor which has led to the growth of Administrative Law.

2. A private hospital receives significant funding from the government to provide subsidised health care services to the poor. The hospital's management is supervised by government officials, and it performs functions similar to those of government hospitals.
Would this private hospital be considered as 'State' under Article 12 of the Constitution? Give reasons. Competency Based Que

Ans. Yes, the private hospital would be considered as 'State' under Article 12. This is because it receives significant government funding, is supervised by government officials, and performs functions similar to those of government hospitals, making it an instrumentality of the state.

3. What does Constitutional Law clarify?

Ans. Constitutional Law clarifies the scope of rights and duties of citizens and the government.

4. State the types of Administrative Law.

Ans. Administrative action can be of four types
(i) Administrative Legislative Action
(ii) Quasi-judicial Action
(iii) Simply Administrative Action
(iv) Ministerial Action/Purely Administrative Action

5. What is meant by Administrative Legislative Action?

Ans. When administration exercises law-making power delegated to it by the legislature, it is referred to as an administrative legislative action. The power is delegated because it is not practically possible for any legislature in the word to legislate so perfectly that their laws are able to cover the possibility of all kinds of conflicts, which can arise out of a decision.

6. Simran learnt in his school that delegated legislation is important in the present scenario. What do you understand by delegated legislation? Competency Based Que

Ans. 'Delegated legislation' means exercising of legislative power by an agent who is lower in rank to the legislature, or who is subordinate to the legislature. Delegated legislation is an enactment made by an individual or body other than Parliament. Parliament, through an Act, can allow someone else or some body to make enactment.

7. What does separation of power refer to?

Ans. Separation of powers refers to the division of a State's Government into branches, each with separate, independent powers and responsibilities, so that the powers of one branch are not in conflict with those of the other branches. 'Separation of powers' was meant to create divisions within the government setup to create better administration within the state.

8. 'The principles of natural justice recognised by English Law'. Explain. Competency Based Que

Ans. The principles of natural justice are based on two Latin maxims. In simple words, English law recognises two principles of natural justice as stated below
(i) NemoJudex in Causasua or Nemodebetessejudex in Propriacausa or Rule against bias which means no man shall be a judge in his own cause.
(ii) Audi Alteram Partem or the rule of fair hearing (hear the other side) which means no one shall be unheard, both the parties have an opportunity of being heard.

9. What is natural justice? Write a note on its principles.

Ans. Natural justice is an expression of English common law and involves a procedural requirement of fairness.

The principles of natural justice have great significance in the study of Administrative Law. It is also known as substantial justice or fundamental justice or universal justice or fair play in action.

- The principles of natural justice are not embodied rules and are not codified.
- They are judge made rules and are regarded as counterparts of the American procedural due process.

10. 'Post decisional hearing means to supplement the latter whenever the case demands'. Examine.

Competency Based Que

Ans. Post decisional hearing can be identified as a harmonising tool to balance between administrative efficacy and fair procedures governing an individual.

Post decisional hearing is a demand when immediate decisions are to be taken in relation to the public interest. In the case of post decisional hearing, an individual is provided with an opportunity to be heard after a decision has been adopted by the concerned authorities, within a specific time frame.

Short Answer Type Questions

1. 'Administrative law is the body of law that governs the administration and regulation of authorities created by the government'. With reference to the statement state the different types of Administrative Law.

Competency Based Que

Ans. The different types of Administrative Law are

(i) **Administrative Legislative Action** When the administration exercises law-making power delegated to it by the legislature, it is referred to as an administrative legislative action. The power is delegated because it is not practically possible for any legislature in the world to legislate so perfectly that their laws are able to cover the possibility of all kinds of conflicts, which can arise out of a decision. Administrative legislative action includes rule-making action as well as delegated legislation.

(ii) **Quasi-judicial Action or Administrative adjudicatory Action** When the administration exercises judicial powers, it is referred to as quasi-judicial action, e.g. Tribunals.

(iii) **Simply Administrative Action** The simply administrative action deal with execution of crucial administrative decisions. In simply administrative action, there is discretion to the administrative authority i.e. the authority has the right to exercise his/her own understanding and discretion in dealing with the matter.

(iv) **Ministerial Action/Purely Administrative Action** Actions which are copybook action and actions in which no discretion is vested with the authority i.e. there is only one way of performing that action, such actions are referred to as purely administrative action or ministerial action.

For example, the law which created a university, mandates that the university open a bank account with a particular bank. This is a purely administrative action or a ministerial action as there is no scope of any discretion in its performance.

2. In the case of Kesavananda Bharati Vs. State of Kerala, 'Rule of Law was categorised as a 'Basic Structure' of the Constitution. Discuss about Rule of Law.

Competency Based Que

Ans. Rule of law is an essential tool to protect the freedom and dignity of individuals against organised powers.

In the case of Kesavananda Bharati Vs. State of Kerala, 'Rule of Law' was categorised as a 'Basic Structure' of the Constitution. Basic structure means those basic characters/attributes which are enshrined in the heart of the Constitution and which cannot be repealed/replaced by any Parliament.

There was opposition to the doctrine of Rule of Law in the days of monarchy as it limits the powers of the monarch or king to change laws and rules according to his own desire. Hence, Rule of Law as a principle is essentially based only in democratic societies and is not a known feature of monarchies.

3. 'No one shall be unheard, both the parties have an opportunity of being heard'.

(i) Identify the principle of natural justice, stated above.

(ii) Explain this principle of natural justice.

Competency Based Que

Ans. (i) This is the Audi Alteram Partem principle of natural justice.

(ii) Audi Alteram Partem or the rule of fair hearing is the the second fundamental principle of natural justice. It means no one shall be condemned unheard i.e. there must be fairness on the part of the deciding authority. According to this principle, reasonable opportunity must be given to a person before taking any action against him.

This rule insists that the affected person must be given an opportunity to produce evidence in support of his case. He should disclose the evidence to be utilised against him and should be given an opportunity to rebut the evidence produced by the other party.

4. There are three kinds of bias. Explain its each kinds.

Ans. The kinds of bias are

(i) **Pecuniary Bias** Pecuniary bias arises, when the judge has monetary/economic interest in the subject matter of the dispute/case. The judge, while deciding a case should not have any pecuniary or economic interest. In other words, pecuniary interest in the subject matter of litigation disqualifies a person from acting as a judge.

(ii) **Personal Bias** Personal bias arises from near and dear i.e. from friendship, relationship, business or professional association. Such a relationship disqualifies a person from acting as a judge.

(iii) **Bias as to Subject Matter** (official bias) When the judge has general interest in the subject matter in dispute due to his association with the administration or private body, he will be disqualified on the ground of bias if he has personally identified himself with the issues in dispute. There must be intimate and direct connection between the judge and the issues in dispute to disqualify the judge according to this bias.

5. A hearing will be treated as a fair hearing, if it included essentials of hearing. Explain the essentials of hearing. Competency Based Que

Ans. For answer refer to the text under the heading 'Essentials of Fair Hearing on page no. 97 and 98.

6. The government issues an order to demolish a slum area to make way for a new highway project. The residents are not given a prior hearing, but are offered a post-decisional hearing to appeal against the order. The residents claim that the demolition will leave them homeless and affect their livelihood.

What is the significance of post-decisional hearing in this scenario, and what are the exceptional grounds that justify its usage? Competency Based Que

Ans. Post-decisional hearing is significant in this scenario as it provides the residents with an opportunity to be heard and appeal against the demolition order, despite not being given a prior hearing.

The exceptional grounds that justify the usage of post-decisional hearing in this case include deprivation of property, livelihood, and potentially, public interest. The usage of post-decisional hearing is restricted to exceptional cases, and this scenario meets those criteria.

7. A university student is expelled from the institution without being given a prior hearing. The student is later offered a post-decisional hearing to appeal against the expulsion order. The student claims that the expulsion was unfair and affected their academic career. What are the key features of post-decisional hearing, and how does it balance administrative efficacy with fair procedures in this scenario?

Ans. The key features of post-decisional hearing include providing an individual with an opportunity to be heard after a decision has been made, and ensuring that the decision is not permanent or final until the individual has been heard.

In this scenario, post-decisional hearing balances administrative efficacy with fair procedures by allowing the university to take swift action, while also providing the student with a chance to appeal and present their case. This ensures that the student's rights are protected, while also maintaining the university's ability to take decisive action.

Long Answer Type Questions

1. Explain about the growth, development and study of administrative law.

Ans. For answer refer to the text under the heading the Growth, Development and Study of Administrative Law, on page no. 94 and 95.

2. Explain in detail the Droit Administrative Law.

Ans. For answer refer to the text under the heading Droit Administrative Law, on page no. 99.

3. Explain the significant changes introduced by Napoleon in the French judicial administration and how they led to the establishment of a dual system of justice in France. What were the objectives of these reforms, and how did they impact the decision-making process in cases involving private individuals and government departments?

Ans. Napoleon's judicial reforms marked a transformative phase in French administration. Before his rule, the king's court (Conseil du Roi) served merely as an advisory body, while ordinary courts were underfunded and dependent on collected fees, fostering inefficiency and conflict with the government. Napoleon aimed to accelerate socio-economic progress and resolve disputes involving government departments swiftly. To achieve these objectives, he abolished the king's court, restricted judicial interference in administrative affairs, and established specialised courts to handle disputes expeditiously.

This system introduced a dual justice framework. Civil courts managed private disputes, while administrative courts, led by the Conseil d'État, handled cases involving individuals and the government.

Initially, administrative cases required ministerial referral and the court's decisions were advisory. Despite criticisms, the droit system is considered efficient, ensuring that disputes are resolved promptly without hindering governance.

SELF ASSESSMENT TEST

Multiple Choice Questions

1. Which of the following bias arises from near and dear i.e. from friendship, relationship, business or professional association?
   (a) Personal bias (b) Pecuniary Bias (c) Official bias (d) None of these
2. In a democratic society, fundamental principles of Administrative Law are transparency or openness, the principle of participation, of impartiality and objectivity, reasoned decisions, legality, effective review of administrative rules and administrative decisions, accountability and non-arbitrariness. All these principles are broadly encompassed under the **Competency Based Que**
   (a) Rule of law (b) Doctrine of separation of powers
   (c) Principles of natural justice (d) All of these
3. According to this principle, reasonable opportunity must be given to a person before taking any action against him. This rule insists that the affected person must be given an opportunity to produce evidence in support of his case. Which of the following(s) is/are talked about?
   (a) Nemo Judex in Causa Sua (b) Audi Alteram Partem
   (c) Both (a) and (b) (d) Neither (a) nor (b)

Very Short Answer Type Questions

4. State two differences between Administrative Law and Constitutional Law.
5. The Commissioner of Education revokes the teaching licenes of a teacher after conducting a hearing and finding that the teacher had engaged in unprofessional conduct . The teacher had been accussed of physically abusing a student, and the commissioner's dicision was based on evidence presented during the hearing. What type of action is commissioner's decision? **Competency Based Que**
6. Mention the difference between Simply Administrative Action and Ministerial Action/Purely Administrative Action.

Short Answer Type Questions

7. "Rule of law is an essential tool to protect the freedom and dignity of individuals against organised powers". Explain. **Competency Based Que**
8. Analyse which rules made it clear that the judiciary must be free from bias and should deliver pure and impartial justice?

Long Answer Type Questions

9. Post decisional hearing be considered as a harmonising tool. Justify. **Competency Based Que**
10. The Napolean Bonaparte introduced the system of administration of justice. Analyse the statement. **Competency Based Que**

06

CHAPTER

Jurisprudence, Nature and Meaning of Law

In Layman's language, law can be described as "A system of rules and regulations which a country or society recognises as binding on its citizens, which the authorities may enforce, and violation of which attracts punitive action".

YOUR STUDY GOALS

YOUR PRACTICE GOAL

- Objective Type Questions (21 Qs ; MCQs, A-R, Statements, Matching)
- Subjective Questions (7 VSAs, 7 SAs, 4 LAs)

6.1 Introduction and Meaning of Jurisprudence

- Jurisprudence is the **philosophy and theory of law.**
- The law and the legal system are very important in any civilisation.
- Law is not only important for an orderly social life but also essential for the very existence of mankind.
- Therefore, it is important for everyone to understand the meaning of law.
- Jurists and legal scholars have not arrived at a unanimous definition of law.

Definitions of Law

There are many definitions of law given by various jurists. Some jurists consider law as a **divinely**[1] ordered rule or as a reflection of divine reasons. Some of the important definitions of law are

- According to Greek philosopher **Aristotle**, law is 'As an embodiment of reasons whether in individual or the community'.
- According to German jurist and historian **Friendrich Carl Von Savigny**, 'Law is a product of the general consciousness of the people'.

1 **Divinely** It means the power of God.

6.2 Historical Perspective

Case of the Speluncean Explorers

- In 1949, Lon Fuller created a fictitious case for the Harvard Law Review which has been called a **classic in jurisprudence**.
- It is the case of the **Speluncean Explorers**.
- The case takes place in the equally fictitious 'Commonwealth of Newgarth' in the year 4300.
- It offers five possible judicial responses.
- This account of Fuller is an example of mid-20th century legal theory.
- According to British philosopher **Jeremy Bentham**, law is defined as 'A collection of signs declarative of a volition conceived or adopted by the sovereign'.
- According to **John Austin,** law is 'a body of rules determined and enforced by a sovereign political authority'.
- According to Israeli philosopher **Joseph Raz,** 'Law consists of authoritative positivist considerations enforceable by the courts'.
- It is because of these different approaches that different concepts of law and consequently various schools of law have emerged.

Facts

- Five cave explorers (spelunkers) are trapped inside a cave following a landslide, one of them being Roger Whetmore. They have limited food supplies and no source of food inside the cave. The rescue was difficult, time-consuming, and costly due to the remote location. Ten workmen were killed in the rescue. Approaching starvation, a radio contact is eventually established with the rescue team on the 20th day of the cave-in. The explorers learn that another 10 days would be required in order to free them. After consultation with medical experts, they were told that they are unlikely to survive another 10 days without food. The explorers inquire the doctors about their chances of surviving if they killed and ate one of their own.
- The doctors hesitantly stated that they would. No one on the rescue team said yes when asked if they should hold a lottery to decide who to kill and eat. The radio is turned off, and later a lottery is held. The explorers were initially hesitant to use this desperate step, but after hearing the radio chats, they agreed.
- Roger Whetmore proposed casting lots, using a pair of dice he happened to have with him. Roger Whetmore backed out of the deal before the dice were rolled, indicating he would wait another week. The other accused him of betraying their trust and continued to cast the dice.
- The defendants invited Whetmore to announce any concerns to the fairness of the dice throw before throwing it on his behalf. He didn't raise an objection, and the throw went against him. Whetmore was put to death and devoured.

In the case of the Speluncean Explorers, the person to be eaten was chosen by throwing a pair of dice.

- Following their rescue and recovery, the survivors were charged with murder of Roger Whetmore. In the Commonwealth of Newgarth, the mandatory sentence for murder is death by hanging.
- On the facts as found by the jury, the trial judge ruled that the defendants were guilty of murder and sentenced them to be hanged.
- Post-trial, both the trial judge and the jury joined in a petition to the Chief Executive of Newgarth, to commute the death sentence of surviving explorers to six months' imprisonment. The Chief Executive waits for the Supreme Court's disposition of the petition of error before making a decision regarding clemency.

Jury involved in Judgement

- Chief Justice Truepenny
- Justice Foster
- Justice Tatting
- Justice Keen
- Justice Handy
- In this case, several viewpoints were forwarded about the nature of the law.

Viewpoints of Chief Justice Truepenny

- The law is unambiguous (clear) and must be applied by the judiciary.
- The public opinion and sentiment has no influence over the word of the law.
- Granting mercy falls within the scope of the executive and not the judiciary.
- The Chief Justice depends on the **possibility of clemency (forgiveness)** by the executive, to mitigate the word of law.
- The Supreme Court petitions the Chief Executive for clemency. Thus, by relying on the executive, justice can be done without violating the letter or spirit of the law.
- Thus, Truepenny CJ upholds the conviction but recommends clemency.

Viewpoints of Justice Foster

- Within the scope of the **laws of nature**, it is acceptable to sacrifice one person, if it means the others (many) can survive.
- A '**purposive**[2] **approach**' must be taken to the law.
- The main aim of criminal law is **punishing the criminals**, and by that punishment, **warning further offenders**.
- In this case, punishing the offenders will not serve the purpose of deterrence/warning.
- The judges have a certain leeway in interpretation of the law especially in cases that are extraordinary in nature.
- The decision made by the judges in this case would not be going against the will of the legislature, but ensuring that the legislative will is effective.
- Justice foster concludes that the conviction should be set aside.

Viewpoints of Justice Tatting

- He criticises the view under natural law that prioritises freedom of contract to kill above the right to life in the state of nature.
- He also criticises the purposive approach to the criminal law which has multiple purposes, including **retribution**[3] and **rehabilitation**[4].
- The doctrine that is taught in Law Schools is that 'The man who acts to repel an aggressive threat to his own life does not act wilfully, but in response to an impulse deeply ingrained in human nature'.
- The judge cites the case of Commonwealth Vs. Valjean, in which starvation was held not to justify the theft of a loaf of bread, let alone homicide (killing of a person).

Viewpoints of Justice Keen

- He stated that it is not for the judiciary to decide whether executive clemency should be extended to the defendants.
- The Chief Executive should be petitioned for clemency and the decision should be left up to him.
- Judges have to apply the 'law of the land' in a case, instead of their conceptions of morality.

---

2 **Purposive** It means having or done with a purpose.

3 **Retribution** It means punishment for something that was done morally wrong.

4 **Rehabilitation** It means the action of restoring something that has been damaged to its former condition.

- Laws may have many possible purposes, with difficulties arising in assuming the actual purpose of a piece of legislation.
- A hard decision is never a popular decision.
- Justice keen affirms the conviction.

Viewpoints of Justice Handy

- Court should take account of **public opinion** and **'common sense'**.
- Government is 'a human affair' in which people are ruled well when their rulers understand the feelings and conceptions of the masses.
- Judiciary is one branch of the government that is most likely to lose its contact with the common man.
- Taking a common sense approach he concludes that the defendants are innocent and conviction should be set aside.

Quick Test 1

1. How does John Austin define the law?
2. Mention any one viewpoint of Justice Truepenny about the nature of law.
3. What is the main aim of criminal law according to Justice Foster?
4. Who should be petitioned for clemency according to Justice Keen?

6.3 Schools of Law

- On the basis of the definitions of law as provided by jurists and legal philosopher over time, there is no universally accepted definition of law as different schools of law are characteristically different in their approach.
- The various schools of law are

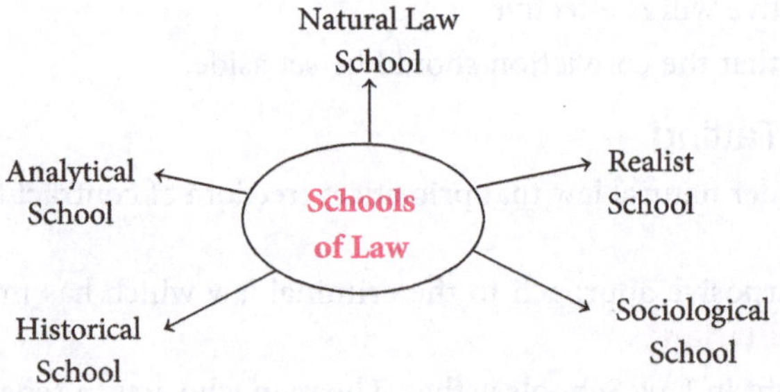

Natural Law School

- Natural law is the law of nature, divine law, a law which is eternal and universal.
- Natural law is believed to exist independent of human will.
- It is not created by man, but is found through nature.

Natural Law Theory

- The central idea of natural law theory states that, there is a higher law based on morality against which the moral or legal validity of human law can be measured.
- It is a belief that there are certain universal moral laws against which no human laws may go, without losing legal or moral force.

- Natural law theory asserts that there is an essential connection between law and morality. The law is not simply what is enacted in statutes. If legislation is not moral, then it is not a law. According to St. Thomas Aquinas a law without moral content is called as **perversion of law.**
- According to natural law theory, law and morality are linked to each other.
- This view is expressed by the maxim **'Lex iniusta non est lex'** (an unjust law is not a true law).
- It was also asserted that, if it is not a true law then there is no need to follow it.
- This view point considers that the concept of law cannot be fully expressed without mentioning morality.
- According to the classical naturalists, the law necessarily includes all moral principles.
- However, this argument does not mean that the law is all about moral principles.
- This is simply to demonstrate that human-made legal rules are only acceptable if they are morally sound.

The Principles of Natural Law

- In the 19th century, jurists such as **Bentham and Austin** has rejected the principles of natural law because of its vague and ambiguous (unclear) character.
- The change in socio-political conditions of the world, like the rise of materialism after the First World War led to the revival of natural law theory in its modified form, which is different from its traditional form. The principles of natural law have been inspired by the emergence of the modern philosophy of human rights.
- The principles of natural law provides guidance for the **protection of human rights** and **fundamental freedoms.**

The Principles of Natural Justice

- In India, the principles of natural justice are mentioned in Articles 14 and 21 of the Constitution.
- The violation of the principles of natural justice results in arbitrariness (unfair).
- Therefore, violation of natural justice is a violation of the equality clause of Article 14.
- The principle of natural justice encompasses the following two rules
  (i) No one should be a judge in his own cause or the rule against bias. (Nemo judex in causa sua)
  (ii) No one should be condemned unheard. (Audi Alteram Partem)
- Generally, the **'rule of law'** and **'due process of law'** are considered as new incarnations of natural justice in the 20th century.

Rule of Law

- 'Rule of Law' means that **law carries supremacy** over all individuals, even those in the position of power.
- According to **Max Weber**, rule of law is characterised as "Legal domination as an idea of government of law rather than an idea of men".
- The beliefs of **equality** and **non-arbitrariness** are also important components of rule of law.
- The rule of law is one of the basic and general principles of the Constitution.
- Rule of law means that everyone from the government to its officials, together with citizens should act according to the law.
- The doctrine of rule of law has been described as supremacy of the law.
- This means that no person is above the law.
- Even the functions and actions of the executive organ of the state shall be within the extent of law.
- Rule of law imposes a duty on all citizens in a Parliamentary democracy to obey the law and for such obedience the law itself must be just law and not arbitrary or oppressive law.

Analytical School

- The aim of this school is to create a scientifically valid system of law, by analysing legal concepts and ideas on the basis of empirical or scientific methods.
- It is also referred to as the **positive** or **imperative**[5] **school** of jurisprudence.
- It came as a reaction against the school of natural law.
- Most of the founders of this school like Jeremy Bentham (1748-1832) and John Austin (1790-1859), **rejected natural law** as 'vague and abstract ideas'.

Positivism

- The idea of positivism emphasises the separation of law and morality.
- Natural law thinkers proposed that if a law is not moral, no one is under any duty to obey it.
- On the other hand, positivists believe that a duly enacted law, remains law and should be obeyed, until it is changed.

John Austin's The Province of Jurisprudence Determined

- John Austin suggested that law is the command of the sovereign, backed by threat of punishment. In his work, The Province of Jurisprudence Determined published in 1832, Austin made an effort to explain the distinction between law and morality.
- According to him, natural law doctrines were responsible for the unclear distinction between law and morality.
- To get rid of this confusion, he defined law as 'species of command of sovereign'.
- According to Austin, command is an expression of desire by a political superior (e.g. king, Parliament, etc.) to a political inferior (e.g. subjects, citizens).
- The political inferior shall commit or omit an act, under an obligation to obey the command and if, the command is disobeyed, then the political inferior is liable for punishment.
- Commands are prescribed modes of conduct by the sovereign.
- He further viewed sovereign as a person or group of persons, to whom a society gives habitual obedience and who gives no such obedience to others.
- The idea of command and punishment for disobeying the command is the most prominent and distinctive character of 'positive law'.
- It differentiates positive law from the 'principles of morality' and from 'positive morality'.
- Principles of morality consider law as 'Law of God' and 'positive morality' considers law as man-made rules of conduct, such as customary rules and international law, etc.
- 'Principles of morality' and 'positive morality' do not originate from a sovereign.

Historical School

- The historical school suggests that the law should conform to the local needs and feelings of the society.
- Its followers believe that laws are the creation of interactions between the local situation and conditions of the people.
- It started as a reaction against natural law and positivism to grow as a form of law.
- It emphasised the irrational, racial and evolutionary character of law.

5 **Imperative** It means something of vital importance.

- **Sir Henry James Sumner Maine,** a British jurist and legal historian, who developed the study of comparative law, primitive law and anthropological[6] jurisprudence, is the main exponent of the British historical school of jurisprudence.
- According to **Friedman,** the main features of **Savigny's** historical school of jurisprudence are
  - Law should be a reflection of the common spirit of the people and their custom.
  - Law is not universal, it is particular like the language of a particular society.
  - Law is not static, it has relationship with the development of the society.
  - Law is not given by a political superior, but is found or given by the people.
- The approach in the historical school is criticised and rejected because of the unclear and unscientific explanation of the law.

Sociological School

- The sociological school considers law as a tool for social change.
- Followers of this school insist on the fact that law exists for the needs of the society.
- The philosophy of the sociological approach provides an opportunity to social and legal reformers.
- Sociological school consider law as a social phenomenon.
- It visualises law from the perceptions of people in the society.
- This approach emphasises on balancing the conflicting interests in society.
- **Roscoe Pound** (1870-1964), an American jurist, was considered as the **chief exponent of sociological jurisprudence** in the United States.
- According to Roscoe Pound, the main features of the sociological school are
  - It highlights the purpose and function of law rather than its content.
  - Law is a social institution designed for social need.
  - Law is a tool to balance conflicting interests of society.

Realist School

- Realists consider laws made by judges as the real law.
- They give less importance to the traditional rules and concepts as real sources of law.
- Realism is contrary to idealism. It is a combination of analytical positivism and sociological jurisprudence.
- Realists do not give much importance to laws enacted by legislative bodies and **consider the judge-made laws as the actual law.**
- Realists place great emphasis on the role of judges in the implementation, interpretation and development of law.
- They believe that the social, economic and psychological background of a judge plays an important part in his decision-making.

Features of Realist School

- **Karl Llewellyn,** an American jurisprudential scholar was associated with the school of legal realism. He had identified some of the main features of the realist school which are
  - Law is not static as it keeps on changing.
  - Law is a means to a social end.
  - Society changes faster than the law.
  - Law cannot be certain.
  - Decisions of the courts depend on many factors like the psychological, social and economic background of the judges.
  - Case studies are important and the court room is a laboratory of law.

6 **Anthropological** It is the study of human kind.

Schools of Law

Schools of Law	Jurists/ Philosophers	Distinguishing Features/Source of Law
Natural Law School	Aristotle, Plato, Thomas Aquinas, Hobbes Montesquieu, Rousseau, etc.	Nature, Human Reasons, Divine Sources
Analytical School of Law	Bentham, Austin, Kelsan, HLA Hart, etc.	Command of the sovereign, Morality ignored
Historical School of Law	Savigny, Henry Maine, etc.	Custom, Common spirit of the people
Sociological School of Law	Roscoe Pound, Duguit, Ihering, Ehrlich, etc.	Purpose of law is to balance conflicting interests in the society
Realist School of Law (American and Scandinavian Realism)	Jerome Frank, O W Holmes Alf Ross, Olivecrona, Hangerstorm, etc.	Judicial decisions are the prime source of law.

6.4 Function and Purpose of Law

- The functions and purpose of law have been changing with time and place.
- They depend on the nature of the state.
- However, in a welfare and democratic state, there are several important functions of law.
- It can be stated that law starts regulating the welfare and other aspects of human life. In fact, the state interacts with and protects its citizens throughout their lives, with the help of law.
- Some of the major functions and purposes of law are
  - To deliver justice
  - To maintain impartiality
  - To maintain social control
  - To provide equality and uniformity
  - To maintain law and order
  - To resolve conflicts
  - To bring orderly change through law and social reform.

Quick Test 2

1. What is the meaning of perversion of law?
2. Who rejected the principles of natural law?
3. Which school of law aims to create a scientifically valid system of law?
4. Who was considered as the chief exponent of sociological jurisprudence in the United States?
5. Mention any two functions of law.

Mind Map

1 Introduction to Jurisprudence

Definition
- The philosophy and theory of law.
- Explores the principles underlying legal systems and their societal impact.

Importance of Law
- Ensures orderly social life and protects civilisation.
- Essential for the existence and governance of mankind.

Definitions by Jurists
- **Aristotle** Law as an embodiment of reason.
- **Jeremy Bentham** A collection of signs declarative of a sovereign's will.
- **John Austin** A command of the sovereign, backed by a threat of sanction.
- **Joseph Raz** Law consists of enforceable authoritative considerations.

2 Historical Perspective

Case of the Speluncean Explorers
- A fictional case illustrating jurisprudential debates.
- Explores legal reasoning in life-and-death scenarios.
- Judges' differing views on law, morality and justice
  - **Chief Justice Truepenny** Law is unambiguous; clemency is executive's domain.
  - **Justice Foster** Advocates natural law; prioritises survival over rigid legalities.
  - **Justice Tatting** Highlights complexity in balancing natural law and state law.
  - **Justice Keen** Emphasises strict adherence to legal provisions.
  - **Justice Handy** Supports common-sense and public opinion in legal decisions.

3 Schools of Law

Natural Law School
- **Key Proponents** Aristotle, Thomas Aquinas, Rousseau.

Principles
- Law is universal, eternal, and rooted in morality.
- Maxim 'Lex iniusta non estlex' (Unjust law is not a true law).
- Connects law and morality; unjust laws lack legitimacy.

Analytical (Positive) School
- **Key Proponents** Jeremy Bentham, John Austin.

Principles
- Focuses on law as it is, not as it ought to be.
- Separates law from morality.
- Law is a command by a sovereign, enforceable through sanctions.

Historical School
- **Key Proponents** Friedrich Carl von Savigny, Henry Maine.

Principles
- Law evolves from societal customs and shared spirit.
- Rejects universal laws; emphasises local traditions.

Sociological School
- **Key Proponents** Roscoe Pound.

Principles
- Law as a social institution addressing societal needs.
- Balances conflicting interests to promote social welfare.

Realist School
- **Key Proponents** Jerome Frank, Karl Llewellyn.

Principles
- Focuses on how judges apply laws in real-life situations.
- Emphasises judicial decisions as primary law sources.

JURISPRUDENCE, NATURE, AND MEANING OF LAW

4 Principles of Natural Justice

Key Rules
- **Nemo Judex in Causa Sua** No one should judge their own case.
- **Audi Alteram Partem** No one should be condemned unheard.

In India
- Articles 14 and 21 of the Constitution uphold natural justice.
- Promotes fairness, non-arbitrariness and equality.

Rule of Law

Definition
- Supremacy of law over individuals and governments.
- **Max Weber** Law governs the state, not men.

Significance
- Ensures equality, impartiality and non-arbitrariness.
- A cornerstone of democratic governance.

Function and Purpose of Law

Key Functions
- Deliver justice.
- Maintain equality, impartiality and social order.
- Resolve conflicts and promote social reform.

Purpose
- Acts as a tool for societal control and orderly change.
- Balances individual rights with collective welfare.

Revival of Natural Law

Causes
- Reaction against positivist theories post-World War I.
- Addressed issues of fascism and totalitarianism.

Modern Natural Law
- Value-oriented and dynamic.
- Upholds human rights and fundamental freedoms.
- Balances individual rights with collective welfare.

6 Key Takeaways

- Jurisprudence bridges law and philosophy.
- Schools of law offer diverse perspectives on legal interpretation.
- The principles of natural justice and the rule of law ensure fairness.
- Law evolves to meet societal, political and cultural needs.

5 Comparative Features of Schools of Law

School	Proponents	Key Features
Natural Law	Aristotle, Aquinas	Morality-based, universal principles.
Analytical Law	Bentham, Austin	Sovereign's command; morality ignored.
Historical Law	Savigny, Maine	Customs and common spirit of people.
Sociological Law	Roscoe Pound	Balances societal needs and conflicting interests.
Realist Law	Jerome Frank, Olive Crona	Judicial decisions as real law, contextual.

CBSE Textbook Folder

1. Provide one point of difference between the following

(i) Natural Law School and Analytical School

(ii) Sociological School and Realist School

(iii) Original and Revived Natural Law School

Ans. (i) Natural law is believed to exist independent of human will and it is not created by man but is found through nature.

On the other hand, the Analytical law school creates a scientifically valid system of law, by analysing legal concepts and ideas on the basis of empirical or scientific methods.

(ii) The Sociological school considers law as a tool for social change. It emphasises on balancing the conflicting interest in society.

On the other hand the realists consider laws made by judges as the real law. They emphasises on the role of judges in the implementation, interpretation and development of law.

(iii) Originally, natural law is the body of universal moral principles which has laid down the ethical and moral guidelines to regulate human conduct. It is also known as the 'Law of Nature'.

The change in socio-political conditions of the world, like the rise of materialism after the First World War led to the revival of natural law theory in its modified form, which is different from its traditional form.

2. Answer the following questions briefly.

(i) On what grounds was the historical approach to law criticised?

(ii) What do you understand by the maxim "Lex iniusta non est lex"?

(iii) State the two important rules of natural justice principles.

(iv) State two examples of the principles of natural justice grounded in the Constitution of India.

Ans. (i) Historical approach to law was criticised on the following grounds

- There are certain non-alignment which are apparently observed in Savigny's theory. He focused upon the national character of law but at the same time suggested a model by which Roman law could be adopted and accepted as the law of Germany.
- Savigny's theory of law is negative, obscure and suffers from narrow sectarian outlook. He was against codification of law which is one of the most accepted forms of modern progressiveness legislation. Following anti-codification attitude of him delayed the codification of Germany law for more than fifty years.
- Savigny asserted that popular consciousness is the sole source of law is not wholly true. There are many areas which would have been left without legal rules because any popular consciousness never existed about them.

(ii) Lex iniusta non est lex, is an expression of natural law, acknowledging that authority is not legitimate unless it is good and right.

(iii) The principle of natural justice encompasses the following two rules which are

(a) Nemo judex in causa sua which means no one should be a judge in his own cause or, the rule against bias.

(b) Audi alteram partem which means no one should be condemned unheard.

(iv) The two examples of the principles of natural justice are

(a) Natural justice allows a person to claim the right to adequate notification of the date, time, place of the hearing as well as detailed notification of the case to be met.

(b) Natural justice allows the person adequate time to effectively prepare his or her own case and to answer the case againt him or her.

3. Answer the following questions in detail.

(i) Explain the purpose of law.

(ii) Explain the viewpoint of Analytical Law School. Also state the reasons for its rejection.

Ans. (i) The purpose of law has been changing with time and place. It depends on the nature of the state. However, in a welfare and democratic state, there are several important functions and purposes of law. These are

- To deliver justice.
- To provide equality and uniformity.
- To maintain impartiality.
- To maintain law and order.

- To maintain social control.
- To resolve conflicts.
- To bring orderly change through law and social reform.

(ii) The aim of Analytical Law School is to create a scientifically valid system of law, by analysing legal concepts and ideas on the basis of empirical or scientific methods. It is also referred to as the positive or imperative school of jurisprudence. It came as a reaction against the school of natural law. But later it was rejected by jurist such as Dworkin, Fuller and Finnis because it gave too much emphasis on 'law as a command' and reject morality and custom as a source of law. It failed to give morality its due importance.

4. Imacia, a country follows laws which appeal to the conscience of people only. They strongly believe in the principles of natural justice and due process of law. Which school of law do they follow? Explain the school.

Ans. The school of law followed in Imacia is Natural Law School. Natural law is generally explained as the law of nature, divine law, a law which is eternal and universal. However, it has been given different meanings at points in time. For instance, it was considered to be associated with theology but at the same time it was also used for secular purposes. Natural law is believed to exist independent of human will.

Natural law theory asserts that there is an essential connection between law and morality. The law is not simply what is enacted in statutes and if legislation is not moral, then it is not law. St. Thomas Aquinas called law without moral content, as 'perversion of law'.

Exponents of natural law believe that law and morality are linked. This view is expressed by the maxim 'Lex iniusta non est lex' (an unjust law is not a true law). It was also asserted that, if it is not a true law then there is no need to follow it. According to this view, the notion of law cannot be fully articulated without some reference to morality.

Exam Pattern Questions

Objective Type Questions

Multiple Choice Questions (MCQs)

1. Which of the following best describes the role of the 'Lady of Justice'?

(a) She symbolises the imposition of punishment without bias.
(b) She represents the fair and equal administration of law without prejudice.
(c) She is depicted as the enforcer of divine laws.
(d) She only appears in legal systems that follow Roman traditions.

2. Which of the following is very important in any civilisation?

(a) Constitutional Monarch (b) Legal System
(c) Media (d) All of these

3. Which of the following is NOT true about the concept of law?

(a) Law is essential for the orderly social life and existence of mankind.
(b) Law can be defined from various philosophical, theological and social perspectives.
(c) Law always reflects divine will or reasoning in every society.
(d) Jurists have different views on what constitutes the law and legal systems.

4. Law is "As an embodiment of reasons whether in individual or the community". **Competency Based Que**
The above mentioned definition of law is given by which of the following?

(a) Jereny Bentham (b) Friedrich Carl von Savigny
(c) Maxim (d) Aristotle

5. According to the ...., law necessarily includes all moral principles.

(a) Principle of Natural Justice
(b) Principle of Analytical Justice
(c) Classical Naturalists
(d) Classical Analytists

6. Which of the following is consider as new incarnations of natural justice?

(a) Procedure established by law (b) Due process of law
(c) Rule of law (d) Both (b) and (c)

7. .... called law without moral content, as 'perversion of law'.
(a) Israeli Philosopher Joseph Raz
(b) St. Thomas Aquinas
(c) Oliver Wendell Holmes
(d) Ronald Dworkin

8. Which of the following Articles of the Indian Constitution deals with the principles of natural justice?
(a) Article 20 (b) Article 21
(c) Article 17 (d) Article 19

9. The principles of natural law have also been inspired by the emergence of the ....
(a) philosophy of human rights
(b) philosophy of legal rights
(c) philosophy of fundamental rights
(d) None of the above

10. "The aim of this school is to create a scientifically valid system of law, by analysing legal concepts and ideas on the basis of empirical or scientific methods".
The above mentioned statement is referred to which of the following school of law? **Competency Based Que**
(a) Natural School of Law
(b) Analytical School of Law
(c) Sociological School of Law
(d) Historical School of Law

11. The theory of sociological jurisprudence was introduced by......... .
(a) Jeremy Bentham (b) John Austin
(c) H.L.A. Hart (d) Roscoe Pound

12. American and Scandinavian are the part of which of the following school?
(a) Realist School (b) Sociological School
(c) Historical School (d) Analytical School

13. Consider the following statements and choose the correct option.
The rule against bias is a fundamental principle of natural justice that ensures a decision maker is impartial and unbiased.
Which of the following statement is TRUE about the purpose of the rule against bias? **Competency Based Que**
(a) To ensure decisions are made quickly and effectively.
(b) To allow decision-makers to show leniency in certain cases.
(c) To prevent decisions being influenced by personal opinion or interest.
(d) To give decision-makers absolute discretion in their decisions.

14. Who among the following was against the analytical school?
I. Jeremy Bentham II. John Austin
III. John Finnis IV. Roscoe Pound
Select the correct option.
(a) I and II
(b) II, III and IV
(c) Only III
(d) II and III

15. Statement I The realist school of law emphasises that law is not just a set of rules and principles, but also a reflection of social and political realities.
Statement II Realists argue that judges decisions are often influenced by their personal values, political beliefs, and social context, rather than just the law itself.
Choose the correct option
(a) Both Statements are correct.
(b) Both Statements are incorrect.
(c) Statement I is correct, but Statement II is not correct.
(d) Statement II is correct, but Statement I is not correct.

16. Match the following.

Column I	Column II
A. Divine sources	1. Historical School of Law
B. Common spirit of the people	2. Realist School of Law
C. Judicial decisions are the prime sources of law	3. Analytical School of Law
D. Morality ignored	4. Natural Law School

Codes

	A	B	C	D		A	B	C	D
(a)	2	1	3	4	(b)	2	3	4	1
(c)	4	3	1	2	(d)	4	1	2	3

17. Match the following.

Column I	Column II
A. Plato	1. Analytical School of Law
B. Kelsan	2. Sociological School of Law
C. Savigny	3. Historical School of Law
D. Ihering	4. Natural Law School

Codes

	A	B	C	D		A	B	C	D
(a)	2	1	3	4	(b)	4	3	2	1
(c)	2	4	3	1	(d)	4	1	2	3

Assertion-Reason Questions

Directions (Q. No. 18-21) In the questions given below, there are two statements. Read the statements and choose the correct option.

Codes

(a) Both A and R are true and R is the correct explanation of A.
(b) Both A and R are true, but R is not the correct explanation of A.
(c) A is true, but R is false. (d) A is false, but R is true.

18. Assertion (A) In India, the principles of natural justice are firmly grounded in Articles 14 and 21 of the Constitution.

Reason (R) The principles of natural law have also been inspired by the emergence of the modern philosophy of human rights.

19. Assertion (A) Ronald Dworkin, Fuller and Finnis has rejected the analytical school of law.

Reason (R) It gave too much emphasis on 'Law as a command' and rejected morality and custom as a source of law.

20. Assertion (A) The analytical school suggests that the law should conform to the local needs and feelings of the society.

Reason (R) Jeremy Bentham and jurist and John Austin credited for founding the analytical school of jurisprudence.

21. Assertion (A) Law is not static as it keeps on changing.

Reason (R) Law is a means to a social end.

Answers

1. (b) She represents the fair and equal administration of law without prejudice.
2. (b) Legal System
3. (c) Law always reflects divine will or reasoning in every society.
4. (d) Aristotle
5. (c) Classical Naturalists
6. (d) Both (b) and (c)
7. (b) St. Thomas Aquinas
8. (b) Article 21
9. (a) philosophy of human rights
10. (b) Analytical School of Law
11. (d) Roscoe Pound
12. (a) Realist School
13. (c) To prevent decisions being influenced by personal opinion or interest.
14. (c) Only III
15. (a) Both Statements are correct.
16. (d) 4 1 2 3
17. (d) 4 1 2 3
18. (b) Both A and R are true, but R is not the correct explanation of A.
19. (b) Both A and R are true, but R is not the correct explanation of A.
20. (a) Both A and R are true and R is the correct explanation of A.
21. (d) A is false, but R is true.

Subjective Questions

Very Short Answer Type Questions

1. 'It is important for everyone to understand the law'. Explain why? **Competency Based Que**

Ans. The law and the legal system are very important in any civilisation. In modern times, no one can imagine a society without law and a legal system. Law is not only important for an orderly social life but also essential for the very existence of mankind. Therefore, it is important for everyone to understand the meaning of law.

2. 'Law is a system of rules'. Justify the statement. **Competency Based Que**

Ans. Law can be described as 'A system of rules and regulations' which a country or society recognises as binding on its citizens. It is a collection of established guidelines and principles that govern behaviour within a society, enforced by a controlling authority, essentially acting as a structured set of rules that everyone is expected to follow'. It regulates, conduct and maintain the order.

3. What is the central idea behind natural law theory?

Ans. The central idea of natural law theory states that there is a higher law based on morality against which the legal validity of human law can be measured.

It is a belief that there are certain universal moral laws that human laws may not go against, without losing legal or moral force.

4. 'Natural law is not created by men, but is found through nature'. Justify this Statement. Competency Based Que

Ans. Natural Law is the law of nature, divine law, a law which is external and universal. It is belived to exist independent of human will.

The central idea of this law states that, there is a higher law based on morality against the legal validity of human can be measured. According to this theory, if legislation is not moral, then it is not a law.

5. Give Jeremy Bentham's views on law.

Ans. British Philosopher Jeremy Bentham's defined law as 'A collection of signs declarative of a volition conceived or adopted by the sovereign'.

6. (i) What is the aim of analytical school?

(ii) Who was the founder of analytical school?

Ans. (i) The aim of analytical school is to create a scientifically valid system of law, by analysing legal concepts and ideas on the basis of empirical or scientific methods.

(ii) Jeremy Bentham (1748-1832) and John Austin (1790-1859) were the founder of analytical school.

7. State any two features of sociological school.

Ans. The two features of sociological school are

(i) They consider law as a social phenomenon.

(ii) It visualises law from the perceptions of people in the society.

Short Answer Type Questions

1. (i) Define law.

(ii) How has Aristotle defined law?

Ans. (i) For answer, Definition or Meaning of Law, refer to Q.No.2 of Very Short Answer Type Questions.

(ii) According to Greek Philosopher Aristotle, law is 'as an embodiment of reasons whether in individual or the community'.

2. 'The principles of natural law was rejected by positivists like Bentham and Austin'? Explain why they rejected? Competency Based Que

Ans. Jurists such as Bentham and Austin in the 19th century has rejected the principles of natural law because of its vague and ambiguous character. It was realised that overemphasis on the historical approaches to law had led to the rise of fascism in Italy and Nazism in Germany.

The change in socio-political conditions of the world, like the rise of materialism after the First World War, shook the conscience of the Western society. These factors led to the revival of natural law theory in its modified form, which is different from its traditional form.

3. State the views of John Austin on law and also describe about his view on natural law.

Ans. John Austin propounded that law is the command of the sovereign, backed by threat of punishment. In his work, 'The Province of Jurisprudence Determined' published in 1832, Austin made an effort to explain the distinction between law and morality.

According to him, natural law doctrines were responsible for blurring the distinction between law and morality. To get rid of this confusion he defined law as species of command of sovereign.

4. A new law is enacted by the legislature, which is morally questionable. Natural law thinkers argue that the law is invalid because it is immoral. However, positivists argue that the law is valid because it was duly enacted by the legislature. John Austin's concept of law as a 'Command of the sovereign' is relevant in this scenario.

Explain Austin's concept and its implications for the validity of the law. Competency Based Que

Ans. John Austin's concept of law as a 'Command of the sovereign' emphasises that law is a man-made rule enacted by a political superior, backed by the threat of punishment. According to Austin, a law is valid if it is duly enacted by the sovereign, regardless of its moral content.

In the illustration, Austin's concept would imply that the law is valid because it was enacted by the legislature, despite being morally questionable. This highlights the positivist separation of law and morality.

5. A group of citizens challenge a newly enacted law, arguing that it violates their moral rights. The court is faced with the decision of whether to uphold the law or declare it invalid. The analytical school of jurisprudence, led by John Austin, would approach this decision differently than natural law thinkers.

Explain the key differences between the analytical school and natural law thinkers in approaching this decision. Competency Based Que

Ans. The analytical school, led by John Austin, would approach this decision by emphasising the separation of law and morality. They would argue that the law is valid because it was duly enacted by the legislature, regardless of its moral content.

In contrast, natural law thinkers would argue that the law is invalid because it violates moral rights. They would emphasise the importance of morality in determining the validity of the law.

This highlights the fundamental difference between the analytical school's positivist approach and natural law thinkers' emphasis on moral principles.

6. Simmi was reading about the law schools. She read about a school which emphasised on the irrational, racial and evolutionary character of law. Competency Based Que

(i) Identify the school about which Simmi was reading.

(ii) Mention the main features of this school.

Ans. (i) Simmi was reading about the Savigny's historical school.

(ii) The main features of Savigny's historical school of jurisprudence are

- Law should be a reflection of the common spirit of the people and their custom.
- Law is not universal; it is particular like the language of a particular society.
- Law is not static; it has relationship with the development of the society.
- Law is not given by a political superior, but is found or given by the people.

7. What were the main features of the sociological school according to Roscoe Pound?

Ans. According to Roscoe Pound, the main features of the sociological school were

- It highlights the purpose and function of law rather than its content.
- Law is a social institution designed for social need.
- Law is a tool to balance conflicting interests of society.

Long Answer Type Questions

1. 'During the end of the 19th century, the natural law theory was revived in its modified from, which is different from its traditional form'. With reference to the statement state, what led to the revival of the natural law theory in its modified form? Competency Based Que

Ans. During the end of the 19th century, we saw the revival of natural law theories mainly due to the following reasons

- It emerged as a reaction against the legal theories which had exaggerated the importance of positive law.
- It was realised that abstract thinking was not completely futile.
- Positivist theories failed to solve the problems created by the changed social conditions.
- The ideologies of fascism and also led to the revival of natural law theories, as at that time during the two world wars, the world witnessed great destruction of human lives and property and principles of natural law were approached in order to attain peace.
- Generally, the 'rule of law' and 'due process of law' are considered as new incarnations of natural justice in the 20th century.
- Natural law in its new form is value-oriented and value conscious. It is neither permanent nor everlasting in character and it is relative, not absolute in nature. For example, in modern times procedural as well as substantive laws have to be just, fair and reasonable.

2. Do a comparative study of main features of Savigny's historical school of jurisprudence and that of Roscoe Pounds sociological school?

Ans. For answer, Savigny's and Roscoe Pound of sociological school, refer to Q. No. 6. (ii) and Q.No. 7 of Short Answer Type Questions.

3. Name the various schools of law, their main proponents and the main features of each school.

Ans. The various schools of law are

(i) **Natural Law School** Jurists and Philosophers such as Rudolf Stammler, John Rawls, Kohler and others has contributed to the revival of natural law in the 20th century.

The main features of natural school are

- Human reason
- Divine source

(ii) **Analytical Law School** The main proponents are Jeremy Bentham (1748-1832), an English philosopher and jurist and John Austin (1790-1859), an English jurist and a student of Bentham.

The main features of analytical school are

- Command of the sovereign
- Morality ignored

(iii) **Historical Law School** German jurist and historian of the 19th century, Friedrich Carl von Savigny is considered as proponent of this school.

The main features of Savigny's historical law school are

- Law should be a reflection of the common spirit of the people and their custom.
- Law is not universal; it is particular like the language of a particular society.

(iv) **Sociological Law School**

Roscoe Pound (1870-1964), an American jurist, is considered as the chief exponent of sociological jurisprudence in the United States.

The main features of the sociological school are

- It highlights the purpose and function of law rather than its content.
- Law is a social institution designed for social need.

(v) **Realist Law School**

Karl Llewellyn (American jurisprudential), is considered as the main proponent of this school.

The main features of the realist school are

- Law is not static as it keeps on changing.
- Law is a means to a social end.

4. List some of the major functions and purposes of law.

Ans. For answer refer to text under the heading Function and Purpose of Law on page no. 114.

SELF ASSESSMENT TEST

Objective Type Questions

1. Which of the following is the correct expression of Lex iniusta non est lex?
   (a) Unjust law is not a true law (b) A reflection of divine reasons
   (c) Nemo judex in causa sua (d) Rule against bias
2. .... is considered as proponent of historical school.
   (a) Sir Henry Sumner Maine (b) Friedrich Carl von Savigny
   (c) Themis (d) D. Rudolf von Ihering
3. 'The Province of Jurisprudence Determined' was published by .... in 1832.
   (a) Jeremy Bentham (b) John Austin
   (c) Leon Duguit (d) Eugene Ehrlic

Very Short Answer Type Questions

4. 'Jurisprudence is the philosophy and theory of law'. Analyse the statement. **Competency Based Que**
5. Write a short note on Justitia.
6. 'Natural law believed to exist independent of human will'. Justify the statement. **Competency Based Que**
7. State why Roscoe Pound was considered as the chief exponent of sociological jurisprudence in the USA.

Short Answer Type Questions

8. What are 'Principles of Natural Justice'? Explain in the context of Indian Constitution.
9. Discuss principles of 'Morality' and 'Positive Morality'.
10. Explain the features of the sociological school of law.
11. 'Realist consider laws made by judges as the real law'. Comment. **Competency Based Que**

Long Answer Type Questions

12. Why there is no universal definition of law? Explain the views of different jurist and scholar on law.
13. Who was the founder of analytical school of law? What were the main features of this school? Discuss.
14. Who was the jurist and legal scholar of sociological school of law? Describe the philosophy of this school.
15. 'Case studies are important and the court room is a laboratory of law'. **Competency Based Que**
    (i) Identify the school as discussed in the above statement.
    (ii) Explain its features and limitations.
16. 'The functions and purpose of law have been changing with time and place'. Justify the statement. **Competency Based Que**

07

CHAPTER

Classification of Laws

There are several ways of classifying law with respect to time and place. Classification of law is important to ensure a correct and comprehensive understanding of law.

YOUR STUDY GOALS

- 7.1 Classification of Law on the Basis of Subject Matter
- 7.2 Classification of Law on the Basis of Scope of Law
- 7.3 Classification of Law on the Basis of Jurisdiction

YOUR PRACTICE GOAL

- Objective Type Questions (32 Qs ; MCQs, A-R, Statements, Matching)
- Subjective Questions (10 VSAs, 9 SAs, 3 LAs)

Benefits of Classification of Law

Laws can be classified into several ways and has the following benefits

- It helps in understanding the interrelation of rules.
- It helps in the systematic arrangements of rules.
- It is useful for students and professionals in law.

7.1 Classification of Law on the Basis of Subject Matter

On the basis of subject-matter, laws are classified into the following

Criminal Laws

- Any act which is considered to be an offence/prohibited by the laws in force in India is covered under criminal laws.
- Crimes affect the society as a whole and not just the victim.
- In crimes, action is initiated by the state on behalf of the individual.
- According to criminal laws, the punishment for committing a crime include imprisonment of the accused or fine or both.
- Some examples of crimes are theft, murder, rape, etc.

Civil Laws

- All acts which are not specifically defined as a crime are civil in nature.

- These acts only affect an individual and not the society as a whole.
- A civil action is initiated by the individual himself/herself.
- According to civil laws, the punishment for a civil action include compensation, damages (monetary relief) and injunction (an official order from a court of law to do/not to do something).
- Some examples of civil actions are property disputes, family matters, etc.

7.2 Classification of Law on the Basis of Scope of Law

On the basis of scope, laws are classified into the following

Substantive Laws

- Substantive laws are the laws that define the **rights and liabilities** of an individual.
- The legislative acts that are classified on the basis of subject matter of the law are substantive acts.
- Some examples of substantive laws are consumer protection act, right to information act, etc.

Procedural Laws

- Laws that define the **procedures and protocols** for enforcing substantive law or filing a case are called procedural laws.
- The legislative acts that are classified on the basis of procedure to be followed by the executive and judiciary in implementation of laws, are procedural acts.
- Some examples of procedural laws are code of civil procedure for civil cases, code of criminal procedure for criminal cases, etc.

7.3 Classification of Law on the Basis of Jurisdiction

On the basis of jurisdiction, laws are classified into the following

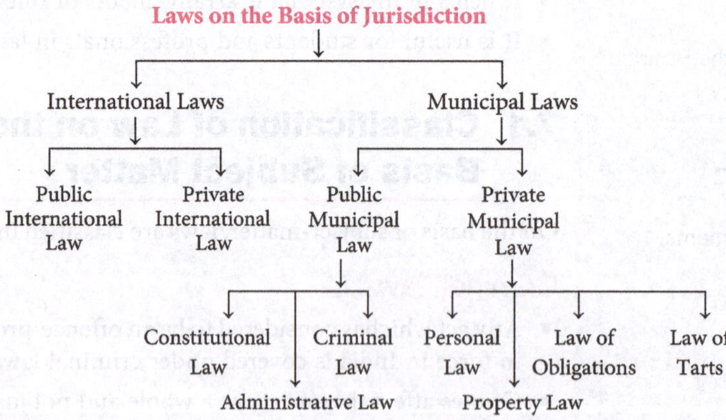

International Law

- International law deals with those rules and regulations which govern the relations among different nations or states in the international domain.
- These rules and regulations of nation are recognised and are binding upon each other through **reciprocity**[1].

1 **Reciprocity** It means the practice of enchanging things with other for mutal benefit.

- International law has been further classified into

Public International Law

- This law is related to the rules and regulations which governs the relationship between nations.
- Countries mutually recognise these sets of rules on a reciprocal basis.
- Public international law is also known as the Law of Nations.

Private International Law

- This law is related to the rights of private citizens of different countries.
- It deals with the **relationship of private persons** who belong to two different legal systems.
- Marriages and adoption of individuals are included in this branch of law.

Municipal Law

- Municipal laws are basically domestic or national laws.
- They regulate the relationship between the **state and its citizens** and determine the relationship among citizens.
- Municipal law has been further classified into public law and private law.

Public Law

- Public law includes the rules and regulations that regulates the relationship between the state and its subjects.
- Public law provides the structure and functioning of the organs of states.
- This law can be further classified into

  (i) **Constitutional Law** This law is considered to be the basic as well as the **supreme law** of the country. The nature of any state is basically determined by its Constitution. It also provides the structure of the government. All the organs of states derive their powers from the Constitution. Some countries, such as India, have a written Constitution, while countries such as the United Kingdom have an '**un-codified**[2] Constitution'.

  (ii) **Administrative Law** This law mainly deals with the powers and functions of administrative authorities like government departments, authorities, bodies, etc. It deals with the mechanism through which their actions can be controlled. It also provides for legal remedies in case of any violation of the rights of the people.

  (iii) **Criminal Law** This law is very important for maintaining order in the society, and for maintaining peace. It is considered a part of public law, as crime is not only against the individual but against the whole society. **Indian Penal Code, 1860** (also known as IPC) is an example of a criminal law legislation, in which different kinds of offences are defined and punishments are prescribed.

Private Law

- Private law includes the rules and regulations that regulates, governs and enforces relationships between individuals and associations and corporations.
- In other words, private law deals with the definition, regulation and enforcement of mutual rights and duties of individuals.
- The state settle the dispute between the parties by intervening through its judicial organs (e.g. courts).
- Private or civil law confers civil rights which are administered and judged by civil courts.
- Much of the life of a society is regulated by the set of private laws or civil rights.

---

2 Un-codified It means something is not written in a law or statute, but instead exists by virtue of common law or other practices and traditions.

- This law can be further classified into the following
  - (i) **Personal Law** This law is related to matters of religion, rituals, customs of marriage, divorce and inheritance. In such matters, people are mostly governed by the personal laws laid down by their religions. For example, the marriage of Hindus is governed by personal laws like the Hindu Marriage Act, 1955 while Muslim marriages are governed by a Muslim customary law[3], which is largely un-codified.
  - (ii) **Property Law** This law deals with the ownership of immovable and movable properties. For example, the Transfer of Property Act, 1882, deals with transfer of immovable property whereas the Sales of Goods Act, 1930, deals with movable property.
  - (iii) **Law of Obligations** This law is related to a person's legal duty to do something. It puts an obligation on the person to perform certain actions which generally arise as a consequence of an enforceable promise or agreement. If someone violates his promise, that promise may be enforced in a court of law.

    According to the **Indian Contract Act, 1872**, a contract is an agreement which is enforceable by law. In other words, a contract is an agreement with specific terms between two or more persons in which there is a **promise to do something** in lieu of a valuable profit, known as consideration. For example, 'A' has offered his mobile phone to 'B' for an amount of money. 'B' agreed to purchase the same. This has created a legal relationship where both have made a promise which is enforceable by law.
  - (iv) **Law of Torts Tort is a civil wrong.** This law creates and provides remedies for civil wrongs that do not arise out of contractual duties. A tort deals with negligence cases as well as intentional wrongs which cause harm. An aggrieved person may use law of tort to claim damages from someone who has caused the wrong or legal injury to him/her. Torts cover intentional acts and accidents.

    For example, if 'A' throws a stone and it hits another person namely 'B' on the head, 'B' may sue 'A' for the injury caused by the accident.

Quick Test 1

1. Mention any one benefit of classification of law.
2. Give two examples of civil laws.
3. Which country have an uncodified Constitution?
4. What do you understand by the term law of obligations?

3 **Customary Law** It is a set of unwritten rules that are based on the traditions, customs and beliefs of a community.

Mind Map

CLASSIFICATION OF LAWS

1 Introduction

Definition
- Classification of laws refers to organising laws into various categories based on subject matter, scope, or jurisdiction.

Importance
- Helps understand the interrelation between rules.
- Aids in systematic arrangement of legal principles.
- Useful for legal professionals and students.

2 Benefits of Classification

- Promotes a systematic understanding of legal rules.
- Simplifies study and application of laws.
- Provides clarity on overlapping and distinct legal areas.

3 Classification Based on Subject Matter

Criminal Laws
- Deals with acts prohibited by law (e.g., murder, theft).
- Crimes are against society; punishment includes imprisonment or fines.
- **Example** Indian Penal Code, 1860.

Civil Laws
- Concerns disputes between individuals or organisations.
- Focus on compensation or injunctions.
- **Examples** Property disputes, family matters.

4 Classification Based on Scope

Substantive Laws
- Define rights and liabilities.
- **Examples** Consumer Protection Act, Right to Information Act.

Procedural Laws
- Specify procedures to enforce substantive laws.
- **Examples** Code of Civil Procedure, Code of Criminal Procedure.

5 Classification Based on Jurisdiction

International Law
- Governs relationships among nations.

Public International Law
- Deals with rules governing states and international organisations.
- **Example** Treaties, agreements.

Private International Law
- Resolves disputes involving private individuals across nations.
- **Example** Marriage or adoption involving different nationalities.

Municipal Law
- Governs relationships within a state.

Public Municipal Law
- Focuses on state-citizen relationships.

Includes
- **Constitutional Law** Supreme law defining state structure.
- **Administrative Law** Regulates powers of administrative bodies.
- **Criminal Law** Maintains order and peace.

Private Municipal Law
- Deals with relationships among individuals.

Includes
- **Personal Law** Marriage, divorce, inheritance based on religion.
- **Property Law** Ownership and transfer of movable and immovable property.
- **Law of Obligations** Enforceable agreements or promises.
- **Law of Torts** Civil wrongs, including negligence and intentional harm.

6 Key Legal Examples

Indian Contract Act, 1872
- Governs enforceable agreements.
- Defines consideration and obligations.

Property Law
- Transfer of Property Act, 1882 (immovable property).
- Sale of Goods Act, 1930 (movable property).

Law of Torts
- Provides remedies for civil wrongs and negligence.

7 Key Statements

- Criminal law is part of public law because crimes affect society as a whole.
- Public international law governs relationships between nations through reciprocal agreements.

8 Key Takeaways

- Classification aids in clarity and better legal practice.
- Highlights the interdependence of laws across domains.
- Essential for understanding and applying legal principles.

CBSE Textbook Folder

1. Provide brief answers for the following

(i) Why is classification of law important? What are its benefits?

(ii) What is international law? Explain the two types of international law.

(iii) Differentiate between international and municipal law.

(iv) What is a contract?

(v) Discuss the different types of public and private municipal laws.

Ans (i) Classification of law is important to ensure a correct and comprehensive understanding of law. Laws can be classified into several ways and has the following benefits

- It helps in understanding the inter-relation of rules.
- It helps in the systematic arrangements of rules.
- It is useful for students and professionals in law.

(ii) International law is an important branch of law. It deals with those rules and regulations which govern the relations among different nations or states in the international domain. Such rules are thus termed as international laws.

The two types of International law are

(a) **Public International Law** This branch of law relates to the body of rules and regulations which governs the relationship between nations. Countries mutually recognise these sets of rules which are binding on them in their transactions on a reciprocal basis. Public international law is also known as the 'Law of Nations.'

(b) **Private International Law** The private international law relates to the rights of private citizens of different countries. It deals with the relationship of private persons who belong to two different legal systems. Marriages and adoption of individuals fall within its domain.

(iii) International law is a set of generally accepted rules and regulations controlling the conduct of nations, international organisations and individuals.

On the other hand, municipal law deals with the relationship between the individuals and their organisation within a state.

While each state has its own municipal laws, the international law is common to all states and individuals. The international court of justice is charged with the responsibility of adjudicating the controversies arising under international law.

(iv) According to the Indian Contract Act, 1872 an agreement enforceable by law is called a contract.

(v) The different types of public and private municipal laws are

(a) **Public Law** Public law chiefly regulates the relationship between the state and its subjects. The three important branches of public law are

- **Constitutional Law** Constitutional law is considered to be the basic as well as the supreme law of the country. The nature of any state is basically determined by its Constitution. It also provides the structure of the government.
- **Administrative Law** Administrative law mainly deals with the powers and functions of administrative authorities like government departments, bodies, etc. It deals with the mechanism by which their actions can be controlled.
- **Criminal Law** Criminal law generally deals with acts which are prohibited by law and defines the prohibited act as an offence. It also prescribes punishments for criminal offences. **Indian Penal Code**, 1860 (also known as IPC) is an example of a criminal law legislation, in which different kinds of offences are defined and punishments prescribed.

(b) **Private Law** This law defines, regulates, governs and enforces relationships between individuals and associations and corporations. Private or civil law confers civil rights which are administered and adjudicated by civil courts. Much of the life of a society is regulated by this set of private laws or civil rights.

This branch of law can be further classified into the following

- **Personal Law** These laws are based on religion, ritual and customs of marriage, divorce and inheritance. In such matters, people are mostly governed by the personal laws laid down by their religions.
- **Property Law** This law deals with the ownership of immovable and movable properties.

- **Law of Obligations** This law is related to a person's legal duty to do something. It puts an obligation on the person to perform certain actions which generally arise as a consequence of an enforceable promise or agreement. If someone violates his promise, that promise may be enforced in a court of law.
- **Law of Torts** Tort is a civil wrong. This law creates and provides remedies for civil wrongs that do not arise out of contractual duties. An aggrieved person may use law of tort to claim damages from someone who has caused the wrong or legal injury to him/her.

2. Identify the branch of law and define

(i) Antilla and Portico are two countries which have a border dispute.

(ii) Shefali was angry because her passport was refused by the Passport Department without any reason.

(iii) Gita died without a will and her kids don't know how to divide the property.

(iv) Ajit was in an agreement to supply 50 kgs of rice to Bittu but did not do so. **Competency Based Que**

Ans (i) The branch of law in this condition is public international law. This branch of law relates to the body of rules and regulations which governs the relationship between nations. Countries mutually recognise these sets of rules which are binding on them in their transactions on a reciprocal basis.

(ii) The branch of law in this condition is administrative law. This mainly deals with the power and functions of adminstrative authorities like government departments, authorities, bodies etc. It deals with the mechanism through which their actions can be controlled.

(iii) The branch of law in this condition is personal law. These laws are based on religion, ritual and customs of marriage, divorce and inheritance. In such matters, people are mostly governed by the personal laws laid down by their religions.

(iv) The branch of law in this condition is law of obligations. This law is related to a person's legal duty to do something. It puts an obligation on the person to perform certain actions which generally arise as a consequence of an enforceable promise or agreement. If someone violates his promise, that promise may be enforced in a court of law.

3. Sheena was a victim of sexual harassment at workplace. Explain why her criminal case is a part of public municipal law. **Competency Based Que**

Ans. Sheena's criminal case is a part of public municipal law. Because crime is not only against the individual but against the whole society.

4. Halestina and Xina, two countries are bound by some laws which foster their relations by following some rules based on reciprocity. Identify the branch of law and explain its two sub types. **Competency Based Que**

Ans. For answer refer to CBSE text book folder Q.No.1(ii) Types of internal laws.

5. The Government of India introduced a new law whereby the passport of any person could be revoked on mere suspicion of fraudulent financial transactions without providing a chance of hearing.

Identify and define the branch of law under which such a law can be challenged.

Ans. This law can be challenged under administrative law. Administrative law provides for legal remedies in case of any violation of the rights of the people.

It means an individual can file a petition in court to contest the decision to revoke their passport, arguing that the process was unfair or lacked proper justification.

Exam Pattern Questions

Objective Type Questions

Multiple Choice Questions (MCQs)

1. Which of the following is true about Civil Laws?

(a) Civil laws deal with crimes affecting society as a whole.
(b) A civil action is initiated by the state on behalf of the individual.
(c) The remedy in civil law typically includes compensation or damages.
(d) Civil laws deal with public offenses and prescribe imprisonment.

2. Which of the following is an example of a Substantive Law?

(a) Code of Criminal Procedure
(b) Consumer Protection Act
(c) Code of Civil Procedure
(d) Indian Penal Code

3. "It deals with those rules and regulations of a nation which are recognised and are binding upon each other through reciprocity". The above mentioned statement is related to which of the following laws? **Competency Based Que**

(a) Administrative Law (b) Municipal Law
(c) Criminal Law (d) International Law

4. Marriages and adoption of individuals belonging to different nations fall within .... domain.

(a) Private International Law (b) Law of Obligations
(c) Public International Law (d) Property Law

5. India and Pakistan has not maintained good relation since its inception. They have more disagreements than agreements over many issues. Which branch of law is applicable that governs the relationship between nations? **Competency Based Que**

(a) Bilateral International Law
(b) Private International Law
(c) Public International Law
(d) Mutual International Law

6. Which of the following laws regulates the relationship between the state and its citizens?

(a) Private International Law (b) Law of Obligations
(c) Property Law (d) Municipal Law

7. .... is considered to be the basic as well as the supreme law of the country.

(a) Criminal Law (b) Constitutional Law
(c) Law of Obligations (d) Administrative Law

8. Which of the following low maintains order in the society?

(a) Criminal Law
(b) Constitutional Law
(c) Public Law
(d) Administrative Law

9. .... are based on religion, ritual and customs of marriage, divorce and inheritance.

(a) Personal Law (b) Law of Obligations
(c) Property Law (d) Law of Torts

10. Indian Contract Act was passed in which of the following years?

(a) 1876 (b) 1872 (c) 1976 (d) 1972

11. 'A' having a matrimonial dispute with her husband 'B', approaches the court for divorce. Which law shall govern this situation? **Competency Based Que**

(a) Personal Law (b) Law of Obligations
(c) Property Law (d) Law of Torts

12. 'A' has offered his mobile phone to 'B' for ₹ 15,000. 'B' agreed to purchase the same.
Which of the following laws will govern this situation? **Competency Based Que**

(a) Law of Contract (b) Law of Torts
(c) Property Law (d) Constitutional Law

13. Rustam and Shyam were arguing over the property ownership in an area. In the meantime Rustam has planned to kill Shyam to get rid of him. Any act which is considered to be an offence/prohibited by the laws in force in India is called? **Competency Based Que**

(a) Public law
(b) Private law
(c) Civil law
(d) Criminal law

14. Rahul Sharma, who attended his first day in the court as an advocate, observed that the honourable judge delivered judgement related to RTI as a part of substantive law. Identify among the following, which is not a substantive law? **Competency Based Que**

(a) Indian Penal Code
(b) Code of Civil Procedure
(c) Indian Contract Act, 1872
(d) Transfer of Property Act, 1882

15. This branch of law creates and provides remedies for civil wrongs that do not arise out of contractual duties. It deals with negligence cases as well as intentional wrongs which cause harm. An aggrieved person may use it to claim damages from someone who has caused the wrong or legal injury to him/her. Identify this branch of law.

(a) Personal Law (b) Law of Obligations
(c) Property Law (d) Law of Torts

16. If 'A' throws a stone and it hits another person namely 'B' on the head, 'B' may sue 'A' for the injury caused by the accident. **Competency Based Que**

Which law shall govern this situation?

(a) Personal Law (b) Law of Obligations
(c) Property Law (d) Law of Torts

17. Which of the following is NOT a part of Public Law under Municipal Law?

(a) Constitutional Law (b) Administrative Law
(c) Criminal Law (d) Law of Torts

18. Reshma is not happy with her husband because of various differences lies between them. Her parents suggest Reshma to file divorce petition in as per civil laws. Which among the following is the branch of civil law? **Competency Based Que**

(a) Contract Law (b) Business Law
(c) Union Law (d) Transfer Law

19. Dr. Satya Prakash sends his servant Aditya to receive the guests at railway station and however the driver accidentally injured a pedestrian. Name the law that shall be imposed by the injured or the aggrieved party against the accused in this situation. **Competency Based Que**

(a) Personal Law (b) Law of Obligations
(c) Constitutional Law (d) Law of Torts

20. Rohan sells his motorcycle to Karan for ₹ 50,000. The motorcycle is delivered to Karan, but the registration paper are still in Rohan's name. Later, Rohan discovers that there is some defect in the motorcycle, which he was awareof before the sale. Karan wants to return the motorcycle and get full refund. Under the Sale of Goods Act, which of the following is true? **Competency Based Que**

(a) Rohan is not liable for the defect in the engine as the motorcycle was sold 'as is'.
(b) Karan has the right to return the motorcycle and get a full refund.
(c) Rohan is liable for the defect, but only if Karan had expressly informed him about the defect before the sale.
(d) The sale is void as the registration papers are still in Rohan's name.

21. The law of obligations is a branch of private law that deals with the legal relationships between parties who have assumed obligations or duties towards each other. Which of the following statement is a key principle of the law of obligations?

(a) The parties to an obligation have complete freedom to contract as they wish.
(b) Obligations can only be created by formal written agreements/contracts.
(c) Parties to an obligation must act in good faith and fair dealing.
(d) Obligations are only enforceable if they are registered with a government agency.

22. Consider the following statements and choose the correct option.

Statement I Municipal laws are laws enacted by national governments, such as cities or countries, to govern matters within their jurisdiction.

Statement II These laws typically relate to issues such as zoning, public health, safety and welfare, and are enforceable within the boundaries of the municipality.

Choose the correct option

(a) Both Statements are correct.
(b) Both Statements are incorrect.
(c) Statement I is correct, but Statement II is incorrect.
(d) Statement I is incorrect, but Statement II is correct.

23. Which of the following are classifications of public law?

I. Criminal Law **II. Constitutional Law**
III. Law of Obligations **IV. Administrative Law**

Codes

(a) I, II and IV (b) II, III and IV
(c) II and III (d) I and IV

24. Which of the following is/are the parts of private law?

I. Personal Law **II. Law of Obligations**
III. Property Law **IV. Administrative Law**

Codes

(a) I and II (b) II, III and IV
(c) Only III (d) I, II and III

25. Kindly arrange the following laws in chronological order as per their year of establishment.

I. Sales of Goods Act
II. Transfer of Property Act
III. Hindu Marriage Act
IV. Indian Penal Code

Choose the correct Code

(a) IV, II, I, III (b) IV, I, III, II
(c) IV, I, III, II (d) III, II, IV, I

26. Match the following

Column I	Column II
A. Supreme Law of the country	1. Personal Law
B. Deals with the powers and functions of government departments	2. Constitutional Law
C. Considered a part of public law	3. Administrative Law
D. Laws are based on religion	4. Criminal Law

Codes

	A	B	C	D		A	B	C	D
(a)	2	1	3	4	(b)	4	1	2	3
(c)	3	4	2	1	(d)	2	3	4	1

27. Match the following.

Column I	Column II
A. Written Constitution	1. UK
B. Unwritten Constitution	2. IPC
C. Criminal Law	3. Contract Law
D. Law of Obligations	4. India

Codes

	A	B	C	D		A	B	C	D
(a)	4	1	2	3	(b)	1	2	3	4
(c)	2	1	3	4	(d)	4	2	3	1

Assertion-Reason Questions

Directions (Q. Nos. 28-32) In the questions given below, there are two statements. Read the statements and choose the correct option.

Codes

(a) Both A and R are true and R is the correct explanation of A.

(b) Both A and R are true, but R is not the correct explanation of A.

(c) A is true, but R is false.

(d) A is false, but R is true.

28. Assertion (A) International law regulates the relationship between the state and its citizen, and determines the relationship among citizens.

Reason (R) Municipal laws are basically domestic or national laws.

29. Assertion (A) Public international law relates to the body of rules and regulations which governs the relationship between nations.

Reason (R) Countries mutually recognise these sets of rules which are binding on them in their transactions on a reciprocal basis.

30. Assertion (A) Constitutional law also provides for legal remedies in case of any violation of the rights of the people.

Reason (R) In India, the Fundamental Rights are granted and protected under Articles 32 and 226 of the Indian Constitution.

31. Assertion (A) Criminal law is part of public law.

Reason (R) A crime is not only against the individual but against the whole society.

32. Assertion (A) Law of torts creates and provides remedies for civil wrongs that do not arise out of contractual duties.

Reason (R) A tort deals with negligence cases as well as intentional wrongs which cause harm.

Answers

1. (c) The remedy in civil law typically includes compensation or damages.
2. (b) Consumer Protection Act
3. (d) International Law
4. (a) Private International Law
5. (c) Public International Law
6. (d) Municipal Law
7. (b) Constitutional Law
8. (a) Criminal law
9. (a) Personal Law
10. (b) 1872
11. (a) Personal Law
12. (a) Law of Contract
13. (d) Criminal law
14. (b) Code of Civil Procedure
15. (d) Law of Torts
16. (d) Law of Torts
17. (d) Law of Torts
18. (a) Contract Law
19. (d) Law of Torts
20. (b) Karan has the right to return the motorcycle and get a full refund.
21. (c) Parties to an obligation must act in good faith and fair dealing.
22. (c) Statement I is correct, but Statement II is incorrect.
23. (a) I, II and IV
24. (d) I, II and III
25. (a) IV, II, I, III
26. (d) 2 3 4 1
27. (a) 4 1 2 3
28. (d) A is false, but R is true.

29. (a) Both A and R are true and R is the correct explanation of A.

30. (a) Both A and R are true and R is the correct explanation of A.

31. (a) Both A and R are true and R is the correct explanation of A.

32. (b) Both A and R are true, but R is not the correct explanation of A.

Subjective Questions

Very Short Answer Type Questions

1. What are the two major classifications of law on the basis of jurisdiction?

Ans. Law may be broadly divided into the following two classes in terms of its jurisdiction
(i) International law
(ii) Municipal law

2. What is municipal law?

Ans. Municipal laws are basically domestic or national laws. They regulate the relationship between the state and its citizens, and determine the relationship among citizens.

3. Alxania and Cynthia, two countries are bound by some laws which foster their relations by following some rules based on reciprocity.
(i) Which branch of law would regulate the relation between the two nations?
(ii) Which branch of law would regulate the relation between the individuals of these two nations?

Ans. (i) Public International Law
(ii) Private International Law

4. What is public international law?

Ans. Public international law relates to the body of rules and regulations which governs the relationship between nations. Countries mutually recognise these sets of rules on a reciprocal basis.

5. 'Much of the life of a society is regulated by the set of private laws'. With reference to this statement explain the private law? **Competency Based Que**

Ans. Private law includes the rules and regulations that regulates, governs and enforces relationships between individuals and associations and corporation. In private law states have the authority to settle the dispute between the parties by intervening through its judicial organs. For example, courts.

6. Marriage of Hindus is governed by some laws like the Hindu Marriage Act 1955. **Competency Based Que**
(i) Identify marriage of Hindu related to which law?
(ii) Explain this law.

Ans. (i) The marriage of Hindus related to personal law.
(ii) Personal law is related to matters of religion, rituals, customs of marriage, divorce and inheritance.
In such matters, people are mostly governed by the personal laws laid down by their religions.

7. The low deals with the ownership of immovable and moveable assets.
(i) Identify which law has been discussed here?
(ii) This law will become a part of which division of law, based on usage?

Ans. (i) Property law
(ii) Municipal law

8. A Hindu woman wants to divorce her husband, but is unsure about the laws governing divorce in her community. What branch of law is applicable in this case? **Competency Based Que**

Ans. Personal Law, specifically the Hindu Marriage Act, 1955, is applicable in this case, as it deals with marriage, divorce, and succession laws for Hindus.

9. A person enters into a contract with a builder to construct a house. The builder fails to complete the construction on time, causing financial losses to the person. The person wants to sue the builder for damages. What branch of law is applicable in this case? **Competency Based Que**

Ans. Law of Obligations, specifically the Indian Contract Act, 1872, is applicable in this case, as it deals with enforceable agreements and promises.

10. A person is injured in a road accident caused by the negligence of another driver. The person wants to claim damages from the driver. What branch of law is applicable in this case? **Competency Based Que**

Ans. Law of Torts is applicable in this case, as it deals with civil wrongs, including negligence, and provides remedies for damages.

Short Answer Type Questions

1. Why there is a need for the classification of low?

Ans. The classification of law was required for a proper understanding of law and its features. Classification of law makes clear the relation between different rules and their effect on each other. It also helps in providing justice to the victim and affected ones in a concise and systematic manner.

2. **(i) What does criminal law deal with?**

(ii) Why is it considered a part of public law?

Ans. (i) Criminal law generally deals with acts which are prohibited by law and defines the prohibited act as an offence. It also prescribes punishments for criminal offences. Criminal law is very important for maintaining order in the society and for maintaining peace.

(ii) It is considered a part of public law as crime is not only against the individual but against the whole society.

Indian Penal Code, 1860 (also known as IPC) is an example of a criminal law legislation, in which different kinds of offences are defined and punishments prescribed.

3. **Sujata Mahajan is very excited after her enrollment in city's prestigious law institute. She has planned to pursue International law as her specialisation. What are the two classes of International law? Describe each briefly.** Competency Based Que

Ans. The two classes of International Law are

(i) **Public International Law** This branch of law relates to the body of rules and regulations which governs the relationship between nations.

Countries mutually recognise these sets of rules which are binding on them in their transactions on a reciprocal basis.

(ii) **Private International Law** It is that part of law of the state which deals with cases having a foreign element. Private international law relates to the rights of private citizens of different countries. Marriages and adoption of individuals belonging to different nations fall within its domain.

4. **Ritika in her first lecture of law class has learnt that the Constitutional law is supreme law of the country. Explain how Constitutional law is the basic structure of the government?** Competency Based Que

Ans. Constitutional law is considered to be the basic as well as the supreme law of the country.

The nature of any state is basically determined by its Constitution. It also provides the structure of the government. All the organs of states derive their powers from the Constitution. Some countries, such as India, have a written Constitution, while countries such as the United Kingdom have an 'uncodified Constitution'. In India, the Fundamental Rights are granted and protected under the Constitution.

5. **Administrative law is an important part of public law. Explain the administrative law with reference to the statement.** Competency Based Que

Ans. Administrative law mainly deals with the powers and functions of administrative authorities like government departments, bodies etc.

- It deals with the extent of powers held by the administrative bodies and the mechanism whereby their actions can be controlled.
- It also provides for legal remedies in case of any violation of the rights of the people.

6. **Ravi Shankar while reading newspaper, found that there is a mention of Kiran Kumari Vs. Government of India. Why there is always action is initiated by the state on behalf of the individual?** Competency Based Que

Ans. In criminal matters, the aggrieved party is called the state, which is the custodian of the social interests of the community at large, and so it is necessary for the state to take all steps necessary for bringing the person who has acted against the social interests of the community.

7. **The British Government while rule in India has brought several laws, based on universal principles of justice. One of the best example of such legal development was introduction of public and private laws. Explain private law with its types.**

Ans. Private law applies to any circumstances relating to relationships between individuals in a legal system. In other words, this branch of law deals with the definition, regulation and enforcement of mutual rights and duties of individuals.

Types of private law are

(i) **Personal Law** This law is related to matters of religion, rituals, customs of marriage, divorce and inheritance. In such matters, people are mostly governed by the personal laws laid down by their religions.

(ii) **Property Law** This law deals with the ownership of immovable and movable properties.

(iii) **Law of Obligations** This law is related to a person's legal duty to do something. It puts an obligation on the person to perform certain actions which generally arise as a consequence of an enforceable promise or agreement.

(iv) **Law of Torts** This law creates and provides remedies for civil wrongs that do not arise out of contractual duties.

8. **Rammohan a small businessman had taken 5 lakh loan from a private loan provider. However, Rammohan died after 2 years of due period and his law of obligation has ended with it. What do you understand by law of obligation?** Competency Based Que

Ans. Law of obligations is related to a person's legal duty to do something. It puts an obligation on the person to perform certain actions which generally arise as a consequence of an enforceable promise or agreement. If someone violates his promise, that promise may be enforced in a court of law.

9. Anil has acquired a building premises for lease with the purpose of opening of a Business Process Outsourcing (BPO). However within a span of 6 months there were several issues related to building maintenance arouse, which was ratified by the tenant as per the contract. Explain the term contract. **Competency Based Que**

Ans. A contract is an agreement with specific terms between two or more persons in which there is a promise to do something in lieu of a valuable profit known as consideration. The Indian Contract act, 1872 is applicable to all the states of India.

The Act determines the circumstances in which promises made by the parties to a contract shall be legally binding.

For example, 'A' has offered his mobile phone to 'B' for an amount of money. 'B' agreed to purchase the same. This has created a legal relationship where both have made a promise which is enforceable by law.

Long Answer Type Questions

1. Sudhakar is explaining to his friend Ravi how the state plays a larger role in ensuring the well-being of its people through public law. To make Ravi understand better, Sudhakar describes how public law is divided into three main branches. Ravi listens carefully and asks Sudhakar to elaborate on these branches in more detail.

Identify and describes the three main branches of public law in the situation above. **Competency Based Que**

Ans.
- Sudhakar explains the three main branches of public law to his friend Ravi.
- Public law includes the rules and regulations that regulates the relationship between the state and its subjects.
- Public law provides the structure and functioning of the organs of states.
- This law can be further classified into

(i) **Constitutional Law** This law is considered to be the basic as well as the supreme law of the country. The nature of any state is basically determined by its Constitution. It also provides the structure of the government. All the organs of states derive their powers from the Constitution. Some countries, such as India, have a written Constitution, while countries such as the United Kingdom have an 'un-codified Constitution'.

(ii) **Administrative Law** This law mainly deals with the powers and functions of administrative authorities like government departments, authorities, bodies, etc. It deals with the mechanism through which their actions can be controlled. It also provides for legal remedies in case of any violation of the rights of the people.

(iii) **Criminal Law** This law is very important for maintaining order in the society, and for maintaining peace. It is considered a part of public law, as crime is not only against the individual but against the whole society.

Indian Penal Code, 1860 (also known as IPC) is an example of a criminal law legislation, in which different kinds of offences are defined and punishments are prescribed.

2. What do you understand by the term private law? How has private law been classified?

Ans. For answer refer to text under the heading Private Law on page no. 125 and 126.

3. A person, Rohan, enters into a contract with a builder, Kumar, to construct a house. The contract specifies that the house will be completed within two years. However, Kumar fails to complete the construction on time, causing financial losses to Rohan. Rohan wants to sue Kumar for damages. Kumar argues that the contract is not enforceable as it was not registered.

Identify the applicable law and discuss the rights of the parties in this case. **Competency Based Que**

Ans. In this case, the applicable law is the Indian Contract Act, 1872, which governs contracts and agreements between parties. According to the Act, a contract is an agreement with specific terms between two or more persons, in which there is a promise to do something in lieu of a valuable profit, known as consideration.

In this case, Rohan and Kumar entered into a contract, which is enforceable under the Act. Kumar's argument that the contract is not registered is not valid, as registration is not mandatory for all contracts. Rohan has the right to sue Kumar for damages for breach of contract. Kumar, on the other hand, has the obligation to complete the construction of the house as per the contract.

SELF ASSESSMENT TEST

Objective Type Questions

1. Which of the following laws regulates the relationship between the state and its citizen and determines the relationship among citizens?

(a) International law (b) Municipal law (c) Constitutional law (d) Criminal law

2. Public municipal law are classified into .... parts.

(a) two (b) three (c) four (d) five

3. Which of the following acts has defined a contract as an agreement which is enforceable by law?

(a) Transfer of Property Act (b) Indian Contract Act

(c) Sale of Goods Act (d) None of the above

Very Short Answer Type Questions

4. Discuss the benefits of classification of law.

5. The law is related to the rights of private citizens of different countries. Identify the law and explain its features. **Competency Based Que**

6. Give two examples of property law and explain.

7. Define a contract with the help of an example.

Short Answer Type Questions

8. State any three differences between public international law and private international law.

9. Give any three points of difference between private municipal and public municipal law?

10. With the help of an example, explain the law of torts.

Long Answer Type Questions

11. How has municipal law been classified? Give a brief description of each category.

12. State the various categories of private municipal law.

13. Neha throws a stone and it hits to Meenakshi on the head, Meenakshi may sue Neha for the injury caused by the accident.

(i) Identify the law in the above situation.

(ii) Explain the features of this law.

(iii) Neha throws a stone and injuries Meenakshi, what legal action can Meenakshi take under this law?

(iv) Explain the concept of negligence under this law.

(v) Explain the concept of intentional wrong under this law.

08

CHAPTER

Sources of law refer to the sources from where law or the binding rules of human conduct originate.

Sources of Laws

▼ **YOUR STUDY GOALS**

8.1 Meaning and Origin of Sources of Law
8.2 Major Sources of Law
8.3 Importance of Custom as a Source of Law in India
8.4 Judicial Precedent
8.5 Legislation

▼ **YOUR PRACTICE GOAL**

– Objective Type Questions (21 Qs ; MCQs, A-R, Statements, Matching)
– Subjective Questions (13 VSAs, 7 SAs, 4 LAs)

8.1 Meaning and Origin of Sources of Law

- As the term 'law' has several meanings, legal experts also view the sources of law from various aspects.
- Jurists have different views on the origin, definitions and sources of law.
- For example,
    - **Austin** considers sovereign as the source of law.
    - **Savigny** and **Henry Maine** consider custom as the most important source of law.
    - **Natural law school** considers nature and human reason as the sources of law.
    - Theologians[1] consider the religious scriptures as sources of law.
- There are various claims and counter claims regarding the sources of law, but in almost all societies, law has been derived from similar sources.

1 Theologians is a person who engages or is an expert in theology (the study of nature of God).

8.2 Major Sources of Law

In a modern society, there are **three** major sources of law. These are

(i) Customs (ii) Judicial precedents (iii) Legislation

Customs

- Customs are those **long established practices** or **unwritten rules** which have acquired binding or obligatory character.
- A custom becomes valid if it is observed continuously for a very longtime without any interruption.
- Further, a practice must be supported not only for a very long time, but it must also be supported by the opinion of the general public and morality to become a custom.
- Every custom does not become a law. For example, the **Hindu Marriages Act, 1955** prohibits marriages which are within the prohibited degrees of relationship.
- However, the act still permits marriages within the prohibited degree of relationship, if there is a **proven custom** within a certain community.
- Saptapadi is an example of customs as a source of law.
- It is the most important rite of a Hindu marriage ceremony.
- The word, **Saptapadi** means **'Seven steps'.**
- This has been incorporated in **Section 7 of Hindu Marriage Act, 1955.**

Can Customs be Law?

- There is no doubt about the fact that custom is an important source of law.
- Jurists such as Austin opposed custom as law because it did not originate from the will of the soverign.
- Jurists like savigny consider custom as the main source of law.
- The will of the people has always been reflected in the customs and traditions of the society.

Kinds of Customs

Customs can broadly be classified into two classes

(i) **Customs without Sanction** These customs are **not binding in nature.** They are only followed because of public opinion acceptance.

(ii) **Customs with Sanction** These customs are **binding in nature** because they are enforced by the state. They can further be divided into

(a) **Legal Custom** It refers to a custom that has **absolute authority**. In other words, it has the force of law and is recognised and enforced by the courts. Legal customs are further sub-divided into

- **General customs** that prevailed throughout the territory of the state.
- **Local customs** that are applicable locally, i.e. to a particular region of the country.

(b) **Conventional Customs** These customs are **binding on the parties** to an agreement. When two or more persons enter into an agreement related to a trade, it is assumed in law that they make the contract according to the established convention or usage of that trade. For example, an agreement between a landlord and tenant regarding the payment of rent will be governed by convention prevailing in this regard.

Essentials of a Valid Custom

In order to become valid sources of law, a custom must fulfill the following essentials

Antiquity

- In order to become legally valid, customs should have been in **existence for a longtime**, even beyond human memory.
- In England, the year **1189** i.e. the reign of **Richard I King of England**, has been fixed to determine the validity of customs.
- However, in India there is no such time-limit for deciding the antiquity of the customs.
- The only condition is that customs should have been in practice since time immemorial.

Continuous

- A custom, must have been in **continuous practice**, to become valid.
- It should have been in practice without any kind of interruption.

Exercised as a Matter of Right

- A custom must be **enjoyed openly** and **with the knowledge** of the community.
- It should not have been practiced secretly.
- A custom must be proved to be a matter of right.
- A mere doubtful exercise of a right is not sufficient to claim a custom to be valid.

Reasonableness

- A custom **must not be against the norms of justice and public utility.**
- A custom should be based on rationality and reason.
- If a custom is likely to cause more inconvenience and mischief than convenience, then it will not be valid.

Morality

- A custom which is **immoral or opposed to public policy cannot be a valid** custom.
- Courts have declared many customs as invalid as they were practiced for immoral purposes, or were opposed to public policy. For example, Bombay High Court in the case of **Mathura Naikon Vs. Esu Naekin (1880)** decided that the custom of adopting a girl for immoral purposes is illegal.

Custom's Status with Regard to a Legislation

- In any modern state, when a new legislation is enacted, it is generally preferred to the custom.
- Therefore, a **custom must not be opposed or contrary to legislation.**
- Many customs have been repealed by laws that are enacted by the legislative bodies in India.
- For example, the customary practice of child marriage has been declared as an offence. Similarly, adoption laws have been changed by legislation in India.

8.3 Importance of Custom as a Source of Law in India

- Custom was the most important source of law in ancient India.
- It was considered as a **real source of law.**
- Even the British adopted the policy of non-intervention in personal matters of Hindus and Muslims.
- Customs were not uniform or universal throughout the country.
- Some regions of the country had their own customs and usages.

- These variances in customs were considered a hindrance in the integration of various communities of the country.
- During India's freedom struggle, there were parallel movements for social reform in the country.
- Social reformers raised many issues related to women and children such as widow re-marriage and child marriage.
- After independence and with the enactment of the Constitution, the Indian Parliament took many steps and repealed many old customary practices with some progressive legislation.
- Hindu personal laws were codified and the Hindu Marriage Act, 1955 and the Hindu Adoption Act, 1955, were adopted.
- The Constitution of India provided a positive environment for these social changes.
- With the passage of time and advent of modern civilisation, the importance of custom as a source of law diminished and other sources such as judicial precedent and legislation gained importance.
- However, a large part of Indian law, especially personal laws, is still governed by customs.

Check Point 1

1 What do you understand by customs?
2 State any one difference between 'Local Customs' and 'General Customs'.
3 Give an example of conventional custom.
4 What is morality in order to become valid source of law?

8.4 Judicial Precedent

- Judicial precedents refer to **previously decided judgments of the superior courts,** such as the High Courts and the Supreme Court, which judges are bound to follow.
- The binding character of the previously decided cases is important, considering the hierarchy of the courts established by the legal systems of a particular country.
- In India, this hierarchy has been established by the Constitution.
- Judicial precedent is an important source of law, but it is neither as modern like legislation and nor as old like custom.
- It is an important feature of the English legal system and other common law countries which follow the English legal system.
- In most of the developed legal systems, judiciary is considered to be an important organ of the state.
- In modern societies, rights are generally granted to the citizens by legislation and the main function of the judiciary is to adjudicate upon these rights.
- The judges decide matters on the basis of the legislation and prevailing custom.
- In this process, they play a creative role by interpreting the law.
- They lay down new principles and rules which are generally binding on lower courts within a legal system.
- It was not bound by its own decisions, or decisions of Privy Council or Federal Court.

Hierarchy of Courts in British India

- Before Independence, Privy Council was supreme judicial authority in India. According to **Section 212** of the **Government of India Act, 1919,** the law laid down by the Federal Court and any judgement of the Privy Council was binding on all courts of British India.
- After Independence, the Supreme Court (SC) became the supreme judicial authority in India and an organised system of courts was established.
- It is important to understand the hierarchy of courts in order to understand judicial precedent. Every legal system has its own distinct features.
- Therefore, the doctrine of precedent is applied differently in different countries. In India, the doctrine of precedent is based on the concept of hierarchy of courts.

Hierarchy of Courts in British India

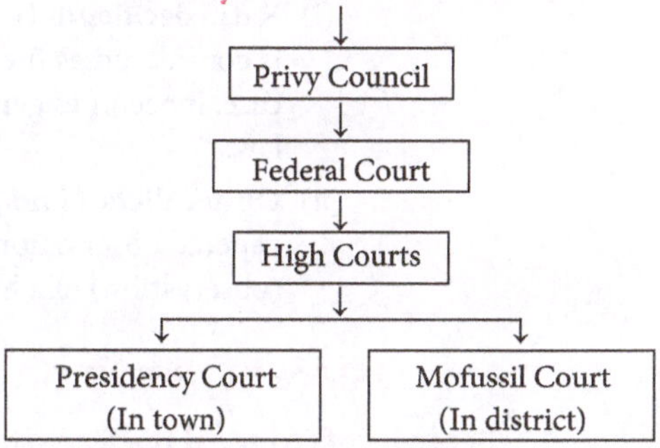

Hierarchy of Courts in India after Independence

- After independence, India adopted its own Constitution, which provided for a hierarchical judicial system that is pyramidal in nature.
- The Supreme Court of India, came into existence on **26th January, 1950** under **Article 124(1)** of the Constitution of India.
- The **Supreme Court replaced the Federal Court** established by the Government of India Act,1935.
- The Supreme Court of India, thus, became the supreme judicial authority with an organised system of courts working under it.
- Today, it is the Apex Court in the hierarchy of courts, followed by the High Courts at the state level.
- The District Courts and Sessions Court are below the High Courts.
- The hierarchy of Indian judicial system is as follows
  - (i) **Supreme Court**
    - The decisions given by the Supreme Court are binding on all the courts throughout the territory of India.
    - The Supreme Court is not bound by its own decisions; however a smaller **bench**[2] is bound by the decision of the larger bench, and the co-equal bench.
  - (ii) **High Courts**
    - The decisions given by the High Courts are binding on the Subordinate Courts within its jurisdiction.
    - The decisions of the High Courts are not binding beyond their respective jurisdictions.
    - However, the decisions of the High Courts, have **persuasive**[3] value for the other High Courts and the Subordinate Courts beyond their jurisdiction.
  - (iii) **Lower Courts**
    - These court are bound to follow decisions of higher courts in its own state, in preference to High Courts of other states.

2 **Bench** The bench is a court of law or the place where a judge or judges sit in court.

3 **Persuasive** It means something that can be used to influence a court's decision-making process, but the court is not required to follow it.

Judicial Decisions

Judicial decisions can be divided into following two parts

(i) **Ratio decidendi (Reason of Decision)** 'Ratio decidendi' refers to the binding part of a judgment. It is considered as the general principle which is assumed by the courts from the facts of a particular case. It becomes generally binding on the lower courts in future cases involving similar questions of law.

(ii) **Obiter dicta (Said by the Way)** An 'obiter dictum' refers to parts of judicial decisions which are general observations of the judge and do not have any binding authority. However, obiter (observation) of a higher judiciary is considered by lower courts and has persuasive value.

Different Views on Making of Laws by Judges

Hierarchy of Criminal Justice System

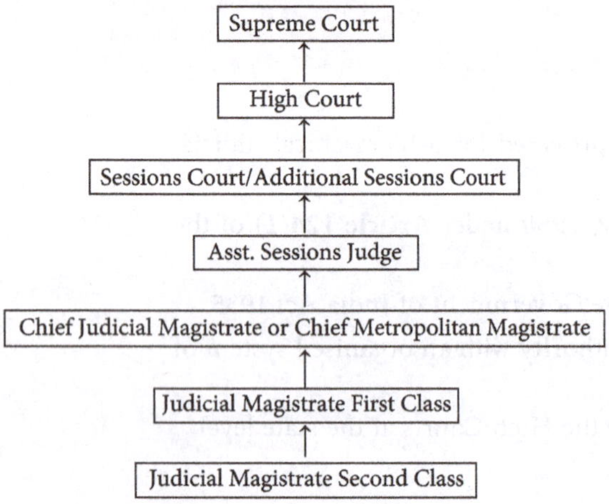

Hierarchy of Civil Judicial System

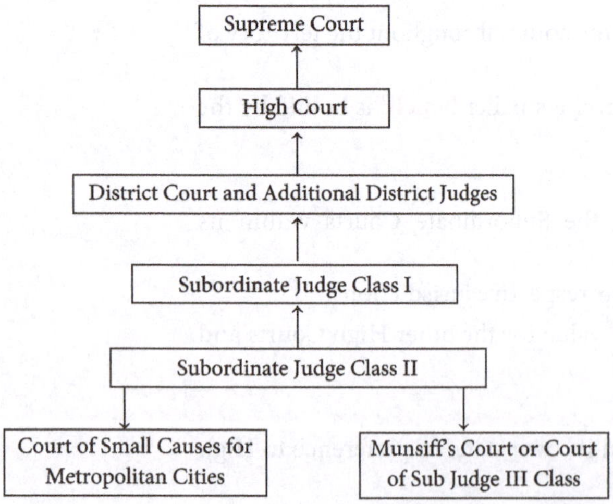

- The Constitution of India grants power to the legislature to make law, while the judiciary has the power to examine the Constitutionality of the laws enacted by the legislature.
- The courts also decides the rights and duties of citizens, and further interprets the provisions of the Constitution and other statutes.
- Through these processes, the courts create new rights for the citizens. By this exercise, the judiciary makes additions to the existing laws of the country.
- Thus, it is argued that during this exercise, judges actually make law.

  There are two different views regarding making of laws by judges

  (i) Some jurists like **Edward Coke** and **Mathew Hale** believe that **judges do not make the law** but that they simply declare the existing law. According to them, judicial decisions are not sources of law but they are simply the proof of what the law is. Judges are not law-givers, but they discover law.

  (ii) Other jurists like **Dicey, Gray, Salmond** believe that **judges do make law**. They believe that, while interpreting the law enacted by the legislative bodies, judges contribute to the existing body of law. A large part of the English law is judge-made law.
- Thus, it can be inferred that judges do not make the law in the same manner like legislative bodies.
- Judges work on a given legal material, passed as law by the legislature.
- While declaring the law, judges interpret the 'legislation' in question and play a creative role.
- By this creative role, judges have contributed significantly to the development of law.
- In the Indian context, former judges of the Supreme Court of India like **Justice P.N. Bhagwati and Justice Krishna Iyer** enlarged the meaning and scope of various provisions of the Constitution, through their creative interpretation of the legal text.
- The Supreme Court also has created many new rights such as the right to privacy, right to live in a pollution free environment, right to livelihood, etc.

- These new rights were created only by way of interpreting Article 21 (Right to life) of the Consitution of India. These rights developed by the courts are not in any sense lesser than the laws enacted by the legislative bodies.
- Therefore, it can be concluded that the judicial precedents are important sources of law in modern society and judges do play a significant role in law-making.

Check Point 2

1 Which part of judicial decisions, refers that judges do not have any binding authority?
2 Who introduced the system of courts in India?
3 What was the hierarchy of courts in British India?
4 Which courts lies just below the Session Court in the criminal court hierarchy?

8.5 Legislation

- Legislation means **laws enacted by the sovereign** or any other person or institution authorised by him.
- In modern times, legislation is considered as the most important source of law.
- The term legislation is derived from the Latin word 'legis' which means 'law' and 'lactum' which means 'to make' or 'set'.
- Therefore, the word legislation means the 'making of law'.

The importance of legislation as a source of law can be measured from the fact that it is backed by the authority of the sovereign, and it is directly enacted and recognised by the state. The expression 'legislation' has been used in various ways and includes every method of law-making.

Kinds of Legislation

There are two kinds of legislation. These are

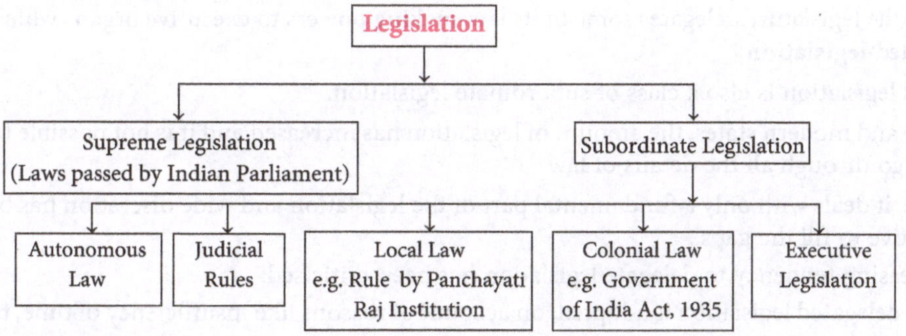

Supreme Legislation

- When the laws are **directly enacted** by the sovereign, it is considered as supreme legislation.
- One of the features of supreme legislation is that **no other authority** except the sovereign itself **can control or check it.**
- The laws enacted by the British Parliament fall in this category, as the British Parliament is considered sovereign. The law enacted by the Indian Parliament also falls in the supreme legislation.
- In India, powers of the Parliament are regulated and controlled by the Constitution but, the laws enacted by it are not under the control of any other legislative body.

Subordinate Legislation

- Subordinate legislation is made by any authority which is subordinate to the supreme or sovereign authority.
- It is **enacted under the delegated authority of the sovereign.**
- The origin, validity, existence and continuance of subordinate legislation totally depends on the will of the sovereign authority.
- Subordinate legislation further can be classified into the following types
  - **Autonomous Law** When a group of individuals recognised or incorporated under the law as an autonomous body, it is granted the power to make rules and regulation. The laws made by such a body are called autonomous laws, e.g. laws made by the bodies like Universities, incorporated companies etc.
  - **Judicial Rules** When the judiciary is granted the power to make rules for their administrative procedures, such rules are called judicial rules. Under the Constitution of India, the Supreme Court and High Courts have been granted such kinds of power to regulate procedure and administration.
  - **Local Laws** When the local bodies are recognised and granted the law-making powers, then the laws made by them are called local laws. They are entitled to make bye-laws in their respective jurisdictions (part of Laws made by the Executive). In India, local bodies like Panchayats and Municipal Corporations have been recognised by the Constitution, through the **73rd and 74th Constitutional Amendments.**
  - **Colonial Law** Laws made by colonial countries for their colonies or the countries controlled by them are known as colonial laws. This types of legislation is losing its importance as most countries of the world have gained independence from the colonial powers.
  - **Laws made by the Executive** In most of the modern states, sovereignty is generally divided among the three organs of the state. The three organs of the state namely legislature, executive and judiciary are provided three different functions. The **legislature has the responsibility of law-making**, while the executive has the responsibility to implement the laws enacted by the legislature.
- However, the legislature delegates some of its law-making powers to executive organs which are termed as **delegated legislation.**
- Delegated legislation is also a class of subordinate legislation.
- In welfare and modern states, the amount of legislation has increased and it is not possible for legislative bodies to go through all the details of law.
- Therefore, it deals with only a fundamental part of the legislation and wide discretion has been given to the executive to fill the gaps.
- This increasing tendency to delegate legislation has been criticised.
- However, delegated legislation is adopted, on account of reasons like insufficiency of time, technicalities of law and emergency.
- Therefore, delegated legislation is sometimes considered necessary.

Check Point 3

1. In modern times, which body is considered as the most important source of law?
2. Name the two local bodies that are formed by 73rd and 74th Constitutional Amendments.
3. How are Colonial Laws losing importance?
4. What is Delegated legislation?

Mind Map

SOURCES OF LAW

1 Meaning and Origin of Sources of Law

Definition
- Sources of law refer to origins from which binding rules of human conduct arise.

Perspectives
- **Austin** Sovereign as the source of law.
- **Savigny and Maine** Custom is the most important source.
- **Natural Law School** Nature and human reason.
- **Theologians** Religious scriptures.

Three Major Sources of Law
- Custom
- Judicial Precedent
- Legislation

2 Custom as a Source of Law

Customs
- Long-established practices with obligatory character.
- **Example** Saptapadi in Hindu marriages.

Types
- **Customs without Sanction** Followed due to public opinion.
- **Customs with Sanction** Enforced by the state.

Categories of Customs
- **Legal Customs**
  - **General** Applicable across the state.
  - **Local** Specific to regions.
  - **Conventional Customs** Bind specific agreements, e.g., landlord-tenant agreements.
- **Essentials for Valid Custom**
  - Antiquity, continuity, exercised as a matter of right, reasonableness and morality.

3 Role of Custom in Indian Legal System

- Prevalent in ancient India and British India.

Reforms
- Codification post-independence (e.g., Hindu Marriage Act, 1955).
- Modern civilisation reduced its importance.

Current Scenario
- Personal laws largely governed by customs.

4 Judicial Precedents as a Source of Law

- Decisions by superior courts binding lower courts.

Parts
- **Ratio Decidendi** Binding principle.
- **Obiter Dicta** Persuasive remarks.

Hierarchy of Courts
- **Supreme Court** Apex authority.
- **High Courts** Jurisdiction-specific binding.
- **Lower Courts** Bound by decisions of higher courts.

5 Judicial Precedents in Indian Context

Evolution
- Introduced during British rule.
- Privy council as the final appellate body.

Post-Independence
- Supreme Court became the apex judicial body in 1950.

Impact
- Creative role in law interpretation.
- Development of new rights (e.g., Right to Privacy, Pollution-free Environment).

6 Legislation as a Source of Law

Legislation
- Laws enacted by sovereign or authorised entities.

Types
- **Supreme Legislation** Enacted by sovereign, e.g., Indian Parliament.
- **Subordinate Legislation**
  - Autonomous (e.g., university rules).
  - Judicial (court procedures).
  - Local (Panchayats, Municipalities).
  - Colonial (laws by colonial rulers).
  - Executive (delegated powers for detailed rules).

Significance
- Directly enacted and recognised by the state.

Features
- Backed by sovereign authority.
- Adapts to modern needs and emergencies.

Subordinate Legislation Criticism
- Delegated powers may lead to misuse.
- Necessary due to technicalities and limited legislative time.

7 Comparison of Sources

Source	Characteristics	Examples
Customs	Long-established practices, binding under specific conditions.	Saptapadi, local marriage customs.
Precedents	Court rulings creating binding laws.	Vishaka Guidelines, Right to Privacy.
Legislation	Enacted by sovereign/Parliament.	Indian Penal Code, Consumer Protection Act.

8 Key Takeaways

- Sources of law evolve with societal needs.
- Balance between traditional customs, judicial creativity, and formal legislation is vital.
- Judicial precedents and legislation dominate modern legal systems.

CBSE TEXTBOOK Folder

1. Write one point of difference between the following

(i) **Ratio Decidendi and Obiter Dicta**
(ii) **Custom and legislation as a source of law**
(iii) **Supreme legislation and Subordinate legislation**
(iv) **Judgments of Supreme Court and High Court**
(v) **General customs and Local customs**

Ans. (i) 'Ratio Decidendi' refers to the binding part of a judgment while an 'obiter dictum' refers to parts of judicial decisions which are general observations of the judge and do not have any binding authority.

(ii) Custom can be explained as those long established practices or unwritten rules which have acquired binding or obligatory character.

On the other hand legislation refers to laws enacted by the sovereign or any other person or institution authorised by him. The term legislation is derived from the Latin which means the 'making of law'.

(iii) When the laws are directly enacted by the sovereign, it is considered as supreme legislation while subordinate legislation is a legislation that is made by any authority which is subordinate to the supreme or sovereign authority.

(iv) The judgements given by the Supreme Court are binding on all the courts throughout the territory of India. The Supreme Court is not bound by its previous decisions; however a smaller bench is bound by the decision of the larger bench, and the co-equal bench.

While, the judgements given by the High Courts are binding on the subordinate courts within the jurisdiction of that particular High Court.

The judgements of the High Courts are not binding beyond their respective jurisdictions.

(v) General customs are customs prevailing throughout the territory of the state. On the other hand, local customs are applicable locally, i.e, to a particular region of the country.

2. Write short notes on the following

(i) **Custom as a source of law**
(ii) **Subordinate legislation**
(iii) **Parts of judicial decision**

Ans. (i) Customs are those long established practices or unwritten rules which have acquired binding or obligatory character.

A custom becomes valid if it is observed continuously for a very long time without any interruption. Further, a practice to become custom must be supported not only for a very long time but, it must also be supported by the opinion of the general public and morality.

Every custom is not required to become a law. For example, the Hindu Marriages Act, 1955 prohibits marriages which are within the prohibited degrees of relationship. However, the act still permits marriages within the prohibited degree of relationship, if there is a proven custom within a certain community.

(ii) Subordinate legislation is a legislation which is made by any authority which is subordinate to the supreme or sovereign authority. It is enacted under the delegated authority of the sovereign. The origin, validity, existence and continuance of such legislation totally depends on the will of the sovereign authority.

(iii) Judicial decisions can be divided into following two parts

(a) **Ratio Decidendi (Reason of Decision)** 'Ratio Decidendi' refers to the binding part of a judgment. 'Ratio Decidendi' literally means reasons for the decision.

It is considered as the general principle which is deduced by the courts from the facts of a particular case.

It becomes generally binding on the lower courts in future cases involving similar questions of law.

(b) **Obiter Dicta (Said by the Way)** An 'Obiter Dictum' refers to parts of judicial decisions which are general observations of the judge and do not have any binding authority. However, obiter of a higher judiciary is considered by lower courts and has persuasive value.

3. Identify the following legislations

(i) **Law made by sovereign**
(ii) **Law made by municipal corporation**
(iii) **Law made by universities**
(iv) **Law made by executive**
(v) **Law made by colonial rulers**

Ans. (i) Supreme legislation
(ii) Subordinate legislation
(iii) Autonomous legislation
(iv) Delegated legislation
(v) Colonial legislation

4. Provide brief answers for the following.

(i) **How did Austin and Savigny view custom as a source of law?**

(ii) **What are the two parts of judicial decisions?**

(iii) **Do judges make law? Comment.**

(iv) **What is the importance of custom as a source of law in India?**

(v) **Enumerate the legislations that are based on customs.**

(vi) **What is the hierarchy of the civil and criminal justice system in India?**

Ans (i) Both Austin and Savigny has opposing views when it comes to custom as a source of law.

Austin opposed custom as law because it did not originate from the will of the sovereign, whereas savigny considered custom as the main source of law.

(ii) Refer to Q. 2 (iii) of CBSE Textbook Folder.

(iii) There are two different views regarding making of laws by judges

(a) Some jurists like Edward Coke and Mathew Hale believe that judges do not make the law but that they simply declare the existing law. According to them, judicial decisions are not sources of law but they are simply the proof of what the law is. Judges are not law-givers, but they discover law

(b) Other jurists like Dicey, Gray, Salmond believe that judges do make law. They believe that, while interpreting the law enacted by the legislative bodies, judges contribute to the existing body of law. A large part of the English law is judge-made law.

Thus, it can be inferred that judges do not make the law in the same manner like legislative bodies. Judges work on a given legal material, passed as law by the legislature. While declaring the law, judges interpret the 'legislation' in question and play a creative role. By this creative role, judges have contributed significantly to the development of law.

(iv) Custom has played as significant role as a source of law in India, especially in its historical and cultural context. The importances of customs as a source of law are

- Custom was the most important source of law in ancient India. Even the British initially adopted the policy of non-intervention in personal matters of Hindus and Muslims. The British courts, in particular, the Privy Council, in cases such as Mohammad Ibrahim Vs. Shaik Ibrahim (AIR 1922 PC59) observed and underlined the importance of custom in moudling the law. At the same time, it is important to note that customs were not uniform or universal throughout the country. Some regions of the country had their own customs and usages. These variances in customs were also considered a hindrance of the integration of various communities of the country.
- During our freedom struggle, there were parallel movements for social as widow re-marriage and child marriage. After independence and with the enactment of the Constitution, the India Parliament took many steps and abrogated many old customary practices with some progressive legislation. Hindu personal laws were codified and the Hindu Marriage Act, 1955 and the Hindu Adoption Act, 1955, were adopted. The Constitution of India provided a positive environment for these social changes.
- After independence, the importance of custom has definitely diminished as a source of law and judicial precedent, and legislation has gained a more significant place. A large part of Indian law, especially personal laws, however, is still government by customs.

(v) Some legislations which are based on customs are

(a) Hindu Marriage Act (b) Hindu Adoption Act

(vi) **Hierarchy Of Criminal Justice System**

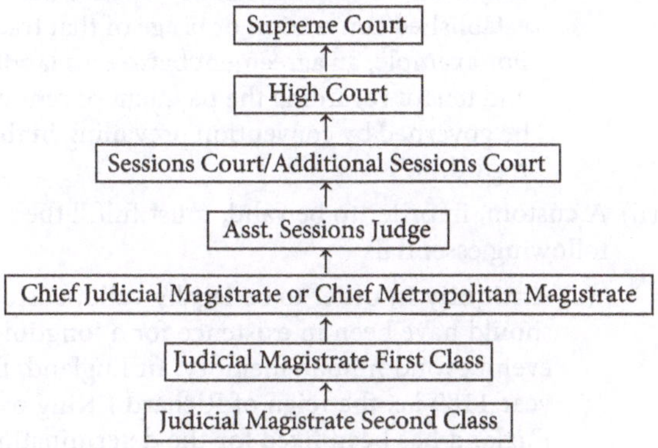

Hierarchy of Civil Judicial system

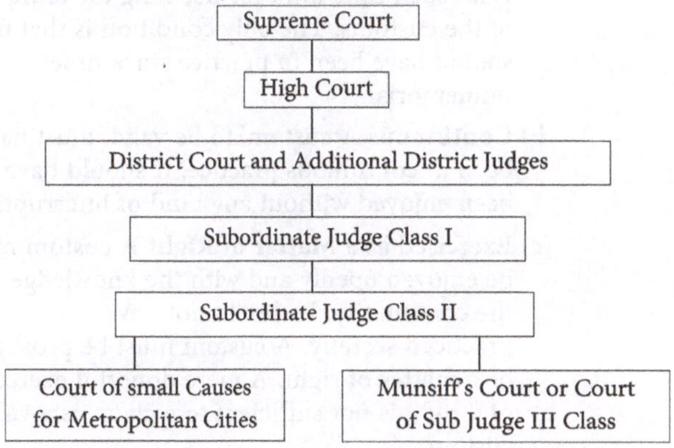

5. Provide detailed answers for the following.

(i) Explain different kinds of customs.

(ii) What are the essentials of a valid custom?

(iii) Explain legislation as a source of law.

(iv) Explain different kinds of legislation.

Ans (i) Customs can broadly be classified into two classes

(a) **Customs without Sanction** These customs are not binding in nature. They are only followed because of public opinion.

(b) **Customs with Sanction** These customs are binding in nature because they are enforced by the state. They can further be divided into

- **Legal Custom** It refers to a custom that has absolute authority. In other words, it has the force of law and is recognised and enforced by the courts. Legal customs are further subdivided into general customs (prevailing throughout the territory of the state) and local customs (applicable locally, i.e, to a particular region of the country).
- **Conventional Customs** These customs are binding on the parties to an agreement. When two or more persons enter into an agreement related to a trade, it is presumed in law that they make the contract in accordance with established convention or usage of that trade. For example, an agreement between a landlord and tenant regarding the payment of rent will be governed by convention prevailing in this regard.

(ii) A custom, in order to be valid, must fulfill the following essentials

(a) **Antiquity** In order to be legally valid, customs should have been in existence for a longtime, even beyond human memory. In England, the year 1189 i.e. the reign of Richard I King of England has been fixed for the determination of validity of customs. However, in India there is no such time limit for deciding the antiquity of the customs. The only condition is that those should have been in practice since time immemorial.

(b) **Continuous** A custom, to be valid, must have been in continuous practice. It should have been enjoyed without any kind of interruption.

(c) **Exercised as a Matter of Right** A custom must be enjoyed openly and with the knowledge of the community. It should not have been practiced secretly. A custom must be proved to be a matter of right. A mere doubtful exercise of a right is not sufficient to a claim as a valid custom.

(d) **Reasonableness** A custom must not be against the norms of justice and public utility. A custom, to be valid, should be based on rationality and reason. If a custom is likely to cause more inconvenience and mischief than convenience, such a custom will not be valid.

(e) **Morality** A custom which is immoral or opposed to public policy cannot be a valid custom. Courts have declared many customs as invalid as they were practised for immoral purposes or were opposed to public policy. For example, Bombay High Court in the case of Mathura Naikon Vs. EsuNaekin, decided that the custom of adopting a girl for immoral purposes is illegal.

(iii) In modern times, legislation is considered as the most important source of law. The term legislation is derived from the Latin word legis which means 'law' and latum which means 'to make' or 'set'. Therefore, the word 'legislation' means the 'making of law'.

The importance of legislation as a source of law can be measured from the fact that it is backed by the authority of the sovereign and it is directly enacted and recognised by the state.

The expression 'legislation' has been used in various ways. It includes every method of law-making. In the strict sense, it means laws enacted by the sovereign or any other person or institution authorised by him.

(iv) The different kinds of legislation are

(a) **Supreme Legislation** When the laws are directly enacted by the sovereign, it is considered as supreme legislation. One of the features of supreme legislation is that no other authority except the sovereign itself can control or check it.

(b) **Subordinate Legislation** Subordinate legislation is a legislation which is made by any authority which is subordinate to the supreme or sovereign authority. It is enacted under the delegated authority of the sovereign. The origin, validity, existence and continuance of such legislation totally depends on the will of the sovereign authority.

Subordinate legislation further can be classified into the following types

- **Autonomous Law** When a group of individuals recognised or incorporated under the law as an autonomous body, is conferred with the power to make rules and regulation, the laws made by such body fall under autonomous law. For example, laws made by the bodies like universities, incorporated companies etc. fall in this category of legislation.

- **Judicial Rules** In some countries, the judiciary is conferred with the power to make rules for their administrative procedures. For example, under the Constitution of India, the Supreme Court and High Courts have been conferred with such kinds of power to regulate procedure and administration.
- **Local Laws** In some countries, local bodies are recognised and conferred with the law-making powers. They are entitled to make bye-laws in their respective jurisdictions. In India, local bodies like Panchayats and Municipal Corporations have been recognised by the Constitution through the 73rd and 74th Constitutional Amendments. The rules and bye-laws enacted by them are examples of local laws.
- **Colonial Law** Laws made by colonial countries for their colonies or the countries controlled by them are known as colonial laws. For a long time, India was governed by the laws passed by the British Parliament. However, as most countries of the world have gained independence from the colonial powers, this legislation is losing its importance and may not be recognised as a kind of legislation.
- **Laws made by the Executive**
  In most of the modern states, sovereignty is generally divided among the three organs of the state. The three organs of the state namely legislature, executive and judiciary are vested with three different functions. The prime responsibility of law-making vests with the legislature, while the executive is vested with the responsibility to implement the laws enacted by the legislature.

6. Why is delegated legislation sometimes considered as a necessary evil?

Ans. Delegated legislation is sometimes considered a necessary evil because while it can be criticised for undermining the legislature's role and serves practical purposes. The primary reasons for this view are

(i) **Efficiency** The legislature cannot handle all the details of every law due to time constraints. Delegated legislation allows the executive to address specific issues or make detailed rules quickly, ensuring smooth implementation of laws.

(ii) **Expertise** Certain laws require technical or specialised knowledge that the legislature may not have. The executive or specialised bodies are better equipped to create regulations based on this expertise.

(iii) **Flexibility** Delegated legislation provides flexibility to adapt laws to changing circumstances without needing a full legislative process, which can be slow and cumbersome.

(iv) **Emergency Situations** In cases of urgency or crisis, delegated legislation allows the executive to act swiftly to address issues without waiting for legislative approval.

7. Which is the most relevant source of law in today's time? Define.

(i) Give any two differences between its two types.

(ii) Also explain which of its forms is a necessary evil and why?

Ans. For answer, refer to Q 5(iii) of CBSE Textbook Folder.

(i) For answer, refer to Q 5(iv) of CBSE Textbook Folder.

(ii) For answer, refer to Q 6 of CBSE Textbook Folder.

8. What are judicial precedents? Also answer the following questions

(i) The Chennai High Court gave a decision in the year 2005 which was overturned by Supreme Court in 2011. Which of the two decisions should be followed by a District Court in Chennai.

(ii) Kerala High Court and Calcutta High Court gave contradicting decisions in the year 2009 and 2017 respectively. Which decision should the Kerala District Court follow?

(iii) In the year 2018, a division bench of Supreme Court and Constitutional bench of Supreme Court gave two contradicting decisions. Which decision should be followed?

Ans. Judicial precedents refer to previously decided judgments of the superior courts, such as the High Courts and the Supreme Court, which judges are bound to follow.

(i) The decision of the Supreme Court should be followed by the district court as the High Court's decision has been overturned by the Supreme Court.

(ii) The Kerala District Court will follow the decision given by the Kerala High Court because it's the Kerala High Court that has jurisdiction over the District Courts in Kerala.

(iii) In the year 2018, if the Constitutional bench of Supreme Court and the division bench of Supreme Court gave two contradicting decisions, the decision of the Constitutional bench is to be followed because the number of judges in a Constitutional bench is higher.

9. The Supreme Court of India passed a judgment in the year 2015 which banned diesel cars registered before the year 2005 from plying on the road. The rationale behind the judgment was the deterioration of the engine and hence poor performance and increased pollution.

While writing the judgment the judges made many remarks on other sources of pollution too like construction, fires, etc.

(i) What is the relevance of this judgment in the creation of laws?

(ii) What two parts of this judgment are being talked about above?

(iii) Can the Delhi High Court overturn this judgment?

Ans. (i) This judgment will propel the legislature to create laws that aim at curbing pollution and ensuring better quality of vehicles which are environment friendly.

(ii) The two parts of the judgment are
(a) Obiter Dicta
(b) Ratio Decidendi

(iii) No, a High Court cannot overturn the judgment of the Supreme Court.

10. 'All customs cannot be accepted as sources of law, nor can all customs be recognised and enforced by the courts'.

(i) Explain any three factors which are taken into consideration for deciding any custom as a valid source of law.

(ii) What is the relevance of customs as a source of law in the present day context?

Ans. (i) For, answer, refer to Q. 5 (ii) of CBSE Textbook Folder.

(ii) After independence and with the enactment of the Constitution, the Indian Parliament took many steps and repealed many old customary practices with some developing legislation.

Hindu personal laws were codified and the Hindu Marriage Act, 1955 and the Hindu Adoption Act, 1955, were adopted. The Constitution of India provided a positive environment for these social changes.

With the passage of time and advent of modern civilisation, the importance of custom as a source of law diminished and other sources such as judicial precedent and legislation gained importance. However, a large part of Indian law, especially personal laws, is still governed by customs.

Exam Pattern Questions

Objective Type Questions

Multiple Choice Questions (MCQs)

1. Rajan lost his job without being served the notice. He filed a petition to put a hold over the employee's action. Rajan curiously asked the advocate about the meaning of sovereign in the Constitution. Competency Based Que

Who among the following considers sovereign as the source of law?

(a) Austin
(b) Savigny
(c) Henry Maine
(d) All of these

2. Rhea told her daughter Shea that the customs are most important role in law-making process. Name the thinker who stated that custom is the most important source of law. Competency Based Que

(a) Austin
(b) Savigny
(c) Henry Maine
(d) Both (b) and (c)

3. Which of the following statements is TRUE about the nature of custom as a source of law?

(a) Custom is always preferred over legislation in modern states.
(b) Custom can become law only if it is supported by public opinion and morality.
(c) Custom can override statutory law without any restrictions.
(d) All customs regardless of their nature are enforceable by the courts.

4. Which of the following is NOT a requirement for a custom to be recognised as a valid source of law?

(a) Antiquity
(b) Continuous practice without interruption
(c) Reasonableness and morality
(d) The custom must be widely opposed by the public

5. "These kinds of customs are non-obligatory in nature and are followed because of public opinion". The above-mentioned statement is related to ....

(a) customs without sanction
(b) customs with sanction
(c) general customs
(d) local customs

6. **In England, the year 1189 i.e. the reign of Richard I, King of England has been fixed for the determination of validity of customs. However, in India there is no such time limit for deciding it. This passage is related to ....**
(a) antiquity
(b) reasonableness
(c) exercised as a matter of right
(d) morality

7. **Gaurav and Abishek were talking about the uniqueness of India's Constitution. Both agreed that the various personal laws of different sects must have been included in the Constitution like the Hindu personal laws. Identify among the following that are the parts of Hindu personal laws.** Competency Based Que
I. Hindu Marriage Act, 1955
II. Hindu Succession Act, 1956
III. Hindu Minority and Guardianship Act, 1956
IV. Hindu Adoptions and Maintenance Act, 1956
Codes
(a) I, II and IV (b) I and II
(c) II, III and IV (d) All of these

8. **............ refers to previously decided judgments of the superior courts, such as the High Courts and the Supreme Court, which judges are bound to follow.**
(a) Judicial precedent
(b) Antiquity
(c) Morality
(d) Ratio decidendi

9. **It is considered as the general principle which is deduced by the courts from the facts of a particular case. It becomes generally binding on the lower courts in future cases involving similar questions of law.**
(a) Ratio decidendi (b) Obiter dictum
(c) Doctrine of precedent (d) None of these

10. **The Supreme Court, too in its role as through an activist, has created many new rights such as the right to privacy, right to live in a pollution free environment, right to livelihood. These rights are a part of which of the following Articles of the Indian Constitution?**
(a) Article 36 (b) Article 51
(c) Article 18 (d) Article 21

11. **Which of the following are the major sources of law in modern society?**
I. Custom **II. Judicial Precedent**
III. Legislation
Codes
(a) Both I and II (b) Only III
(c) Only II (d) All of these

12. **According to the hierarchy, arrange the court as per superior to inferior**
I. District Court **II. Subordinate judge class II**
III. Munsiff Court **IV. High Court**
Choose the correct option
(a) IV, I, II, III (b) III, II, I, IV
(c) III, IV, II, I (d) IV, I, III, II

13. **Ved Prakash, a law student was asked in the campus placement about the subordinate legislation and its origin is India. Which of the following is/are the parts of Subordinate Legislation?** Competency Based Que
I. Obiter dicta **II. Judicial Rules**
III. Colonial Law **IV. Local Law**
Codes
(a) I, II and IV (b) II, III and IV
(c) I, II and III (d) All of these

14. **This type of legislation is also known as subordinate legislation, and is typically used to supplement or implement primary legislation.**
Which of the following is a true characteristic of delegated legislation?
(a) It is made by the legislature itself.
(b) It is only used for minor or trivial matters.
(c) It is subject to strict parliamentary control.
(d) It is made by an executive authority under the authority of legislature.

15. **Match the following.**

	Column I		Column II
A.	Autonomous Law	1.	Judicial Decisions
B.	Ratio Decidendi	2.	Customs
C.	Antiquity	3.	Subordinate legislation
D.	Saptapadi	4.	Essentials of a valid custom

Codes

	A	B	C	D		A	B	C	D
(a)	3	1	4	2	(b)	1	2	3	4
(c)	2	1	4	3	(d)	4	1	3	2

16. **Statement I** Obiter dictum refers to the remark opinion made by a judge that is not essential to the decision in a particular case.
Statement II Obiter dictum is binding on lower courts, but may be considered persuasive authority in future cases.
Choose the correct options
(a) Both the Statement are correct.
(b) Both the Statement are incorrect.
(c) Statement I is correct, but Statement II is not correct.
(d) Statement I is not correct, but Statement II is correct.

Assertion-Reason Questions

Directions (Q. Nos. 17-21) In the questions given below, there are two statements. Read the statements and choose the correct option.

Codes

(a) Both A and R are true and R is the correct explanation of A.

(b) Both A and R are true, but R is not the correct explanation of A.

(c) A is true, but R is false.

(d) A is false, but R is true.

17. Assertion (A) Customs fall under formal sources of law.

Reason (R) Formal sources of law are the sources from which law derives its force and validity.

18. Assertion (A) Austin considers sovereign as the source of law and opposed custom as law.

Reason (R) It did not originate from the will of the sovereign.

19. Assertion (A) Saptapadi is an example of customs as a source of law.

Reason (R) The word Saptapadi means 'Seven steps'.

20. Assertion (A) The laws enacted by the British Parliament fall in supreme legislation.

Reason (R) The British Parliament is considered sovereign.

21. Assertion (A) In India, the doctrine of precedent is based on the concept of hierarchy of courts.

Reason (R) In India, hierarchy has been established by the British Parliament.

Answers

1. (a) Austin
2. (d) Both (b) and (c)
3. (b) Custom can become law only if it is supported by public opinion and morality.
4. (d) The custom must be widely opposed by the public.
5. (a) customs without sanction
6. (a) antiquity
7. (d) All of these
8. (a) Judicial precedent
9. (a) Ratio decidendi
10. (d) Article 21
11. (d) All of these
12. (a) IV, I, II, III
13. (b) II, III and IV
14. (d) It is made by an executive authority under the authority of legislature.
15. (a) 3 1 4 2
16. (c) Statement I is correct, but Statement II is not correct.
17. (a) Both A and R are true and R is the correct explanation of A.
18. (d) A is false, but R is true.
19. (b) Both A and R are true, but R is not the correct explanation of A.
20. (a) Both A and R are true and R is the correct explanation of A.
21. (c) A is true, but R is false.

Subjective Questions

Very Short Answer Type Questions

1. What is the meaning of source of law?

Ans. Sources of law refers to the sources from where law or the binding rules of human conduct originate.

2. What is custom?

Ans. Customs are those long established practices or unwritten rules which have acquired binding or obligatory character.

3. Saptapadi is an example of customs as a source of law. **Competency Based Que**

(i) What is Saptapadi?

(ii) Saptapadi incorporated in which act?

Ans. (i) The word, Saptapadi means 'Seven steps'. It is an important custom recognised in Hindu marriages.

(ii) Saptapadi incorporated in Section 7 of Hind Marriage Act, 1955.

4. Can a custom be a main source of law?

Ans. Yes, according to Savigny and Henry Maine consider custom as the most important source of law. According to them, the real source of law is the will of the people and not the will of the sovereign.

The will of the people has always been reflected in the customs and traditions of the society.

5. What are the different kinds of customs?

Ans. Customs can be broadly divided into two classes

(i) **Customs without Sanction** These customs are not binding in nature. They are only followed because of public opinion acceptence.

(ii) **Customs with Sanction** These customs are binding in nature because they are enforced by the state. They are two types-legal customs and conventional customs.

6. Briefly explain the legal custom.

Ans. Legal custom is a custom whose authority is absolute, it possesses the force of law. It is recognised and enforced by the courts.

7. It is a custom whose authority is absolute; it possesses the force of law. It is recognised and enforced by the courts. Competency Based Que

(i) What does the given statement about?

(ii) Give the classification of the mentioned custom.

Ans. (i) The above statement talks about legal customs.

(ii) A legal customs can be classified into general custom and local custom.

- **General Customs** These customs are prevailed throughout the territory of the state.
- **Local Customs** These customs are applicable locally, i.e., to a particular region of the country.

8. State the main function of the judiciary.

Ans. The main function of the judiciary is to adjudicate the rights which are generally conferred on the citizens by legislation.

9. Why is the British Parliament considered as a part of the supreme legislation?

Ans. The laws enacted by the British Parliament fall under supreme legislation as the British Parliament is considered as sovereign.

10. What is meant by legislation?

Ans. The term legislation is derived from the Latin word 'legis' which means 'law' and 'latum' which means 'to make' or 'set'. Therefore, the word legislation means the 'making of law'.

11. Rahul, a citizen of India, challenges the validity of a law enacted by the Indian Parliament, arguing that it violates the principles of the Constitution. The Parliament claims that as the supreme legislative body, its laws cannot be checked or controlled by any other authority. However, Rahul contends that the Constitution regulates and controls the powers of the Parliament. Write any one feature of supreme legislation. Competency Based Que

Ans. One of the features of supreme legislation is that no other authority except the sovereign itself can control or check it.

12. (i) The Calcutta High Court gave a decision in the year 2008 which was overturned by Supreme Court in 2011. Which of the two decisions should be followed by a District Court in Kolkata.

(ii) Will the decision of Calcutta Hight Court or Madras High Court be binding on a district court in Calcutta in case of a contradiction between the two? Competency Based Que

Ans. (i) The District Court in Kolkata will actually be following the decision of the Supreme Court in this case because in case of a dispute between the decision of the High Court and the Supreme Court, the decision of the Supreme Court will prevail.

(ii) The decision of the Calcutta High Court will be binding on the District Court in Calcutta.

13. The Supreme Court gave a judgment on the re-productive right of women in India in the year 2022. The Delhi High Court gave a decision contrary to this decision. Decide. Competency Based Que

(i) Will the decision of the Delhi Hight Court prevail?

(ii) Can the Supreme Court overturn the decision of the Delhi High Court?

Ans. (i) The decision of the Delhi High Court will not prevail because it is not in alignment with the Supreme Court decision.

(ii) Yes, the Supreme Court can overturn the decision of the Delhi High Court because it is the apex court in the country.

Short Answer Type Questions

1. What is Antiquity? Explain with the help of an example.

Ans. In order to be legally valid, customs should be antiquity which means they should have been in existence for a long time. In England, the year 1189 i.e., the reign of Richard I King of England, has been fixed for the determination of validity of customs.

However, in India, there is no such time limit for deciding the antiquity of the customs. The only condition is that those should have been in practice since time immemorial.

2. Judicial decisions can be divided into two parts. Explain each part in brief.

Ans. For answer refer to the text under the heading Judicial Decisions on page no. 142.

3. Briefly explain about the jurisdiction of the Supreme Court and High Court.

Ans. For answer, refer to Q.No. 1 (iv) of CBSE Textbook Folder.

4. In India, there is not only legislature but the judiciary has played an active role for the enactment of law. Do judges make laws? Elaborate. Competency Based Que

Ans. The Indian Constitution confers power on the legislature to make law, while the judiciary has the power to examine the Constitutionality of the law enacted by the legislature. The courts also adjudicate upon the rights and duties of citizens, and further interpret the provisions of the Constitution and other laws. Through these processes, the courts create new rights for the citizens. By this exercise, the judiciary makes additions to the existing laws of the country.

It can be inferred that judges do not make the law in the same manner in which legislative bodies do. Judges work on a given legal material passed as law by the legislature. While declaring the law, judges interpret the 'legislation' in question and play a creative role. By this creative role, judges have contributed significantly to the development of law.

Therefore, it can be concluded that the judicial precedents are important sources of law in modern society and judges do play a significant role in law-making.

5. Garima after completion of her law degree, has planned for practice in High Court. She is eager to witness the various process of legislation making. Discuss the different types of legislation.

Ans. For answer refer to the text under the heading Types of Legislation, on page no. 143 and 144.

6. The Supreme Court of India made guidelines for sexual harassment of women at workplace in the famous Visakha case. However, there was no such law governing the sexual harassment of women at workplace back then. Decide.

(i) Do judges have the power to make law?

(ii) What is the relevance of this judgment in the creation of laws? Competency Based Que

Ans. (i) Judges do not have the formal power to make laws like lawmakers (Parliament), but they can interpret existing laws and fill in gaps when needed. This is called judicial law-making. Judges can create guidelines or principles through their decisions, which can have the effect of law in certain situations.

(ii) In the Visakha case, the Supreme Court created guidelines to prevent sexual harassment at the workplace because there was no law on the issue at that time. These guidelines helped fill the legal gap and later became the basis for the Sexual Harassment of Women at Workplace Act, 2013. The judgment highlighted the need for specific legislation and protected women's rights at work. It shows how court decisions can influence the creation of laws when there is a gap in existing legal frameworks.

7. The Constitution of India confers power on the legislature to make law, while the judiciary has the power to examine the Constitutionality of the laws enacted by the legislature.

(i) How Supreme Court of India has played its role as an activist in many instances?

(ii) Discuss the role of custom in the formulation of laws.

Ans. (i) In India, Supreme Court has played an active role through its activism to restore the rights of disadvantaged sections of the society. The Apex Court has created many new rights such as the right to privacy, right to live in a pollution free environment, right to livelihood, etc. These new rights were created only by way of interpreting Article 21 (Right to Life) of the Constitution of India.

(ii) The Custom is considered to be the most important source of law in ancient India. Even the British initially adopted the policy of non-intervention in personal matters of Hindus and Muslims.

The customs were not uniform or universal throughout the country. Some regions of the country had their own customs and usages. After independence, the importance of custom has definitely diminished as a source of law, though large part of Indian law, especially personal laws, however, are still governed by customs.

Long Answer Type Questions

1. State the essential tests for customs to be recognised as valid sources of law.

Ans. For answer refer to the text under the heading the Essentials of a Valid Custom, on page no. 139.

2. Imagine a situation where a well-known restaurant in Delhi refuses entry to a group of women because they are wearing traditional Indian attire, stating that it does not meet the "modern" dress code of the restaurant. The women are shocked and file a complaint with the authorities, arguing that their cultural attire should not be used to discriminate against them.

(i) How can the state intervene to ensure that such practices do not violate Fundamental Rights?

(ii) What categories of customs enforced by the state would apply to prevent such discrimination?

Ans. (i) In this situation, the state can intervene by ensuring that the restaurant's actions do not violate the women's Fundamental Rights, particularly the right to equality and non-discrimination under the Constitution of India. The state can investigate the restaurant's dress code policy and assess whether it unfairly targets or discriminates against any specific cultural or gender group.

(ii) To prevent such discrimination, the following categories of customs enforced by the state would apply.

- **Legal Custom** It refers to a custom that has absolute authority. In other words, it has the force of law and is recognised and enforced by the courts. Legal customs are further sub-divided into
  - (i) General customs that prevailed throughout the territory of the state.
  - (ii) Local customs that are applicable locally, i.e. to a particular region of the country.
- **Conventional Customs** These customs are binding on the parties to an agreement. When two or more persons enter into an agreement related to a trade, it is assumed in law that they make the contract according to the established convention or usage of that trade. For example, an agreement between a landlord and tenant regarding the payment of rent will be governed by convention prevailing in this regard.

3. **"The doctrine of precedent in India is a British Legacy". Explain.** **Competency Based Que**

Ans. The system of precedent is based on the hierarchy of courts. Therefore, it becomes important to understand the hierarchy of courts in order to understand precedent. Every legal system has its own distinct features. Therefore, the doctrine of precedent is applied differently in different countries.

In India, the doctrine of precedent is based on the concept of hierarchy of courts. The modern system of precedent developed in India during the British rule. It was the British who introduced the system of courts in India by the Regulating Act of 1773 and a Supreme Court was established at Calcutta (Kolkata).

Later on, other Supreme Courts were established in other presidency towns also. After that, High Courts were established in provinces. However, there was no hierarchy of courts between the Supreme Court and High Courts, and they were independent of one another. The hierarchy of courts could be established only when the judicial committee of the Privy Council became the final appellate tribunal. Another milestone regarding the hierarchy of courts was the Government of India Act, 1935, which established the Federal Court.

Hence, as far as hierarchy of courts in India before Independence was concerned, the Privy Council was the final appellate court. Other courts like the Federal Court, High Court, the Presidency and Mofussil (district) Courts were bound to follow the decisions of their Superior Courts.

4. **Priyanka and Supriya moved to session court for the legal dispute over the property. The advocate of each client informed them that the case shall proceed under the subordinate legislation. Discuss the four main classification of subordinate legislation.** **Competency Based Que**

Ans. For answer, refer to Q.No. 5 (iv) of CBSE Textbook Folder.

SELF ASSESSMENT TEST

Objective Type Questions

1. Which of the following customs is/are not binding in nature?
   (a) Customs without sanction (b) Customs with sanction
   (c) Both (a) and (b) (d) None of these
2. When a group of individuals recognised or incorporated under the law as an autonomous body, it is called............ .
   (a) Autonomous law (b) Judicial rules (c) Local customs (d) None of these
3. By the Regulating Act of 1773, a Supreme Court was established at ....
   (a) Bombay (b) Delhi (c) Calcutta (d) Chennai
4. Judicial decisions are divided into ....
   (a) obiter dicta (b) ratio decidendi (c) local custom (d) Both (a) and (b)
5. The prime responsibility of law-making vests with the ....
   (a) bureaucracy (b) legislature (c) executive (d) judiciary

Very Short Answer Type Questions

6. Discuss the views of Austin on sources of law.
7. What is the classification of customs with sanction?
8. State the importance of custom as a source of law in India.
9. Mention the three main sources of law in modern society.
10. What do you mean by judicial precedent? Why is it considered an important source of law?
11. Define you mean by obiter dicta.

Short Answer Type Questions

12. Give any three difference between the will of the people and the will of the sovereign.
13. Explain the hierarchy of courts in India.
14. Was there a hierarchy of courts in British India?
15. Mention the two parts into which judicial decisions can be divided.
16. 'There ane two kinds of legislation.' **Competency Based Que**
    (i) State their names.
    (ii) Explain these legislations with examples.

Long Answer Type Questions

17. 'A custom must have been in continuous practice, to become valid.' Justify the statement. **Competency Based Que**
18. Explain the different views on making of laws by judges.
19. 'Legislation means laws enacted by the sovereign or any other person or institution authorised by him.' Comment. **Competency Based Que**

09

CHAPTER

Law reform refers to the process by which the law is adapted and advanced over a period of time in response to changing social values and priorities.

YOUR STUDY GOALS

YOUR PRACTICE GOAL

- Objective Type Questions (16 Qs ; MCQs, A-R, Statements)
- Subjective Questions (6 VSAs, 5 SAs, 3 LAs)

Law Reforms

9.1 Need for Law Reform

- Law reform is a strong relationship between law and society. Law and society act and react upon each other. **Law cannot be static[1]** as it has to change with the needs of time.
- Law has to respond to the social concerns and has to provide easy solutions to the problems that keep coming up before the society.
- It has to respond to social, economic or technological developments.
- Law reforms are also necessary as they help to shape democracies to suit changing political and legal environments. It is not a one-time process but a slow and gradual process.

9.2 Law Reforms in India

Law reforms in India can be broadly classified into two periods

- Pre-independent India law reforms
- Post-independent India law reforms

Pre-independent India Law Reforms

Law Reforms in Ancient and Medieval India

- Before the advent of British rule, Indian society was governed by its **customary law,** either based on Hindu Dharmashastra or Islamic religious scripts.

1 **Static** It means something lacking in movement, action or change, especially in an undesirable or uninteresting way.

- These customary laws were followed by the rulers and the people who were ruled.
- Customary laws were considered as rigid and against the idea of social change.

Law Reforms During British Rule

- Before the First War of Independence in 1857, the East India Company ruled India under the permission of the British crown and later on the British crown governed India till from 1600 AD to 1947 AD.
- During this period, there were major changes in political, economic, administrative and legal fields.
- The law reforms during British rule were
  - The East India Company introduced the Western Legal System as well as legal reforms in India.
  - There were major changes in political, economic, administrative and legal fields.
  - Modern courts were established by the enactment of various acts such as the Regulating Acts 1773, the Government of India Act 1935, etc.
  - Principles of English law like justice, equity and good conscience were used by the courts in India for their decisions.
- The administrators who played cruical roles in the reforms in the judicial system in pre-independent India were
  - **Warren Hastings** (1732-1818), the first Governor-General of India.
  - **Charles Cornwallis** (1738-1805), a British Army Officer and Colonial Administrator, who served as a civil and military governor in India and is known for his contribution to the policy for permanent settlement.
  - **William Bentinck** (1774-1839), a British statesman, who served as Governor- General of India from 1828 to 1835. Played crucial role in reforming judicial system.

Law Commission

- A major milestone in law reform during the British Raj, was the establishment of the law commission.
- The first law commission was established in 1834 under the Charter Act of 1833, under the chairmanship of **Thomas Babington Macaulay**.
- The second, third and fourth law commissions were established in the years 1853, 1861 and 1879 respectively.
- The major contribution of the law commission were

(i) It recommended the codification of the penal code and the criminal procedure code.

(ii) It also contributed in the Indian Code of Civil Procedure 1908, the Indian Contract Act 1872, the Indian Evidence Act 1872 and the Transfer of Property Act 1882.

Post-Independent India Law Reforms

- The laws reforms after Independence of India were
  - The newly enacted Constitution and principles enshrined under it were the main guiding forces of law.
  - The Fundamental Rights and Directive Principles of State Policies became the basis for any social change.
  - The Constitution, under **Article 372**, recognised the pre-Constitutional laws. However, there were demands from various quarters to review the colonial laws.
  - The Indian Government constituted the first law commission of independent India under the chairmanship of the then Attorney General, **Mr. M.C. Setalvad.**
  - Since then, twenty law commissions have been constituted.
  - The law commission of India has dealt with a wide range of issues.

- However, in recent years, economic reforms have brought about many changes in the Indian society. New categories of crimes including white collar-crimes, crimes against women and economic inequality in particular, have to be tackled on an urgent basis. The law commission therefore occupies a central role in law reforms in India.

Quick Test 1

1 Name the two customary laws that were followed before the advent of British in India.
2 Name the two British administrators who brought various socio-political and administrative changes in India.
3 When did the first law commission established under the Charter Act of 1833?
4 Which article of Indian Constitution recognised the pre-Constitutional laws?

9.3 Recent Law Reforms in Independent India

The Right to Information Act, 2005

- The Right to Information Act, also known as **RTI Act** came into existence in 2005 after continuous struggle by anti-corruption activists.
- It aims to promote transparency in government institutions in India.
- It is a **revolutionary**[2] act as it opens public authority for scrutiny by an ordinary citizen.
- Under this act, an Indian citizen can demand information from any government agency, which in turn is bound to provide the information within 30 days. If such agency fails, then the officer concerned is fined.

Information Technology Act, 2000

- The Information Technology Act, 2000 is based on the **UNCITRAL** (United Nations Commission on International Trade Law) Model Law on Electronic Commerce, 1996.
- It deals with cybercrime and e-commerce.
- It provides legal recognition for transactions carried out by means of electronic data interchange and other means of electronic communication, commonly referred to as electronic commerce.

Muslim Women (Protection of Rights on Marriage) Act, 2019

- Muslim Women (Protection of Rights on Marriage) Act, 2019 was passed by the Parliament of India to protect the rights of married Muslim women and to prohibit divorce by pronouncing talaq by their husbands.
- In 2017, the Supreme Court of India declared **Triple Talaq**, which enables Muslim men to instantly divorce their wives, to be **unconstitutional**[3].

The Consumer Protection (Amendment) Act, 2019

- The Consumer Protection (Amendment) Act, 2019 came into effect in July, 2020.
- It repeals and replaces the Consumer Protection Act, 1986.
- The purpose of the amendment act is to **prevent unfair trade practices** in e-commerce to protect consumers.

2 **Revolutionary** It means involving or causing a complete or dramatic change.
3 **Unconstitutional** It means something which is not in accordance with the Constitution or with procedural rules.

- The Consumer Protection (Amendment) Act, 2019 provides greater transparency and gives more power to the customer for redressal of disputes in the following ways
  - This act protects the consumers from misleading and deceptive[4] advertisements.
  - Now, an advertising code gives protection to customers against false advertisements, especially protecting them from celebrities, who do paid reviews of the products and services.
  - The advertising code is applicable throughout all mediums of communication like social media, print media, etc.
- This act also provides for settlement of consumer disputes in India.
- It imposes strict penalties, including jail terms for adulteration and for misleading advertisements.
- It now prescribes rules for the sale of goods through e-commerce.

Highlights of the Act

Important highlights of the Consumer Protection Act, 2019 are

- An aggrieved consumer can file complaints about a defect in goods or deficiency in services from where she/he lives, instead of the place of business or residence of the seller or service provider. Hence, it brings e-filing of consumer complaints.
- No fees are required to be paid if the claim is within ₹ 5 lakh.
- The consumer is **not required to engage a lawyer** and can conduct her/his own case via video conferencing.
- A concept of product liability allows aggrieved consumers to claim compensation due to the negligence of the manufacturer or service provider.
- A class-action suit can be filed by a group of aggrieved consumers who can unite to reduce costs and improve chances of redressal or settlement (like in the US).
- Producers of false or fake goods may be punished with imprisonment.
- Those celebrities who endorse[5] a product can be barred from endorsing, if the advertisement is misleading.
- E-commerce is tightly regulated. E-commerce companies have to disclose all relevant product information, including country of origin, and address all consumer grievances within prescribed timelines.
- Settlement of consumer disputes through mediation is encouraged which saves time as well as resources of disputing parties.

Quick Test 2

1 How does RTI bring and promote transparency?
2 Which act is based on UNCITRAL Model Law on Electronic Commerce?
3 Write a feature of Information Technology Act, 2000.
4 Mention the act which protects consumers from misleading and deceptive advertisements.

4 **Deceptive** It means giving an impression or appearance different from true one.
5 **Endorse** It means to declare one's public approval.

Mind Map

1 Introduction to Law Reforms

Definition
- Process of adapting and advancing laws over time to address changing societal values, needs and priorities.

Importance (Need)
- Reflects the dynamic relationship between law and society.
- Responds to social, economic and technological developments.
- Shapes democracies and ensures governance aligns with evolving environments.

2 Phases of Law Reforms in India

Pre-Independent India
- Governed by customary laws based on
  – Hindu Dharmashastra
  – Islamic Religious Scripts
- Rigid laws resistant to social change.
- Key Developments during British Rule
  – Introduction of the Western Legal System.
  – Enactment of **Regulating Acts (1773), Government of India Act (1935).**
  – **Use of English principles** justice, equity, and good conscience.
  – Establishment of modern courts.

Prominent administrators
- **Warren Hastings** First Governor-General of India.
- **Cornwallis** Reformed land revenue and judiciary.
- **William Bentinck** Reformed civil and military administration.

Law Commission
- Established in 1834 under **Charter Act of 1833.**

Contributions
- Codification of **Indian Penal Code, Criminal Procedure Code, Indian Evidence Act,** etc.

Post-Independent India
- Constitution as the guiding force for law reforms.
- Principles of **Fundamental Rights** and **Directive Principles of State Policy.**
- First Law Commission of Independent India:
- Established under **M.C. Setalvad.**
- Addressed colonial laws and societal demands.

Modern Challenges
- Tackling new crimes like white-collar crimes and crimes against women.
- Adapting laws to economic and social reforms.

LAW REFORMS

3 Recent Law Reforms in Independent India

Right to Information Act, 2005
- Promotes transparency in governance.
- Empowers citizens to seek information from government bodies.
- Ensures accountability by imposing penalties for non-compliance.

Information Technology Act, 2000
- Based on **UNCITRAL Model Law.**
- Legalises e-commerce and addresses cybercrime.

Muslim Women (Protection of Rights on Marriage) Act, 2019
- Declares Triple Talaq void and unconstitutional.
- Imposes penalties for instant divorce practices.

Consumer Protection (Amendment) Act, 2019
- Addresses consumer rights in e-commerce.
- Penalises misleading advertisements and unfair trade practices.
- Introduces grievance redressal mechanisms for consumers.

4 Role of Law Commission in India

- Established under **Charter Act of 1833.**

Key contributions
- Codification of essential laws.
- Reforms in criminal justice, civil procedure and evidence laws.

Central role in addressing societal needs
- Tackling economic inequality.
- Addressing new categories of crimes.
- Aligning laws with technological advancements.

5 Challenges in Law Reforms

- Resistance from traditional systems.
- Balancing societal values with modernity.
- Need for timely implementation and enforcement.

6 Key Takeaways

- Law reforms are continuous and adapt to societal evolution.
- Historical and modern contributions of law commissions are pivotal.
- Recent reforms emphasise transparency, accountability and consumer protection.

CBSE TEXTBOOK Folder

1. What is the need for Right to Information Act in today's context?

Ans. The RTI Act is importance in today's context because it

(i) **Empowers Citizens** It allows citizens to access information about the government, which helps them make informed decisions and hold public officials accountable.

(ii) **Promotes Transparency and Accountability** The RTI Act makes the government more transparent and accountable to its citizens.

(iii) **Controls Corruption** The RTI Act helps control corruption by making it harder for corruption to happen when citizen are informed about important thing.

(iv) **Improves the Functioning of Public Authorities** The RTI Act helps to improve the functioning of public authorities by making them more responsible and sensitive to the development process.

(v) **Helps with the Implementation of Government Progress** The RTI Act helps with the implementation of government programmes by controlling delays.

Exam Pattern Questions

Objective Type Questions

Multiple Choice Questions (MCQs)

1. The process by which a law is adapted and advanced over a period of time in response to changing social values and priorities is known as ....

(a) progress (b) law development
(c) law reform (d) legislation

2. Sanjay is very radical about the fundamental changes in the legal system of India and actively asks for reforms in laws as it was brought in the past. Who has introduced legal reform in India? Competency Based Que

(a) British East India Company (b) Mughal Era
(c) Harsha Dynasty (d) Dutch

3. Which of the following act(s) was/were responsible for the establishment of Modern Courts in India?

I. Regulating Acts, 1773
II. Government of India Act, 1935
III. Charter Act of 1833

Codes

(a) Both I and II (b) Only II
(c) Both I and III (d) All of these

4. Sulekha Sharma in her history lecture explained the class how Warren Hastings established the real authority of the East India Company over Bengal. Who was Warren Hastings? Competency Based Que

(a) First Governor-General of India
(b) British Army Officer
(c) Colonial Administrator
(d) Governor-General of Bombay

5. He is a British Army Officer and Colonial Administrator who also served as a civil and military governor in India and is known for his contribution to the policy for permanent settlement. This information is related to whom?

(a) Lord Macaulay (b) William Bentinck
(c) Cornwallis (d) Warren Hastings

6. Which among the given statements is TRUE regarding the Right to Information (RTI) Act, 2005?

(a) The RTI Act allows only government officials to access information from public authorities.
(b) Government agencies must provide requested information within 60 days.
(c) The RTI Act was enacted to promote transparency and accountability in government institutions.
(d) An RTI application can only be filed in person, not online.

7. Meera, a social activist suspects that a local government office is misusing public funds allocated for rural development. She wants to access official records to verify how the funds are being utilised. Which legal provision allows her to obtain this information? Competency Based Que

(a) The Indian Contract Act, 1872
(b) The Right to Information Act, 2005
(c) The Information Technology Act, 2000
(d) The Government of India Act, 1935

8. **Which among the following is NOT a feature of the Consumer Protection (Amendment) Act, 2019?**
(a) E-commerce platforms must disclose product information, including the country of origin.
(b) Consumers can file complaints from their place of residence.
(c) Lawyers are mandatory for consumer dispute cases.
(d) Misleading celebrity endorsements can result in penalties.

9. **Arrange the following Acts as per their year of enforcement**
I. The Information Technology Act
II. Consumer Protection Act
III. Muslim Women (Protection of rights on marriage) Act
IV. The Right of Information Act

Choose the Correct option
(a) III, II, IV, I (b) II, IV, I, III
(c) II, I, IV, III (d) III, I, II, IV

10. **Statement I** The first law commission was established in India in 1934 under the Charter Act of 1933.

Statement II The main objective of the law commission was to codify and improve the Indian Legal system, which was a mix of Hindu, Muslim and British Laws.

Choose the correct option
(a) Both the Statement are correct.
(b) Both the Statement are incorrect.
(c) Statement I is correct, but Statement II is not correct.
(d) Statement I is not correct, but Statement II is correct.

11. **Statement I** The first law commission of independent India was established in 1955 under the Government of India Act.

Statement II The commission was chaired by Mr. M.C. Setalvad, the then Solicitor General of India, and was tasked with reviewing and revising the Indian Legal System.

Choose the correct option
(a) Both the Statement are correct.
(b) Both the Statement are incorrect.
(c) Statement I is correct, but Statement II is not correct.
(d) Statement I is not correct, but Statement II is correct.

Assertion-Reason Questions

Directions (Q. Nos. 12-16) In the questions given below, there are two statements. Read the statements and choose the correct option.

Codes
(a) Both A and R are true and R is the correct explanation of A.
(b) Both A and R are true, but R is not the correct explanation of A.
(c) A is true, but R is false.
(d) A is false, but R is true.

12. **Assertion** (A) Law reform has to respond to social, economic or technological developments.
Reason (R) Law reform is not a one-time process but a slow and gradual process.

13. **Assertion** (A) Indian society was governed by its customary law, either based on Hindu Dharmashastra or Islamic religious scripts.
Reason (R) Customary laws were considered as rigid and averse to the idea of social change.

14. **Assertion** (A) Warren Hastings (1732-1818) was the first Governor-General of India.
Reason (R) He is known for his contribution to the policy for permanent settlement.

15. **Assertion** (A) The East India Company played crucial roles in improving the Civil and Criminal Justice System in pre-independent India.
Reason (R) They introduced the Western Legal System as well as legal reforms in India.

16. **Assertion** (A) The second law commission was established in 1834 under the Charter Act of 1853, under the chairmanship of Thomas Babington Macaulay.
Reason (R) The major contribution of the law commission was the recommendation on the codification of the penal code and the criminal procedure code.

Answers

1. (c) law reform
2. (a) British East India Company
3. (a) Both I and II
4. (a) First Governor-General of India
5. (c) Cornwallis
6. (c) The RTI Act was enacted to promote transparency and accountability in government institutions.
7. (b) The Right to Information Act, 2005
8. (c) Lawyers are mandatory for consumer dispute cases.
9. (c) II, I, IV, III
10. (d) Statement I is not correct, but Statement II is correct.
11. (b) Both the Statement are incorrect.
12. (a) Both A and R are true but R is not the correct explanation of A.
13. (b) Both A and R are true, but R is not the correct explanation of A.
14. (c) A is true, but R is false.
15. (a) Both A and R are true and R is the correct explanation of A.
16. (d) A is false, but R is true.

Subjective Questions

Very Short Answer Type Questions

1. What do you mean by law reforms?

Ans. Law reform is the process by which a law is adapted and advanced over a period of time in response to changing social values and priorities.

2. What is the need for law reforms?

Ans. Law has to respond to the social concerns and has to provide amicable solutions to the problems that keep coming up before the society.

It has to respond to social, economic or technological developments. Law reforms also help to shape democracies to suit changing political and legal environments.

3. What are the two periods into which law reforms can be classified?

Ans. Law reforms in India can be broadly classified into two periods, which are

(i) Pre-independent India law reforms

(ii) Post-independent India law reforms

4. What were the major contributions of the law commission in pre-independence India?

Ans. A major milestone in law reform during the British Raj, was the establishment of the law commission.

The major contribution of the law commission were

(i) It recommended the codification of the penal code and the criminal procedure code.

(ii) It also contributed in the Indian Code of Civil Procedure 1908, the Indian Contract Act 1872, the Indian Evidence Act 1872 and the Transfer of Property Act 1882.

5. During his civil services exam preparations, Jayant has learnt that the various acts passed by the British government were based on the English laws. How is the Regulating Act of 1773 considered to be a milestone in the British administration in India? Competency Based Que

Ans. The Regulating Act of 1773 was introduced to establish a central administrative system in British India. The major purpose of the act was to regulate the activities of the British East India Company and allow them to retain its territorial possessions in India. The act for the first time gave the British cabinet the right to exercise control over Indian affairs.

6. Hansika, Jyotika and Samar are three youngsters who bought a product from different stores located in the same city. The products that they bought does not function effectively and is faulty.

(i) In such a scenario, identify which act/law can help them?

(ii) Explain this act. Competency Based Que

Ans. (i) In this scenario, Hansika, Jyotika and Samar can seek protection under the Consumer Protection Act, 2019. This law safeguards the rights of consumers and addresses issues related to faulty or defective products.

(ii) According to the Consumer Protection Act, consumers have the right to file complaints if they purchase a product that is defective or does not perform as expected. The law allows for the following actions

(a) **Replacement of the Faulty Product** The store or manufacturer can be asked to replace the product.

(b) **Refund of the Purchase Price** If the product is defective and cannot be replaced, they are entitled to a full refund.

(c) **Compensation** If the faulty product caused harm or loss, they can seek compensation for damages.

The consumers can approach the Consumer Court or the Consumer Disputes Redressal Forum to file a complaint and seek redress for the issue under this law.

Short Answer Type Questions

1. Why law reforms are important? Were there any law reforms before the advent of Britishers?

Ans. Law reforms are important because they provide easy solutions to the problems that keep coming up before the society. These are also necessary as they shape democracies with the changing political and legal environments.

Before the advent of British rule, Indian society was governed by its customary law, either based on Hindu Dharmashastra or Islamic religious scripts. These customary laws were followed by the rulers and the ruled. Customary laws were considered as rigid and averse to the idea of social change. So, these laws did not change.

2. The East India Company first came to India as a trader group, but within a span of time captured many provinces in India. However, the company has brought several new elements in India. Discuss the role of East India Company in introducing the law reform in India. Competency Based Que

Ans. The East India Company introduced the Western Legal System as well as legal reforms in India. Prior to the First War of Independence in 1857, the East India Company ruled India under the permission of the British crown and later on the British crown governed India till 1947.

During the British Raj, i.e. from 1600 AD to 1947 there were major changes in political, economic, administrative and legal fields as follows

- Modern courts were established by the enactment of various acts such as the Regulating Acts, 1773, the Government of India Act, 1935, etc.
- Further, well accepted principles of English law like justice, equity and good conscience were used by the courts in India for their decisions.

3. A major milestone in law reform during the British Raj, was the establishment of the law commission.
(i) When was the first law commission established and who was the chairman of the first law commission?
(ii) Mentioned the name of the acts which were passed as a response to the law commission.
Competency Based Que

Ans. (i) The First Law Commission was established in 1834 under the Charter Act of 1833, under the chairmanship of Thomas Babington Macaulay.
(ii) The Indian Code of Civil Procedure, 1908; the Indian Contract Act, 1872; the Indian Evidence Act, 1872 and the Transfer of Property Act, 1882, were the major contributions of the law commission.

4. How does the law commission occupy a central role in law reforms in India?

Ans. The Law Commission occupies a central role in law reforms in India. It indicates that the government is aware and concerned about the need for timely law reform, so that laws may respond to the changing needs of society. This is especially true in recent years wherein economic reforms have brought about many changes in Indian society.

New categories of crimes including white-collar crimes, crimes against women and economic inequality in particular have to be tackled on an urgent basis.

5. Yasmeen is divorced by her husband through Triple Talaq. She came back to her parents' home and worried about her future. However her friend Sunanda took her to police station and helped lodge a case against her husband. Mention any two provisions of Muslim Women Act, 2019. Competency Based Que

Ans. The Muslim Women (Protection of Rights on Marriage) Act was passed in the year 2019 by the Indian Parliament. Its most important provisions are
(i) The act declares the instant divorce granted by pronouncement of Talaq three times as void and illegal.
(ii) It provides for imprisonment for a term up to 3 years and fine to the husband who practiced instant Triple Talaq.

Long Answer Type Questions

1. What is the meaning of law reform? Discuss the law reforms in pre-independence India.

Ans. For answer refer to text under the heading Law Reform and Law Reforms in Pre-independence India, on page no. 157 and 158.

2. In 2008, Tapas was appointed to work in the Indian Railways. However, due to some administrative issues related to her appointment, she was not allowed to join the office, and she was neither informed nor given any explanation. After years of uncertainty, Tapas has decided to file a Right to Information (RTI) request to seek clarification about her situation.
(i) What is RTI Act?
(ii) Mention the significance of the Right to Information Act in this case.
(iii) State its major characteristics. Competency Based Que

Ans. (i) The Right to Information (RTI) Act, enacted in 2005 empowers citizens to request information from public authorities, ensuring transparency and accountability in government operations.
(ii) In Tapas's case, the RTI Act would allow her to inquire about the reasons behind her delayed appointment and the administrative issues that prevented her from joining her office.
The significance of the RTI Act lies in its ability to give ordinary citizens access to information that was previously often hidden, promoting transparency in government processes.
(iii) The major characteristics of the RTI Act include
- **Public Access** Any citizen can request information from government bodies.
- **Time-bound Response** Authorities must respond within 30 days.
- **Appeal Mechanism** If the response is unsatisfactory, the applicant can appeal.
- **Exemptions** Some information related to national security or personal privacy is not disclosed.

3. Narendra is a tech savvy person who orders most of his goods and necessary items through various e-commerce platforms. One day, one of his ordered items was received in a spoilt condition, but the seller refused to resolve his problem and denied to exchange it with other one. What do you understand by e-commerce? Does the Consumer Protection Act, 2019 address such e-commerce entities? Competency Based Que

Ans. For answer refer to text under the heading The Consumer Protection (Amendment) Act, 2019 on page no. 159 and 160.

SELF ASSESSMENT TEST

Objective Type Questions

1. Who served as Governor-General of India from 1828 to 1835?
   (a) Warren Hastings (b) William Bentinck (c) Cornwallis (d) Macaulay
2. The law commission works in close co-ordination and under the general instruction of ....
   (a) Ministry of Personnel and Grievance (b) Comptroller and Auditor General
   (c) Ministry of Law and Justice (d) Ministry of Social Justice and Empowerment

Very Short Answer Type Questions

3. 'Law reforms is not a one-time process but a slow and gradual process.' Comment. **Competency Based Que**
4. Analyse the law reforms in India, before the advant of the Britishers. **Competency Based Que**
5. What are the different periods of law reforms in India?
6. Who was William Bentinck?
7. Write a short note on the law commission.
8. Explain the Muslim Women (Protection of Rights on Marriage) Act, 2019.

Short Answer Type Questions

9. Who were the important personalities during British rule?
10. Explain the law reforms during British rule.
11. Give three differences between pre-independent India law reforms and post-independent India law reforms.

Long Answer Type Question

12. Elaborate upon the two phases of law reforms in the Indian context.
13. Write a note on The Consumer Protection (Amendment) Act, 2019.
14. Law reforms refer to the process by which the law is adopted and advanced over a period of time in response to changing social values and priorities. **Competency Based Que**
    (i) State how law reforms has to respond to the social concerns.
    (ii) What is Article 372?
    (iii) With reference to law reforms how IT Act, 2000 deals with cybercrime and e-commerce.

10

CHAPTER

People from all over the world are provided with new opportunities to connect and communicate through the emergence of advanced digital innovations.
All these opportunities and advances are possible because of the internet.

Cyber Laws, Safety and Security in India

YOUR STUDY GOALS

10.1 Introduction
10.2 Cyber Law
10.3 Cyber Crime
10.4 Cyber Law in India
10.5 Scope and Extent of the Information and Technology Act, 2000 (IT Act)

YOUR PRACTICE GOAL

- Objective Type Questions (14 Qs ; MCQs, A-R, Statements, Matching)
- Subjective Questions (7 VSAs, 7 SAs, 3 LAs)

10.1 Introduction

- The internet is defined as, 'A system architecture that has revolutionised communications and methods of commerce by allowing various computer networks around the world to interconnect'.
- The computer-generated world of the internet that involves interactions between people, software and services is known as **cyberspace**. It is a dynamic, exponential and undefined space.
- The internet was initially developed as a research and information sharing tool and was **unregulated**[1].
- With time, it became more transactional with e-business, e-commerce, e-governance and e-procurement, etc.
- As the number of internet users is increasing, the need for cyber laws and their application has also increased.

10.2 Cyber Law

- Cyber law is the law governing computers and the internet.
- Cyber law deals with legal issues related to use of inter-networked information technology.
- It provides the legal rights and restrictions governing technology.

1 **Unregulated** It means not controlled or supervised by laws.

- Cyber law include laws relating to cyber crimes, electronic and digital signatures, intellectual property, data protection and privacy, etc.
- All legal issues related to internet crime are dealt with through cyber laws.

Need for Cyber Laws

Cyber laws are needed due to the following reasons

- The **anonymous nature** of the internet makes it possible for it to be used for many criminal activities due to which cyber laws are needed.
- Cyber law is important because it handles almost all aspects of transactions and activities on the internet.
- Every action and every reaction in cyberspace has cyber legal perspectives.
- Cyber law **examines every individual** using the internet like booking a domain name, disputes relating to online, intellectual property, etc.

10.3 Cyber Crime

- Cyber crime refers to an activity done with **criminal intent** in cyberspace.
- In other words, any offence or crime in which a computer is used is a cyber crime.
- Even a small offence like stealing can be considered a cyber crime, if the basic data or aid in that offence is a computer or information stored in a computer used (or misused) by the fraudster.
- Cyber crimes can be against persons, property or government.
- It includes many offences some of which are
    - **Cyber stalking** (using of internet or other technology to harass another person online)
    - **Computer vandalism** (getting some one's passwords or important data through a programme)
    - **Phishing** (stealing user data including personal information such as login credentials, bank information, etc.)
    - Some other offences are: Stealing of data, hacking, mail fraud, etc.

Definition of Cyber Crime

- The term cyber crime is not defined in Information Technology Act, 2000 or the National Cyber Security Policy, 2013 or in any other regulation in India.
- Cyber crime has been defined by the **National Cyber Crime Reporting Portal** as any unlawful act where a computer or communication device or computer network is used to commit or facilitate the commission of crime.
- National Cyber Crime Reporting Portal is a body set up by the government to facilitate reporting of cyber crime complaint.
- The courts in India have recognised cyber crime as "The offences that are committed against individuals or groups of individuals with a criminal motive **to intentionally harm** the reputation of the victim or cause physical or mental harm, or loss, to the victim directly or indirectly, **using modern telecommunication networks** such as internet and mobile phones (Bluetooth/SMS/MMS)".

Categories of Cyber Crime

Cyber crimes can be divided into the following categories

- **Cyber Crime against Person** It includes crimes like cyber stalking, cyber harassment, transmission of child pornography, etc.
- **Cyber Crime against Property** It includes computer trespassing, vandalism and unauthorised possession of computerised information, etc.

- **Cyber Crime against Government Cyber terrorism** is a distinct kind of crime in this category.
- **Cyber Harassment** Various kinds of harassment can occur in cyber space or by use of cyberspace. It can be sexual, racial, religious or others. It can also include violation of privacy of netizens (online citizens). The **internet makes it easy to violate the privacy** of any person which can result in harassment.
- **Cyber Bullying** Cyber bullying is bullying with the help of cyberspace and use of devices like cell phones, tablets, laptops, etc. It can occur through SMS, email, social forums as well as gaming.
  - It means **sending, sharing or posting** false, derogatory, harmful or negative content about any person.
  - It includes sharing personal information about a person without his/her consent causing humiliation. Cyber bullying can even result in unlawful or criminal behaviour online.

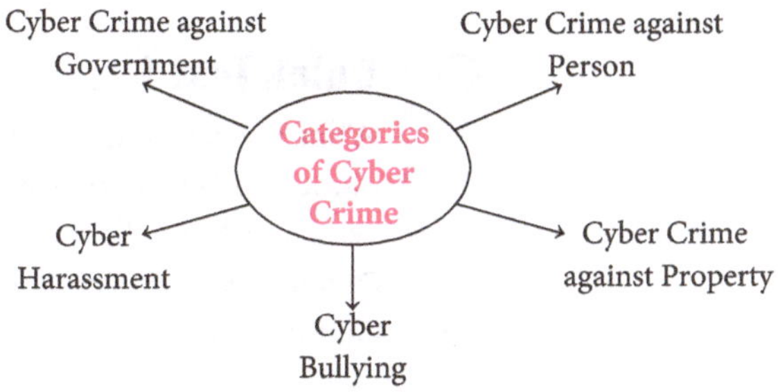

▲ *Categories of Cyber Crime*

Cyber Bullying and Online Gaming

- Playing video games is a popular pastime for children these days.
- It, therefore, becomes a platform for cyber bullying.
- If someone doesn't perform well in a game, he/she becomes a victim of negative remarks and can even be excluded from the game altogether.
- Sometimes, the bully may use the game as a medium to obtain personal information of the gamers, thereby compromising not just the child's information but also their parents. This tactic is known as Doxing which makes children more vulnerable to harassment by the bully.

Hacking as a Cyber Crime

- It happens when a stranger breaks into a person's computer system without that person's knowledge or consent and interferes with confidential information.
- Hacking into government or military owned website results in **Cyber Terrorism.**

Example of Cyber Terrorism

The attack on the Pentagon and the World Trade Centre, USA on 11th September, 2001 demonstrated the use of cyber space for terrorism. The terrorists gained access to intellectual resources of the government and used it as weapons of destruction. The terrorists **hijacked**[2] the flight procedures, and schedules, and executed the attack.

Cyber Safety and Security

- Cyber safety is the safe and responsible use of information and communication technology.
- Cyber security means protecting information, equipment, devices, computers, computer resources, communication devices and information stored therein from unauthorised access, use, disclosure, **disruption**[3], modification or destruction.
- Cyber safety is not only about keeping information safe and secure, but also about being responsible with that information and being respectful of other people online.
- Cyber safety and security can be ensured by enacting laws.
- It can also be ensured by use of technologies, processes and practices that are designed to protect networks, computers, programmes and data from attack, damage or unauthorised access.

---

2 **Hijacked** It means to seize possession or control of a vehicle from another person by force or threat of force.
3 **Disruption** It means disturbance or problems which interrupt an event, activity or process.

Quick Test 1

1. What do you understand by cyberspace?
2. Mention a feature of National Cyber Crime Reporting Portal.
3. What is cyber bullying?
4. Define how online gaming and doxing are interrelated?
5. Give one example of cyberspace attack that occurred in the past.

10.4 Cyber Law in India

- In India, cyber laws are included in the **Information Technology Act, 2000** which came into force on 17th October, 2000.
- The main purpose of the act is to provide legal recognition for transactions carried out by means of electronic data interchange and other means of electronic communication, commonly referred to as electronic commerce.
- It also aims to facilitate filing of electronic records with the government.

History of Cyber Law in India

- In 1996, the United Nations Commission on International Trade Law (UNCITRAL) adopted the **Model Law on Electronic Commerce**, to bring uniformity in the law in different countries.
- The Model Law on Electronic Commerce aims to enable and facilitate commerce conducted by electronic means.
- It provides a set of universally acceptable rules to the countries that are aimed at removing legal obstacles and increasing legal predictability for electronic commerce.
- This model law provides for equal treatment which is essential for enabling paperless communication and fostering[4] efficiency in international trade.
- India became the 12th **country** to **enable cyber law** after it passed the Information Technology Act, 2000.

10.5 Scope and Extent of the Information and Technology Act, 2000 (IT Act)

- The Information Technology Act, 2000 extends to the whole of India.
- It also applies to any offence committed outside India by any person irrespective of his/her nationality, if such offence involves a computer, computer system or network located in India.
- The features of the act are
  - The act provides legal infrastructure for e-commerce, electronic records (like online contracts) and other activities carried out by electronic means. It also deals with electronic governance and cyber crimes.
  - The act defines **digital signature** as authentication of any electronic record by a subscriber by means of electronic method or procedure.
- The courts in India have also recognised cyber crime (e.g., the Gujarat High Court in the case of Jaydeep Vrujlal Depani Vs. State of Gujarat) to mean the offences that are committed against individuals or group of individuals with a criminal motive to intentionally harm the reputation of the victim or cause physical or mental harm, or loss, to the victim directly or indirectly.

4 Foster It means to encourage the development of something.

Section 66 A of IT Act, 2000

- According to **Section 66 A** of the IT Act, 2000, if any person sends a 'grossly offensive' or 'menacing information' using a computer resource or communication device, then it is a punishable offence.
- Section 66 A was inserted by an amendment in the act in 2009.
- The reason behind the amendment was to address new forms of cyber crimes such as
  - Publishing sexually explicit materials in electronic form.
  - **Video voyeurism** (secretly capturing or recording private image or video of an individual without his/her consent) and breach of confidentiality[5].
  - Leakage of data by intermediary, e-commerce frauds like personation[6] commonly known as phishing.
  - Identity theft and offensive messages through communication services.
- Therefore, the Section 66 A, IT Act, 2000 **imposed punishment** and criminalised the sending of offensive messages through a computer or other communication devices.

Limitations of the IT Act and Section 66 A

- The IT Act used wide terms in Section 66 A which were not defined under the act.
- This caused a lot of confusion as the perception of an individual in defining 'grossly offensive' and 'menacing information' varies from one individual to another.
- This point was highlighted in the petitions of **Shreya Singhal Vs. Union of India**, in the year 2012 filed under Article 32.
- The petitioners argued for the following
  - The wordings of the section were too wide and ambiguous leading to misuse.
  - Most of the terms used in the section had not been specifically defined under the act.
  - The section restricted the right to free speech and expression prescribed under Article 19(1)(a) of the Constitution of India.
- On 24th March, 2015, the Supreme Court declared **Section 66 A of the IT Act, 2000 unconstitutional** for being violative of Article 19(1)(a) of the Constitution of India.

Quick Test 2

1. In which year Information Technology Act passed in India?
2. Name any one clause of Model Law on Electronic Commerce.
3. Write any one feature of Information Technology Act, 2000.
4. What is Digital Signature?
5. Why the Supreme Court declared Section 66 A of the IT Act, 2000 unconstitutional?

5 **Confidentiality** It means the stage of keeping or being kept secret.

6 **Personation** It means to assume the identity of another person with intent to deceive.

Mind Map

CYBER LAWS, SAFETY, AND SECURITY IN INDIA

1 Introduction

Internet Definition
- A system architecture enabling communication and commerce by interconnecting computer networks globally.

Cyberspace
- A dynamic virtual world involving people, software and services.
- Initially for research and information sharing; evolved into e-commerce, e-governance, etc.

Need for Cyber Laws
- The growing internet user base necessitates laws to address misuse and ensure security.

2 Cyber Law

Definition
- Governs computers, the internet, and related technology.
- Covers legal rights and restrictions related to digital activities.

Scope
- Addresses cybercrimes, digital signatures, intellectual property, data protection and privacy.

Importance
- Handles internet-based transactions.
- Governs domain disputes and online intellectual property issues.

3 Cyber Crimes

Definition
- Criminal activities using computers or networks.
- Recognised as offenses against individuals, property, or governments.

Examples
- Cyberstalking, phishing, hacking, cyberbullying, and vandalism.

Categories

Against Persons
- Cyberstalking, harassment, child pornography.

Against Property
- Hacking, unauthorised access, data theft.

Against Government
- Cyberterrorism, targeting government resources.

4 Cyber Bullying and Harassment

Definition
- Using cyberspace to harm or humiliate others.

Forms
- Derogatory remarks, sharing personal data without consent, exclusion from online forums.

Example
- **Doxing** Revealing private information online for malicious intent.

Online Gaming as a Platform
- A medium for bullying and unauthorised data collection.

5 Cyber Safety and Security

Definition
- Protecting information, systems, and networks from unauthorised access or damage.

Importance
- Ensures safe use of communication technology.
- Protects sensitive data from cyber threats.

6 Cyber Law in India

Information Technology Act, 2000
- Provides legal recognition to digital transactions.
- Facilitates electronic record filing with the government.

History
- Derived from the **UNCITRAL Model Law on Electronic Commerce** (1996).
- India became the 12th country to adopt cyber laws.

Key Provisions
- Legal framework for e-commerce.
- Recognition of digital signatures as electronic authentication.

7 Section 66A of IT Act

Overview
- Criminalised sending offensive or menacing information online.

Challenges
- Ambiguity in defining terms like "offensive."
- Restricted freedom of speech (Article 19 of the Constitution).

Shreya Singhal Case (2015)
- Supreme Court declared Section 66A unconstitutional for violating free speech.
- Highlighted the misuse of vague legal terminology.

8 Examples of Cyber Threats

Cyberterrorism
- Attacks like 9/11 demonstrate the use of cyberspace for malicious activities.

Phishing
- Fraudulent practices to obtain sensitive data (e.g., credit card details).

Hacking
- Unauthorised access to systems, sometimes escalating to national security risks.

9 Key Takeaways

Need for Cyber Laws
- Protect users and address crimes in cyberspace.

Cyber Safety
- Advocates responsible use of technology.

Judicial Interpretation
- Courts in India have defined cybercrime broadly, encompassing harm to individuals and institutions.

CBSE TEXTBOOK Folder

1. Answer the following questions briefly

(i) Explain the importance of cyber laws in current times.

(ii) What are the various categories of cyber crime? Give examples.

(iii) What is cyber bullying? How does it take place?

Ans. (i) The importance of cyber laws in current times is

- The anonymous nature of the internet makes it possible for it to be used for many criminal activities due to which cyber laws are needed.
- Cyber law is important because it handles almost all aspects of transactions and activities on the internet. Every action and every reaction in cyberspace has cyber legal perspectives.
- Cyber law examines every individual using the internet like booking a domain name, disputes relating to online, intellectual property, etc.

(ii) Cyber crimes can be divided into the following categories

(a) **Cyber Crime against Person** It includes crimes like cyber stalking, cyber harassment, transmission of child pornography, etc.

(b) **Cyber Crime against Property** It includes computer trespassing, vandalism and unauthorised possession of computerised information, etc.

(c) **Cyber Crime against Government** Cyber terrorism is a distinct kind of crime in this category.

(d) **Cyber Harassment** Various kinds of harassment can occur in cyber space or by use of cyberspace.

It can be sexual, racial, religious or others. It also include violation of privacy of netizens (online citizens).

(iii) Cyber bullying is a form of bullying that occurs through the use of digital platforms such as cell phones, tablets, laptops, or other electronic devices. It involves using the internet, social media, or other online communication tools to harass, threaten, or hurt someone.

Cyber bullying can happen in many different ways. Some common methods include

(i) **Sending Harmful Messages** Bullying through text messages, emails, or social media posts that include false, derogatory, or hurtful content.

(ii) **Sharing Personal Information** Posting personal details, pictures, or private information about someone without their permission, often to embarrass or humiliate them.

(iii) **Public Humiliation** Posting negative comments, rumours, or inappropriate content about a person on social forums or social media platforms.

(iv) **Exclusion** Intentionally excluding someone from online groups or activities, often to isolate or make them feel rejected.

(v) **Cyber Stalking or Threatening** Sending repeated, threatening, or abusive messages that may make the victim feel scared or unsafe.

2. Answer the following questions in about 150 words

(i) Trace the evolution of cyber laws in India.

(ii) Critically analyse the importance of Section 66A of the Information Technology Act, 2000.

Ans. (i) In 1996, the United Nations Commission on International Trade Law (UNCITRAL) adopted the Model Law on Electronic Commerce to bring uniformity in the law in different countries.

The Model Law on Electronic Commerce aims to enable and facilitate commerce conducted by electronic means by providing countries with a set of universally acceptable rules that are aimed at removing legal obstacles and increasing legal predictability for electronic commerce.

This model law provides for equal treatment which is essential for enabling paperless communication and fostering efficiency in international trade.

India became the 12th country to enable cyber law after it passed the Information Technology Act, 2000.

(ii) According to Section 66 A of the IT Act, 2000, if any person sends 'grossly offensive' or 'menacing information' using a computer resource or communication device, then he/she is committing a punishable offence.

Section 66 A was inserted by an amendment in the act in 2009. The reason behind the amendment was to address new forms of cyber crimes such as

- Publishing sexually explicit materials in electronic form.
- Video voyeurism (secretly capturing or recording private image or video of an individual without his/her consent) and breach of confidentiality.
- Leakage of data by intermediary, e-commerce frauds like personation commonly known as phishing.
- Identity theft and offensive messages through communication services.

Therefore, the Section 66 A IT Act, 2000 imposed punishment and criminalised the sending of offensive messages through a computer or other communication devices.

Exam Pattern Questions

Objective Type Questions

Multiple Choice Questions (MCQs)

1. Which of the following is best described as 'A system architecture that has revolutionised communications and methods of commerce by allowing various computer networks around the world to interconnect'?

(a) Internet (b) Cyberspace
(c) Cyber law (d) Cyber crime

2. Which among the given statements is TRUE for Cyber Law?

(a) Cyber Law only deals with criminal activities conducted online.
(b) Cyber Law encompasses laws related to cyber crimes, electronic signatures, intellectual property and data protection.
(c) Cyber Law is not necessary because the internet was initially developed as an unregulated research tool.
(d) Cyber Law applies only to businesses and not to individuals using the internet.

3. Rehman, a retired school teacher, was cheated while he was withdrawing his pension through a UPI app. He had received a call requesting the OTP which he had unknowingly provided leading to a loss of a large amount of his pension. This act comes under .... **Competency Based Que**

(a) cyber bullying (b) doxing
(c) cyber crime (d) cyber terrorism

4. Sweta has lodged a written complaint against two young boys who always keep on sending her messages on her social media handles. Which of the following cyber crimes are the boys committing? **Competency Based Que**

(a) Cyber theft
(b) Cyber harassment
(c) Transmission of child pornography
(d) All of the above

5. Which among the following can be a part of cyber bullying?

(a) Death threat (b) Online gaming
(c) Stalking (d) Unwarranted mails

6. Which among the following is NOT a method of ensuring cyber safety and security?

(a) Enacting cyber laws
(b) Using secure technologies and practices
(c) Encouraging unauthorised access to networks for ethical hacking
(d) Protecting data from unauthorised access

7. Rajini has just downloaded few UPI apps regarding the online payments and cashless transactions. However, her father adviced her to use those application with precautions. Which of the following refers to the safe and responsible use of information and communication technology? **Competency Based Que**

(a) Cyber safety (b) Cyber law
(c) Cyber crime (d) None of these

8. Akshara went on a holiday to Dubai with some of her friends. While enjoying her vacation, she noticed a boy following them and video taping everything that the girls did. Akshara, after talking to her friends, goes to the police. What will be the charge against this crime in India? **Competency Based Que**

(a) Cyber bullying (b) Video voyeurism
(c) Computer trespassing (d) Mail fraud

9. Match the following

	Column-I		Column-II
A.	One of the gravest cyber crimes	1.	Cyber terrorism
B.	Crime against government	2.	IT Act
C.	United Nations Commission on International Trade Law (UNCITRAL)	3.	Hacking
D.	Legal infrastructure for electronic records	4.	1996

Codes

	A	B	C	D		A	B	C	D
(a)	3	1	4	2	(b)	1	2	3	4
(c)	2	1	4	3	(d)	4	2	3	1

10. Under Indian cyber laws, doxing is considered a form of cyber harassment and is punishable.
Which of the following statement is true about doxing under Indian cyber laws?

(a) Doxing is not specifically mentioned in Indian cyber laws.
(b) Doxing is considered a form of cyber harassment and is punishable.
(c) Doxing is only punishable if it leads to physical harm.
(d) Doxing is only punishable if it involves sharing financial information.

11. **Statement I** Section 66 A of IT Act, 2000 was a controversial provision that criminalised sending offensive messages through computer resources.

Statement II In 2015, the Supreme Court of India struck down Section 66 A as unconstitutional, holding that it violated the right to freedom of speech and expression.

Choose the correct option

(a) Both the Statement are correct.
(b) Both the Statement are incorrect.
(c) Statement I is correct but, Statement II is not correct.
(d) Statement I is not correct, but Statement II is correct.

Assertion-Reason Questions

Directions (Q. Nos. 12-14) In the questions given below, there are two statements. Read the statements and choose the correct option.

Codes

(a) Both A and R are true and R is the correct explanation of A.
(b) Both A and R are true, but R is not the correct explanation of A.
(c) A is true, but R is false.
(d) A is false, but R is true.

12. **Assertion** (A) Playing video games becomes a platform for cyber bullying.

Reason (R) If someone doesn't perform well in a game, he/she becomes a victim of negative remarks and can even be excluded from the game altogether.

13. **Assertion** (A) Cyber bullying is bullying with the help of cyberspace and use of devices like cell phones, tablets, laptops, etc.

Reason (R) It can occur through SMS, email, social forums as well as gaming.

14. **Assertion** (A) 'Cyber security' means protecting information, equipment, devices, computers and information stored therein from unauthorised access.

Reason (R) Cyber terrorism is a distinct kind of crime in crimes against government.

Answers

1. (a) Internet
2. (b) Cyber Law encompasses laws related to cyber crimes, electronic signatures, intellectual property and data protection.
3. (c) cyber crime
4. (b) Cyber harassment
5. (b) Online gaming
6. (c) Encouraging unauthorised access to networks for ethical hacking
7. (a) Cyber safety
8. (b) Video voyeurism
9. (a) 3 1 4 2
10. (b) Doxing is considered a form of cyber harassment and is punishable.
11. (a) Both the Statement are correct.
12. (a) Both A and R are true and R is the correct explanation of A.
13. (a) Both A and R are true and R is the correct explanation of A.
14. (b) Both A and R are true, but R is not the correct explanation of A.

Subjective Questions

Very Short Answer Type Questions

1. **Urvashi has just been promoted to class 11 and her parents has provided a desktop with internet connection for enhancement in studies. What do you understand by the term 'internet'?** **Competency Based Que**

Ans. The internet is defined as 'A system architecture that has revolutionised communications and methods of commerce by allowing various computer networks around the world to interconnect'.

2. **Gautami has cleared the law entrance exam and decided to pursue cyber law as her specialisation. Why is cyber law important?** **Competency Based Que**

Ans. Cyber law is important because it handles almost all aspects of transactions and activities on the internet. Every action and every reaction in cyberspace has cyber legal perspectives.

3. What is cyber crime?

Ans. Cyber crime refers to an activity done with criminal intent in cyberspace. In other words, any offence or crime in which a computer is used is a cyber crime.

4. Give some examples of cyber crime against property.

Ans. Cyber crime against property includes computer trespassing, vandalism and unauthorised possession of computerised information, etc.

5. Amit, a skilled computer programmer, hacked into the Indian Army's website and accessed classified information without authorisation. He did not tamper with the data but revealed the vulnerability of the website to the authorities. Classify Amit's actions and explain the consequences of his action into a government-owned website, citing relevant details from the passage. Competency Based Que

Ans. Amit's actions can be classified as hacking, which is a grave cyber-crime. Although he did not tamper with the data, hacking into a government-owned website like the Indian Army's can be considered cyber terrorism, which has severe consequences. It compromises national security and confidentiality.

6. Vikul, a 15 years old student, created a fake social media profile of his classmate, Rohit, and posted derogatory comments and personal information about him. Rohit felt humiliated and threatened to report the incident to the authorities. Identify the type of behaviour exhibited by Vikul and explain the consequences of such behaviour. Competency Based Que

Ans. Vikul exhibited cyber bullying behaviour by creating a fake profile and posting derogatory comments and personal information about Rohit. This behaviour can result in unlawful or criminal behaviour online, causing humiliation and harm to Rohit. It violates Rohit's consent and can have severe consequences.

7. What is cyber safety?

Ans. Cyber safety is the safe and responsible use of information and communication technology. It is not only about keeping information safe and secure, but also about being responsible with that information and being respectful of other people online.

Short Answer Type Questions

1. Cyber crime has emerged as the most important challenge in front of the world. Many countries have various robust mechanisms to tackle such menace. How have courts in India defined cyber crime?

Ans. The courts in India have defined cyber crime as 'The offenses that are committed against individuals or groups of individuals with a criminal motive to intentionally harm the reputation of the victim or cause physical or mental harm, or loss, to the victim directly or indirectly, using modern telecommunication networks such as internet (networks including but not limited to chat rooms, emails, notice boards and groups) and mobile phones (Bluetooth/SMS/MMS)'.

2. In the present times, man has become more and more dependent upon the computer and its related networks. Although persistence threats of cyber crimes has increased tremendously as well. Discuss the different categories of cyber crime.

Ans. For answer refer to text under the heading Categories of Cyber Crime on page no. 168.

3. One day, Rakshita returned home from school with great sadness. When her mother consoled her she confessed that one of her classmate always teases her and make immoral comments about her body shape at social networking platforms. The family in a state of dilemma. On relation to this case, write a short note on cyber bullying and online gaming. Competency Based Que

Ans. For answer refer to text under the heading Cyber Bullying and Online Gaming on page no. 169.

4. What do you understand by hacking? Give an example of hacking as a cyber crime.

Ans. Hacking is one of the gravest cyber crimes known. It happens when a stranger breaks into a person's computer system without that person's knowledge or consent and tampers with confidential information. Hacking into government or military owned website results in cyber terrorism.

For example, the attack on the Pentagon and the World Trade Centre, USA on 11th September, 2001 demonstrated the use of cyber space for terrorism.

The terrorists gained access to intellectual resources of the government and used it as weapons of destruction. The terrorists, hijacked the flight procedures and schedules, and executed the attack.

5. 'Cyber crime' has been defined by the National Cyber Crime Reporting Portal (a body set up by the government to facilitate reporting of cyber-crime complaints) to 'mean any unlawful act where a computer or communication device or computer network is used to commit or facilitate the commission of crime'.

(i) Give some examples of cyber crime against a person.
(ii) Give some examples of cyber bullying.

Ans. (i) It includes crimes like cyber stalking, cyber harassment, transmission of child pornography, etc.

(ii) Cyber bullying can occur through SMS, email, social forums as well as gaming. It means sending, sharing or posting false, derogatory, harmful or negative content about any person.

6. **'X' indulges in the practice of sending fraudulent emails to people claiming that they have won a lottery worth ₹ 1 crore. The mails claim to be from reputable companies to induce people to reveal their credit card details.**

(i) What is 'X' guilt of ? Competency Based Que

(ii) Define the practice mentioned in (i).

Ans. (i) 'X' is guilty of phishing in this case.

(ii) Phishing refers to the fraudulent practice of sending emails that seems to come from reputable companies in order to induce individuals to reveal personal information, such as passwords, credit card numbers, etc.

7. **In the year 2012, in the matter of Shreya Singhal Vs. Union of India, a batch of writ petitions were filed under Article 32 of the Constitution of India.**

(i) What was the matter raised in this case?

(ii) What was the immediate cause of concern in these petitions?

Ans. (i) The matter raised in the case of Shreya Singhal Vs. Union of India was primarily about the Constitutionality of Section 66A of the Information Technology Act, 2000. This section criminalised the sending or posting of offensive, inflammatory, or annoying content online through messages, emails, or social media. The petitioners arguing that it violated the right to freedom of speech and expression guaranteed under Article 19(1)(a) of the Indian Constitution.

(ii) The immediate cause of concern in these petitions was the misuse of Section 66A, which led to the arrest of individuals for merely expressing their opinions on social media.

The petitioners sought to have Section 66A struck down as unconstitutional for violating the right to free speech and expression. The Supreme Court of India in 2015 ruled in favor of the petitioners and declared Section 66A unconstitutional, as it was found to be vague, overbroad, and inconsistent with the Constitution.

Long Answer Type Questions

1. Ratikant Shukla, a vigilant social worker and RTI activist always keenly informs people about their rights and especially about the IT Act which came into force to provide legal recognition to electronic commerce and to facilitate filing of electronic records with the government.

Which legislation provides the framework for cyber laws in India? Trace the historical evolution of cyber laws as well. Competency Based Que

Ans. In India, cyber laws are contained in the Information Technology Act, 2000 which came into force on 17th October, 2000. The main purpose of the act is to provide legal recognition for transactions carried out by means of electronic data interchange and other means of electronic communication, commonly referred to as electronic commerce and to facilitate filing of electronic records with the government.

For answer refer to text under the heading historical Evolution of Cyber Laws in India, on page no. 170.

2. **The city police arrested four women for posting allegedly offensive and objectionable comments on social networking sites about the god like treatment of a political leader. However, later police relased them on the ground of previous judgement of honourable Supreme Court regarding the Shreya Singhal case. Discuss the issue in Shreya Singhal case.** Competency Based Que

Ans. In the year 2012, in the matter of Shreya Singhal Vs. Union of India, a batch of writ petitions were filed under Article 32 of the Constitution of India raising an important question relating primarily to the Fundamental Right of free speech and expression guaranteed by Article 19 of the Constitution of India.

The immediate cause for concern in these petitions was Section 66 A of the Information Technology Act of 2000. The petitioners argued for the following

- The wordings of the section were too wide and ambiguous leading to misuse.
- Most of the terms used in the section had not been specifically defined under the act.
- The section restricted the right to free speech and expression prescribed under Article 19(1)(a) of the Constitution of India.

On 24th March, 2015, the Supreme Court declared Section 66 A of the IT Act, 2000 unconstitutional for being violative of Article 19(1)(a) of the Constitution of India.

3. In the case of Shreya Singhal Vs. Union of India (2012), the petitioners challenged the Constitutional validity of Section 66 A of the IT Act, 2000, arguing that it restricted the right to free speech and expression. Examine the key arguments raised by the petitioners and the implications of the section on individual freedoms.

Discuss how the section's vague terminology contributed to its misuse and the potential consequences of such a provision on the Fundamental Rights guaranteed under Article 19(1)(a) of the Constitution of India.

Ans. The petitioners in Shreya Singhal Vs. Union of India (2012) argued that Section 66 A of the IT Act, 2000, was unconstitutional as it restricted the right to free speech and expression guaranteed under Article 19(1)(a) of the Constitution of India. They contended that the section's wide and ambiguous terminology, such as 'grossly offensive' and 'menacing information', led to its misuse and arbitrary application. The petitioners also pointed out that the section's vagueness allowed for subjective interpretation, which could result in the suppression of legitimate online expression. The implications of such a provision were far-reaching, as it could stifle online dissent and creativity. The case highlighted the need for clear and specific legislation to balance individual freedoms with the need to regulate online content. Ultimately, the Supreme Court struck down Section 66 A as unconstitutional, upholding the Fundamental Right to free speech and expression.

SELF ASSESSMENT TEST

Objective Type Questions

1. In India, electronic governance is dealt with by............... .

   (a) IT Act (b) IPC (c) CrPC (d) All of these

2. Which model law provides for equal treatment which is essential for enabling paperless communication and fostering efficiency in international trade?

   (a) UNCITRAL (b) UNHRC (c) Geneva Declaration (d) All of these

Very Short Answer Type Questions

3. Explain the need for cyber laws.
4. How has playing video games become a popular platform for cyber bullying?
5. What is the main purpose of the IT Act?
6. Define digital signature.

Short Answer Type Questions

7. Why is it important to have cyber laws in the current scenario?
8. 'The aims of cyber law in India is to facilitate filing of electronic records with the government'. Comment.
9. What was the need behind the evolution of UNCITRAL laws?
10. Discuss the application of the IT Act.

Long Answer Type Questions

11. Stealing user data including personal information is a type of a cyber crime. **Competency Based Que**

    (i) Identify the cyber crime as discussed in the above statement.

    (ii) Analyse any two categories of cyber crime.

    (iii) How cyber security protects the information from unauthorised access and use?

12. Discuss in detail the striking down of Section 66 A of the IT Act by the Supreme Court.
13. Why is the Shreya Singhal case important?

11

CHAPTER

The judiciary is the final authority in interpreting legal issues and Constitutional arrangements. The nature of democracy and development of the state depends upon how the legal system conducts itself to sustain the overall socio-economic and political environment.

YOUR STUDY GOALS

11.1 Indian Legal System and Judiciary
11.2 Role of Constitution and Impartiality of Judiciary
11.3 Establishment of Supreme Court
11.4 Establishment of High Courts
11.5 Subordinate Courts in India
11.6 Civil Court Structure

YOUR PRACTICE GOAL

- Objective Type Questions (31 Qs ; MCQs, A-R, Statements, Matching)
- Subjective Questions (12 VSAs, 11 SAs, 4 LAs)

Judiciary : Constitutional and Civil Courts

11.1 Indian Legal System and Judiciary

- The Indian legal system derives its authority from the **Indian Constitution** and is deeply rooted in the Indian political system.
- The presence of judiciary supports the concept of separation of powers in which the other two organs (Legislature and Executive) are different from it.
- In a Parliamentary democracy, the judiciary safeguards the interest of the citizens by not allowing the other organs to go beyond their role assigned in the Constitution.
- The Supreme Court of India is the logical and primary custode on of the Constitution of India, while also being its interpreter and guardian.
- Parliament enjoys the authority to amend the Constitution and Supreme Court has the authority to examine those Constitutional amendments.

Judicial System in India

- India is a Parliamentary democracy having a federal Constitution system.
- Parliamentary democracy works at the **Union and State level.**

- There is **direct participation** of the legislature and the executive, especially in the making of law.
- The Indian Constitution has not provided for a dual system of courts.
- There is a single integrated system of courts for the union as well as the states which administers both union and state laws.
- **Dr. B.R. Ambedkar**, the architect of the Indian Constitution gave his support for establishing **one single integrated judiciary** in the Constituent Assembly which is capable of providing remedies in civil, criminal and Constitutional law matters.
- Thus, India has a unified judicial system with the Supreme Court at the apex.
- There are High Courts below the Supreme Court and under each High Court, there exists a system of subordinate courts.

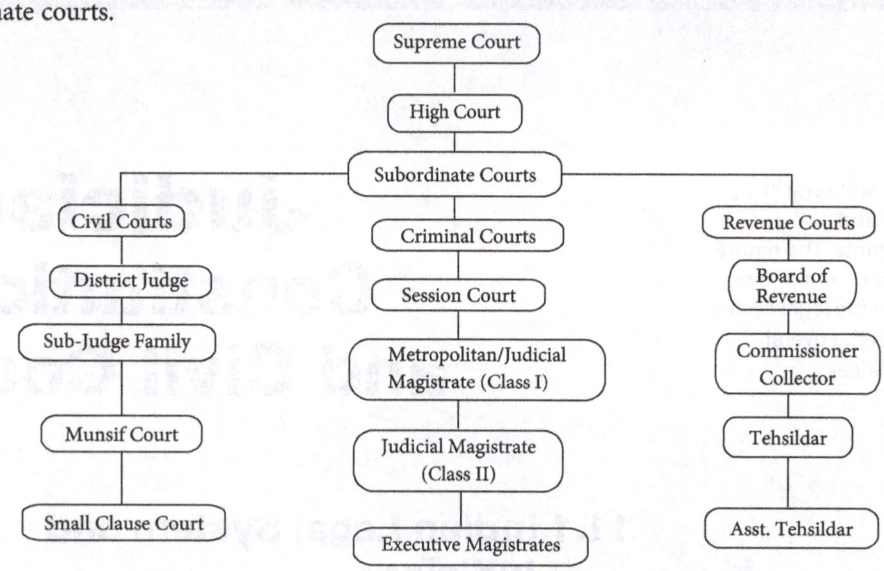

▲ *Structure and Hierarchy of the Courts in India*

11.2 Role of Constitution and Impartiality of Judiciary

Constitution of Judiciary

- The judiciary in India is an extension of the British Legal System.
- The Supreme Court is the apex body in the judiciary, followed by 25 High Courts, which supervise and govern numerous District Courts.

Role of Indian Judiciary

- Judiciary in India plays an important role in **interpreting** and **applying** the law and decide upon controversies between the citizens, the states and various other parties.
- It is the function of the courts to uphold the rule of law in the country and to safeguard civil and political rights.
- The courts have the function of safeguarding the supremacy of the Constitution by interpreting and applying its provisions and limiting the functioning of all authorities within the Constitutional framework.
- In a **federation**[1], the judiciary has a meaningful assignment, legally known as **Original Jurisdiction** of the Supreme Court of India.

1 **Federtion** It means union of states.

- It means to **decide controversies between** the constituent states as well as between the union and the states. A federal government is a legislative government, in which the powers are allocated between centre and states.
- The judiciary has been made the watchdog of Indian democracy.
- The role of the judiciary has been ever changing and has evolved based on the Constitution of India and the socio-economic needs of the country.

Judicial Review

- The judiciary has the power of judicial review. It implies that every part of the legislation passed by the Parliament is subject to judicial scrutiny by the Supreme Court of India.
- There are no specific provisions for this arrangement, however, the power and extent of judicial review has been clarified through judicial pronouncements.
- The Supreme Court of India has the power to abolish any part of legislation, aimed at amending the Constitution of India on two grounds
  (i) First, if the procedure prescribed under Article 368 is not followed
  (ii) Second, if the amending act seeks to violate one or more basic features of the Constitution.

Impartiality and Independence of the Judiciary

- 'Independence' and 'impartiality' are the most crucial concepts for any court.
- These two concepts are read together but they are separate and distinct.
- Impartiality refers to a state of mind and attitude of the court or tribunal in relation to the issues and the parties in a particular case.
- Independence refers to the state of mind or attitude and to a status or relationship to others, particularly to the executive branch of government that rests on objective conditions or guarantees.
- In simple words, impartiality means that the court is supposed to be neutral and not biased towards any party.
- On the other hand, independence means the freedom to act in the right manner without any constraint from any other organ of the government.
- The Constitution of India has ensured independence of the judiciary through a number of provisions. These provisions are
  - Subscribing to an oath or affirmation.
  - Providing security of tenure for judges by ensuring that judges cannot be removed except through a special impeachment procedure.
  - Retirement at the age of 65 years for judges of Supreme Court and 62 for judges of High Court, which is significantly higher than the retirement age in other public services.
  - Protection of privileges, allowances, perks and **emoluments**[2] by charging them to the Consolidated Fund of India.
  - The power to punish for their contempt.
  - Not being subject to discussion in a legislature for their conduct in judicial matters, etc.

Judges Standards and Accountability Act

- It has been reported that the Government of India has initiated various measures to introduce reforms in the judiciary.
- It has proposed to enact a new law, 'the Judges Standards and Accountability Act', which seeks to introduce greater accountability in judiciary.

2 **Emoluments** It is the returns arising from office or employment usually in the form of compensation or prerequisites.

Quick Test 1

1 Which organs of the government get direct participation in the making of law?
2 Why Dr. B.R. Ambedkar gave his support to one single integrated judiciary?
3 On what basis has the role of the judiciary evolved?
4 State any one provision through which independence of the judiciary has been ensured.

11.3 Establishment of Supreme Court

- After India attained independence in 1947, the Constitution of India came into being on 26th January, 1950.
- There was a smooth transition from the Federal Court to the Supreme Court of India (SCI).
- **Justice Hiralal J. Kania** became the first Chief Justice of India.
- The original Constitution of India proposed a Supreme Court with **a Chief Justice** and **seven** puisne[3] judges, while empowering the Parliament to increase the number of judges.
- Subsequently, the Parliament has the power to increase the number of judges of Supreme Court.
- The judges generally sit in smaller benches of twos or threes.
- They form larger benches of five or more only when required to do so or to settle a difference of opinion or controversy.

Appointment of Judges of Supreme Court

- The judges of the Supreme Court are appointed by the President of India.
- The Constitutional provisions regarding the appointment of a judge is that only those persons can be appointed as a judge of the Supreme Court who
  - are citizens of India.
  - have been the judge of a High Court or of two or more courts in succession at least for five years.
  - have been an advocate of a High Court or of two or more such courts in succession at least for ten years.
  - is a **distinguished jurist** in the opinion of the President.
- However, most of the appointments to the Supreme Court have been made from sitting judges or Chief Justices of High Courts.
- The judiciary enjoys considerable powers in the appointment of judges to the higher Constitutional Courts.
- According to **Article 124 (4)**, the President has the power to remove the judges if a motion is passed by a special majority of each House of Parliament, on the basis of proved misbehaviour or incapacity to discharge their duties.

Jurisdictions of Supreme Court

Supreme Court has a three fold jurisdiction

As a Federal Court

Supreme Court exercises **exclusive** jurisdiction over matters of dispute between

- The Central Government and one or more states.
- The Central Government and one or more states on one side and some states on the other.

3 Pulsne It is a term used to denote a judge of a superior court inferior in rank to Chief Justices.

As an Appellate Court

- Supreme Court can hear appeals against the judgements of the High Courts on civil, criminal and Constitutional matters.
- The Supreme Court also has a very wide appellate jurisdiction under **Article 136**, as it can grant special leave to appeal from any judgement, decree, determination or sentence or order against any court or Tribunal in India.
- The Supreme Court also hears a number of statutory appeals (appeals allowed under different legislations).
- The appellate jurisdiction of Supreme Court in different cases is
  - (i) Appeal in Constitutional Matters Under **Article 132 (1)** of the Constitution of India, an appeal can be made to the Supreme Court from any judgement of a High Court in civil, criminal or other proceedings if the High Court under **Article 134-A** certifies that the case involves a substantial question of law regarding the interpretation of the Constitution.
  - (ii) Appeal in Civil Cases Under **Article 133** of the Constitution of India, an appeal can be made to the Supreme Court from any judgement in civil proceeding of a High Court only if High Court under **Article 134-A** certifies that
    - the case involves a substantial question of law of general importance.
    - in the opinion of the High Court, such question needs to be decided by the Supreme Court.
  - (iii) Appeal in Criminal Cases Under **Article 134** of the Constitution of India, an appeal can be made to the Supreme Court from any judgement of a High Court in a **criminal** proceeding. This appeal can be in **two** ways, which are without a certificate of High Court and with a certificate of the High Court.

    An appeal can be made without the certificate if
    - (a) The High Court has reversed an order of acquittal of an accused person on appeal and sentenced him to death.
    - (b) The High Court has withdrawn any case from any subordinate court before it for trial and has convicted the accused person in such trial and sentenced him to death.

Under Advisory Jurisdiction

- The Supreme Court has advisory jurisdiction under **Article 143** in matters specifically referred to it by the President of India.
- According to Article 143, the President may refer any question for the advisory opinion of the court, if he/she thought that the question is of such a nature and public importance that it is beneficial to obtain the opinion of the Supreme Court upon it.
- After such hearing, the Supreme Court may report its opinion to the President.
- The Supreme Court laid down following principles related to its advisory jurisdiction in **re Kerala Education Bill Case** (1958).
  - (a) The Supreme Court has the choice to refuse to express any opinion on the question submitted to it.
  - (b) The President is responsible to decide what question should be referred to the court and if he/she does not entertain any serious doubt on the other provisions, it is not for any party to say that doubts arise also out of them.
  - (c) The advisory opinion of the Supreme Court is **not binding** on courts because it is not a law within meaning of **Article 141**.
- However, in re Special Court Bill Case (1979), the Supreme Court decided that its advisory jurisdictions are binding on all courts in the territory of India.

- It also decided that under **Article 143**, the Supreme Court is under duty to give its advisory opinion if questions referred to it are not indefinite and are of political nature.
- The Parliament has the **power to extend the jurisdiction** of the Supreme Court but **cannot reduce it**.
- According to **Article 141** of the Indian Constitution, a law declared by the Supreme Court shall be binding on all the courts within the territory of India.

Original Jurisdiction of Supreme Court

- The Supreme Court has a concurrent original jurisdiction with the High Courts for the enforcement of Fundamental Rights under **Article 32**.
- These are in the nature of the **writs** of Habeas Corpus, Mandamus, Prohibition, Certiorari and Quo-Warranto.
- These writs make the Supreme Court a **protector and guarantor** of Fundamental Rights.
- The Supreme Court has the power to declare a law passed by the legislature as invalid, if it violates the Fundamental Rights.
- Thus, the Supreme Court serves as the guardian of Fundamental Rights.

Role of Supreme Court in Disputes relating to Distribution of Power

- Disputes usually arise between the governments relating to distribution of power and function between them.
- Thus, a mediator is required to examine laws to see whether they fall within the allotted legislative domain of the enacting legislature.
- This function is usually performed by the judiciary.
- In this connection, the Supreme Court of India uses the following principles of interpretation of law
  - Doctrine of pith and substance
  - Doctrine of severability
  - Doctrine of colourable legislation
  - Doctrine of basic structure

Doctrine of Pith and Substance

- It states that when there is a question of determining whether a particular law relates to a particular subject, the court looks into the substance of the matter.
- This principle is applied when the law made by the legislature is trespassed by other legislatures.
- In order to determine the true character of a law, one must consider the enactment, objectives, scope and effect of the provisions of that law.

Doctrine of Severability

- It separates repugnant (contradictory or violative) provisions of law from others that are Constitutional.
- The **violating part** of any provision of a law is declared unconstitutional and invalid, but the remaining parts or provisions remain enforceable and valid.

Doctrine of Colourable Legislation

- It **prevents legislatures** from making laws that are not created according to the Constitutional restrictions.
- The whole doctrine of colourable legislation is based upon the principle that you cannot do indirectly what you are not allowed to do directly.

Doctrine of Basic Structure

- The phrase 'basic structure' was introduced first time in the **Golaknath case** (Golaknath Vs. State of Punjab, 1967).
- It was used by the Supreme Court only in **1973**.

- It means and includes those features of the Indian Constitution which are basic, require much more than the usual procedures to change them.
- It was decided in the **Kesavananda Bharati case** that any amendment which aims at violating the basic structure of the Constitution would be unconstitutional.
- Hence, every proposed amendment is subject to judicial scrutiny if it is aimed at violating the basic structure of the Constitution.
- The constituent elements of the basic structure include
  - the supremacy of the Constitution
  - republican and democratic form of government
  - secular character of the Constitution
  - separation of powers between the legislature, executive and the judiciary
  - the federal character of the Constitution
- Basic structure of the Indian Constitution cannot be altered or amended by the legislature.

Public Interest Litigation (PIL)

- The Supreme Court has assumed additional duties under a concept called 'Public Interest Litigation' (PIL).
- Under PIL, **any citizen can bring any matter of general importance** to the general public for consideration of the Supreme Court.
- If the Supreme Court finds that the executive has been failing to perform its duties, it passes the required directions to the concerned authorities in government.

Important Case Laws of Supreme Court

State of Maharashtra Vs. F.N. Balsara

- The state of Maharashtra passed a law **putting a cap**[4] on the maximum amount of liquor (both domestic and imported) that could be held by any dealer/wholesaler.
- The petitioner, F.N. Balsara, was aggrieved by this law and challenged it in the Supreme Court as the law was putting a cap on quantity of imported liquor which was a topic in union list and hence State Government was incompetent to make such a law.
- The state government asserted that the purpose of law was to regulate consumption of liquor in the state and not regulation of import and export. The cap was on both domestic and foreign liquor.
- The question before to court was that the law made by State Government was valid or violative of Article 246?

Decision

- The Supreme Court decided in this case that when judging the validity of any law, the act should be read as a whole to get its essence.
- The essence of law is reglation of liquor consumption in a state, which is a topic in the state list and hence the law is valid.

Balaji Vs. State of Mysore

- The Mysore Government introduced reservations to the extent of 51 per cent under **Article 16** of the Constitution.
- This was challenged in the Supreme Court as being violative of **Article 14**.
- The government asserted that it did not make reservations under Article 14 but made them only under Article 16.
- Constitutional validity of the Mysore governments' order on reservation.

4 Putting a cap It means to establish a clear upper limit on something.

Decision

- The Supreme Court decided in this case that a law made should be legal under all provisions.
- By resorting to one provision only, the government cannot ignore another provision by applying the doctrine of colourable legislation.
- By applying doctrine of severability, the court upheld 49 per cent of reservations but invalidate the excess reservation of 2 per cent.

Quick Test 2

1 Which institution of India is the logical and primary custodian of the Constitution?
2 Name the threefold jurisdiction of Supreme Court.
3 Under which article of the Constitution of India, an appeal can be made to the Supreme Court.
4 What is PIL?

11.4 Establishment of High Courts

- The High Court stands at the **head of the judiciary in a state.**
- The institution of the High Court dates back to 1862 when High Courts were established at Calcutta, Bombay and Madras under the **Indian High Court Act, 1861.**
- In course of time, other High Courts have also been established.
- According to **Article 214**, there shall be a High Court for each state.
- There are currently **25 High Courts** in India.
- There is a High Court for each of the states, except
  - Mizoram, Arunachal Pradesh and Nagaland which have the High Court of Assam at Guwahati as their common High Court.
  - Haryana which has a common High Court (at Chandigarh) with Punjab.
  - Goa which is under Bombay High Court.
- The maximum part of the work of the High Courts consists of appeals from lower courts and writ petitions under **Article 226 and 227** of the Constitution of India.
- Apart from writ petitions, any civil or criminal case which does not fall within the purview of the subordinate courts of that state, due to lack of economic or territorial jurisdiction, can be heard by the High Court of that state.
- Some other matters or issues may also be heard by the High Court as part of its original jurisdiction, if the law laid down by the legislature provides to that effect.

Jurisdictions of High Courts

- The High Courts enjoy civil as well as criminal, ordinary as well as extraordinary and general as well as special jurisdiction.
- They enjoy original jurisdiction in respect of **testamentary**[5], matrimonial and guardianship matters.
- Original jurisdiction is conferred on the High Courts under various laws.
- They enjoy extraordinary jurisdiction under Article 226 to issue various writs.
- Each High Court has **supervisory**[6] power over subordinate courts under it.
- Each High Court, being a court of record (under Article 215) enjoys the power to punish for its contempt as well as its subordinate courts.

5 **Testamentary** It means relating to or bequeathed or appointed through a will.
6 **Supervisory** It means the power to monitor the acts of inferiors.

11.5 Subordinate Courts in India

- The subordinate courts, at district and lower levels, have almost similar structure all over the country with slight variation. They deal with civil and criminal cases in accordance with their respective jurisdictions.
- The two branches of judicial system, **civil** and **criminal,** are bifurcated at the lowest stage.
- The **Munsiff's Courts** are the lowest civil courts. Subordinate Judges are above the Munsiffs.
- The District Judge hears first appeals from the decisions of Subordinate Judges and also from the Munsiffs (unless they are transferred to a Subordinate Judge). He possesses **unlimited original jurisdiction**, both civil and criminal.
- Appeals can be made from the District Court to the High Court.
- The **District and Sessions Judge** is the highest judicial authority (civil and criminal) in the district since the enactment of the Code of Criminal Procedure, 1973 (CrPC). The criminal trials are conducted exclusively by Judicial Magistrates.
- The Chief Judicial Magistrate is the head of the criminal courts in a district. In metropolitan areas, there are Metropolitan Magistrates.

Appointment of Subordinate Judges

- The subordinate judiciary in each district is headed by a District and Sessions Judge.
- The usual designations on the civil side are District Judge, Additional District Judge and Civil Judge.
- The designations on the criminal side are Sessions Judge, Additional Sessions Judge, Chief Judicial Magistrate, Judicial Magistrate, etc.
- The District Judges are appointed by the Governor in consultation with the High Court of that particular state.
- According to **Article 233,** to become eligible for the position of a District Judge, a person shall not be in Government Service and should have at least seven years experience at the bar.
- The appointment of persons other than District Judges to the judicial service of a state shall be made by the Governor in accordance with rules made thereunder.
- According to **Article 234,** the State Public Service Commission and the High Court have to be consulted in the matter of such appointments.

Types of Jurisdiction

Jurisdiction means the **extent of power** of a court to consider law suits and applications. The types of jurisdiction in subordinate courts are

- **Territorial Jurisdiction** The physical area or local limits within which a court exercises its jurisdiction is known as territorial jurisdiction.
- **Pecuniary Jurisdiction** Jurisdiction defined on the basis of **money claims** that can be heard by a court is known as pecuniary jurisdiction.
- **Original Jurisdiction** The power of a court to hear and try a case for the first time is known as original jurisdiction.
- **Appellate Jurisdiction** The power of the court to hear appeals from decisions of a lower court is known as appellate jurisdiction.
- **Jurisdiction as to Subject Matter** This jurisdiction is defined on the basis of types of cases that can be heard by a court, e.g., family law, criminal law, etc.

11.6 Civil Court Structure

- Civil cases are those which are **not criminal in nature.** The Civil Court decides disputes relating to property, breach of contracts, wrongs committed in money transactions, minor omissions, etc. These are categorised as **civil wrongs** and are subject to a civil process.
- The Civil Courts administer justice by considering the nature of the wrong done.
- Civil wrongs are redressed before civil courts by granting orders or by payment of damages or compensation to the aggrieved party.

Civil Process and Functioning of Civil Courts

- The CPC regulates the functioning of civil courts.
- The Code of Civil Procedure, 1908 (CPC) is a procedural law.
- It is intended to regulate the procedure to be followed by civil courts.
- The first Uniform Code of Civil Procedure was enacted in 1859.
- The objective of the Code is to consolidate and amend the laws relating to procedure of civil judicature.
- CPC lays down the following
  - Procedure of filing a civil case
  - Powers of court to pass various orders
  - Court fees and stamps involved in filing of a case
  - Rights of the parties to a case (plaintiff and defendant)
  - Jurisdiction and parameters of civil courts functioning
  - Specific rules for proceedings of a case
  - Right of appeals, review or reference
- The CPC can be divided into two parts
  - The main body of the CPC containing **158 sections.**
    - The sections deal with matters of a **substantive**[7] **nature** laying down the general principles of jurisdiction.
    - The body of the CPC containing sections is fundamental and cannot be amended except by the legislature.
  - The **First Schedule, containing 51 Orders and Rules**, relates to the **procedure**[8] and the method, manner and mode in which the jurisdiction may be exercised. The First Schedule of the CPC, containing orders and rules can be amended by High Courts.

Res Sub Judice and Res Judicata in Code of Civil Procedure, 1908

- Res judicata refers to **matters already decided** whereas res sub-judice applies to **matters pending** in a court of law.
- Res sub judice (**Sec 10** of Code of Civil Procedure, 1908) implies that if a subject matter is pending in a court of law for decision between the parties, any other court is barred from considering that case as long as the first suit is going on.

  For example, 'X' files a case for negligence in service against 'Y', his employee. While this suit is pending, he also files another suit for claiming accounts from his employee. The subsequent suit is stayed as the matter is res sub-judice.
- Res judicata (**Sec 11** of Code of Civil Procedure, 1908) literally means a thing which has been decided.

7 Substantive laws means the statutory laws which define and determine both the rights and obligations of the citizens to be protected by the law.
8 Procedural laws prescribes the means of enforcing rights or providing redress of wrongs.

- This doctrine is based on the principle of **finality of litigation** and conclusiveness of a decision.
- It is founded on the principle of justice, equity and good conscience.

  For example, 'X' sues 'Y' for breach of contract. The suit gets dismissed. 'X' now files a suit for damages for breach of contract. The suit for damages is **barred** as it is res judicata.

Common Legal Terminologies

Term	Meaning
Plaintiff	Person who files the civil case against another.
Defendant	Person against whom the case has been filed.
Plaint	Document filed by the plaintiff containing his version of the case.
Written Statement	Reply to the plaint, filed by the defendant.
Appellant	One who files the appeal.
Respondent	Other party against whom appeal has been filed.
Prosecution	A person or group of people who try to show that somebody is guilty of a crime in a court of law.
Defence	A person or group of people who try to show that the defendant is not guilty of a crime in a court of law.
Application	Document seeking an urgent instant relief. It can be filed by the plaintiff or the defendant. It can be filed with the plaint/written statement or even in between the proceedings. An application is always filed under a plaint (after a case has been filed).
Interim	It means in between the proceedings. (An interior order is a temporary decision made by a judge.)
Arrested and Accused Person	When a person is arrested by the police during investigation merely on the basis of suspicion that he/she has committed an offence, the person is known as an arrested person. Arrest of a person does not necessarily amount to conviction. When solid evidence is gathered against an arrested person and a trial is initiated against the person, the person becomes an accused.

Quick Test 3

1. Mention the act under which the High Courts were established at Calcutta, Bombay and Madras.
2. What do you understand by the Munsiff Court?
3. How many years of experience is required to become a District Judge?
4. Mention any two features of the Code of Civil Procedure (CPC), 1908.
5. Identify the term which is based on the principle of 'finality of litigation'.

Mind Map

JUDICIARY: CONSTITUTIONAL AND CIVIL COURTS

1 Indian Legal System and Judiciary

Foundation
- Rooted in the **Indian Constitution**.
- Reflects the principle of **separation of powers** among Legislature, Executive and Judiciary.

Role in Democracy
- Acts as a guardian of **citizens' rights**.
- Ensures the Constitution's supremacy.

Structure
- Unified judiciary with the **Supreme Court** at the apex, followed by High Courts and subordinate courts.
- No dual system of courts; a single integrated system administers both union and state laws.

2 Role of Constitution and Impartiality of Judiciary

Constitutional Role
- Judiciary interprets and applies laws, safeguarding civil and political rights.
- Ensures all authorities operate within Constitutional limits.

Independence and Impartiality
- **Independence** Judges act free from executive and legislative interference.
- **Impartiality** Judges maintain neutrality in cases.

Provisions Ensuring Independence
- Security of tenure and special impeachment procedures.
- **Retirement Age** 65 years for Supreme Court judges, 62 years for High Court judges.
- Privileges, emoluments, and protection against contempt of court.

3 Supreme Court of India

Establishment
- Transitioned from the Federal Court in 1950.
- Justice Hiralal J. Kania: First Chief Justice of India.

Composition
- Initially, Chief Justice and seven puisne judges; Parliament empowered to increase the number of judges.

Appointment
- Judges appointed by the President based on specific qualifications.
- **Removal** Requires special majority in Parliament (Article 124).

Jurisdiction

Original Jurisdiction
- Concurrent with High Courts to enforce Fundamental Rights (Article 32).
- Writs include Habeas Corpus, Mandamus, Prohibition, Certiorari, Quo-Warranto.

Appellate Jurisdiction
- Hears appeals from High Courts on civil, criminal and Constitutional matters (Articles 132–134).
- Special leave under Article 136.

Advisory Jurisdiction
- Provides opinions on matters referred by the President (Article 143).

4 High Courts in India

Historical Background
- Established under the **Indian High Courts Act, 1861** (Calcutta, Bombay, Madras).
- Governed by Article 214.

Jurisdiction
- Supervisory powers over subordinate courts.
- Original jurisdiction in testamentary, matrimonial and guardianship matters.
- Extraordinary jurisdiction under Article 226 to issue writs.

5 Subordinate Courts

Structure
- Includes District and Sessions Courts, Civil and Criminal Courts.
- **Munsiff's Courts** Lowest civil courts.
- **District Judge** Highest authority in a district.

Appointment
- District judges appointed by the Governor in consultation with the High Court.
- **Eligibility** Minimum seven years at the bar (Article 233).

Jurisdictions
- **Territorial** Defined geographical areas.
- **Pecuniary** Monetary claims within specified limits.
- **Subject-Matter** Family law, criminal law, etc.

6 Key Doctrines Used by Judiciary

- **Doctrine of Pith and Substance** Focuses on the substance of law when determining its validity.
- **Doctrine of Severability** Separates unconstitutional provisions from valid ones.
- **Doctrine of Colourable Legislation** Prevents legislatures from bypassing Constitutional restrictions.
- **Doctrine of Basic Structure** Fundamental principles like Constitutional supremacy, secularism, and separation of powers cannot be altered (Kesavananda Bharati case).

7 Judicial Review

- Power to examine and invalidate laws violating Fundamental Rights or the Constitution.
- Ensures legislation adheres to Constitutional provisions.
- Protects democratic principles and rights of citizens.

8 Public Interest Litigation (PIL)

Legal mechanism enabling citizens to approach the judiciary on matters of public importance.

Impact
- Strengthens accountability of government bodies.
- Expands access to justice for marginalised communities.

9 Civil Court Procedures

Code of Civil Procedure (CPC), 1908 Regulates the functioning of civil courts.

Divided into
- **Substantive Sections** General principles of jurisdiction.
- **Schedules** Procedural aspects like filing, orders and appeals.

Key Legal Doctrines
- **Res Sub Judice** Bars multiple suits on the same matter.
- **Res Judicata** Prevents re-litigation of decided matters.

CBSE TEXTBOOK Folder

1. Answer the following questions briefly

(i) What are the two grounds on which the Supreme Court can strike down a legislation aimed at amending the Constitution?

(ii) What were the principles laid down by the Supreme Court regarding advisory jurisdiction of the Supreme Court in (a) re Kerala Education Bill case (1958), (b) re Special Court Bill case (1979)?

(iii) Give the Constitutional provisions regarding the appointment of a judge to the Supreme Court.

(iv) Write a short note on the Code of Civil Procedure, 1908.

(v) What is jurisdiction? Explain any two types of jurisdiction.

Ans. (i) The two grounds on which the Supreme Court can strike down a legislation aimed at amending the Constitution are

(a) if they are violative of the Fundamental Rights

(b) if they violate the basic structure of the Constitution

(ii) (a) In re Kerala Education Bill case (1958), the Supreme Court laid down the following principles

- The Supreme Court has the choice to refuse to express any opinion on the question submitted to it.
- The President is responsible to decide what question should be referred to the court and if she does not entertain any serious doubt on the other provisions, it is not for any party to say that doubts arise also out of them.
- The advisory opinion of the Supreme Court is not binding on courts because it is not a law within meaning of Article 141.

(b) In re Special Court Bill case (1979), the Supreme Court held that its advisory jurisdiction is binding on all courts in the territory of India. It also held that under Article 143, the Supreme Court is under duty to give its advisory opinion if questions referred to it are not indefinite and of political nature.

(iii) The Constitutional provisions regarding the appointment of a judge is that only those persons can be appointed as a judge of the Supreme Court who

- are citizens of India and have been the judge of a High Court or of two or more courts in succession at least for five years.
- have been an advocate of a High Court or of two or more such courts in succession at least for ten years.
- is a distinguished jurist in the opinion of the President.

(iv) The Code of Civil Procedure, 1908 (CPC) is a procedural law. It is intended to regulate the procedure to be followed by civil courts.

The objective of the code is to consolidate and amend the laws relating to procedure of civil judicature.

CPC lays down the following

- Procedure of filing a civil case
- Powers of court to pass various orders
- Court fees and stamps involved in filing of a case
- Rights of the parties to a case (plaintiff and defendant)
- Jurisdiction and parameters of civil courts functioning
- Specific rules for proceedings of a case
- Right of appeals, review or reference

(v) Jurisdiction refers to the power of the courts to consider law suits and applications.

Two types of jurisdictions are

(a) **Territorial Jurisdiction** The physical area or local limits within which a court exercises its jurisdiction is known as territorial jurisdiction.

(b) **Pecuniary Jurisdiction** Jurisdiction defined on the basis of money claims that can be heard by a court is known as pecuniary jurisdiction.

2. Explain the appellate jurisdiction of the Supreme Court of India.

Ans. The appellate jurisdiction of Supreme Court in different cases is

- **Appeal in Constitutional Matters** Under Article 132 (1) of the Constitution of India, an appeal can be made to the Supreme Court from any judgement of a High Court in civil, criminal or other proceedings if the High Court under Article 134-A certifies that the case involves a substantial question of law regarding the interpretation of the Constitution.
- **Appeal in Civil Cases** Under Article 133 of the Constitution of India, an appeal can be made to the Supreme Court from any judgement in civil

proceeding of a High Court only if High Court under Article 134-A certifies that

- the case involves a substantial question of law of general importance.
- in the opinion of the High Court such question needs to be decided by the Supreme Court.

- **Appeal in Criminal Cases** Under Article 134 of the Constitution of India, an appeal can be made to the Supreme Court from any judgement of a High Court in a criminal proceeding. This appeal can be in two ways which are without a certificate of High Court and with a certificate of the High Court.

3. Mr. Ranjeet Sahay, a journalist, was unhappy over a judgement given by the Supreme Court. In his TV programme, he openly criticised the judgement given by the Supreme Court. Is it allowed? Can the Supreme Court take any action against him? If so, mention the relevant article. **Competency Based Que**

Ans. Yes, the Supreme Court can take action against him under the Article 129 of the Constitution which gives the Supreme Court to punish for its contempt. As the dignity of the Judiciary is of the utmost importance, the Supreme Court has the power to punish any person for the contempt of court.

Exam Pattern Questions

Objective Type Questions

Multiple Choice Questions (MCQs)

1. Ratikant and Gauri were in discussion about the India Laws and Philosophy. Ratikant has said that Indian legal system is one of the oldest in the world. The Indian legal system derives its authority from the .... **Competency Based Que**

(a) Modern Hindu Law (b) Uniform Civil Code
(c) Constitution of India (d) Parliament of India

2. Tajvinder taught his daughter about the importance of separation of power. The presence of .... substantiates the theory of separation of powers.

(a) judiciary (b) executive
(c) legislature (d) All of these

3. Who is the final authority in interpreting legal issues and Constitutional arrangements?

(a) Parliament (b) Executive
(c) President of India (d) Judiciary

4. Harishanker is a vigilant social workers. He gives advices and gives information about the significance of Fundamental Rights of every individual. Who acts as the guardian of Fundamental Rights? **Competency Based Que**

(a) Parliament (b) Supreme Court
(c) High Court (d) President

5. Who has the authority to amend the Constitution?

(a) President (b) Supreme Court
(c) Parliament (d) High Court

6. Which of the following is TRUE about the authority to remove a judge of the Supreme Court of India?

(a) President, after consulting the Chief Justice of India.
(b) Parliament, by passing a motion with a special majority.
(c) Prime Minister, after consultation with the Cabinet.
(d) The Judiciary itself, in cases of misbehaviour or incapacity.

7. Which of the following organs of the government is not involved in the process of appointment of judges?

(a) Executive
(b) Legislature
(c) Judiciary
(d) None of the above

8. Which of the following is NOT a part of the Supreme Court of India's jurisdiction only?

(a) Exclusive original jurisdiction in disputes between the Government of India and states.
(b) Appellate jurisdiction for civil, criminal and Constitutional matters.
(c) Advisory jurisdiction in matters referred by the President of India.
(d) Jurisdiction over cases related only to Fundamental Rights violations.

9. The National Judicial Appointment Commission (NJAC) Act, 2014 was Constitutional amendment that amend to replace the collegium system for appointing judges with a more transparent and accountable process. **Competency Based Que**

Which of the following statement is true about the appointment of High Court and Supreme Court judges in India?

(a) The President has sole discretion to appoint judges.
(b) The Chief Justice of India has a veto power over appointments.
(c) The NJAC Act, 2014 is currently in force.
(d) Consultation with the Chief Justice of India is mandatory.

10. Who has the power to deal with cases that are arising between the union and the states and among the states themselves?

(a) Civil Court (b) District Court
(c) Supreme Court (d) High Court

11. Who among the following has the power to issue writs for enforcement of Fundamental Rights?

(a) Supreme Court (b) High Court
(c) President (d) Both (a) and (b)

12. Indrani, a law faculty in the Vedanta College, in her class lecture explained about the advisory jurisdiction of the Apex Court. It is quite unique, as provided by the Indian Constitution. Which of the following Articles contains advisory jurisdiction of the Supreme Court?

Competency Based Que

(a) Article 133 (b) Article 143
(c) Article 134 (d) Article 152

13. Article .... of the Constitution of India provides that the law declared by Supreme Court is binding on all courts.

(a) 141 (b) 129 (c) 121 (d) 137

14. The President of India seeks to obtain a legal opinion on a particular issue.

Identify which of the following article falls under this issue?

(a) Article 128 (b) Article 129
(c) Article 141 (d) Article 143

15. .... separates repugnant provisions of a statute or law from others that are Constitutional.

(a) Doctrine of Pith and Substance
(b) Doctrine of Severability
(c) Doctrine of Colourable Legislation
(d) Doctrine of Basic Structure of the Constitution

16. The violating part of any provision of a statute is declared unconstitutional and void to the extent of such inconsistency, but the remainder remains enforceable and valid.

The above statement is related to

(a) Judicial Overreach
(b) Doctrine of Severability
(c) Doctrine of Basic Structure
(d) Judicial Review

17. The true object of the legislation or a statute, relates to a matter with the competence of the legislature which enacted it. In order to ascertain the true character of the legislation one must have regard to the enactment as a whole, to its object and to the scope and effect of its provisions.

The above statements are related to

(a) Doctrine of Pith and Substance
(b) Doctrine of Severability
(c) Doctrine of Colourable Legislation
(d) Doctrine of Basic Structure

18. In which of the following cases has the phrase 'basic structure' been introduced for the first time?

(a) Kesavananda Bharati case (b) Maneka Gandhi case
(c) Golaknath case (d) Minerva Mill case

19. Any citizen can bring any matter of general importance to the general public for consideration of the Supreme Court. If the Supreme Court finds that the executive has been failing in due discharge of its duties, it passes the required directions to the concerned authorities in government. The above statements implies

Competency Based Que

(a) Judicial Overreach (b) Public Interest Litigation
(c) Judicial Review (d) None of these

20. Disputes relating to property, breach of contracts, wrongs committed in money transactions, minor omissions are categorised as ....

(a) Civil wrongs (b) Court of law
(c) Munsiff's Court (d) None of these

21. An appeal from the decision of the Munsiff's Court is filed before the ....

(a) High Court (b) Supreme Court
(c) District Court (d) Both (a) and (c)

22. Consider the following statement regarding the role and function of judiciary and choose the correct option.

I. Parliament in India plays an important role in interpreting and applying the law.

II. Courts have an additional function of safeguarding the supremacy of the Constitution by interpreting.

Codes

(a) Only I (b) Only II
(c) Both I and II (d) None of these

23. Arrange the following cases in chronological order.

I. President's Rule case
II. Golaknath Vs. state of Punjab
III. In Re Kerala Education Bill case
IV. In Re special Court Bill Case

Choose the correct option

(a) III, IV, I, II (b) III, II, IV, I
(c) IV, II, III, I (d) IV, III, I, II

24. Match the following

Column-I	Column-II
A. Supreme Court's judgements binding on all courts	1. Article 136
B. Appellate jurisdiction of Supreme Court	2. Article 141
C. Removal of judges	3. Article 32
D. Writ jurisdiction of Supreme Court	4. Article 124(4)

Codes

	A	B	C	D
(a)	2	1	4	3
(b)	1	2	4	3
(c)	2	1	3	4
(d)	1	2	3	4

25. Match the following

Column-I	Column-II
A. Plaintiff	1. Person who files the civil case against another.
B. Defendant	2. Person against whom the case has been filed.
C. Plaint	3. Document filed by the plaintiff containing his version of the case.
D. Written Statement	4. Reply to the plaint, filed by the defendant.

Codes

	A	B	C	D
(a)	2	1	4	3
(b)	1	2	4	3
(c)	2	1	3	4
(d)	1	2	3	4

26. **Statement I** The Re-special Court Bill case (1932) was a landmark judgement of the Supreme Court of India that dealt with the Constitutionality of the special courts bill, 1992.

Statement II The Supreme Court held that the Re-special Court Bill case was Constitutional as it did not violated the principles of separation of powers and delegated excessive power to the executive.

Choose the correct option

(a) Both the Statement are correct.
(b) Both the Statement are incorrect.
(c) Statement I is correct, but statement II is not correct.
(d) Statement I is not correct, but statement II is correct.

Assertion-Reason Questions

Directions (Q. Nos. 27-31) In the questions given below there are two statements. Read the statements and choose the correct option.

Codes

(a) Both A and R are true and R is the correct explanation of A.
(b) Both A and R are true, but R is not the correct explanation of A.
(c) A is true, but R is false.
(d) A is false, but R is true.

27. **Assertion** (A) The Indian legal system derives its authority from the Constitution of India and is deeply embedded in the Indian political system.

Reason (R) Judiciary is the final authority in interpreting legal issues and Constitutional arrangements.

28. **Assertion** (A) The judiciary provides a mechanism for the resolution of disputes arising in any society between groups or individuals.

Reason (R) The Supreme Court has the original jurisdiction.

29. **Assertion** (A) The Constitution of India provides for a single integrated judicial system.

Reason (R) Supreme Court decisions are binding precedent for lower subordinate courts.

30. **Assertion** (A) The citizens of India are secure as far as Fundamental Rights are concerned.

Reason (R) The Supreme Court has concurrent jurisdiction with the High Courts to issue directions, orders and writs for enforcement of Fundamental Rights.

31. **Assertion** (A) 'Independence' and 'impartiality' are the most crucial concepts for any court.

Reason (R) 'Impartiality' refers to a state of mind and attitude of the court or tribunal in relation to the issues and the parties in a particular case.

Answers

1. (c) Constitution of India **2.** (a) judiciary
3. (d) Judiciary **4.** (b) Supreme Court
5. (c) Parliament
6. (b) Parliament, by passing a motion with a special majority.
7. (b) Legislature
8. (d) Jurisdiction over cases related only to fundamental rights violations.
9. (d) Consultation with the Chief Justice of India is mandatory.
10. (c) Supreme Court **11.** (d) Both (a) and (b)
12. (b) Article 143 **13.** (a) 141
14. (d) Article 143
15. (b) Doctrine of Severability
16. (b) Doctrine of Severability
17. (a) Doctrine of Pith and Substance
18. (c) Golaknath case
19. (b) Public Interest Litigation
20. (a) Civil wrongs **21.** (c) District Court
22. (b) Only II **23.** (b) III, II, IV, I
24. (a) 2 1 4 3 **25.** (d) 1 2 3 4
26. (d) Statement I is not correct, but Statement II is correct.
27. (b) Both A and R are true, but R is not the correct explanation of A.
28. (b) Both A and R are true, but R is not the correct explanation of A.
29. (a) Both A and R are true and R is the correct explanation of A.
30. (a) Both A and R are true and R is the correct explanation of A.
31. (b) Both A and R are true, but R is not the correct explanation of A.

Subjective Questions

Very Short Answer Type Questions

1. What do you understand by the term 'integrated judiciary'?

Ans. 'Integrated judiciary' means that the decisions of the Higher Courts of a State are binding on all its subordinate courts. The Supreme Court is the supreme of all courts and its decisions are binding on all.

2. Who is the supreme interpreter of the Constitution of India?

Ans. The Supreme Court is the supreme interpreter of the Constitution of India and the guardian of Fundamental Rights guaranteed by the Constitution. The Supreme Court also helps in maintaining uniformity of law throughout the country.

3. What do you understand by the term 'impartiality'?

Ans. Impartiality refers to a state of mind and attitude of the court or tribunal in relation to the issues and the parties in a particular case.

4. The President of India sought the advisory jurisdiction of the Supreme Court on a matter of public importance. Decide. Competency Based Que

(i) In which case was the advisory opinion of the Supreme Court declared to be binding on all Courts in India?

(ii) When is the Court under a duty to render advisory opinion?

Ans. (i) In re Special Court Bill case (1979), the Supreme Court held that its advisory jurisdiction is binding on all courts in the territory of India.

(ii) The Supreme Court under Article 143 is under duty to give its advisory opinion if questions referred to it are not indefinite and of a political nature.

5. What are the different kinds of writs mentioned under Article 32 of the Indian Constitution?

Ans. The Supreme Court has concurrent jurisdiction with the High Courts to issue directions, orders and writs for enforcement of Fundamental Rights (Article 32 of Constitution of India). These are in the nature of the writs of Habeas Corpus, Mandamus, Prohibition, Certiorari and Quo-Warranto.

6. State the principles of interpretation used by the Supreme Court.

Ans. The following are principles of interpretation of law which are used by the Supreme Court

(i) Doctrine of pith and substance
(ii) Doctrine of severability and
(iii) Doctrine of colourable legislation

7. What is the doctrine of colourable legislation?

Ans. Doctrine of colourable legislation prevents legislatures from making laws that are not created according to the Constitutional restrictions. The whole doctrine of colourable legislation is based upon the principle that you cannot do indirectly what you are not allowed to do directly.

8. Explain the concept of the doctrine of pith and substance.

Ans. Doctrine of pith and substance states that when there is a question of determining whether a particular law relates to a particular subject, the court looks into the substance of the matter. This principle is applied when the law made by the legislature is trespassed by other legislatures.

9. What is the doctrine of severability?

Ans. Doctrine of severability separates repugnant (contradictory or violative) provisions of law from others that are Constitutional. The violating part of any provision of a law is declared unconstitutional and invalid, but the remaining parts or provisions remain enforceable and valid.

10. 'The Supreme Court has assumed additional duties under a concept called Public Interest Litigation'. Explain PIL with regards to the statement. Competency Based Que

Ans. Under Public Interest Litigation (PIL), any citizen can bring any matter of general importance to the general public for consideration of the Supreme Court. If the Supreme Court finds that the executive has been failing to perform its duties, it passes the required directions to the concerned authorities in government.

11. What legal term refers to a civil wrong?

Ans. The legal term for a civil wrong is a tort. It occurs when a person's legal rights are violated. Disputes relating to property, breach of contracts, wrongs committed in money transactions, minor omissions, etc, are categorised as civil wrongs.

12. How can a person redress civil wrongs?

Ans. Civil wrongs are redressed before civil courts by granting orders or by payment of damages or compensation to the aggrieved party.

Short Answer Type Questions

1. In the entire world, the function of democracy highly relies upon the smooth functioning of the three organs of the government. If one organ fails or get paralysed then entire democracy can collapse. State the importance of the judicial organ of government in the Indian context. Competency Based Que

Ans. Judiciary plays an important role in providing/offering justice to people. It also performs the following functions

- The judiciary acts as the guardian of the Constitution by interpreting it in a proper manner as it can declare any law passed by legislature unconstitutional if it is inconsistent with the Constitution.
- The judiciary performs administrative functions by keeping check on the functioning of each court.
- The judiciary acts as the protector of Fundamental Rights in case of its violation and issues orders for its implementation.
- The judiciary performs legislative functions by giving judgements and making laws to fill up the gap between the legislature and society.

2. India has 'a single integrated judiciary'. Explain. Competency Based Que

Ans. The Indian Constitution has not provided for a dual system of courts. There is a single integrated system of courts for the union as well as the states which administers both union and state laws.

Dr. B.R. Ambedkar, the architect of the Indian Constitution, gave his support for establishing 'one single integrated judiciary' in the Constituent Assembly which is capable of providing remedies in civil, criminal and Constitutional law matters.

3. Geetu told her friend Jaspreet that Indian Constitution is much more flexible than that of the United States. However, she maintained that the basic structure of Indian Constitution cannot be changed or modified. Discuss the doctrine of basic structure of the Constitution. Competency Based Que

Ans. The phrase 'basic structure' was introduced in the Golaknath case (Golaknath Vs. State of Punjab, 1967) but it was only in 1973 that this phrase was used by the Supreme Court.

It means and includes those features of the Constitution which lay at its core and require much more than the usual procedures to change them.

It was held in the historic Kesavananda Bharati case that any amendment which aims at abrogating the basic structure of the Constitution would be unconstitutional. Hence, every proposed amendment is subject to judicial scrutiny if it is aimed at abrogating the basic structure of the Constitution.

Constituent elements of the basic structure include the supremacy of the Constitution, republican and democratic form of government, secular character of the Constitution, separation of powers between the legislature, executive and the judiciary and primarily the federal character of the Constitution.

4. Ishwar Sainath has been appointed as the new District Judge in Agra district. His father has advised him to work towards truth and justice, and one day he can be promoted to Supreme Court. Who is eligible to appoint the judges of the Supreme Court? Competency Based Que

Ans. The judges of the Supreme Court are appointed by the President of India.

The Constitutional provisions regarding the appointment of a judge is that only those persons can be appointed as a judge of the Supreme Court who

- are citizens of India and have been the judge of a High Court or of two or more courts in succession at least for five years.
- have been an advocate of a High Court or of two or more such courts in succession at least for ten years is a distinguished jurist, in the opinion of the President.

5. Raman believes that many judgements of the Supreme Court have been criticised on several occasions. However, the Supreme Court has always served as the guardian of Fundamental Rights. Elaborate. Competency Based Que

Ans. The Supreme Court has concurrent jurisdiction with the High Courts to issue directions, orders and writs for enforcement of Fundamental Rights. These are in the nature of the writs of Habeas Corpus, Mandamus, Prohibition, Certiorari and Quo-Warranto. These writs make the Supreme Court a protector and guarantor of Fundamental Rights. The idea is that in case of violation of a law or right, the court may issue directions for compliance with the Constitution.

Thus, the citizens of India are secure as far as Fundamental Rights are concerned. The Supreme Court has the power to declare a law passed by the legislature null and void if it violates the Fundamental Rights. It has exercised this power on several occasions. This shows how the Supreme Court has always served as the guardian of Fundamental Rights.

6. The Supreme Court of India also has advisory jurisdiction.

(i) Which article provides for advisory jurisdiction?

(ii) Briefly discuss the provision on advisory jurisdiction in the Constitution. Competency Based Que

Ans. (i) Article 143 provides for advisory jurisdiction.

(ii) The Supreme Court has advisory jurisdiction under Article 143 in matters specifically referred to it by the President of India.

According to Article 143, the President may refer any question for the advisory opinion of the court, if he/she thought that the question is of such a nature and public importance that it is beneficial to obtain the opinion of the Supreme Court upon it. After such hearing, the Supreme Court may report its opinion to the President.

7. Shanti Devi, an old aged widow was removed by her children from ancestral home. However, the lower court did not grant her any relief. Her brother advised her to move High Court. Write a short note on the establishment of High Courts. Competency Based Que

Ans. The High Court stands at the head of the judiciary in a state. The institution of the High Court dates back to 1862 when High Courts were established at Calcutta, Bombay and Madras under the Indian High Court Act, 1861.

In course of time, other High Courts have also been established. According to Article 214, there shall be a High Court for each state.

There are currently 25 High Courts in India. There is a High Court for each of the states, except

- Mizoram, Arunachal Pradesh and Nagaland which have the High Court of Assam at Guwahati as their common High Court
- Haryana which has a common High Court (at Chandigarh) with Punjab
- Goa which is under Bombay High Court

8. Discuss the concepts of res sub judice and res judicata.

Ans. Res sub judice (Sec 10 of Code of Civil Procedure, 1908) implies that if a subject matter is pending in a court of law for decision between the parties, any other court is barred from considering that case as long as the first suit is going on.

Res judicata refers to matters already decided (Sec 11 of Code of Civil Procedure, 1908). It means a thing which has been decided. This doctrine is based on the principle of finality of litigation and conclusiveness of a decision.

9. The phrase 'basic structure' was introduced in the Golaknath case (Golaknath Vs. State of Punjab, 1967) but it was only in 1973 that this phrase was used by the Supreme Court and it means and includes those features of the Constitution which lay at its core requiring much more than the usual procedures to change them. Competency Based Que

(i) What is 'basic structure'?

(ii) What constitutes the basic structure according to the Supreme Court?

Ans. (i) The 'basic structure' includes the feature of the Indian Constitution which cannot be amended or changed by the legislature.

(ii) Constituent elements of the basic structure include the supremacy of the Constitution, republican and democratic form of government, secular character of the Constitution, separation of powers between the legislature, executive and the judiciary and primarily the federal character of the Constitution.

10. Abhimanyu sues Yagavendra for breach of contract. The suit gets dismissed. Abhimanyu now files a suit for damages for breach of contract. Decide.
(i) Will the suit for damages be allowed?
(ii) Which concept has been applied in the given situation? Elaborate. **Competency Based Que**

Ans. (i) No, the suit for damages is barred by res judicata.
(ii) The concept of res judicata has been applied in the given situation. It is provided under Sec 11 of Code of Civil Procedure, 1908. It literally means a thing which has been decided.
This doctrine operates as a bar to the trial of a subsequent suit on the same cause of action between the same parties. It is based on the principle of finality of litigation and conclusiveness of a decision. It is founded on the principle of justice, equity and good conscience.

11. 'A', an Indian citizen, is 62 years old. He has been a High Court judge for 5 years and wants to become a judge of the Supreme Court. Decide. **Competency Based Que**
(i) What are qualifications prescribed in the Indian Constitution to become a Supreme Court judge?
(ii) Will 'A' be eligible to become a Supreme Court judge?

Ans. (i) The Constitutional provisions regarding the appointment of a judge is that only those persons can be appointed as a judge of the Supreme Court who
- are citizens of India, and have been the judge of a High Court or of two or more courts in succession at least for five years.
- have been an advocate of a High Court or of two or more such courts in sucession at least for ten years.
- is a distinguished jurist, in the opinion of the President.

(ii) Yes, 'A' will be eligible to become a Supreme Court judge.

Long Answer Type Questions

1. Monica attended a group discussion in a company interview where various aspects of the Indian judiciary system were discussed. She has noticed that everyone has agreed upon the versatility of Indian judiciary. In this relation, discuss the functions of the judiciary in India. **Competency Based Que**

Ans. For answer refer to text under the heading Role of Indian Judiciary, on page no. 180 and 181.

2. Shekhar has explained to his friend Sameer how Supreme Court uses its jurisdiction over inter-state disputes or Union Vs. State disputes. Describe the various jurisdictions of the Supreme Court.

Ans. For answer refer to text under the heading Jurisdictions of Supreme Court, on page no. 182 and 183.

3. What is the Code of Civil Procedure? Explain its, composition.

Ans. The CPC regulates the functioning of civil courts. The Code of Civil Procedure, 1908 (CPC) is a procedural law. It is intended to regulate the procedure to be followed by civil courts.
The first Uniform Code of Civil Procedure was enacted in 1859.
The objective of the code is to consolidate and amend the laws relating to procedure of civil judicature.
The CPC can be divided into two parts
(i) The main body of the CPC containing 158 sections. The sections deal with matters of a substantive nature laying down the general principles of jurisdiction.
The body of the CPC containing sections is fundamental and cannot be amended except by the legislature.
(ii) The First Schedule, containing 51 orders and rules, relates to the procedure and the method, manner and mode in which the jurisdiction may be exercised.
The First Schedule of the CPC, containing orders and rules can be amended by High Courts.

4. 'X' files a case for negligence in service against 'Y', his employee. Whilst this suit is pending, he also files another suit for claiming accounts from his employee. **Competency Based Que**
(i) What happens to the subsequent suit?
(ii) Elaborate the concept discussed in (i).

Ans. (i) The subsequent suit is stayed as the matter is res sub judice.
(ii) For answer refer to text under the heading Res Sub Judice, on page no. 188 and 189.

SELF ASSESSMENT TEST

Objective Type Questions

1. .... of the Indian Constitution contains the writs provisions of the High Court.
   (a) Article 32 (b) Article 226 (c) Article 141 (d) Article 129
2. Which of the following statements is correct related to the eligibility to appoint a judge of the Supreme Court?
   (a) He has been a judge of a High Court or of two or more courts in succession at least for five years.
   (b) He has been an advocate of a High Court or of two or more such courts in succession at least for ten years.
   (c) He is a distinguished jurist, in the opinion of the President. However, most of the appointments to the Supreme Court have been made from sitting judges or Chief Justices of High Courts.
   (d) All of the above
3. Identify the writ that can be issued against any private individual.
   (a) Habeas Corpus (b) Certiorari (c) Prohibition (d) Quo-Warranto
4. Which among the following sections defines judgment?
   (a) Section 2 (2) (b) Section 2 (9) (c) Section 33 (d) Section 134

Very Short Answer Type Questions

5. Justice 'X' is a High Court Judge who is known for his bold decisions and independent decisions. He has a reputation for standing up to the government and corporate interests even if it means going against the popular opinion. How ever in a recent, Justice 'X' was heard making comments that suggested a bias towards a particular political party. What are the majar differences between independence and impartiality of judiciary? **Competency Based Que**
6. What are the two grounds on which the Supreme Court can strike down any piece of legislation?
7. Can the Supreme Court review its own judgment? Explain.
9. What is the classification of Code of Civil Procedure?
8. Discuss the jurisdiction of the High Court.
10. Discuss the hierarchy of the civil court in India.

Short Answer Type Questions

11. Write a short note on Supreme Court and Judicial review.
12. Discuss the appellate jurisdiction of the Supreme Court.
13. Explain the meaning of the term 'basic structure'. When was it first used?
14. 'The High Court stands at the head of the judiciary in a state'. Comment. **Competency Based Que**
15. Write a short note on the Code of Civil Procedure, 1908.

Long Answer Type Questions

16. How has the Constitution of India ensured the independence of the judiciary?
17. 'Jurisdiction means the extent of power of a court to consider law suits and applications'. Explain the types of jurisdication.

12

CHAPTER

Structure and Fuctioning of Criminal Courts in India

Administration of criminal justice is carried out through Magistrate Courts and Sessions Courts.
The Indian Penal Code (IPC), 1860 together with other penal laws constitutes India's substantive criminal law.

YOUR STUDY GOALS

12.1 Operating Criminal Laws
12.2 Categories of Criminal Courts in India
12.3 Types of Offences
12.4 Criminal Investigation Prosecution and First Information Report (FIR)
12.5 Role and Function of Police
12.6 Other Courts in India

YOUR PRACTICE GOAL

- Objective Type Questions (27 Qs ; MCQs, A-R, Statements, Matching)
- Subjective Questions (14 VSAs, 9 SAs, 3 LAs)

12.1 Operating Criminal Laws

- The IPC is inspired from the English criminal law. However, it cannot be self-operative. A Code of Criminal Procedure, 1861 was enacted as a sequel to the IPC.
- The 1861 Code was repealed after which a new Code of Criminal Procedure **(CrPC)**, 1973 was enacted to carry out the process of the administration and enforcement of the substantive criminal law.
- The CrPC also controls and regulates the working of the machinery set-up for the investigation and trial of the offences.
- In addition to the CrPC, the **Indian Evidence Act of 1872** was enacted to guide the process of investigation and trial.

12.2 Categories of Criminal Courts in India

The criminal court system in India is structured in a tiered system with each level having its own jurisdiction and authority.

Courts of Session

- As per Section 9 of CrPC, the Sessions Court is established by the State Government for every sessions division.

- The court is presided over by a judge, appointed by the High Court of that particular state.
- The High Court may also appoint Additional Sessions Judges and Assistant Sessions Judges in this court. It has the power to impose any sentence including capital punishment.

Courts of Judicial Magistrates

- As per **Section 11** of CrPC, Courts of **Judicial Magistrate of the First Class and the Second Class** shall be established in every district (except a metropolitan area).
- The number of courts and their location that shall be established may be specified by the State Government after consultation with the High Court, through a notification.
- Courts of Judicial Magistrate of First Class are at the **second lowest level** of the Criminal Court structure in India.
- According to **Section 15** of the CrPC, a Judicial Magistrate is under the general control of the Sessions Judge and is subordinate to the Chief Judicial Magistrate.
- According to **Section 29** of the CrPC, a Judicial Magistrate of First Class **can pass a sentence** of imprisonment for a term not exceeding three years or impose a fine not exceeding ₹ 10,000, or both.
- The court at the lowest level is called Judicial Magistrate of the Second Class.
- This court is competent to try the case if the offence is punishable with imprisonment for a term not exceeding one year or with fine not exceeding ₹ 5,000, or both.
- The First Class Magistrate is competent to try offences punishable with imprisonment for a term not exceeding three years or with fine up to ₹ 10,000.

- In states such as Kerala, the Second and the First Class Magistrate Courts have been unified.

- The **Assistant Sessions Judge** is competent to impose punishments of up to ten years imprisonment and impose any fine.
- The **Sessions Judge** can impose any punishment authorised by law but the sentence to death passed by him should be subject to the High Court's final decision.

Chief Judicial Magistrate

- In every district (except a metropolitan area), the High Court shall appoint a Judicial Magistrate of the First Class to be the Chief Judicial Magistrate.
- A Chief Judicial Magistrate may impose a sentence except
  - sentence of death
  - imprisonment of life
  - imprisonment for a term exceeding seven years
- A Chief Judicial Magistrate shall be subordinate to the Sessions Judge.
- Every other Judicial Magistrate shall subject to the general control of the Sessions Judge, and be subordinate to the Chief Judicial Magistrate.

Metropolitan Magistrates

- The Courts of Metropolitan Magistrates were created by **Section 16** of the Code of Criminal Procedure.
- The Court of Chief Metropolitan Magistrate and those of the Additional Chief Metropolitan Magistrates were created by **Section 17** of the code.
- **Section 18** of the code also provided for Special Metropolitan Magistrates.

  The towns having population exceeding one million could be declared metropolitan areas.

- Metropolitan Magistrate is under the general control of the Sessions Judge and is subordinate to the Chief Metropolitan Magistrate.
- Courts of Metropolitan Magistrates were created by Section 16 of the code.

Executive Magistrates

- In every district and metropolitan area, the **State Government** may appoint persons (as many as it thinks fit) to be Executive Magistrates and appoint one of them to be the **District Magistrate.**
- These officers work in **tandem**[1] with the police to maintain law and order in the city. They are also responsible for some judicial acts like traffic challans, registration of documents (like sale deeds, wills, marriage certificates, birth and death certificates).
- They are known as **District Magistrates** (DM), **Sub Divisional Magistrate** (SDM), **Executive Magistrate, Special Executive Magistrates.**

12.3 Types of Offences

Based on nature and gravity of offences, they can be classified into three different categories

Bailable and Non-bailable Offences

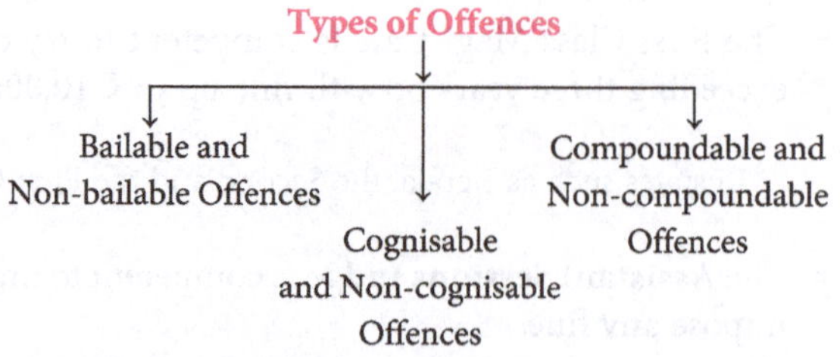

- There is no definition of 'bail' under CrPC.
- The objective of the bail is to **secure the physical appearance** of a person at the time of trial and at the time of sentence, if found guilty.
- According to the Supreme Court of India, bail covers release on one's own bond, with or without sureties.
- CrPC has classified all offences into 'bailable' and 'non-bailable' offences.
- According to the **First Schedule of Section 2(a)** of the CrPC, all serious offences, i.e. offences punishable with imprisonment for three years or more have been considered as non-bailable offences.
- This general rule can be suitably modified according to specific needs.
- If the offence is **non-bailable,** it does not mean that the person accused of such offence shall not be released on bail.
- Bail is not a matter of right, but only a privilege to be granted at the discretion of the court.
- If a person accused of a **bailable offence** is arrested or detained without warrant, he/she has the right to be released on bail (Section 436 of CrPC).
- The **power to cancel bail** has been given to the court and not to a police officer.
- The court which granted the bail can alone cancel it.

Anticipatory Bail

- **Section 438** of the CrPC enables the superior courts to grant anticipatory bail. An anticipatory bail can be applied for when the person has reason to believe that he/she may be arrested.
- An application for anticipatory bail can be made to the Sessions Court, the High Court or even the Supreme Court.
- However, normally the **Court of Sessions** would be **first approached** for grant of anticipatory bail.

1 **Tandem** It means group of two people or things that work together or are associated with each other.

- The court may consider the following aspects when considering an application for anticipatory bail
  - the nature and gravity of accusation.
  - the antecedents[2] of the applicant.
  - the possibility that the accused may escape from justice.
  - the accusation appears to be aimed at humiliating the applicant.

Cognisable and Non-cognisable Offences

- There is no test or criterion[3] given by the CrPC to determine cognisable or non-cognisable offences.
- However, the First Schedule of CrPC indicates that all offences punishable with imprisonment of **not less than three years** are taken as serious offences and are **treated as cognisable.**
- Offences such as murder, robbery, dacoity, rape and kidnapping are cognisable offences.
- Offence of bigamy (multiple marriages) is punishable with more than five years imprisonment but it has been included in the category of non-cognisable offences.
- The classification of offences as 'cognisable' and 'non-cognisable' is essentially intended to indicate whether the arrest in respect of an offence can be made with or without a warrant [Section 2 (c) and (l)]. The classification requires the need of immediate action in respect of every cognisable offence.
- However, in the case of non-cognisable offences, warrant is required for the arrest of the accused.

Compoundable and Non-compoundable Offences

- The offences in which the accused can come to an arrangement, where instead of being imprisoned the accused can pay a fine, are called compoundable offences.
- The most common example of this is where you get caught without a ticket on a bus or a train and have to pay a fine.
- In this case, the officer fining you is in fact compounding your offence.
- However, all the offences are not compoundable. It would not be desirable that murderers should be able to compound their offences.

Quick Test 1

1. Mention the new Code of Criminal Procedure which repealed the 1861 Code.
2. As per which Section of CrPC is the Session Court established by the State Government?
3. Why is the Judicial Magistrate of the Second Class known as the 'court at the lowest level'?
4. Mention any one power of Metropolitan Magistrate.
5. State ceny one example of compoundable offence.

12.4 Criminal Investigation Prosecution and First Information Report (FIR)

The investigation in a criminal case starts after an FIR or a private complaint is recorded.

First Information Report (FIR)

- FIR is the information recorded by the police officer on duty, given either by the aggrieved person or any other person, about the commission of **cognisable offence**.
- The statement of the informant as recorded under **Section 154** will be treated as the FIR.

---

2 Antecedents It means a person's ancestors, family and social background.

3 Criterion It means a principle or standard by which something may be judged or decided.

- The main objective of the FIR from the informant's perspective is to set the criminal law in motion (Hasib Vs. State of Bihar, AIR 1972 SC 283).
- The **police cannot refuse to register** the complaint.
- The power of police to lodge an FIR cannot be assumed by the Magistrate.
- If the police officer (incharge of police station) refused to record FIR of any person, then such person may send such information in writing by post to the **Superintendent of Police** concerned **[Section 154(3)]**.
- **Section 154** of the CrPC provides for the manner in which such information is to be recorded.

Some important facts about FIR are

- Information of cognisable offence can be given by any person to police having jurisdiction in the area where the commission of crime took place.
- **FIR is not a substantive piece of evidence.** It has to be duly proved by evidence. It can be **used as relevant fact** in order to prove the substantive issue.
- Police officers shall reduce such information in writing. Informant's signature must be obtained.
- Contents of such information should be **read over to informant** and must be entered in record by a police officer.
- Police officers shall **give a copy** of such information to the informant immediately.
- The **original FIR** must be sent to the Magistrate immediately.
- FIR must be made to the officer incharge of the police station. If a police officer refused to register an FIR, the aggrieved person can send such information to the Superintendent of Police by post.
- FIR is **to be made immediately** after the occurrence of an incident when the memory of the informant is fresh in his/her mind about the occurrence.
- Telephonic information from a person which discloses commission of the cognisable offence would also constitute FIR.
- The government has formulated the provisions of **Zero FIR** in adverse situations, in order to protect the rights of the people. According to this, the victim can file his/her complaint in **any police station** for any offence for a quick action and the case can be transferred to the concerned police station thereafter.

Information to the Police about Non-cognisable Offence

- According to **Section 155** of CrPC, if a person gives information about a non-cognisable offence to an officer in charge of a police station, the officer shall enter such information in a book prescribed for this purpose.
- The police officer has no further duty unless the Magistrate directs the police officer to investigate the case.
- Generally, non-cognisable offences are more or less considered as private criminal wrongs.
- No police officer shall investigate a non-cognisable case and have power to try such a case or commit the case for trial without the order of a Magistrate.
- In a situation where a criminal case consists of both cognisable and non-cognisable offences, the case shall be deemed to be a cognisable case even if the other offences are non-cognisable.

Private Complaint

- Private complaint basically means a complaint which is directly filed by the complainant in the court.
- The private parties can conduct the cases through their own lawyers in respect of private complaints. **Section 138** of the Negotiable Instruments Act, 1881 mentions private complaint.
- The Magistrate has the power to take cognisance of such private complaint under **Section 190(1) (a)** of the CrPC.

Process of Investigation, Inquiry and Trial

- For every offence under the Indian Penal Code, 1860, the CrPC elaborates the procedure to be followed in every investigation, inquiry and trial.
- It divides the procedure to be followed for administration of criminal justice into **three stages,** namely **investigation, inquiry** and **trial**.

Investigation

- The objective of investigation is to collect evidence for the purpose of any inquiry or trial.
- Investigation is a **preliminary stage** enquiry conducted by the police.
- It usually starts after the recording of the First Information Report (FIR) in the Police Station (Sections 154-155 of the Code).
- After an FIR is made, the police officer incharge or any subordinate officer is duty-bound to proceed to the spot to investigate the facts and circumstances of the case.
- If necessary, the officer can take measures for the discovery and arrest of the offender.
- Investigation primarily consists of finding facts and circumstances of the case. It includes
  - The collection of evidence.
  - Inspection of the place of occurrence of the crime.
  - Ascertainment (verification) of facts and circumstances.
  - Discovery of any article or object used for the commission of the crime.
  - Arrest of the suspected offender.
  - Interrogation and examination of various persons including the accused and taking of their statements in writing.
  - Search of places or seizure of things considered necessary for the investigation, and considered to be material at the time of the trial, etc.
- Investigation is completed when a police officer submits the report to the Magistrate.
- After that, the matter is brought before the Magistrate or the concerned court.
- If the police officer finds that no offence has been committed, the officer reports the fact to the Magistrate who drops the proceedings.
- If the Magistrate is of a contrary opinion, the matter is taken up for further inquiry.

Inquiry

- Inquiry is the second stage of the process where in a Magistrate seeks to find out whether the accused should be committed to the sessions or discharged.
- **Section 2 (g)** of the CrPC defines inquiry as every inquiry which is conducted by a Magistrate or court and which is not a trial.
- If **no prima facie[4] case is made out,** the Magistrate **dismisses the complaint** or discharges the accused. If a prima facie case is **made out**, the Magistrate **frames the charges**.

Trial

- Trial is **judicial determination** of a person's guilt or innocence.
- Trial is a proceeding which involves examination and determination of the cause by a judicial tribunal.
- It ends in **conviction or acquittal** (release) of the accused.
- In cases of serious offences such as murder or dacoity, the trial takes place before the Sessions Court.

4 Prima facie It is something based on the first impression.

- In India, the system of criminal trial proposed by the CrPC is the **adversary system** based on the accusatorial method.
- In this system, the prosecutor representing the state (or the people) accuses the defendant (the accused person) of committing some crime and tries to prove it, and the defendant's lawyer argues for the defendant's release.
- The accused person is presumed to be innocent unless his/her guilt is proved beyond reasonable doubt (presumption of innocence).

- Presumption of innocence is one of the fundamental principles of the Indian criminal justice system.

Warrant, Summons and Summary Trials

Under the CrPC, criminal trials have been categorised into two types. These are

(i) **Warrant case Section 2(x)** of the CrPC defines 'warrant-case' as a case relating to an offence punishable with death, imprisonment for life or imprisonment for a term exceeding two years.

- The CrPC provides for two types of procedure for the trial of warrant cases by a Magistrate. These are
  (a) those instituted upon **a police report** (Sections 238-243)
  (b) those instituted otherwise than on police report, i.e. upon complaints (Sections 238-243)
- With respect to cases instituted on police report, the Magistrate is required to **discharge** the accused person upon consideration of the police report and attached documents if there is no legal basis for the case.
- With respect to the cases instituted otherwise than on police report, the Magistrate hears the prosecution and takes the evidence. If there is no case, the accused is **discharged.**
- If the accused is not discharged, the Magistrate holds regular trial after framing the charge, etc.
- With respect to offences punishable with death, life imprisonment or imprisonment for a term exceeding seven years, the trial is conducted in a Sessions Court after being committed or forwarded to the court by a Magistrate.

(ii) **Summons Case** It relates to all offences punishable with **imprisonment not exceeding two years.**

- With respect to summons cases, there is no need to frame a charge. The court gives substance of the accusation called **notice** to the accused when the person appears in execution of the summons.
- The **court has the power** to convert a summons case into a warrant case if the Magistrate thinks that it is in the interest of justice.

Summary Trial

- Summary trial is the name given to trials where cases are disposed of speedily and the procedure is simplified.
- In a summary trial, only **small offences are tried** and complicated cases are reserved for summons or warrant trial.
- **Sections 260 to 265** of the Code of Criminal Procedure, 1973 (CrPC) deal with the provisions relating to summary hearings.

Distinct Stages in a Criminal Trial

A criminal trial will have the following district stages.

Framing of Charge or Issuance of Notice

- Framing the charges and issuing notice indicates the beginning of a trial.
- At this stage, the judge is required to examine the evidence for the purpose of finding out whether or not a prima facie case against the accused has been made out or not.
- If the materials placed before the court discloses the commission of an offence, the court frames the charge and proceeds with the trial.
- On the other hand, if the judge considers that there is no sufficient ground for proceeding, the judge discharges the accused and records the reasons for doing so.
- The charge shall be read out and explained to the accused and the accused shall be asked whether he/she pleads guilty of the offence charged with or claims to be tried.

Recording of Prosecution Evidence

- After the charge is framed, the prosecution is asked to examine its witnesses before the court. The statement of witnesses is taken under an oath.
- This is called **examination-in-chief**. The accused has a **right to cross-examine** all the witnesses presented by the prosecution.
- **Section 309** of the CrPC provides that the proceeding shall be held as quickly as possible.
- It also provides that when the examination of witnesses has once begun, the same shall be continued day-to-day until all the witnesses in attendance have been examined.

Statement of Accused

- The court has powers to examine the accused at any stage of inquiry or trial for the purpose of obtaining any explanation against incriminating circumstances appearing before it.
- However, it is mandatory for the court to **question the accused** after examining the evidence of the prosecution if it incriminates the accused.
- This examination is **without oath** and before the accused enters a defence.
- The purpose of this examination is to **give the accused a reasonable opportunity** to explain the incriminating facts and circumstances in the case.

Defence Evidence

- After taking the evidence for the prosecution, examining the accused and hearing the prosecution and defence, if the judge considers that there is no evidence of the accused committing the offence, then the judge is required to record the **order of acquittal** (release).
- However, when the accused is not acquitted for absence of evidence, a defence must be entered and evidence must be given in its support.
- The accused may produce witnesses who may be willing to depose in support of the defence.
- The accused is also a competent witness under the law.
- The accused may apply for the issue of process for attendance of any witness or the production of any document or thing. The witnesses produced by the accused are cross-examined by the prosecution.
- The accused person is entitled to present evidence after recording of the statement.
- Most accused persons do not lead defence evidence. One of the major reasons for this is that India follows the **common law system** where the burden of proof is on the prosecution and the degree of proof required in a criminal trial is beyond reasonable doubt.

Final Arguments

- This is the final stage of the trial.
- The provisions of the CrPC provide that when examination of the witnesses for the defence is complete, the prosecutor shall sum up the prosecution case and the accused is entitled to reply.

Judgement

- After conclusion of arguments by the prosecutor and defence, the judge pronounces his judgement in the trial.
- After hearing the prosecution and the defence, if the judge considers that there is **no evidence** for the accused committing the offence with which he/she is charged, the judge can record an order of **acquittal.**
- If the judgement is one of conviction and the judge does not proceed to invoke the **benevolent**[5] provisions of the Probation of Offenders Act, 1958 and the judge shall hear the accused on the question of the appropriate sentence.
- Under the CrPC, an accused can also be withdrawn from prosecution at any stage of trial with the permission of the court. If the accused is allowed to be withdrawn from prosecution prior to framing of charge, it will be considered as a discharge.
- On the other hand, if such withdrawal is allowed **after framing of charge,** it will be treated as an **acquittal.**

Accused and the Right against Self-incrimination

The right against self-incrimination is provided under **Article 20(3)** of the Constitution of India. It states that **'No person accused of an offence shall be compelled to be a witness against himself'**.

However, the following restrictions are placed on the exercise of this right

- Only such documents/statements are protected which are within the personal knowledge of the accused. The records that are maintained in fulfillment of a statutory requirement may not be protected. Further, the accused can be required to give a handwriting sample/blood/DNA sample as they are not within the 'personal knowledge' of the accused.
- **Article 20(3)** protects the accused only against being compelled to produce documents. The Supreme Court has ruled that a search and seizure is not considered to be 'compulsion to produce', and is thus outside the protection of Article 20(3).
- Summons under **Section 91 of CrPC** cannot be issued to an accused person. However, a general search warrant under **Section 93(1)(c)** CrPC is not protected under Article 20(3) of the Constitution of India.

Prosecution

- Prosecution is conducted by the Director of Public Prosecution through public prosecutors.
- **Section 225** of the CrPC provides that every trial before a Sessions Court shall be conducted by a public prosecutor.

Arrest and Rights of the Arrested Person

- Under **Section 57/167** of the CrPC, the accused must be produced before a Magistrate **within 24 hours of arrest.**
- If the investigation cannot be concluded within this time, a Magistrate may order for the remand of the arrested person to police custody under **Section 167(3)** of the CrPC.
- The rights of the arrested person are
  (i) Under **Section 50** of the CrPC, the arrested person is **to be informed** of the particulars of the offence or any other grounds for arrest.
  (ii) If a person is arrested without a warrant for an offence which is bailable, he/she **must be informed that** he/she is **entitled to be released on bail.**

5 **Benevolent** It means well meaning and kindly.

(iii) Under **Section 50A** of the CrPC, the arrested person is entitled to inform a person nominated by him about the arrest. The Supreme Court has also recognised the right of the arrested person to have access to a lawyer in the case of **Nandini Satpathy (1978) and D.K. Basu (1997).**

(iv) Under **Section 51** of the CrPC, a person who is arrested **may be searched** and a list shall be prepared of any articles found from the person.
- This personal search memo is especially important if there is any allegation of recovery of incriminating material from the accused person.

(v) Under **Section 54** CrPC, the arrested person can request to be examined by a medical practitioner.

(vi) Under **Section 53 and 53A** of the CrPC, the police can send the arrested person for medical examination.

Age and Criminal Liability

Age	Whether liable
Upto 7 years	No criminal liability.
7-12 years	Mental agility of child is assessed.
12-16 years	A child is liable under the Juvenile Justice Act.
16-18 years	Child is liable under Juvenile Justice Act but if the crime committed is **heinous in nature,** then the child **can be tried as an adult under IPC** and other criminal legislations.
Above 18 years	**Criminally liable** under IPC and other criminal legislations.

Doctrine of Autrefois Acquit and Autrefois Convict

- Autrefois acquit means **previously aquitted** and autrefois convict means **previously convicted.**
- According to this doctrine, if a person is tried and acquitted or convicted of an offence, he/she cannot be tried again for the same offence or on the same facts for any other offence.
- This doctrine has been substantially incorporated in the **Article 20(2)** of the Constitution of India and is also mentioned in **Section 300** of CrPC.
- Instances where the accused may raise certain preliminary requests, the court does not have the jurisdiction or competence to try the accused person or is restricted by the limitation of time prescribed by law.

12.5 Role and Functions of Police

- Police force comes under the State Government and the executive realm[6].
- The **Police Act, 1861** describes the structure and function of the police in general.
- The police are expected to be the most accessible, interactive and dynamic organisation of any society.
- Their roles, functions and duties in the society are natural to be varied, and diversified on the one hand; and complicated, knotty and complex on the other.
- The twin roles, which the police are expected to play in a society are **maintenance of law** and **maintenance of order.**
- However, the consequences of these two duties are numerous, which result in making a large inventory of duties, functions, powers, roles and responsibilities of the police organisation.
- The role and functions of the police in general are
  - to uphold and enforce the law impartially, and to protect life, liberty, of the public.
  - to promote and preserve public order.

6 Realm It means a field or domain of activity or interest.

- to protect internal security, to prevent and control terrorist activities, breaches of communal harmony, militant activities and other situations affecting internal security.
- to protect public against acts of vandalism[7], violence or any kind of attack.
- to prevent crimes, and reduce the opportunities for the commission of crimes through their own preventive action and measures, as well as by aiding and co-operating with other relevant agencies.
- to accurately register all complaints brought to them by a complainant or his representative.
- to register and investigate all cognisable offences coming to their notice through such complaints or otherwise.
- to create and maintain a feeling of security in the community.
- to provide, (as first responders) all possible help to people in situations arising out of natural or man-made disasters.
- to collect intelligence relating to matters affecting public peace, and all kind of crimes including social offences, communalism, extremism, terrorism and other matters relating to national security, and disseminate the same to all concerned agencies.
- to take charge (as a police officer on duty) of all unclaimed property and take action for their safe custody and disposal according to the procedure prescribed.
- to train, motivate and ensure welfare of police personnel.

Quick Test 2

1. Write any one objective behind the First Information Report (FIR).
2. Whose order is prerequisite for a police officer to investigate a non-cognisable cases?
3. Name the section which deal with the provisions relating to summary hearing.
4. Mention the section under CrPC which provides every trial in a Session Court shall be conducted by a public prosecutor.
5. Which act describes the structure and function of the police in India?

12.6 Other Courts in India

In addition to the civil and criminal courts, there are a number of **special courts and tribunals established in India** to govern specific areas of law. A few such examples include

- Motor Accidents Claims Tribunal (MACT)
- Rent Control Tribunal
- Railway Claims Tribunal
- Debt Recovery Tribunal (DRT)
- Income Tax Appellate Tribunal (ITAT)
- National Green Tribunal (NGT)
- Central Excise and Service Tax Appellate Tribunal (CESTAT)

The purpose of these special courts is to bring efficiency in the judiciary by lowering the case burdens on the traditional courts and providing a quick relief to the parties involved.

Family Courts

- The **Family Courts Act, 1984** in India was enacted on **14th September, 1984.**
- It provides for the establishment of family courts with a view to **promoting conciliation** and secure speedy settlement of disputes relating to marriage and family affairs.
- The Family Courts in India deal with matters related to the following
  - Matrimonial relief which includes nullity of marriage, judicial separation, divorce, restitution of conjugal rights.

7 Vandalism It means willful or malicious destruction or damage of public or private property.

- The validity of marriage and matrimonial status of the person, property of the spouses or any of them.
- The legitimacy of any person, guardianship of a person or custody of any minor, maintenance including the proceedings under the CrPC.

- The objective of the Family Courts Act is to take family and marital disputes away from the overcrowded and congested traditional courts of law, and bring them to **congenial** (pleasant) and sympathetic surroundings.
- The aim of this is 'conciliation' (ending the argument) between the family members and not **'confrontation'**.
- The emphasis is on a non-adversarial method of resolving family disputes.
- The act states that a party is not entitled to be represented by a lawyer without the express permission of the court.
- However, generally the court grants this permission and usually it is a lawyer which represents the parties.
- The most unique aspect regarding the proceedings before the family court is that they are first referred to conciliation and if the conciliation proceedings fail to resolve the issue successfully, the matter will be taken up for trial by the court.
- The conciliators are professionals who are appointed by the court.
- Once a final order is passed, the aggrieved party has an option of filing an appeal before the High Court.
- Such appeal is to be heard by a bench consisting of **two judges**.

Administrative Tribunals

- The Parliament enacted the **Administrative Tribunals Act, 1985** with a view to ease the congestion of pending cases in various High Courts and other courts in the country. It came into force in **July, 1985**.
- Central Administrative Tribunals were established in **November, 1985** at Delhi, Mumbai, Calcutta and Allahabad.
- Currently, there are **17 Benches** of the Tribunal located throughout the country with **33 Division Benches.**
- In addition, circuit sittings are held at Nagpur, Goa, Aurangabad, Jammu, Shimla, Indore, Gwalior, Bilaspur, Ranchi, Pondicherry, Gangtok, Port Blair, Shillong, Agartala, Kohima, Imphal, Itanagar, Aizawl and Nainital.
- The Central Administrative Tribunal (CAT) has been established for deciding disputes with respect to
  - recruitment and conditions of service of persons appointed to public services.
  - posts in connection with the affairs of the union or other local authorities within the territory of India or under the control of Government of India.
  - The conditions of service of Chairman, Vice-Chairmen and members are governed by the provisions of the Central Administrative Tribunal (Salaries and Allowances and conditions of service of Chairman, Vice-Chairmen and members), Rules, 1985, as amended from time to time.

Quick Test 3

1. Mention any two special courts and tribunals established in India to govern specific areas of law.
2. In which year was Family Courts Act enacted?
3. What is the objective of Family Courts Act?
4. Why has the CAT been established?
5. How many benches of Administrative Tribunals are located throughout the country?

Mind Map

STRUCTURE AND FUNCTIONING OF CRIMINAL COURTS IN INDIA

1 Introduction to Criminal Justice System

Purpose

- Administration of justice through **Magistrate** and **Sessions Courts.**
- Guided by **Indian Penal Code (IPC), 1860, Code of Criminal Procedure (CrPC), 1973** and **Indian Evidence Act, 1872.**

2 Criminal Laws Operating in India

Indian Penal Code (IPC), 1860

- Defines substantive criminal law.

Code of Criminal Procedure (CrPC), 1973

- Governs the investigation, trial, and punishment of crimes.

Indian Evidence Act, 1872

- Guides admissibility and evaluation of evidence.

3 Categories of Criminal Courts

Sessions Court

- Established under Section 9 of CrPC.
- Presided over by a Sessions Judge.

Powers

- Can impose any sentence, including capital punishment.
- Death sentences require High Court confirmation.

Judicial Magistrates

- Established under Section 11 of CrPC.

Categories

First Class Magistrate Can impose imprisonment up to 3 years or a fine up to ₹10,000.

Second Class Magistrate Can impose imprisonment up to 1 year or a fine up to ₹5,000.

Chief Judicial Magistrate Authority to impose imprisonment up to 7 years.

- Subordinate to Sessions Judge.

Metropolitan Magistrates

- Created under Section 16 of CrPC.
- Chief and Additional Chief Metropolitan Magistrates oversee operations.

Executive Magistrates

- Appointed by the state for maintaining law and order.
- Includes District Magistrates (DM) and Special Executive Magistrates.

4 Types of Offences

Bailable Vs. Non-Bailable

- **Non-bailable** Serious crimes requiring judicial discretion for bail.
- **Bailable** Right to bail granted for minor offenses.

Anticipatory Bail Allows a person to seek bail from a court before he/she is arrested.

Cognisable Vs. Non-Cognisable

- **Cognisable** Police can arrest without warrant (e.g., murder, robbery).
- **Non-Cognisable** Requires prior Magistrate approval. (e.g. trespassing, misbehaviour).

Compoundable Vs. Non-Compoundable

- **Compoundable** Settled between parties (e.g., defamation).
- **Non-Compoundable** Requires court adjudication (e.g., murder).

5 Criminal Procedures

First Information Report (FIR)

- Recorded under Section 154 of CrPC.
- Sets the criminal law process in motion.
- Police cannot refuse to register an FIR.
- Provisions for **Zero FIR** Filing at any police station regardless of jurisdiction.

Investigation

- Conducted after FIR registration.
- Includes evidence collection, interrogation and arrests.

Inquiry

- Preliminary examination by a Magistrate.
- Determines whether charges should be framed.

Trial

- Judicial determination of guilt or innocence.

Types

- **Warrant Trial** For serious crimes.
- **Summons Trial** For minor crimes.
- **Summary Trial** Simplified for petty offenses.

6 Rights of the Accused

Against Self-Incrimination

- Protected under Article 20 (3) of the Constitution.

Fair Trial

- Accused presumed innocent until proven guilty.
- Legal representation and opportunity to cross-examine witnesses.

Arrest Rights

- Right to be informed of charges.
- Right to bail for bailable offenses.
- Right to consult a lawyer (recognised in cases like D.K. Basu).

7 Role of Police

- Enforce law and maintain order.
- Prevent crime through proactive measures.
- Investigate offenses and ensure community security.
- Facilitate disaster response and collect intelligence.

8 Special Courts and Tribunals

Examples

- Family Courts, National Green Tribunal, Debt Recovery Tribunal.

Purpose

- Relieve traditional courts and ensure efficient adjudication of specialised disputes.

9 Key Features of the Judiciary

- Ensures justice and Constitutional supremacy.
- Acts as a watchdog of Indian democracy.
- Provides remedies for civil, criminal and Constitutional grievances.

CBSE TEXTBOOK Folder

1. Discuss the three stages in the procedure for administration of criminal justice in India.

Ans. The procedure of administration of criminal justice in our country is divided into three stages namely investigation, inquiry and trial. The three terms denote three different stages of a criminal case. These are

(i) The first stage is reached when a police officer either by himself or under order of a Magistrate investigates a case. If the police officer finds that no offence has been committed, the officer reports the fact to the Magistrate who drops the proceedings. If the Magistrate is of a contrary opinion, the matter will be taken up for further inquiry.

(ii) In the second stage, an inquiry into the case by the Magistrate is done. If no prima facie case is made out, the Magistrate dismisses the complaint or discharges the accused. If a prima facie case is made out, the Magistrate frames the charges.

(iii) The third and final stage is reached when the charge is framed and the trial begins. The Magistrate may conduct the trial and may either convict the accused, or acquit him/her. In cases of serious offences, such as murder or dacoity the trial takes place before the Sessions Court.

2. Elaborate the six stages in a criminal trial.

Ans. The six stages in a criminal trial are given below

(i) **Framing of Charge or Issuance of Notice** Framing the charges and issuing notice indicates the beginning of a trial. At this stage, the judge is required to examine the evidence for the purpose of finding out whether or not a prima facie case against the accused has been made out or not.

(ii) **Recording of Prosecution Evidence** After the charge is framed, the prosecution is asked to examine its witnesses before the court. The statement of witnesses is taken under an oath. This is called examination in chief. The accused has a right to cross-examine all the witnesses presented by the prosecution.

(iii) **Statement of Accused** The court has powers to examine the accused at any stage of inquiry or trial for the purpose of obtaining any explanation against incriminating circumstances appearing before it. However, it is mandatory for the court to question the accused after examining the evidence of the prosecution if it incriminates the accused. This examination is without oath and before the accused enters a defence. The purpose of this examination is to give the accused a reasonable opportunity to explain the incriminating facts and circumstances in the case.

(iv) **Defence Evidence** After taking the evidence for the prosecution, examining the accused and hearing the prosecution and defence, if the judge considers that there is no evidence of the accused committing the offence, then the judge is required to record the order of acquittal (release). However, when the accused is not acquitted for absence of evidence, a defence must be entered and evidence must be given in its support.

(v) **Final Arguments** This is the final stage of the trial. The provisions of the CrPC provide that when examination of the witnesses for the defence is complete, the prosecutor shall sum up the prosecution case and the accused is entitled to reply.

(vi) **Judgement** After conclusion of final arguments by the prosecutor and defence, the judge pronounces his judgement in the trial. After hearing the prosecution and the defence, if the judge considers that there is no evidence for the accused committing the offence with which he/she is charged, the judge can record an order of acquittal.

3. Discuss the functions performed by police.

Ans. The role and functions of the police in general are

- to uphold and enforce the law impartially, and to protect life, liberty, of the public.
- to promote and preserve public order.
- to protect internal security, to prevent and control terrorist activities, breaches of communal harmony, militant activities and other situations affecting internal security.
- to protect public against acts of vandalism, violence or any kind of attack.
- to prevent crimes, and reduce the opportunities for the commission of crimes through their own preventive action and measures, as well as by aiding and co-operating with other relevant agencies.
- to accurately register all complaints brought to them by a complainant or his representative.
- to register and investigate all cognisable offences coming to their notice through such complaints or otherwise.

- to create and maintain a feeling of security in the community.
- to provide, (as first responders) all possible help to people in situations arising out of natural or man-made disasters.
- to collect intelligence relating to matters affecting public peace, and all kind of crimes including social offences, communalism, extremism, terrorism and other matters relating to national security, and disseminate the same to all concerned agencies.
- to take charge (as a police officer on duty) of all unclaimed property and take action for their safe custody and disposal according to the procedure prescribed.
- to train, motivate and ensure welfare of police personnel.

4. Ms. Anukriti went to the police station to get an FIR filed in relation to her chain snatching. The officer in charge of the police station was not available.

(i) Who is competent to file the FIR in absence of the officer in charge?

(ii) What if the officer in charge was present but refused to file the FIR? What remedy is available to Ms. Anukriti? **Competency Based Que**

Ans. (i) If the officer incharge of a police station is absent, than any other police officer on duty at the station is competent to file an FIR.

(ii) If Anukriti is aggrieved by a refusal on the part of the police officer in charge of the police station to record the information, she may send the substance of such information in writing by post to the Superintendent of Police concerned [Section 154(3)].

5. Varun is 9 years old. While playing with his friends, there was a quarrel amongst them and he ended up hitting one of the boys with a rock on the head. He is very young and lacks maturity to understand the gravity and consequences of his actions.

(i) Would Varun be punished for the Criminal Act?

(ii) Discuss the relation between age and criminal liability. **Competency Based Que**

Ans. (i) No, Varun will not be punished for the Criminal Act in this case.

(ii) The relation between age and criminal liability is discussed in the table given below

Age	Whether liable
Upto 7 years	No criminal liability.
7-12 years	Mental agility of child is assessed.
12-16 years	A child is liable under the Juvenile Justice Act.
16-18 years	Child is liable under Juvenile Justice Act but if the crime committed is heinous in nature, then the child can be tried as an adult under IPC and other criminal legislations.
Above 18 years	Criminally liable under IPC and other criminal legislations.

6. In 2010, Madhu was arrested for attempt to murder. After the trial, she was acquitted by the court due to lack of evidence. In 2021, can Madhu be tried again for the same offence in which she was earlier acquitted? Discuss with relevant doctrine and provision of law. **Competency Based Que**

Ans. No, Madhu cannot be tried again in 2021 for the offence she committed in 2010 because of the doctrine of autrefois acquit.

According to this doctrine, if a person is tried and acquitted or convicted of an offence, he/she cannot be tried again for the same offence or on the same facts for any other offence. This doctrine has been substantially incorporated in the Article 20(2) of the Constitution of India and is also mentioned in Section 300 of CrPC.

7. Sanjay is arrested in relation to a case of theft. The police asks him to submit the following

(a) DNA sample

(b) Handwriting sample

(c) His personal diary

(d) He is forced to be a witness against himself.

(i) Which among the above mentioned he cannot be asked to submit?

(ii) Discuss in context the rights of the accused and arrested. **Competency Based Que**

Ans. (i) Sanjay cannot be forced to be a witness against himself and cannot be asked to submit his personal diary.

(ii) The right against self-incrimination is provided under Article 20(3) of the Constitution of India, which provides that no person accused of an offence shall be compelled to be a witness against himself/herself. However, the following restrictions are placed on the exercise of this right.

(a) Only such documents/statements are protected which are within the personal knowledge of the accused. The records that are maintained in fulfillment of a statutory requirement may not be protected. Further, the accused can be required to give a handwriting sample/blood/DNA sample as they are not within the 'personal knowledge' of the accused.

(b) Article 20(3) protects the accused only against being compelled to produce documents. The Supreme Court has ruled that a search and seizure does not considered to be 'compulsion to produce', and is thus outside the protection of Article 20(3).

(c) Summons under Section 91 of CrPC cannot be issued to an accused person. However, a general search warrant under Section 93(1)(c) CrPC is not protected under Article 20(3) of the Constitution of India.

8. There is criminal dispute where the maximum punishment could be capital punishment.

(i) Which court is competent to hear the case?

(ii) Make a flow chart of the hierarchy of criminal courts in India.

Ans. (i) Sessions Court is competent to hear such case.

(ii) The flow chart of the hierarchy of criminal courts in India is given below

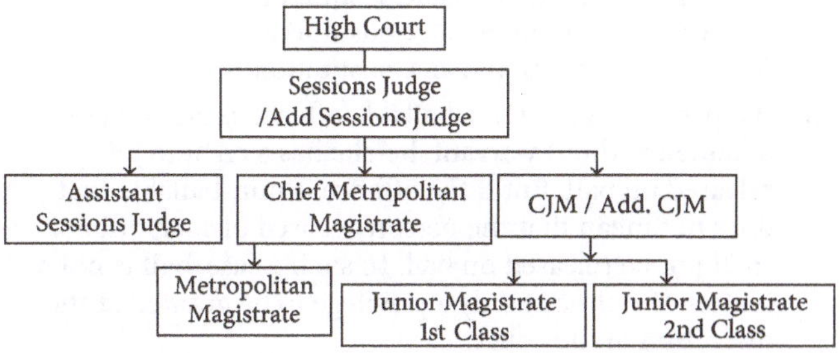

Exam Pattern Questions

Objective Type Questions

Multiple Choice Questions (MCQs)

1. British regime had passed various laws and acts for the better administration and law and order. When was the Indian Evidence Act enacted?

(a) 1861 (b) 1860 (c) 1872 (d) 1974

2. Which section of the Code of Criminal Procedure established courts of session by the State Government?

(a) Section 7 (b) Section 9
(c) Section 11 (d) Section 15

3. Gaurav has told his cousin Mohan that India's judiciary system is an hierarchy model where upward it goes to Supreme Court. Who can appoint additional judges in the Court of Session? **Competency Based Que**

(a) Governor (b) High Court
(c) Supreme Court (d) President

4. In every district (not being a metropolitan area), the High Court shall appoint a Judicial Magistrate of the First Class to be the ....

(a) Chief Judicial Magistrate
(b) Metropolitan Magistrate
(c) Special Executive Magistrate
(d) Executive Magistrate

5. Which of the following sections of the Criminal Procedure Code established Courts of Metropolitan Magistrates?

(a) Section 16 (b) Section 12
(c) Section 17 (d) Section 21

6. Under Section 21 of the ...., the State Government may appoint Executive Magistrates.

(a) IPC
(b) CrPC
(c) Indian Evidence Act
(d) None of the above

7. Which of the following is TRUE about the constitutes India's substantive criminal law?

(a) Indian Penal Code, 1860
(b) Code of Criminal Procedure, 1973
(c) Indian Evidence Act of 1872
(d) All of the above

8. Sulekha has completed her law studies and is planning to join law firm for the initial years of practice in criminal law. The ...., along with other penal laws, constitutes India's substantive criminal law. **Competency Based Que**

(a) CrPC, 1973 (b) IPC, 1860
(c) CPC, 1908 (d) The Police Act, 1861

9. According to Section 154-155 of the code, ... is a preliminary stage enquiry conducted by the police and usually starts after the recording of a First Information Report (FIR) in the police station.

(a) investigation (b) inquiry
(c) trial (d) All of these

10. **No person accused of an offence shall be compelled to be a witness against himself/herself.**

This sentence is related to which of the following articles of the Indian Constitution?

(a) Article 21 of the Indian Constitution
(b) Article 20 of the Indian Constitution
(c) Article 22 of the Indian Constitution
(d) Article 19 of the Indian Constitution

11. If a person accused of a bailable offence is arrested or detained without warrant, he/she has a right to be released on bail. But if the offence is non-bailable that does not mean that the person accused of such offence shall not be released on bail. In such a case, bail is not a matter of right but only a privilege to be granted at the discretion of the court.

Which of the following statement is NOT true regarding anticipatory bail? **Competency Based Que**

(a) Section 480 of the CrPC enables the superior courts to grant anticipatory bail.
(b) An anticipatory bail can be applied for when the person has reason to believe that he/she may be arrested.
(c) An application for anticipatory bail can be made to the Sessions Court.
(d) The nature and gravity of accusation is an important aspect of anticipatory bail.

12. **According to this doctrine, if a person is tried and acquitted or convicted of an offence, he/she cannot be tried again for the same offence or on the same facts for any other offence. This doctrine has been substantially incorporated in the Article 20(2) of the Constitution of India and is also embodied in Section 300 of CrPC.**

Which of following option is TRUE in reference to the above texts?

(a) Doctrine of autrefois acquit and auterfois convict
(b) Doctrine of pith and substance
(c) Doctrine of severability
(d) Doctrine of colourable legislation

13. **Saumya is 10 years old. While playing with her friends, there was a quarrel amongst them and she ended up hitting one of the girls with a rock on the head. She is very young and lacks maturity to understand the gravity and consequences of her actions.** **Competency Based Que**

Will Saumya be held liable for her action here?

(a) Yes (b) No
(c) Depends on the situation (d) None of these

14. **Rohan was addicted to gambling and drugs. Mostly, he used to borrow money from friends and local people to fulfill his desires. One day, he was murdered by the same people who gave him money. A murder case lodged against them. What is the punishment prescribed in the case of death?** **Competency Based Que**

(a) Life Imprisonment (b) 7 Years
(c) Both (a) and (b) (d) Life Imprisonment or 10 years

15. **The statement of the informant as recorded under .... will be treated as the FIR.**

(a) Section 152 (b) Section 153
(c) Section 154 (d) Section 155

16. **Hansika was severely beaten up by her husband. After some hesitancy, she agreed to file an FIR against her husband. Consider the following statements related to the First Information Report.**

I. The police cannot refuse to register the complaint.
II. The power of police to lodge an FIR cannot be usurped by the Magistrate. **Competency Based Que**

Choose the correct option

(a) Only I (b) Only II
(c) Both I and II (d) None of these

17. **Consider the following statements related to Judicial Magistrate and identify the correct sentence.**

I. The court at the lowest level is called Judicial Magistrate of the First Class.
II. The Sessions Judge can impose any punishment authorised by law but the sentence of death passed by him should be subject to confirmation by the High Court.

Choose the correct option.

(a) Only I (b) Only II
(c) Both I and II (d) None of these

18. **Arrange the following in a chronological order.**

I. Recording of prosecution evidence
II. Framing of charge or issuance of notice
III. Final arguments IV. Statement of accused
V. Defense evidence VI. Judgement

Codes

(a) II, I, IV, V, III, VI (b) I, II, III, V, IV, VI
(c) V, VI, II, I, III, IV (d) IV, I, V, II, VI, III

19. **Arrange the following provisions of the CrPC in chronological order.**

I. Judicial Magistrate First Class may pass a sentence of imprisonment.
II. Judicial Magistrate is under the general control of session judge.
III. The Courts of Metropolitan Magistrates.
IV. Special Metropolitan Magistrates.

Choose the correct option

(a) I, II, III, IV (b) II, III, IV, I
(c) II, IV, I, III (d) I, IV, II, III

20. **Statement I** An assistant session judge is a judicial officer who has the power to try cases and pass judgements, but only upto certain limit of sentence, typically 10 years.

Statement II The competency of an assistant session judge is limited to trying offences that are punishable with imprisonment for a term not exceeding 10 years.

Choose the correct option
(a) Statement I is correct, but Statement II is incorrect.
(b) Statement I is incorrect, but Statement II is correct.
(c) Both the Statement are correct.
(d) Both the Statement are incorrect.

21. **Statement I** Anticipatory bail is a type of bail that is granted to an individual before they are arrested or taken into custody.

Statement II The purpose of anticipatory bail is to protect the individual from being denied bail after arrest, and to ensure that they have a fair opportunity to prepare their defense.

Choose the correct option
(a) Statement I is correct, but Statement II is incorrect.
(b) Statement I is incorrect, but Statement II is correct.
(c) Both the Statement are correct.
(d) Both the Statement are incorrect.

22. **Match the following.**

	Column I (Age)	Column II (Whether liable)
A.	Upto 7 years	1. No criminal liability
B.	7-12 years	2. Mental agility of child is assessed
C.	12-16 years	3. A child is liable under the Juvenile Justice Act
D.	16-18 years	4. Child is liable under Juvenile Justice Act but if the crime committed is heinous in nature, then the child can be tried as an adult under IPC and other criminal legislations.

Codes

	A	B	C	D
(a)	1	2	3	4
(b)	2	1	3	4
(c)	4	2	3	1
(d)	3	4	1	2

Assertion-Reason Questions

Directions (Q. Nos. 23-27) In the questions given below, there are two statements. Read the statements and choose the correct option.

Codes
(a) Both A and R are true and R is the correct explanation of A.
(b) Both A and R are true, but R is not the correct explanation of A.
(c) A is true, but R is false.
(d) A is false, but R is true.

23. **Assertion** (A) The 1861 Code was repealed after which a new Code of Criminal Procedure, 1973 (CrPC) was enacted to carry out the process of the administration and enforcement of the substantive criminal law.

Reason (R) The CrPC controls and regulates the working of the machinery setup for the investigation and trial of the offences.

24. **Assertion** (A) The towns having population exceeding one million could be declared as metropolitan areas.

Reason (R) A Metropolitan magistrate is under the general control of the Sessions Judge and is subordinate to the Chief Metropolitan Magistrate.

25. **Assertion** (A) Inquiry is the first stage of the process wherein a Magistrate seeks to find out whether the accused should be committed to the sessions or discharged.

Reason (R) Section 2 (g) of the CrPC, 'inquiry' means every inquiry, other than a trial, conducted under this code by a Magistrate or court.

26. **Assertion** (A) No person accused of an offence shall be compelled to be a witness against himself.

Reason (R) The right against self-incrimination is provided under Article 21(3) of the Constitution of India.

27. **Assertion** (A) The overall administration of the police in a state is vested with the Director-General of Police.

Reason (R) The Police Act, 1861 describes the structure and function of the police in general.

Answers

1. (c) 1872
2. (b) Section 9
3. (b) High Court
4. (a) Chief Judicial Magistrate
5. (a) Section 16
6. (b) CrPC
7. (d) All of the above
8. (b) IPC, 1860
9. (a) investigation
10. (b) Article 20 of the Indian Constitution
11. (a) Section 480 of the CrPC enables the superior courts to grant anticipatory bail.
12. (a) Doctrine of autrefois acquit and auterfois convict
13. (a) Yes
14. (c) Both (a) and (b)
15. (c) Section 154
16. (c) Both I and II
17. (b) Only II
18. (a) II, I, IV, V, III, VI
19. (b) II, III, IV, I
20. (c) Both the Statement are correct.
21. (a) Statement I is correct, but Statement II is incorrect.

22. (a) 1 2 3 4
23. (b) Both A and R are true, but R is not the correct explanation of A.
24. (b) Both A and R are true, but R is not the correct explanation of A.
25. (d) A is false, but R is true.
26. (c) A is true, but R is false.
27. (a) Both A and R are true and R is the correct explanation of A.

Subjective Questions

Very Short Answer Type Questions

1. Write a short note about the Court of Judicial Magistrates.

Ans. As per Section 11 of CrPC, Courts of Judicial Magistrate of the First Class and the Second Class shall be established in every district (except a metropolitan area). The number of courts and their location that shall be established may be specified by the State Government after consultation with the High Court, through a notification.

2. What does Section 29 of the Code of Criminal Procedure say?

Ans. According to Section 29 of the CrPC, a Judicial Magistrate of First Class may pass a sentence of imprisonment for a term not exceeding three years, or fine not exceeding ₹ 5,000, or both.

3. State the exceptions mentioned for the Chief Judicial Magistrate to impose sentences.

Ans. A Chief Judicial Magistrate may impose a sentence except
- sentence of death
- imprisonment of life
- imprisonment for a term exceeding seven years

4. Who is a Chief Judicial Magistrate?

Ans. A chief Judicial Magistrate is a First Class Magistrate appointed by the High Court in each district (except metropolition areas) to oversee judicial matterl at the district level.

5. Write a short note on Metropolitan Magistrates.

Ans. The Courts of Metropolitan Magistrates were created by Section 16 of the Criminal Procedure Code. A Metropolitan Magistrate is under the general control of the Sessions Judge and is subordinate to the Chief Metropolitan Magistrate.

6. Explain the powers assigned to a First Class Magistrate.

Ans. The First Class Magistrate is competent to try offences punishable with imprisonment for a term not exceeding three years or fine up to ₹ 10,000. In states such as Kerala, the Second and the First Class Magistrate Courts have been unified.

7. Who is a Judicial Magistrate?

Ans. The court at the lowest level is called Judicial Magistrate of the Second Class. This court is competent to try the case if the offence is punishable with imprisonment for a term not exceeding one year, or fine not exceeding ₹ 5,000, or both.

8. Define trial and inquiry.

Ans. Trial is judicial determination of a person's guilt or innocence. Trial is a proceeding which involves examination and determination of the cause by a judicial tribunal.

It ends in conviction or acquittal of the accused.
Inquiry refers to proceedings before a Magistrate prior to the framing of the charge which does not result in conviction of the accused.

9. What is the examination-in-chief?

Ans After the charge is framed, the prosecution is asked to examine its witnesses before the court. The statement of witnesses is taken under an oath. This is called examination-in-chief.

10. Manish Kumar Singh lost his original passport, PAN card and passbook at Patna railway station around 4:30 PM on November 2, 2024. He has filed a complaint with the officer-in-charge of Muffassil police station in Patna requesting that an FIR be registered for the loss and to obtain an attested copy of complaint. What is the First Information Report? **Competency Based Que**

Ans. First Information Report (FIR) is the information recorded by the police officer on duty, given either by the aggrieved person or any other person about the commission of cognisable offence.

11. The right against self-incrimination is provided under Article 20(3) of the Constitution of India.
(i) What does Article 20(3) stipulate?
(ii) What is this doctrine called? **Competency Based Que**

Ans. (i) This article stipulates that no person accused of an offence shall be compelled to be a witness against himself.
(ii) This doctrine is called the doctrine of autrefois acquit.

12. Discuss the different aspects of anticipatory bail.

Ans. The different aspects for anticipatory bail are

- The nature and gravity of accusation.
- The antecedents of the applicant.
- The possibility that the accused may escape from justice.
- The accusation appears to be aimed at humiliating the applicant.

13. Sheila is a 30 years old woman. She was walking back to her home from work when two men threatened her with a knife, trying to rob her. As soon as the started screaming for help, they stabbed her to death and took all her jewellery and money. These men were found and arrested by the police.

Will they be able to get bail from the court? Give reasons to support your answer. Under which section of the CrPC does their offence fall? **Competency Based Que**

Ans. No, they will not be able to get bail from the court because their offence is a non-bailable offence. Under Section 2(a) of the CrPC, it is generally stated that all serious offences, i.e., offences punishable with imprisonment for three years or more have been considered as non-bailable offences.

14. A case of fraud and felony was filed against Suraj by his friend and business partner, Vishal. The police has to start the process of criminal prosecution. What is the first stage of this procedure? Explain in brief. Also mention the other steps.

Ans. The first stage of this procedure is investigation. It is a preliminary stage enquiry conducted by the police and usually starts after the recording of a First Information Report (FIR) in the police station. The other steps in the process are inquiry and trial.

Short Answer Type Questions

1. What are the different laws enacted for criminal justice?

Ans. The different laws enacted for criminal justice are

- The Indian Penal Code, 1860 (IPC) together with other penal laws constitutes India's substantive criminal law.
- As a sequel to the IPC, a Code of Criminal Procedure, 1861 was enacted. The 1861 Code was repealed after which a new Code of Criminal Procedure, 1974 (CrPC) was enacted to carry out the process of the administration and enforcement of the substantive criminal law.
- In addition to the CrPC, the Indian Evidence Act of 1872 was enacted to guide the process of investigation and trial.

2. Sudeep became a newly appointed Judicial Magistrate in Indore. His parents advised him to honestly exercise his jurisdiction in criminal matters arising in the District. Briefly explain about the Courts of Judicial Magistrates. **Competency Based Que**

Ans. As per Section 11 of CrPC, Courts of Judicial Magistrate of the First Class and Second Class shall be established in every district, (except a metropolitan area). The number of courts and their location that shall be established may be specified by the State Government after consultation with the High Court, through a notification.

Courts of Judicial Magistrate of First Class are at the second Lowest Level of the Criminal Court structure in India.

According to Section 15 of the CrPC, a Judicial Magistrate is under the general control of the Sessions Judge and is subordinate to the Chief Judicial Magistrate.

3. Garu was sentenced for two years by the Chief Judicial Magistrate for illegal mining in the Haldwani area. Discuss the position of Chief Judicial Magistrate.

Ans. In every district (not being a metropolitan area), the High Court shall appoint a Judicial Magistrate of the First Class to be the Chief Judicial Magistrate. A Chief Judicial Magistrate may impose a sentence except

- sentence of death
- imprisonment of life
- imprisonment for a term exceeding seven years

A Chief Judicial Magistrate shall be subordinate to the Sessions Judge. Every other Judicial Magistrate shall subject to the general control of the Sessions Judge and be subordinate to the Chief Judicial Magistrate.

4. Tina was killed by her husband and in-laws for non-payment of said amount as dowry. The grieved family has lodged complaint and police filed a case as cognisable offence. What is cognisable and non-cognisable offence? Explain with an example. **Competency Based Que**

Ans. The First Schedule of CrPC indicates that all offences punishable with imprisonment of not less than three years are taken as serious offences and are treated as cognisable.

Cognisable offences are crimes that police can investigate and arrest without a warrant. Examples of this offences are-murder, robery, dacoity, rape and kidnapping.

Non-cognisable offences are crimes that require a warrant and sometimes a complaint. Examples of this offences are-bigamy, public nuisance, defamation etc.

5. What is a warrant case? Explain two types of procedure for the trial of warrant cases.

Ans. Section 2(x) of the CrPC defines 'warrant-case' as a case relating to an offence punishable with death, imprisonment for life or imprisonment for a term exceeding two years.

The CrPC provides for two types of procedure for the trial of warrant cases by a Magistrate. These are

- those instituted upon a police report (Sections 238-243) and the defendant's lawyer argues for the defendants release.
- those instituted otherwise than on police report, i.e. upon complaints (Sections 238-243).

6. Roshni was served summon by the local court for making allegedly hate speech against a particular community. What do you understand by the summons case? **Competency Based Que**

Ans. Summons case relates to all offences punishable with imprisonment not exceeding two years.

With respect to summons cases, there is no need to frame a charge. The court gives substance of the accusation called notice to the accused when the person appears in execution of the summons.

The court has the power to convert a summons case into a warrant case if the Magistrate thinks that it is in the interest of justice.

7. Nayantara a 16 years old girl was abducted and physically tortured by a group of three people. However, the police managed to capture the culprits and imposed charge-sheet as non-bailable offence. Discuss non-bailable offences. **Competency Based Que**

Ans. According to the First Schedule of Section 2(a) of the CrPC, all serious offences, i.e. offences punishable with imprisonment for three years or more have been considered as non-bailable offences.

This general rule can be suitably modified according to specific needs. If the offence is non-bailable, it does not mean that the person accused of such offence shall not be released on bail.

Bail is not a matter of right, but only a privilege to be granted at the discretion of the court in such a case. If a person accused of a bailable offence is arrested or detained without warrant, he/she has the right to be released on bail (Section 436 of CrPC).

8. What is anticipatory bail? Also, explain the different aspects of anticipatory bail.

Ans. An anticipatory bail can be applied for when the person has reason to believe that he/she may be arrested.

An application for anticipatory bail can be made to the Sessions Court, the High Court or even the Supreme Court. However, normally the Court of Sessions would be the first approached for grant of anticipatory bail.

The court may consider the following aspects when considering an application for anticipatory bail

- the nature and gravity of accusation
- the antecedents of the applicant
- the possibility that the accused may escape from justice
- the accusation appears to be aimed at humiliating the applicant

9. "Arrested person has certain rights under CrPC in order to present their view in the court".

(i) Elaborate on the given statement.

(ii) Discuss the doctrine of autrefois convict.

Ans. (i) Some rights of the arrested person are

- Under Section 50 of the CrPC, the arrested person is to be informed of the particulars of the offence or any other grounds for arrest.
- If a person is arrested without a warrant for an offence which is bailable, he/she must be informed that he/she is entitled to be released on bail.

(ii) According to doctrine of autrefoies, if a person is tried and acquitted or convicted of an offence, he/she cannot be tried again for the same offence or on the same facts for any other offence. This doctrine has been substantially incorporated in the Article 20(2) of the Constitution of India and is also mentioned in Section 300 of CrPC.

Long Answer Type Questions

1. Among all the democracies in the world, India has the different categories of justice system. In the criminal courts itself, there are several hierarchy exists in India. Discuss the different categories of Criminal Courts in India.

Ans. For answer refer to text under the heading Different Categories of Criminal Courts in India, on page no. 200 and 201.

2. What is FIR? Discuss the important facts about FIR.

Ans. For answer refer to text under the heading First Information Report, on page no. 203 and 204.

3. Kamal Tripathi is an honest and disciplined police officer in Kanpur region. He also motivates his colleagues and peer groups to be more people centric and betterment of the society.
Elaborate the function and role of police.

Ans. For answer refer to text under the heading Role and Functions of Police, on page no. 209 and 210.

SELF ASSESSMENT TEST

Objective Type Questions

1. Which among the following sections of CrPC provided for Special Metropolitan Magistrates?
   (a) Section 32 (b) Section 18 (c) Section 17 (d) Section 31
2. What is the criteria to declare a town as metropolitan areas?
   (a) Towns having population exceeding one million. (b) Towns having population exceeding two million.
   (c) Towns having population exceeding one billion. (d) Towns having population exceeding two billion.
3. Which among the following sections define inquiry as means every inquiry, other than a trial, conducted under this code by a Magistrate or court?
   (a) Section 2(e) (b) Section 2(d) (c) Section 3(g) (d) Section 2(g)
4. What is the punishment mentioned in Section 29 of the CrPC?
   (a) 3 years (b) ₹ 5,000 (c) Both (a) and (b) (d) None of these
5. What is the time duration given to the police to produce an accused before the Magistrate?
   (a) Within 12 hours of arrest (b) Within 24 hours of arrest
   (c) Within 48 hours of arrest (d) None of these

Very Short Answer Type Questions

6. What are the two types of criminal trials?
7. Define warrant case. Which section of CrPC, 1973 defines it?
8. Mention any two rights of an arrested person.
9. At what age does criminal liability arise according to the IPC, 1860?

Short Answer Type Questions

10. Write a short note on the hierarchy and categories of criminal courts in India.
11. Article 20(3) of the Constitution of India provides the right against self-incrimination. Explain this right. What are the restrictions on the exercise of this right? **Competency Based Que**
12. Rajesh is accused of stealing a bike worth ₹ 5,000. The police can arrest him without a warrant and need a magistrate's permission to investigate the case. What are the major differences between cognisable and non-cognisable offences? **Competency Based Que**
13. Discuss the doctrine of autrefois acquit and autrefois convict, giving the relevant provisions of the Constitution of India and CrPC, 1973.

Long Answer Type Questions

14. Explain in detail the three stages involved in the criminal justice administration system.
15. What are the six distinct stages of a criminal trial? Discuss.
16. The Central Administrative Tribunal (CAT) has been established for deciding disputes'. Analyse the statement. **Competency Based Que**

13
CHAPTER

Family laws or personal laws consist of family or personal matters like marriage, dowry, dis-solution of marriage, guardianship, adoption, maintenance, gifts, wills, inheritance, succession, etc.

▼ **YOUR STUDY GOALS**

▼ **YOUR PRACTICE GOAL**

- Objective Type Questions (35 Qs ; MCQs, A-R, Statements, Matching)
- Subjective Questions (15 VSAs, 13 SAs, 6 LAs)

Institutional Framework, Marriage and Divorce

13.1 Nature of Family Law in India

- **Family laws in India are not uniform,** unlike other laws in India such as criminal and civil laws.
- In India, religion and personal laws are largely interlinked. So, Hindus, Sikhs, Jains and Buddhists follow Hindu family laws.
- Sikhs have their own marriage law but their other family matters are covered under Hindu law.
- Muslims, Christians and Parsis have their own laws. Other traditional communities, like the tribal groups, follow their own customary practices or customary laws.
- The Hindu law, the Sikh marriage law, the Parsi law and the Christian law are codified[1] or passed by the Indian Parliament as acts or laws.
- **The Muslim law is uncodified** and is based on the Sharia which is the moral and religious law.
- It is primarily based on the principles of the Islamic religious text, the holy Quran and the examples laid down in the Sunnah by the Islamic Prophet Muhammad.
- India follows a concept of a secular state, i.e, it has no state religion. The different communities in India live independently and separately when it comes to family laws.

1 **Codified** It means the rules and regulations that have been collected, restated and written down for the purpose of providing civil order to a society.

- However, the Constitution of India in **Article 44**, provides for a goal or aspiration for achieving a **uniform civil code** in family and personal matters.
- This provision is only a directive and is not enforceable by a court of law.

13.2 Historical Background of Laws

Ancient Period

- The laws in ancient India were primarily based on religious texts such as **Dharmashastras** and **Dharmasutras**. They are texts written in Sanskrit on religious and legal duties.
- They provided rules for the life of an ideal householder and contained Hindu knowledge about religion, law, ethics and so on.

Medieval Period

- The Hindu legal system in the medieval period was based on the **Smriti literature** and the **Dharmashastra**, as well other later texts.
- Two major schools of personal laws have been followed since the medieval period from 8th century. These are
  (i) **Mitakshara** It is followed in North and South India.
  (ii) **Dayabhaga** It is followed in the Bengal region.
- The Hindu law and the Muslim Shariat covered all aspects of life and did not differentiate much between morals, customs and laws.
- During the Mughal period (16th and 18th centuries) in the Indian sub-continent, Hindus and Muslims were ruled largely by their own sets of local customs and personal laws.

British India

- The British came to the Indian sub-continent in the early 17th century.
- In the initial years, they were not concerned with the various regional and local laws practiced in the sub-continent.
- In 1772, when the East India Company established themselves as the civil administrators, **Warren Hastings,** the first Governor-General of Bengal, introduced the **uniform criminal law**.
- It provides the idea of equality before the law for both Hindus and Muslims.
- However, in matters of personal law, the laws of the holy Quran would be applicable to the Muslims and the Shastras for the Hindus.
- As the British had no knowledge of the personal laws, they appointed Hindu pandits and Muslim jurists as consultants in their courts.
- This led to the administration and development of the Anglo-Hindu and the Anglo-Islamic personal laws.
- After 1864, the system of court Hindu pandits and Muslim jurists was abolished.
- This was due to dissimilar interpretations, suspicions of corruption and the interpretation of the personal laws by the court judges themselves.
- During British rule, both the Anglo-Hindu personal law and the Anglo-Islamic personal laws continued to develop through reforms, law commissions, and mainly through case laws.

Post-Independence

- After India's independence in 1947, efforts were made to develop a uniform civil code for dealing with matters of personal law.
- The uniform Hindu Code Bill, which attempted to combine the different regional customs and usages was started. However, **it was rejected in 1951,** due to much opposition.
- In 1955-56, the Parliament adopted and codified the four different major legislations which governed the family and personal law matters of the **Hindu community**.
- These were
  - Hindu Marriage Act (1955)
  - Hindu Succession Act (1956)
  - Hindu Minority and Guardianship Act (1956)
  - Hindu Adoptions and Maintenance Act (1956).
- Accordingly, Christians, Parsis and Sikhs have their own codified marriage acts, Muslims are governed by the Sharia, and the traditional communities continue to practice their uncodified customary laws.

Quick Test 1

1. Name the religious law that is uncodified in nature.
2. Which article of the Constitution provides for a goal for achieving a uniform civil code?
3. 'Dayabhaga' is followed in which region?
4. In which year, the British East India Company established themselves as civil administrators?
5. Who introduced the Criminal Law?

13.3 Human Rights and Gender Perspective

- Many provisions are specified for gender equality in the Indian Constitution. Some of these are
  - The Preamble to the Constitution of India resolves to secure justice, liberty, equality and dignity of all.
  - **Article 14** provides equal treatment before the law for every person.
  - **Article 15** prohibits discrimination based on religion, race, caste, sex or place of birth.
- However, there are also some exceptions like **Articles 25 and 26** of the Constitution **provide for freedom of religion.**
- It includes freedom of conscience[2] and free profession, practice and propagation[3] of religion, as well as freedom to manage religious affairs.
- The religious communities have used these provisions to argue that modifying their family laws would be interfering with their freedom of religion.
- For those who promote the traditional religious values, the gender equality provisions are contrary to their customary methods of law.
- For example, the traditional Hindu religious legal methods found in **'The Laws of Manu'** provide for unequal treatment of law and punishment based on gender as well as caste.
- Gender inequalities also exist within the Islamic legal traditions.
- These gender inequalities of the two communities prevented the adoption of a uniform civil code.
- The modern Hindu family laws were adopted on the basis of modern Constitutional values and by reconfiguring the traditional religious laws.
- However, complete gender equality has not been achieved.
- The instances of **gender inequality** existing in the present day **Hindu family law** include

2 Conscience It is a person's moral sense of right or wrong.
3 Propagation It is an action of widely spreading and promoting an idea.

- The Hindu Marriage Act [Section 5(3)] prescribes marriageable age for girls as 18 and boys as 21. Recently, the government has proposed the marriageable age of girls to be increased from 18 to 21 years.
- The Hindu Succession Act provides different methods of succession of property for male and female without a will.
- **The Hindu Minority and Guardianship Act (Section 6)** prohibits a mother to act as a child's natural guardian[4], unless the father is dead or otherwise disqualified.
- **The Hindu Adoptions and Maintenance Act (Section 6)** prohibits a mother to give her child in adoption, unless the father is dead or otherwise disqualified.

- Some instances of **gender inequalities** in the Islamic family laws include
  - The practice of polygamy is permitted in Islamic law.
  - A husband can divorce his wife by the Triple Talaq.
  - A Muslim husband is to pay maintenance to a divorced wife, only during the iddat[5] period of three months.
- There are other challenges in achieving gender equality in the realm of family laws like lack of information about family laws that are applicable to respective communities.
- Most residents of rural India does not know about the minimum age of marriage and that dowry is prohibited.
- They are also unaware about legal grounds of divorce and prohibition of the practice of bigamy or polygamy.

Three Types of Divorce in Islamic Law

- **Talaq-e-Ahsan** It is a form of divorce in Muslims by which a man can divorce his wife by pronouncing 'talaq', followed by a period of abstinence[6].
- **Talaq-e-Hasan** In Talaq-e-Hasan, a man can dissolve the marriage by **pronouncing the word 'talaq', once every month** over a period of three months.
- **Talaq-e-Biddat or Instant Triple Talaq** It was an Islamic practice that allowed men to divorce their wives immediately by pronouncing the word **'talaq' three times.**
  - The pronouncement to end the marriage could be oral or written, or by electronic means, i.e., telephone, SMS, email or social media.
  - Under the new law, Talaq-e-Biddat or Instant Triple Talaq in any form, is **illegal and void,** with up to three years in jail for the husband.
  - The other two forms of talaq (divorce), Talaq-e-Ahsan and Talaq-e-Hasan **remain valid** under the Muslim law.

13.4 Institutional Framework : Family Courts

- **In 1984, the Family Courts Act was enacted** for the creation and functioning of family courts with expertise to deal with matrimonial and family law matters.
- The act is procedural and does not override the family laws.
- Accordingly, the rights and obligations of parties in disputes are based on the family, personal or matrimonial laws.

4 Natural guardian It is a child's biological or adopted parents who has the legal right to make decisions for the child.
5 Iddat It is a period of waiting after a divorce or the death of a spouse in which Muslim woman is not allowed to remarry.
6 Abstinence It means the practice of restraining oneself from indulging in something.

- During the late 1980s and 1990s, many family courts were established in most major cities in India. The matrimonial and family law cases were shifted from the district, civil and criminal courts to the newly created special courts.
- Family courts were created with many distinct features and goals including
  - Reduction in formality and pressure in litigation process
  - Speed in justice delivery
  - Facilitation in conciliation and settlements
- The subject matters of personal or family law that fall within the jurisdiction of family courts include the following
  - Validity of marriage
  - Matrimonial status
  - Disputes regarding property of either of the parties or joint property
  - Threat arising out of marital relations
  - Legitimacy of any person
  - Maintenance
  - Guardianship, custody and access to any minor
  - Nullity of marriage that is to declare a marriage as null and void.
  - If either of the spouse leaves the common matrimonial home without any reasonable excuse, then the aggrieved spouse can file a petition for **restoration of marital rights**. By this, the courts asks the spouse to return back to the common matrimonial home.
  - Judicial separation in which the marriage is not dissolved but the marital rights and obligations are suspended.
- The Family Courts Act provides **mandatory powers to the State Governments** to set up family courts in cities and towns with a population over one million, and discretionary powers for areas with less than one million.
- However, some states have failed to create family courts due to financial and space constraints to the lawyers.

Acts under the Scope of Family Courts Act

The acts under the purview of Family Courts Acts are

- **The Hindu Marriage Act, 1955** This act **codifies** the marriage law of the Hindus. It primarily deals with the validity and conditions for invalidity and applicability of marriage.
- **Special Marriage Act, 1954** The act provides a special method of civil contractual marriage (and divorce) for all Indian nationals regardless of religion or faith followed by the parties. This act does not require the customary or religious rites or ceremonies of marriage to be observed.
- **Dissolution of Muslim Marriage Act, 1939** This act explains the dissolution of marriage by women married under Muslim law and the effects of the renunciation (rejection) of Islam by a married Muslim woman.
- **Foreign Marriages Act, 1969** This act deals with marriages of citizens of India living outside the nation.
- **The Indian Divorce Act, 1869** This act relates to the divorce of persons professing the Christian religion.
- **The Parsi Marriage and Divorce Act, 1936** This act deals with marriage and divorce among the Parsis.
- **Muslim Women (Protection of Rights on Divorce) Act, 1986** This act deals with the matters of the divorced Muslim women and governs their right to maintenance from their former husband.

- **Muslim Personal Law/Application of Shariat Act, 1937** This act requires the application of the Islamic Law Code of Shariat to Muslims in India in their family or personal matters.
- **Hindu Adoption and Maintenance Act, 1956** This act deals with the legal process of adopting children by a Hindu adult and the legal obligations to provide maintenance to the various family members.
- **The Indian Christian Marriage Act, 1872** This act regulates the formalisation of marriages among Indian-Christians.
- **Hindu Minority and Guardianship Act, 1956** This act explains the guardianship or relationship of Hindus involving the adults and minors as well as between people of all ages and their respective properties.
- **Guardian and Wards Act, 1890** This is a non-religious and universally applicable law regarding the issues relating to guardianship of a child in India.
- **Chapter IX of the Criminal Procedure Code, 1973 (S-125 to 128)** This law deals with the issues of maintenance of wives, children and parents.
- **Protection of Women from Domestic Violence Act, 2005** This act provides safeguards to the wife or female live-in partner against domestic violence by husband or male live-in partner or his relatives. This act also provides protection to other women living in a household including sisters, widows, or mothers.
- **Muslim Women (Protection of Rights on Marriage) Act, 2019** This act made Triple Talaq a cognisable offence and punishable.

Role of Women in the Creation of Family Courts

- Women associations and organisations have played a critical role in the creation of family courts.
- In the 1980s, the women's rights movement groups spoke about legislative reforms, which included the creation of special courts dealing with family matters to curb violence against women including murder of wife.
- These issues of gender justice were an important factor for the creation of family courts.
- Thus, family courts aimed at creating **women-friendly court** procedures that were less formal and more accessible to women, especially those from the marginalised section.
- For achieving this aim, the family courts intended to depend less on the traditional lawyers and more on counselors to help the parties in the dispute.
- The conciliators or mediators were involved to **increase the power of negotiation** of women in settlement in issues such as quantum of maintenance upon divorce, custody and access of children, protection against domestic violence, and right of residence in the matrimonial home.
- The need to establish the family courts was first emphasised by late **Smt. Durga Bai Deshmukh** after her visit of China in the year 1953.

Role of Lawyers and Counselors in Family Courts

- The Family Courts Act restricts the role of lawyers and increases the role of counselors in dispute resolution to encourage mutually peaceful settlements.
- This is different from the practices of other courts which commonly employ the English legal method of practice called the **adversarial system of adjudication.**
- In this system, the judge plays the role of a neutral mediator.
- He/she takes the decision on the basis of merits of the case presented to him/her by the lawyers of the opposing parties.
- The Family Courts Act limits the role of the lawyers as legal experts or 'amicus curiae' to whom the courts may consult for opinion.

- This is done to prevent excessive litigation costs, corruption, manipulative[7] and subversive[8] tactics, extended and bitter court battles, refusal to settle or compromise, etc.
- However, these restrictions on the lawyers are criticised in the following ways
  - Critics have argued that lawyers are necessary to help clients with complex cases and court procedures in which the counselors may not have that kind of expertise.
  - There is no mechanism to ensure the availability of 'amicus curiae' or 'legal experts' for the constant requirements of courts.
- Thus, family courts have routinely allowed lawyers to represent clients.
- The Family Courts Act has given the **counselors high preference over lawyers** in the family courts in order to promote efforts for settlement between the parties.
- However, in practice, the **role of counselors is insignificant** due to following reasons
  - Majority of the states do not adequately integrate[9] the requirement of counselors with the legal practice of family courts.
  - The role of the counselors is limited to the task of deciding if the dispute can be resolved.
  - The role of counselors in court practice is a new idea and neither the judges nor the lawyers are oriented to this concept.
  - There are differences among states with respect to the process adopted to appoint the counselors, their qualifications and remunerations, their role, and the counseling techniques. Thus, while some states have used non- governmental organisations as counselors, others have used trained personnel, individual volunteers, as well as lawyers.
- There are a few states such as Maharashtra, where counselors play a considerable role in promoting negotiations and settlements.

Role of Counselors and Gender Issues

The women groups have criticised the role of counselors on the basis of gender issues in the following ways

- The women groups have argued that **counselors should be trained with gender-sensitivity**. This is because the unbiased opinions of counselors are usually anti-women and influenced by patriarchal biases against women.
- The women groups have demanded clearly defined frameworks for gender justice in the practice of the family courts, especially with respect to the roles of counselors. The objective of this is to avoid gender biases in the process of fulfilling the 'speedy settlement' and 'protect and preserve' the family.
- In order to accomplish the mandate of reconciliation or settlement, some counselors force women to return to the spousal home, disregarding their human dignity, physical safety and economic rights.
- In some cases, where women have been physically abused and thrown out of their matrimonial homes and have demanded maintenance (**under Section 125 of the Criminal Procedure Code)**, the counselors and lawyers have regularly and successfully sought maintenance, which is argued to be a legal trick that reduces women's claim to maintenance.
- There are legal complexities[10] in family issues. Thus, gender-sensitivity may help counselors to not only take neutral positions, but also consider the unequal power relationships between men and women in settlement processes.
- One of the major criticisms by the women groups about the Family Courts Act and the family justice system is that the conceptual basis of 'gender justice', which is the prime objective of the women's movement, is not included.

7 Manipulative It means exercising unscrupulous control or influence over a person or situation.
8 Subversive, It means seeking or intended to subvert on established system or institution.
9 Integrate It means to combine one thing with other to make a whole.
10 Complexities It means the state or quality of being intricate or complicated.

- Instead, the Family Courts Act focuses on 'preservation of the family' through resolution in a speedy manner. Women groups have always maintained that 'preservation of family' is not synonymous with 'gender justice' or 'rights of women'.

Quick Test 2

1. Name any two articles of the Indian Constitution that are specified for gender equality.
2. Why was the Family Courts Act enacted in India?
3. Name any two law cases that were shifted from the district, civil and criminal courts to the newly created special courts.
4. Which act provides a special method of civil contractual marriage?
5. Which Marriage Act is considered as the oldest law that regulates the formalisation of marriages among Indian-Christians?

13.5 Marriage

- Marriage is defined as a **social and legal union** between a man and a woman.
- The spouses create kinship through the institution of marriage.
- Kinship is a system of social organisation between people who are related by blood, marriage or adoption. Marriage is a social union because both the spouses are entitled to each other's company and conjugal rights.
- Conjugal rights are mutual rights and privileges between two individuals that arise from the state of being married. These rights and privileges include affection, companionship, co-habitation, joint property rights and sexual relations.
- If either of the spouses separates herself/himself from the social and emotional companionship of her/his spouse without reasonable cause (i.e. sound judgement, which is just, fair and rational), then the aggrieved party can approach the court for relief.
- In such cases, the court may direct the accused spouse to return with the other spouse to their matrimonial home. This is called as restitution of conjugal rights.
- Marriage is also a **legal union** as certain legal consequences follow after marriage. For example,
  - Parties get the status of husband and wife.
  - Legitimacy is conferred on children who are born after marriage.
  - The rights of maintenance and inheritance of property are conferred on husband and wife.
- Different laws of marriage govern people belonging to different religions. For example, the Hindu Marriage Act, 1955, governs a Hindu marriage; the Parsi Marriage and Divorce Act of 1936 governs the marriage between Parsees; and the Christian Marriage Act, 1872, governs the Christian marriage. Muslims do not have any codified law for marriage. They are governed by their religious texts.

Forms of Marriage

The different forms of marriage are

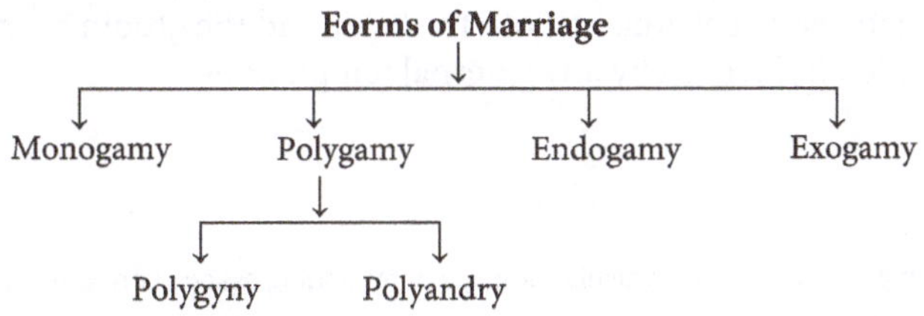

- **Monogmy** The majority of marriages are based on monogamy. It refers to a union between one woman and one man.
- **Polygamous Marriage** It refers to multiple spouses or multiple marriages that include either multiple husbands or multiple wives. It is of two types based on the purpose it serves
  - **Polygyny** The practice of polygyny (or multiple wives) was often a strategy for increasing the population size. It also ensured that all women in the society were taken care of when men were in short numbers.
  - **Polyandry** Polyandry (or multiple husbands) is associated with shortage of women may be due to female infanticide and poverty.
- **Endogamy** It is about marriage to a person **within one's own group**. Such group may be based on
  - **caste** for example a Brahmin will marry a Brahmin; a Kshatriya will marry a Kshatriya, etc.
  - **class** i.e. social categories based on economic and educational status.
  - **ethnic group** i.e. socially defined category based on common culture or nationality.
  - a religious group
  - a village
- **Exogamy** It is a rule that requires an individual to marry outside the tribe, family, clan or other social unit. It is especially with regard to descent groups, on the basis of descent from a common ancestor or ancestress. The group can consist of children of the same father/mother, grandchildren of the same grandmother/father, great- grandchildren of the same great- grandparent etc., or of the descendants of these persons.

  In exogamy, a certain degree of social or relationship distance must exist. If it is not the case, exogamic **taboo**[11] is attached to such marriages that take place within close social or relationship **proximity**[12].

Conditions of a Valid Marriage

For a valid marriage, certain conditions are to be fulfilled by the parties to the marriage. These conditions may vary from religion to religion. These are

- There is a rule of monogamy among Hindus, Parsis and Christians according to which they can marry only once. Their **first marriage must be dissolved** if they want to **marry again**. The **dissolution of marriage** can take place either by divorce (i.e., dissolution of marriage by the court) or by death of another spouse. However, Muslim law permits 'polygamy' where a Muslim man can have four wives.
- No religious ceremony is required to constitute a valid marriage under the Muslim law. The offer and acceptance to marry is often required of a Muslim couple. However, this is not so among the other religious groups like Hindus, Parsis or Christians. If any Hindu marriage has been solemnised (formalised) without the performance of customary rites on ceremonies prevailing in the community of either of the parties, such marriage is legally void.
- The religious communities other than Muslims solemnised their marriages in the following ways
  - Hindus follow the ceremony of **'Saptapadi'** or taking of seven steps before a sacred fire.
  - Sikhs solemnise their marriage by **'Anandkaraj'** ceremony where Lavan or the four hymns of Laav are performed during the four nuptial (matrimonial) rounds.
  - Parsi marriage must be solemnised in accordance with a ceremony called **'Ashirwad'**. This ceremony binds the couple in matrimony spiritually. Both the bride and the groom promise to remain faithful to each other and not be led influenced by any external temptations.

11 **Taboo** It is a social or religious custom prohibiting or restricting a particular practice or forbidding association with a particular person.
12 **Proximity** It is nearness is space time or relationship.

- For Christians in India, certain people are recognised as authorities under the Christian law who can perform the marriage, otherwise the marriage is void. These include any of the following persons to solemnise marriage
  - persons who have received episcopal ordination (consecration[13] or installation by authority)
  - any Clergyman of the Church of Scotland
  - any Minister (or priest) of Religion licensed under this law.
  - Such persons grant certificates of marriage to the Christian couples.
- Different religions prescribe different age for marriage. For example, Hindu, Christian and Parsi law prescribe age of 18 years for girls and 21 years for boys. On the other hand, Muslim law mentions **age of puberty,** which is generally attained at 15 years of age.
- A person cannot marry anyone who belongs to his or her close relations. All the religions recognise that parties should not marry within certain blood relations or certain persons with whom relationship has arisen by marriage. For example, a person cannot marry his or her brother or sister.
- A person must be of sound mind at the time of marriage. The sound mind refers to the ability of individuals to understand the nature of marriage, and responsibilities towards their spouses, once they get married.

Concept of Void and Voidable Marriage

- When all the conditions prescribed by the personal laws are fulfilled and there is **no legal restriction**, the marriage is considered as valid.
- If a party contravenes any of these conditions, then the marriage would be ascribed to the status of void or voidable marriage.
- Such status of void or voidable marriage is dependent upon the nature of conditions that are violated.
- A voidable marriage is a perfectly valid marriage as long as it is not annulled (legally invalid) by any court of law. Only the aggrieved party to the marriage can file the petition for annulment.
- The court can annul a voidable marriage by passing a decree of nullity.
- The word 'marriage' describes that the two persons have undergone the ceremonies of marriage that are prerequisite for a valid marriage.
- A void marriage is no marriage.

Hindu Law

- The Hindu Marriage Act, 1955 makes the distinction between void and voidable marriage. It provides three basis for void marriage that are
  - **Sapinda Relationship** Marriage with any person falling within sapinda relationship is void. A sapinda relationship is one in which a person is lineal descendent of the other person with respect to third generation in the line of family through mother or fifth generation in the line of family through father. Blood relations are covered under it. For example, a person cannot marry his maternal or paternal uncle's daughter.
  - **Prohibited Relationship** One cannot marry with any person with whom a relationship has arisen by marriage. For example, there cannot be marriage between uncle and niece or aunt and nephew. The concept of prohibited relationship is wider than sapinda relationship as it covers relationship by blood as well as by marriage.
  - If any Hindu re-marries during the lifetime of his/her spouse, then the second marriage is void.

---

13 Consecration It is the action of making or declaring something sacred.

- The Hindu Marriage Act also provides four basis for voidable marriages that are
  - If marriage cannot be completed to perfection due to the inability of one spouse, then the other spouse can get it annulled. Here, impotency does not mean barrenness or sterility (inability to have child), rather it is failure to have sexual intercourse.
  - When the consent for marriage is obtained by force or fraud, then the aggrieved party can get the marriage annulled.
  - The **pre-marriage pregnancy** of a wife is another ground for voidable marriage. It is the condition when the wife is pregnant before marriage by some person other than the husband. However, the husband must be ignorant of this fact at the time of marriage.
  - **Unsoundness of mind** is also a basis for voidable marriage.

Muslim Law

- Under Muslim law, void marriage is known as **Batil marriage.**

  Marriage is void on the basis of the following
  - **Polyandry** It means that a married woman cannot contract a second marriage during the subsistence of the first marriage.
  - **Consanguinity** It means prohibition of marrying certain blood relations. For example, a Muslim cannot marry his mother, grandmother, daughter, granddaughter, paternal and maternal uncles and aunts, etc.
  - **Affinity** It means prohibition of marrying certain persons with whom relationship has arisen by marriage. For example, a Muslim cannot marry wife's mother or grandmother, wife's daughter (from another husband) or granddaughter, if his marriage with wife is completed to perfection.
  - **Fosterage** It means when a woman, (other than the mother of the child) has suckled (feed) a child under the age of two years, then the woman becomes the foster mother of the child. A man cannot marry his foster-mother or her daughter, or his foster sister.
  - There is no concept of voidable marriage under Muslim law rather they recognise concept of irregular (Fasid) marriages.
  - Irregular marriage is that which can become valid, if the defect is cured. For example, marriage with a fifth wife is irregular and can be regularised if any of the earlier four wives either dies or obtains divorce from the husband.
  - Irregular marriages are recognised only by the Sunnis and not by the Shia sect among the Muslims.

Christian Law

- The Indian Divorce Act, 1869, governs the Christians.
- It also provides for nullity of marriage but the act does not distinguish between void and voidable marriage.
- It only states that marriage may be declared as null and void on certain basis which are
  - An aggrieved party can get the decree of nullity on the basis of **inability of other spouse** at the time of marriage.
  - Decree of nullity can be obtained if parties are within the **prohibited degrees** of affinity or blood relationship.
  - Marriage may be annulled if the former husband or wife of either party was living at the time of marriage.
  - Marriage may be annulled if either party was of unsound mind at the time of marriage.

Parsi Law

- Parsis do not recognise the distinction between void and voidable marriage. Under the Parsi Marriage and Divorce Act, 1936, declaration to nullity of the marriage can be obtained in one situation where **completion of marriage is impossible due to natural causes.**

Essentials for Marriage in Different Religions

Criteria	Hindu	Muslim	Christian	Parsi	Sikh
Age	Girls - 18 years Boys - 21 years	Age of puberty-15 years	Girls - 18 years Boys- 21 years	Girls - 18 years Boys- 21 years	Girls - 18 years Boys- 21 years
Monogamy	Essential	Polygamy upto 4 wives are allowed. Polyandry is not allowed.	Essential	Essential	Essential
Prohibited relationships	Sapinda relationships, consanguinity and affinity	Consanguinity and affinity based	Consanguinity and affinity	Consanguinity and affinity	Consanguinity and affinity
Sound mind	Both parties	Both parties	Both parties	Both parties	Both parties
Religious ceremonies	Saptapadi (seven steps around the fire)	Civil contract offer, acceptance and consideration (husband pays a sum of money-mehr/dower; in return wife promises to follow the husband)	Priest-certificate of marriage	Ashirwad ceremony	Four Laav

Quick Test 3

1. Which religious community does not haveany codified law for marriage?
2. Name the religious ceremony practiced in the Hindu religion.
3. Who is recognised as an authority to perform Christian marriages in India?
4. Who can file petition to annul a voidable marriage?
5. Which sect of Muslims recognises the concept of irregular marriages?

13.6 Divorce

- Divorce is the **termination of a marital union.**
- Divorce results in the break of matrimonial tie between husband and wife.
- The status of husband and wife ceases after divorce.

Theories of Divorce

- The concept of divorce has evolved in the form of different theories.
- Situations like adultery (sexual intercourse outside marriage), cruelty and desertion (when one spouse leaves the other spouse and never return), affects the foundation of marriage.
- The divorce on these conditions only enables the other party to put an end to the marriage.

Guilt or Offense Theory of Divorce

- According to this theory, a marriage can be dissolved only if one of the parties to marriage has, committed some matrimonial offense, after its solemisation.
- The offense must be one that is recognised as a ground of divorce.
- This theory implies that there is a guilty party, i.e. a party who has committed a matrimonial offense, and an innocent party who is a victim.
- Insanity was added later in this theory as a ground of divorce.
- However, it did not fit within the framework of this theory as the party suffering from insanity could hardly be called a guilty party. This led to renaming of the Guilty Theory as **Fault Theory**.
- If one of the parties has some fault in him/her, marriage could be dissolved, whether that fault is his/her conscious act or providential.

Mutual Consent Theory of Divorce

- This theory originated due to the shortcomings of the Fault Theory of Divorce.
- The biggest limitation of the Fault Theory has been the presumption that there is one innocent party and one guilty party.
- Sometimes, husband and wife are not able to live together and there is no fault in either of them.
- In that case, both of them are left with no remedy.
- Thus, a new theory of mutual consent developed where marriage could be dissolved by mutual consent of both the husband and the wife where they are not able to live together.
- Divorce by mutual consent means that the law recognises the situation, where parties can also obtain divorce by mutual consent.
- But only the mutual consent will not automatically terminate the relationship. It is essential to obtain a decree of the court.
- Divorce by mutual consent requires the consent of both the parties, and if one of the parties withholds his/her consent, divorce can never be obtained.

Theory of Mutual Consent in Hindu Law

- Under the Hindu Marriage Act, 1955, parties must live separately for a period of one year or more before filing a joint petition. Then, after filing of petition, there will be a cooling off period for six months during which the court will not examine the petition.
- Thereafter, the parties have to file a joint motion to initiate the divorce proceedings.
- In the case of **Amardeep Singh Vs. Harveen Kaur,** the Supreme Court stated that it is **not compulsory to wait** for a cooling off period of 6 months, as proposed **under Section 13 B (2)** of the Hindu Marriage Act.
- The Parsi Marriage and Divorce Act, 1936 has provided this ground.

Theory of Mutual Consent in Muslim Law

- The concept of divorce by mutual consent is also recognised under Muslim law in the form of **Mubarat** (mutual release) and **Khula** (redemption).
- In Mubarat, both the parties mutually decide to release each other from marriage bond.
- In Khula, the wife offered to dissolve marriage, and she has to pay consideration (something of monetary value in exchange for a promise) to the husband, in lieu of acceptance.

Theory of Irretrievable Breakdown of Marriage

- According to this theory, if a marriage has broken down without possibility of repair (or ir-retrievable), then it should be dissolved without looking at the fault of either party.
- In 1964, the Archbishop of Canterbury appointed a committee under the chairmanship of Dr. Mortimer Bishop of Exeter to look into the matter.
- The **Mortimer Committee** in its report recommended that the 'breakdown of marriage' should be the **sole ground of divorce** replacing all the fault grounds of divorce.
- The Committee defined such breakdown of marriage a failure in the matrimonial relationship that offers no reasonable probability of comfort and support.
- **The Matrimonial Causes Act, 1959** of the commonwealth of Australia, provides that if a decree of restitution of conjugal rights is not complied with for a period of one year, then either party may seek divorce.
- Further, a divorce could also be obtained on the basis that the parties have not resumed cohabitation for a period of one year or more after a decree of judicial separation.
- **The Parsi Marriage and Divorce Act, 1936;** Hindu Marriage Act, 1955 and Special Marriage Act, 1954 also has this ground.
- In the 1960s, an agitation started to reform English law of divorce.
- This agitation produced a rapid response in India which led to the 1964 amendment in the Hindu Marriage Act, 1955.
- It tried to introduce the 'breakdown principle' along the lines of Australian Matrimonial Causes Act, 1959.
- This basis has not been specifically included in the Hindu Marriage Act, 1955.
- However, the Supreme Court in the case of **Naveen Kohli Vs. Neelu Kohli, 2006,** strongly recommended that irretrievable breakdown of marriage should be made a basis for divorce.
- The Indian Parliament has introduced Marriage Laws Amendment Bill 2010, with the aim of making irretrievable breakdown of marriage as a basis for divorce in the Hindu Marriage Act, 1955.

Grounds for Divorce

- In Muslim law, husband enjoys special privilege in the area of divorce. He can divorce his wife at his will without citing any reason.
- Earlier, the Muslim wife had no corresponding right of divorce. It is only after passing of Dissolution of Muslim Marriage Act, 1939 that wife has been conferred right to obtain divorce.
- According to Hindu Marriage Act, 1955, both husband and wife are entitled to file a petition for dissolution of marriage.
- This petition can be filed on grounds of adultery, cruelty, desertion, unsoundness of mind, etc.
- Parsis as well as Christians recognise adultery, cruelty, desertion and unsoundness of mind as grounds of divorce.
- The Indian Divorce Act, 1869 governs Christians in matters of divorce.
- Under this act, the husband can file a petition of divorce **only on the grounds of adultery** on the part of the wife, whereas the wife can file a petition on any of the mentioned grounds.
- If husband is guilty of rape or sodomy or anal intercourse, then wife can file petition for divorce.
- This remedy is available to Hindu, Parsi and Christian wife.

13.7 Matrimonial Rights and Obligations

- There are certain marital rights and obligations that marriage confers on husband and wife.
- These are conjugal rights, rights of maintenance and inheritance.

Conjugal Rights

- These are the rights and privileges arising from the **marital relation,** especially the mutual rights of companionship, aid and sexual relations. The basis of this right is **'consortium'** (an association or alliance, or a legal right of one spouse to have comradeship and support with the other).
- Under these rights, parties get right of cohabitation.
- The living together of a man and woman is supposed to be the quintessence sexual relationship.
- It means an emotional and physical intimate relationship, which includes a common living place known as 'matrimonial home'.

Right of Maintenance

- According to this right, a man takes on an obligation to support his wife out of his earnings or other income according to his total income. This obligation remains in force for the duration of the marriage and sometimes even if the wife has an adequate income of her own.
- The right of maintenance under the laws of different religious communities are

  (i) **Under Hindu law,** the wife has an absolute right to claim maintenance from her husband. Her right to maintenance is codified in the **Hindu Adoptions and Maintenance Act, 1956**. For assessing the amount of maintenance, the court considers various factors like financial position and liabilities of the husband.

  - The right of maintenance does not exist for the husband. However, if any matrimonial dispute is brought before the court, then the Hindu Marriage Act, 1955 provides that either husband/wife who has insufficient means can claim maintenance **pendente lite** or **permanent alimony.**
  - Pendente lite refers to maintenance during pendency of the proceedings. Permanent alimony refers to maintenance at the time of final disposal of the case.
  - For fixing the amount of permanent alimony, the court will determine the amount according to the ability of husband to pay, wife's own assets and conduct of the parties.
  - The order will remain in force as long as the wife remains chaste and unmarried.

  (ii) **The Parsi Marriage and Divorce Act, 1936** also recognises the right of husband as well as of the wife to claim maintenance i.e. both pendente lite as well as permanent alimony. The parameter for granting the maintenance is the same as in the case of Hindus.

  (iii) **Under the Muslim law,** the Muslim Women (Protection of Rights on Divorce) Act, 1986 protects the rights of Muslim women who have been divorced by or have obtained divorce from their husbands. If the husband fails to pay maintenance to the wife then she is entitled to obtain divorce from the husband.

  (iv) **The Indian Divorce Act, 1869** governs maintenance rights of a Christian wife. This act does not apply to Hindus, Muslims and Parsees. The provisions of this act are same as those under the Parsi law, and the same considerations are applied in granting maintenance i.e. both pendente lite and permanent alimony.

Right of Inheritance

- According to this right, when one person dies without making a will, his property devolves (passes on), under the law of succession.
- When two persons get married, they get mutual rights of inheritance.

- Different laws of succession govern persons belonging to different religions. These are
  - Under the Undivided Hindu Family, if a male or female dies without making a will, then the property is distributed as per rules of succession prescribed in the Hindu Succession Act, 1956.
  - Under the act, both husband and wife are included in the category of most preferred heirs.
  - Both of them can make a will of his/her separate properties and can give them to anyone.
  - But, the ancestral property has to be disposed off according to the Hindu Succession Act, 1956.
  - Under Muslim law, in the case of death of wife, the share of husband is 1/4th of the property when there is a son or child of a son.
  - However, when there is no such child, then husband is entitled to 1/2 of the property of wife.
  - In case of the death of the husband, the share of the wife is 1/8th when there are children; but if there are no children, then her share increases to 1/4th.
  - Under the Muslim law, there is a restriction that a Muslim cannot dispose off more than 1/3rd of his property by a will.

Matrimonial Property

- Property and gifts received at or about the time of marriage, belong jointly to the husband and wife.
- But there are certain properties belonging exclusively to each one of them. For example, there is a concept of 'stridhan' in the Hindu law. Any gifts given to the wife by her parents and in-laws exclusively belong to her.
- Concept of 'dower' under Muslim law is another example of matrimonial property which belongs exclusively to the wife.
- Dower is a sum of money or property that the wife is entitled to receive from the husband, in consideration of marriage.

The Prohibition of Child Marriage Act, 2006

- Minor is a person who has **not completed the age of 18 years** under the Indian Majority Act, 1875.
- With respect to the age of marriage, the Hindu Marriage Act, 1955, the Parsi Marriage and Divorce Act, 1936 and the Christian Marriage Act, 1872 has prescribed the age of 18 years for girls and 21 years for boys. In India, child marriages were prevalent.
- These included marriages which takes place before a girl attains the age of 18 years, and 21 years in case of boys. When the Hindu Marriage Act, 1955 was drafted, it did not affect the validity of child marriages.
- Only some minor penalties were imposed. The Prohibition of Child Marriage Act, 2006 has changed the position in this regard.
- It has made child marriage voidable. Rigorous imprisonment of 2 years or fine, which may extend up to one lakh rupees, may be imposed in case of violation of any provision of this act. But even now, child marriage is valid.
- The Prohibition of Child Marriage (Amendment) Bill, 2021 proposes to increase the marriageable age of girls from 18 to 21 years, to bring parity in the marriageable age of the girls and boys.
- The bill also provides that the provisions of the act shall dominate over any other law, custom, usage or practice that governs the parties to the marriage.

Quick Test 4

1. What is required for divorce by mutual consent to be legally valid?
2. Mention the purpose of the cooling-off period under Section 13 B(2) of Hindu Marriage Act
3. What is the concept of divorce by mutual consent recognised under Muslim law?
4. Who has the absolute right to claim maintenance from the other party under Hindu law?
5. Under the Hindu Marriage Act, 1955, what penalty was imposed for child marriages?

Mind Map

INSTITUTIONAL FRAMEWORK, MARRIAGE, AND DIVORCE

1 Nature of Family Law in India

Key Characteristics
- Family laws are **not uniform** across religions.

Personal laws are religion-specific
- **Hindus, Sikhs, Jains and Buddhists** Governed by Hindu family laws.
- **Muslims, Christians and Parsis** Have separate laws.
- **Tribes** Follow customary practices.

Codified Laws
- Hindu, Parsi, Christian family laws codified by Indian Parliament.
- **Muslim Law** Based on **Sharia**, uncodified and drawn from the Quran and Sunnah.

Secular Framework
- Article 44 promotes the aspiration of a **Uniform Civil Code (UCC)**.

2 Historical Background of Family Laws

Ancient Period
- Based on **Dharmashastras** and **Dharmasutras**.
- Rules derived from Sanskrit texts on religion and ethics.

Medieval Period
- **Two major schools of Hindu laws**
  – **Mitakshara** (North and South India).
  – **Dayabhaga** (Bengal region).
- **Mughal Rule** Personal laws for Hindus and Muslims administered locally.

British Period
- Development of **Anglo-Hindu** and **Anglo-Islamic** personal laws.
- Introduction of reforms via law commissions.

Post-Independence
- Efforts to establish a **Uniform Civil Code**.
- Codification of Hindu family laws (1955-56)
  – Hindu Marriage Act.
  – Hindu Succession Act.
  – Hindu Minority and Guardianship Act.
  – Hindu Adoptions and Maintenance Act.

3 Human Rights and Gender Perspective

Constitutional Provisions
- **Article 14** Equality before the law.
- **Article 15** Prohibition of discrimination.

Challenges
- Gender inequalities in religious traditions.
- **Example** Unequal inheritance rights, polygamy in Islamic law, and restrictions on women in Hindu laws.

Modern Reforms
- Promotion of gender justice in family laws.
- Opposition from religious groups citing freedom of religion (Articles 25 and 26).

4 Institutional Framework: Family Courts

Creation
Family Courts Act, 1984
- Specialised courts for matrimonial and family disputes.
- Procedural law, not overriding personal laws.

Goals
- Speedy justice.
- Informal and conciliatory procedures.

Jurisdiction
- Marriage validity, property disputes, maintenance, guardianship and nullity.

Acts Under Family Courts
- Hindu Marriage Act, Special Marriage Act, Dissolution of Muslim Marriage Act, etc.

Role of Counselors
- Promote settlement and reduce adversarial litigation.
- Criticised for lack of uniform training and patriarchal biases.

5 Marriage

Definition
- Social and legal union with rights like companionship, cohabitation and inheritance.

Forms
- **Monogamy** Union between one man and one woman.
- **Polygamy** Multiple spouses, including
  – **Polygyny** Multiple wives.
  – **Polyandry** Multiple husbands.
- **Endogamy** Marriage within the same group.
- **Exogamy** Marriage outside the group.

Conditions
- Monogamy, sound mind, age requirements (18 for women, 21 for men).
- Prohibition of close blood relations.

6 Divorce

Theories
- **Fault Theory** Dissolution based on matrimonial offense (e.g., adultery, cruelty).
- **Mutual Consent Theory** Agreement of both parties.
- **Irretrievable Breakdown** Marriage fails beyond repair.

Religion-Specific Grounds
- **Hindu Marriage Act** Adultery, cruelty, desertion.
- **Muslim Law** Husband's unilateral right (Talaq) balanced by **Dissolution of Muslim Marriage Act.**
- **Christian Law** Adultery, cruelty, desertion.

7 Matrimonial Rights

Conjugal Rights
- Rights to companionship and cohabitation.

Maintenance
- Obligation to support a spouse.
- Permanent alimony under Hindu and Parsi laws.

Inheritance
- Governed by religion-specific laws.

For examples
- Hindu Succession Act.
- Restrictions on disposal under Muslim law.

8 Child Marriage

Prohibition of Child Marriage Act, 2006
- Declares child marriages voidable.
- Proposed amendment to raise the marriageable age for women to 21.

CBSE TEXTBOOK Folder

1. Give one point of difference between the following

(i) Exogamy and endogamy

(ii) Void and voidable marriage

(iii) Monogamy and polygamy

(iv) Marriage and divorce

Ans. (i) Endogamy refers to marriage to a person within one's own group while in exogamy, an individual marries outside the tribe, family, clan or other social unit.

(ii) A voidable marriage is a perfectly valid marriage as long as it is not annulled or legally invalid by any court of law. Only the aggrieved party to the marriage can file the petition for annulment. While a void marriage illegal under the law of jurisdiction. This concept of marriage never existed in the eyes of law.

(iii) Monogamy refers to the practice of having only wife while polygamy refers to the practice of having more than one wife.

(iv) Marriage is an institutional framework that unites two individuals and forms the basis of kinship. On the other hand, divorce refers to the dissolution of marriage.

2. Write brief notes on

(i) Fosterage

(ii) Significance of Article 44

(iii) Role of lawyers and counselors in family courts

(iv) Gender inequality in Hindu family law

(v) Objectives of family court

Ans. (i) Fosterage means when a woman, other than the mother of the child, has suckled (feed) a child under the age of two years, the woman becomes the foster mother of the child. A man cannot marry his foster mother or her daughter, or his foster sister.

(ii) Article 44 is a part of Directive Principles of State Policy which states that state shall provide a Uniform Civil Code (UCC) for its citizens throughout the territory of India.

The Uniform Civil Code (UCC) intends to give protection to weaker sections including women and religious minorities.

(iii) The Family Courts Act has given the counselors high preference over lawyers in the family courts in order to promote efforts for settlement between the parties. However, in practice, the role of counselors is insignificant due to following reasons

- Majority of the states do not adequately integrate the requirement of counselors with the legal practice of family courts.
- The role of the counselors is limited to the task of deciding if the dispute can be resolved.
- There are differences among states with respect to the process adopted to appoint the counselors, their qualifications and remunerations, their role, and the counseling techniques. Thus, some states have used non-governmental organisations as counselors, while others have used trained personnel, individual volunteers, as well as lawyers.

(iv) The instances of gender inequality existing in the present day Hindu family law include

(a) The Hindu Marriage Act prescribes marriageable age for girls as 18 and boys as 21. Recently the government has proposed the marriageable age of girls to be increased from 18 to 21 years.

(b) The Hindu Succession Act provides different methods of succession of property without a will for male and female.

(c) The Hindu Minority and Guardianship Act prohibits a mother to act as a child's natural guardian unless the father is dead or otherwise disqualified.

(d) The Hindu Adoptions and Maintenance Act prohibits a mother to give her child in adoption unless the father is dead or otherwise disqualified.

(v) Family courts were created with many distinct features and goals including

- Reduction in formality and intimidation in litigation process
- Speed in justice delivery
- Facilitation in conciliation and settlements

3. Answer the following questions

(i) Give any two examples of gender inequality in the Islamic family law.

(ii) Explain the grounds for voidable marriage provided in the Hindu Marriage Act.

(iii) What is divorce? What are the various grounds for divorce?

(iv) What are the conditions for a valid marriage?

Ans. (i) Two examples of gender inequality in the Islamic family law are

(a) The practice of polygamy is permitted in Islamic law.

(b) A Muslim husband has to pay maintenance to a divorced wife only during the iddat period of three months.

(ii) The Hindu Marriage Act aprovides four grounds for voidable marriages

(a) If marriage cannot be completed to perfection due to the impotency of one spouse, then, the other spouse can get it annulled. Here, impotency does not mean barrenness or sterility (inability to have child), rather it is failure to have sexual intercourse.

(b) When the consent for marriage is obtained by force or fraud, then the aggrieved party can get the marriage annulled.

(c) The pre-marriage pregnancy of a wife is another ground for voidable marriage. It is the condition when the wife is pregnant before marriage by some person other than the husband. However, the husband must be ignorant of this fact at the time of marriage.

(d) Unsoundness of mind is also a basis for voidable marriage.

(iii) Divorce is the termination of a marital union. Divorce results in the break of matrimonial tie between husband and wife. The status of husband and wife ceases after divorce.

The various grounds fer divorce are

- In Muslim law, husband enjoys special privilege in the area of divorce. He can divorce his wife at his will without citing any reason. Earlier, the Muslim wife had no corresponding right of divorce. It is only after passing of Dissolution of Muslim Marriage Act, 1939 that wife has been conferred right to obtain divorce.
- According to Hindu Marriage Act, 1955, both husband and wife are entitled to file a petition for dissolution of marriage. This petition can be filed on grounds of adultery, cruelty, desertion, unsoundness of mind, etc.
- Parsis as well as Christians recognise adultery, cruelty, desertion and unsoundness of mind as grounds of divorce. The Indian Divorce Act, 1869 governs Christians in matters of divorce.

Under this act, the husband can file a petition of divorce only on the grounds of adultery on the part of the wife, whereas the wife can file a petition on any of the mentioned grounds. If husband is guilty of rape or sodomy or bestiality, then wife can file petition for divorce. This remedy is available to Hindu, Parsi and Christian wife.

(iv) For a valid marriage, certain conditions are to be fulfilled by the parties to the marriage. These conditions may vary from religion to religion. These are

- There is a rule of monogamy among Hindus, Parsis and Christians according to which they can marry only once. Their first marriage must be dissolved if they want to marry again. The dissolution of marriage can take place either by divorce (i.e., dissolution of marriage by the court) or by death of another spouse. However, Muslim law permits 'polygamy' where a, Muslim man can have four wives.
- No religious ceremony is required to constitute a valid marriage under the Muslim law. The offer and acceptance to marry is often required of a Muslim couple. However, this is not so among the other religious groups like Hindus, Parsis or Christians. If any Hindu marriage has been solemnised (formalised) without the performance of customary rites on ceremonies prevailing in the community of either of the parties, such marriage is legally void.
- A person cannot marry anyone who belongs to his or her close relations. All the religions recognise that parties should not marry within certain blood relations certain persons with whom relationship has arisen by marriage. For example, a person cannot marry his or her brother or sister.
- A person must be of sound mind at the time of marriage. The sound mind refers to the ability of individuals to understand the nature of marriage, and responsibilities towards their spouses, once they get married.

4. Identify the marital right and explain

(i) The obligation of a man to support his wife out of his income.

(ii) Devolution of property after the death of spouse in Hindu and Muslim laws.

Ans. (i) **Right of Maintenance** According to this right, a man takes on an obligation to support his wife out of his earnings or other income according to his total income. This obligation remains in force for the duration of the marriage and sometimes even if the wife has an adequate income of her own.

(ii) **Right of Inheritance** According to this right, when one person dies without making a will, his property devolves (passes on), under the law of succession. When two persons get married, they get mutual rights of inheritance. Different laws of succession govern persons belonging to different religions.

Exam Pattern Questions

Objective Type Questions

Multiple Choice Questions (MCQs)

1. In which year did the Family Courts Act come into force?

(a) 1980 (b) 1981 (c) 1983 (d) 1984

2. Which act was enacted by the Indian Parliament to lay down procedures for the creation and functioning of family courts with expertise to deal with matrimonial and family law matters?

(a) The Family Courts Act, 1984
(b) The Matrimonial Act of India, 1980
(c) The Divorce Act, 1999
(d) All of the above

3. What is NOT an objective for establishing family courts?

(a) Reduction in informality and intimidation
(b) Speed in justice delivery
(c) Increase in divorce rates
(d) Facilitation in conciliation and settlements

4. Which of the following act(s) codifies the marriage law of the Hindus and primarily deals with the validity and conditions for invalidity and applicability of marriage?

(a) Special Marriage Act, 1954
(b) The Hindu Marriage Act, 1955
(c) The Indian Divorce Act, 1969
(d) None of the above

5. Haroon and Shanti has decided to get married but due to their parents' disapproval they approached to court for marriage registration under Special Marriage Act.

When was the Special Marriage Act enacted?

Competency Based Que

(a) 1950 (b) 1954 (c) 1955 (d) 1969

6. Name the act which requires the application of the Islamic Law Code of Shariat to Muslims in India in their family or personal matters?

(a) Hindu Adoption and Maintenance Act, 1956
(b) Indian Christian Marriage Act, 1956
(c) Muslim Women (Protection of Rights on Divorce) Act, 1986
(d) Muslim Personal Law/Application of Shariat Act, 1937

7. The .... Act provides mandatory powers to the State Governments to set up family courts in cities and towns with a population over one million and discretionary powers.

(a) Civil Courts (b) Family Courts
(c) Criminal Courts (d) None of these

8. The Family Courts Act restricts the role of .... and enhances the use of .... in the dispute resolution to encourage mutually amicable settlements.

(a) lawyers, counselors (b) counselors, lawyers
(c) police, courts (d) None of these

9. "Critics have argued that lawyers are necessary to help clients with complex cases and court procedures in which the counselors may not have that kind of expertise. Moreover, there has been no mechanism created to ensure the availability of 'amicus curiae' for the constant needs of courts".

What does the term 'amicus curiae' mean?

Competency Based Que

(a) Legal experts (b) Law mechanism
(c) Civil court (d) Criminal court

10. In which of the following Indian states does a counselor play a considerable role in promoting negotiations and settlements?

(a) Bihar (b) Maharashtra
(c) Rajasthan (d) Uttar Pradesh

11. Which section of the Criminal Procedure Code is a safeguard that makes maintenance mandatory for neglected children and women?

(a) Section 120 (b) Section 123
(c) Section 124 (d) Section 125

12. Preeti is getting married next week but she is curios and nervous about the institution called 'marriage'. A legal and .... union between a man and woman is known as marriage.

Competency Based Que

(a) valid (b) social
(c) family (d) void

13. In the earliest period, many civilisations across the world, began with social interaction of an organisations.

Competency Based Que

What is the system of social organisation between people who are related by blood, marriage or adoption called?

(a) Divorce (b) Kinship
(c) Marriage (d) Ethnicity

14. **Rohan read in the newspaper that a person in the Middle-East has record of marrying 60 women. However, marrying multiple women is quite normal in many society.** Competency Based Que

A marital union between one man and one woman is known as ....

(a) monogamy (b) bigamy
(c) polygamy (d) polyandry

15. **The type of marriage which is conducted within one's own social group is known as ....**

(a) endogamy (b) exogamy
(c) monogamy (d) All of these

16. **Which religion solemnises their marriage by 'Anandkaraj' ceremony where Lavan or the fours hymns of Laav are performed during the four nuptial rounds?**

(a) Hinduism (b) Zoroastrianism
(c) Sikhism (d) Jainism

17. **Name the religion that does not have monogamy as an essential condition for designating a marriage as valid.**

(a) Hinduism (b) Islam
(c) Parsi (d) Christianity

18. **George Mathew and Rosy were a married couple but during the Covid pandemic in 2020, George lost his job and therefore his wife deserted him and filed a divorce affidavit.** Competency Based Que

Which act provides for provisions pertaining to nullity of Christian marriages?

(a) Christian Divorce Act, 1870
(b) The Indian Divorce Act, 1869
(c) Indian Marriage Act, 1859
(d) None of the above

19. **Which theory of divorce originated from the drawbacks of Fault Theory of Divorce?**

(a) Divorce by mutual consent
(b) Guilt Theory of Divorce
(c) Irretrievable breakdown of marriage
(d) None of the above

20. **Which of the following theories of divorce originated from the drawbacks of Mutual Consent Theory of Divorce?**

(a) Divorce by mutual consent
(b) Guilt Theory of Divorce
(c) Irretrievable breakdown of marriage
(d) None of the above

21. **The dissolution of Muslim Marriage Act, 1939 provides grounds for a Muslim woman to seek divorce, including cruclty, abandonment and importance.**

Which of the following statement is TRUE about the Dissolution of Muslim Marriage Act, 1939?

(a) It only applies to Muslim men and not Muslim women.
(b) It allows a Muslim woman to seek divorce and Khula.
(c) It does not provide any grounds for divorce other than adultery.
(d) It is applicable to all citizens of India, regardless of religion.

22. **'X' and 'Y' are united in matrimonial obligations under Hindu law. Soon after, differences arose between them on account of which 'Y' filed a suit for divorce against her husband. Decide.** Competency Based Que

The obligation of a man to support his wife out of his income.

(a) Right of maintenance (b) Right of inheritance
(c) Matrimonial right (d) None of the above

23. **In which case did the Supreme Court hold that irretrievable breakdown of marriage should be made a ground of divorce?**

(a) Kesavananda Bharati Case
(b) Indrani Majumdar Case
(c) Neelu Kohli Case
(d) A.K. Gopalan Case

24. **Which of the following is not a conjugal or company rights to which any of the individuals belonging to a marital union is entitled?**

(a) Affection (b) Companionship
(c) Cohabitation (d) Hostility

25. **The mutual rights of companionship, aid, and sexual relations in a marital union are known as.............. .**

(a) maintenance rights (b) inheritance rights
(c) conjugal rights (d) None of these

26. **The concept of 'stridhan' is followed in which of the following religions?**

(a) Islam (b) Hinduism
(c) Christianity (d) Buddhism

27. **Match the following.**

Column I	Column II
A. Polygamy	1. A union between one woman and one man.
B. Monogamy	2. Referred to multiple spouses or multiple marriages that include either multiple husbands or multiple wives.
C. Polyandry	3. A man have many wives.
D. Polygyny	4. A woman have many husbands.

Codes

	A	B	C	D		A	B	C	D
(a)	1	2	3	4	(b)	2	1	3	4
(c)	2	1	4	3	(d)	4	2	3	1

28. **Match the following.**

Column I	Column II
A. Hinduism	1. Episcopal ordination
B. Sikhism	2. Saptapadi
C. Parsi	3. Anandkaraj
D. Christians	4. Ashirwad

Codes

	A	B	C	D		A	B	C	D
(a)	2	3	4	1	(b)	1	2	3	4
(c)	3	2	1	4	(d)	4	2	3	1

29. **Match the following.**

Column I	Column II
A. This act requires the application of the Islamic Law Code of Shariat to Muslims in India in their family or personal matters.	1. Muslim Women (Protection of Rights and Divorce) Act, 1986
B. This statute provides safeguards to the wife or female live-in partner against domestic violence by husband or male live-in partner or his relatives.	2. Protection of Women from Domestic Violence Act, 2005
C. The law codifies the legal process of adopting children by a Hindu adult and the legal obligations to provide maintenance to the various family members.	3. Hindu Adoption and Maintenance Act, 1956
D. The act deals with the matters of the divorced Muslim women and restricts their right to maintenance from their former husband.	4. Muslim Personal Law/Application of Shariat Act, 1937

Codes

	A	B	C	D		A	B	C	D
(a)	4	2	3	1	(b)	1	2	3	4
(c)	3	2	4	1	(d)	2	4	3	1

30. **Arrange the following statutes that come under the purview of Family Courts Act in chronological onder**

I. The Hindu Marriage Act
II. Special Marriage Act
III. Dissolution of Muslim Marriage Act
IV. Foreign Marriages Act

Choose the correct option

(a) I, II, III, IV (b) II, I, IV, III
(c) III, II, I, IV (d) III, IV, II, I

31. **Statement I** The Family Courts Act, 1984 provides for the establishment of Lok Adalat to deal with matrimonial disputes and related matters.

Statement II The act emphasises reconciliation and settlement of disputes through counselling and mediation and provides for the appointement of counselors and mediators to assist in this process.

Choose the correct option

(a) Both Statements are correct.
(b) Both Statements are incorrect.
(c) Statement I is correct but, Statement II is not correct.
(d) Statement II is correct but, Statement I is not correct.

Assertion-Reason Questions

Directions (Q. Nos. 32-35) In the questions given below, there are two statements. Read the statements and choose the correct option.

Codes

(a) Both A and R are true and R is the correct explanation of A.
(b) Both A and R are true, but R is not the correct explanation of A.
(c) A is true, but R is false.
(d) A is false, but R is true.

32. **Assertion** (A) In the 1980s, the women's rights movement groups were vocal about legislative reforms.

Reason (R) These issues of gender justice were an important motivating factor for the creation of family courts.

33. **Assertion** (A) The Family Courts Act was passed by the Indian Parliament in 1984.

Reason (R) Family Courts Act was passed to lay down procedures for the creation and functioning of family courts with expertise to deal with matrimonial and family law matters.

34. **Assertion** (A) Hindu Marriage Act was passed in 1955.

Reason (R) Special Marriage Act was passed in 1954.

35. **Assertion** (A) In the adversarial system of adjudication, the judge plays the role of a neutral arbiter and decides based on the merits of the case presented to him/her by the lawyers of the opposing parties.

Reason (R) Adversarial method of adjudication has originated in India.

Answers

1. (d) 1984
2. (a) The Family Courts Act, 1984
3. (c) Increase in divorce rates
4. (b) The Hindu Marriage Act, 1955
5. (b) 1954
6. (d) Muslim Personal Law/Application of Shariat Act, 1937
7. (b) Family Courts
8. (a) lawyers, counselors
9. (a) Legal experts
10. (b) Maharashtra
11. (d) Section 125
12. (b) social
13. (b) Kinship
14. (a) monogamy
15. (a) endogamy
16. (c) Sikhism
17. (b) Islam
18. (b) The Indian Divorce Act, 1869
19. (b) Guilt Theory of Divorce.
20. (c) Irretrievable breakdown of marriage
21. (b) It allows a Muslim woman to seek divorce and Khula.
22. (a) Right of maintenance
23. (c) Neelu Kohli Case
24. (d) Hostility
25. (c) conjugal rights
26. (b) Hinduism
27. (c) 2 1 4 3
28. (a) 2 3 4 1
29. (a) 4 2 3 1
30. (c) III, II, I, IV
31. (d) Statement II is correct, but Statement I is not correct.
32. (a) Both A and R are true and R is the correct explanation of A.
33. (a) Both A and R are true and R is the correct explanation of A.
34. (b) Both A and R are true, but R is not the correct explanation of A.
35. (c) A is true, but R is false.

Subjective Questions

Very Short Answer Type Questions

1. What was the aim behind creating women friendly court procedures?

Ans. Family courts aimed at creating women- friendly court procedures that were less formal and more accessible to women, especially those from the marginalised section.

2. A husband who is of short tempered in nature and the wife who is of soft nature are married. The wife was brought-up in a soft atmosphere. The husband's short temper is exposed in due course of time. The husband, shouts, abuses, throws away things and his behaviour becomes unpleasant. Such matrimonial cases are taken up in family courts.

What were the objectives behind creation of family courts? **Competency Based Que**

Ans. Family courts were created with many distinct features and goals including

(i) Reduction informality and intimidation in the litigation process. The process was made less formal and intimidating.

(ii) Speed in justice delivery.

(iii) Facilitation in conciliation and settlements.

3. Which situations affect the very foundations of a marriage?

Ans. The situations that affect the very foundations of a marriage are adultery, cruelty and desertion.

4. Define the institution of marriage.

Ans. Marriage is defined as a social and legal union between a man and a woman. Marriage is a social union because both the spouses are entitled to each other's company and conjugal rights.

These are mutual rights and privileges between two individuals that arise from the state of being married.

5. What do you understand about conjugal rights?

Ans. Conjugal rights are mutual rights and privileges between two individuals that arise from the state of being married. These rights and privileges include affection, companionship, co-habitation, joint property rights and sexual relations.

6. What are the grounds on which a marriage can be declared void?

Ans. A marriage can be declared void on the grounds of polyandry, consanguinity, affinity and fosterage.

7. John is married to Emily and they have two children together John and Emily have a loving relationship and are committed to each other. On the other hand, Michael has three wives. Rachel, Sophia and Olivia. He married Rachel first, then Sophia and later Olivia. All three wives live together with Michael in same household.

What do we call both the scenarios kindly define the kind of marriages they are in. **Competency Based Que**

Ans. John and Emily are in a monogamous marriage, which means they are married to each other and both are committed to the single relationship on the other hand, Michael is in a polygamous marriage, as he has many wives.

Monogamy is defined as a union between one woman and one man. Polygamy is referred to multiple spouses or multiple marriages that include either multiple husbands or multiple wives.

8. 'The Special Marriage Act was enacted in 1954'. Explain this act. **Competency Based Que**

Ans. The Special Marriage Act was enacted in 1954. The act was enacted to afford a special method of civil contractual marriage (and divorce) for all Indian nationals regardless of religion or faith followed by the parties. This act does not require the customary or religious rites or ceremonies of marriage to be observed.

9. A Kayastha man marries a Brahmin woman.

(i) Which rule of marriage is broken in such a case?

(ii) Define the rule of marriage in (i). **Competency Based Que**

Ans. (i) Endogamy

(ii) Endogamy is about marriage to a person within one's own group.

10. What are the grounds of divorce prescribed under Christian law?

Ans. The grounds of divorce prescribed under Christian law are

(i) Agrricved party can get the decree of nullity on ground of impotency of other spouse at the time of marriage.

(ii) Decree of nullity can be obtained if parties are within the prohibited degrees of consanguinity or affinity.

(iii) Marriage may be revoked if the former husband/wife of either party was living at the time of marriage.

(iv) It may be annulled if either party was of unsound mind at the time of marriage.

11. What was the subject matter of Foreign Marriages Act and Indian Divorce Act?

Ans. The subject matter of these acts are

(i) **Foreign Marriages Act, 1969** This act deals with marriages of citizens of India living outside India.

(ii) **The Indian Divorce Act, 1869** This act is related to the divorce of persons professing the Christian religion.

12. Define Fasid. Which religion has the concept of Fasid?

Ans. Fasid is defined as an 'irregular marriage'. It is the marriage which can become valid, if the defect is cured.

The concept of Fasid has emanated from Islam.

13. What is divorce? What does divorce result in?

Ans. Divorce is the termination of a marital union. It results in the cessation of matrimonial ties between husband and wife. The status of husband and wife ceases after divorce.

14. "It results in the cessation of matrimonial ties between husband and wife. The status of husband and wife ceases after this phenomena. This concept has evolved in the form of different theories". **Competency Based Que**

(i) Which phenomena is being discussed here?

(ii) What are the two prominent theories of (i)?

Ans. (i) Divorce

(ii) The two prominent theories of divorce are

(a) Guilt theory (b) Divorce by mutual consent

15. How is a minor defined as per law? Which act made child marriage voidable?

Ans. A minor is a person who has not completed the age of 18 years under the Indian Majority Act, 1875. The Prohibition of Child Marriage Act, 2006 made child marriage voidable.

Short Answer Type Questions

1. Raj and Anand were discussing about the judicial structure of India and both were surprised to learn that in India there are around 743 family courts are functional across the country. **Competency Based Que**

List out the various subjects which fall under the jurisdiction of family courts.

Ans. The subject matters of personal or family law that fall within the jurisdiction of family courts include

- Nullity of marriage
- Restoration of marital rights
- Judicial separation
- Validity of marriage

- Matrimonial status
- Disputes regarding property of either of the parties or joint property
- Command arising out of marital relations
- Legitimacy of any person
- Maintenance
- Guardianship custody and access to any minor

2. Describe the critical role played by women associations and organisations in the creation of family courts.

Ans. For answer refer to text under the heading Role of Women in the Creation of Family Courts, on page 227.

3. Rama has filed for divorce due to continuous tortures and mental trauma given by her husband. She hired an advocate for her case. Competency Based Que

How did the Family Courts Act define the role of lawyers and counselors in family courts?

Ans. The Family Courts Act defines the role of lawyers and counselors in family courts in following ways

- It restricts the role of lawyers and enhances the use of counselors in the dispute resolution, to encourage mutually peaceful settlements.
- It limits the role of the lawyers as legal experts or 'amicus curiae' who the courts may consult for opinion.
- It prevent excessive litigation costs, corruption, manipulative and subversive tactics, extended and bitter court battles, and refusal to settle or compromise, etc.
- It has given the counselors high preference over lawyers in the family courts in order to promote efforts for settlement between the parties.

4. What are the actual and ground level conditions of counselors in the majority of Indian states?

Ans. The actual and ground level conditions of counselors in the majority of Indian states are

- In practice, the role of counselors is more superficial.
- Majority of the states do not adequately integrate the requirement of counselors with the legal practice of family courts.
- The role of the counselors is limited to the task of deciding if the dispute can be resolved.
- The role of counselors in court practice is a new idea and both the judges and the lawyers are oriented to this concept.
- There are differences among states with respect to the process adopted to appoint the counselors, their qualifications and remunerations, their role and the counseling techniques. Thus, some states have used non- governmental organisations as counselors, while others have used trained personnel, individual volunteers, as well as lawyers.

5. Which identities define an endogamous group?

Ans. Endogamous groups may be based on the

(i) caste e.g. a Brahmin will marry a Brahmin; a Kshatriya will marry a Kshatriya, etc.
(ii) class, i.e. social categories based on economic and educational status.
(iii) ethnic group i.e. socially defined category based on common culture or nationality.
(iv) a religious group
(v) a village

6. Simranjeet has informed her fiancé Dilpreet that how the marriage ceremony in Sikhism and Hinduism are similar. Competency Based Que

In this context, describe the different kinds of marriage ceremonies practiced by different religions.

Ans. The different kind of marriage ceremonies practiced in different religions are

- Hindus follow the ceremony of 'Saptapadi' or taking of seven steps before a sacred fire.
- Sikhs solemnise their marriage by 'Anandkaraj' ceremony where Lavan or the fours hymns of Laav are performed during the four nuptial rounds.
- Parsi marriage must be solemnised in accordance with a ceremony called Aashirwad. This ceremony binds the couple in matrimony spiritually. Both the bride and the groom promise to remain faithful to each other and not to be influenced by any external temptations.
- For Christians in India, certain people are recognised as authorities under the Christian law who can perform the marriage, otherwise the marriage is void. These include following persons
  (i) Persons who have received episcopal ordination (consecration or installation by authority).
  (ii) Any Clergyman of the Church of Scotland.
  (iii) Any Minister (or priest) of religion licensed can solemnise marriages.

7. 'X', a Christian, wants to marry 'Y', a Hindu.

(i) Which legislation can be used to solemnise this marriage? Competency Based Que

(ii) What is the purview of the act mentioned in (i)?

Ans. (i) Special Marriage Act.

(ii) The act affords a special method of civil contractual marriage (and divorce) for all Indian nationals regardless of religion or faith followed by the parties. This act does not require the customary or religious rites or ceremonies of marriage to be observed.

8. Explain the grounds based on which a marriage under Hindu Marriage Act can be declared void.

Ans. For answer refer to text under the heading Hindu Marriage Act void, on page no. 231 and 232.

9. Jiwan and his wife want to take divorce through free will. There is no dispute between them except the views, which are different. When they contacted an advocate for divorce on the free consent of the parties, the lawyer stated that without proving the guilt of opposite party, there is no divorce. What do you understand by the Guilt Theory of Divorce? Competency Based Que

Ans. According to Guilt Theory of Divorce, a marriage can be dissolved only if one of the parties to marriage has, committed some matrimonial offense, after its solemisation. The offense must be one that is recognised as a ground of divorce. This theory on the one hand implies that there is a guilty party, i.e. a party who has committed a matrimonial offense, and on the other an innocent party who is a victim.

Insanity was added later in this theory as a ground of divorce but it did not fit within the framework of this theory, as the party suffering from insanity could hardly be called a guilty party. This led to renaming of the Guilty Theory as Fault Theory.

If one of the parties has some fault in him/her, marriage could be dissolved, whether that fault is his/her conscious act or providential.

10. Explain the theory of divorce by mutual consent.

Ans. Theory of divorce by mutual consent originated due to the shortcomings of the Fault Theory of Divorce. The biggest limitation of the Fault Theory has been the presumption that there is one innocent party and one guilty party. Sometimes, husband and wife are not able to live together and there is no fault in either of them. In that case both of them are left with no remedy.

Thus, a new theory of mutual consent develop where marriage could be dissolved by mutual consent of both the husband and the wife where they are not able to live together. Divorce by mutual consent means that the law recognises the situation, where parties can also obtain divorce by mutual consent. But only the mutual consent will not automatically terminate the relationship. It is essential to obtain a decree of the court.

Divorce by mutual consent requires the consent of both the parties, and if one of the parties withholds his or her consent, divorce can never be obtained.

11. What are the laws of divorce in Islam?

Ans. Laws of divorce prescribed in Islam are

- Muslims do not have a codified law for marriage and divorce. They are governed by their religious texts.
- Generally, decree of court is required for dissolution of marriage by divorce. But Muslims are an exception to this rule.
- In Muslim law, husband enjoys special privilege in the area of divorce. He can divorce his wife at his will without citing any reason.
- Earlier, the Muslim wife had no corresponding right of divorce. It is only after passing of Dis-solution of Muslim Marriage Act, 1939 that wife has been conferred right to obtain divorce.

12. Different laws of divorce govern people belonging to different religions. Decree of court is required for dissolution of marriage by divorce.

(i) Which religion has an exception to the said rule?

(ii) Which legislation governs Hindus in matters of marriage and divorce? Competency Based Que

Ans. (i) Decree of court is required for dis-solution of marriage by divorce. But Muslims are an exception to this rule. In Muslim law, husband enjoys special privilege in the area of divorce. He can divorce his wife at his will without citing any reason. Earlier, the Muslim wife had no corresponding right of divorce. It is only after passing of Dissolution of Muslim Marriage Act, 1939 that wife has been conferred right to obtain divorce.

(ii) The Hindu Marriage Act, 1955 governs Hindus in matters of marriage and divorce. Both husband and wife are entitled to file a petition for dissolution of marriage. The petition can be filed on grounds of adultery (sexual intercourse outside wedlock), cruelty (conduct of such a nature that it is not possible for the aggrieved party to live with the spouse who has committed that act), desertion (physical separation as well as intention to leave the matrimonial home permanently on the part of deserter), unsoundness of mind (mental disorder of such a kind that it is not possible for the petitioner to live with the respondent) and so on.

13. Radheyshyam and Bansilal were two sons of Mukundlal. Being an elder son Radheyshyam was Mukundlal's first choice to inherit all of his property. However, his younger Bansilal filed a case against his father and elder brother. Competency Based Que

Describe the provisions of Hindu Succession Act.

Ans. The provisions of Hindu Succession Act are

(i) Under Hindu family, if a male or female dies without making a will, then the property is distributed as per rules of succession prescribed in the Hindu Succession Act, 1956.

(ii) Under the act, both husband and wife are included in the category of most preferred heirs. Both of them can make a will of his or her separate properties and can give them to anyone. But, the ancestral property has to be disposed off according to the Hindu Succession Act, 1956.

Long Answer Type Questions

1. What are the different statutes which come within the purview of the Family Courts Act? Describe.

Ans. The relevant statutes or acts that come within the purview of Family Courts Act include

- **The Hindu Marriage Act, 1955** This act codifies the marriage law of the Hindus. It primarily deals with the validity and conditions for invalidity and applicability of marriage.
- **Special Marriage Act, 1954** This act provides a special method of civil contractual marriage (and divorce) for all Indian nationals, regardless of religion or faith followed by the parties. This act does not require the customary or religious rites or ceremonies of marriage to be observed.
- **Dissolution of Muslim Marriage Act, 1939** This act explains the dissolution of marriage by women married under Muslim law and the effects of the renunciation (rejection) of Islam by a married Muslim woman.
- **Foreign Marriages Act, 1969** This act deals with marriages of citizens of India, living outside India.
- **The Indian Divorce Act, 1869** This act is relates to the divorce of persons professing the Christian religion.
- **The Parsi Marriage and Divorce Act, 1936** This act deals with marriage and divorce among the Parsis.
- **Muslim Women (Protection of Rights and Divorce) Act, 1986** This act deals with the matters of the divorced Muslim women and restricts their right to maintenance from their former husband.
- **Muslim Personal Law/Application of Shariat Act, 1937** This act deals with the application of the Islamic Law Code of Shariat in India in their family or personal matters.
- **Hindu Adoption and Maintenance Act, 1956** This act codifies the legal process of adopting children by a Hindu adult and the legal obligations to provide maintenance to the various family members.
- **The Indian Christian Marriage Act, 1872** This act regulates the formalisation of marriages among Indian Christians.
- **Hindu Minority and Guardianship Act, 1956** This act explains the guardianship relationships of Hindus involving the adults and minors as well as between people of all ages and their respective property.
- **Guardian and Wards Act, 1890** This is a non-religious and universally applicable law regarding the issues relating to guardianship of a child in India.
- **Chapter IX of the Criminal Procedure Code, 1973** This act deals with the issues of maintenance of wives, children and parents.
- **Protection of Women from Domestic Violence Act, 2005** This act provides safeguards to the wife or female live-in partner against domestic violence by husband or male live-in partner or his relatives. This law also provides protection to other women living in a household including sisters, widows, or mothers.

2. Shabana became a family court lawyer in Lokhandwala area of Mumbai. While dealing in her first case, her client Mamta was accused by her husband of being infidel and both don't want to live together anymore. Competency Based Que

Describe in detail the role played by lawyers and counselors in family courts. What is the criticism of the existing status of lawyers pertaining to family courts ?

Ans. For answer refer to text under the heading Role of Lawyers and Counselor in Family Courts, on page no. 227 and 228.

3. There are a few states such as Maharashtra, where counselors play a considerable role in promoting negotiations and settlements'. Based on the above statement describe the role of women's organisations, counselors and issues pertaining to them around gender sensitivity.

Ans. For answer refer to text under the heading Role of Counselors and Gender Issues, on page no. 228 and 229.

4. Tannu and Siddhartha are married for 10 years but both lives separately for almost 5 years or more. Parents of Siddhartha now counseling an advocate for formal divorce, so that their son can get remarry another girl. In this context, describe in detail the necessary conditions of a valid marriage. Competency Based Que

Ans. For answer refer to text under the heading Conditions of a Valid Marriage, on page no. 230 and 231.

5. Define divorce. Explain in detail the different theories of divorce.

Ans. Divorce is the termination of a marital union. It results in the end of matrimonial ties between husband and wife. The status of husband and wife ceases after divorce.

For Different Theories of Divorce, refer to text on page no. 233 and 234.

6. Muskan, a 12 years old girl was kidnapped from Hisar while her family members left her in the hotel room. Later the police rescued her from a marriage ceremony. All the accused were sent to jail. In this context, describe the various provisions of Child Marriage Act, 2006. Competency Based Que

Ans. For answer refer to text under the heading The Prohibition of Child Marriage Act, 2006, on page no. 237.

SELF ASSESSMENT TEST

Objective Type Questions

1. Marriage is a social union because both the spouses are entitled to each other's company and .... rights.
   (a) hostile (b) conjugal (c) literal (d) None of these
2. Which of the following means the act or state of dwelling together, or in the same place with one another?
   (a) Consummation (b) Conference (c) Cohabitation (d) All of these
3. There is no concept of voidable marriage under Muslim law rather they recognise concept of irregular or .... marriage.
   (a) Iftar (b) Fasid (c) Iddat (d) None of these
4. In which of the following religious communities, there is no codified law for marriage and guardianship?
   (a) Hindu (b) Sikh (c) Parsi (d) Muslim
5. .... is a sum of money or property that the wife is entitled to receive from the husband in consideration of marriage.
   (a) Donor (b) Doer (c) Doher (d) Dower

Very Short Answer Type Questions

6. Specify the major aims and objectives behind the establishment of a system of family courts to settle domestic disputes.
7. How is the Family Court Act's system of adjudication different from English family law?
8. The Family Courts Act does away with lawyers to prevent certain malpractices. List out which malpractices are prevented through reduction of the role of lawyers in matters pertaining to family law. **Competency Based Que**
9. What are the mutual rights and privileges between two individuals that arise from the state of being married?
10. Define the theory of divorce by mutual consent.

Short Answer Type Questions

11. Briefly explain the crucial role played by women's associations in making family courts a reality of the Indian judicial system. **Competency Based Que**
12. Chart out the crucial subjects which fall under the jurisdiction of Family Courts Act of 1984.
13. Describe the conditions of a valid marriage among Hindus, Parsis and Christians.
14. State the different ages prescribed for marriage by different religions.
15. 'The Hindu Marriage Act, 1955 makes the distinction between void and voidable marriage'. Mention the three grounds for void marriage provided by Hindu Marriage Act. **Competency Based Que**
16. Describe the theory of irretrievable breakdown of marriage.

Long Answer Type Questions

17. When was the Family Court Act passed? Discuss the aims and objectives behind settlement of such courts. What is the extent of their jurisdiction?
18. Discuss in detail the contemporary debate going on around gender justice and family laws.
19. Explain the concept of void and voidable marriage. Also explain the laws prescribed by various religions pertaining to void and voidable marriages.
20. 'Different laws of divorce govern people belonging to different religions'. Describe in detail these different laws. **Competency Based Que**

14

CHAPTER

Child Rights

According to the Convention on the Rights of the Child of 1989, a child is any human being below the age of eighteen years, unless under the law applicable to the child, majority is attained earlier.

YOUR STUDY GOALS

YOUR PRACTICE GOAL

- Objective Type Questions (26 Qs ; MCQs, A-R, Statements, Matching)
- Subjective Questions (9 VSAs, 5 SAs, 6 LAs)

14.1 Rights of Child

- The term 'child' is derived from the Latin word 'infans', which means the **one who does not speak.**
- In India, a person is deemed to be a major on attaining the age of 18 years under the Indian Majority Act, 1875.
- The law, policy and practice of child welfare has undergone a significant change from a historical perspective.
- Earlier, there was the concept of authority and control where the father had absolute rights over his children.
- Later, the welfare principle was reflected in the dominant[1] ideology of the family.
- The Indian traditional view of welfare is based on daya, dana, dakshina, bhiksha, ahimsa and tyaga.
- It was believed that welfare of children depended upon these values.
- The concept of children's right emerged only during the 20th century.
- The rights approach is primarily concerned with issues of social justice, non-discrimination, equity and empowerment.
- The rights perspective is embodied in the **United Nations Convention on the Rights of the Child 1989,** which is a landmark in international human rights legislation.

1 Dominant It means having power of influence over others.

Convention on the Rights of Child

- In **December 1992,** India ratified the Convention on the Rights of the Child.
- This convention gives all those basic human rights to children that will enable them to achieve their full potential.
- These rights include civil, economic, social, cultural and political rights.
- The civil rights include protection from torture and maltreatment.
- It also include making of special rules that control the circumstances under which children may be deprived of their liberty.
- The economic rights include the right to ensure proper development and protection from exploitation at work.
- The social rights include the right to the highest attainable standard of health services, protection from sexual exploitation and the regulation of adoption.
- The cultural rights include **Right to Education.**

Right to Education

- Education is the transmission of the values and accumulated knowledge of a society.
- It helps children in knowing their culture, moulding their behaviour in the ways of adulthood and directing them towards their future role in society.
- Right to education is one of the Fundamental Rights in the Indian Constitution (**Article 21A inserted by 86th Constitutional Amendment**).
- It provides that the state shall provide free and compulsory education to all children between the age of **6 to 14 years.**
- The state also has the power to promote the educational and economic interests of the weaker sections of the society and particularly the Scheduled Castes and the Scheduled Tribes.
- It is the mandatory duty of the state to make effective provisions for securing the right to education according to its economic capacity and development. Moreover, it is also the duty of the parents or guardian to provide opportunities for education to his child or ward between the age of 6 to 14 years.

Salient Features of the Right to Education Act

Some of the salient features of Right to Education Act are

- The Right of Children to Free and Compulsory Education Act was passed by the Parliament in 2009.
- The act ensures that children get education irrespective of their economic condition.
- The financial burden for the implementation of the act is to be shared by State and the Central Government on the basis of the **Sarva Shiksha Abhiyan** programme of the Central Government.
- It also provides for 25 per cent reservation for economically disadvantaged communities in all private and minority schools.
- The private schools have to face penalty for violating any provision of this act.
- The act prohibit physical punishment and mental harasssment.

Right to Health

- Health is a state of complete physical, mental and social well-being.
- The enjoyment of the highest attainable standard of health is one of the Fundamental Rights of every human being without distinction of race, religion and political belief, economic or social condition.
- Healthy development of the child is one of the basic needs, and the ability to live harmoniously in a changing environment is essential for such development.

- The extension of the benefits of medical, psychological and related knowledge to all the people, is essential for the most comprehensive attainment of health.
- The **World Health Organisation (WHO)** is a specialised agency of the United Nations that is concerned with international public health.

Important Case Laws

- **Consumer Education and Research Centre Vs. Union of India, (1995).** Right health and medical care is Fundamental Right under Article 21 read with Article 39 (c), 41 and 43 of the Constitution.
- **Paschim Banga Khet Mazdoor Sanity Vs. State of West Bengal, (1996).** Article 21 imposes and delegation on the state to safeguard the right ot life of every person. Preservation of human life is, thus, of paramount importance.

Provisions regarding Right to Health

Following are the provisions for health

- A Constitutional duty has been imposed on the state to ensure that the health and strength of workers, men and women and the tender age of children are not abused.
- The state has to ensure that children are given opportunities and facilities to develop in a healthy manner and in conditions of freedom and dignity.
- Childhood will be protected against exploitation.
- The health of infant and mother has to be protected by maternity benefit.
- It is the primary duty of the state to
  - improve public health.
  - secure justice and humane conditions for works.
  - provide of sickness, old age, disablement and maternity benefits.
  - prohibit the consumption of intoxicating drinking and drugs that are injurious to health.
  - protect and impose a pollution free environment for the good health of its citizens.

Right to Shelter

- Shelter is a place where a person has opportunities to grow physically, mentally, intellectually and spiritually.
- Shelter includes the entire infrastructure necessary to enable an individual to live and develop as a human being.

  Right to shelter includes
  - Adequate living space
  - Clean and hygienic surroundings
  - Pure air and water
  - Sanitation
  - Safe and repeatable structure
  - Sufficient light
  - Electricity
  - Other civic amenities like roads.
- The components of shelter are discussed by the Supreme Court in the case of **Chameli Singh Vs. State of UP, (1996).**
- In **Shantistar Builders Vs. Narayan Khimalal Totame,** (1990) the Supreme Court decided that the right to life would include the right to food, the right to clothing, the right to decent environment and a reasonable accommodation to live in, within its scope.
- There is a difference between the need of an animal and a human being for shelter.
- For the animal, it is the bare protection of the body whereas for a human being it has to be a suitable accommodation, which would allow him to grow in every aspect i.e., physical, mental and intellectual.
- Thus, right to shelter has become an integral part of the right to life.

Quick Test 1

1 What is the provision of Indian Majority Act, 1875?
2 When did India ratified the Convention on the Rights of the Child?
3 Mention any one provision regarding health.
4 In which case, the Supreme Court decided that the right to life would include right to food, right to clothing, right to decent environment and a reasonable accommodation to live in?

14.2 Child Labour (Right Against Exploitation)

- Child Labour means labour by the child i.e., when the child is made to work.
- There are a number of factors to determine whether a particular form of 'work' can be called as 'child labour' or not.
- These factors include child's age, nature, hours of work and the conditions under which such work is performed, etc.
- The labour that threatens the physical, mental or moral well-being of a child is known as **hazardous work.**
- Such labour deprives children of their childhood, potential and dignity.

Indian Constitution and Right Against Exploitation

The Indian Constitution has provided the right against exploitation as a Fundamental Right. The provisions of this right are

- A child who is **below the age of 14 years** cannot be employed in any factory or mine or engage in any other hazardous employment.
- A duty has been imposed on the state to ensure that tender age of children is not abused.
- The state has to ensure that the children are not forced by economic necessity to enter into any occupation unsuited to them.
- The **Child Labour (Prohibition and Regulation) Act** was enacted in 1986.
- The objective of this act are
  - Banning the employment of children, who have not completed their 14 years, in specified occupations and processes.
  - Laying down procedures to decide modifications to the schedule of banned occupations or processes.
  - Regulating the conditions of work of children in employment where they are not prohibited from working.
- In 2006, legislature had brought child domestic workers upto 14 years of age working in hotels, dhabas, eateries and in the entertainment industry within the purview of the Child Labour (Prohibition and Regulation) Act, 1986.

International Labour Organisation

- The International Labour Organisation (ILO) was founded in 1919. It was the first specialised agency of the United Nations to deal with the labour issue.
- ILO started the **International Programme on the Elimination of Child Labour** (IPEC) in 1992.
- Its main objective is progressive elimination of child labour.

National Policy on Child Labour

- A national policy on child labour was formulated in 1987.
- This policy provides for strict enforcement of Child Labour Laws.
- The focus under this policy is on the general developmental programmes on child labour.
- It provides for starting of projects in the areas having high concentration of child labour.
- In pursuance to this policy, the **National Child Labour Project (NCLP)** scheme was launched in 1988.
- The scheme proposes to run special schools for children withdrawn from work.

14.3 Sexual Abuse

- Child sexual abuse involves any sexual activity with a child.
- It is interaction between a child and an adult or older child in which child is used for the sexual stimulation of the perpetrator (wrong doer).
- It includes fondling (touching) of a child's genitals, making the child to fondle the perpetrator is genitals, intercourse, incest, rape, sodomy, exhibitionism and sexual exploitation.
- A person **under the age of 18 years** may also commit sexual abuse.
- There is significant disparity in age, development, or size, rendering the victim incapable of giving consent.
- Child sexual abuse include extra-familial (outside a family) abuse as well as inter-familial (within family) abuse. The **Protection of Children from Sexual Offences Act, 2012** was passed by the Parliament in 2012 to deal with this problem.

  This act protects children from
  - offences of penetrative sexual assault.
  - offences of sexual assault.
  - offences of sexual harassment.
  - use of child for pornographic purposes.

Programmes for Mitigating Sexual Abuse

- Education programmes for children are created to create awareness among children. These programmess focus on two main goals
  (i) **Primary Prevention** Preventing the abuse from occurring.
  (ii) **Detection** Encouraging children to report past and current abuse.
- The parents play an important role in empowering their children to protect themselves.
- Accordingly, the prevention of child sexual abuse begins with social awareness, and the recognition that expertise, energy and money are needed to alleviate (mitigate) the conditions that produce child sexual abuse.
- School based sex education for children is important because it has the potential to reach large numbers of young people.
- Parental competency programmes target at risk parents (poor, young, single) and at risk children, with the goal of providing training and social support before any abuse can occur.

14.4 Juvenile Justice

- The word 'juvenile' has originated from the Latin word 'juvenilis', which means 'of or **belonging to youth**'.
- Juvenile justice is the area of criminal law applicable to persons who are not old (mature) enough to be held responsible for criminal acts.
- The environmental factors that have awakened criminal tendencies in the child should be held responsible for the criminal acts.
- The removal of these factors might turn the juvenile into a person of stature and excellence.

History of Juvenile Justice System in India

- The primary legal framework of juvenile justice law in India was the **Juvenile Justice Act, 1986**.
- This act provided protection, treatment and rehabilitation of children and criminal juveniles and for deciding of certain matters related to the disposition of criminal juveniles.
- On **20th November, 1989** the General Assembly of the United Nations adopted a Convention on the Rights of Child.
- This convention seeks to protect the best interest of juvenile offenders.
- The convention states that to protect the social reintegration of juveniles, there shall be no judicial proceedings and court trials against them.
- The convention led the Indian legislation to repeal the Juvenile Justice Act, 1986 and to make a new law.
- Thus, Indian legislation came up with a new Act which was called the **Juvenile Justice (Care and Protection of Children) Act, 2000.**
- It was amended twice first in 2006 and later in 2011.
- The amendments were made to address the gap and defects in the implementation.
- The increasing number of cases of juvenile crimes in recent years and frightful incident of Delhi Gang Rape case, **Mukesh & Anr Vs. State for Nct of Delhi & Ors (2017)** encouraged major changes in the criminal justice system of India.
- The Juvenile Justice (Care and Protection of Children) Act, 2000 was replaced by the **Juvenile Justice (Care and Protection) Act, 2015.**

Juvenile Justice (Care and Protection of Children) Act, 2015

- It is the primary legal framework for juvenile justice in India. It has brought 'children in need of care and protection' and 'children in conflict with law', within its scope.
- A 'child in need of care and protection' means a child who is found without any home and ostensible (presumed) means of subsistence. It includes the following
  - A child who is mentally or physically challenged or suffering from terminal or incurable diseases, with no one to look after him/her.
  - Children who are likely to be grossly abused, tortured or exploited for the purpose of sex or other illegal acts.
  - Children having parents who are unfit to exercise control over them.
  - Children who do not have parents and no one is willing to take care of them.
  - A child who is found vulnerable and is likely to be
    - inducted into drug abuse or trafficking
    - abused for unconscionable gains
    - a victim of any armed conflict, civil commotion or natural calamity.
  - A child who is found begging or a child living on the streets, or a working child.

- A **'child in conflict with law'** means a juvenile who is alleged to have committed an offence but has **not completed 18 years of age** as on the date of commission of such offence.
- The Juvenile Justice (Care and Protection of Children) Act also provides for proper care, protection and treatment to juveniles by catering to their developmental needs.
- It also aims at ultimate rehabilitation through various institutions established under this enactment.
- It has tried to lay down a uniform framework for juvenile justice in the country.

Salient Features of the Juvenile Justice (Care and Protection of Children) Act, 2015

- The Juvenile Justice Act divided the crimes into three different categories i.e. petty offences, serious offences and heinous offences.
- **Juvenile Justice Boards are constituted in every district** to deal with children in conflict with law. The board comprises a Metropolitan Judge and Judicial Magistrate with two social workers.
- For all cases, excluding the offence of heinous crimes, the juvenile will get institutional care for a maximum of three years by the Juvenile Justice Board.
- If a minor between the age of 16-18 years is accused of committing a heinous crime then under the amended law, the minor can be tried as an adult.

Important Decisions in Cases regarding Juvenile Justice

- The Supreme Court in the case of **Sheela Barse Vs. Secretary, Children's Aid Society** decided that children should not be made to stay in observation homes for too long and as long as they are there, they should be kept occupied. The occupations should be **congenial**[2] and intended to bring about adaptability in life, self-confidence and development of human values.
- In the case of **Sanjay Suri Vs. Delhi Administration**, a news report described the ill treatment suffered by minors in the Tihar Jail in Delhi with the assistance of the jail staff. In this case, the Supreme Court ordered to release some juvenile undertrial prisoners immediately. Some convicted minors were freed on parole (conditional release of a prisoner) for one month. The judgement stressed the need to generate a sense of humanism in jail administration.

Quick Test 2

1. What do you mean by child labour?
2. When did International Labour Organisation came into existence?
3. Mention any one objective of education programme to mitigate sexual abuse.
4. What is meant by a 'child in conflict with law' according to Juvenile Justice (Care and Protection of Children) Act, 2015?
5. Mention any one feature of Juvenile Justice (Care and Protection of Children) Act, 2015.

2 **Congenial** It means pleasing or liked on account of having qualities or interests that are similar to one's own.

Mind Map

CHILD RIGHTS

1 Introduction to Child Rights

Definition

- Derived from the Latin word **"infans"**, meaning "one who does not speak."
- **Child** Any human below 18 years unless majority is attained earlier (as per Indian Majority Act, 1875).

Evolution

- **Earlier focus** Paternal authority and control.
- **Modern focus** Welfare and rights.
- Influenced by values like **daya, dana, ahimsa, tyaga** in Indian tradition.
- Shift towards rights-based approach focusing on justice, non-discrimination, equity and empowerment.

International Landmark

United Nations Convention on the Rights of the Child (1989)

- India ratified it in 1992.
- Recognised children's civil, economic, social, cultural and political rights.

2 Key Rights of Children

Right to Education

- Recognised as a Fundamental Right (Article 21A).

Right of Children to Free and Compulsory Education Act, 2009

- Free and compulsory education for children aged 6–14.
- 25% reservation for economically disadvantaged communities in private schools.
- Prohibits physical punishment and harassment in schools.

Right to Health

- Protected under Article 21 and related provisions.

Ensures

- Healthy development.
- Maternity benefits for mothers and children.
- Prohibition of drug and alcohol abuse among children.

Landmark Cases

- **Consumer Education & Research Centre Vs. Union of India (1995)** Declared health as a Fundamental Right.
- **Paschim Banga Khet Mazdoor Samity Vs. State of West Bengal (1996)** Highlighted the state's duty to safeguard life.
- Right to Shelter
- Integral part of the Right to Life (Article 21).

Includes

- Adequate living space.
- Hygienic surroundings.
- Clean water, sanitation, and other civic amenities.

3 Child Labour

Definition

- Employment of children in work detrimental to their physical or mental health.

Legal Provisions

- **Child Labour (Prohibition and Regulation) Act, 1986**
  - Prohibits employment of children below 14 in hazardous industries.
  - Regulates working conditions where employment is permitted.
- **National Policy on Child Labour (1987)**
  - Focus on strict enforcement of child labour laws.
  - Special projects in high child-labour areas (e.g., National Child Labour Project).
- **International Efforts**

International Labour Organisation (ILO)

- Founded in 1919, started International Programme on the Elimination of Child Labour (IPEC) in 1992.

4 Child Sexual Abuse

Definition

- Any sexual activity involving a child, including exploitation and harassment.

Legislation

- Protection of Children from Sexual Offences (POCSO) Act, 2012 cover:
  - Penetrative and non-penetrative sexual assault.
  - Sexual harassment.
  - Use of children for pornography.

Mitigation Measures

- Education and awareness programmes for children and parents.
- School-based sex education.
- Social and legal support systems.

5 Juvenile Justice System

Definition

- Criminal law applicable to persons not old enough to be held responsible for crimes.

Historical Context

- **Juvenile Justice Act, 1986** Initial framework.
- **Juvenile Justice (Care and Protection of Children) Act, 2000** Amended to align with UN conventions.
- **Juvenile Justice (Care and Protection of Children) Act, 2015** differentiates offenses into **petty, serious and heinous.**
- **Juvenile Justice Boards**
  - Handle children in conflict with the law.
  - Includes judicial and social work experts.
- Minors (16–18) accused of heinous crimes can be tried as adults.

Landmark Cases

- **Sheela Barse Vs. Secretary, Children's Aid Society**
  Highlighted humane treatment and engagement of children in observation homes.
- **Sanjay Suri Vs. Delhi Administration**
  Addressed ill-treatment of minors in custody.

6 Role of Constitution

Key Provisions

- **Article 21A** Right to Education.
- **Article 24** Prohibition of child labour in hazardous industries.
- **Articles 39(e) and (f)** Protects children from abuse and promotes development in a dignified environment.

7 Key Takeaways

- The chapter highlights the **progressive development** of child rights in India.
- Emphasises the role of **education, health, and protection** as foundational rights.
- Calls for stronger enforcement of laws to safeguard children's welfare.

CBSE TEXTBOOK Folder

1. The United Nations Convention on the Rights of Child gives all basic rights to a child that will enable them to achieve their full potential. Explain the cultural and social rights available to a child.

Ans The United Nations Convention on the Rights of the Child recognises the cultural and social rights of every child. These rights are essential for children to grow and develop in a healthy and positive way and to fully realise their potential.

Cultural and social rights include

- **The Right to Express their Views** Children have the right to express their opinions and ideas on all matters that affect them and their views should be given due weight and consideration.
- **The Right to Education** Children have the right to education that promotes their personal development and prepares them for responsible citizenship. Education should be free, compulsory and accessible to all children.
- **The Right to Play and Rest** Children have the right to engage in play and recreational activities and to rest and leisure time.
- **The Right to Participate in Cultural Activities** Children have the right to participate in cultural life, including the arts and to access and enjoy cultural heritage.
- **The Right to Freedom of Thought, Conscience and Religion** Children have the right to freedom of thought, conscience and religion and to express their beliefs and values.
- **The Right to Freedom of Association** Children have the right to freedom of association, to form and join groups and to participate in peaceful assembly.
- **The Right to be Protected from Exploitation and Abuse** Children have the right to be protected from all forms of exploitation, abuse, neglect and violence, including trafficking, sexual exploitation and harmful traditional practices.

These cultural and social rights are crucial for the development of a child's personality, creativity, and full potential. They help children to engage with their communities and the wider world, and to become active and responsible citizens.

2. What is the status of education as a right? How did it acquire this status?

Ans. The status of education as a right varies by country and region. However, education has been recognised as a Fundamental Human Right by International Organisations and many countries around the world.

The Universal Declaration of Human Rights, adopted by the United Nations General Assembly in 1948, states that 'everyone has the right to education', and that 'education shall be free, at least in the elementary and fundamental stages'. This declaration has been followed by several international treaties and agreements that reinforce education as a human right, including the International Covenant on Economic, Social and Cultural Rights and the Convention on the Rights of the Child.

Education has acquired the status of right in India through the 86th Constitutional Amendment which inserted Article 21A in the Constitution of India. It provides for free and compulsory education of all children in the age group of 6 to 14 years.

3. Is there any legislation in India dealing with child labour? Name the relevant legislation. Aditi hired a 12 years old girl to help her with the domestic household chores. Can she be prosecuted for child labour? Explain giving legal reasons. **Competency Based Que**

Ans. Yes, there is legislation in India dealing with child labour. The relevant legislation is the Child Labour (Prohibition and Regulation) Act, 1986, which aims to prohibit the engagement of children in certain types of employment and to regulate the conditions of work for children in other occupations.

In the case of Aditi hiring a 12 years old girl to help with domestic household chores, Aditi could be prosecuted for violating the Child Labour (Prohibition and Regulation) Act, 1986. Under this act, a child is defined as a person who has not completed 14 years of age. It is illegal to employ a child in any occupation or process, and it is also illegal to employ an adolescent (between the ages of 14-18 years) in hazardous occupations and processes.

In this case, Aditi has employed a child to work in her household, which is a violation of the act. Domestic household chores are not considered hazardous, but it is still illegal to employ a child below 14 years of age for such work. Aditi could face prosecution for employing a child in violation of the Child Labour (Prohibition and Regulation) Act, 1986, and may be subject to a fine and imprisonment.

Exam Pattern Questions

Objective Type Questions

Multiple Choice Questions (MCQs)

1. **The term 'child' is derived from the word 'infans'. This word belongs to which language?**
(a) German (b) Greek (c) Latin (d) Roman

2. **The Indian traditional view of welfare is based on six principles. Which one of the following is NOT one of them?** **Competency Based Que**
(a) Daya (b) Dakshina
(c) Tapa (d) Ahimsa

3. **According to which convention, a child is defined as any human being below the age of eighteen years, unless under the law applicable to the child, majority is attained earlier?**
(a) Convention on the Rights of the Child of 1989
(b) Convention on Children, 1990
(c) Child Rights Covenant, 2002
(d) None of the above

4. **When did the United Nations Convention on the Rights of the Child came into existence?**
(a) 1985 (b) 1989
(c) 1990 (d) 1992

5. **When did India ratified the Convention on the Rights of the Child?**
(a) April, 1981 (b) March, 2002
(c) June, 2003 (d) December, 1992

6. **Right to Education is enshrined in which Article of Indian Constitution?**
(a) Article 20 (b) Article 21
(c) Article 21 A (d) Article 22

7. **Which amendment of Indian Constitution inserted Article 21 A in Indian Constitution?**
(a) 85th Amendment Act
(b) 88th Amendment Act
(c) 80th Aamendment Act
(d) 86th Amendment Act

8. **In which year did The Right of Children to Free and Compulsory Education Act was passed by the Parliament?**
(a) 2001 (b) 2002
(c) 2008 (d) 2009

9. **In .... programme of Central Government, the financial burden for the implementation is to be shared by State and the Central Government?**
(a) Sarva Shiksha Abhiyan
(b) Sustainable Education
(c) Shiksha and Education
(d) None of the above

10. **Which act provides for 25 per cent reservation for economically disadvantaged communities in all private and minority schools?**
(a) Right to Schooling
(b) Right of Children to Free and Compulsory Education
(c) Right to Siksha
(d) None of the above

11. **'The article imposes an obligation on the state to safeguard the right to life of every person'. Identify the article.**
(a) Article 20 (b) Article 22
(c) Article 21 (d) Article 25

12. **In which case did Supreme Court held that the right to life would take within its scope the right to food, the right to clothing, the right to decent environment and a reasonable accommodation to live in?** **Competency Based Que**
(a) Shantistar Builders Vs. Narayan Khimalal Totame, (1990)
(b) Kesavanada Bharati Case Vs. State of Kerala, (1993)
(c) Maneka Gandhi Vs. Union of India, (1985)
(d) None of the above

13. **In which case did the Supreme Court held that children should not be made to stay in the observation homes for too long and as long as they are there, they should be kept occupied?**
(a) Sheela Barse Vs. Secretary, Children's Aid Society
(b) Ashutosh Varshney Vs. Children's Aid Society
(c) Both of the above
(d) None of the above

14. **When was International Labour Organisation founded?**
(a) 1920 (b) 1921
(c) 1922 (d) 1919

15. Which act was enacted to ban the employment of children, who have not completed their 14th years, in specified occupations and processes?

(a) The Child Labour (Prohibition and Regulation) Act, 1986
(b) Child Protection Act, 1990
(c) Child Labour Prevention Act, 1992
(d) None of the above

16. In which year did the Protection of Children from Sexual Offences Act pass?

(a) 2010 (b) 2011
(c) 2012 (d) 2013

17. It has adopted a child-friendly approach in the adjudication and disposition of matters in the best interest of children. It also aims at ultimate rehabilitation through various institutions established under this enactment.

The above mentioned provisions are engrained in which act? **Competency Based Que**

(a) Children Protection Act, 2006
(b) Juvenile Justice (Care and Protection of Children) Act, 2000
(c) Life and Property maintenance Act, 1992
(d) None of the above

18. Which of the following is TRUE regarding the minimum age of a child who can be held criminally liable in India?

(a) 12 years (b) 16 years
(c) Below 7 years (no criminal liability)
(d) 18 years (with no exceptions)

19. Kindly arrange the following events as per its year of happening.

I. The Rights of Children to free and compulsory education Act.
II. National Policy on child labour.
III. Protection of Children from sexual offences Act.
IV. India ratified the Convention on the Rights of the Child.

Choose the correct option

(a) II, I, III, IV (b) II, IV, I, III
(c) IV, II, III, I (d) IV, III, II, I

20. What is the primary objective of the International Labour Organisation (ILO)?

Statement I The ILO promotes personal and economic progress by setting international labour standards.

Statement II The ILO aims to achieve full employment and improve working conditions worldwide.

Choose the correct option

(a) Both the Statements are correct.
(b) Both the Statements are incorrect.
(c) Statement I is correct but, Statement II is incorrect.
(d) Statement I is incorrect but, Statement II is correct.

21. Match the following.

	Column I (Acts Policies)		Column II (Year)
A.	Right to Education	1.	1890
B.	Indian Majority Act	2.	2009
C.	Sarva Shiksha Abhiyan	3.	2001

Codes

	A	B	C		A	B	C
(a)	1	2	3	(b)	2	1	3
(c)	2	3	1	(d)	1	3	2

22. Match the following.

	Column I		Column II
A.	National Policy on Child Labour	1.	2000
B.	Juvenile Justice (Care and Protection of Children) Act	2.	2012
C.	Protection of Children from Sexual Offences Act	3.	1987

Codes

	A	B	C
(a)	3	1	2
(b)	1	2	3
(c)	2	1	3
(d)	2	3	1

Assertion-Reason Questions

Directions (Q.Nos. 23-26) In the questions given below, there are two statements marked as Assertion (A) and Reason (R). Read the statements and choose the correct options.

Codes

(a) Both A and R are true and R is the correct explanation of A.
(b) Both A and R are true, but R is not the correct explanation of A.
(c) A is true, but R is false.
(d) A is false, but R is true.

23. Assertion (A) The rights approach is primarily concerned with issues of social justice, non-discrimination, equity and empowerment.

Reason (R) The rights perspective is embodied in the United Nations Convention on the Rights of the Child 1990.

24. Assertion (A) Education is the transmission of the values and accumulated knowledge of a society.

Reason (R) It helps children in knowing their culture, moulding their behaviour in the ways of adulthood and directing them towards their eventual role in society.

25. **Assertion** (A) The Right of Children to Free and Compulsory Education Act was passed by the Parliament in 2015.

Reason (R) The act ensures that children get education irrespective of their economic condition.

26. **Assertion** (A) A child is any human being below the age of eighteen years, unless under the law applicable to the child, majority is attained earlier.

Reason (R) In India, a person is deemed to be a major on attaining the age of 18 years.

Answers

1. (c) Latin
2. (c) Tapa
3. (a) Convention on the Rights of the Child of 1989
4. (b) 1989
5. (d) December, 1992
6. (c) Article 21 A
7. (d) 86th Amendment Act
8. (d) 2009
9. (a) Sarva Shiksha Abhiyan
10. (b) Right of Children to Free and Compulsory Education
11. (c) Article 21
12. (a) Shantistar Builders Vs. Narayan Khimalal Totame, (1990)
13. (a) Sheela Barse Vs. Secretary, Children's Aid Society
14. (d) 1919
15. (a) The Child Labour (Prohibition and Regulation) Act, 1986
16. (c) 2012
17. (b) Juvenile Justice (Care and Protection of Children) Act, 2000
18. (d) 18 years (with no exceptions)
19. (b) II, IV, I, III
20. (c) Statement I is correct, but Statement II is not correct.
21. (c) 2 3 1
22. (a) 3 1 2
23. (c) A is true, but R is false.
24. (a) Both A and R are true and R is the correct explanation of A.
25. (d) A is false, but R is true.
26. (b) Both A and R are true, but R is not the correct explanation of A.

Subjective Questions

Very Short Answer Type Questions

1. What are the principles on which traditional view of welfare is based?

Ans. The Indian traditional view of welfare is based on daya, dana, dakshina, bhiksha, ahimsa and tyaga.

2. How does Convention on the Rights of the Child, 1989 defines 'Child'?

Ans. According to the Convention on the Rights of the Child of 1989, a child is any human being below the age of 18 years, unless under the law applicable to the child, majority is attained earlier.

3. What are the issues with which rights framework is primarily concerned?

Ans. The rights approach is primarily concerned with issues of social justice, non-discrimination, equity and empowerment.

4. Ramesh, a 10 years old boy from a rural village, was working in his family's farm to support his family financially. However, with the help of a local NGO, Ramesh enrolled in a nearby school. He learned to read, write, and acquired skills in mathematics, science and technology. He also gained knowledge about health, nutrition and environmental conservation.

Briefly describe the significance of education.

Competency Based Que

Ans. Education is the transmission of the values and accumulated knowledge of a society.

It helps children in knowing their culture, moulding their behaviour in the ways of adulthood and directing them towards their eventual role in society.

5. What is the subject matter of Article 21 A of Indian Constitution?

Ans. Article 21 A provides that the state shall provide free and compulsory education to all children between the age of 6-14 years.

6. What are the basic constituents of Right to Shelter?

Ans. Right to shelter includes adequate living space, safe and repeatable structure, clean and hygienic surroundings, sufficient light, pure air and water, electricity, sanitation and other civic amenities like roads.

7. How is the term 'child labour' defined?

Ans. Child Labour means labour by the child i.e., when the child is made to work.

There are a number of factors to determine whether a particular form of 'work' can be called as 'child labour' or not.

8. A teenager, a few months shy of 18, allegedly drove a luxury car at high speed under the influence of alcohol and crashed into a motorcycle, causing the death of a man and a women. An FIR against the minor was registered under sections 304, 304 A of the IPC. There is little to no possibility that the alleged offendor would be tried as an adult, as the Juvenile Justice Act only tries Juveniles as adults in henious offences.

What is meant by Juvenile Justice? **Competency Based Que**

Ans. The word 'juvenile' has originated from the Latin word 'Juvenilis', which means 'of or belonging to youth'. Juvenile justice is the area of criminal law applicable to persons who are not old (mature) enough to be held responsible for criminal acts.

9. What is meant by child in conflict by Law?

Ans. A 'child in conflict with law' means a juvenile (person who has not attained the age of 18 years) who is alleged to have committed an offence (violation or breach of law) and has not completed 18 years of age as on the date of commission of such offence.

Short Answer Type Questions

1. The children rights perspective is embodied in which convention? What are its basic characteristics?

Ans. The children rights perspective is embodied in the United Nations Convention on the Rights of the Child 1989, which is a landmark in international human rights legislation. India ratified the Convention on the Rights of the Child in December, 1992.

The characteristics of the convention are

This convention gives all those basic human rights to children that will enable them to achieve their full potential. These include civil, economic, social, cultural and political rights.

- The civil rights include protection from torture and maltreatment. It also include making of special rules that control the circumstances under which children may be deprived of their liberty.
- The economic rights include the right. to ensure proper development and protection from exploitation at work.
- The social rights include the right to attain standard of health services, protection from sexual exploitation and the regulation of adoption.
- The cultural rights include right to education.

2. What are the different kind of rights mentioned in the United Nations Covenants on Rights of Child?

Ans. The United Nations Covenants on Rights of Child include following kind of rights

(i) **Civil Rights** The civil rights include protection from torture and maltreatment. Making of special rules governing the circumstances under which children may be deprived of their liberty also constitutes part of civil rights.

(ii) **Economic Rights** The economic rights include the right to ensure proper development and protection from exploitation at work.

(iii) **Social Rights** The social rights include the right to the highest attainable standard of health services, protection from sexual exploitation and the regulation of adoption.

(iv) **Cultural Rights** Right to education is included in the cultural rights.

3. 'The Protection of Children from Sexual Offences Act, 2012 provides protection to children from various kind of sexual offences'. List out what kinds of sexual offences fall under the ambit of this act? **Competency Based Que**

Ans. The Protection of Children from Sexual Offences Act protects children from following kinds of sexual offences

- Offences of penetrative sexual assault (penetration of penis or any object or part of body into the vagina, mouth, urethra or anus of child or makes the child to do so with him or any other person. It also includes manipulation of any part of the body of the child so as to cause such penetration).
- Sexual assault (touching vagina, penis, anus or breast of child with sexual intent or making a child to do so).
- Sexual harassment (uttering words, making sounds or gesture or exhibiting any body part or making a child to do so).
- Use of child for pornographic purposes (using a child in any form of media for the purposes of sexual gratification).

4. 'Juvenile Justice is the primary legal framework in India. Explain the salient features of the Juvenile Justice Act, 2015. Competency Based Que

Ans. The salient features of the the Juvenile Justice (Care and Protection) Act, 2015 are
- The Juvenile Justice Act divided the crimes into three different categories i.e. petty offences, serious offences and heinous offences.
- Juvenile Justice Boards are constituted in every district to deal with children in conflict with law. The board comprises a Metropolitan Judge and Judicial Magistrate with two social workers.
- For all cases excluding the offence of heinous crimes, the juvenile will get institutional care for a maximum of three years by the Juvenile Justice Board.
- If a minor between the age of 16-18 years is accused of committing a heinous crime (whether a crime is heinous or not is determined by the Juvenile Justice Board on a case to case basis), then under the amended law, the minor can be tried as an adult.

5. "Juvenile Justice Boards are constituted in every district to deal with children in conflict with law". Elaborate. Competency Based Que

Ans. Juvenile Justice Boards are constituted in every district to deal with children in conflict with law. The board comprises a Metropolitan Judge and Judicial Magistrate with two social workers. For all cases, excluding the offence of heinous crimes, the juvenile will get institutional care for a maximum of three years by the Juvenile Justice Board.

If a minor between the age of 16-18 years is accused of committing a heinous crime (whether a crime is heinous or not is determined by the Juvenile Justice Board on a case to case basis), then under the amended law, the minor can be tried as an adult.

Long Answer Type Questions

1. Describe the concept of Education. Mention the salient features of the Right to Education.

Ans. Education is the transmission of the values and accumulated knowledge of a society. It helps children in knowing their culture, moulding their behaviour in the ways of adulthood and directing them towards their eventual role in society.

Some of the salient features of Right to Education Act are
- The Right of Children to Free and Compulsory Education Act was passed by the Parliament in 2009.
- The Act ensures that children get education irrespective of their economic condition.
- It provides for free and compulsory education to all children in the age group of six to fourteen years (6 -14 years).
- The financial burden for the implementation is to be shared by State and the Central Government on basis of the Sarva Shiksha Abhiyan programme of the Central Government.
- It also provides for 25 per cent reservation for economically disadvantaged communities in all private and minority schools.
- The private schools have to face penalty for violating any provision of this act.

2. (i) What are the provisions in Indian Constitution pertaining to Right to Health?

(ii) Enumerate the primary duty of state pertaining to public health.

Ans. (i) Various provisions pertaining to Right to Health in Indian Constitution are
- A Constitutional duty has been imposed on the state to ensure that the health and strength of workers, men and women and the tender age of children are not abused.
- It has to ensure that children are given opportunities and facilities to develop in a healthy manner and in conditions of freedom and dignity.
- Childhood will be protected against exploitation.
- The health of infant and mother has to be protected by maternity benefit.

(ii) The primary duty of state related to public health are
- Improve public health.
- Secure justice and humane conditions for works.
- Extension of sickness, old age, disablement and maternity benefits.
- Prohibition of consumption of intoxicating drinking and drugs that are injurious to health.
- Protect and impose a pollution free environment for the good health of its citizens.

3. (i) Describe the concept of 'Child Labour'.

(ii) Describe the Constitutional provisions mentioned in Indian Constitution pertaining to child labour.

(iii) Explain the provisions of national policy on child labour, 1987.

Ans. (i) Child labour means labour by the child i.e., when the child is made to work. There are a number of factors to determine whether a particular form of 'work' can be called as 'child labour' or not. These factors include child's age, nature, hours of work and the conditions under which such work is performed, etc.

(ii) The provisions in the Indian Constitution and child labour are
- The Indian Constitution has provided the right against exploitation as a Fundamental Right.
- A child who is below the age of 14 years cannot be employed in any factory or mine or engage in any other hazardous employment.
- A duty has been imposed on the state to ensure that tender age of children is not abused.
- The state has to ensure that these children are not forced by economic necessity to enter into any occupation unsuited to them.
- The Child Labour (Prohibition and Regulation) Act was enacted in 1986.

(iii) The provisions of national policy on child labour are
- This policy provides for strict enforcement of Child Labour Laws.
- The focus under this policy is on the general developmental programmes on child labour.
- It provides for starting of projects in the areas having high concentration of child labour.
- In pursuance to this policy, the National Child Labour Project (NCLP) scheme was launched in 1988.
- The scheme envisages running of special schools for children withdrawn from work.

4. 'Juvenile Justice is the area of criminal law applicable to persons who are not old (mature) enough to be held responsible for criminal acts'.
(i) What are the provisions of Juvenile Justice Act, 2000?
(ii) How is a 'child in need of protection and care' and 'a child in conflict with law' defined?

Competency Based Que

Ans. (i) The various provisions of Juvenile Justice (Care and Protection of Children) Act, 2000 are
- Indian Constitution enables the state to make special provisions for children.
- The Juvenile Justice (Care and Protection of Children) Act, 2000 is the primary legal framework for juvenile justice in India.
- It has brought within its ambit 'children in need of care and protection' and 'children in conflict with law'.
- This act also provides for proper care, protection and treatment to juveniles by catering to their developmental needs.
- It has adopted a child-friendly approach in the adjudication and disposition of matters in the best interest of children.
- It also aims at ultimate rehabilitation through various institutions established under this enactment.
- It has tried to lay down a uniform framework for juvenile justice in the country.

(ii) A 'child in need of care and protection' means a child who 'is found without any home and ostensible means of subsistence. It include the following
- A child who is mentally or physically challenged or suffering from terminal or incurable diseases with no one to look after him/her.
- Children who are likely to be grossly abused, tortured or exploited for the purpose of sex or other illegal acts.
- Children having parents who are unfit to exercise control over them.
- Children who do not have parents and no one is willing to take care of them.
- A child who is found vulnerable and is likely to be inducted into drug abuse or trafficking.

A 'child in conflict with law' means a juvenile (person who has not attained the age of 18 years) who is
- Alleged to have committed an offence (violation or breach of law).
- Not completed 18th years of age as on the date of commission of such offence.

5. Explain in detail the History of the Juvenile Justice System.

Ans. For answer refer to text under the heading History of Juvenile Justice System in India, on page no. 255.

6. Explain in detail about the Juvenile Justice (Care and Protection of Children) Act, 2015.

Ans. For answer refer to text under the heading Juvenile Justice (Care and Protection of Children) Act, 2015, refer to text on page no. 255 and 256.

SELF ASSESSMENT TEST

Objective Type Questions

1. Who among the following has the Constitutional duty to promote the educational and economic interests of the weaker sections of the society?
(a) State (b) Population (c) Territory (d) All of these

2. The financial burden for the implementation is to be shared by State and the Central Government on basis of the Sarva Shiksha Abhiyan programme of the Central Government. Which principle of governance is being followed here? **Competency Based Que**
(a) Unionism (b) Federalism (c) Capitalism (d) None of these

3. Right to health and medical care is a Fundamental Right under which article of Indian Constitution?
(a) Article 20 (b) Article 21 (c) Article 21 A (d) Article 22

4. Which among the following does not fall under Right to Shelter?
(a) Adequate living space (b) Clean surroundings
(c) Sufficient air (d) None of these

5. In which year did the International Labour Organisation started the International Programme on the Elimination of Child Labour (IPEC)?
(a) 1990 (b) 1991 (c) 1992 (d) 1993

Very Short Answer Type Questions

6. How do you define the terms education and health?
7. Mention the characteristic features of International Labour Organisation.
8. How does law define child sexual abuse?
9. "Juvenile justice is the area of criminal law applicable to persons who are not old (mature) enough to be held responsible for criminal acts". Explain in brief. **Competency Based Que**
10. Write in brief about the Juvenile Justice (Care and Protection of Children) Act, 2000.

Short Answer Type Questions

11. Describe the different facets of Right to Shelter in India.
12. Does Indian Constitution have laws which prohibits child labour? If yes, explain.

Long Answer Type Questions

13. 'Health is a state of complete physical, mental and social well-being.
(i) State the provisions regarding right to health.
(ii) Mention any two judgements of the Supreme Court on health.
(iii) Explain how health is the primary duty of the state. **Competency Based Que**
14. Describe the various dimension pertaining to child sexual abuse. What steps can be taken to prevent it?
15. "Juvenile Justice (Care and Protection of Children) Act, 2015 also embraces those children who are likely to be grossly abused, tortured or exploited for the purpose of sex or other illegal acts". Elaborate. **Competency Based Que**

15

CHAPTER

Adoption is the act of establishing a person as parents to one who is not in fact or in law his child.

Adoption

▼ **YOUR STUDY GOALS**

15.1 Meaning of Adoption

15.2 Minor Custody and Guardianship

▼ **YOUR PRACTICE GOAL**

- Objective Type Questions (18 Qs ; MCQs, A-R, Statements, Matching)
- Subjective Questions (6 VSAs, 6 SAs, 3 LAs)

15.1 Meaning of Adoption

- Adoption is the means by which a legal relationship is established between the parents and children who are **not related biologically**.
- It is also defined as a process by which people take a child who was not born to them and raise him/her as a member of their family.
- Earlier, the objective of adoption was mainly to secure performance of funeral rites and to preserve the continuance of one's **lineage**[1].

Laws Governing Adoption

The operation of adoption is governed by many statutes

The Hindu Adoption and Maintenance Act, 1956

- In India, the only law governing adoption for Hindus is the **Hindu Adoption and Maintenance Act, 1956.** Its scope is confined only to Hindus.
- The law codifies the legal process of adopting children by a Hindu adult and the legal obligations to provide maintenance to the various family members.

1 **Lineage** It means direct descent from an ancestor.

Law on Adoption for other Religions/Communities

- There is no law on adoption for Christians, Parsis and Muslims.
- A person belonging to these communities has to get himself appointed as guardian under the Guardians and Wards Act, 1890.
- This act applies to all communities and castes.
- The court will consider the personal law of the minor while appointing or declaring a person as guardian, under the Guardians and Wards Act, 1890.
- Once a person is appointed or declared as a guardian, he has to abide by the provisions of the Guardians and Wards Act, 1890.

15.2 Minor Custody and Guardianship

- Minor is a person who has not completed the age of 18 years under the Indian Majority Act 1875.
- A guardian is a person who has rights and duties with respect to the care and control of a minor's person in relation to body or property (estate or wealth of minor).
- The rights of guardians include the right to determine the child's upbringing in regard to religion, education and other matters such as the disposal of properties, etc.
- A guardian has the duty to act for the welfare of the minor.
- The welfare of the child is the supreme concern for the court in matters related to custody and guardianship of the child.
- In matters of custody and guardianship every community has its own laws.

The Guardians and Wards Act, 1890

- This is a **non-religious and universally applicable law** regarding the issues relating to guardianship of a child in India.
- The Guardians and Wards Act, 1890 was passed during the British period.
- This act has **authorised the court to appoint guardians** for a minor child.
- The child may belong to any community.

The Hindu Minority and Guardianship Act, 1956

- The Hindu Minority and Guardianship Act was enacted in 1956.
- This act has codified the law relating to custody and guardianship of children belonging to the Hindu community.
- According to this act, guardian includes the following
  - A **natural guardian**[2]
  - A guardian appointed by the will of the minor's father or mother
  - A guardian appointed or declared by a court

De-jure and De-facto Guardians

- A guardian can be de-jure when the authority of guardianship is provided by law.
- A guardian can be de-facto when a person power without being legally established.

---

2 **Natural Guardian** It menas a child's mother on father, biological or adopted, natural Guardian has the legal right to mmake decisions for a minor child.

Types of De-jure Guardians

De-jure guardians can be of three types, they are

(i) **Natural guardians (by birth)** Generally, father and mother are recognised as natural guardians of the child.

(ii) **Testamentary Guardians** These are guardians appointed by will.

(iii) **Certificated Guardians** These are guardians appointed by the court under the Guardians and Wards Act, 1890.

Natural Guardian under Hindu Law

- **Section 6** of Hindu Minority and Guardianship Act, 1956 provides that the natural guardian of a Hindu minor boy or unmarried girl is the father, and after him, only the mother.
- The mother is entitled to guardianship 'after' the father.
- Here, the term after means in the absence of.
- Ordinarily, the custody of a minor child who is **below the age of 5 years** is given to the mother.
- Thus, a functional guardian i.e. (person who is looking after the welfare of the child and actually taking care of him), will be given responsibility of the guardianship.

Natural Guardian under Muslim Law

- Muslims do not recognise mother as a guardian, whether natural or otherwise.
- But she has the **Right of Hizanat** means the right of the mother **to have custody** of the child during early childhood.

Testamentary Guardian under Hindu and Muslim Law

- Under the Hindu Minority and Guardianship Act, 1956, both the parents can appoint a testamentary guardian for the child.
- However, in Muslim law, only the father has power to appoint a testamentary guardian. The mother has no such power.

Mind Map

ADOPTION

1 Meaning of Adoption

Definition
- Legal relationship established between parents and a child who is not biologically related.
- Process by which a child becomes a member of a family not born into.

Historical Objective
- Secure performance of funeral rites.
- Preserve the continuance of one's lineage.

2 Laws Governing Adoption

Hindu Adoption and Maintenance Act, 1956
- Governs adoption among Hindus, Jains, Buddhists and Sikhs.
- Codifies the legal process and maintenance obligations.

Other Religions
- Christians, Parsis, and Muslims do not have codified laws on adoption.
- Governed by the **Guardians and Wards Act, 1890**
  – Court-appointed guardians manage the welfare of the child.
  – Personal laws of the minor are considered during guardianship appointments.

3 Minor Custody and Guardianship

Definition of a Minor
- Person below 18 years as per the Indian Majority Act, 1875.

Definition of a Guardian
- Person responsible for care and control of the minor's body and property.

Types of Guardians

De-jure Guardians
- Natural guardians (father and mother).
- Testamentary guardians (appointed by will).
- Certificated guardians (appointed by court).

De-facto Guardians
- Individuals acting as guardians without legal authority.

4 Custody Laws by Religion

Hindu Law
- Governed by the **Hindu Minority and Guardianship Act, 1956.**
- Natural guardianship lies with the father, followed by the mother.
- For minors below 5 years, custody usually given to the mother.

Muslim Law
- Does not recognise the mother as a guardian.
- Grants **Hizanat (custody rights)** to the mother during early childhood.
- Father can appoint a testamentary guardian.

Guardians and Wards Act, 1890
- Non-religious and universally applicable.
- Authorises courts to appoint guardians for minors from any community.

5 Key Provisions of Adoption and Guardianship

Natural Guardianship
- Defined under Section 6 of the Hindu Minority and Guardianship Act.
- Recognises father and, in his absence, mother as natural guardians.

Testamentary Guardianship
- **Hindu law** Both parents can appoint a guardian through a will.
- **Muslim law** Only fathers have testamentary authority.

Custody Decisions
- Welfare of the child is the paramount consideration for courts.

6 Landmark Acts

Hindu Adoption and Maintenance Act, 1956
- Focuses on legal processes for Hindus.
- Covers rights and obligations of adopted children.

Guardians and Wards Act, 1890
- Provides for court-appointed guardians.
- Applicable to all communities.

7 Rights and Duties of Guardians

Responsibilities
- Ensure minor's welfare, including education and health.
- Manage minor's property and estate.

Limitations
- Guardians must act in the best interest of the child.
- Guardianship can be revoked if duties are not fulfilled.

8 Key Takeaways

- Adoption ensures children are provided with familial care and legal rights.
- Guardianship emphasises the welfare of minors in matters of custody and property management.
- Laws vary significantly across religions, with personal laws and court intervention playing a significant role.

CBSE TEXTBOOK Folder

1. The act that codified the law relating to custody and guardianship of children belonging to the Hindu community is known as ....

(a) The Guardians and Wards Act, 1890
(b) The Hindu Minority and Guardianship Act, 1956
(c) The Hindu Adoption and Maintenance Act, 1956
(d) The Hindu Marriage and Divorce Act

Ans. (b) The Hindu Minority and Guardianship Act, 1956

2. Which of the following communities has a law on adoption?

(a) Christians
(b) Parsis
(c) Hindus
(d) Muslims

Ans. (c) Hindus

3. Anisha's (a minor) father appointed Anisha's aunt as her guardian in his will under the Hindu Minority and Guardianship Act, 1956. Anisha's aunt is a ....

(a) testamentary Guardian
(b) natural Guardian
(c) de facto Guardian
(d) certificated Guardian

Ans. (a) testamentary Guardian

4. Shanaya is a 5 years old Muslim girl. Her parents are separated. Which parent will get custody of the child and why? Competency Based Que

Ans. As per Hizanat under the Muslim personal law, the child's custody rights rest solely with the mother till the child is 7 years of age, except if she is considered unfit or incapable of raising the child.

5. Anuj is the son of Neeta and Neelesh Pandey. The couple separated and both are eager to seek the custody of Anuj. Who will be Anuj's guardian under Hindu law? Explain the position of both the mother and father. Competency Based Que

Ans. Anuj's guardian under Hindu law will be his father Neelesh Panday. Section 6 of Hindu Minority and Guardianship Act, 1956 provides that the natural guardian of a Hindu minor boy or unmarried is the father and only after him, the mother. The mother is entitled to guardianship 'after' the father. Here, the term 'after' means 'in the absence of'.

Ordinarily, the custody of a minor child who is below the age of five years is given to the mother. Thus, a functional guardian (person who is looking after the welfare of the child and actually taking care of him) will be given responsibility of the guardianship.

6. Angad, a minor Sikh was staying in Delhi with his parents who were involved in a bitter battle over his custody. Explain with relevant provisions as to who will get his custody. Competency Based Que

Ans. A guardian appointed by the will of Angad, or his natural guardian, or the guardian appointed by the court will get the custody of Angad. The law pertaining to the custody of children in India is determined by the Guardian and Wards Act,1890. However, it may also vary from case to case depending upon the religion of both the parties as the personal laws for every religion is different.

Hindu, Jain, Buddhist and Sikh are governed by the Hindu Minority and Guardian Act,1956 whereas Muslims and Christians are governed by their respective personal laws.

Exam Pattern Questions

Objective Type Questions

Multiple Choice Questions (MCQs)

1. **Which of the following means a person who has not completed the age of 18 years?**

(a) Guardian (b) Minor
(c) Both (a) and (b) (d) Majority

2. **There is no law of adoption for which of the following?**

(a) Christians (b) Muslims
(c) Parsis (d) All of these

3. **Once a person is appointed or declared as a guardian, he has to abide by the provisions of which of the following acts?**

(a) Guardians and Wards Act, 1890.
(b) The Hindu Minority and Guardianship Act
(c) The Hindu Adoption and Maintenance Act
(d) None of the above

4. **Under which of the following acts, both the parents can appoint a testamentary guardian for the child?**

(a) Hindu Minority and Guardianship Act, 1956
(b) The Hindu Adoption and Maintenance Act
(c) Both (a) and (b)
(d) Neither (a) nor (b)

5. **Minor is a person who has not completed the age of 18 years under the ....**

(a) Indian Majority Act, 1875
(b) Indian Majority Act, 1872
(c) Indian Majority Act, 1882
(d) Indian Majority Act, 1885

6. **Ordinarily, the custody of a minor child who is below the age of .... years is given to the mother.**

(a) 5 (b) 6 (c) 2 (d) 1

7. **The law codifies the legal process of adopting children by a Hindu Adult.**

Which of the following statement is TRUE regarding adoption.

(a) In India, the only law governing adoption for Hindus is the Hindu Adoption and Maintenance Act.
(b) In India, the only law governing adoption for hindus is the Guardians and Wards Act.
(c) In India, the only law governing adoption for Hindus is the Guardians and Wards Act.
(d) In India, the only law governing adoption for thindus is Indian Majority Act.

8. **Which among the following is Not a feature of Guardianship Act.**

(a) The Guardians and Wards Act, 1890 was passed during the British period.
(b) The child may belong to any community.
(c) A guardian has the duty to act for the welfare of the minor.
(d) The Hindu Minority and Guardianship Act was enacted in 1954.

9. **In Muslim law, which of the following has power to appoint a testamentary guardian?**

(a) Father (b) Mother
(c) Both (a) and (b) (d) Court

10. **The court appointed Kavya's uncle as her guardian under the Guardians and Wards Act, 1890. Kavya's uncle is a ....**

(a) testamentary guardian (b) natural guardian
(c) de-facto guardian (d) certificated guardian

11. **Alia is a 5 years old Muslim girl. Her parents are separated. Which parent will get custody of the child?**

(a) Mother (b) Father
(c) Joint custody (d) None of these

12. **Arrange the following acts as per the year of enactment.**

I. The Hindu Minority and Guardianship Act
II. The Guardians and Wards Act,
III. Hindu Adoption and Maintenance Act
IV. Indian Majority Act

Choose the correct option

(a) IV, II, I, III (b) III, IV, II, I
(c) IV, III, II, I (d) III, II, IV, I

13. **Statement I** The Hindu Adoption and Maintenance Act, 1956, allows for the adoption of a child by a Hindu male or female.

Statement II The act provides that a married Hindu woman can adopt a child only with the consent of her husband.

Which of the following is true about the Hindu Adoption and Maintenance Act, 1956?

(a) Statement I is true, but Statement II is false.
(b) Statement I is false, but Statement II is true.
(c) Both Statement I and Statement II are true.
(d) Both Statement I and Statement II are false.

14. **Statement I** The Right of Hizanat is the custody of a child, typically granted to the mother in Islamic law.

Statement II The father's Right to Hizanat is absolute and cannot be denied under any circumstances.

Which of the following is true about the Right of Hizanat?

(a) Statement I is true, but Statement II is false.
(b) Statement I is false, but Statement II is true.
(c) Both Statement I and Statement II are true.
(d) Both Statement I and Statement II are false.

15. **Match the following.**

	Column I		Column II
A.	Act of establishing a person as parent to one who is not in fact or in law his child.	1.	Guardian
B.	A person who has rights and duties with respect to the care and control of a minor's person in relation to body or property.	2.	Testamentary guardian
C.	A guardian appointed by 'will'	3.	Adoption
D.	Authority vested by law	4.	De-jure

Codes

	A	B	C	D
(a)	3	4	2	1
(b)	1	4	3	2
(c)	2	3	1	4
(d)	3	1	2	4

Assertion-Reason Questions

Directions (Q. Nos. 16-18) In the questions given below, there are two statements marked as Assertion (A) and Reason (R). Read the statements and choose the correct option.

Codes

(a) Both A and R are true and R is the correct explanation of A.
(b) Both A and R are true, but R is not the correct explanation of A.
(c) A is true, but R is false.
(d) A is false, but R is true.

16. **Assertion** (A) The primary objective of adoption earlier was to provide a loving home to orphaned children.

Reason (R) Adoption was mainly done to secure performance of funeral rites and to preserve the continuance of one's lineage.

17. **Assertion** (A) The primary consideration of the court in matters of custody and guardianship is the welfare of the child.

Reason (R) The court's main objective is to ensure the child's property and estate are protected.

18. **Assertion** (A) For a Hindu minor boy or unmarried girl, the mother is the natural guardian in respect of the minor's person and property.

Reason (R) The father is not available to take care of the minor.

Answers

1. (b) Minor
2. (d) All of these
3. (a) Guardians and Wards Act, 1890.
4. (b) The Hindu Adoption and Maintenance Act
5. (a) Indian Majority Act, 1875
6. (a) 5
7. (a) In India, the only law governing adoption for Hindus is the Hindu Adoption and Maintenance Act.
8. (d) The Hindu minority and Guardianship Act was to enacted in 1954.
9. (a) Father
10. (d) certificated guardian
11. (a) Mother
12. (a) IV, II, I, III
13. (c) Both Statement I and Statement II are true.
14. (a) Statement I is true, but Statement II is false.
15. (d) 3 1 2 4
16. (d) A is false, but R is true.
17. (c) A is true, but R is false.
18. (c) A is true, but R is false.

Subjective Questions

Very Short Answer Type Questions

1. What was the main objective of adoption earlier?

Ans. Earlier, the objective of adoption was mainly to secure performance of funeral rites and to preserve the continuance of one's lineage.

2. There is no law on adoption for Christian, Parsis and Muslims. Identify and explain under which act they appoint guardians. **Competency Based Que**

Ans. There is no law on adoption for Christians, Parsis and Muslims. A person belonging to these communities has to get himself appointed as guardian under the Guardians and Wards Act, 1890. This act applies to all communities and castes. The court will take into consideration the personal law of the minor while appointing or declaring a person as guardian under the Guardians and Wards Act, 1890.

3. What is the difference between a minor and a guardian?

Ans. Minor is a person who has not completed the age of 18 years under the Indian Majority Act, 1875, whereas, a guardian is a person who has rights and duties with respect to the care and control of a minor's person in relation to body or property (estate or wealth of minor).

4. State about the Hindu Adoption and Maintenance Act, 1956.

Ans. In India, the only law governing adoption is the Hindu Adoption and Maintenance Act, 1956. Its scope is confined only to Hindus.

The law codifies the legal process of adopting children by a Hindu adult and the legal obligations to provide maintenance to the various family members.

5. Ramesh is the biological father of 8 years old Rohan. However, due to his busy work schedule, Rohan has been living with his grandparents, Ravi and Sarita, since he was a toddler. Ravi and Sarita have been taking care of Rohan's daily needs, education, and well-being. In fact, Rohan considers Ravi and Sarita as his parents. Who is the de-jure guardian of Rohan?

What do you mean by de-jure and de-facto guardian? **Competency Based Que**

Ans. A guardian can be de-jure when the authority of guardianship is provided by law. A guardian can be de-facto when a person power without being legally established.

6. Leela, a 75 years old widow, is suffering from dementia and requires constant care. Her son, Raghav, is a busy professional and cannot take care of her full-time. Leela's family approaches a professional caregiver agency, which assigns a trained caregiver, Suman, to take care of Leela's daily needs. Suman is authorised to make medical decisions on Leela's behalf and manages Leela's finances.

Who is the certified guardian in this scenario? What do you mean by certified guardian? **Competency Based Que**

Ans. In the above case Suman is performing caregiving duties and she is not a certified guardian. Because a certified guardian means a person who is legally appointed by the court to make decisions on behalf of another person, under the Guardianship and Wards Act, 1890.

Short Answer Type Questions

1. 'The Hindu Adoption and Maintenance Act, 1956 different from the laws on adoption for other religions/communities'. Explain how they are different. **Competency Based Que**

Ans. **The Hindu Adoption and Maintenance Act, 1956** In India, the only law governing adoption is the Hindu Adoption and Maintenance Act, 1956. Its ambit is confined only to Hindus. The law codifies the legal process of adopting children by a Hindu adult and the legal obligations to provide maintenance to the various family members.

Law on Adoption for Other Religions/Communities

There is no law on adoption for Christians, Parsis and Muslims. A person belonging to these communities has to get himself appointed as guardian under the Guardians and Wards Act, 1890. This act applies to all communities and castes. The court will take into consideration the personal law of the minor while appointing or declaring a person as guardian under the Guardians and Wards Act, 1890. Once a person is appointed or declared as a guardian, he has to abide by the provisions of the Guardians and Wards Act, 1890.

2. (i) 'A guardian has rights and duties to care of a minor's person'. Comment.

(ii) What does the Guardians and Wards Act, 1890 state?

Ans. (i) A guardian is a person who has rights and duties with respect to the care and control of a minor's person in relation to body or property.

- The rights of guardians include the right to determine the child's upbringing in regard to religion, education and other matters such as the disposal of properties etc.
- A guardian has the duty to act for the welfare of the minor.

(ii) This is a non-religious and universally applicable law regarding the issues relating to guardianship of a child in India.

- The Guardians and Wards Act, 1890 was passed during the British period.
- This act has authorised the court to appoint guardians for a minor child. The child may belong to any community.

3. Explain the differences between The Guardians and Wards Act, 1890 and The Hindu Minority and Guardianship Act, 1956.

Ans. **The Guardians and Wards Act, 1890**

This is a non-religious and universally applicable law regarding the issues relating to guardianship of a child in India. The Guardians and Wards Act, 1890 was passed during the British period. This act has authorised the court to appoint guardians for a minor child. The child may belong to any community.

The Hindu Minority and Guardianship Act, 1956 The Hindu Minority and Guardianship Act was enacted in 1956. This act has codified the law relating to custody and guardianship of children belonging to the Hindu community.

Under this act, the guardian includes the following

- A natural guardian.
- A guardian appointed by the will of the minor's father or mother.
- A guardian appointed or declared by a court.

4. What are the different types of de-jure guardians?

Ans. De-jure guardians can be of three types, they are

- **Natural guardians (by birth)** Generally, father and mother are recognised as natural guardians of the child
- **Testamentary guardians** These are guardians appointed by will.
- **Certificated guardians** These are guardians appointed by the court under the Guardians and Wards Act, 1890.

5. What does the natural guardian under Muslim law and Hindu law state?

Ans. Muslims do not recognise mother as a guardian, whether natural or otherwise. But she has the 'Right of Hizanat', which is the right of the mother to have custody of the child during early childhood.

Whereas the Hindu law on Natural Guardian States that the natural guardian of a Hindu minor boy or unmarried girl is the father and after him, only the mother. The mother is entitled to guardianship after the father (Here, the term after means in the absence of).

6. Amisha's mother, a Muslim, wanted to appoint a guardian for her through a will. Is this possible? Explain this type of guardianship. Competency Based Que

Ans. No, under Muslim law, the mother cannot appoint a testamentary guardian. Testamentary guardians refer to those guardians that are appointed by will.

Under the Hindu Minority and Guardianship Act, 1956, both the parents can appoint a testamentary guardian for the child. But it is not so among Muslims.

In Muslim law, only the father has power to appoint a testamentary guardian. The mother has no such power.

Long Answer Type Questions

1. What do you mean by adoption and what are the laws governing adoption?

Ans. For answer refer to text under the heading Adoption and Laws Governing Adoption, on page no. 266, 267.

2. Explain in detail minor custody and guardianship.

Ans. For answer refer to text under the heading Minor Custody and Guardianship, on page no. 267.

3. Raj is a Hindu minor boy has been living with his parents in Mumbai. His parents are currently separated and involved in a legal dispute regarding his custody. Explain based on relevant legal provisions about who will have custody of Raj? Competency Based Que

Ans. As per Section 6 of the Hindu Minority and Guardianship Act, 1956, the natural guardian of a Hindu minor boy is the father. The mother can only be considered the guardian in the absence of the father.

However, when determining custody, the paramount consideration is the welfare of the child. In the case of a minor boy, the father generally holds the custodial rights unless he is unfit to take care of the child.

If the father is not present or deemed unfit, the mother may be granted custody, but only in the absence of the father. But if the child is below the age of five years, the custody is typically granted to the mother, as per the welfare principle.

Therefore, in the case of Raj the father is entitled to custody unless he is unavailable or unfit and if not the mother would be granted custody, keeping in mind the best interests of the child.

SELF ASSESSMENT TEST

Objective Type Questions

1. Once a person is appointed or declared as a guardian, he has to abide by the provisions of which of the following acts?
   (a) Guardians and Wards Act, 1890.
   (b) The Hindu Minority and Guardianship Act, 1956
   (c) Both (a) and (b)
   (d) Neither (a) nor (b)
2. Which of the following is a non-religious and universally applicable law regarding the issues relating to guardianship of a child in India?
   (a) The Guardians and Wards Act, 1890
   (b) The Hindu Minority and Guardianship Act, 1956
   (c) Both (a) and (b)
   (d) Neither (a) nor (b)
3. A person belonging to which of the following communities has to get himself appointed as guardian under the Guardians and Wards Act, 1890?
   (a) Christians (b) Hindus (c) Parsis (d) Only (a) and (c)
4. Which of the following is a type of de-jure guardian?
   (a) Natural guardians
   (b) Testamentary guardians
   (c) Certificated guardians
   (d) All of these
5. Which of the following is the right of the mother to have custody of the child during early childhood, under Muslim law?
   (a) Right of Hizanat (b) Right to Nafaqah (c) Both (a) and (b) (d) Neither (a) nor (b)

Very Short Answer Type Questions

6. "A Guardian is a person who has rights and duties with respect to the care and control of a minor's person in relation to body or property (estate or wealth of minor)". Explain. **Competency Based Que**
7. "The mother is entitled to guardianship 'after' the father". What does 'after' mean here? **Competency Based Que**
8. Highlight the meaning and importance of the 'Right of Hizanat' under Muslim law.

Short Answer Type Questions

9. "There is no law on adoption for Christians, Parsis and Muslims". Explain. **Competency Based Que**
10. "It is also defined as a process by which people take a child who was not born to them and raise him or her as a member of their family". Explain what is talked about here. **Competency Based Que**

Long Answer Type Questions

11. 'Every community has its own laws in matters of custody and guardianship'. Explain. **Competency Based Que**
12. What are de-jure and de-facto guardians? State the type of de-jure guardians.

16

CHAPTER

The term property is derived from the Latin term 'propertietat' and the French equivalent 'proprious' which means a thing owned.

Property, Succession and Inheritance

▼ **YOUR STUDY GOALS**

16.1 Concept of Property

16.2 Inheritance and Succession

▼ **YOUR PRACTICE GOAL**

- Objective Type Questions (25 Qs ; MCQs, A-R, Statements, Matching)
- Subjective Questions (8 VSAs, 8 SAs, 4 LAs)

16.1 Concept of Property

- Property is any interest or right in a thing that is legally recognised as belonging to a person, group or entity. Property can be physical or intangible.
- There are two kinds of property

(i) **Joint Family Property** Property acquired by joint funds of the family is known as joint family property. All the needs of the family are fulfilled from it.

(ii) **Self-acquired Property** Property acquired by self-exertion or labour is known as self-acquired property. Thus, it includes property by one's own learning.

According to Gains of Learning Act, 1930 learning is the education whether elementary, technical, scientific and special or general.

16.2 Inheritance and Succession

Inheritance

- Inheritance means the right of an heir by way of succession.
- Inheritance is one of the means of acquisition of property.
- There are different laws of succession for governing persons belonging to different religions.

- After the death of the owner, all rights belonging to the deceased with regard to the property are divisible into two classes, namely
  - (i) **Inheritable Rights** A right is inheritable if it survives its owner. It remains functional even after the death of the person to whom it belongs and devolves on his legal representative. **Proprietary rights** (rights attached to property) like debts are inheritable.
  - (ii) **Uninheritable Rights** A right is not inheritable if it dies with its owner. **Personal rights** (rights associated with the person) are not inheritable as they extinguish with the death of the deceased.

Passive Euthanasia

- On 9th **March, 2018,** the Supreme Court of India made a landmark judgement permitting passive euthanasia under strict guidelines in the country.
- The judgement was delivered on a **PIL filed by NGO Common Cause** for an individual's right to make a living will document for passive euthanasia.
- However, the judgement to legalise passive euthanasia was delivered in 2011 by the Supreme Court in the case of Mumbai nurse **Aruna Shanbaug**, who was in a permanent vegetative state for more than 40 years.
- The Supreme Court of India legalised passive euthanasia by means of withdrawal of life support to patients in a permanent vegetative state.
- Passive euthanasia allows withdrawal of medical treatment with the intention to execute the death of a terminally-ill patient.
- The Supreme Court also ruled that in specific circumstances, a person has the right to decide against artificial life support by creating a living will.
- The Supreme Court has attached strict conditions for executing a living will that was made by a person in his normal state of health and mind.
- The Supreme Court declared the right to die with dignity as a Fundamental Right within the scope of the right to live with dignity. It ruled that the right to life and liberty under **Article 21** of the Constitution of India also includes **the right to die peacefully and with dignity.**

Succession

Succession is the process in which property is transferred upon someone's death. It is also used to refer to the estate a person leaves behind after death.

Testamentary Succession

- When a person disposes off his property by making a will, it is known as testamentary succession.
- Testamentary succession is governed by the **Indian Succession Act, 1925.**
- In testamentary succession, the law empowers a person to determine, (during his lifetime) the disposition of the property that he leaves behind after his death.
- The law respects the will of the deceased and secures its enforcement.
- Will is a **legal declaration of a person's wish** regarding the disposal of his/her property or estate after death. A person who has made a legally valid will before death is called a **Testator.**

Testamentary Succession under Muslim Law

- A Muslim who is of sound mind and who is not a minor, may make a valid will.
- In Muslim or Mohammedan law, a will is known as **'wassiyat'** and the executor or the person who is appointed by a testator to execute the testator's will, is known as **wasi.**
- No particular form is required to make a valid will nature will suffice.
- A will may be made either verbally or in writing. Any property which is capable of being transferred and which exists at the time of the testator's death, may be disposed of by a will.
- A Muslim can dispose off **only one-third** of his property, which is left after the payment of his funeral expenses and his debts. The **balance two-third** of the property goes to the heirs of the deceased.

Testamentary Succession among Hindus, Parsis and Christians

- The rules relating to testamentary succession among **Hindus, Parsis and Christians** are contained in the Indian Succession Act, 1925.
- This act does not deal with substantive law, such as what property may be transferred or what estates and interest may be created.
- The Indian Succession Act, 1925 primarily deals with formalities related to the following matters
  - **Execution** Validation of a legal document by the performance of all necessary formalities.
  - **Revocation** To recall, withdraw or reverse the will.
  - **Revival** Restoration to use, acceptance, activity or vigor after a period of obscurity (uncertainty).
  - **Interpretation** An explanation or conceptualisation of will.
  - **The Grant of Probate** The process of legally establishing the validity of a will before a judicial authority and other legal representations, powers and duties of the executors.

Intestate Succession

A person who dies **without making a will** is known as intestate and succession to his property is known as intestate succession.

Heirs

- The person/persons on whom the property devolves after the death of the deceased are called the heirs of the deceased.
- A person who is entitled to inherit property after the death of the intestate is known as heir.
- These heirs could be of three types
  (i) **Ascendants** They are the ancestors of a person both on the paternal and maternal side. There is no limit to degrees of ascent. The immediate ascendants are father and mother. It includes Father (F), Mother (M), Paternal Grandfather (FF), Paternal Grandmother (FM), Maternal Grandfather (MF), Maternal Grandmother (MM), etc.

  (ii) **Descendants** It means the offspring of a person. There is no limit to degree of descent. The immediate descendants of a person are his or her sons and daughters. It includes Son (S), Daughter (D), Grandson (SS), Granddaughter (SD), Great grandson (SSS), Great granddaughter (SSD), etc.

  (iii) **Collaterals** They are **descendants in parallel lines** i.e., from a common ancestor or ancestress. For example, brothers, sisters and their children, paternal and maternal uncles and aunts and their children, are all collaterals. These heirs can relate to each other by full blood, half blood or uterine blood as follows
  - **Relation by Full Blood** Two persons are related to each other by full blood when they have same father and same mother.
  - **Relation by Half Blood** Two persons are related to each other by half blood when they have the same father, but different mothers.
  - **Relation by Uterine Blood** Two persons are related to each other by uterine blood when they have same mother, but different fathers.

Rules Relating to Intestate Succession

- The rules related to intestate succession are more or less similar in all the communities.
- According to these rules, the first preference is given to the husband/wife of the deceased and their descendants.
- In their absence, the preference is given to the collaterals that are close to the deceased.
- In their absence, property goes to remote male heirs and then to female heirs.

- A rule of **escheat** is applicable in all the communities. If no heir is present then **property goes to the government** by this rule.
- In every religion, the way of determining the **disposition**[1] of property is different.

Rules of Intestate Succession among Hindu Male

- The intestate succession among the Hindus is governed by the Hindu Succession Act, 1956.
- According to it, if a Hindu dies intestate i.e. without making a will, then both the separate property and joint family property passes on to his heirs.
- Heirs belonging to a Hindu male are classified into **four categories** i.e., Class I, Class II, agnates and cognates.
- **Class I** heirs are the **most preferred heirs,** which includes mother, wife, son as well as daughter and their descendants upto the third generation.
- **Class II** heirs include father, brother as well as sister and their children, maternal and paternal uncles and aunts, maternal and paternal grandfather and grandmother, etc. Class II heirs will inherit property only in absence of Class I heirs.
- If there are no heirs belonging to Class I or Class II then property goes to **agnates**. When two persons are related by blood or adoption wholly through males, they are called agnates.

  For example, the son of a great grandson (son, grandson, great grandson being dead).

  P-----> S-----> SS ------> SSS ------->SSSS1

  In the above diagram

  - S is son of P
  - SS is son of S and grandson of P
  - SSS is son of SS and great grandson of P
  - SSSS1 is son of SSS and great great grandson of P.

  Here, SSSS1 is agnate to P as he is tracing relation wholly through males i.e., his father (SSS), grandfather (SS) and great grandfather (S). **No female has intervened** in between them.
- In case, all the heirs i.e., Class I, Class II and agnates are absent then property will go to **cognates**. When two persons are related by blood or adoption, but not wholly through males, they are called cognates.

  For example, the father of paternal grandmother (FMF1)

  P ----> F -----> FM ------> FMF1

  In the above diagram

  - F is father of P
  - FM is mother of F and paternal grandmother of P
  - FMF1 is father of FM.

  Here, FMF1 is cognate to P as a **female has intervened** in between, i.e., Father's Mother (FM).

Rules of Intestate Succession among Hindu Female

- Under Hindu law, a son had a birthright in joint family property.
- The Hindu Succession (Amendment) Act, 2005 was enacted to **remove gender discriminatory** provisions in the Hindu Succession Act, 1956.
- Now, according to this amendment, the daughters also have inheritance rights equal to those of sons from the properties of their fathers, grandfathers and great grandfathers.
- If a female Hindu dies intestate, then heirs are divided into five categories. These are
  - (i) The first category includes husband, son, daughter and children of predeceased son and daughter.
  - (ii) The second category includes heirs of husband.
  - (iii) The third category includes father and mother.
  - (iv) The fourth and fifth category includes heirs of father and mother respectively.

1 **Disposition** It means a person's inherent qualities of mind and character.

Rules of Intestate Succession among Muslims

- There is no codified law for Muslims related to intestate succession.
- They are governed by their religious texts.
- They do not make any distinction between ancestral and self-acquired property.
- The right of an heir comes into existence on the death of the ancestor.
- Among Sunnis, heirs are divided into three categories
  (i) Sharers (Quranic heirs) (ii) Residuaries (agnatic heirs)
  (iii) Distant kindred (uterine heirs)
- Sharers are the most preferred heirs. First of all, sharers are allotted their Quranic shares.
- If something is left behind after allotting shares to them, then it goes to residuaries.
- If their shares exhaust the entire estate, then sharers exclude residuaries and distant kindred.
- The distant kindred are not entitled to succeed as long as there is any heir belonging to the class of sharers or residuaries.
- However, the distant kindred will inherit with the sharer, when there is only one sharer i.e., the wife/husband of the deceased and no other sharer or residuary exist.
- Among Shias, heirs are divided into two categories
  (i) Heirs by **consanguinity** (ii) Heirs by **marriage** i.e., husband and wife.
- Heirs by consanguinity are further sub-divided into three classes
  (i) **Class I** includes parents and children.
  (ii) **Class II** includes grandparents, brothers and sisters and their descendants, etc.
  (iii) **Class III** includes paternal and maternal uncles and aunts of the deceased and of his parents, grandparents, etc.
- Among the heirs by consanguinity, the first group excludes the second and the second group excludes the third.
- The claimants in both the categories i.e., heirs by consanguinity and heirs by marriage succeed together, if there are heirs of both the categories.

Rules of Intestate Succession among Christians and Parsis

- Christians and Parsis are governed by the **Indian Succession Act, 1925**.
- Among Christians, the first preference is given to the **spouse** of the deceased and his lineal descendants i.e., children, grand children, great grand children or their remote lineal descendants.
- When there are **no lineal descendants,** then property passes on to the spouse of the deceased and those who are kindred (relations) to him.
- If there are no lineal descendants or one who is kindred to him, then entire property goes to his/her spouse.
- In the absence of spouse, property passes on to lineal descendants or to those who are kindred to him.

Mind Map

PROPERTY, SUCCESSION, AND INHERITANCE

1 Concept of Property

Definition
- Legally recognised interest or right in tangible or intangible assets.
- Derived from Latin 'propertietat' and French 'proprious', meaning 'a thing owned.'

Types

Joint Family Property
- Acquired using family funds; fulfills collective family needs.

Self-Acquired Property
- Gained through personal effort or labour.
- Defined by the Gains of Learning Act, 1930, including education-related acquisitions.

2 Inheritance and Succession

Inheritance
- Rights passed to heirs after a person's death. Classified into.
- **Inheritable Rights** Persist after the owner's death (e.g., debts, property).
- **Uninheritable Rights** End with the owner's death (e.g., personal rights).

Succession
- Transfer of property upon death.

Types

Testamentary Succession
- Based on a valid will.
- Governed by the Indian Succession Act, 1925.
- Includes formalities like execution, revocation and probate.

Intestate Succession
- Without a will; property distributed per laws of succession.

3 Testamentary Succession

Hindus, Parsis, Christians
- Governed by Indian Succession Act, 1925.
- Allows individuals to willfully distribute property.

Muslim Law
- Will known as 'wassiyat', executor called wasi.
- Conditions
  - Verbal or written will valid.
  - Can dispose of up to one-third of property (post-expenses).
  - Remaining two-thirds go to heirs.

4 Intestate Succession

Definition
- Succession when no will exists.

Hindu Succession Act, 1956.
- Property devolves based on Classes
  - **Class I Heirs** Mother, wife, children (most priority).
  - **Class II Heirs** Siblings, grandparents, uncles/aunts.
  - **Agnates** Related wholly through males.
  - **Cognates** Related not wholly through males.

Muslim Law
- Categorised into
  - **Sharers** Quranic heirs with fixed shares.
  - **Residuaries** Receive remaining estate.
  - **Distant Kindred** Claim in absence of others.

Christian and Parsi Law
- Governed by Indian Succession Act, 1925.
- Priority Spouse and lineal descendants.

5 Landmark Concepts

Heirs
- **Ascendants** Ancestors (parents, grandparents).
- **Descendants** Offspring (children, grandchildren).
- **Collaterals** Relatives in parallel lines (siblings, cousins).
- **Types of relationships**
  - **Full Blood** Same parents.
  - **Half Blood** Same father, different mothers.
  - **Uterine Blood** Same mother, different fathers.

Escheat Rule
- Property passes to government if no heirs exist.

6 Passive Euthanasia and Property Rights

Landmark Judgements
- **ArunaShanbaug Case (2011)** Legalised passive euthanasia.
- **2018 Judgment**
  - Declared 'right to die with dignity' as Fundamental Right.
  - Living wills allowed under strict conditions.

Impact on Inheritance
- Rights of terminally ill individuals to manage property.

7 Rights and Duties of Guardians

Key Provisions of Indian Succession Act, 1925
- Execution, validation, revocation, and interpretation of wills.
- Legal framework for administrators and executors of estates.

8 Summary of Inheritance Rules

Laws tailored by religion
- **Hindus** Detailed classification under Succession Act.
- **Muslims** Specific categories governed by Shariat.
- **Christians and Parsis** Formalised through Indian Succession Act.

CBSE TEXTBOOK Folder

1. 'X', a Hindu male, dies leaving behind a farm house that he purchased out of his own earnings and a flat that he acquired from his father. The heirs left behind after him included his mother, wife, brother and two sons. He bequeathed the house and farm house by way of a will in favour of his younger son and nothing for his elder son. Answer the following. **Competency Based Que**

(i) Identify the two types of properties and the mode of disposing off both the types.

(ii) Is the above will valid? If not, distribute the property of 'X' amongst his heirs giving all the applicable rules.

Ans. (i) The two types of properties are

(a) **Joint Family Property** Property acquired by joint funds of the family is known as joint family property. All the needs of the family are fulfilled from it.

(b) **Self-acquired Property** Property acquired by self-exertion or labour is known as self-acquired property. Thus, it includes property by one's own learning.

(ii) Yes, the above will is valid. Section 8 groups the heirs of a male intestate into four groups and lays down that the property first devolves upon the heirs of Class I of the Schedule. They are the son, daughter, widow, mother, son of a predeceased son, daughter of a predeceased son, son of a predeceased daughter, daughter of a predeceased daughter, widow of a predeceased son, son of a predeceased son of a predeceased son, daughter of a predeceased son of a predeceased son and widow of a predeceased son of a predeceased son.

All these heirs inherit simultaneously. If heirs of Class I are not available, the property goes to the enumerated heirs specified in Class II of the Schedule, wherein an heir in a higher entry is preferred over an heir in a lower entry.

2 What do you mean by inheritance? Differentiate between inheritable and uninheritable rights with relevant examples.

Ans. Inheritance is one of the means of acquisition of property. Inheritance means the right of an heir by way of succession.

Inheritable Rights A right is inheritable if it survives its owner. It remains functional even after the death of the person to whom it belongs and devolves on his legal representative. For example, rights attached to property like debts are inheritable rights.

Uninheritable Rights A right is not inheritable if it dies with its owner. For example, personal rights such as right to vote, the right to reputation are uninheritable rights.

3. Differentiate between Testamentary and Intestate Succession.

Ans. When a person disposes off his property by making a will, it is known as testamentary succession. Testamentary succession is governed by the Indian Succession Act, 1925. In testamentary succession, the law empowers a person to determine, (during his lifetime) the disposition of the property that he leaves behind after his death.

On the other hand, a person who dies without making a will is known as intestate and succession to his property is known as intestate succession.

The rules related to intestate succession are more or less similar in all the communities. According to these rules, the first preference is given to the husband or wife of the deceased and their descendants.

In their absence, the preference is given to the collaterals that are close to the deceased. In their absence, property goes to remote male heirs and then to female heirs.

4. A dies without an heir. She has left behind substantial property that is self-acquired through her own learning. By what rule will her property be disposed of and who will acquire the property? **Competency Based Que**

Ans. According to the Indian Succession Act, 1925, in the case where a person dies without leaving a will and without any legal heirs, their property will be disposed of according to the rules of intestate succession.

In the case of a woman who dies without leaving any legal heirs, her property will be inherited by her husband's relatives if she was married at the time of her death. However, if she was not married, then her property will be inherited by her own relatives.

The specific rules for inheritance depend on the personal law applicable to the deceased person. For example, if the deceased person was Hindu, then the Hindu Succession Act, 1956 would apply and if the deceased person was Muslim, then the Muslim Personal Law (Shariat) Application Act, 1937 would apply.

5. You are a practicing lawyer who is an expert in creating wills. Draft a will for your client who is a senior Vice-President in a company. She is married with two daughters. She owns a house in a posh locality in South Delhi, has share holdings, jewellery and fixed deposits and money in the savings account.

She has two cars. She also has an old help who has been working for her for the past 25 years. She wants to divide her property equally between her husband and children. She also wants to ensure that she provides for some amount to her old help in her will.

Competency Based Que

Ans. I, [Client's Name], residing at [Client's Address], being of sound mind, hereby declare this to be my last will and testament, revoking all prior wills and codicils made by me.

Executor I appoint my spouse [Spouse's Name] as the executor of my estate. If my spouse is unable or unwilling to serve, I appoint my daughter [Daughter's Name] as the alternate executor.

Bequests I direct that all of my just debts and funeral expenses be paid as soon as practicable after my death.

(i) I give, devise and bequeath my house located at [Address] to my husband [Spouse's Name] absolutely and forever.

(ii) I give, devise, and bequeath all of my shares and investments to be divided equally between my husband [Spouse's Name], and my two daughters [Daughter 1's Name] and [Daughter 2's Name].

(iii) I give, devise, and bequeath all of my jewellery and valuable personal effects to be divided equally between my two daughters [Daughter 1's Name] and [Daughter 2's Name].

(iv) I give, devise, and bequeath the sum of [Amount] to my loyal and dedicated helper [Helper's Name], who has been in my service for the past 25 years.

(v) I give, devise, and bequeath all of my remaining property, real and personal, to be divided equally between my husband [Spouse's Name], and my two daughters [Daughter 1's Name] and [Daughter 2's Name].

Guardian I appoint my husband [Spouse's Name] as the guardian of my two daughters [Daughter 1's Name] and [Daughter 2's Name]. In the event my husband predeceases me, I appoint [Alternate Guardian's Name] as the alternate guardian.

Residuary Clause

I hereby give, devise and bequeath all the rest, residue, and remainder of my estate, of whatever nature and wherever situated, to be divided equally among my husband [Spouse's Name], and my two daughters [Daughter 1's Name] and [Daughter 2's Name].

IN WITNESS WHERE OF, I have hereunto set my hand and seal this [Date] day of [Month], [Year].

[Client's Signature]

[Client's Name]

Exam Pattern Questions

Objective Type Questions

Multiple Choice Questions (MCQs)

1. The term property is derived from which word?
(a) Propertietat (b) Propertat
(c) Propertiat (d) None of these

2. Which among the following is not a kind of property?
(a) Joint Family Property (b) Self-Acquired Property
(c) Mixed Property (d) All of these

3. How is 'self-acquired' property acquired?
(a) Heredity (b) Inheritance
(c) Royalty (d) Labour

4. Which act defines learning as education whether elementary, technical, scientific and special or general?
(a) Gains of Learning Act, 1930
(b) Learning Act, 1935
(c) Forensic Act, 1940
(d) None of the above

5. The kind of succession in which a person can make a will only of his/her separate property is known as …… .
(a) related succession (b) testamentary succession
(c) will succession (d) All of these

6. Which act governs testamentary succession in India?
(a) Succession Act, 1750
(b) Law of Succession, 1850
(c) Indian Law of Succession, 1925
(d) Indian Succession Act, 1925

7. Which among the given statements is TRUE regarding intestate succession under Hindu law?
(a) A person who dies after making a will is called intestate.
(b) Hindu intestate successions is governed by the Muslim personal law.
(c) The Hindu Succession (Amendment) Act, 2005 grants daughters equal inheritance rights as sons.
(d) Only male heirs can inherit property under Hindu law.

8. Under Mohammedan law, the term 'will' is known as……… .
(a) talaq (b) wassiyat
(c) mehar (d) None of these

9. Which religion does not have a law for intestate succession?
(a) Hinduism (b) Islam (c) Christianity (d) Parsis

10. According to which kind of succession, the property devolves according to the law or custom by which the deceased is governed?
(a) Testamentary (b) Intestate
(c) Interstate (d) Intrastate

11. Descendants from parallel lines are known as ……….. .
(a) collaterals
(b) ascendants
(c) will keepers
(d) All of the above

12. Two persons are related to each other by …… blood when they have same father and same mother.
(a) full (b) half
(c) empty (d) None of these

13. When two persons are related by blood or adoption wholly through males, they are known as ……….. .
(a) collaterals (b) agnates
(c) cabinets (d) heirs

14. P ---->S----> SS---->SSS---->SSSS1

The above-mentioned pattern describes.
(a) Collaterals (b) Cabiners
(c) Heirs (d) Agnates

15. P---->F---->FM---->FMF1

The above mentioned pattern describes.
(a) Cognates (b) Agnates
(c) Collaterals (d) Heir

16. When did daughter got birth right to property according to Hindu Succession Act, 1925?
(a) 1925 (b) 1950
(c) 2000 (d) 2005

17. Arrange the following act as per the year of enactment.
I. Hindu Succession Act
II. Hindu Succession (Amendment) Act
III. Indian Succession Act
IV. Gains of Learning Act
Choose the correct option
(a) IV, III, I, II
(b) III, II, I, IV
(c) III, IV, I, II
(d) IV, I, III, II

18. **Succession is the process in which property is transferred upon someone's death. Choose the statement which is NOT TRUE regarding succession**

(a) When a person disposes off his property by making a will is known as testamentary succession.

(b) Testamentary succession is governed by the India Succession Act.

(c) In intestate succession, the property devolves according to the will by the deceased.

(d) If a Hindu dies without making a will, then, both separate property as well as joint family property passes on to his heirs.

19. **Statement I** Self-acquired property is a property that an individual owns solely, without any share or interest from others.

Statement II Self-acquired property can be acquired through inheritance, gift, or partition of ancestral property.

Which of the following is true about self-acquired property?

(a) Statement I is true, but Statement II is false.

(b) Statement I is false, but Statement II is true.

(c) Both Statement I and Statement II are true.

(d) Both Statement I and Statement II are false.

20. **Statement I** Intestate succession occurs when a person dies without leaving a valid will, and their property is distributed according to the laws of succession.

Statement II In intestate succession, the deceased person's property is always divided equally among their heirs.

Which of the following is true about intestate succession?

(a) Statement I is true, but Statement II is false.

(b) Statement I is false, but Statement II is true.

(c) Both Statement I and Statement II are true.

(d) Both Statement I and Statement II are false.

21. **Match the following.**

	Column I (Term)		Column II (Meaning)
A.	Collaterals	1.	The ancestors of a person both on the paternal and maternal side.
B.	Agnates	2.	It mean the offspring of a person.
C.	Ascendants	3.	They are descendants in parallel lines.
D.	Descendants	4.	When two persons are related by blood or adoption wholly through males.

Codes

	A	B	C	D		A	B	C	D
(a)	1	3	2	4	(b)	4	3	2	1
(c)	3	4	1	2	(d)	1	4	2	3

22. Match the following.

	Column I (Term)		Column II (Definition)
A.	Inheritance	1.	When a person disposes off his property by making a will.
B.	Intestate succession	2.	Two persons having the same father, but different mothers.
C.	Relation by half blood	3.	The property devolves according to the law or custom by which the deceased is governed.
D.	Testamentary succession	4.	One of the means of acquisition of property.

Codes

	A	B	C	D		A	B	C	D
(a)	4	2	3	1	(b)	1	2	3	4
(c)	3	2	1	4	(d)	1	4	2	3

Assertion-Reason Questions

Directions (Q. Nos. 23-25) In the questions given below there are two statements marked as Assertion (A) and Reason (R). Read the statements and choose the correct option.

Codes

(a) Both A and R are true and R is the correct explanation of A.

(b) Both A and R are true, but R is not the correct explanation of A.

(c) A is true, but R is false.

(d) A is false, but R is true.

23 **Assertion** (A) There is one kind of property i.e. joint family property.

Reason (R) The French equivalent of the term property is 'proprious' which means a thing owned.

24. **Assertion** (A) Inheritance is one of the means of acquisition of property.

Reason (R) Proprietary rights (rights attached to property) like debts are inheritable.

25. **Assertion** (A) A person who dies without making a will is known as intestate.

Reason (R) There are no common rules of intestate succession.

Answers

1. (a) Propertietat
2. (c) Mixed Property
3. (d) Labour
4. (a) Gains of Learning Act, 1930
5. (b) testamentary succession
6. (d) Indian Succession Act, 1925
7. (c) The Hindu succession (Amendment) Act, 2005 grants daughters equal inheritance rights as sons.
8. (b) wassiyat
9. (b) Islam
10. (a) Testamentary
11. (a) collaterals
12. (a) full
13. (b) agnates
14. (d) Agnates
15. (a) Cognates
16. (d) 2005
17. (c) III, IV, I, II
18. (c) In intestate succession, the property devolves according to the will by the deceased.
19. (a) Statement I is true, but Statement II is false.
20. (a) Statement I is true, but Statement II is false.
21. (c) 3 4 1 2
22. (a) 4 2 3 1
23. (d) A is false, but R is true.
24. (b) Both A and R are true, but R is not the correct explanation of A.
25. (c) A is true, but R is false.

Subjective Questions

Very Short Answer Type Questions

1. What is the origin of the term 'property'?

Ans. The term property is derived from the Latin term 'propertietat' and the French equivalent 'proprious' which means a thing owned.

2. Amit, a renowned painter, passes away. Can his right to sue for defamation be inherited by his legal heirs? **Competency Based Que**

Ans. No, Amit's right to sue for defamation cannot be inherited by his legal heirs.

This is because personal rights, such as the right to sue for defamation, are not inheritable and extinguish with the death of the person.

3. Rahul, a property owner, passes away leaving behind a debt of ₹ 5 lakhs. Who will be responsible for paying off this debt, and why? **Competency Based Que**

Ans. Rahul's legal representative will be responsible for paying off the debt. This is because proprietary rights, such as debts, are inheritable rights that survive their owner and devolve on their legal representative.

4. What is meant by a testator?

Ans. A testator is a person who has made a legally valid will before death.

5. What is the difference between an heir and a testator?

Ans. The person/persons on whom the property devolves after the death of the deceased are called the heirs of the deceased.

A person who is entitled to inherit property after the death of the estate is known as heir.

On the other hand, a testator is a person who has made a legally valid will before death.

6. Based on the rules of intestate succession among Hindus, specify the which heir of a Hindu male belong to these classes **Competency Based Que**

(i) Class I **(ii) Class II**

Ans. (i) **Class I** Class I heirs include mother, wife, son as well as daughter and their descendants up to the third generation.

(ii) **Class II** Class II heirs include father, brother as well as sister and their children, maternal and paternal uncles and aunts, maternal and paternal grandfather and grandmother.

7. Based on the rules of intestate succession among Hindus, define the following terms

(i) Agnates **(ii) Cognates**

Ans. (i) **Agnates** When two persons are related by blood or adoption wholly through males, they are called agnates. For example, the son of a great grandson.

(ii) **Cognates** When two persons are related by blood or adoption, but not wholly through males, they are called cognates. For example, father of paternal grandmother.

8. Rahul dies intestate (without a will), leaving behind a property worth ₹10 lakhs. His family consists of his widow, Rukmini and two children, Rohan and Rhea. Meanwhile, his friend, Raj, dies leaving behind a will that bequeaths his entire property to his friend, Ramesh. What is the key difference between succession and will? **Competency Based Que**

Ans. Succession is the process in which property is transferred upon someone's death. It is also used to refer to the estate a person leaves behind at death. On the other hand, a legal declaration of a person's wish regarding the disposal of his/her property or estate after death.

Short Answer Type Questions

1. Define the term 'inheritance'. Elucidate the difference between 'inheritable' and 'uninheritable rights'.

Ans. Inheritance is one of the means of acquisition of property. After the death of the owner, all rights belonging to the deceased with regard to the property are divisible into two classes

(i) Inheritable rights (ii) Uninheritable rights

The differences between inheritable and uninheritable rights are

Inheritable Rights	Uninheritable Rights
A right is inheritable if it survives its owner.	A right is uninheritable right if it doesn't survive its owner.
It remains functional even after the death of the person to whom it belongs and devolves on his legal representative.	It doesn't remain functional after the death of the person.
Proprietary rights (rights attached to property) like debts are inheritable.	Personal rights are not inheritable as they extinguish with the death of the deceased.

2. Define testamentary succession. Describe the rules of testamentary succession in Mohammedan law.

Ans. When a person disposes off his property by making a will, it is known as testamentary succession.

The Mohammedan law has following rules for testamentary succession

- A Muslim who is off sound mind and who is not a minor, may make a valid will. No particular form is required to make a valid will nature will suffice.
- A will may be made either verbally or in writing. Any property which is capable of being transferred and which exists at the time of the testator's death, may be disposed of by a will.
- A Muslim can dispose of only one-third of his property, which is left after the payment of his funeral expenses and his debts. The balance two-thirds of the property goes to the heirs of the deceased.

3. Explain Testamentary Succession among Hindus, Parsis and Christians.

Ans. For answer refer to text under the heading Testamentary Succession among Hindus, Parsis and Christians, on page no. 278.

4. Elucidate the meaning of following terms in the context of intestate succession

(i) Ascendants (ii) Descendants (iii) Collaterals

Ans. (i) **Ascendants** They refer to the ancestors of a person both on the paternal and maternal side. The immediate ascendants are father and mother.

(ii) **Descendants** They refer to the offsprings of a person. The immediate descendants of a person are his or her sons and daughters.

(iii) **Collaterals** They are descendants in parallel lines meaning the offspring from a common ancestor or ancestress.

5. Mention how are two individuals related by

(i) Full Blood (ii) Half Blood

(iii) Uterine Blood

Ans. (i) **Relation by Full Blood** Two persons are related to each other by full blood when they have same father and same mother.

(ii) **Relation by Half Blood** Two persons are related to each other by half blood when they have the same father, but different mothers.

(iii) **Relation by Uterine Blood** Two persons are related to each other by uterine blood when they have same mother, but different fathers.

6. Heirs can be related by full blood, half blood and uterine blood. Explain the difference between the three.

Ans. Difference between various kinds of relations are

Relation by Full Blood	Relation by Half Blood	Relation by Uterine Blood
Two persons are related to each other by full blood when they have same father and same mother.	Two persons are related to each other by half blood when they have the same father, but different mothers.	Two persons are related to each other by uterine blood when they have same mother, but different fathers.

7. In condition of the death of an intestate Hindu female, in how many categories are heirs of such a female divided?

Ans. If a female Hindu dies intestate then heirs are divided into five categories. These are

(i) The first category includes husband, son, daughter and children of predeceased son and daughter.

(ii) The second category includes heirs of husband.

(iii) The third category includes father and mother.

(iv) Fourth and fifth category includes the heirs of father and mother.

8. What do you mean by 'consanguinity'. In which classes do heirs by consanguinity divided?

Ans. Consanguinity refers to the characteristic of having a kinship with another person.

Heirs by consanguinity are divided into three classes

(i) **Class I** This class includes parents and children.

(ii) **Class II** This class includes grandparents, brothers and sisters, and their descendants.

(iii) **Class III** This class includes paternal and maternal uncles and aunts of the deceased and of his parents, grandparents.

Long Answer Type Questions

1. Bhavana is in a permanent vegetative state for more than 20 years. She wanted withdrawal of life support or medical treatment with the intention to execute her death. Explain if Bhavana can do so. Is there any law for this? If yes, explain it. Competency Based Que

Ans. Yes, Bhavana can demand the withdrawal of life support or medical treatment, according to the law of passive euthanasia. Passive euthanasia allows withdrawal of medical treatment with the intention to execute the death of a terminally-ill patient.

On 9th March, 2018, the Supreme Court of India made a landmark judgement permitting passive euthanasia under strict guidelines in the country. The judgement was delivered on a PIL filed by NGO Common Cause for an individual's right to make a living will document for passive euthanasia.

However, the judgement to legalise passive euthanasia was delivered in 2011 by the Supreme Court in the case of Mumbai nurse Aruna Shanbaug, who was in a permanent vegetative state for more than 40 years.

The Supreme Court of India legalised passive euthanasia by means of withdrawal of life support to patients in a permanent vegetative state. The Supreme Court also ruled that in specific circumstances, a person has the right to decide against artificial life support by creating a living will. The Supreme Court has attached strict conditions for executing a living will that was made by a person in his normal state of health and mind.

2. (i) What is intestate succession.

(ii) Explain in detail the various kinds of heirs recognised under intestate succession with examples.

(iii) Explain various kinds of relationships existing in intestate succession.

Ans. (i) A person who dies without making a will is known as intestate and succession to his property is known as intestate succession.

(ii) Refer to text under the heading Heir on page no. 278.

(iii) Refer to text under the heading Heir (iii) on page no. 278.

3. Describe the rules pertaining to intestate succession among Hindus.

Ans. The intestate succession among the Hindus is governed by the Hindu Success Act, 1956. According to it, if a Hindu dies intestate i.e. without making a will, then both the separate property and joint family property passes on to his heirs.

Heirs belonging to a Hindu male are classified into four categories i.e., Class I, Class II, agnates and cognates.

Class I heirs are the most preferred heirs and include mother, wife, son as well as daughter and their descendants upto the third generation.

Class II heirs include father, brother as well as sister and their children, maternal and paternal uncles and aunts, maternal and paternal grandfather and grandmother, etc. Class II heirs will inherit property only in absence of Class I heirs.

If there are no heirs belonging to Class I or Class II then property goes to agnates. When two persons are related by blood or adoption wholly through males, they are called agnates.

For example, the son of a great grandson (son, grandson, great grandson being dead).

P----> S---> SS ----> SSS ----->SSSS1

In the above diagram

- S is son of P.
- SS is son of S and grandson of P.
- SSS is son of SS and great grandson of P.
- SSSS1 is son of SSS and great great grandson of P.

Here, SSSS1 is agnate to P as he is tracing relation wholly through males i.e., his father (SSS), grandfather (SS) and great grandfather (S). No female has intervened in between them.

In case, all the heirs i.e., Class I, Class II and agnates are absent then property will go to cognates.

When two persons are related by blood or adoption, but not wholly through males, they are called cognates.

For example, the father of paternal grandmother (FMF1)

P ----> F -----> FM -------> FMF1

In the above diagram

- F is father of P.
- FM is mother of F and paternal grandmother of P.
- FMF1 is father of FM.

Here, FMF1 is cognate to P as a female has intervened in between, i.e., Father's Mother (FM).

4. What does the Indian Succession Act, 1925 primarily deal with?

Ans. Refer to text under the heading Testamentary succession among Hindu, Parsis and Christians.

SELF ASSESSMENT TEST

Objective Type Questions

1. A right is inheritable if it survives its owner. What kind of right is being talked about here? **Competency Based Que**

   (a) Uninheritable (b) Real (c) Partial (d) Inheritable

2. Which among the following is not a type of devolution of property?

   (a) Testamentary succession (b) Intestate succession
   (c) Both (a) and (b) (d) None of these

3. The ancestors of a person both on the paternal and maternal side are known as ....

   (a) ascendants (b) agantes (c) descendants (d) collaterals

4. A legal declaration of a person's wish regarding the disposal of his or her property or estate after death is known as ....

   (a) will (b) succession (c) Both (a) and (b) (d) Neither (a) nor (b)

Very Short Answer Type Questions

5. Define the terms 'self-acquired' as well as 'joint family property'.
6. What are the different kinds of heirs of property?
7. Which religion does not have defined laws for succession?
8. In relation to the formalities dealt by the Indian Succession Act, what is the difference between Execution and Revival?
9. 'Succession is the process in which property is transferred upon someone's death'.With reference to the statement explain the testamentary successions. **Competency Based Que**

Short Answer Type Questions

10. Explain the various provisions of testamentary succession in case of Mohammedan law.
11. State the provisions of Indian Succession Act of 1925.
12. 'Heirs by consanguinity are sub-divided into three classes'. Identify the three classes and explain them. **Competency Based Que**

Long Answer Type Questions

13. Define the terms 'inheritance' and 'succession'. Describe various types of successions.
14. 'On 9th March, 2018, the Supreme Court of India made a landmark judgement permitting passive euthanasia under strict guidelines in the country'.

    (i) Identify the case in which the above given judgement was delivered.
    (ii) State the ruling of the Supreme Court in the above landmark judgement.
    (iii) Analyse the ruling of the Supreme Court given in the above case.

15. How is the testamentary succession among Muslims different from those among the Hindus, Parsis and Christians?
16. How do different religions regulate their intestate succession?

17

CHAPTER

Prevention of Violence Against Women

Domestic abuse or 'domestic violence' is a pattern of behaviour in any domestic relationship that is used to gain or maintain power and control over another.

YOUR STUDY GOALS

17.1 Domestic Abuse/Violence
17.2 International Legal Framework
17.3 Laws in India on Prevention of Violence Against Women

YOUR PRACTICE GOAL

- Objective Type Questions (22 Qs ; MCQs, A-R, Statements, Matching)
- Subjective Questions (6 VSAs, 3 SAs, 3 LAs)

17.1 Domestic Abuse/Violence

- Abuse is physical, sexual, emotional, economic or psychological actions or threats of actions that influence another person.
- This includes any behaviour that frightens, intimidates, terrorises, manipulates, hurts, humiliates, blames, injures, or wounds someone.
- The features of domestic abuse or violence are
  - Domestic abuse can happen to anyone of any race, age, sexual orientation, religion, or gender.
  - It can occur within a range of relationships including couples who are married, living together or dating.
  - Domestic abuse affects people of all socio-economic backgrounds and education levels.
  - It is largely forbidden in Western countries.
- However, in many countries, domestic abuse is either legally recognised or socially acceptable. For example, the **United Arab Emirates'** laws allow the man to use limited physical means to discipline his wife and children.
- Domestic abuse is a socially acceptable practice in many developing countries like Jordan, Guinea, Zambia, Sierra Leone, Laos and Ethiopia.

17.2 International Legal Framework

The concern for 'violence against women' including violence in **intimate**[1] relationships, has significantly existed in international discourses and legal frameworks. These include

- **The Convention on the Elimination of All Forms of Discrimination Against Women (CEDAW), 1979**
  - It is a United Nations treaty that defines what constitutes discrimination against women.
  - It also sets up an agenda for national action to end such discrimination.
  - CEDAW is often referred to as the **international bill of rights for women** and has 99 countries, including India, as signatories.
  - These have committed themselves to undertake various measures to end discrimination against women in all forms.
  - In 1992, the CEDAW Committee recommended that any form of discrimination or violation of women's rights is considered to be violence and state is responsible for such violence committed both by state as well as private individuals.
- **The UN Declaration on Elimination of Violence Against Women**
  - It was adopted in 1993.
  - It defines 'violence against women' as any gender-based violence act that results in, or is likely to result in, physical, sexual or psychological harm or suffering to women.
  - **India is a party to this declaration.**
- **The UN Model Legislation on Domestic Violence**
  - It was created by the UN Commission on Human Rights in 1996 with the objective of serving as a drafting guide for comprehensive legislation on domestic violence at states levels.
  - It defines domestic violence as all acts of gender-based physical, psychological and sexual abuse by a family member against women in the family, ranging from
    - kidnapping
    - threats
    - humiliating verbal abuse
    - stalking
    - destruction of property
    - arson
    - dowry or bride-price related violence
    - female genital **mutilation**[2]
    - simple assaults to aggravated physical battery
    - violence related to exploitation through prostitution
    - violence against household workers and attempts to commit such acts
  - These acts may occur either in public or in private life.
  - Violence may occur outside the family in the general community.
  - Such violence may include rape, sexual abuse, sexual harassment and intimidation at work, in educational institutions and elsewhere, trafficking in women and forced prostitution.

Quick Test 1

1. What do you understand by the term 'abuse'?
2. In which country, laws allow the man to use limited physical means to discipline his wife and children?
3. Why CEDAW is often referred to as the international bill of rights for women?
4. How many nations have signed the CEDAW?

1 **Intimate** It means closely acquinated or familiar.

2 **Mutilation** It means an act of destroying, removing or severely damaging a lamb or other body part of a person or animal.

17.3 Laws in India on Prevention of Violence Against Women

The laws in India for prevention of women against violence are

Protection of Women from Domestic Violence Act (PWDVA), 2005

- **Before 2005,** the concept of 'domestic violence' was not recognised under the Indian law as a special category.
- **In 2005,** the Indian Parliament adopted the Protection of Women from Domestic Violence Act (PWDVA). The objective of this act is to provide effective protection to women who are victims of violence occurring within the family or anyway connected with the family sphere.
- The idea of 'domestic violence' in India was borrowed mostly from the international legal framework.
- The adoption of PWDVA addresses two important concerns
  (i) **Firstly,** the family law reforms of the 1980s like the Family Courts Act, focus more on the need to **preserve the family** at all costs. Hence, it does not emphasise on ending violence against women in the private sphere. PWDVA helps to address violence occurring in the private sphere.
  (ii) **Secondly, before 2005,** domestic violence against women was considered 'cruelty'. It was punishable under the criminal law. However, there was no comprehensive law providing civil remedies for domestic violence for women like monetary reliefs or compensation as well as other services that aid women who are sufferers of domestic violence.
- PWDVA recognises how domestic violence affects women at multiple levels and provides various support services to women to help deal with the situation. They are
  - Mandatory assistance by medical facilities and shelter homes
  - Provision for legal aid
  - Counseling on the direction of the court
  - Protection officers and service providers to maintain a list and facilitate access

Definition of Violence According to PWDVA

- PWDVA adopts a comprehensive definition of domestic violence and includes physical abuse as well as other forms of violence within the family that is manifested and affects the woman.
- According to **Section 3** of the PWDVA, any act, omission or commission or conduct of the respondent shall constitute domestic violence in case it
  - harms or injures or endangers the health, safety, life, **limb**[3] or well-being, whether mental or physical, of the aggrieved person or tends to do so.
  - includes causing physical abuse, sexual abuse, verbal and emotional abuse and economic abuse.
  - harasses, harms, injures or endangers the aggrieved person with a view to coerce her or any other person related to her, to meet any unlawful demand for any dowry or other property or valuable security.
  - has the effect of threatening the aggrieved person or any person related to her by any conduct mentioned in clause (a) or clause (b).
  - injures or causes harm, whether physical or mental, to the aggrieved person.

3 **Limb** It is an arm or leg of a person or four-legged animal or a bird's wing.

Features of PWDVA

The salient features of PWDVA are

- The PWDVA is a civil law, except **Section 31 and 33** where criminal proceedings are involved.
- Its primary objective is to provide compensation as well as support to the woman. This is contrary to criminal law, which intends to primarily punish the executors. Enforcing criminal laws depends on the state, the police and the prosecution lawyer.
- As a civil law, PWDVA is victim-driven and has direct access to the court.
- The rights and reliefs under PWDVA can only be initiated with the consent of the woman.
- PWDVA describes **domestic relationships** broadly to include, wives, mothers, sisters, daughters and live-in partners. All of these are provided protection by the PWDVA.
- The protection under the PWDVA is not limited to the matrimonial home but covers 'shared householder' to include mothers, sisters and daughters as well.
- PWDVA provides for **stop violence** orders that offer emergency reliefs to stop violence immediately.
- PWDVA is an additional law and allows women to enforce other laws, such as the divorce laws as well.
- PWDVA offers both access to justice as well as access to support systems. It provides for protection officers to operate as a **nexus**[4] between the court and the woman to ensure accessibility to the justice system. These protection officers are usually women. Their role includes
  - assisting women in filing for applications seeking various reliefs.
  - assisting the magistrate in discharge of his functions.
  - making women aware about their right to get free legal aid.
  - providing women shelter homes, medical services, etc.
- PWDVA involves **service providers**, i.e. non-governmental organisations who voluntarily register under the act, to deliver it with essential support such as shelter and medical facilities.
- Service providers are crucial as women often would feel more comfortable approaching an NGO rather than the police or state authorities.
- PWDVA involves the **single window clearance system** to aid women in accessing the justice system.
- For example, a woman use one PWDVA suit to enforce her right to not be dis-possessed when a divorce petition is pending (**Section 498 A** of the Indian Penal Code).
- PWDVA provides that the magistrate may, direct either one or both the parties to the suit to undertake counseling with any member of the service provider, who holds the required qualification and experience of counseling.
- Women groups are critical to the counseling provision as it is often seen as a tool for preserving marriage.

Protection of Women from Sexual Harassment Act, 2013 (POSH Act)

- POSH Act was enacted on 9th December, 2013 by the Ministry for Women and Child Development.
- It was enacted with the objective of making workplaces safer for women by preventing, prohibiting and redressing acts of sexual harassment against them in the workplace.
- Many women's rights groups and non-governmental organisations filed a case **Vishakha and Others** Vs. **State of Rajasthan** in the Supreme Court in the interest of women's protection, as a Public Interest Litigation or Social Action Litigation.
- The origin of this case dates back to 1992 and it demanded action against sexual harassment towards women at the workplace.

4 **Nexus** It means a connection or a series of connection linking two or more things.

Facts

- Then, a low-caste women in the 50s. Bhanwari Devi, who was working as a social or grass roots worker with the Rajasthan Government's women development project, was gang-raped by a group of upper-caste men because she tried to stop the devious practice of child marriage.
- The trial court acquitted the accused offenders stating also that upper caste men could not have raped a low-caste woman, and also because all, including the village authorities, doctors and the police rejected her alligation.

- In the absence of any Indian law dealing specifically with violence against women, the Supreme Court referred to the UN Convention on the Elimination of All Forms of Discrimination against Women and delivered a set of standards, also called the **Vishakha Guidelines.**
- The guidelines included the following
  - It is the responsibility of the employer to include a rule in the company code of conduct for preventing sexual harassment.
  - Organisations must establish complaint committees that are headed by women.
  - Initiate disciplinary actions against offenders and safeguard the interests of the victim.
  - Female employees shall be made aware of their rights.
- Vishakha Guidelines established by **Article 32** of the Constitution have the force of law and must be obeyed by organisations in both the commercial and public sectors.
- The **Sexual Harassment of Women at Workplace** (Prevention, Prohibition and Redressal) Act of 2013 is based on Vishakha Guidelines.
- It aims to create a mechanism for redressal of sexual harassment complaints at workplace.

Quick Test 2

1. In which year, India adopted PWDV Act?
2. Give any one provision for legal aid under the PWDVA.
3. Which UN Convention was referred by the Supreme Court to issue set of guidelines?
4. What are Vishakha Guidelines?

Mind Map

PREVENTION OF VIOLENCE AGAINST WOMEN

1 Definition and Nature of Domestic Abuse

- India abuse encompasses physical, sexual, emotional, economic, or psychological actions or threats that influence another person.
- It includes behaviours that frighten, intimidate, manipulate, hurt, humiliate, blame, injure, or wound someone.

Characteristics of Domestic Abuse

- Domestic abuse can affect anyone regardless of race, age, sexual orientation, religion, or gender.
- It occurs in various relationships, including married couples, cohabiting partners and dating.
- The impact of domestic abuse spans all socio economic backgrounds and education levels.
- It is largely forbidden in Western countries.

Global Perspectives on Domestic Abuse

- Abuse while largely forbidden in Western countries, domestic abuse is legally recognised or socially acceptable in many nation.
- For instance, in the United Arab Emirates, laws permit limited physical discipline of wives and children.
- Countries like Jordan, Guinea, Zambia, Sierra Leone, Laos, and Ethiopia view domestic violence as socially acceptable.

2 International Legal Framework

Key International Treaties and Declarations

- The Convention on the Elimination of All Forms of Discrimination against Women (CEDAW) was adopted in 1979 and serves as a foundational treaty defining discrimination against women.
- CEDAW sets an agenda for national action to eliminate discrimination, with 99 countries, including India, as signatories.

UN Declaration on Elimination of Violence against Women

- Adopted in 1993, this declaration defines violence against women as any gender based act likely to result in physical, sexual, or psychological harm.
- India is a party to this declaration, committing to its principles.

UN Model Legislation on Domestic Violence

- Created in 1996, this legislation serves as a drafting guide for comprehensive domestic violence laws at the state level.
- It defines domestic violence broadly, including various forms of abuse such as physical, psychological and sexual violence.

3 Laws to Prevent Violence Against Women

Protection of Women from Domestic Violence Act (PWDVA), 2005

- Prior to 2005, domestic violence was not recognised as a distinct legal category in India.
- The PWDVA aims to provide effective protection to women facing violence within the family or related contexts.
- The act addresses the shortcomings of family law reforms from the 1980s, which prioritised family preservation over addressing violence.

Features of PWDVA

- PWDVA is primarily a civil law, focusing on compensation and support for victims than punishment of offenders.
- It allows women to initiate legal action with their consent and includes a broad definition of domestic relationships, covering wives, mothers, sisters, daughters, and live-in partners.
- The act provides for emergency reliefs, such as 'Stop Violence' orders, and recognises the need for support services like legal aid and counseling.

Support Service Under PWDVA

- The act mandates assistance from medical facilities and shelter homes for victims.
- Legal aid provisions are established to help women navigate the legal system.
- Protection officers and service providers are designated to facilitate access to necessary services and support.

Sexual Harassment and Legal Protections

The Protection of Women from Sexual Harassment Act (POSH Act), 2013

- Enacted on December 9, 2013, the POSH Act aims to create safer workplaces for women by preventing and addressing sexual harassment.
- The act emerged from the Vishakha case, which highlighted the need for legal protections against workplace harassment.

Vishakha Guidelines

- The Supreme Court established the Vishakha Guidelines in 1997, mandating employers to create a code of conduct for preventing sexual harassment.
- Organisations are required to form complaint committees headed by women and take disciplinary action against offenders
- The guidelines emphasise the importance of informing female employees of their rights.

Implementation and Impact

- The POSH Act provides a framework for addressing complaints of sexual harassment workplaces.
- It aims to empower women and create a culture of safety and respect in professional environments.

4 Conclusion

Ongoing Challenges and Future Directions

- Despite legal frameworks, domestic violence and abuse remain pervasive issues in society.
- Continuous efforts are needed to raise awareness, provide support, and enforce laws effectively to protect victims and prevent violence against women.
- Collaboration between government, NGOs, and communities is essential to create a safer environment for all individuals.

CBSE TEXTBOOK Folder

1. Briefly answers the following questions.

(i) What is CEDAW?

(ii) What is PWDVA? State the support services provided to women under PWDVA.

(iii) What guidelines were issued by the Supreme Court in Vishakha & others vs State of Rajasthan?

(iv) Trace the evolution of POSH Act, 2013 in India.

Ans. (i) The Convention on the Elimination of All Forms of Discrimination Against Women, 1979 (CEDAW) is a United Nations treaty that defines what constitutes discrimination against women. It also set up an agenda for national action to end such discrimination. CEDAW is often referred to as the international bill of rights for women and has 99 countries, including India, as signatories. These have committed themselves to undertake various measures to end discrimination against women in all forms.

(ii) In 2005, the Indian Parliament adopted the Protection of Women from Domestic Violence Act (PWDVA) with the objective of providing effective protection to women who are victims of violence occurring within the family or anyway connected with the family sphere.

PWDVA provides various support services to women to help deal with the situation. They are

- Mandatory assistance by medical facilities and shelter homes.
- Provision for legal aid.
- Counseling on the direction of the court.
- Protection Officers and Service Providers to maintain a list and facilitate access.

(iii) The following guidelines were issued by the Supreme Court in Vishakha Vs. State of Rajasthan

- It is the responsibility of the employer to include a rule in the company code of conduct for preventing sexual harassment.
- Organisations must establish complaint committees that are headed by women.
- Initiate disciplinary actions against offenders and safeguard the interests of the victim.
- Female employees shall be made aware of their rights.

(iv) POSH Act was enacted on 9th December, 2013 by the Ministry for Women and Child Development. It was enacted with the objective of making workplaces safer for women by preventing, prohibiting and redressing acts of sexual harassment against them in the workplace.

Many women's rights groups and non-governmental organisations filed a case Vishakha & others Vs. State of Rajasthan in the Supreme Court in the interest of women's protection, as a Public Interest Litigation or Social Action Litigation.

The origin of this case dates back to 1992 and it demanded action against sexual harassment towards women at the workplace.

In the absence of any Indian law dealing specifically with violence against women, the Supreme Court referred to the UN Convention on the Elimination of All Forms of Discrimination against Women and delivered a set of standards, also called the Vishakha Guidelines.

2. The concern for 'violence against women' including violence in intimate relationships has significantly existed in international discourse and legal frameworks.

(i) Which United Nations treaty defines violence against women?

(ii) How has the Indian Parliament reacted to the rising cases of domestic violence?

(iii) State a few salient features of the act.

Ans. (i) The Convention on the Elimination of All Forms of Discrimination against Women, 1979 (CEDAW) is a United Nations treaty that defines what constitutes discrimination against women.

(ii) In response to the rising cases of domestic violence, the Indian Parliament enacted the Protection of Women from Domestic Violence Act (PWDVA) in 2005. Before this law, domestic violence was not recognised as a special legal issue in India.

The PWDVA was introduced to protect women from violence occurring within the family or related to family matters. It draws inspiration from international frameworks, such as the Convention on the Elimination of All Forms of Discrimination Against Women (CEDAW) and the UN declaration on the elimination of violence against women.

The act provides legal remedies and protection for women, aiming to ensure their safety and well-being within the home.

(iii) The salient features of PWDVA are as follows
- The PWDVA is a civil law, except Sections 31 and 33 where criminal proceedings are involved. Its primary objective is to provide compensation as well as support to the woman. This is contrary to criminal law, which intends to primarily punish the executors.
The rights and reliefs under PWDVA can only be initiated with the consent of the woman.
- PWDVA describes 'domestic relationships' broadly to include, wives, mothers, sisters, daughters and live-in partners. All of these are provided protection by the PWDVA.
- The protection under the PWDVA is not limited to the matrimonial home but covers 'shared householder' to include mothers, sisters and daughters as well.
- PWDVA provides for 'stop violence' orders that offer emergency reliefs to stop violence immediately. PWDVA is an additional law and allows women to enforce other laws, such as the divorce laws as well.

Exam Pattern Questions

Objective Type Questions

Multiple Choice Questions (MCQs)

1. Tanvi has newly joined a government institution and she was secretly informed by her female colleagues that there are certain officers who most of the time asks for sexual favour in promotion and recognition.
Which among the following is a United Nations treaty that defines norms and standards of discrimination against women and set up an agenda for national action to end such discrimination? **Competency Based Que**
(a) UN Convention on Climate Change, 1992
(b) The Convention on the Elimination of All Forms of Discrimination against Women, 1979 (CEDAW)
(c) UN Convention on Women's Development, 1984
(d) None of the above

2. In ...., the CEDAW Committee recommended that any form of discrimination or violation of women's rights amounts to violence and the State is responsible for such violence committed both by state as well as private individuals.
(a) 1990 (b) 1992 (c) 1995 (d) 1998

3. How many countries are signatory to the Convention on the Elimination of All Forms of Discrimination against Women?
(a) 90 (b) 92 (c) 99 (d) 199

4. Harish has informed his son Gautam that the United Nations has taken various steps to prevent women harassment and domestic violence, which became the standard parameters for all the nations including India.
When was the UN Declaration on Elimination of Violence against Women adopted? **Competency Based Que**
(a) 1993 (b) 1992 (c) 1991 (d) 1990

5. Subsidiary organ of the United Nations created the UN Model Legislation on Domestic Violence with the objective of serving as a drafting guide for comprehensive legislation on domestic violence at states levels'. Identify the subsidiary organ.
(a) UN Commission on Women
(b) UN Commission on Domestic Violence
(c) UN Commission on Human Rights
(d) None of the above

6. It defines domestic violence as all acts of gender-based physical, psychological and sexual abuse by a family member against women in the family, ranging from simple assaults to aggravated physical battery, kidnapping, threats, intimidation, coercion, stalking, humiliating verbal abuse, forcible or unlawful entry, arson, destruction of property, sexual violence, marital rape, dowry or bride-price related violence, female genital mutilation, violence related to exploitation through prostitution, violence against household workers and attempts to commit such acts. **Competency Based Que**
Which law/convention/declaration provides the above mentioned definition of 'domestic violence'?
(a) UN Model Legislation on Domestic Violence
(b) Protection of Women from Domestic Violence Act
(c) Convention on the Elimination of All Forms of Discrimination against Women
(d) The UN Declaration on Elimination of Violence against Women

7. Indian Parliament adopted the Protection of Women from Domestic Violence Act (PWDVA). Which of the following statement is NOT True regarding PWDVA?

(a) The protection under the PWDVA is not limited to the matrimonial home but covers 'shared householder'.
(b) PWDVA puts responsibility on the local governments for training of general public.
(c) PWDVA also envisages service providers, i.e NGOs.
(d) PWDVA stipulates for the 'single window clearance system'.

8. When did the Indian Parliament adopt the Protection of Women from Domestic Violence Act (PWDVA)?

(a) 2002 (b) 2003 (c) 2004 (d) 2005

9. Protection of Women from Domestic Violence Act (PWDVA) is a .... law.

(a) civil (b) criminal
(c) international (d) All of these

10. The Protection of Women from Domestic Violence Act (PWDVA) adopts a comprehensive definition of domestic violence. Identify which among the following is TRUE about the primary objective of PWDVA.

(a) To eliminate violence against women in public spaces.
(b) To provide protection to women victims of violence within the family.
(c) To protect women from workplace harassment.
(d) To regulate domestic issues between married couples.

11. Which act puts responsibility on the Central and State Governments for training and sensitisation of the general public as well as the state authorities including the judiciary?

(a) UN declaration against domestic violence
(b) Protection of Women from Domestic Violence Act
(c) Both of the above
(d) None of the above

12. Yamini is too much scared of her husband who most often beat her for smaller mistakes and non-fulfilment of dowry amount. Luckily her friend has helped her to lodge a formal complaint against her husband.

Which section of the Indian Penal Code deals with the cases related to domestic violence? **Competency Based Que**

(a) 490 (b) 490 A
(c) 488 (d) 498 A

13. Protection of Women from Domestic Violence Act recognises how domestic violence affects women at multiple levels and provides various support services to women to deal with the situation.

Which among the following is NOT a level described in PWDVA?

(a) Mandatory assistance by medical facilities and shelter homes
(b) Provision for legal aid
(c) Counseling on the direction of the court
(d) All of the above

14. In the absence of any Indian law dealing specifically with violence against women, the Supreme Court referred to the UN Convention and delivered a set of standards, called the Vishakha Guidelines, which directed that the organisations must establish .... that must be headed by women.

(a) Social Committee
(b) Complaint Committee
(c) Women Committee
(d) Gender Sensitive Committee

15. Statement I The Protection of Women against Domestic Violence Act, defines domestic violence to include physical, sexual, verbal, emotional and economic abuse.

Statement II The act only provides for criminal proceedings against the perpetrator and does not offer any civil remedies for the victim.

Choose the correct statement

(a) Both Statement are correct.
(b) Both Statement are incorrect.
(c) Statement I is correct, but Statement II is not correct.
(d) Statement II is correct, but Statement I is not correct.

16. Statement I The CEDAW Committee recommends that states parties ensure women's equal rights to ownership, management and access to land and natural resources.

Statement II The CEDAW Committee suggests that states parties should only provide protection to women who have experienced extreme forms of gender-based violence.

Choose the correct statement

(a) Both Statement are correct.
(b) Both Statement are incorrect.
(c) Statement I is correct, but Statement II is not correct.
(d) Statement II is correct, but Statement I is not correct.

17. Arrange the following frameworks and policies as per the year in chronological order

I. Vishakha and Others Vs. State of Rajasthan and Others

II. UN Declaration on Elimination of Violence against Women was adopted.

III. Indian Parliament adopted the Protection of Women from Domestic Violence Act.

IV. Protection of Women from Sexual Harassment Act.

Choose the correct arrangement

(a) IV, III, II, I (b) IV, I, II, III
(c) I, II, III, IV (d) II, I, III, IV

18. Match the following.

Column-I	Column-II
A. Vishakha Guidelines	1. 1979
B. Protection of Women from Domestic Violence Act	2. 1997
C. UN Model Legislation on Domestic Violence	3. 2005
D. The Convention on the Elimination of All Forms of Discrimination against Women	4. 1996

Codes

	A	B	C	D		A	B	C	D
(a)	1	2	3	4	(b)	4	2	3	1
(c)	4	1	2	3	(d)	2	3	4	1

Assertion-Reason Questions

Directions (Q. Nos. 19-22) In the questions given below, there are two statements. Read the statements and choose the correct option.

Codes

(a) Both A and R are true and R is the correct explanation of A.
(b) Both A and R are true, but R is not the correct explanation of A.
(c) A is true, but R is false.
(d) A is false, but R is true.

19. **Assertion** (A) The nature of violence against women varies based on the particular socio-cultural as well as political and economic contexts.

Reason (R) Domestic violence against women happens in the private space.

20. **Assertion** (A) UN Declaration on Elimination of Violence against Women defines discrimination against women and set up an agenda for national action to end such discrimination.

Reason (R) UN Declaration on Elimination of Violence against Women was adopted in 1993.

21. **Assertion** (A) Protection of Women from Domestic Violence Act adopts a comprehensive definition of domestic violence only including physical abuse.

Reason (R) The definition of domestic violence is provided in Section 3 of the Protection of Women from Domestic Violence Act.

22. **Assertion** (A) The concept of 'domestic violence' was not recognised under the Indian law as a special category.

Reason (R) The Protection of Women from Domestic Violence Act (PWDVA) was adopted in 2010.

Answers

1. (b) The Convention on the Elimination of All Forms of Discrimination against Women, 1979 (CEDAW)
2. (b) 1992
3. (c) 99
4. (a) 1993
5. (c) UN Commission on Human Rights
6. (a) UN Model Legislation on Domestic Violence
7. (b) PWDVA puts responsibility on the local governments for training of general public.
8. (d) 2005
9. (a) civil
10. (b) To provide protection to women victims of violence within the family.
11. (b) Protection of Women from Domestic Violence Act
12. (d) 498 A
13. (d) All of the above
14. (b) Complaint Committee
15. (c) Statement I is correct, but Statement II is not correct.
16. (c) Statement I is correct, but Statement II is not correct.
17. (c) I, II, III, IV
18. (d) 2 3 4 1
19. (b) Both A and R are true, but R is not the correct explanation of A.
20. (d) A is false, but R is true.
21. (d) A is false, but R is true.
22. (c) A is true, but R is false.

Subjective Questions

Very Short Answer Type Questions

1. Which international treaty is known as the international bill for rights of women?

Ans. The Convention on the Elimination of All Forms of Discrimination against Women, 1979 (CEDAW) is known as the International Bill for Rights of Women. It is a United Nations treaty that defines the norms and standard of discrimination against women and sets up an agenda for national action to end such discrimination.

2. What is the objective of UN Model Legislation on Domestic Violence?

Ans. The UN Commission on Human Rights created the UN Model Legislation on Domestic Violence with the objective of serving as a drafting guide for comprehensive legislation on domestic violence at states levels.

3. How does the UN Declaration on Elimination of Violence against Women describe 'violence against women'?

Ans. The UN Declaration on Elimination of Violence against Women was adopted in 1993 and defines 'violence against women' as any gender-based violence acts that result in, or are likely to result in, physical, sexual or psychological harm or suffering to women.

4. State some international laws of rights for women in which India is a signatory.

Ans. India is signatory to the following international laws

- The Convention on the Elimination of All Forms of Discrimination against Women, 1979 (CEDAW).
- The UN Declaration on Elimination of Violence against Women, 1993.
- UN Model Legislation on Domestic Violence.

5. 'PWDVA recognises that domestic violence affects women at multiple levels'. Mention these levels. Competency Based Que

Ans. PWDVA recognises the different levels at which domestic violence affects women.

These are

- Mandatory assistance by medical facilities and shelter homes.
- Provision for legal aid.
- Counseling on the direction of the court.
- Protection officers and service providers to maintain a list and facilitate access.

6. The origin of this case dates back to 1992 and it demanded action against sexual harassment towards women at the workplace. Competency Based Que

(i) Identify the case.

(ii) Government passed an act called POSH Act, 2013 based on the above case explain the act.

Ans. (i) The above discussed case is Vishakha and Others Vs. State of Rajasthan.

(ii) POSH Act was enacted in 2013 and it was enacted by the Ministry for Women and Child Development. This act was enacted with the objective of making workplace safer for women by preventing, prohibiting and redressing acts of sexual harassment against them in workplace.

Short Answer Type Questions

1. Saraswati S and Teena Bala were discussing how UN and India has transformed common people's life in the larger extend. Many laws or set of directions has given the way forward for women and child safety and welfare.

What are the major features of Convention on the Elimination of All Forms of Discrimination against Women? Competency Based Que

Ans. For answer refer to text under the heading International Legal Framework on page no. 291.

2. Many women in India suffers cruelty and domestic violence on regular basis. Many of them are aware of women's right but they hesitate to report or inform their family members regarding the same.

What are the two important concerns addressed by the Protection of Women from Domestic Violence Act, 2005? Competency Based Que

Ans. The adoption of Protection of Women from Domestic Violence Act, 2005 addresses the following two important concerns

(i) Firstly, the family law reforms of the 1980s like the Family Courts Act, focus more on the need to 'preserve the family' at all costs. In that, they do not emphasise on ending violence against women in the private sphere. PWDVA addresses violence occurring in the private sphere.

(ii) Secondly, before 2005, domestic violence against women was considered 'cruelty' and was punishable under the criminal law and they formed grounds for divorce under the family laws.

3. Raman and Madhu has now developed bitter and harsh relationship while staying together as a live-in partners. One day, Raman smashed on Madhu's face. When he was confronted the police he simply denied by stating that they both aren't a married couple. However police arrested him. Which forms of violence are included under the Protection of Women from Domestic Violence Act, 2005? Competency Based Que

Ans. Following forms of violence are included under the Protection of Women from Domestic Violence Act, 2005

- harms or injures or endangers the health, safety, life, limb or well-being, whether mental or physical, of the aggrieved person or tends to do so.
- includes causing physical abuse, sexual abuse, verbal and emotional abuse and economic abuse.
- harasses, harms, injures or endangers the aggrieved person with a view to coerce her or any other person related to her, to meet any unlawful demand for any dowry or other property or valuable security.
- the effect of threatening the aggrieved person or any person related to her by any conduct mentioned in clause (a) or clause (b).
- injures or causes harm, whether physical or mental, to the aggrieved person.

Long Answer Type Questions

1. Savita a house-help in the Rajnagar area was known for her honesty and determination. One day, her husband beat her mercilessly and thrown out of his house. She was thankfully helped by some generous people. What do you understand by 'domestic violence' and what are the international legal framework established for the same? Competency Based Que

Ans. UN Model Legislation on Domestic Violence defines domestic violence as 'all acts of gender-based physical, psychological and sexual abuse by a family member against women in the family, ranging from

- kidnapping
- threats
- intimidation
- coercion
- stalking
- humiliating verbal abuse
- forcible or unlawful entry
- arson
- destruction of property
- sexual violence
- marital rape
- simple assaults to aggravated physical battery
- dowry or bride-price related violence
- female genital mutilation
- violence related to exploitation through prostitution
- violence against household workers and attempts to commit such acts.'

These acts may occur either in public or in private life. Violence may occur outside the family in the general community.

The international legal frameworks regarding the concern for 'violence against women' include

- **The Convention on the Elimination of All Forms of Discrimination against Women, 1979 (CEDAW)** It is a United Nations treaty that defines what constitutes discrimination against women and sets up an agenda for national action to end such discrimination.
- **The UN Declaration on Elimination of Violence against Women** It was adopted in 1993. It defines violence against women as any gender-based violence acts that result in, or are likely to result in, physical, sexual or psychological harm or suffering to women.
- **UN Model Legislation on Domestic Violence** It was created in 1996 with the objective of serving as a drafting guide for comprehensive legislation on domestic violence at states levels.

2. Describe the major features of protection of women from Domestic Violence Act, 2005.

Ans. For answer refer to text under the heading Protection of Women from Domestic Violence Act (PWDVA), 2005 on page no. 293.

3. Hari attended a group discussion session where the importance of preventing sexual harassment was the topic. Hari gave his view point with the Supreme Court's historic Vishakha Guidelines, which changed the whole work culture in India.

Describe in detail the Vishakha Case. What are the major guidelines provided in the Supreme Court judgement of the case? Competency Based Que

Ans. The case of Vishakha and Others Vs. State of Rajasthan was decided by the Supreme Court of India in 1997. This case is a landmark judgement on sexual harassment of women at workplace. Many women's rights groups and non-governmental organisations filed a case Vishakha and Others Vs. State of Rajasthan in the Supreme Court in the interest of women's protection, as a Public Interest Litigation or Social Action Litigation. The origin of this case dates back to 1992 and it demanded action against sexual harassment towards women at the workplace.

Thus, in the absence of any Indian law dealing specifically with violence against women, the Supreme Court referred to the UN Convention on the Elimination of All Forms of Discrimination against Women and delivered a set of standards, also called the Vishakha Guidelines.

The provisions of the Vishakha Guidelines are

- It is the responsibility of the employer to include a rule in the company code of conduct for preventing sexual harassment.
- Organisations must establish complaint committees that are headed by women.
- Initiate disciplinary actions against offenders and safeguard the interests of the victim.
- Female employees shall be made aware of their rights.

SELF ASSESSMENT TEST

Objective Type Questions

1. .... against women happens in the private space.
   (a) Domestic violence (b) International violence (c) Statutory violence (d) None of these
2. The law of which country allows the man the use of limited physical means to discipline his wife and children?
   (a) India (b) United States (c) Britain (d) United Arab Emirates
3. .... is a United Nations treaty that defines what constitutes discrimination against women and sets up an agenda for national action to end such discrimination.
   (a) Protection of Women from Domestic Violence Act, 2005
   (b) The UN Declaration on Elimination of Violence against Women, 1993
   (c) UN Model Legislation on Domestic Violence, 1996
   (d) Convention on the Elimination of All Forms of Discrimination against Women, 1979
4. Which act was passed by the Government of India with the objective of providing effective protection to the women victims of violence occurring within the family or anyway connected with the family sphere?
   (a) Protection of Women from Domestic Violence Act, 2005
   (b) The UN Declaration on Elimination of Violence against Women, 1993
   (c) UN Model Legislation on Domestic Violence, 1996
   (d) Convention on the Elimination of All Forms of Discrimination against Women, 1979

Very Short Answer Type Questions

5. Define 'Domestic Violence' and 'Violence against Women'.
6. How does the nature of violence against women varies?
7. Mention the features of Convention on the Elimination of All Forms of Discrimination against Women, 1979.
8. What is the effect of domestic violence on women?

Short Answer Type Questions

9. Explain the various kinds of domestic violence described in the Section 3 of Protection of Women from Domestic Violence Act.
10. Vishakha case is a landmark judgement on sexual harassment of women at work place. Explain the guidelines provided in this judgement. **Competency Based Que**

Long Answer Type Questions

11. Write short notes on
    (i) Convention on the Elimination of All Forms of Discrimination against Women.
    (ii) Protection of Women Against Domestic Violence Act.
12. Describe the International Legal Framework on Domestic Violence and Violence against Women.
13. 'According to Section 3 of the PWDVA, any act, omission or commission shall constitute domestic violence in case it injures or cause harm etc'. **Competency Based Que**
    (i) State the two concerns related to this act.
    (ii) Explain the features of PWDVA Act, 2005.

PROJECT WORK

Uniform Civil Code

Declaration

I hereby declare that this document, titled "Uniform Civil Code," is an original work completed by me. The information presented has been gathered from various sources, including textbooks, online research, and official reports, to provide an insightful understanding of the Uniform Civil Code.

I affirm that this work has not been copied from any existing material, and all sources of information have been duly acknowledged.

Signature: ________________

Name: ________________

Date: ________________

Certificate

This is to Certify that the project work

.... is the bonafide

work of .... (Name of the student) who

carried out the work under my supervision

....

Name and Signature of
Teacher/Supervisor

Acknowledgement

I want to sincerely thank to Mr. / Mrs. _______________, my Legal Studies instructor, for her direction and assistance with my paper. I was able to better organise and explain my ideas as a result of her insightful criticism and recommendations. Their ongoing encouragement has always encouraged me to aim high and follow my passions.

I also want to express my gratitude to the library personnel for giving me access to a variety of books on legal studies and tools. This project would not have been possible without their help.

Finally, I want to highlight the importance of Uniform Civil Code as it examines the potential impact on ensuring equality, justice and national unity in a diverse country like India. The goal of this project is to investigate the need for a common set of laws for all citizens and address potential challenges to its implementation and propose solutions for overcoming them.

Date...........

....
Name of Student

Contents

Uniform Civil Code

Introduction

The Uniform Civil Code (UCC) has been a longstanding and complex issue within India's legal and social framework. It proposes to replace the current system, where different religious communities are governed by their own personal laws for matters such as marriage, divorce, inheritance and adoption with a single set of laws applicable to all citizens. Supporters of the UCC argue that it would foster national unity which ensures gender justice and establishes equality before the law. On the other hand, critics voice concerns about safeguarding India's religious and cultural diversity.

The concept of a UCC has been enshrined in India's Constitutional framework since independence, as part of the Directive Principles of State Policy. However, its implementation has remained a controversial topic for decades. The debate over the UCC involves sensitive issues such as religious freedom, the protection of minority rights, and the challenge of balancing uniform civil laws with the preservation of India's rich cultural and religious diversity.

Purpose of The Project

The purpose of this project is to explore the concept of the Uniform Civil Code (UCC) and examine its potential impact on ensuring equality, justice and national unity in a diverse country like India. The project aims to investigate the need for a common set of laws for all citizens, irrespective of their religion, in areas like marriage, divorce, inheritance and adoption. By providing a comprehensive understanding of the UCC, the project seeks to support its implementation with research evidence, focusing on its benefits in promoting gender equality, legal transparency, and social harmony. The project will also address potential challenges to its implementation and propose solutions for overcoming them.

The Uniform Civil Code

The Uniform Civil Code refers to a single set of laws governing personal matters such as marriage, divorce, adoption, inheritance and succession for all citizens of India.

The concept of UCC is mentioned in **Article 44** of the **Indian Constitution as a Directive Principle of State Policy,** which states that the state shall endeavor to secure a uniform civil code for citizens throughout the territory of India. However, it's important to note that this is not a legally enforceable right but a guiding principle for the state.

Historical Context And Background

Personal family laws govern matters like marriage, divorce, inheritance, adoption, and maintenance based on religious customs. Different communities in India (Hindus, Muslims, Christians, Parsis, etc.) follow distinct personal laws rooted in their traditions and beliefs.

- **Ancient Period** In ancient period Hindu laws were based on texts like the **Dharmashastras,** while Muslims followed **Sharia.** These laws were rooted in religion and custom.
- **Medieval Period** In the medieval period two main schools of Hindu law emerged-Mitakshara (North and South India) and Dayabhaga (Bengal). Muslims continued to follow Sharia.
- **British Period** In 1772, Warren Hastings introduced uniform criminal laws but allowed Hindus and Muslims to follow their personal laws for family matters. Courts relied on Hindu pandits and Muslim jurists to interpret these laws but later replaced them with judges due to inconsistencies and corruption.
- **Post-independence Efforts** After 1947, attempts were made to introduce a UCC, but opposition led to its delay.

The concept of the Uniform Civil Code has its roots in colonial India. During British rule, personal laws were respected to maintain peace among different communities. However, reformers like Raja Ram Mohan Roy argued for uniformity in certain areas, especially concerning women's rights.

After independence in 1947, India's leaders had debates on UCC while drafting the Constitution. **Dr. B.R. Ambedkar,** the architect of the Constitution, supported the idea but faced opposition from religious groups who wanted to preserve their customs. As a compromise, UCC was included in the Directive Principles of State Policy, meaning it would not be mandatory.

Sub-Committee on Fundamental Rights

The Sub-committee on Fundamental Rights was responsible for drafting the Fundamental Rights of the Constitution. Eminent leaders like Dr. B.R. Ambedkar, K.M. Munshi, and Minoo Masani included the idea of the Uniform Civil Code (UCC) in their drafts.

The Sub-committee divided Fundamental Rights into two categories i.e. justiciable (enforceable by courts) and non-justiciable (not enforceable by courts but guiding principles for governance). The UCC was placed in the non-justiciable section.

Constituent Assembly Debates

During the Constituent Assembly debates, the idea of the UCC was extensively discussed. Dr. B.R. Ambedkar introduced Draft Article 35, which eventually became Article 44 of the Indian Constitution.

Defense of the UCC

Supporters of the UCC presented strong arguments in its favour, which are as follow

- **K.M. Munshi** He advocated for the UCC as a means to ensure national unity and secularism. Munshi also acknowledged concerns within Hindu communities but emphasised the broader need for uniform laws.
- **Alladi Krishnaswamy Iyer** He argued that a UCC would promote harmony and questioned why there was resistance to a common civil code when a common criminal code was already in place without controversy.
- **Dr. B.R. Ambedkar** Ambedkar defended the inclusion of the UCC in the Directive Principles as a practical compromise. He stressed that the UCC would remain optional, allowing individuals and communities time to adapt to the idea.

Opposition of the UCC

- Leaders like **Ismail Sahab** and **Pocker Sahib Bahadur** expressed strong opposition, stating that the UCC would infringe on religious freedom and disrupt communal harmony.
- This debate reflects the complexities of balancing religious diversity, individual rights, and national unity in the framing of India's Constitution.

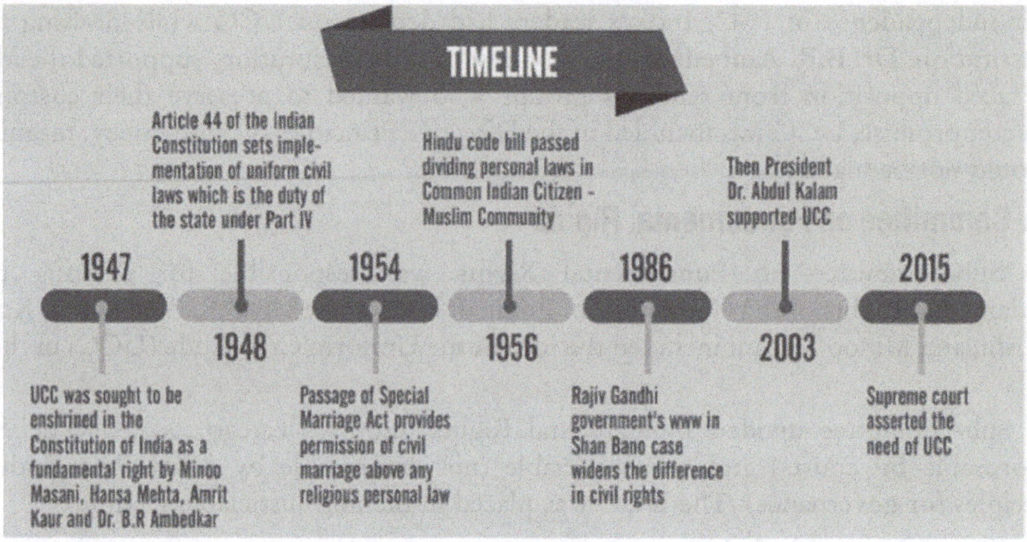

Importance of the Uniform Civil Code (UCC) in India

The Uniform Civil Code (UCC) holds significant importance in India for various reasons.

Equality

One of the most important benefits of the UCC is that it ensures equality for all citizens under the law. Currently, different religious communities follow different personal laws for matters like marriage, divorce, and inheritance. For example, Hindus, Muslims, Christians, and Parsis each have their own sets of laws. This creates inequality because people are treated differently depending on their religion.

Secularism

India is a secular country, which means that the government treats all religions equally and does not favor any one religion. In a secular state, religion and law should be separate. Laws should be made for everyone, not based on religious beliefs. However, personal laws in India are often tied to religion, which sometimes creates bias and conflicts.

Women's Rights

Personal laws in India often treat women unfairly. Many personal laws are outdated and based on traditional customs that do not give women equal rights. For example, in some personal laws, women do not get equal inheritance rights compared to men. Some laws allow practices like triple talaq (instant divorce), which are unfair to women. The UCC would replace these unequal personal laws with a single set of laws that ensures fairness for women. It would guarantee equal rights in property, marriage, divorce, and other legal matters. This would empower women and promote gender equality.

Inheritance and Property Laws

- Before the **Hindu Succession Act (2005)** was amended, Hindu daughters did not have equal rights to inherit ancestral property. Sons were given preference, while daughters had limited rights.
- Muslim women are entitled to inherit only half the share of property compared to male relatives.
- Christian women were earlier restricted from inheriting equal property under the **Indian Succession Act (1925).**

Divorce Laws

- Muslim men could previously divorce their wives instantly through **triple talaq** (saying 'etalaq' three times), leaving women vulnerable. This practice was abolished by the Supreme Court in 2017 in the **Shayara Bano Case,** which again showed the need for uniform and equal laws.

These inequalities in personal laws demonstrate the urgent need for a UCC to ensure all citizens have the same rights in matters like property, marriage and divorce.

National Unity

The UCC can help bring the nation together by creating a sense of equality and reducing conflicts between communities. In a diverse country like India, having different personal laws for each community sometimes causes disputes and divisions. These differences can lead to misunderstandings and feelings of inequality among citizens.

Modernisation

As society evolves, laws must also adapt to meet the changing needs of people. Many personal laws in India are based on old traditions and customs that no longer fit in today's society.

For example, modern families are more likely to see women as equals, but some personal laws do not reflect this change. Issues like divorce, adoption, and inheritance are handled differently in different communities, creating confusion and delays in justice.

The UCC would update and standardise these laws to match the modern values of justice, equality and fairness. It would make the legal system more effective and relevant for today's citizens.

Constitutional Provisions

India's judiciary has played a crucial role in highlighting the importance of the Uniform Civil Code (UCC) over the years. Through various landmark judgements, the courts have consistently emphasised the need for a common legal framework to ensure justice, equality and national integration.

Shah Bano Case (1985)

In this case, a woman named Shah Bano was divorced by her husband using triple talaq and was also denied maintenance. The District Court & the High Court ruled in her favour. However, the husband appealed to the Supreme Court where he contended that he had fulfilled all his obligations under the Muslim law, where the maintenance was to be paid only till the iddat period i.e. three lunar cycles.

Court Judgement The Supreme Court ruled in Shah Bano's favour under **Section 125 of Criminal Procedure Code 1973,** which deals with the maintenance of wives, children and parents. Since Criminal Procedure Code is a public law, it is applicable to all the citizens irrespective of religion. The Supreme Court further recommended that a Uniform Civil Code should be enforced

Importance The court linked the case to the need for the UCC, stating that a uniform law for all citizens would help ensure justice, especially for women. It also highlighted that a UCC could promote national integration by reducing legal inequalities based on religion.

Jorden Diengdeh Case (1985)

Ms. Jordan Diengdeh, a Christian woman, initiated legal proceedings in the Delhi High Court, seeking the annulment of her marriage based on her husband's impotence. The High Court declined her request for annulment but granted a decree for judicial separation on the grounds of cruelty.

Ms. Diengdeh appealed to the Supreme Court, asserting that the Christian Marriage Act, 1872, provided limited grounds for divorce and did not encompass the concept of irretrievable breakdown of marriage.

This case dealt with inconsistencies in divorce laws across different religions. The petitioner argued that the absence of uniform divorce laws caused confusion and unfairness.

Court Judgement In a unanimous decision articulated by, the Supreme Court acknowledged the lack of uniformity in divorce laws and advocated for reform.The Supreme Court pointed out that different personal laws for divorce were creating legal challenges and inconsistencies. It strongly recommended the need for a UCC to simplify and standardise divorce laws for all citizens.

Importance The case emphasised the need for legal uniformity in personal matters, such as marriage and divorce. It showed how inconsistent personal laws could lead to injustice, further strengthening the argument for a UCC.

Sarla Mudgal Case (1995)

This case focused on issues related to polygamy among Hindus who converted to Islam to marry a second time without divorcing their first wife.

The court held that the Hindu marriage solemnised under Hindu law can only be dissolved on any of the grounds specified under the Hindu Marriage Act 1955. Conversion to Islam and marrying again, would not by itself dissolve the Hindu marriage under the Act and therefore, a second marriage solemnised after converting to Islam would be an offense under section 494 (Bigamy) of the Indian Penal Code(IPC).

Court Judgement The Supreme Court criticised the misuse of personal laws and strongly supported the implementation of a UCC. It argued that uniform laws would prevent such legal loopholes and promote fairness.

Importance The court questioned why there was a delay in implementing the UCC, especially for the Hindu majority population. It highlighted the need for a single legal framework to prevent exploitation and misuse of personal laws.

Pannalal Bansilal Pitti Case (1996)

This case addressed the challenges of India's diverse religious and cultural practices in the context of implementing a UCC.

Court Judgement The Supreme Court acknowledged India's cultural diversity and stated that implementing the UCC should be done gradually and with sensitivity. It emphasised that the UCC must not be imposed hastily but should be achieved through consensus and public acceptance.

Importance The case recognised the complexities of India's pluralistic society and called for a balanced approach to the UCC. It showed that while the UCC is important, its implementation must respect India's diversity.

Sushmita Ghosh Case (2000)

The case revolves around the offence of bigamy. It refers to marrying another person while still legally married to someone else.

Sushmita Ghosh filed a petition before the Supreme Court mentioning about her marriage with Mr. G.C. Ghosh as per Hindu rituals, in 1984. She further stated that her husband said that she should agree to give him divorce by mutual consent. And since Hindu Marriage Act, 1955 does not allow bigamy, he converted to Islam to remarry a woman named Ms. Vinita Gupta.

Court Judgement The Supreme Court of India ruled that a Hindu man cannot marry again if he is still legally married to his first wife. If a person marries another while their first marriage is valid and not legally dissolved, the second marriage is invalid and considered bigamy under the law. The court also clarified that a person must follow proper legal procedures to divorce their first spouse before marrying again.

Importance The case helped strengthen marriage laws in India by protecting women from being unfairly treated in cases of bigamy, ensuring that the marriage laws are followed properly.

John Vallamattom Case (2003)

A Christian priest named John Vallamattom filed this writ petition before the Honorable Supreme Court of India. Through this writ petition, he challenged Section 118 of the Indian Succession Act of 1925. The petitioner contended that this Section discriminates against Christians who want to leave their property for religious and charitable purposes.

This case challenged discriminatory provisions in law that restricted the rights of Christian clergy to write wills.

Court Judgement The Supreme Court ruled that Section 118 of the Indian Succession Act was unconstitutional, as it unfairly restricted Indian Christians from leaving property for charitable or religious purposes. The court stated this violated Article 14 of the Constitution, which guarantees equality.

Importance The case highlighted that even within specific communities, personal laws could be discriminatory. It strengthened the argument for a common legal framework like the UCC to ensure fairness and equality.

Shabnam Hashmi Case (2014)

Shabnam Hashmi, a prominent human rights activist, began her advocacy work in 1981, focusing on adult literacy. She adopted a girl but faced the issue of not being recognised as the child's parents. According to Islamic law, a biological relationship is necessary to be called a parents. She filed a writ petition, not only to address her own situation but to represent all citizens facing similar challenges when adopting children.

In her petition, she highlighted the need for a change in personal laws to ensure that childless couples, irrespective of their religious backgrounds could adopt children and provide them with proper care, emotional support and a nurturing environment.

This case revolved around the adoption rights of a Muslim woman under the Juvenile Justice Act, which provides for secular adoption laws.

Court Judgement The Supreme Court ruled that Shabnam Hashmi could adopt a child under the secular Juvenile Justice Act, even if her personal laws did not permit it. The court linked the need for uniform adoption laws to the broader issue of implementing a UCC.

Importance The case emphasised that secular laws like the Juvenile Justice Act could be a model for the UCC. It showed how secular legal frameworks promote equality and justice for all citizens, regardless of their religion.

Shayara Bano Case (2017)

This case dealt with the practice of triple talaq (instant divorce) in Muslim personal law. Shayara Bano, a Muslim woman, challenged the Constitutionality of triple talaq. The contention of the petitioner was that this type of divorce (talaq) is violative of Fundamental Rights and further argued that these practices were not protected under Articles 25(1), 26(b) and 29 of the Constitution.

Court Judgement The Supreme Court declared triple talaq unConstitutional, stating that it was discriminatory and violated the right to equality. However, the court separated the issue of triple talaq from the broader debate on the UCC, focusing instead on human rights.

Importance The case reignited the debate on the UCC by showing how certain personal laws are discriminatory and unjust. It highlighted the need for a common legal framework to ensure justice for all, especially women.

These judicial pronouncements illustrate the challenges posed by India's diverse personal laws and highlight the judiciary's support for a Uniform Civil Code. Each case emphasises how the UCC can ensure justice, equality, and fairness while addressing issues of discrimination, legal inconsistencies and outdated practices. However, the courts also recognise the importance of implementing the UCC gradually, with sensitivity to India's cultural diversity.

Law Commission of India Report

21st Report (2018)

The Law Commission of India, in its 21st report, studied whether a Uniform Civil Code was necessary in India or not. This report said that the formulation of UCC is neither necessary nor desirable at this stage, rather reforms must be undertaken on family laws of every religion to make them gender-just.

Research Evidence Supporting the Uniform Civil Code (UCC)

Research-based evidence that supports the implementation of the UCC are as follow

Equality and Gender Justice

The UCC is crucial for achieving equality, particularly gender equality. It seeks to standardise laws across all religions in matters like marriage, divorce, and inheritance to ensure that no gender is treated unfairly.

Research Evidence

- Currently, many personal laws, especially in Hindu, Muslim and Christian communities, do not treat women equally. For example, under **Muslim personal law**, a woman is entitled to only half of what a man inherits. This creates a situation where women are not given the same rights as men, which is unfair and discriminatory.

- Under **Hindu personal law**, daughters were not given equal inheritance rights until the amendment of the Hindu Succession Act in 2005. While this amendment was a step toward gender equality, similar reforms have not been made in other personal laws.
- Studies by organisations such as the **National Commission for Women** (NCW) highlight that existing personal laws continue to reinforce gender biases. They emphasise that the UCC would eliminate these inequalities and guarantee equal rights for women.

National Unity and Social Cohesion

The UCC can unify the country by applying the same set of legal rules to all citizens, regardless of their religion, thus promoting a sense of belonging and national integration.

Research Evidence

- India is a diverse country with multiple religions, and having separate personal laws for each group has often caused divisions among communities.
- A study by the **Indian Social Institute** highlights that religious-based personal laws create confusion and disparity. It concludes that a common set of laws under the UCC would remove these legal inconsistencies and promote unity among citizens.
- Countries like **France** and **Turkey** have implemented uniform civil codes to eliminate religious distinctions in their legal systems. This has helped these nations achieve national cohesion and reduce conflicts caused by differing religious practices in personal laws.

Legal Transparency and Simplification

A UCC would make the legal system simpler and more transparent, helping citizens understand the laws better and reducing confusion.

Research Evidence

- The current system of multiple personal laws is overly complicated. For example, different rules apply to marriage and divorce for Hindus, Muslims, Christians and Parsis. This makes legal processes confusing, especially for ordinary citizens who are not well-versed in legal matters.
- Research conducted by **National Law School of India University (NLSIU)** indicates that these complexities lead to delays in justice and inconsistencies in judgements. A UCC would simplify the legal framework, making it easier for everyone to access justice.

- Countries like **Belgium** and **Switzerland** have uniform civil codes that make their legal systems straightforward. Citizens in these countries benefit from greater legal certainty and faster resolution of disputes because everyone is governed by the same laws.

Secularism and State Neutrality

A UCC ensures that the state remains neutral by not favoring any particular religion in its legal system. This promotes fairness and strengthens the secular character of the country.

Research Evidence

- Legal scholars, like Professor **S. P. A. S. R. M.**, argue that the UCC will provide equal legal rights without interfering in religious practices. For example, it would govern matters like marriage and divorce but would not affect how people pray, celebrate festivals, or follow other religious customs.
- In Turkey, a secular civil code replaced religious laws in personal matters, creating equality among citizens while allowing them to continue practicing their religious traditions freely.

Uniform Civil Code : Goa and Uttarakhand

Goa

In 1867 Portugal introduced a Civil Code and by 1869 it was extended to its overseas provinces, including Goa. This code is considered a form of Uniform Civil Code.

While there is not complete uniformity in areas like marriage and adoption, the Goa Civil Code is generally more **gender-equal** compared to other laws in India. It does not recognise bigamy or polygamy, even for Muslims. Although it allows a Hindu man to remarry, if his wife fails to conceive a child by the age of 21 or a male child by the age of 30.

Features of the Goa Civil Code include

- **Mandatory marriage registration** before a civil authority, ensuring equal inheritance rights for the wife, who is entitled to half of the 'common assets,' including those inherited by her husband in case of divorce.
- Parents must share at least half of their property with their children, including daughters.

Uttarakhand

Uttarakhand government officially implemented the Uniform Civil Code (UCC) on January 27, 2025, making it the first Indian state to adopt the UCC post-independence.

- The Uniform Civil Code (UCC), as a Constitutional measure, aims to eliminate discrimination and promote women's empowerment.

- It ensures equality, treating all individuals equally regardless of gender, caste, or religion.
- However, **Scheduled Tribes,** as defined under **Article 342** of the Constitution, are exempted from the UCC to protect their unique rights and traditions.

Features of the Uttarakhand Civil Code include

- **Banned Practices** The law bans halala, iddat, and talaq as part of Muslim Personal Law.
- **Equal Rights for Women** It guarantees equal rights for women in terms of property and inheritance.
- **Mandatory Online Registrations** All marriages, divorces, and live-in relationships must be registered on the government portal **ucc.uk.gov.in.**

Global Perspective on Uniform Civil Code

The concept of a Uniform Civil Code is not unique to India. Many countries have implemented similar codes to ensure equality and fairness in their legal systems. The examples from other countries are

- **France** France follows the Napoleonic Code, which introduced a uniform legal system for all citizens regardless of religion or background. It is known for promoting secularism and equality.
- **United States** The U.S. has a uniform set of federal laws that apply to all citizens. While there are state-level differences, Fundamental Rights and equality are ensured at the federal level.
- **Turkey** Under Mustafa Kemal Ataturk, Turkey adopted a civil code in 1926 based on the Swiss model. It replaced Islamic laws with a secular legal system and promoted gender equality.
- **Indonesia** Despite being a predominantly Muslim country, Indonesia has a civil code for its citizens. However, Sharia-based laws are also allowed in certain areas, creating a dual legal system.
- **South Africa** South Africa has a unified legal system but recognises customary laws for certain communities. It is an example of balancing diversity with a unified legal framework.

Arguments in Favour of Uniform Civil Code

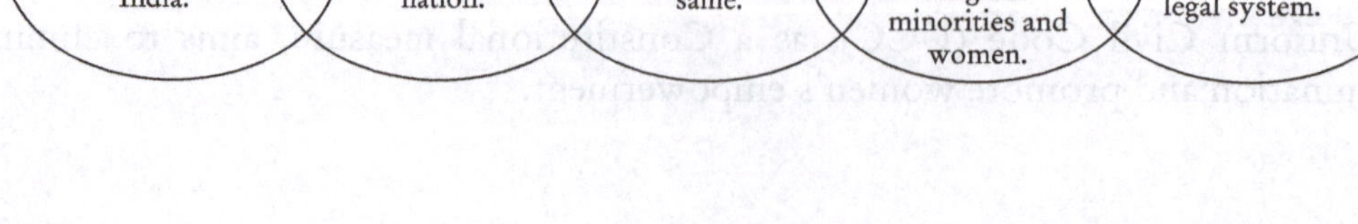

Arguments Against Uniform Civil Code

Many communities feel UCC may override their religious practices. For instance, Christians might fear that their unique marriage and divorce laws will be replaced by generic rules.
India's strength lies in its cultural variety. A single law might fail to respect customs like Hindu joint family property traditions or Muslim inheritance rules.
Minorities worry that UCC might reflect Hindu customs more than their own. For example, they fear laws like those in Hindu marriage practices might dominate.
Implementing UCC across millions of citizens with varied traditions is difficult. Goa's success, though admirable, is in a small state, and applying it to all of India could lead to unrest.

Challenges in Implementation

- **Diversity of Traditions** India's strength lies in its diversity. Different communities follow unique traditions that have been passed down for generations. Tribal groups, for instance, have their own customary practices, which may not align with a uniform law.
- **Lack of Awareness** In rural areas, many people are unaware of the benefits of UCC. They may view it as an attack on their religion or culture rather than as a step toward equality.
- **Political Sensitivity** UCC is a politically charged issue. Political parties often use it to gain votes, which makes meaningful discussions difficult. This politicisation divides communities further.
- **Legal Challenges** Replacing existing personal laws with a uniform code is a complex process. It requires revising hundreds of laws, training legal professionals, and ensuring smooth transitions in courts.
- **Practical Implementation Issues** Implementing UCC in a large and diverse country like India requires extensive planning. This includes addressing conflicts that may arise during the transition and ensuring proper representation of all communities.

Recommendations and Way Forward

To successfully implement the Uniform Civil Code (UCC) in India, careful planning and a phased approach are required. Some recommendations and way forward are as follows

- **Public Awareness Campaigns** Educate people about the benefits of UCC. Campaigns should focus on clearing misconceptions, highlighting how UCC promotes equality and unity without undermining religious freedom.

For example, use media platforms, workshops, and community events to inform citizens, especially in rural areas, about how UCC can ensure gender justice and reduce legal complexities.

- **Community Involvement** Include leaders and representatives from various religious and tribal communities in discussions. This will help address their concerns and ensure their voices are heard.
  For example, form a special committee with members from different religious groups, legal experts and women's rights activists to draft a UCC that respects diversity while ensuring equality.
- **Gradual Implementation** Introduce UCC in stages, starting with areas where consensus is easier to achieve.
  For example, reforms in inheritance or adoption laws can be introduced first, as these often face less resistance.
- **Protect Cultural Diversity** While drafting the UCC, ensure that the unique cultural practices of different communities are respected as long as they do not conflict with Fundamental Rights like gender equality.
  For example, allow certain customary practices to coexist with the UCC, provided they are not discriminatory.
- **Strengthening Women's Rights** Focus on addressing gender-based inequalities in personal laws. This will not only promote justice but also gain support from progressive sections of society.
  For example, ensure that women across all religions have equal rights in matters of marriage, divorce and maintenance.
- **Pilot Projects** Test the implementation of UCC in states or regions that are more open to reform, such as Goa, which already has a form of a Uniform Civil Code. This can serve as a model for the rest of the country.
  For example, use Goa's experience with a common family law as a reference to understand the challenges and benefits of UCC.
- **Political Consensus** Encourage political parties to work together on UCC as a national goal rather than a divisive issue. This can be done by forming an all-party Parliamentary committee to discuss and draft the UCC.
- **Judicial Support** Work closely with the judiciary to ensure smooth implementation. Training judges and lawyers to handle cases under the UCC is essential.
  For example, create specialised training programmes for legal professionals to familiarise them with the changes brought by UCC.
- **Use International Examples** Study and adapt successful practices from countries that have implemented uniform legal codes. Ensure that the Indian version is tailored to the country's unique needs and challenges.

Project Work

For example, refer to Turkey's experience in replacing religious laws with a secular civil code to understand how to address resistance.

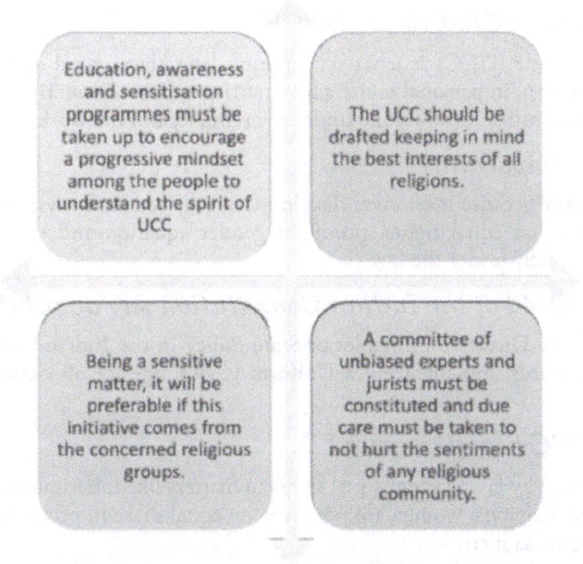

Suggestions for Implementation of UCC

Conclusion

The Uniform Civil Code is an important step towards ensuring equality, justice, and national unity in India. While there are challenges to its implementation, the potential benefits in terms of gender equality, legal transparency, and social cohesion are significant. A UCC can help ensure that all citizens are treated equally under the law, regardless of their religious background, while also maintaining the secular nature of the state.

Sources

- National Commission for Women (NCW) Report on Gender Justice and Personal Laws
- Indian Social Institute (ISI) Report on Legal Reforms and National Unity
- National Law School of India University (NLSIU) Study on Legal Reforms
- Professor S. P. A. S. R. M. Comparative Law on Secular Civil Codes
- Research on Secular Civil Codes in different countries such as France, Turkey etc.
- The Hindu Succession Act (Amendment) 2015
- Indian Law Commission Reports on UCC

Viva Voce Questions

1. ***What is the Uniform Civil Code (UCC)?***

Ans. The Uniform Civil Code (UCC) is a set of common laws that would apply to all citizens of India, regardless of their religion, in personal matters like marriage, divorce, inheritance and adoption. Its goal is to ensure equality and justice for everyone under the same legal framework.

2. ***Why is the UCC important?***

Ans. The UCC is important because it removes discrimination in personal laws, especially against women. It ensures that everyone has equal rights, promotes gender equality, and strengthens national unity by treating all citizens equally under the law.

3. ***What does Article 44 of the Indian Constitution say about the UCC?***

Ans. Article 44 is part of the Directive Principles of State Policy in the Indian Constitution. It says that the state should work towards implementing a Uniform Civil Code for all citizens to ensure equality and justice.

4. ***How does the UCC benefit women?***

Ans. The UCC helps women by giving them equal rights in matters like inheritance, divorce and maintenance. For example, in some religions, women are not given an equal share in property. The UCC would ensure they get the same rights as men.

5. ***What are the main challenges in implementing the UCC?***

Ans. The main challenges in implementing the UCC are as follow

- Many communities fear that the UCC will interfere with their traditions.
- Opposition from religious groups who believe personal laws are tied to their identity.
- Lack of awareness among people about how the UCC can promote equality.

6. ***Can you give examples of countries that have implemented uniform civil laws?***

Ans. Yes, countries like Turkey and France have implemented uniform civil laws. In Turkey, they abolished religious laws for personal matters in 1926 and introduced common laws for everyone. France has had a uniform legal system for marriage, divorce, and inheritance for a long time.

7. ***What are the main personal laws in India right now?***

Ans. In India, different religions have their own personal laws, such as

- **Hindu Law** Governs Hindus, Sikhs, Jains and Buddhists.
- **Muslim Law** Based on Sharia law for Muslims.
- **Parsi Law** Governs Parsis.
- **Christian Law** Governs Christians.

Each law has different rules for marriage, divorce, inheritance, etc.

8. ***What are some important Supreme Court cases related to the UCC?***

Ans. Some important Supreme Court cases related to UCC are

- **Shah Bano Case** (1985) The court highlighted the need for a UCC to protect women's rights.
- **Sarla Mudgal Case** (1995) The court again stressed the importance of implementing the UCC for national integration.

9. ***Does the UCC affect religious practices?***

Ans. No, the UCC does not affect religious practices like prayers, festivals, or rituals. It only deals with personal legal matters like marriage, divorce and inheritance. People can still follow their traditions and ceremonies.

SAMPLE QUESTION PAPER 1

A Highly Simulated Sample Question Paper for CBSE Class XI

LEGAL STUDIES

General Instructions

- This question paper contains 4 sections – A, B, C and D.
- Section A contains 20 multiple choice questions for 20 marks.
- Section B contains 8 short answer type questions for 2 marks each.
- Section C contains 8 questions for 3 marks each.
- Section D contains 4 long answer type questions for 5 marks each.

Time : 3 hours ***Max. Marks : 80***

SOLVED

SECTION A

1 A Law student, Manu, has briefed his junior fellows about the concepts of Locke, that laws could only be designed in the name of the common good. Identify the related concept, as given by Locke. (1)

(a) Divine Power
(b) Limited Government
(c) Sovereign Government
(d) Self-Preservation

2 Which of the following deals with legal issues related to use of inter-networked information technology? (1)

(a) Cyber crime (b) Cyber law
(c) Internet (d) None of these

3 Which act was enacted to ban the employment of children, who have not completed their fourteenth year, in specified occupations and processes? (1)

(a) The Child Labour (Prohibition and Regulation) Act, 1986
(b) Child Protection Act, 1990
(c) Child Labour Prevention Act, 1992
(d) None of the above

4 Sanjay is very radical about the fundamental changes in the legal system of India and actively asks for reforms in laws as it was brought in the past. Who has introduced legal reform in India? (1)

(a) British East India Company
(b) Mughal Era
(c) Harsha Dynasty (d) Dutch

5 Dr. Satya Prakash sends his servant Aditya to receive the guests at railway station and however the driver accidentally injures a pedestrian. Name the law that shall be imposed by the injured or the aggrieved party against the accused in this situation. (1)

(a) Personal Law (b) Law of Obligations
(c) Constitutional Law (d) Law of Torts

6 Which of the following best describes the concept of sources of law? (1)

(a) The theoretical foundation that defines the nature of law.
(b) The fundamental origins from which legally binding rules are derived.
(c) The chronological development of legal systems across history.
(d) The mechanisms through which laws are enforced and penalties are imposed.

7 Ved Prakash, a law student was asked in the campus placement about the subordinate legislation and its origin is India. Which of the following is/are the parts of subordinate legislation? (1)

I. Obiter dicta II. Judicial rules
III. Colonial law IV. Local law

Codes

(a) I, II and IV (b) II, III and IV
(c) I, II and III (d) All of these

8 "Law is an embodiment of reasons whether in individual or the community".
The above mentioned definition of law is given by which of the following? (1)
(a) Jereny Benthan
(b) Friendrich Carl Von Savigny
(c) Maxim
(d) Aristotle

9 In which of the following cases the Supreme Court held that its advisory jurisdiction is binding on all courts in the territory of India? (1)
(a) In re Kerala Education Bill case
(b) In re Special Court Bill case
(c) Balaji Vs. State of Mysore
(d) State of Maharashtra Vs. F.N. Balsara

10 "Critics have argued that lawyers are necessary to help clients with complex cases and court procedures in which the counselors may not have that kind of expertise. Moreover, there has been no mechanism created to ensure the availability of 'amicus curiae' for the constant needs of courts". What does the term 'amicus curiae' mean? (1)
(a) Legal experts (b) Client
(c) Litigation (d) None of these

11 Which of the following is NOT a criticism of the Patriarchal and Matriarchal Theories? (1)
(a) The authority of the state is not naturally derived from family roles.
(b) The state is created based on the individuals choice and not by blood relations.
(c) The state and family share the same purpose of governance.
(d) The authority in the state is conferred based on the competence of the ruler.

12 Which of the following countries does not follow a Parliamentary form of government? (1)
(a) United States (b) United Kingdom
(c) India (d) Nepal

13 Rehana, who just turned eighteen years this year, is very excited about her role in voting and election procedures. Which among the following articles, states about Adult Suffrage?
(a) Article 321 (b) Article 324 (1)
(c) Article 326 (d) Article 327

14 **Assertion** (A) Protection of Women from Domestic Violence Act adopts a comprehensive definition of domestic violence only including physical abuse.
Reason (R) The definition of domestic violence is provided in Section 3 of the Protection of Women from Domestic Violence Act. (1)
Codes
(a) Both A and R are true and R is the correct explanation of A.
(b) Both A and R are true, but R is not the correct explanation of A.
(c) A is true, but R is false.
(d) A is false but R is true.

15 **Assertion** (A) According to Zero FIR, the victim can file complaint in any police station for any offence for quick action and the case can be transferred to the concerned police station thereafter.
Reason (R) The Government has formulated the provisions of Zero FIR in adverse situations, in order to protect the rights of the people. (1)
Codes
(a) Both A and R are true and R is the correct explanation of A.
(b) Both A and R are true, but R is not the correct explanation of A.
(c) A is true, but R is false.
(d) A is false, but R is true.

16 In a monarchy, the king or queen holds supreme power, often inherited through family lineage. The monarch serves as head of state, making key decisions on laws, foreign policy and governance. Which of the following best describe the characteristic of a Constitutional monarchy? (1)
(a) The monarch has absolute power.
(b) The monarch's powers are limited by laws or Parliaments.
(c) The monarch is elected by citizens.
(d) The monarch serves as head of government.

17 Which among the following statements is TRUE for the Social Contract Theory? (1)
(a) The Social Contract Theory emphasises protecting the ruler's authority.
(b) The primary purpose of the state is to protect the natural rights of individuals.
(c) It focuses on preserving religious values above all.
(d) It aims to maintain social hierarchy as a priority.

18 **Statement I** In a democratic system, citizens have the right to participate in free and fair elections.

SOLVED

Statement II The protection of individual rights and freedoms is a fundamental principle of democracy. (1)

Choose the correct statement

(a) Both Statement are correct.

(b) Both Statement are incorrect.

(c) Statement I is correct, but Statement II is not correct.

(d) Statement II is correct, but Statement I is not correct.

19 **Statement I** Montesquieu's doctrine of separation of power divides government into three branches: legislative, executive and judicial.

Statement II This division aims to provide checks and balances, preventing any one branch from abusing its authority. (1)

Choose the correct statement

(a) Both Statement are correct.

(b) Both Statement are incorrect.

(c) Statement I is correct, but Statement II is not correct.

(d) Statement II is correct, but Statement I is not correct.

20 **Statement I** Critics argue that the doctrine of separation of powers leads to inefficiency and delays due to inter-branch conflicts and overlapping responsibilities.

Statement II The strict separation of powers can also hinder co-ordination and co-operation among the branches, making it difficult to address complex national issues. (1)

Choose the correct statement

(a) Both Statement are correct.

(b) Both Statement are incorrect.

(c) Statement I is correct, but Statement II is not correct.

(d) Statement II is correct, but Statement I is not correct.

SECTION B

21 Hansika, Jyotika and Samar are three youngsters who bought a product from different stores located in the same city. The products that they bought does not function effectively and is faulty. In such a scenario, which act/law can help them? (2)

22 How does the UN Declaration on Elimination of Violence against Women describe 'violence against women'? (2)

Or 'The origin of this case dates back to 1992 and it demanded action against sexual harassment towards women at the workplace'.

(i) Identify the case.

(ii) Government passed an act called POSH Act, 2013 based on the above case. Explain the act?

23 The President of India sought the advisory jurisdiction of the Supreme Court on a matter of public importance. Decide. (2)

(i) In which case was the advisory opinion of the Supreme Court declared to be binding on all courts in India?

(ii) When is the court under a duty to render advisory opinion?

24 Alxania and Cynthia, two countries are bound by some laws which foster their relations by following some rules based on reciprocity. (2)

(i) Which branch of law would regulate the relation between the two nations?

(ii) Which branch of law would regulate the relation between the individuals of these two nations?

25 Urvashi has just been promoted to class 11 and her parents has provided a desktop with internet connection for enhancement in studies. What do you understand by the term 'internet'? (2)

26 How does the state originate as per the divine theory? (2)

Or How Hobbes' Social Contract Theory is criticised by R.G. Gettle?

27 A case of fraud and felony was filed against Suraj by his friend and business partner, Vishal. The police has to start the process of criminal prosecution. What is the first stage of this procedure? Explain in brief. Also mention the other steps. (2)

28 Country 'X' was primarily a federal state with a Parliamentary form of government wherein the powers were divided between the centre and states. However, certain provisions in the Constitution empowered the President to run the state in a unitary manner in certain cases.

(i) Identify, which provisions are being discussed here?

(ii) Which part of the Constitution contains such provisions? (2)

Or These provisions are not enforceable by any court of law, but provide guidance in carrying out and drafting laws regarding human and social development.

(i) Which provisions are being discussed here?

(ii) These provisions are contained in which part of the Constitution?

SECTION C

29 "The government is the sum total of Legislative, Executive and Judicial activities of a state". (3)

(i) What is the role of government?

(ii) Also explain the other three elements of state.

Or Discuss the concept of checks and balances as propounded by Montesquieu. Also explain its impact.

30 In the year 2012, in the matter of Shreya Singhal Vs. Union of India, a batch of writ petitions were filed under Article 32 of the Constitution of India. (3)

(i) What was the matter raised in this case?

(ii) What was the immediate cause of concern in these petitions?

31 A major milestone in law reform during the British Raj, was the establishment of the law commission. (3)

(i) When was the first law commission established and who was the chairman of the first law commission?

(ii) Mentioned the name of the acts which were passed as a response to the law commission.

32 "Power corrupts and absolute power corrupts absolutely". (3)

(i) Who made the above statement?

(ii) This theory is in support of which doctrine?

(iii) Why is the doctrine a protest against absolute power?

33 "Juvenile Justice Boards are constituted in every district to deal with children in conflict with law". Elaborate. (3)

Or 'The Protection of Children from Sexual Offences Act, 2012 provides protection to children from various kind of sexual offences'. List out what kinds of sexual offences fall under the ambit of this act?

34 Before Independence India was under the control of the British Government. During their time, the British Parliament has enacted several legislations. (3)

(i) Name any few laws enacted by the British Parliament.

(ii) State any two features of the Government of India Act, 1858.

(iii) Which act is known as Act for the Better Government of India?

35 'In India, there is not only legislature but the judiciary has played an active role for the enactment of law'. Do judges make laws? Elaborate. (3)

36 'Govind has acquired a building premises for lease with the purpose of opening of a Business Process Outsourcing (BPO). However within a span of 6 months there were several issues related to building maintenance arouse, which was ratified by the tenant as per the contract'. Explain the term contract. (3)

Or What are the main features of Savigny's historical school?

SECTION D

37 In a debate organised in a law school, a group of students were agruing and trying to explain the origin of state, though there was no valid answer regarding the same. Like them, political philosophers and thinkers have also tried and attempted to trace out and explain the origin of the state in various methods. There were various beliefs regarding the origin of the state, some believe that the origin of the state lie in the 'hands of God' whereas others believe that they are based on social contract and some trust on single force, the family, etc.

(i) Explain the origin of the state by the 'hands of God'.

(ii) How is population an important element of state?

(iii) What are the functions of a government in a state? (5)

38 There are three countries 'A', 'B' and 'C' all of them are democracies but differ in the forms of government that exist in these countries. In country 'A', the Presidential form of government is followed, while in the other two countries 'B' and 'C', Parliamentary form of government exists.

While one of the countries is located in the sub-continent of Asia, the other one is located in North America and Europe. One of the countries 'A' is the oldest democracy of the world while the other 'C' is the largest democracy of the world. The other one 'B' is a Constitutional monarchy.

(i) Identify the three countries discussed in the case.

(ii) How is power separated in the country 'A'. Explain? (5)

39 'Priyanka and Supriya moved to session court for the legal dispute over the property. The advocate of each client informed them that the case shall proceed under the subordinate legislation'. Discuss the four main classification of subordinate legislation. (5)

Or Imagine a situation where a well-known restaurant in Delhi refuses entry to a group of women because they are wearing traditional Indian attire, stating that it does not meet the 'modern' dress code of the restaurant. The women are shocked and file a complaint with the authorities, arguing that their cultural attire should not be used to discriminate against them.

(i) How can the state intervene to ensure that such practices do not violate Fundamental Rights?

(ii) What categories of customs enforced by the state would apply to prevent such discrimination?

40 Briefly describe different forms of governments that exist at different locations in the world. (5)

Or

There are two countries, one of which is located in Europe and the other one in North America. Historically, one of them has been the colony of the other. The political systems existing in these two countries are two of the most widely prevalent form of governments in modern times. The political system followed in one of these is also practiced in India.

(i) Identify the two countries and explain the forms of governments which are prevalent in these countries.

(ii) Give any three differences between the two distinct forms of government that prevail in these countries.

Answers

1. (b)	**2.** (b)	**3.** (a)	**4.** (a)	**5.** (d)	**6.** (b)	**7.** (b)
8. (d)	**9.** (b)	**10.** (a)	**11.** (c)	**12.** (a)	**13.** (c)	**14.** (d)
15. (a)	**16.** (b)	**17.** (b)	**18.** (a)	**19.** (a)	**20.** (a)	

21. In the given scenario, the Consumer Protection (Amendment) Act, 2019 can help Hansika, Jyotika and Samar. Under this act, they can come together to reduce costs and improve chances of redressal or settlement.

22. The UN Declaration on Elimination of Violence against Women was adopted in 1993 and defines 'violence against women' as any gender-based violence acts that result in, or are likely to result in, physical, sexual or psychological harm or suffering to women.

Or (i) The above discussed case is Vishakha and Others Vs. state of Rajasthan.

(ii) POSH Act was enacted in 2013 and it was enacted by the Ministry for Women and Child Development. This act was enacted with the objective of making workplaces safer for women by preventing, prohibiting and redressing acts of sexual harassment against them in workplace.

23. (i) In re Special Court Bill case (1979), the Supreme Court held that its advisory jurisdiction is binding on all courts in the territory of India.

(ii) The Supreme Court under Article 143 is under duty to give its advisory opinion when the President of India refers a matter of public importance to the Supreme Court. However, the Supreme Court is not obliged to give an opinion. It may choose to give one if it deems the issue significant enough.

24. (i) Public international law

(ii) Private international law

25. The internet is defined as 'A system architecture that has revolutionised communications and methods of commerce by allowing various computer networks around the world to interconnect'.

26. According to the divine theory, state is established and governed by God or some superior power or king as the agent of God and the religious scriptures.

The supporter of divine theory believed that the state doesn't come into being by the people but it is the handwork of God on the Earth.

Or Hobbes' theory was criticised by R.G. Gettle in the following ways

- Hobbes created an all-powerful sovereign on the belief that law, order, peace and security could not be maintained in society without such sovereign power.
- He deprived the people of their right to revolt against the sovereign.

27. The first stage of this procedure is investigation. It is a preliminary stage enquiry conducted by the police and usually starts after the recording of a First Information Report (FIR) in the police station. The other steps in the process are inquiry and trial.

Inquiry It is the second stage of the process wherein a Magistrate seeks to find out whether the accused should be committed to the sessions or discharged.

Trial It is the third stage of the process. It is the judicial determination of a person's guilt or innocence.

28. (i) Emergency provisions are being discussed here.

(ii) Part XVIII of the Constitution contains the emergency provisions.

Or (i) Directive Principles of State Policy are being discussed here.

(ii) These provisions are contained in Part IV of the Constitution.

29. (i) The roles of government are

- The government of a state makes provisions for the services of defence, foreign relations, levy of taxes, issue of currency, building of roads, bridges, transportation, communication, water supply, electricity, health education, and other types of social and physical infrastructure.
- The government of a state enforces law to maintain order, peace and security.

(ii) The other three elements of state include

(a) **Sovereignty** It is an important factor that distinguishes the state from other associations without sovereignty, there is no existence of a state.

(b) **Territory** It is a geographical area that is owned and controlled by a government or country to exercise state sovereignty.

(c) **Population** It is an essential element of a state as it is the people who make a state and there con be no state without them.

Or Montesquieu is credited with the origin of the system of checks and balances. This system provides for a system based regulation wherein one branch is allowed to limit the other.

The impact of his concept are

- This doctrine was adopted by Montesquieu in his country's political system. His teachings also gave a boost to the French Revolution and further led to the adoption of the Declaration of Rights in 1789.
- The Declaration provided that every society in which separation of powers is not determined, has no Constitution.
- The French Constitution, 1791 made executive, legislative and judiciary independent of one another'. The doctrine of separation of powers forms the foundation on which the entire structure of the US Constitution 1787 is based.

30. (i) The matter raised an important question relating primarily to the Fundamental Right of free speech and expression guaranteed by Article 19 of the Constitution of India.

(ii) The immediate cause for concern in these petitions was Section 66A of the Information Technology Act of 2000.

The petitioner argued argued that wordings of the section were too wide and ambiguous, which leads to misuse. Most of the term used in the section had not been specifically defined under the act. Further, the petitioners argued that the section restricted the right to free speech and expression prescribed under Article 19 (1) (a) of the Constitution of India.

31. (i) The first law commission was established in 1834 under the Charter Act of 1833, under the chairmanship of Thomas Babington Macaulay.

(ii) The Indian Code of Civil Procedure, 1908; the Indian Contract Act, 1872; the Indian Evidence Act, 1872 and the Transfer of Property Act, 1882, were the major contributions of the law commission.

32. (i) Lord Acton made the above statement.

(ii) This theory is in support of the doctrine of separation of powers.

(iii) Separation of powers is in itself a protest against power. Its meaning can be better analysed if the use of the word powers of the organs is substituted by functions. The word 'functions' implies the attitude of service while the word 'powers' implies force.

The government performs activities to serve the purpose of the state and its individuals through its classified functions for which the different organs are created.

33. Juvenile Justice Boards are constituted in every district to deal with children in conflict with law. The board comprises a Metropolitan Judge and Judicial Magistrate with two social workers. For all cases, excluding the offence of heinous crimes, the juvenile will get institutional care for a maximum of three years by the Juvenile Justice Board.

If a minor between the age of 16-18 years is accused of committing a heinous crime (whether a crime is heinous or not is determined by the Juvenile Justice Board on a case to case basis), then under the amended law, the minor can be tried as an adult.

Or The Protection of Children from Sexual Offences Act protects children from following kinds of sexual offences

- Offences of penetrative sexual assault (penetration of penis or any object or part of body into the vagina, mouth, urethra or anus of child or makes the child to do so with him or any other person.
- It also includes manipulation of any part of the body of the child so as to cause such penetration).
- Sexual assault (touching vagina, penis, anus or breast of child with sexual intent or making a child to do so).
- Sexual harassment (uttering words, making sounds or gesture or exhibiting any body part or making a child to do so).
- Use of child for pornographic purposes (using a child in any form of media for the purposes of sexual gratification).

34. (i) Some of the significant legislations of the British Parliament responsible for the Governance of India were

- Government of India Act, 1858
- Indian Councils Act, 1861
- Indian Councils Act, 1892
- Indian Councils Act, 1909
- Government of India Act, 1919
- Government of India Act, 1935

(ii) The two features of Government of India Act, 1858 are

(a) It ended the dual government scheme initiated due to Pitt's India Act.

(b) The powers of the Company's Court of Directors were transferred to the Secretary of State for India. He was going to be a member of the British Parliament.

(iii) The Government of India Act, 1858

35. The Indian Constitution confers power on the legislature to make law, while the judiciary has the power to examine the Constitutionality of the law enacted by the legislature.

The courts also adjudicate upon the rights and duties of citizens, and further interpret the provisions of the Constitution and other laws. Through these processes, the courts create new rights for the citizens. By this exercise, the judiciary makes additions to the existing laws of the country. It can be inferred that judges do not make the law in the same manner in which legislative bodies do. Judges work on a given legal material passed as law by the legislature.

While declaring the law, judges interpret the 'legislation' in question and play a creative role. By this creative role, judges have contributed significantly to the development of law.

Therefore, it can be concluded that the judicial precedents are important sources of law in modern society and judges do play a significant role in law-making.

36. A contract is an agreement with specific terms between two or more persons in which there is a promise to do something in lieu of a valuable profit known as consideration. The Indian Contract Act, 1872 is applicable to all the states of India. The act determines the circumstances in which promises made by the parties to a contract shall be legally binding.

For example, 'A' has offered his mobile phone to 'B' for an amount of money. 'B' agreed to purchase the same. This has created a legal relationship where both have made a promise which is enforceable by law.

Or The main features of Savigny's historical school of jurisprudence are

- Law should be a reflection of the common spirit of the people and their custom.
- Law is not universal; it is particular like the language of a particular society.
- Law is not static; it has relationship with the development of the society.
- Law is not given by a political superior, but is found or given by the people.

37. (i) The origin of the State by the 'hands of God' is based on the divine theory of state. It states that state is established and governed by God and the king as its agent to rule over its subjects.

(ii) Population is an essential element of a state as it is the people who make a state and without them, there can be no state. The people also maintain the resources, live on the land, and form the government. The population must be large enough to make a state and sustain it.

(iii) The functions of a government in a state are

- Government is the political and administrative organ of a state. The state operates through its government.
- The government is the sum total of legislative, executive and Judicial activities of a state.

  It also includes internal bodies and sub-state governing authorities at the local and regional levels, such as the municipal corporations, municipal councils, panchayats and gram sabhas in India.
- The government of a state makes provisions for the services of defense, foreign relations, levy of taxes, issue of currency, building of roads, bridges, transportation, communication, water supply, electricity, health education, and other types of social and physical infrastructure.
- The government of a state shall be so organised that it enforces law to maintain order, peace and security.

38. (i) Based on the above description, the three countries are

(a) America (b) UK (c) India

(ii) The power separated in America is as follow

- The US Constitution has adopted the presidential form of government wherein the theory of separation of powers has been adopted in letter and spirit.
- The American Constitution did not mention that the powers must be separated. It simply distributed the powers among the three organs of the government i.e. the executive organ, judicial organ and legislative organ.
- While it give a major share of powers to one organ of government, instead smaller shares of powers to each of the other organs. This was done to avoid concentration and consequent abuse of power.
- The fathers of the Constitution considered that power should be limited, controlled and diffused.

39. Subordinate legislation can be classified into the following types

(i) **Autonomous Law** When a group of individuals recognised or incorporated under the law as an autonomous body, is conferred with the power to make rules and regulation, the laws made by such body fall under autonomous law. For example, laws made by the bodies like Universities, incorporated companies etc. fall in this category of legislation.

(ii) **Judicial Rules** In some countries, the judiciary is conferred with the power to make rules for their administrative procedures. For example, under the Constitution of India, the Supreme Court and High Courts have been conferred with such kinds of power to regulate procedure and administration.

(iii) **Local Laws** In some countries, local bodies are recognised and conferred with the law-making powers. They are entitled to make bye-laws in their respective jurisdictions. In India, local bodies like panchayats and municipal corporations have been recognised by the Constitution through the 73rd and 74th Constitutional Amendments. The rules and bye-laws enacted by them are examples of local laws.

(iv) **Colonial Law** Laws made by colonial countries for their colonies or the countries controlled by them are known as colonial laws. For a long time, India was governed by the laws passed by the British Parliament. However, as most countries of the world have gained independence from the colonial powers, this legislation is losing its importance and may not be recognised as a kind of legislation.

Or (i) In this situation, the state can intervene by ensuring that the restaurant's actions do not violate the women's Fundamental Rights, particularly the right to equality and non-discrimination under the Constitution of India. The state can investigate the restaurant's dress code policy and assess whether it unfairly targets or discriminates against any specific cultural or gender group.

(ii) To prevent such discrimination, the following categories of customs enforced by the state would apply.

Legal Custom It refers to a custom that has absolute authority. In other words, it has the force of law and is recognised and enforced by the courts. Legal customs are further subdivided into

(i) General customs that prevailed throughout the territory of the state.

(ii) Local customs that are applicable locally, i.e. to a particular region of the country.

Conventional Customs These customs are binding on the parties to an agreement. When two or more persons enter into an agreement related to a trade, it is assumed in law that they make the contract according to the established convention or usage of that trade. For example, an agreement between a landlord and tenant regarding the payment of rent will be governed by convention prevailing in this regard.

40. The different forms of government that exist in the world are as below

(i) **Monarchy** It is the oldest form of government. In a monarchy, the state machinery functions according to the commands and rule of the monarch. Monarchy, thus, refers to a rule by one. It is the will of one person which ultimately prevails in all matters of governance.

(ii) **Aristocracy** It is a form of government in which political powers of the state are vested in the hands of a few people. It is a form of government in which a relatively small proportion of people determine the policies of the government.

(iii) **Dictatorship** In this form of government, a single person or a small group of people exercise complete authority over others. The dictator controls and exercises the political powers of the state. He does not come to power through elections, instead he occupies the position by force, invasion, intervention and militarism, in contrast to a monarch.

His dictates are the laws of the country. He implements them and pass judgement according to his will. He holds absolute power.

He is not accountable or answerable to the citizens of the state.

(iv) **Democracy** It is form of government in which people are powerful. According to Abraham Lincoln democracy is a government of the people, by the people and for the people. 'Government of the people' means equal distribution of political powers and influence among the citizens of the state.

'Government by the people' means participation of all citizens in forming a government. 'Government for the people' means the rule of government for the promotion of public welfare.

Or (i) These two countries are the United Kingdom, situated in Europe and the United States, situated in North America. The United Kingdom follows a Parliamentary form of government while the United States follows the Presidential form of government.

(ii) Differences between a Presidential and a Parliamentary form of government are

Parliamentary form of Government	Presidential form of Government
The President is indirectly elected.	People directly elect the President.
The President is the nominal head of the state while the Prime Minister is the head of the government as well as the state.	The President is the real head of the state and the government.
The Prime Minister and the Council of Ministers are answerable to the legislature.	The President and the Secretaries are not answerable to the legislature.

SAMPLE QUESTION PAPER 2

A Highly Simulated Sample Question Paper for CBSE Class XI

LEGAL STUDIES

General Instructions

- This question paper contains 4 sections – A, B, C and D.
- Section A contains 20 multiple choice questions for 20 marks.
- Section B contains 8 short answer type questions for 2 marks each.
- Section C contains 8 questions for 3 marks each.
- Section D contains 4 long answer type questions for 5 marks each.

Time : 3 hours ***Max. Marks : 80***

UNSOLVED

3SECTION A

1 Kavya, an MBA aspirant, has learnt that England shall be the best place since it is most liberal and citizens enjoys larger freedom right at there, which was also described by Montesquieu. Name the despotic ruler, who was contemporary of Montesquieu. (1)

(a) Louis XIV

(b) Louis XV

(c) Louis XVI

(d) Louis XVII

2 Which of the following statements best describes the role of the judiciary in the system of Separation of Powers within a government? (1)

(a) The judiciary only acts as an advisory body to the legislature and executive in legal matters.

(b) The judiciary has the power to create new laws in the absence of legislative action.

(c) The judiciary interprets the law and adjudicates disputes, ensuring that laws are applied correctly and fairly across cases.

(d) The judiciary enforces laws directly, alongside the executive, when there is a legal vacuum.

3 The origin of state is traced to the authority of the eldest male descendant of the family in which of the following theories? (1)

(a) Matriarchal theory

(b) Patriarchal theory

(c) Divine theory

(d) Kinship theory

4 "The aim of this school is to create a scientifically valid system of law, by analysing legal concepts and ideas on the basis of empirical or scientific methods".

The above mentioned statement is referred to which of the following school of law? (1)

(a) Natural School of Law

(b) Analytical School of Law

(c) Sociological School of Law

(d) Historical School of Law

5 Akshara went on a holiday to Dubai with some of her friends. While enjoying her vacation, she noticed a boy following them and video taping everything that the girls did. After talking to her friends Akshara, goes to the police. What will be the charge against the boy? (1)

(a) Cyber bullying (b) Video voyerism

(c) Computer trespassing (d) Mail fraud

UNSOLVED

6 **Assertion** (A) Dictatorial form of government respects individual liberty.
Reason (R) In a democracy, people have a huge say in decision-making of the government. (1)

Codes
(a) Both A and R are true and R is the correct explanation of A.
(b) Both A and R are true, but R is not the correct explanation of A.
(c) A is true, but R is false.
(d) A is false, but R is true.

7 Which among the given statements is TRUE regarding the challenges in defining law unanimously? (1)
(a) Law is an ambiguous and impractical concept, making it difficult to define.
(b) Law has been interpreted through various lenses, including philosophical, theological and social perspectives, leading to multiple definitions.
(c) Each government establishes its own definition of law, making a universal definition impossible.
(d) The discipline of legal studies is relatively new, lacking sufficient historical context for a definitive explanation.

8 Harishanker is a vigilant social workers. He gives advices and gives information about the significance of Fundamental Rights of every individual. Who acts as the guardian of Fundamental Rights? (1)
(a) Parliament (b) Supreme Court
(c) High Court (d) President

9 Which of the following is NOT a part of public law? (1)
(a) Constitutional Law
(b) Administrative Law
(c) Criminal Law
(d) Civil Law

10 Right to Education is enshrined in which Article of Indian Constitution? (1)
(a) Article 20 (b) Article 21
(c) Article 21 A (d) Article 22

11. The court appointed Lavanya's uncle as her guardian under the Guardians and Wards Act, 1890. Identify the type of guardianship of Lavanya's uncle given by the court. (1)
(a) Testamentary Guardian
(b) Natural Guardian
(c) De-facto Guardian
(d) Certificated Guardian

12 Which of the following constitutes India's substantive criminal law? (1)
(a) Indian Penal Code, 1860
(b) Code of Criminal Procedure, 1973
(c) Indian Evidence Act of 1872
(d) All of the above

13 Yamini is too much scared of her husband who most often beat her for smaller mistakes and non-fulfillment of dowry amount. Luckily her friend has helped her to lodge a formal complaint against her husband.
Which section of the Indian Penal Code deals with the cases related to domestic violence? (1)
(a) 490 (b) 490 A
(c) 488 (d) 498 A

14 **Assertion** (A) Colonial Government conceded that the Constitution of India would be framed by an elected Constituent Assembly consisting of Indian people.
Reason (R) Growing dissatisfaction over limited governing rights granted to Indians under 1935 Act led to widespread protests. (1)

Codes
(a) Both A and R are true and R is the correct explanation of A.
(b) Both A and R are true, but R is not the correct explanation of A.
(c) A is true, but R is false.
(d) A is false, but R is true.

15 Which among the following act is TRUE to governs testamentary succession in India? (1)
(a) Succession Act, 1750
(b) Law of Succession, 1850
(c) Indian Law of Succession, 1925
(d) Indian Succession Act, 1925

16 For a marriage to be valid, certain conditions must be met. Which of the following is NOT a condition for a valid marriage? (1)
(a) Parties must have attained the minimum age.
(b) Parties must have similar religious beliefs.
(c) Parties must be mentally capable of giving consent.
(d) Marriage must be performed with free consent.

17 Which among the given statements is TRUE regarding the drafting of the Objectives Resolution? (1)
(a) The Objectives Resolution was drafted by Dr. B.R. Ambedkar to define the Fundamental Rights of citizens.